P9-AOW-135

WITHDRAWN

High-Performance Networking

*Mark Sportack,
Frank C. Pappas,
Emil Rensing,
et al.*

sams.net

201 West 103rd Street
Indianapolis, IN 46290

UNLEASHED

Copyright © 1997 by Sams.net Publishing

FIRST EDITION

International Standard Book Number: 1-57521-187-4

Library of Congress Catalog Card Number: 96-69715

2000 99 98 97   4 3 2 1

Interpretation of the printing code: the rightmost double-digit number is the year of the book's printing; the rightmost single digit, the number of the book's printing. For example, a printing code of 97-1 shows that the first printing of the book occurred in 1997.

Composed in AGaramond and MCPdigital by Macmillan Computer Publishing

Printed in the United States of America

Trademarks

President, Sams Publishing	*Richard K. Swadley*
Publishing Manager	*Dean Miller*
Director of Editorial Services	*Cindy Morrow*
Managing Editor	*Kitty Wilson Jarrett*
Director of Marketing	*Kelli S. Spencer*
Product Marketing Manager	*Wendy Gilbride*
Assistant Marketing Managers	*Jennifer Pock, Rachel Wolfe*

Acquisitions Editor
Cari Skaggs

Development Editor
Jeffrey J. Koch

Production Editor
Mary Ann Abramson

Copy Editor
Margaret Berson
Mary Ann Faughnan

Indexer
John Sleeva

Technical Reviewer
Dennis Teague

Editorial Coordinators
Mandie Rowell
Katie Wise

Technical Edit Coordinator
Lynette Quinn

Resource Coordinator
Deborah Frisby

Editorial Assistants
Carol Ackerman
Andi Richter
Rhonda Tinch-Mize

Cover Designer
Jason Grisham

Cover Production
Aren Howell

Book Designer
Gary Adair

Copy Writer
David Reichwein

Production Team Supervisors
Brad Chinn
Charlotte Clapp

Production
Rick Bond
Georgiana Briggs
Betsy Deeter
Mark Walchle

Overview

13 ISDN 233

Foreword

Business and business processes are becoming increasingly information intensive. The marketplace is responding to this need with never-ending increases in computational ability and application software sophistication. These evolutionary changes in processors and applications impose challenging and variegated performance requirements on the networks that support them. Consequently, data communications and networking are becoming increasingly vital to the success of information users.

Networking technologies, historically, have been largely regarded as the proverbial black box. Few, if any, people really understood the mechanics of these vital technologies. As information technologies become more complex, they will require very different levels of network performance. Networks will continue to evolve in response to these technological innovations. They will continue to become faster and more feature-rich.

The key to success will be to match the features and functionalities of networks to the attributes and performance requirements of the networked processors and applications. This requires everyone, from IT executives and managers to application programmers and network administrators, to understand the abilities, limitations, and performance requirements of each piece of the IT infrastructure, and to work together to craft cohesive solutions.

High-Performance Networking Unleashed demystifies networking technologies through a step-by-step introduction to their underlying components. This provides the context for a more specific examination of how networking can satisfy the requirements of emerging information technologies and applications.

Dedication

To my precious wife, Karen. Thank you for your unwavering love and support.
I couldn't have done this without you.

To my son Adam, who doesn't want to write books when he gets older
because it is too much work. You are wise beyond your years.

To my infant daughter Jennifer, thank you for sleeping so much. That made me feel much less guilty.

And lastly, to Louis C. Masters for introducing me to Cari Skaggs
and Sams Publishing. I'll get you for this! :)

Mark Sportack

My work is dedicated to my parents, whose love, patience, and sacrifice have given me the world.

Frank C. Pappas

Things happen. People change. Life goes on. My work is dedicated to my dad, who recently
demonstrated how not to give up—even when the going gets the worst.

Emil Rensing

Acknowledgments

I would like to extend my deepest gratitude to my boss, Portia Johnson, for her support of this effort, and to my friends and co-workers Stan Griff, Dave Kurtiak, Rex Avery, Jim Hinman, and Tom Papazian for their insight, assistance, and reference materials.

—Mark Sportack

My personal cast of characters has a number of superstars who deserve special recognition. I'd especially like to thank my parents for sticking with me through thick and thin (and everything in between); Uncle John, for setting me straight when I've needed it; Bob Samaniego, my favorite sixth grade teacher, who taught me all about the wide world of computing way back in the age of the Apple II; Jim Fry, for always giving me great advice; Professor John Morgan, for refusing to accept anything but my best; Emil "The Pterodactyl" Rensing, for his writing skill, soda runs, and spare change; and Agador Spartacus, for making me laugh.

—Frank C. Pappas

Mr. Rensing would like to acknowledge the assistance and support of Greenhouse Networks, a business unit of America Online, Inc. His contribution would not have been made possible without the additional support of Keri Rensing (his wife), John Merz (his boss), Spif (some guy), Jon Jackson (his other boss), The Notorious FCP (his editor), Eric Newman (his new and improved Yoda), Jim Hoare (his director), and Gene Fennel (his 9th grade English teacher). Additionally, he would like to thank Frank Bottiglieri (for having a cool computer back in 1992), The George Washington University (for having labs to learn in and servers to crash on, but no curriculum to keep his interest), David Hostetter (for just always being interesting), and Joe Carabillo (for giving an ungrateful, irresponsible kid a chance), whose help and encouragement kept him out of the booth.

—Emil Rensing

About the Authors

Mark A. Sportack is an experienced Information Technology (IT) management professional with approximately 14 years of experience in many facets of IT. His experience includes project management, forecasting and managing multi-million dollar capital budgets, expense budgets, design of internal billing systems, short-and long-range IT infrastructure planning, systems and applications design/development, directing implementation teams, and management of both technology and technical personnel. He is currently working in the Consumer Operations and Technology (CO&T) Department of the Consumer and Small Business (C&SB) unit at AT&T where he leads a group of technical professionals and is responsible for Technology Planning and Strategy.

Frank Charles Pappas sang and danced his way through his early years, though innate good sense prompted him to escape the natural—and not so natural—disasters of southern California for a new and exciting life in our nation's capital. Since then, Frank has devoted himself to working for politicians and technology firms, dodging Secret Service vehicles while playing roller hockey in front of the White House, and reading 500-year-old Spanish literature. Frank graduated with degrees in Political Science and Spanish Language and Literature from the George Washington University in Washington, DC. He is currently pursuing a Masters Degree in Latin American Studies at GW's Elliott School of International Affairs. He can be reached via e-mail at `fcpappas@aol.com`.

Emil Rensing is a native New Yorker now living in the northern Virginia suburbs of Washington, D.C. He is currently employed as a Web Developer for Greenhouse Networks, the original content arm of AOL Studios and a division of America Online, Inc. As a perpetual student at The George Washington University, Emil hopes to one day never be *required* to set foot on campus again. He can be reached via e-mail at `emil@aol.net`.

Louis C. Masters is an applications/communications/systems programmer with multiple years experience in the Information Technology field. He teaches classes on applications/systems development, programming for the Internet, and client/server architecture. Louis has an M.B.A. from Rutgers University with a concentration in Information Technology and the Management of Innovation. He is currently employed at AT&T and works for the Consumer and Small Business unit, leading a team of application developers in developing networked applications.

Martin J. Bligh is a communications specialist working for Sequent Computer Systems in the United Kingdom. He has experience in planning, designing, and implementing networks, specializing in UNIX and Windows NT communications and LAN/WAN technologies. He holds a degree in Mathematics and Computing from Oxford University, England, and his research interests include distributed operating systems and the application of neural networks to playing the game of Go. He can be contacted via e-mail at `mbligh@sequent.com`.

Michael R. Starkenburg is the Manager of Development and Operations for Digital City, Inc., where he leads a team of engineers creating online content delivery systems and tools. Previously, he was responsible for the creation of the Internet's largest Web site, `www.aol.com`, and several other high-profile Web sites. He holds degrees in business from The George Washington University and Saddleback College. Mike can be reached at `http://www.starkenburg.com` or `stark@aol.net`.

Arthur B. Cooper Jr. has over 19 years of network experience. He was a military technician between 1978 and 1982. Following that, he spent five years working for Honeywell and General Electric repairing data and voice network impairments. From 1987 until early 1997, Mr. Cooper worked in network management for the U.S. Air Force. Currently, he is working for Lanier Worldwide, Inc. as a Systems Engineer. He has an AA in Computer Science, an AAS in Electronic Systems Technology, a BS in Organizational Management, and he is completing an MA in Curriculum and Instruction. He is married, has two sons, and makes his home in Colorado Springs.

Richard J. Maring is a Senior Programmer/Analyst for the National Association of Securities Dealers (NASD). He is currently tasked with the design and development of an enterprise scale, Web-based OLAP solution for the internal Executive Information System. He is also a freelance Microsoft Certified Trainer specializing in all 32-bit Microsoft operating systems. His extensive background includes LAN/MAN/WAN construction, capacity planning, performance tuning, database design, and system development/integration as well as extensive project management/budgeting experience. Richard has recently been acquired by Microsoft to serve in their elite Internet Infrastructure and Architecture division as the Site Architect and QA Manager for all Microsoft.com Web sites throughout the world. He can be reached via e-mail at `rmaring@microsoft.com`.

James F. Causey is an Intel Systems Specialist for Indiana University Computing Services. He performs high-level support, development, and administration tasks for NT-centric networks, with clients ranging from NT and 95 to DOS/Windows and MacOS. He also teaches courses on networking and the Microsoft suite of operating systems, as well doing freelance software development. Originally trained as a Military Historian, his interests include music, sports cars, history, and any other recreational task that takes him as far from computers as possible. He has occasionally been known to pine for the days when VMS was king and Commodores were cool from his home in Bloomington, Indiana. He lives with his partner, Tina, and his cat, Gabby. James can be reached via e-mail at `jcausey@bluemarble.net`.

Dave Welk has been working in the networking industry for over ten years with extensive telecommunications and LAN/WAN experience. Many years spent administering Novell networks allowed Dave to complete the set of seven CNE tests within an eighteen-day time period in March 1994. Today, he routinely assists in analyzing and designing networks that include thousands of computers and rooms full of servers. Dave has a bachelors degree in Management and recently completed his Master of Project Management Degree. He has been certified by just about every major manufacturer of networking products, including Bay Networks, 3COM, Fore Systems, and Network General.

Phillip T. Rawles is a professor of Telecommunications and Networking Technologies in the Department of Computer Information Systems and Technology at Purdue University. Professor Rawles teaches Network and Systems Administration, Enterprise Network Management, and Manufacturing Information Systems. His other academic interests include Network Security and Simulation.

Tell Us What You Think!

As a reader, you are the most important critic and commentator of our books. We value your opinion and want to know what we're doing right, what we could do better, what areas you'd like to see us publish in, and any other words of wisdom you're willing to pass our way. You can help us make strong books that meet your needs and give you the computer guidance you require.

Do you have access to CompuServe or the World Wide Web? Then check out our CompuServe forum by typing GO SAMS at any prompt. If you prefer the World Wide Web, check out our site at http://www.mcp.com.

> **NOTE**
>
> If you have a technical question about this book, call the technical support line at 317-581-3833.

As the team leader of the group that created this book, I welcome your comments. You can fax, e-mail, or write me directly to let me know what you did or didn't like about this book—as well as what we can do to make our books stronger. Here's the information:

Fax: 317-581-4669

E-mail: opsys_mgr@sams.mcp.com

Mail: Dean Miller
          Comments Department
          Sams Publishing
          201 W. 103rd Street
          Indianapolis, IN 46290

IN THIS PART

Planning Your Infrastructure: What You Need to Know

PART

I

CHAPTER 1

Introduction to High-Performance Networks

by Mark Sportack
and Keith Johnson

IN THIS CHAPTER

The past decade has been witness to the radical evolution of data networks from their humble origins to their current forms. The original Local Area Networks (LANs), were nothing more than coaxial cabling, strung from terminal servers to desktop terminals whose users were treated to monochromatic text displayed on low-resolution cathode ray tubes (CRTs).

In the mid-1980s, wide area networks (WANs), too, were slow and crude. Terminal servers multiplexed access for dozens of users to 9.6Kbps circuits. These circuits connected users to mainframe-based applications that lay hidden in a remote data center.

Today, LANs have metamorphosed into high-bandwidth, high-performance, local area networks that support bandwidth- and CPU-intensive client applications such as live, interactive voice and videoconferencing, as well as e-mail and some of the more traditional forms of data processing.

WANs, too, have experienced radical, evolutionary change. Today, 9.6Kbps is deemed inadequate for most of the needs of even a single user. Just try to give a user a 9.6Kbps modem for use as anything but a paperweight!

It is important to recognize that the impetus for all these changes has been, and remains, the user's business requirements. The competitive environment of most business entities ensures that any technological innovations that offer competitive advantages—that is, better, cheaper, and/or faster—get accepted. For example, the introduction of the mouse facilitated access to computing by obviating the need for typing skills. Suddenly, almost everyone could use a computer! Personal computers, too, offered countless advantages by distributing intelligence down to the desktop.

Software developers also drove changes by constantly upgrading a dizzying array of increasingly complex products that enabled users to actually use the newly distributed processing power at their fingertips. Together, these innovations quickly made hard-wired connections to terminal servers obsolete.

Into this void came the first generation of LANs. These networks offered almost obscene amounts of bandwidth, such as 1 or 4Mb per second (Mbps), depending on whose network you purchased. Initially, these LANs were used as a more flexible means of connecting users with terminal servers. After all, the users' basic requirements hadn't changed all that much, and the increased bandwidth was more than adequate to support terminal emulation.

Towards the end of the 1980s, this first generation of LANs began to show its age. Once the user community understood that the distributed microprocessors on their desktops could do more than just terminal emulation, their quest for even more bandwidth and for higher performance networking began.

The second generation of LANs were little more than faster versions of their predecessors. 1Mbps Ethernets grew into 10Mbps Ethernets. Similarly, 4Mbps Token Rings were accelerated to 16Mbps. This increase in the clock rates would keep users somewhat satisfied up to the middle of the 1990s.

The mid-1990s witnessed the maturation of both Ethernet and Token Ring. Unlike the first generation LANs, however, the resulting performance crisis was not caused solely by a lack of bandwidth. On Ethernet networks, in particular, insufficient bandwidth was not the problem. Rather, performance degradation was typically due more to either

- Excessive competition for access to the LAN, or
- Saturation of the available bandwidth with unnecessary broadcasts.

In either event, an increase in the clock rate would only have masked the problem and postponed its solution. A better and more cost-effective approach would be to create more available bandwidth per user by installing switching hubs. Switching hubs segment a LAN's collision domain. That is, within the network's broadcast domain, switching hubs create multiple collision domains, each with their own bandwidth. This proved a more effective solution.

New application types also demonstrated the limitations of the embedded base of networks. They demanded different performance parameters than their supporting networks were designed to provide. For example, in a traditional Ethernet-to-MVS (Multiple Virtual Storage, an IBM mainframe operating system) connection that traversed an Internet Protocol (IP) WAN, the data inside each packet had to be good. Corrupted data meant that the packet had to be present. New time-sensitive applications such as voice or videoconferencing, however, placed a higher importance on the timeliness of delivery than on data integrity. If the packet arrived intact, but two seconds late, it was discarded. Thus, traditional LANs show their maturity by failing to accommodate latency-sensitive traffic.

User requirements are driving innovations in network protocols, too. Networking protocols are adding capabilities such as Quality of Service (QoS) support, bandwidth reservation, and so on, that allow today's networks to become truly high-performance networks by supporting time-sensitive applications as handily as they accommodate traditional bulk data requests.

One of the more significant network protocols, IP, is about to receive its first major update in twenty years. The new protocol will be called IPv6, and will enable networks to adequately support evolving business requirements for many years to come.

IPv6 and other network protocols are adding security features at the network layer. Features such as authentication and encryption that previously could only be implemented at the host level, will now be a native part of the network. This will allow networks to be interconnected in ways that were previously unthinkable. "Open" IP networks of different companies will be directly internetworked in "extranets." These extranets will be functional extensions of corporate intranets that link business partners together in a secure, controlled fashion.

As today's networks become faster and more feature rich, one other important change must occur. Traditionally, data communications experts stayed in the network layer, arrogantly dismissing applications, data, protocols, and so on, as nothing more than 1s and 0s in the stream. The increasing variety of applications, and the subsequent variety of network performance requirements, leaves no room for such aloofness. Today, data communications experts must venture further up the "stack," sometimes as far as the application layer. Their network skills must be augmented with at least a working knowledge of the applications that rely upon networks. More importantly, the specialized performance needs of these applications must be understood in order to unleash the power of high-performance networks.

This book will take you step by step through all of the components that comprise a high-performance network, and provide you with everything you will need to begin building and running your own high-performance network. The Open Systems Interconnection (OSI) 7-layer reference model is used throughout this book as a context for examining the various components and functions of a network. This examination begins with the physical layer.

Networking Glossary: 150+ Words You Should Know

There are a lot of terms used in this book that many of our readers may not be familiar with. To help get you started, we are offering definitions of about 150 networking terms that you should be familiar with.

10base-2

The version of Ethernet that uses thin coaxial cable. The name is derived from the speed of the network (10Mbps), the signaling type (baseband), and the maximum cable length (almost 200 meters).

10base-T

The version of Ethernet that uses twisted-pair cabling. The name is derived from the speed of the network (10Mbps), the signaling type (baseband), and the cable type (twisted pair).

100base-T

An extension to the 10base-T standard describing twisted-pair networks that operate at 100Mbps.

802.3

The IEEE standard that describes the CSMA/CD medium access method used in Ethernet networks.

802.5

The IEEE standard that describes the medium access method used in Token Ring networks.

ADSI (Analog Display Services Interface)

A service allowing voice mail to be viewed on your PC screen. Instead of pressing number keys on the telephone to access voice mail functions, you can use your PC to view and control incoming voice mail. A special communications server on the network handles the incoming voice mail.

ADSL (Asymmetrical Digital Subscriber Line)

A high-speed modem technology that provides data services, such as Internet access, over existing telephone lines. ADSL has a downstream (to the subscriber) data transfer rate of at least 1.5Mbps. Subscribers located within two miles of the telephone office can attain downstream speeds as high as 6.2Mbps. Upstream data rates vary from 16Kbps to 640Kbps, depending on line distance. See also asymmetrical transmission.

ANSI (American National Standards Institute)

A private organization involved with setting US standards, often referred to as ANSI standards.

anonymous FTP (Anonymous File Transfer Protocol)

A protocol that allows users to transfer files between TCP/IP-connected computers. A user will log in to an FTP server using anonymous as the user ID and guest as the password. This process gets a user into a special, usually restricted, area of the FTP server.

AppleTalk

A seven-layer protocol stack designed by Apple Computers that allows the sharing of files and printers and the sending of traffic between computers. Its primary design goal was to give the AppleTalk user a simple plug-and-play environment in which the user does not need to be concerned with the details of network configuration.

application layer

Layer 7 of the seven-layer OSI model. The application layer is responsible for interfacing with the user and directing input from the user to the lower OSI layers. It is the part of the OSI model the user interacts with directly.

ARP (Address Resolution Protocol)

A protocol, described in RFC 826, used to determine the hardware address of another computer on a network. ARP is used when a computer may know the destination computer's IP address, but does not know the destination computer's hardware address. The sender broadcasts an ARP packet and the device that recognizes its own IP address responds with the unknown hardware address.

ASCII (American Standard Code for Information Interchange)

A character set in which each letter, number, or control character is made up of a 7-bit sequence. The term ASCII is sometimes erroneously used when referring to Extended ASCII, an 8-bit character set.

asymmetrical transmission

A transmission method developed to overcome the high cost of high-speed full-duplex transmission. In essence, a line's bandwidth is broken up into two subchannels: the main channel and the secondary channel. The main channel contains the majority of the line's bandwidth, the secondary channel contains only a small portion. The unequal division of bandwidth results in an unequal data transfer rate, but allows service providers to overcome signal-coupling problems in large telephone cable plants.

asynchronous communications

A type of data transmission in which each character transmitted (8 bits) is framed by a start and stop bit. These two control bits delineate the beginning and end of a character. Though there is more flexibility with asynchronous transmission, it is much less efficient because the addition of the control bits increases the packet size by 25percent.

AT command set

The modem command set developed by Hayes, Inc. that has become the de facto standard for programming modems.

ATM (Asynchronous Transfer Mode)

A high-speed connection-oriented switching technology that uses 53-byte cells (packets) to simultaneously transmit different types of data, including video and voice. ATM is an attractive technology because it provides dedicated bandwidth at speeds ranging from 25Mbps to 655Mbps.

AUI (Attachment Unit Interface)

The cable that attaches from a MAU or transceiver to a computer. The AUI cable consists of 15-pin D-shell type connectors, female on the computer end and male on the transceiver end.

authentication

The computer security process of verifying a user's identity or the user's eligibility to access network resources. See also public key encryption.

autonomous system

A group of routers or networks that fall under one network administrative organization. Autonomous systems usually run on a single routing protocol.

B-channel

A 64Kbps ISDN channel used to transmit voice or data. The standard BRI connection contains two B-channels, for a total uncompressed capacity of 128Kbps.

backbone

A network that interconnects individual LANs and that typically has a higher capacity than the LANs being connected. One exception is a T-1 backbone connecting a WAN connecting two 100Mbps Ethernet LANs at either end of the backbone. In this case, the LANs have a much higher capacity than the backbone.

backoff

From CSMA/CD, when a collision occurs on a network, the computer sensing the collision calculates a time delay before trying to transmit again. This time delay is referred to as backoff.

balun

An impedance-matching device used when connecting different types of cable to each other. For example, a balun is required to connect twisted pair cable to coaxial cable on an Ethernet network.

bandwidth

The width of the passband or the difference between the highest and lowest frequencies in a given range. For example, the human voice has a passband of approximately 50Hz to −15,000Hz, which translates to a bandwidth of 14,950Hz.

baseband

A type of transmission that uses digital signals to move data. Because the signal is digital, the entire bandwidth of the cable is used.

BER (Bit Error Rate)

The ratio of received bits that are in error. Diagnostic cable-checking tools sense BER by transmitting a stream of data on one end of a cable and reading the output from the other end.

best-effort delivery

A network function where an attempt is made at delivering data; however, if an error such as line failure occurs, it does not attempt recovery. There is no mechanism in best-effort delivery to buffer data then retransmit it once the failure has been resolved.

BISDN (Broadband ISDN)

The next generation of ISDN service. BISDN is a fiber-optic–based service using asynchronous transfer mode (ATM) over SONET-based transmission circuits. The service is designed to handle high-bandwidth applications, such as video, at rates of 155Mbps, 622Mbps, and higher.

BONDING (Bandwidth ON Demand INteroperability Group)

An ISDN consortium name and the technique of inverse multiplexing they developed. Data is broken up into a stream of frames, each stream using a portion of the total available bandwidth. If your ISDN configuration has two B-channels, each with 64Kbps, your equipment will allow a data rate of 128Kbps by splitting the data.

BOOTP (BOOTstrap Protocol)

A protocol designed to allow diskless workstations to boot onto an IP network. A single BOOTP message contains many pieces of information needed by a workstation at startup, such as an IP address, the address of a gateway, and the address of a server. A workstation that boots up requests this information from a BOOTP server.

BRI (Basic Rate Interface)

The ISDN interface often comprised of two B-channels and one D-channel for circuit-switched communications of voice, data, and video. Depending on connection requirements and the local telephone company, it is possible to purchase just one B-channel.

bridge

A device that interconnects two or more LANs. A bridge is often used to segment a LAN to increase bandwidth on the new segments. Although the segments operate logically as one LAN, the repartitioning prevents data from being broadcast indiscriminately across the entire network.

broadband

A type of transmission using coaxial cable and analog or radio-frequency signals. Broadband uses a frequency band that is divided into several narrower bands, so different kinds of transmission (data, voice, and video) can be transmitted at the same time.

brouter

This term has various definitions, but it usually refers to a device that performs the functions of both a bridge and a multiprotocol router. The term is often misused to describe a bridge with more than two LAN connections.

buffer

A location in memory set aside to temporarily hold data. It is often used to compensate for a difference in data flow rates between devices or skews in event timings; many network devices such as network interface cards (NIC) and routers have integrated buffer storage.

cable modem

A specialized, currently experimental modem service offered by cable companies that provides Internet access at speeds of 10Mbps downstream (to the subscriber) and 768Kbps upstream. The cabling infrastructure is already in place, but the service requires the cable company to replace existing equipment with expensive two-way transmission hardware.

capacity planning

The process of determining the future requirements of a network. An important process, if a network is to function properly and at peak performance, especially when users or equipment is added to the network.

category cable

Cable that complies with standard network cable specifications and is rated category 1 through 5. The higher the number, the higher the speed capability of the cable. The wire may be shielded or unshielded and always has an impedance of 100 ohms.

CAT-5 (Category 5)

A cabling standard for use on networks at speeds of up to 100 Mbits, including FDDI and 100base-T. The 5 refers to the number of turns per inch with which the cable is constructed. See also category cable.

CERT (Computer Emergency Response Team)

Formed in 1988 by the Defense Advanced Research Projects Agency (DARPA) to help facilitate and resolve Internet security issues. CERT was formed in response to the Internet worm written by Robert Morris, Jr., which infected thousands of Internet computers in 1988.

circuit switching

A method of transmission in which a fixed path is established between the nodes communicating. This fixed path permits exclusive use of the circuit between the nodes until the connection is dropped. The public telephone network uses circuit switching.

client/server model

> A common way to describe the rules and concepts behind many network protocols. The client, usually a user's computer and its software, makes requests for information or programs from a server located somewhere on the network.

collision

> The result of two or more computers trying to access the network medium at the same time. Ethernet uses CSMA/CD to handle collisions and to coordinate retransmission.

community string

> A password used by the Simple Network Management Protocol (SNMP) that allows an SNMP manager station access to an agent's Management Information Base (MIB) database.

configuration management

> The process of retrieving data from network devices and using the information to manage the setup of the devices. For example, SNMP has the ability to automatically or manually retrieve data from SNMP-enabled network devices. Based on this data, a network manager can decide whether configuration changes are necessary to maintain network performance.

connection-oriented communications

> The transmission of data across a path that stays established until one of the nodes drops the connection. This type of logical connection guarantees that all blocks of data will be delivered reliably. Telnet is an example of connection-oriented communications.

connectionless communications

> The transmission of data across a network in which each packet is individually routed to its destination, based on information contained in the packet header. The path the data takes is generally unknown because there is no established connection between the computers that are communicating. Connectionless services can drop packets or deliver them out of sequence if each of the packets gets routed differently.

cookie

> A piece of information sent by content providers on the Internet that gets written to the user's local disk. The content providers often use this information to track where visitors link to on their Web site. Most browsers can be configured to disallow the writing of such data to user's disks.

CSMA/CD (Carrier Sense, Multiple Access with Collision Detection)

The medium access method used in Ethernet to avoid having more than one host transmitting on a LAN segment at a time. The transmitting host first *listens* for traffic on the cable and then transmits, if no traffic is detected. If two hosts transmit at the same time, a collision occurs. Each host then waits for a random length of time before listening and transmitting again.

CSU (Channel Service Unit)

The hardware interface to a Digital Data Service, for example, a T-1 line. The CSU provides line termination, signal amplification, and has the diagnostic ability to loop a signal back to its source. See also DSU (Data Service Unit).

datagram

A method of sending data in which some parts of the message are sent in random order. The destination computer has the task of reassembling the parts in the correct sequence. The datagram is a connectionless, single packet message used by the Internet Protocol (IP). A datagram is comprised of a source network address, a destination network address, and information.

D-channel

The ISDN channel used to deliver network control information; often referred to as out-of-band signaling. Because many telephone companies are not configured for out-of-band signaling, they combine the D-channel information with a B-channel. The result of this combination is lower data rates, 56Kbps and 112Kbps, because of the overhead added to the B-channel.

data link layer

Layer 2 of the seven-layer OSI model. The data link layer is concerned with managing network access, for example, performing collision sensing and network control. Also, if the data link layer detects an error, it arranges to have the sending computer resend the corrupt packet.

DDS (Digital Data Service)

A leased digital transmission line offering speeds ranging from switched 56Kbps, to T-1 (1.544Mbps), or to T-3 service operating at 44.736Mbps. When DDS is employed, special digital modems called CSUs and DSUs are used to interface between the DDS line and the LAN.

DES (Data Encryption Standard)

An encryption algorithm based on a 64-bit key. DES is considered the most secure encryption algorithm available, but not the easiest to implement and maintain.

digital ID

An emerging technology using public-key cryptography to make Internet and intranet transactions secure.

DLCI (Data Link Connection Identifier)

A Frame Relay term describing the identifier given to each connection point. The DLCI is used so a node can communicate with the first Frame Relay machine. Then that machine maps the data to another DLCI it uses for its link with the next Frame Relay machine, and so on, until the destination node is reached.

DN (Directory Number)

The directory number is the address for the ISDN line assigned by the telephone company. The type of equipment the telephone company uses at its central office determines whether each of the two B-channels will be assigned their own directory numbers.

DNS (Domain Name Server)

A computer used to map IP addresses to computer system names. A network administrator creates a list on the domain name server where each line contains a specific computer's IP address and a name associated with that computer. When someone wants to access another computer, either the IP address or the name of the computer is used. Using names is easier than remembering scores of IP addresses.

domain

Part of the naming hierarchy used on the Internet and syntactically represented by a series of names separated by dots. Take, for example, the domain name CATJO.BONZO.BOBO.COM. Read right-to-left, the address provides the path to a company (COM) named BOBO, to a company network named BONZO, and finally to the destination computer named CATJO.

DS 1-4 (Digital Services 1-4)

The connection services offered by the telephone companies through T-carriers, more commonly known as T-1, T-2, T-3, and T-4.

Service	T-Carrier	Voice Channels	Rate (Mbps)
DS-1	T-1	24	1.544
DS-2	T-2	96	6.312
DS-3	T-3	672	44.736
DS-4	T-4	4032	274.176

DSL (Digital Subscriber Line)

Modems on either end of a single twisted-pair wire that deliver ISDN Basic Rate Access. A DSL transmits duplex data at 160Kbps over 24-gauge copper lines at distances up to 18,000 feet. The multiplexing and de-multiplexing of this data stream creates two B-channels (64Kbps each), a D-channel (16Kbps), and some overhead that takes place for attached terminal equipment. DSL employs echo cancellation to separate the transmit signal and the receive signal at both ends.

DSS1 (Digital Subscriber Signaling System No. 1)

A set of protocols in ISDN designed so your equipment can ask for specific services across the network. Directed at the carrier's switching equipment, DSS1 sends message types that provide the specific control (for example, connect, hold, and restart) to be taken.

DSU (Data Service Unit)

A DSU provides the interface between the Data Terminal Equipment (DTE) and the Channel Service Unit (CSU) when a network is connected to a Digital Data Service (DDS). The DSU's primary functions are to properly convert a DTE's output signals to the format required by the DDS and to provide control signaling.

DVMRP (Distance Vector Multicast Routing)

A protocol used to support IP Multicast. As users join or leave multicast groups, data is broadcast to each router in the internetwork. The routers *prune* out the users who do not want further transmissions.

encapsulation

A method of wrapping data in a particular protocol header. For example, Ethernet data is wrapped in a special Ethernet header before transmission. Encapsulation is also used when sending data across dissimilar networks. When a frame arrives at the router, it is encapsulated with the header used by the link-layer protocol of the receiving network before it is transmitted.

encryption

A technique of altering data so it becomes incomprehensible to unintended recipients. Encryption algorithms can be simple (for example, associate each letter in the alphabet to a number) or extremely complex (for example, public-key encryption).

Ethernet

The most widely used type of LAN environment, with common operating speeds of 10Mbps and 100Mbps. Ethernet uses the Carrier Sense, Multiple Access with Collision Detection (CSMA/CD) discipline.

Ethernet switch

> A hub-like device that reads the destination address in the header of an Ethernet packet and redirects the packet to the proper destination port. By sending the packets only to the destination port and not all other ports, an Ethernet switch increases the amount of data that can be transmitted on the network at one time. Contrast a switch with a standard repeating hub, which takes incoming traffic and repeats it across all ports regardless of the intended destination.

fast-Ethernet switch

> An Ethernet switch that operates on a 100Mbps LAN.

fault tolerance

> The ability of a network to function even after some hardware or software components have failed and are not available to the user. Fault-tolerant networks attempt to maintain availability by using component redundancy (hardware and/or software) and the concept of atomicity (that is, either all parts of a transaction occur or none at all).

FDDI (Fiber Distributed Data Interface)

> A 100Mbps fiber-optic LAN standard that operates on Token Ring mechanics and is usually installed as a backbone. A full duplex (send and receive simultaneously) configuration is possible, which doubles the transmission throughput to 200Mbps.

file server

> A computer attached to a network that provides mass disk storage and file services to users. Most often a file server is setup so that only select users or groups of users can access the resource.

firewall

> A hardware and software device that protects and controls the connection of one network to other networks. The firewall prevents unwanted or unauthorized traffic from entering a network and also allows only selected traffic to leave a network.

fractional T-1

> A full T-1 line consists of 24 64Kbps channels. It is possible to purchase only a portion of a T-1 line, depending on resource needs; hence the term fractional T-1.

fragment

> Part of a data packet. If a router sends data to a network that has a maximum packet size smaller than the packet itself, the router is forced to break up the packet into smaller fragments.

Frame Relay

A technique using virtual connections to transport data between networks attached to a WAN. Packets are routed to their destination based on the DLCI number assigned to each of the nodes that are members of the Frame Relay cloud. The cloud is the part of the network the telephone company handles. To the user, it's unknown what happens inside the cloud; data goes in the cloud, then comes out and arrives at the correct destination.

frequency division multiplexing (FDM)

The technique of dividing a specific frequency range into smaller parts, with each part maintaining enough bandwidth to carry one channel.

fubar or foobar

Fouled Up Beyond All Repair. There are also other more colorful versions of this slang term.

full-duplex

The capability of having two-way data transmission in both directions (send and receive) simultaneously. Contrast to half-duplex.

gateway

A network device that performs protocol conversion between dissimilar networks. A gateway is typically used to provide access to wide area networks over asynchronous links from a LAN environment.

half-duplex

A method of two-way transmission, but data can only travel in one direction at a time. Contrast to full-duplex.

hardware address

Also called the physical address, it is a data link address associated with a particular network device.

HDLC (High-Level Data Link Control)

The most widely used synchronous data link protocol in existence. It supports both half-duplex and full-duplex transmission, point-to-point configurations, and switched or non-switched channels.

HDSL (High data rate Digital Subscribe Line)

Modems on either end of one or more twisted-pair wires that deliver T-1 or E-1 transmission speeds. Presently, T-1 service requires two lines and E-1 requires three.

HIPPI (High Performance Parallel Interface)

A standard that extends a computer bus over short distances at speeds of 800 to 1600Mbps. HIPPI is often associated with supercomputers.

hop

A routing term that refers to the number of times data travels through a router before reaching its destination.

hub

A device that connects to several other devices, usually in a star topology. For example, a 12-port hub attached to a 100base-T LAN backbone allows 12 devices or segments to connect to the LAN. There are two type of hubs: Dumb hubs simply act as repeaters and smart hubs have sophisticated features such as SNMP support or built-in bridging or routing functions.

ICMP (Internet Control Message Protocol)

The protocol that handles errors and control messages at the Internet Protocol (IP) layer. For example, when a data packet is transmitted with incorrect destination information, the router attached to the network responds with an ICMP message indicating an error occurred within the transmission.

IGRP (Interior Gateway Routing Protocol)

A protocol developed by Cisco Systems that is used on networks that are under common administration. This protocol was designed to operate on large, complex topology networks with segments that have different bandwidth and delay characteristics. As with other routing protocols, IGRP determines where to send data packets that have destination addresses outside the local network.

interoperability

The ability of applications and hardware combinations on two or more computer systems to communicate successfully with each other. Standards set by groups such as the IEEE are the reason why devices from different vendors operating across multiple platforms are capable of working with each other.

intranet

A term that describes a spin on Web technology that uses servers and browsers to set up a private Internet.

IP (Internet Protocol)

A network layer protocol that contains addressing information and some control information so packets can be routed across an internetwork. The ICMP control and message protocol are integrated within IP, also.

IP Multicast

A method of sending data simultaneously to a selected group of recipients. Multicast makes efficient use of bandwidth because it unicasts to all intended recipients and avoids broadcasting to unnecessary destinations.

Ipng or IPv6

The next generation (ng) of Internet addressing. The current 32-bit Internet addressing scheme (IPv4) is severely strained by current Internet growth. IPv6 (64-bit) is one proposed next generation method of increasing the number of available Internet addresses while also providing additional functionality.

IP switching

An ATM switch capable of routing IP. Standard ATM switches cannot accommodate IP without complicated and difficult-to-manage software translation. By implementing the IP protocol stack on ATM hardware, full compatibility with existing IP networks is maintained while reaping the benefits of the high-speed throughputs associated with ATM.

IPX (Internetwork Packet Exchange)

A protocol suite developed by Novell, Inc. and used by computer systems attached to a network running the NetWare operating system. IPX provides a best-effort delivery service and is equivalent to the IP of TCP/IP.

ISDN (Integrated Services Digital Network)

A type of network provided by the telephone companies that allows both voice and digital services to be combined over a single medium. ISDN services are delivered over standard POTS lines at a speed of 128Kbps.

isochronous service

A transmission service in which the data channel has a guaranteed bandwidth. Bandwidth on an isochronous service is preallocated and stays fixed, whether the bandwidth is used or not, guaranteeing that the required bandwidth is available when it is needed. FDDI and ATM, handling audio and video data, are examples of technologies that support isochronous service.

ISP (Internet service provider)

A company that provides direct access to the Internet as opposed to an online service (for example, America Online or CompuServe) that provides Internet access through a gateway. ISPs usually offer a large range of services, such as Gopher, Archie, Telnet, FTP, or WWW.

jabber

Continuously sent random or garbage data.

jam signal

In Ethernet, a signal generated by a network interface to let other devices know that a collision has occurred.

keep alive

A message sent over an idle network link. The message tells a remote computer that the local computer remains operational and is waiting.

Kerberos

An authentication system used for open systems and networks. Developed at MIT, Kerberos can be added onto any existing protocol. The system uses an adaptation of DES (Data Encryption Standard) and tickets to protect messages sent on a network by a user and by the system. Kerberos never transmits passwords over the network. Contrast Kerberos to public key encryption.

LATA (Local Access Transport Area)

Telephone companies operate within specific geographical regions divided into areas called LATAs. A connection made between two points within the same LATA implies that a connection is local. A connection outside the LATA requires the use of an Interexchange Carrier or long-distance company.

LDAP (Lightweight Directory Access Protocol)

A new protocol, also known as X.500 Lite, that simplifies the complex structure of Internet directories (databases) that handle client information about users and e-mail addresses.

leased line

A permanent circuit provided by the telephone company. Communications on a leased line are not established by dialing and are usually configured as a direct point-to-point connection. A T-1 connection is an example of a leased line.

local loop

The copper twisted-pair cable from the telephone company's central office to an end user's location. The local loop is the determining factor in the data rate associated with your use of the telephone system.

MAC (Media Access Control)

The lower portion of the data link layer responsible for control of access to the physical medium.

MAN (Metropolitan Area Network)

A data network intended to serve an area approximating that of a large city.

managed object

Devices on a network such as workstations, hubs, servers, and routers that are all monitored via SNMP. Each device contains hardware or software that allows it to communicate with the SNMP manager station responsible for tracking all the managed network components.

MAU (Media Attachment Unit)

A device that physically attaches to a LAN and allows the connection of computers or additional LAN segments. A MAU is often referred to as a transceiver and attaches to a computer through an AUI cable.

MIB (Management Information Base)

In SNMP, the MIB is the database where information about the managed objects is stored. The structure of an MIB is complex and can contain information about many aspects of the device being managed.

MIME (Multipurpose Internet Mail Extensions)

A standard set of definitions designed to handle non-ASCII e-mail. MIME specifies how binary data, such as graphical images, can be attached to Internet e-mail. The process of attaching binary data to e-mail requires encoding between two types of data formats. It is MIME's responsibility to handle the encoding and the decoding at the destination.

modem (modulator-demodulator)

A communication device that performs conversion of digital signals into analog signals (transmission) and analog signals into digital signals (receiving). This conversion is necessary if communication over standard POTS is attempted.

multicast

The process of sending messages to a defined set of destinations. Unlike a broadcast, which is read by all destinations that receive them, a multicast is received only by those destinations that are part of a predefined group configured to receive multicast messages.

multicast multimedia transmission

A multicast transmission of video. Rather than sending individual streams of video to each user (unicast), multicast multimedia transmission sends a stream of video that is shared among users assuming the user is configured to receive such transmissions. See also multicast.

multimode fiber

A type of fiber-optic cable. The word mode is synonymous with ray; you can think of multimode fiber as transmitting multiple rays. Multimode fiber typically has a core diameter of 62.5 microns and is usually selected for short haul networks (less than 2km).

multiplexer

A device used to combine data transmitted from many low-to-medium speed devices onto one or more high-speed paths for retransmission. There are various techniques for achieving this, such as time division, frequency division, statistical time division, and wavelength division multiplexing. A multiplexer is sometimes called a concentrator.

multiport repeater

A type of hub used to join multiple LAN segments. When a segment exceeds its maximum allowable nodes, a repeater is often used to expand the network. See also segmentation.

NetBIOS (Network Binary Input Output System)

Software developed by IBM that extends the interface between the PC operating system and the PC I/O bus to include attachment to a network. Since its design, NetBIOS has become a de facto standard, providing the basic framework for PCs to operate on a LAN.

network layer

Layer 3 of the seven-layer OSI model. The network layer plans the routing of packets and is responsible for addressing and delivering messages from the sender to the final destination. A simple network comprised of a few LANs linked by bridges would not need a Layer 3 at all, because there is no routing involved.

network management

The job of controlling a network so it can be used in an efficient manner. Network management is divided into five management categories: performance, fault, accounting, security, and configuration.

NNTP (Network News Transport Protocol)

A protocol that allows Internet users to access Usenet groups.

OC-1 to 48 (Optical Carrier 1–48)

The high-speed optical carrier networks used by the telephone companies. OC services provide much higher speeds than T-carrier services such as T-1 or T-2.

OC Service	Data Rate
OC-1	51.84Mbps
OC-12	622.08Mbps
OC-24	1244.16Mbps
OC-48	2488.32Mbps

OPR (Optical Packet Router)

A device demonstrated by British Telecom that is capable of routing data on fiber-optic cable at 100Gbps. The router works by reading the destination address of the encoded pulses of light and switching the data to the appropriate output path toward the destination. Because the data rates are about 100 times faster than current non-optical routers, this technology has significant implications for high-speed networks in the future.

optical matrix switch

A device that simply cross-connects one or more fiber-optic cables. This type of switch allows a network to be reconfigured quickly and easily to accommodate specific requirements or workgroup moves. For example, an ATM LAN could be connected to other multiple protocol networks within a building by optical switches, if needed.

OSI model

A concept developed by ISO and CCITT used to develop standards for data networking that promote multivendor equipment interoperability. The OSI model is separated into seven layers that relate to the interconnection of computer systems. See also application layer, presentation layer, session layer, transport layer, network layer, data link layer, and physical layer.

OSPF (Open Shortest Path First)

A protocol that routers use to communicate between themselves. OSPF has the ability to configure topologies and adapt to changes in the Internet. It can also balance traffic loads by determining which routes offer the best service.

OTDR (Optical Time Domain Reflectometer)

Diagnostic equipment used to calculate the length and attenuation of a fiber-optic cable. By sending a short duration laser pulse into one end of the fiber, the fiber's length is calculated by measuring the amount of time it takes for a reflection to return from the other end.

packet

A group of bits comprised of address, data, and control information that is combined and transmitted as one unit. The terms frame and packet are often used synonymously.

packet-switched network

A networking technique where data is broken into small packets and then transmitted to other networks over a WAN to computers configured as packet switches where the data is then reassembled. The packets get routed and rerouted, depending on the size of the network or the distance the packets travel to their destination.

passband

The range of frequencies a data line is capable of handling. Passband is often confused with bandwidth, the width of a channel contained within the passband.

peer-to-peer

Communication between computers in which neither computer has control over the other.

performance management

The process of analyzing the characteristics of a network to monitor and increase its efficiency. For example, a network manager may monitor a network using a Sniffer and develop statistics from that data in hopes of finding ways to increase available bandwidth on a crowded network.

physical layer

Layer 1 of the seven-layer OSI model, which specifies the physical medium of a network. It is the wire on which data is transmitted and it is the connectors, hubs, and repeaters that comprise the network. Some refer to the physical layer as the hardware layer.

Ping (Packet Internet Groper)

A utility program used to determine whether a remote computer is reachable by sending it multiple ICMP echo requests and then waiting for a response.

POP (Point Of Presence)

The connection site where entry to a WAN or the public switched network occurs. The term is most often heard when referring to Internet service providers (ISPs) and their dial-up access locations.

POTS (Plain Old Telephone Service)

Single line twisted-pair residential telephone service.

PPP (Point-to-Point Protocol)

A point-to-point circuit is a network configuration where a connection exists only between two points. PPP is the protocol for transmitting routing information over synchronous or asynchronous point-to-point circuits. The routing information allows different vendor's equipment to interoperate over point-to-point circuits.

PPTP (Point-to-Point Tunneling Protocol)

A secure remote access protocol, developed by Ascend Communications, Inc. and touted by Microsoft Corp. for their Windows platforms, that allows remote users to access their corporate network(s) via the Internet. PPTP makes use of encryption to secure the virtual private connection between the user and the corporate network. The tunneling nature of PPTP allows users to piggyback IPX and NetBEUI on IP packets.

presentation layer

Layer 6 of the seven-layer OSI model. The presentation layer makes sure that data sent to the application layer is in the correct format. If some conversion were required between different data types, it would take place at this layer. Translation and byte reordering is sometimes necessary when different computers (for example, IBM, Apple, NeXT) want to share information.

PRI (Primary Rate Interface)

An ISDN interface consisting of 23 B-channels, operating at 64Kbps each, and one 64Kbps D-channel. Companies installing multiple ISDN lines often use PRI to provide sufficient bandwidth for their network(s). PRI service is referred to as 23B+D.

protocol

A set of rules governing how information flows within a network. Protocols control format, timing, and error correction. They are essential for a device to be able to interpret incoming information. Suites of protocols are often used in networks, with each protocol responsible for one part of a communications function.

protocol emulator

A computer that generates the protocols required by another computer. The term, protocol converter, is often used in place of protocol emulator. A converter is slightly different in that it translates data between two dissimilar protocols so that different systems can communicate with each other.

proxy agent

In SNMP, a device that gathers information about other SNMP-enabled devices on the network. At some predetermined time, the proxy agent will relay the stored information to the SNMP management station for analysis.

public key encryption

A form of asymmetric encryption in which encryption and decryption are performed using two separate keys. One key is referred to as the public key, the other as the private key. The public key is made available to everyone and is used to encrypt a message. The owner of the public key receives a message encrypted with his public key and then decrypts the message with his private key, the only key that can decrypt the message.

punch down block

A wire termination device in which wire is placed across a Y-shaped connector and then connected or punched down using a special tool. The connections made on a punch down block are very reliable.

PVC (Permanent Virtual Circuit)

A circuit that is permanently dedicated, such as a leased line. The virtual aspect of PVC is that a user does not know what path the data took to get to its destination after the data has entered the circuits of the telephone company's central office.

RARP (Reverse Address Resolution Protocol)

The logical reverse of ARP. RARP is used to determine the IP address of a computer on a TCP/IP network when only the hardware address is known.

repeater

A device used to increase the length of a LAN or to increase the distance between devices attached to the LAN. The span can be increased because a repeater regenerates the signals before retransmitting them.

RFC (Request For Comments)

Documents outlining standards and procedures for the Internet. These numbered documents are controlled by the Internet Activities Board (IAB) and are available in hard-copy from the Defense Data Network, Network Information Center, (DDN/NIC) or electronically over the Internet.

RG58

50 ohm coaxial cable used in 10base-2 Ethernet networks. Often referred to as ThinNet or CheapNet.

RJ45

A standard 8-pin conductor modular plug. The RJ45 connector is replacing the RJ11 (6-pin) connector for use in 10base-T networks. RJ45 connectors look very similar to the old RJ11 modular jack used on telephones.

RMON MIB (Remote Network Monitoring Management Information Base)

The standard that defines the information sent to and from devices within a network using SNMP. To ease the difficulties in managing networks spanning large geographical areas, remote management devices or probes are placed on remote segments to act as the eyes and ears of the network management system. RMON MIB defines what data passes between the remote devices and the SNMP manager.

1

router

In general terms, a router makes decisions about which of several possible network paths data will follow. In a TCP/IP network, a router reads IP destination addresses to determine routes.

routing table

A directory contained in a router's memory that contains the addresses of other networks or devices and how to reach them.

RPC (Remote Procedure Call)

A complex facility that allows a local process or program to invoke a remote process.

SCSI (small computer systems interface)

A high-performance bus for connecting peripherals to a computer. The SCSI interface, or host card, allows multiple SCSI-compatible devices to attach to the bus. SCSI's design intent is two-fold: increase throughput speed and decrease the number of problems associated with hardware compatibility.

SDSL (Single line Digital Subscriber Line)

HDSL over a single telephone line. This name has not been set by any standards group, and may not stick. SDSL operates over POTS and would be suitable for symmetric services to the premises of individual customers.

segment

A bus LAN term meaning an electrically continuous piece of the bus. Segments can be joined together using repeaters or bridges.

segmentation

The process of splitting a network into multiple segments. A multiport repeater is one device often used to segment LANs. In diagnostic terms, segmenting a network minimizes the difficulty of analyzing network faults. Rather than the whole network being inoperable, only the segment with the fault ceases to function.

serial link

A connection where the data bits are transmitted sequentially over a single channel.

session layer

Layer 5 of the seven-layer OSI model. The session layer defines the session type between two computers and controls the dialogue between the applications on those two computers. For example, when a user accesses another computer, a session that allows computer applications to inform each other of any problems is created and controlled by Layer 5.

singlemode fiber

> A type of fiber-optic cable. Singlemode fiber typically has a core diameter of 8 microns and is usually selected for high bandwidth, long haul networks (greater than 2 km). It is also the most difficult optical cable to splice and terminate because of its small core diameter.

SLIP (Serial Line Internet Protocol)

> An Internet protocol used to run IP over serial lines, such as telephone circuits, and connecting two computers. Though similar to PPP, SLIP supports only IP and is not as efficient as PPP.

SMDS (Switched Multimegabit Data Service)

> Pronounced "smuds," SMDS is a high-speed, datagram-based, public data network. SMDS currently allows several remotely located LANs to communicate with each other at 45Mbps (T-3) speeds.

SMTP (Simple Mail Transfer Protocol)

> The TCP/IP standard protocol used to transfer e-mail from one computer to another. SMTP manages mail functions such as establishing a sender's credentials and ensuring a recipient's mailbox is correct.

Sniffer

> Originally the name for the protocol analyzer from Network General, but now incorrectly used to describe protocol analyzers in general. A Sniffer decodes and interprets frames on LANs with more than one protocol. A user programs the Sniffer with search criteria and starts the packet capture process. When the capture is complete, the results are displayed on the screen.

SNMP (Simple Network Management Protocol)

> A network system framework designed to collect report information, configuration information, and performance data with the use of SNMP managers and agents. An agent is a device such as a hub, a router, or even a computer that has the capability to store SNMP data, such as information about whether the device is functioning properly. A manager is the device that retrieves SNMP data from the agent devices installed on the network.

SONET (Synchronous Optical NETwork)

> A high-speed fiber-optic network used to interconnect high-speed networks. SONET can carry data 50 times faster than T-3 rates while providing higher-quality signals. SONET operates by multiplexing low-speed lines onto high-speed trunk lines.

spanning tree

An algorithm used by bridges to automatically develop routing tables, a list of possible data paths, and update that table anytime the network topology changes. Spanning tree is used to avoid network loops by ensuring there is only one route between any two LANs in the bridged network.

SPID (Service Profile IDentifier)

A number used to identify the ISDN device to the telephone network, much as an Ethernet address uniquely identifies a network interface card. A SPID is assigned to each channel of an ISDN line.

spooling

The process of controlling data, usually to a printer. Spooling uses buffer storage to reduce processing delays when transferring large amounts of data between printers and computers. The term is derived from the expression simultaneous peripheral operation Online.

SS7 (Signaling System 7)

A transmission system based on the use of a *dumb* switch and a *smart* database. By using this database and switch combination, the number of network features is significantly increased. Another advantage of SS7 is that networks can be easily customized because more knowledge can be contained in the database than can be embedded cost effectively in hardware.

subnet mask

A 32-bit mask used to interpret the network address from the host addresses in an IP address.

subscriber loop

The connection between the user's equipment and a telephone company's central office.

switched virtual circuit (SVC)

In packet switching, SVC gives the user the appearance of an actual connection. An SVC is dynamically established when needed.

synchronous transmission

A method of data transfer in which characters are blocked together for transmission as a group. Special synchronization characters are placed at the beginning and end of each block to delineate the start and end of the block. Contrast with asynchronous transmission.

T-1

A T-carrier that operates at 1.544Mbps. See also DS1-4.

T-3

A T-carrier that operates at 44.736Mbps. See also DS1-4.

T-Carrier

The U.S. standard for digital transmission lines. The line types are of the form T-n, as in T-1 or T-3, and the corresponding line signal standards of the form DS-n, as in DS-1 or DS-4.

TA (Terminal Adapter)

The terminal adapter's function is to adapt non-ISDN equipment to ISDN. For example, you will often see a terminal adapter marked with an R interface that is a connection point typically for an analog phone, a modem, or other devices that are not ISDN compliant.

Tap

The connecting device on cable-based LANs, such as Ethernet, linking to the main transmission medium. For example, taps are used to connect multiport repeaters to 10base-5 coaxial cabling.

TCP/IP (Transmission Control Protocol/Internet Protocol)

The two best-known Internet protocols that are often mistaken as a single protocol. TCP corresponds to the transport layer (Layer 4 of the OSI model) and is responsible for the reliable transmission of data. IP corresponds to the network layer (Layer 3) and provides for the connectionless service of data transmission.

terminal server

A device that connects terminals and modems to a network. Terminal server is synonymous with access server.

TFTP (Trivial File Transport Protocol)

A simplified version of FTP that transfers files from one computer to another without the need for authentication. TFTP is sometimes used to help boot diskless workstations by retrieving boot images from a remote server.

Token Ring

A popular LAN type in which access to the network is controlled by use of a token. A computer can transmit only if it has possession of the token. Data is attached to the token and the token is passed to the next computer in the sequence. Token Ring network topology is typically star-shaped but, because of the sequential nature of token passing, the network operates logically as a ring.

topology

The physical structure and organization of a network. The most common topologies are bus, tree, ring, and star.

transport layer

Layer 4 of the seven-layer OSI model. The transport layer is responsible for ensuring that data is delivered reliably between nodes. Also, if more than one packet is in process at any one time, the transport layer sequences the packets to ensure the packets get rebuilt in the correct order.

tunneling

A method of encapsulating data so it can be transmitted across a network that operates with a different protocol.

twisted pair

A transmission media consisting of two shielded or unshielded copper wires that are arranged in a precise spiral pattern. The spiral pattern is an important aspect of twisted-pair cables in order to minimize crosstalk or interference between adjoining wires. See also CAT-5.

UDP (User Datagram Protocol)

A connectionless transport protocol used by IP networks that allows an application program on one computer to send a datagram or packet to an application program on another computer. Unlike IP packets, UDP packets include a checksum (error-checking data) with the data being sent.

Usenet

The large group of computers set up to exchange information in the form of newsgroups. Any user that connects to the Internet and has the proper software can access Usenet. It is not controlled by any person or organization, so the content of each newsgroup is determined by its users.

virtual channel

A channel that appears to the user to be a simple, direct connection, but in fact is implemented in a more complex manner.

WDM (Wavelength Division Multiplexing)

A technique using an optical multiplexer to combine light sources of different wavelengths onto a fiber-optic cable. When the light reaches the end of the cable, an optical demultiplexer separates the original signals by wavelength and passes them to detector circuits for conversion back into electrical signals.

wide area network (WAN)

A data communications network designed to work over a large geographical area. Corporate WANs can connect employees across many branch offices by using various telecommunication link technologies.

wiring closet

A room that often serves as the central location for network devices. For example, a wiring closet could be located in the middle of a small building. All the network wiring would originate from this room and all the connections to the routers, hubs, and other network devices are easily accessed in one location.

worm

A program that copies itself from one computer to another, usually over a network. Like viruses, worms may damage data or degrade performance by overloading system resources. One famous worm in the late 1980s virtually brought down the global WAN of a large computer company by tying up network resources each time unwitting users opened their e-mail.

The Physical Layer

by Louis Masters

IN THIS CHAPTER

CHAPTER 2

This chapter starts with an analysis of the Open Systems Interconnect (OSI) Reference Model and how it relates to data networking. All seven layers (application, presentation, session, transport, network, data link, and physical) are explained, as well as the interaction between the layers. The OSI model gives you a way to visualize the interaction between the many parts of a data transmission.

This chapter concentrates on the physical layer of the OSI model. It covers what types of transmission media are available, gives a comprehensive explanation of how they work, and also provides specific benefits and penalties to using them. A precise comparison table is provided to aid in media analysis. The table is intended to give you an in-depth analysis of most of the better-known physical network transmission methods. This chapter arms you with a healthy knowledge of what certain types of networking media can and cannot do.

The OSI Reference Model

In 1983, the International Standards Organization (ISO) created the OSI, or X.200, model. It is a multilayered model for facilitating the transfer of information on a network. The OSI model is made up of seven layers, with each layer providing a distinct network service. By segmenting the tasks that each layer performs, it is possible to change one of the layers with little or no impact on the others. For example, you can now change your network configuration without having to change your application or your presentation layer. The basic OSI model is depicted in Figure 2.1.

The OSI model was specifically made for connecting *open systems*. These systems are designed to be open for communication with almost any other system. The model was made to break down each functional layer so that overall design complexity could be lessened. The model was constructed with several precepts in mind: 1) Each layer performs a separate function; 2) The model and its levels should be internationally portable; and 3) The number of layers should be architecturally needed, but not unwieldy.

Each layer of the model has a distinct function and purpose:

- Application layer—Provides a means for the user to access information on the network through an application. This layer is the main interface for the user to interact with the application and therefore the network. Examples include file transfer (FTP), DNS, the virtual terminal (Telnet), and electronic mail (SMTP).
- Presentation layer—Manages the presentation of the information in an ordered and meaningful manner. This layer's primary function is the syntax and semantics of the data transmission. It converts local host computer data representations into a standard network format for transmission on the network. On the receiving side, it changes the network format into the appropriate host computer's format so that data can be utilized independent of the host computer. ASCII and EBCDIC conversions, cryptography, and the like are handled here.

FIGURE 2.1.
The basic OSI model.

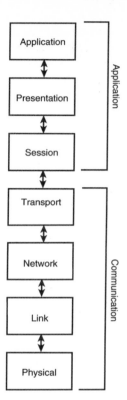

- ▪ Session layer—Coordinates dialogue/session/connection between devices over the network. This layer manages communications between connected sessions. Examples of this layer are token management (the session layer manages who has the token) and network time synchronization.

- ▪ Transport layer—Responsible for the reliable transmission of data and service specification between hosts. The major responsibility of this layer is *data integrity*—that data transmitted between hosts is reliable and timely. Upper layer datagrams are broken down into network-sized datagrams if needed and then implemented using the appropriate transmission control. The transport layer creates one or more than one network connection, depending on conditions. This layer also handles what type of connection will be created. Two major transport protocols are the TCP (Transmission Control Protocol) and the UDP (User Datagram Protocol). IP (Internet Protocol) is a good example of a network layer interface.

- ▪ Network layer—Responsible for the routing of data (packets) to a system on the network; handles the addressing and delivery of data. This layer provides for congestion control, accounting information for the network, routing, addressing, and several other functions.

■ Data link layer—Provides for the reliable delivery of data across a physical network. This layer guarantees that the information has been delivered, but not that it has been routed or accepted. This layer deals with issues such as flow regulation, error detection and control, and frames. This layer has the important task of creating and managing what frames are sent out on the network. The network data frame, or packet, is made up of checksum, source address, destination address, and the data itself. The largest packet size that can be sent defines the maximum transmission unit (MTU).

■ Physical layer—Handles the bit-level electrical/light communication across the network channel. The major concern at this level is what physical access method to use. The physical layer deals with four very important characteristics of the network: mechanical, electrical, functional, and procedural. It also defines the hardware characteristics needed to transmit the data (voltage/current levels, signal strength, connector, and media). Basically, this layer ensures that a bit sent on one side of the network is received correctly on the other side.

Data travels from the application layer of the sender, down through the levels, across the nodes of the network service, and up through the levels of the receiver. Not all of the levels for all types of data are needed—certain transmissions might not be valid at a certain level of the model. A sender-receiver OSI example is shown in Figure 2.2.

Figure 2.2.

An example of an OSI send/receive.

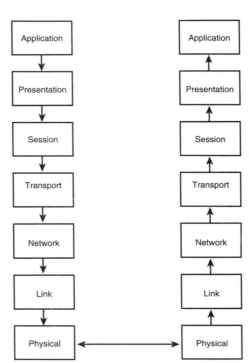

To keep track of the transmission, each layer "wraps" the preceding layer's data and header with its own header. A small chunk of data will be transmitted with multiple layers attached to it. On the receiving end, each layer strips off the header that corresponds to its respective level. Figure 2.3 illustrates how the data is wrapped by the OSI layers.

FIGURE 2.3.
The OSI level wrapper.

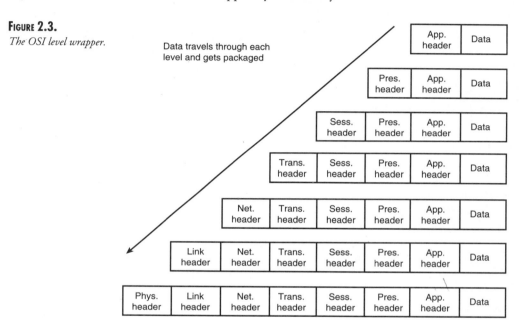

The OSI model should be used as a guide for how data is transmitted over the network. It is an abstract representation of the data pathway and should be treated as such.

Physical Media of Connectivity

For Local Area Networks (LANs), there are three principal connection schemes: twisted pair, coaxial, and fiber optic cable. Satellites, lasers, microwave, and the like can also be used for transmitting network information, but a discussion of those technologies is beyond the scope of this book.

Twisted Pair

Twisted pair (TP) is the most common form of transmission medium in use today. Quite simply, TP is a pair of wires twisted together and combined to form a cable. The entire cable is usually surrounded with a tough PVC sheath to protect it from handling or its environment. Figure 2.4 depicts TP.

Figure 2.4.
Twisted-pair cable.

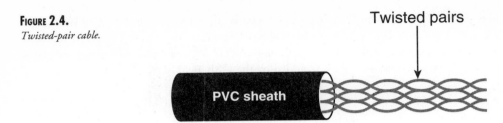

TP is normally used to carry data at speeds from 10Mbps to 100Mbps, but the speed can be decreased by a number of error characteristics: data loss, crosstalk coupling, and electromagnetic interference (EMI).

Shielding (screened twisted-pair cable and foil twisted-pair cable) may be added to TP to confine the wires' electric and magnetic fields. But, when you shield TP, you also increase *attenuation*. Attenuation is the decrease in signal strength from one point to another on the network. The shielding of the cable also causes the resistance, capacitance, and inductance to change in such a way that you may lose data on the line. This loss can make shielded TP undesirable as a reliable transportation medium. Both unshielded and shielded TP can be used in the several hundred meters segment range.

Category Specifications for TP

The five major categories of TP cable are based on specifications designed by the Electronic Industries Association and the Telecommunications Industries Association (EIA/TIA). Please note that the EIA/TIA used only unshielded twisted pair (UTP) when it defined the standard wiring categories for twisted-pair cables.

- Category 1

    Category 1 wiring is mainly used to carry voice. The CAT 1 standard was used primarily for telephone wiring prior to the early 1980s. Category 1 is not certified to carry data of any type and, in most cases, is not implemented as a cable type for data-grade wiring.

- Category 2

    Category 2 wiring is used to carry data at rates up to 4Mbps. This type of wiring is popular for older token-based networks utilizing the 4Mbps specification of the token-passing protocol. It is rated to 1MHz.

- Category 3

    Category 3 wiring is also known as voice-grade cable. It is used primarily in older Ethernet 10base-T LANs and is certified to carry data at 10Mbps. It is rated to 16MHz.

■ Category 4

Category 4 wiring is used primarily when implementing token-based or 10base-T/100base-T networks. CAT4 is certified at 16Mbps and consists of four twisted wires. It is rated to 20MHz.

■ Category 5

Category 5 wiring is the most popular Ethernet cabling category. It is capable of carrying data at rates up to 100Mbps and is used for 100base-T and 10base-T networks. It is rated to 100MHz.

Here are some points to remember:

■ TP is merely copper wires twisted in a spiral along the length of the cable.

■ Two types of TP exist: unshielded and shielded.

■ There are five major categories of TP cable wiring.

Coaxial Cable

Coaxial cable, named from the two cable axes that run the length of the wire, is a versatile and useful transmission medium. The cable consists of a solid or braided outer conductor surrounding either a solid or a stranded inner conductor. The conductors are usually separated by a dielectric material, and the entire wire is covered with an insulating jacket. Coaxial wire allows for greater shielding from interference and greater segment distances. Coaxial 10base-5/2 has a transmission rate of 10Mbps. 10base-5 has a maximum segment length of about 500m/segment, whereas 10base-2 is about 180m/segment. Figures 2.5 and 2.6 show a breakdown of coaxial cable.

FIGURE 2.5.

Cross section of coaxial cable.

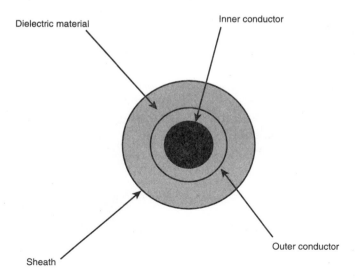

Dielectric material — Inner conductor — Outer conductor — Sheath

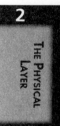

FIGURE 2.6.

Side view of coaxial cable.

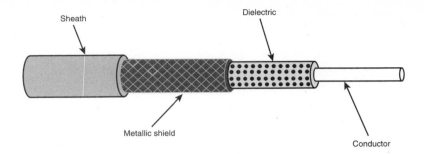

As the diameter of the coaxial cable increases, the data pipeline increases, and so does the transfer rate. But larger wires are also expensive and require special installation tools, thereby making the installation of large-circumference coaxial cable cost-prohibitive.

Here are some points to remember about coaxial cable:

- It has better noise immunity than TP.
- It consists of two pipes separated by dielectric material.
- It comes in two types: 75-ohm ($^1/_2$") and 50-ohm ($^3/_8$").

Optical Fiber

Optical fiber is a thin, flexible medium that carries data in the form of light waves through a glass "wire" or cable. This transfer medium works for distances exceeding the 1-kilometer range and is extremely secure (there is no electric signal to tap). Fiber optic cables come in two varieties: single mode and multimode (graded). The difference between the two will be explained shortly.

Fiber Cable Composition

The composition of fiber optic cable is similar to that of the coaxial cable. It has a solid core made up of one strand of ultra-thin glass or sheathed in a plastic covering (*cladding*), which reflects the light back into the cable's core. The cladding is covered by a concentric layer of thin plastic (jacket) that protects it. When there is more than one fiber, the fibers are grouped together into a bundle and covered with another thin layer of plastic. Figure 2.7 shows a diagram of fiber optic cable.

FIGURE 2.7.

Fiber optic cable.

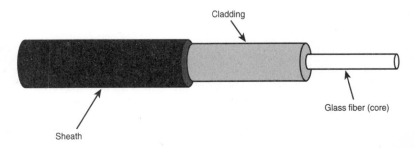

2

Fiber Refresher

As you know, the 0s and 1s your computer uses are merely on and off states. Non-fiber cable transmits this binary-state data by using pulses of electricity. Fiber, utilizing the same principle, uses light pulses to transmit data. A light source sends the data down the fiber "pipe" where, at the terminating point, it is received and converted back into data that the receiving device can use (see Figure 2.8).

FIGURE 2.8.
How fiber works.

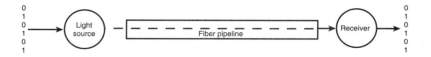

Single Versus Multimode Fiber (Axial Versus Non-Axial Paths)

If you have a thin piece of fiber wire (glass fiber), light will travel down along the axis of the wire. This is known as light traveling along an axial path, which is what happens in single-mode fiber cable (see Figure 2.9).

FIGURE 2.9.
A thin fiber showing a single mode axial path.

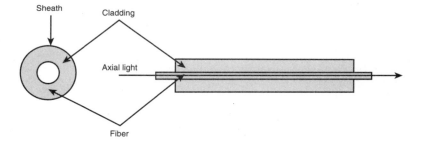

However, the power of this type of transmission is extremely limited. To lessen this limitation, wider cables are implemented. With wider cables, however, you encounter the problem that some of the light waves will enter the pipe at different angles and will travel non-axially down the cable (bouncing from wall to wall). These non-axial waves will travel for a greater distance than the waves that travel axially, causing the light to arrive at the terminating point at different times. This is known as *modal dispersion* (see Figure 2.10).

FIGURE 2.10.
A thick fiber showing non-axial paths and modal dispersion.

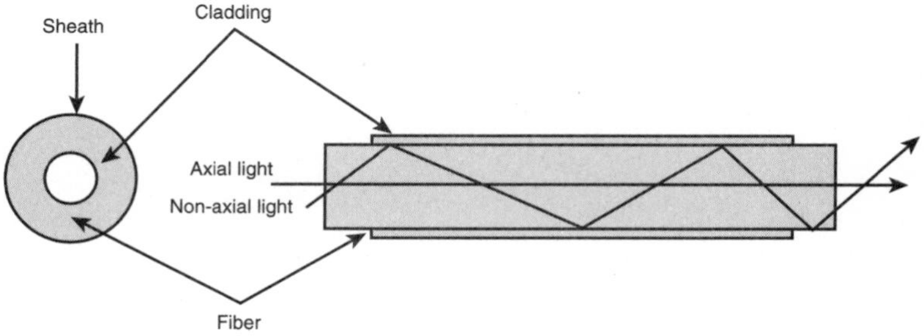

As the number of modes of light down the pipe increases, bandwidth tends to decrease. In addition to different pulses reaching the destination at slightly different times, too much dispersion also results in light pulses overlapping and "confusing" the receiving end. This results in an overall lower bandwidth. Single mode provides only enough of a data pipe for a single mode of light to be transmitted. This results in speeds greater than tens of gigabits per second and can even support multiple gigabit channels by using different wavelengths of light simultaneously. Thus, multimode fiber is slower than single mode.

The easiest way to decrease dispersion is to *grade* the fiber cable. Grading synchronizes the faster and slower light paths so that dispersion at the receiving end is limited. Dispersion can also be lessened by limiting the number of wavelengths of light. Both methods lessen dispersion somewhat but still don't approach the speeds reached by single-mode fiber.

The most popular type of multimode fiber in the United States is 62.5/125. The "62.5" is the diameter of the core, and the "125" is the diameter of the cladding (all in microns). Single-mode fiber is most common in the 5-10/125 micron range. Fiber bandwidth is usually given in MHz-km. The relationship between fiber bandwidth and distance is elastic—as distance increases, bandwidth decreases (and vice versa). At 100 meters, multimode usually reaches about 1600MHz at 850nm. Single-mode fiber reaches about 888GHz for that same 100-meter run.

LED or ILD

The light source of fiber cable may be either a *light-emitting diode* (LED) or an *injection laser diode* (ILD). Single-mode fiber generally uses LEDs as the light-generating device, whereas multimode uses ILDs.

- LED. An LED is a solid-state device that emits light when a current is applied to it. The data rates achieved by this type of signaling are in the range of 12.5Mbps to 25Mbps on distances from 0.5km to 1km, respectively. This light source is considered very weak when compared to a true laser.
- ILD. An ILD is a solid-state device that produces a very intense beam of light over a very narrow bandwidth. This results in higher data rates over longer distances. The data rates offered are between 25Mps and 100Mbps over distances up to 2km.

Here are some points to remember about fiber cable:

- It's immune to EMI.
- Transmission distances up to 10km are possible.
- Up to 4Gbps has been demonstrated in a laboratory.
- Either LED or ILD light sources can be used.

LAN Media Comparison Chart

Table 2.1 shows the advantages and disadvantages of twisted pair, coaxial, and fiber cable. You should weigh each of the advantages and disadvantages relative to the project you have at hand.

Table 2.1. Physical media comparison chart.

Medium	Advantages	Disadvantages
TP	Low cost, easy to install	Unsecure, worst noise immunity
COAX	Relatively fast on short runs	Unsecure, poor noise immunity
Fiber	Voice, data and video, fast, long distance	difficult to install, limited to point-to-point, expensive

An Introduction to LAN Technologies

The choices in the field of high-performance networking have never been as varied as they are today. Newer technologies such as Fast Ethernet, Fibre Channel, FDDI, and ATM have begun replacing their older networking forefathers, such as Token Ring and Ethernet. The following section gives you a sampling of most of the major LAN technology types.

Simple Ethernet (10base-*X*)

Simple Ethernet is one of the oldest, simplest, easiest, and cheapest LAN technologies to implement. Several varieties are available, based on medium type:

- 10base-5 (thick coaxial cable, sometimes called *thicknet*)
- 10base-2 (thin coaxial cable)
- 10base-T (twisted pair)
- 10base-F (fiber)

The architecture for all four types is basically the same. They transmit data on a LAN at speeds up to 10Mbps. They all use the CSMA/CD protocol (see the following section) to send data on the network. Currently, the most popular type of this form of Ethernet is the twisted pair variety.

2

THE PHYSICAL LAYER

CSMA/CD

The heart of the Ethernet technology lies in its Carrier Sense, Multiple Access, Collision Detect (CSMA/CD) protocol. Carrier Sense means that each station will check to see if any other station on the network is transmitting. If so, the station will not detect "carrier" and will not transmit. The station will keep trying to "capture the carrier" until the network becomes idle and the carrier becomes available. Collision Detect means that if two stations transmit at the same time, and their signals collide, they will cease their transmissions and try again at a later time (randomly determined). Multiple Access simply indicates that every station is connected by a single line on the network.

Token Ring

Token Ring is an older LAN technology based on a ring architecture. A control station creates a special entity on the network called a *token* and passes it around the network ring. This token controls which station has the right to transmit on the network. When the token reaches a station on the network that has something to transmit, it "captures" the token and changes the status of the token to busy. It also adds to the token whatever information it wants to transmit and passes it on. It "circulates" through the network until it reaches the station the information was intended for. The receiving station takes the information and passes the token on. When the token reaches the originating station (the station that originally assigned information to it), it is removed from the network and a new token is issued. The cycle begins anew. Figure 2.11 shows the structure of a Token Ring network.

FIGURE 2.11.
A Token Ring network.

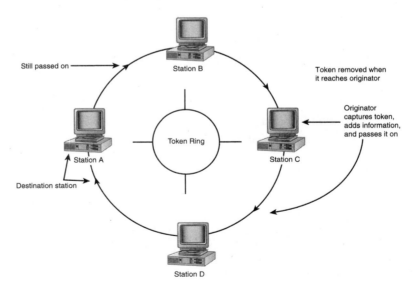

Token Rings are an orderly and efficient network architecture. There are currently two versions available, one running at 4Mbps and one running at 16Mbps.

Fast Ethernet (100base-*XX*)

Several varieties of Fast Ethernet are available, based on medium type:

- 100base-T4 (twisted pair [4 pair])
- 100base-TX (twisted pair [2 pair])
- 100base-FX (fiber)

Thought of as a high-speed cousin to the older 10base-*X* Ethernet, 100base-*XX* is capable of transmitting data over a network at up to 100Mbps.

100VG-AnyLAN

100VG(Voice Grade)-AnyLAN is another version of the 100Mbps network specification. The main difference is that it uses the Demand Priority Access Method (specification 802.12) in place of CSMA/CD to communicate across the network. 100VG-AnyLAN utilizes media types of CAT 3, 4, 5-UTP, 2-STP, in addition to fiber optics. It also supports the 802.3 and 802.5 formats. This support allows for a smooth transition from previous network topologies. Although 100VG runs at almost 100Mbps on copper wire due to its Demand Priority Access method and its use of tiered repeaters and hubs to help network traffic, it has not yet been certified to run on fiber. This makes it a poor choice for running a 100VG network over a long distance (greater than 100m). Also, most of the equipment available for 100VG is from only a few vendors, making this technology proprietary (at least for the time being). Figure 2.12 shows the tiered hub architecture of a VG network. The tiers or branches enable a better distribution of nodes on the network. The topmost, or parent, hub can have zero or more children. Each child can itself have zero or more children and one parent hub. Each hub contains all of the medium rules for network access (not distributed throughout all of the children). Data travels upward throughout the hubs and into the network.

The Demand Priority Access Method or Demand Priority Protocol

The Demand Priority Access method is VG's answer to the CSMA/CD protocol. The client or requester now requests access to the network media for the purpose of transmitting information. The server or granter processes the request and sends a signal back to the client when and if the media is ready to use. At this point, the client has control over the media and may transmit its data. Figure 2.13 shows a diagram of this method.

IsoEthernet

IsoEthernet is unique in that it not only supports the standard 10Mbps Ethernet, but also 96 ISDN B-channels operating at 6.144Mbps, one 64Kbps ISDN D-channel for signaling, and a 96Kbps M-channel for maintenance. The 10Mbps Ethernet channel is used for data packets, and the ISDN B-channel is used for video and audio. IsoEthernet works on existing CAT3 LAN lines and requires no costly cabling upgrades to existing networks.

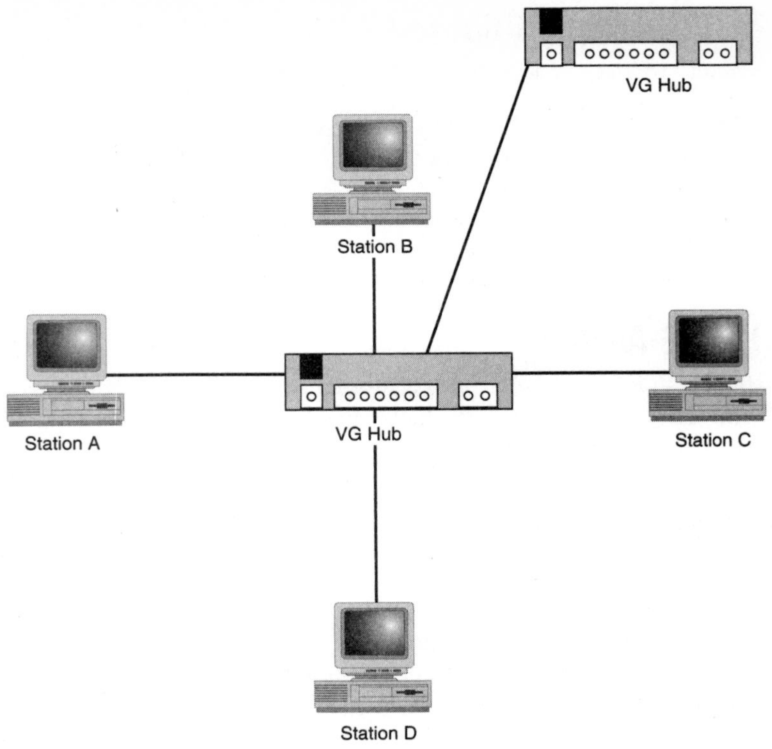

FIGURE 2.12.
VG LAN using tiered hubs.

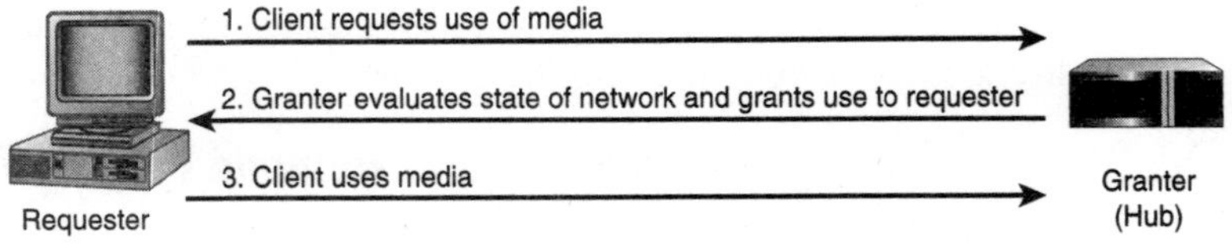

Station B

VG Hub

Station A

VG Hub

Station C

Station D

FIGURE 2.13.
VG request and grant.

1. Client requests use of media

2. Granter evaluates state of network and grants use to requester

3. Client uses media

Requester

Granter
(Hub)

FDDI

FDDI, or *Fiber Distributed Data Interface,* is a stable fiber-based transmission medium capable of speeds up to 100Mbps. It is frequently used as a backbone to large networks, as well as an interim network for connecting LANs to high-speed computers. FDDI is based on a Token Ring topology, but instead of a main single ring to transmit information, it uses two. The first ring is usually the primary ring, and the second is held as a backup. The rings run counter to each other so as to lessen network errors. Future enhancements see the second ring also being used for data transmission, effectively doubling the network transmission rate. Figure 2.14 shows an example.

FIGURE 2.14.
An FDDI dual ring architecture example.

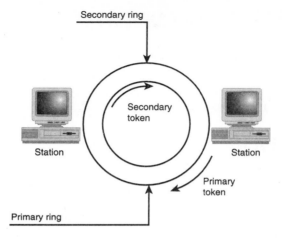

CDDI

CDDI, or *Copper Distributed Data Interface*, was created mainly as an answer to the high cost of fiber optic cable. There is also the need (for better transmission rates)/want (of faster response time) to use existing shielded and unshielded network cables.

Fibre Channel

Fibre Channel (FC) is a new intelligent connection scheme that supports not only its own protocol, but also those of FDDI, SCSI, IP, and several others. This will serve to create a single standard for networking, storage, and general data transfer. Originally meant for WANs, FC can easily be converted to LAN standards by using a switch on the network. FC supports both channel and networking interfaces over one computer port, lessening the network burden on the station. It also supports both electrical and optical media on the network, with speeds ranging from 133Mbps to 1062Mbps. A key piece of FC is the *fabric*—an abstract entity that represents the interim network device, be it a loop, active hub, or circuit switch. FC, for all intents and purposes, is still in the planning stages.

ATM

ATM, or *Asynchronous Transfer Mode*, is the proposed communication standard for broadband ISDN. ATM is a very high performance solution for both local area and wide area networks. ATM makes use of a special high-speed switch that connects to computers by optical fibers (1 for send and 1 for receive). ATM also supports simultaneous transmission of voice, data, and video over one network technology. It is currently available at a speed of 25Mbps, but was originally designed to run at 155Mbps. Future expansion could be in the gigabit or even terabit range. ATM is covered in more detail in Chapter 18, "ATM."

Gigabit Ethernet (1000Mbps??)

Current Ethernet networks are available in either 10Mbps or 100Mbps size. Gigabit networking increases that bandwidth tenfold, allowing speeds of up to 1000Mbps. Existing Ethernet and Fast Ethernet networks are 100% compatible and easily upgradable to the new gigabit networking architecture. This new architecture supports the CSMA/CD protocol and will be available on fiber, coaxial cable, and even UTP.

Summary

This chapter explained the fundamentals of the OSI Reference Model and what it means to a network. Each level of the model was covered along with how they tie together. You reviewed the advantages, disadvantages, and ratings of twisted pair, coaxial, and fiber cable. You learned about older technologies like Token Ring, some common ones like Simple Ethernet (10base-T and so on) and even some fairly uncommon types like Gigabit Ethernet. The chapter ends with a quick reference chart (see Table 2.2) outlining all of the technologies covered, their estimated speeds, and their maximum segment lengths.

Table 2.2. LAN technologies comparison quick reference chart.

Technology	Speed (Mbps)	Maximum Segment Length (meters)
Token-Based		
Token Ring	4, 16	100
Simple Ethernet		
10base-T	10	100
10base-F (multimode)	10	up to 2,000
10base-F (single mode)	10	up to 25,000
10base-5	10	500
10base-2	10	185
10base-36	10	3,600
Fast Ethernet		
100base-T4	100	100
100base-TX	100	100
100base-FX (multimode)	100	412 (½ duplex)
		2,000 (full duplex)
100base-FX (single mode)	100	20,000
100VG	100	media

Technology	Speed (Mbps)	Maximum Segment Length (meters)
Miscellaneous		
ATM	155 to 622	media
FDDI (single mode)	100	40,000-60,000
FDDI (multimode)	100	2,000
FDDI (TP) (CDDI)	100	100
Fibre Channel	133 to 1000 to 1250	10,000
Gigabit Ethernet		
1000base-T (UTP)	1000	100
1000base-T (fiber—single mode)	1000	3,000
1000base-T (fiber—multimode)	1000	500
1000base-T (coax)	1000	25

Frame Types

by Mark Sportack

IN THIS CHAPTER

CHAPTER 3

Frames

Local Area Networks use frames to encapsulate data in a structure that contains all the necessary information required to ship it to its requested destination. This chapter explains the evolution and eventual standardization of frames. Each of the major frame types is examined in detail, as well as the mechanics of their creation and use.

A *"frame"* is a block of data transmitted on a network. The size and structure of the frame is determined by the hardware layer protocol that the network uses, for example, Ethernet, Token Ring, and so on. A frame is directly analogous to an envelope: Everyone can expect that a #10 envelope will be 4 ⅛" × 9 ½". Its payload, however, can vary considerably in size, content, urgency, and so on. Knowing the envelope's size also does not reveal anything about how it will be shipped to its destination. In a network, the mechanics of frame forwarding is called a *protocol*. Protocols also exist at Layer 3 of the OSI Reference Model. These wrap frames in *packets* and provide for their transport beyond the LAN. These protocols are described in Chapter 4, "Internetworking Protocol Stacks."

The envelope can, however, contain enough visible information to identify its originator and its intended recipient. This information is used to either forward the envelope to its intended recipient, or notify the originator that the envelope was undeliverable.

Continuing the analogy, once you know the size of the envelopes, you can begin to deploy an infrastructure for processing them in volume. Thus, standardizing envelope sizes is crucial to ensuring that the forwarding infrastructure can accommodate all envelopes, regardless of who manufactured them.

Networks are, essentially, a frame-forwarding infrastructure, and have the same need for standardization of frames. Standardization ensures that different network components made by different manufacturers can interoperate. These same standards also provide a common basis for the conversion of frame types between dissimilar network types, for example, Ethernet to Token Ring translation.

The body that has been responsible for many of the extant standards that support today's high-performance networks is the Institute of Electrical and Electronics Engineers (IEEE). This standardization work began in February 1980 when the IEEE launched their Local and Metropolitan Area Network Standards Committee, also affectionately referred to as Project 802.

The Committee is chartered with the creation, maintenance, and encouragement of the use of IEEE/ANSI as well as the equivalent Joint Technical Committee 1 (JTC 1) standards established by the International Standards Committee (ISO). The JTC 1 series of equivalent standards are known as ISO 8802-nnn. These standards are basically limited to Layers 1 and 2 of the JTC Open System Interconnection (OSI) Reference Model. Layer 1 defines the physical layer, that is, the media type and the manner in which data is placed on those media. Layer 2 defines the LAN's frame structure and frame-forwarding mechanisms.

Xerox's PARC Ethernet

The world's first LAN was Xerox's PARC Ethernet. This technology originated as an intraoffice, baseband transmission technology for interconnecting workstations. It was cobbled together by researchers at Xerox's Palo Alto Research Center (PARC) for their own use as an expedient alternative to floppy disks for sharing information. In other words, Ethernet was born a fairly crude and simple mechanism.

PARC researchers recognized that Ethernet would be transporting higher-level protocols like the Internet Protocol (IP), Xerox's XNS, and others. Each of these "client" protocols already had their own limitations on data payloads. Thus, rather than put too much effort into defining the hardware layer protocol, it was deemed appropriate to simply provide a two-octet Type field that identified the type of higher-level protocol that the frame contained. This let the more sophisticated client protocol determine overall frame sizes.

> **NOTE**
>
> An octet consists of eight binary digits (bits), regardless of what those bits signify. Beware of the data communications experts who use the less precise "binary term" or "byte" to describe such structures: they have been spending too much time with programmers.

Xerox's home-grown Ethernet lacked sophistication and relied upon client protocols to determine length of data fields.

As illustrated in Figure 3.1, the PARC Ethernet frame consisted of

- An eight octet preamble
- The intended recipient's six-octet MAC address
- The originator's six-octet MAC address
- A two-octet Type field that identified the client protocol embedded in the data field
- A data field of unspecified length

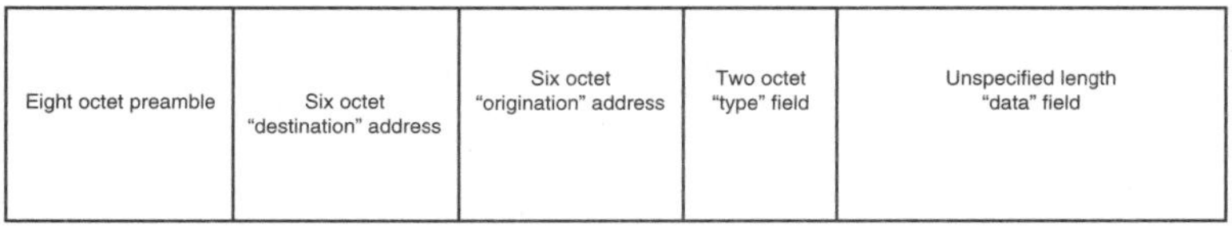

FIGURE 3.1.
Xerox's PARC Ethernet frame.

Eight octet preamble	Six octet "destination" address	Six octet "origination" address	Two octet "type" field	Unspecified length "data" field

This protocol broadcast packets to all devices connected to the LAN. Consequently, all devices had to compete for available packets. A technique known as *Carrier Sense, Multiple Access* was used to facilitate this competition. Recovery of collisions, or other events that resulted in undelivered frames, was left up to the end devices and not handled by the network.

Ethernet II

The commercial potential of Xerox's PARC Ethernet was recognized, and both its frame and protocol were refined to better suit a broader target market. This second-generation LAN, known as Ethernet II, became widely used. (Ethernet II is also sometimes referred to as *DIX Ethernet*, in acknowledgment of its triumvirate of corporate sponsors: Digital, Intel, and Xerox.)

Xerox, the owner of the technology and keeper of its "standards," assigned a two-octet type code to identify client protocols, such as Xerox's XNS, Novell's IPX, IP, and DECNet. These are higher-level protocols than Ethernet, and have different message size requirements. Unlike its predecessor, Ethernet II (illustrated in Figure 3.2), couldn't abdicate control over its frame length and still establish the timing needed to support a more sophisticated access method capable of detecting collisions. Thus frame size limits were defined.

FIGURE 3.2.

Ethernet II (DIX Ethernet) frame.

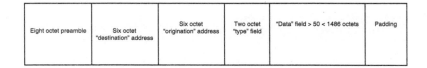

| Eight octet preamble | Six octet "destination" address | Six octet "origination" address | Two octet "type" field | "Data" field > 50 < 1486 octets | Padding |

As illustrated in Figure 3.2, the Ethernet II, or DIX, frame consisted of

- An eight-octet preamble
- The intended recipient's six-octet MAC address
- The originator's six-octet MAC address
- A two-octet Type field that identified the higher-level transport protocol being encapsulated
- A data field of at least 50 octets, but not more than 1486 octets total length.

It is important to note that, despite the definition of a minimum frame length, the Ethernet II standard continued to rely upon PARC Ethernet's two-octet Type field. The client-side transport protocols still had their own frame size requirements but Ethernet II used a more sophisticated access method than its predecessor. The new access method, known as *Carrier Sense, Multiple Access/with Collision Detection*, imposed fairly specific timing requirements.

Without getting too far into the Ethernet II protocol, this access method requires stations to check the "wire" to determine whether any other station is already sending data. If the LAN seems idle, the station is free to transmit. Unfortunately, transmission is not instantaneous over copper transmission facilities. Therefore, it is entirely probable that a station will begin to transmit on what appears to be an idle LAN only to be "hit" with an incoming transmission from another station nanoseconds after initiating its own transmission. This is known as a *collision*. Both stations will detect the collision, "back off" from transmitting, and begin anew after a brief delay.

The way Ethernet II enabled this was by controlling the time required for the worst-case round trip through the LAN. In a 10Mbps Ethernet, this round trip is limited to a maximum of 50 microseconds. Thus, a station would have to continue transmitting until after the worst-case round trip time had expired. This is enough time to transmit 500 bits. Dividing by 8 bits per octet means that packets would have to be a minimum of 62.5 octets in length for collision detection to work. Xerox rounded this up to 64 octets minimum frame size for Ethernet II.

Any frames whose payloads (which was still dictated by the higher-level transport protocol) resulted in an overall frame size of fewer than 64 octets, were padded with zeros by Ethernet II until the frame reached the minimum size. This solved the timing problem of collision detection, but forced each protocol to distinguish data from padding. The Ethernet II frame continued to rely upon the Type field to identify the higher-level protocol and, therefore, its data field length.

Although Ethernet II provided additional functionality intended to make the original Ethernet commercially viable, the only substantive change to the frame was to impose minimum and maximum frame lengths.

Xerox, the originator of Ethernet, retained the rights to the technology and, consequently, established and published its standards. This approach to standardization served its purpose: Ethernet became a commercially available product. Unfortunately, this approach to establishing and maintaining standards for commercial products is not extensible. A competitive corporation cannot be tasked with maintaining the standards for a commodity product. They will be motivated to act on their own behalf. Therefore, for Ethernet to become a truly successful commercial technology, the responsibility for standardization had to be ceded to a neutral entity.

3

FRAME TYPES

IEEE Project 802

In February of 1980, the IEEE launched its Project 802 committee to evaluate and standardize Ethernet as well as the other LAN technologies and protocols that were beginning to emerge. Their objective also included establishing the rules that would enable all types of LANs to easily pass data between them, and to separate the physical media from the LAN protocols. This would permit the implementation of the same LAN on different cable plants, without compromising interoperability.

The committee identified the elements required to support their goals and launched task-specific teams to accomplish them. These teams and their work efforts included

- 802.1: Defined the overview and architecture for interoperability between LANs and MANs. This is the basis for all the 802 initiatives and includes standards for LAN/MAN management and bridging between 802-compliant networks.

- 802.2: Defined the data link layer (Layer 2) standard for telecommunications and information exchange between systems, both LAN and MAN-based. This specification also provided the backward compatibility required to support a transition from the pre-standard versions of Ethernet to the 802.3 standardized version.

■ 802.3: Established the new standard for a LAN that features a Carrier Sense, Multiple Access with Collision Detection (CSMA/CD). This "new" LAN is properly referred to as CSMA/CD, but is more commonly known as "Ethernet."

■ 802.4: Defined a physical layer standard for a bus topology LAN with a token-passing media access method. This LAN is called *Token Bus* and can operate at 1, 2, 5, or 10Mbps.

■ 802.5: Established the standards for Token Ring's access methods and physical signaling techniques.

Though not a complete listing of the Project 802 initiatives, these five items adequately convey the intended benefits of their charter for standardizing Local and Metropolitan Area Networks. Each specification in this "family" can interoperate through unsophisticated frame conversions because they have a common foundation. This charter far exceeded the scope of Xerox's standards and, consequently, made Ethernet II obsolete.

IEEE 802.2 Logical Link Control (LLC)

The IEEE Project 802 organized its standards around a three-tier protocol hierarchy that corresponded to the OSI Reference Model's two bottommost layers: the physical layer and the data link layer. These three tiers are the physical layer, Media Access Control (MAC), and Logical Link Control (LLC). This is valid for all 802-compliant LANs. The MAC layer addressing specification allows for either two-octet or six-octet addresses. The six-octet MAC address is the standard and the two-octet address is rarely used.

As Figure 3.3 shows, the IEEE's 802 Reference Model differs from the OSI Reference Model in two significant aspects. First, 802 Physical Layer is a subset of its OSI counterpart. Second, the OSI's data link layer (Layer 2) is broken into two discrete components: Medium Access Control (MAC) and Logical Link Control (LLC).

Defining the LLC separately from the Media Access Control enabled interoperability of 802-compliant networks, despite differences in topologies, transmission media, and more importantly, media access methodologies. The LLC resides above the MAC and physical layers of the 802 Model. In this model, media access, transmission media, and topology are highly interdependent. Thus, part of the OSI's physical layer was defined as the 802's media access layer.

The LLC uses a subheader to embed the following fields in 802-compliant frames:

■ A one-octet Destination Service Access Point (DSAP) field

■ A one-octet Source Service Access Point (SSAP) field

■ A one-octet Control field.

The Service Access Points, both Destination and Source, indicate which upper-layer protocol the packet is intended for. Protocols are assigned hexadecimal values that are displayed in the DSAP and SSAP fields of a packet.

FIGURE 3.3.

Comparison of the OSI and IEEE 802 reference models.

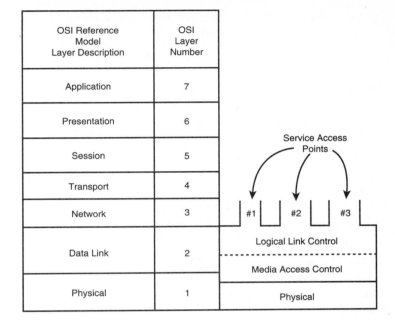

The Logical Link Control (LLC) subframe, or *header*, is prepended to a frame's data field. Its three one-octet fields count as part of the data field's overall length. Figure 3.4 illustrates the structure of the LLC subframe.

FIGURE 3.4.

LLC subframe structure.

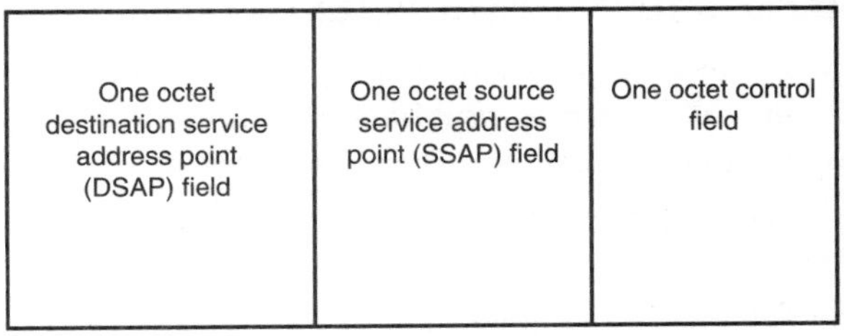

One octet destination service address point (DSAP) field	One octet source service address point (SSAP) field	One octet control field

The LLC provides addressing and control of the data link. It specifies which mechanisms are to be used for addressing stations over the transmission medium, and for controlling the data exchanged between the originator and recipient machines. This is done through the use of three LLC services:

- Unacknowledged connectionless service
- Connection-oriented service
- Acknowledged connectionless service

3

FRAME TYPES

These services are accessed through Service Access Points that are defined between the network and data link layers.

The first LLC service, unacknowledged connectionless service, is a minimal but useful offering. Frequently, Layer 4 protocols such as TCP, SPX, and so on are tasked with providing flow control and other reliability functions. Therefore, it makes sense to have a Layer 2 service that does not redundantly provide the same functions, albeit at a lower level. This cuts down on the communications overhead. Some applications, such as time- and latency-sensitive voice and/ or video conferencing, may actually suffer performance degradation by having to establish and maintain connections at this layer.

The next LLC service, connection-oriented service, provides data link layer mechanisms to establish and maintain connections. This is extremely useful for simple and/or unintelligent devices that may not have Layer 3 or 4 protocols. Thus, they require the ability to provide these functions at Layer 2. This control function requires the link layer to maintain a table that tracks active connections.

The last LLC service, acknowledged connectionless service, is a hybrid of the first two LLC services. This service provides an acknowledgment of receipt without having any of the overhead of connection management. Less overhead directly translates into faster delivery. Adding guaranteed delivery creates a useful service whose applications are almost limitless.

These services tend to be selected per application, and are transparent to application users. As they are part of the 802.2 foundation specification, they are available to all 802-compliant networks and can be used in internetworking different 802-compliant networks.

IEEE 802.2 Sub-Network Access Protocol (SNAP)

As a means of providing backward compatibility with early, non-standardized versions of LANs, like PARC and DIX Ethernet, a subframe structure was developed to provide a mechanism for identifying the upper-layer protocol being transported. The PARC and DIX versions of Ethernet included a Type field in their frame structures. This space was later reallocated by the IEEE in their 802.3 standardized version of Ethernet.

The 802.3 Ethernet was a more sophisticated protocol than its predecessors and eliminated much of the original need for the Type field. Some higher-level protocols, however, relied upon this Layer 2 function. The need to provide compatibility with existing Layer 3 and 4 protocols necessitated the development of a subframe structure that could identify higher-level protocols. The result was the SNAP subframe, illustrated in Figure 3.5.

FIGURE 3.5.

802.2 SNAP frame structure.

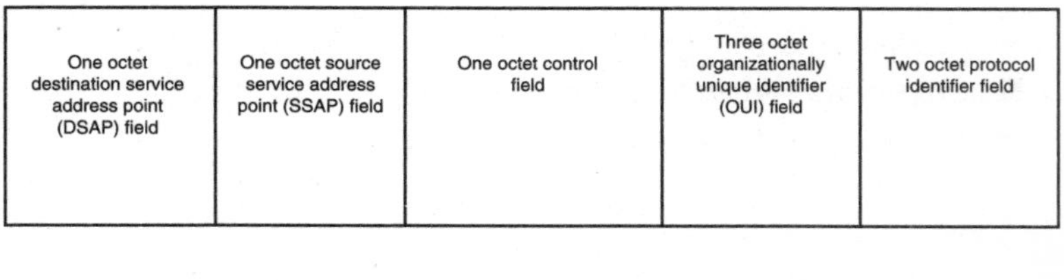

One octet destination service address point (DSAP) field	One octet source service address point (SSAP) field	One octet control field	Three octet organizationally unique identifier (OUI) field	Two octet protocol identifier field

The 802.2 specification also provides a Sub-Network Access Protocol (SNAP) frame structure. This frame builds upon the standard 802.2 frame by adding a five-octet field that contains a three-octet Organizationally Unique Identifier field, and a two-octet Protocol Type field.

The SNAP subframing is an extension of the LLC subframe and must be used with it. It can be used with any 802-compliant LAN.

IEEE 802.3 Ethernet Frame

Project 802 defined a standard basis for all Ethernet frame types. The frames are a minimum of 64 octets, and a maximum of 1500 octets in length, including payload and headers. The headers are used to identify the sender and recipient of each packet. The only limitation on this identification is that each address must be unique and six octets in length.

The first 12 octets of each frame contains the six-octet destination address (the intended recipient's address), and a six-octet source address (the sender's address). These addresses are hardware-level machine address codes, commonly known as MAC addresses. They can either be the unique "universally administered address" that is automatically given to each Ethernet network interface card (NIC) at its manufacture, or they can be customized upon installation. The automatically assigned type of MAC address is represented by six paired hexadecimal numbers, delimited by colons, for example, 99:02:11:D1:8F:19. The first two pairs of numbers are the manufacturer's ID. Each NIC manufacturer must apply to the IEEE for a unique manufacturer's ID and a range of MAC addresses.

Customized addresses are known as *locally administered addresses*. These addresses can be used to identify the room number, department, owner's voice mail extension, and so on. Using locally administered addresses can provide network administrators with vital information that can expedite trouble resolution. Unfortunately, they can also be extremely difficult and time-consuming to maintain.

802-compliant frames may contain a destination address of a single machine, or refer to a group of workstations with a common, identifying characteristic. Transmission to groups of related machines is known as *multicasting*.

Under normal operating circumstances, Ethernet NICs receive only frames whose destination addresses match their unique MAC address, or that satisfy their multicast criteria. Most NICs, however, can be set for *promiscuous mode*, which results in their reception of all frames on the LAN, regardless of addressing. This can pose a security risk for everyone else on the LAN, and a potential performance problem for the user whose machine is operating in that manner.

Although most of the changes from the previous versions of Ethernet that were made to the 802.3 standard were changes to the protocol itself, there was one other significant change to the 802.3 frame. The 802 committee needed a standard that was complete unto itself and not dependent upon the good behavior of other protocols. Therefore, they replaced the two-octet Type field of previous Ethernets with a two-octet Length field.

Having established minimum and maximum field lengths based on a worst-case, round-trip timing window (as previously explained, this was necessary for collision-detection purposes), it was no longer necessary to defer the determination of frame size to client protocols. Instead, the 802.3 working group redefined this two-octet field to explicitly define the length of a frame's data field, and moved protocol identification to the LLC. The structure of the frame is illustrated in Figure 3.6.

FIGURE 3.6.

The IEEE 802.3 Ethernet frame.

Seven octet "preamble"	One octet "start of frame delimiter"	Six octet "destination" address	Six octet "organization" address	Two octet "length" field	Variable length "data" field (> 46 octets < 1482)	Four octet frame check sequence

The IEEE's 802.3 basic Ethernet frame replaced the traditional Type field with a Length field. The 802.2 subframe is used, instead, to identify the type of protocol, if this is necessary. Another change in the 802.3 frame from its predecessors was the requirement for the overall frame size to be between 64 and 1500 octets in length, from the start of the Destination field, through the end of the Frame Check Sequence field.

The preamble is a seven-octet string that precedes each frame, and allows the synchronization of the transmission. This is followed by the Start of Frame Delimiter (SFD). The SFD is fairly self-explanatory: It denotes the start of the frame for all devices in or on the LAN. The SFD is 11 followed by the repeating sequence of 1010101010.

The SFD is sometimes considered an integral part of the preamble, and not a part of the frame itself, thus bringing the preamble up to 8 octets in length. This represents another subtle distinction between the PARC and DIX Ethernet variants and the 802.3 standard. PARC and DIX Ethernets used a consistent, repeating 10101010 pattern for the entire eight-octet preamble. This was used for both synchronization and Start-of-Frame delimiting.

The next mechanism is the Frame Check Sequence (FCS). A mathematically derived value is stored in this field by the frame's originating computer. The destination computer also knows how to calculate this value and does so to verify the integrity of the frame. The frame may be damaged in transit in a variety of ways. Electromagnetic Interference (EMI), cross talk, and so on can all damage the packet without stopping its transmission.

Upon receipt of a frame, its FCS field is checked for damage through a Cyclical Redundancy Check. The destination computer performs the same calculation as the originating computer and compares the resulting value to the one stored in the FCS field. If the values are the same, the destination computer knows the data arrived intact. Otherwise, the destination computer requests a retransmission of the frame.

This basic Ethernet frame is used with either the 802.2 LLC subframe or the SNAP subframe.

Ethernet LLC Frame Structure

The Ethernet LLC frame is a combination of an 802.3 frame and the 802.2 LLC subframe (see Figure 3.7). In this implementation, LLC adds three fields to the basic Ethernet frame: Destination Service Access Port, Source Service Access Port, and Control.

FIGURE 3.7.

The Ethernet LLC frame.

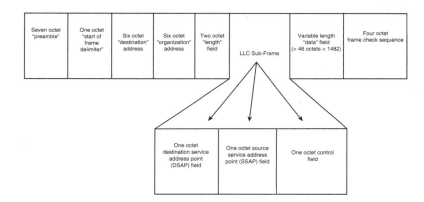

An Ethernet LLC frame has the following structure:

- A seven-octet preamble that signals the start of a frame
- A one-octet Start-of-Frame delimiter that signals the start of the frame's contents
- The intended recipient's six-octet MAC address
- The originator's six-octet MAC address
- A two-octet Length field that identifies the total length of the Data field, including the LLC and SNAP headers
- A one-octet Destination Service Access Point (DSAP) field that identifies, predictably, the LLC's service access point at the destination machine
- A one-octet Source Service Access Point (SSAP) field that identifies the originating machine's LLC service access point
- A one- or two-octet Control field that indicates the type of LLC frame being carried
- A data field that contains either 35 to 1483 octets, or 34 to 1484 octets of data, depending upon the length of the preceding Control field
- A four-octet Frame Check Sequence that is used to check the integrity of the frame

The Ethernet LLC frame integrates the 802.2 subframe structures, or headers, and permits the identification of higher-level protocols that are the intended recipients of the frame's contents. This provides backward compatibility with earlier versions of Ethernet whose frames contained discrete mechanisms for protocol identification.

The total length of an Ethernet LLC frame must be at least 64 octets in length (excluding the preamble and the Start-of-Frame delimiter) to permit proper functioning of the CSMA/CD mechanism. Zeroes are added to the end of the Data field to ensure this minimum length. The upper limit is 1518 octets, including the preamble and the Start-of-Frame delimiter.

Ethernet SNAP Frame Structure

The Ethernet SNAP frame is a combination of an 802.3 frame and the 802.2 Sub-network Access Protocol's subframe (see Figure 3.8). In this implementation, SNAP adds a five-octet Protocol Identification Field. This field is inserted in the frame after the LLC header. It consists of a three-octet Organizationally Unique Identifier (OUI) and a two-octet Type field. These fields identify which upper-layer protocol the frame is intended for.

FIGURE 3.8.

The Ethernet SNAP frame.

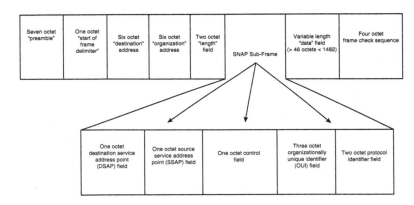

An Ethernet SNAP frame contains the following fields:

- A seven-octet preamble that signals the start of a frame
- A one-octet Start-of-Frame delimiter that signals the start of the frame's contents
- The intended recipient's six-octet MAC address
- The originator's six-octet MAC address
- A two-octet Length field that identifies the total length of the Data field, including the LLC and SNAP headers
- A one-octet Destination Service Access Point (DSAP) field that identifies, predictably, the LLC's service access point at the destination machine
- A one-octet Source Service Access Point (SSAP) field that identifies the originating machine's LLC service access point
- A one- or two-octet Control field that indicates the type of LLC frame being carried
- A five-octet SNAP subframe, including a three-octet Organizationally Unique Identifier field and a two-octet Protocol Type field that identify the upper-level protocol being carried

- A data field that contains either 37 to 1492 octets, or 36 to 1491 octets of data, depending upon the length of the preceding Control field
- A four-octet Frame Check Sequence that is used to check the integrity of the frame

The Ethernet SNAP frame integrates the 802.2 subframe structures, or headers, and permits the identification of higher-level protocols that are the intended recipients of the frame's contents. This provides backward compatibility with earlier versions of Ethernet whose frames contained discrete mechanisms for protocol identification.

The total length of an Ethernet SNAP frame must be at least 64 octets to permit proper functioning of the CSMA/CD mechanism. The upper limit for an Ethernet SNAP frame is 1518 octets, including the preamble and the Start-of-Frame delimiter.

IEEE 802.5 Token Ring

The IEEE also standardized a message format and protocol for a different, more deterministic, LAN known as *Token Ring* in its 802.5 standard. Token ring networks had existed since the mid 1970s and were largely an IBM-specific technology. The 802.5 specification is almost identical to IBM's Token Ring. In fact, the term "token ring" is used indiscriminately to describe both IBM's pre-standard product and IEEE 802.5-compliant products.

IEEE standardization was pushed by several large companies, including IBM (802.5 Token Ring) and General Motors (802.4 Token Bus). Token Ring offered a more timely and deterministic approach to networking than the 802.3 protocol, albeit at a higher per-port cost. Companies whose applications required timely delivery of data found Token Ring to be the only viable solution for their needs. Whereas the 802.3 protocol only assures that the packet has been successfully transmitted, it may require multiple transmission attempts. Therefore, it can't guarantee a timeframe for delivery. The token ring topology can, because of its deterministic, ring-shaped topology and orderly access method.

Understanding Token Passing

In an 802.5-compliant Token Ring network, a special frame (better known as, you guessed it, the "token"!) is passed from device to device, in sequence along the ring. It can only circulate when the ring is idle. This frame, shown in Figure 3.9, is three octets long and contains a special bit pattern. If the token is passed to a device that doesn't need to transmit, it may hold onto the token for 10 milliseconds, or longer if the default value has been changed. If this time expires and the device still doesn't need to transmit, it relinquishes control of the token, which is then sent on to the next device in the ring.

The IEEE's 802.5 Token Ring uses this token to control access to the transmission media. It contains Starting Delimiter, Access Control, and Ending Delimiter fields. The Access Control field contains eight bits, one of which must be inverted to deactivate the token and convert it into a Start-of-Frame sequence.

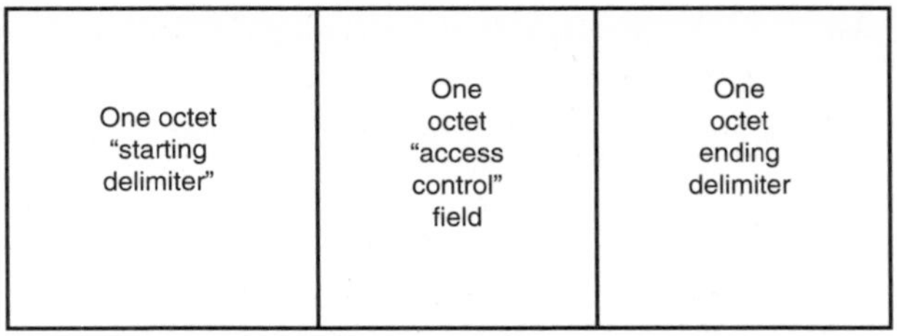

FIGURE 3.9.
*The IEEE 802.5
Token Ring "token"
frame.*

One octet "starting delimiter"	One octet "access control" field	One octet ending delimiter

When this token is passed to a device that needs to transmit, that device seizes the token and inverts a bit value in its frame. This inversion gives that device permission to transmit and is recognized as a Start-of-Frame (SOF) sequence. The data to be transmitted, as well as other important fields, are appended to this modified token frame and put onto the network. As long as a data-bearing frame is traversing the network, no token is being passed.

It is possible to calculate the maximum time that can expire before a device will be able to transmit. This time can be manipulated either upwards or downwards by adding or subtracting nodes from the ring. Token Ring networks are ideal for any application that requires predictable delays.

Understanding Token Ring

Given the previous discussion about the mechanics of token passing, it is obvious that an 802.5-compliant device operates in only one of two modes: transmit or listen. A device that is listening simply forwards the token to the next device in the ring. If the token has been converted to a SOF sequence, a listening device checks to see whether it is the destination of that frame. If it is, it buffers the data and passes the still-modified token back to the originator of the frame that it received it from. The originator then has to acknowledge that the frame was sent successfully, convert the SOF frame back to a token, and put it on the network.

In transmit mode, as previously described, the device alters the token's bit structure to the SOF sequence and appends the necessary data and headers. This methodology, contrary to Ethernet, runs more efficiently under heavy traffic loads because transmission permissions are not chaotic like Ethernet's, and the frame is not limited to a maximum number of octets.

IEEE 802.5 Frame Structure

The 802.5 Token Ring frame structure consists of two parts: the token and the data frame. As previously discussed, the token's frame consists of three one-octet fields.

The token frame and the data frame are illustrated Figure 3.10.

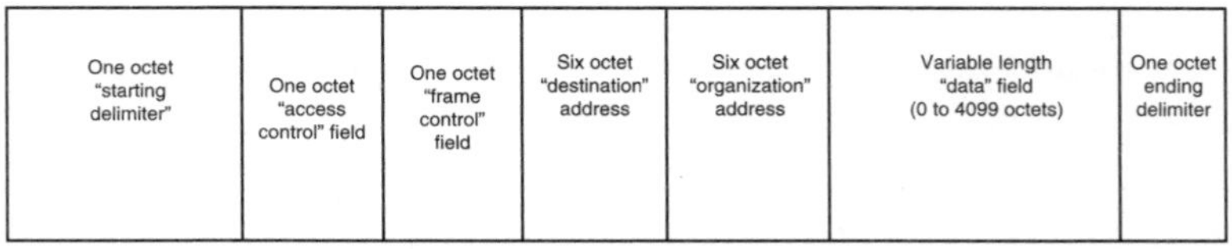

FIGURE 3.10.
*The IEEE's 802.5
Token Ring frame
structure with attached
data field.*

One octet "starting delimiter"	One octet "access control" field	One octet "frame control" field	Six octet "destination" address	Six octet "organization" address	Variable length "data" field (0 to 4099 octets)	One octet ending delimiter

There are three one-octet fields in common between the token and data frames. These are the Starting Delimiter, Access Control, and Ending Delimiter fields. The Access Control field is the key to making a Token Ring work. It contains eight bits, one of which must be inverted to deactivate the token and convert it into a Start-of-Frame sequence.

When the token has been converted to a data frame, it consists of nine different fields and subfields. The first field is the Starting Delimiter, which identifies the beginning of the frame. Next is the Access Control field. This field tells 802.5-compliant devices whether or not they may transmit. This field also contains the bits for Token Ring's priority and reservation system. It is followed by the Frame Control field. This field stores the "type" bits that identify the transport protocol. This field is also used to differentiate between data frames and control frames.

The next two fields are the destination and source MAC addresses. Each one is a six-octet field. These MAC addresses conform to the previously described Project 802 specification, and are identical to those used in Ethernet networks. The data field for a token-based network varies in size from at least 0 octets, up to a maximum of 4099. The last field is the one-octet Ending Delimiter that identifies the end of the frame.

IEEE 802.8 FDDI

The IEEE's 802.8 specification is called the Fiber Distributed Data Interface (FDDI—often pronounced "fiddy"). Although it is widely regarded as merely a higher-speed Token Ring network, FDDI is fundamentally different in its topology, management, and even token and frame structures.

First, unlike Token Ring, which uses a priority/reservation access method, FDDI uses a timed-token protocol to regulate access to the transmission media. This results in a much more deterministic LAN and removes the need for an access control field in its frame.

The IEEE's 802.5 FDDI uses this token to control access to the transmission media. It contains preamble, Starting Delimiter, Frame Control, and Ending Delimiter fields, as shown in Figure 3.11.

FIGURE 3.11.
The IEEE 802.8 FDDI "token" frame.

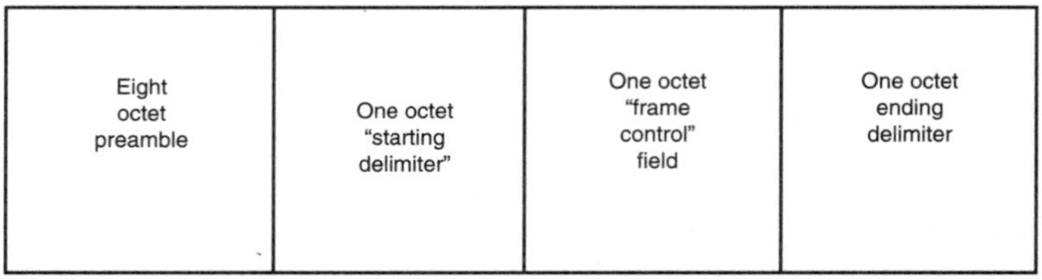

Eight octet preamble	One octet "starting delimiter"	One octet "frame control" field	One octet ending delimiter

The FDDI data-bearing frame is structured as follows:

- An eight-octet preamble that signals the start of the frame.
- A one-octet Start-of-Frame delimiter that signals the start of the frame's contents.

- A one-octet Frame Control field that signals the type of frame, such as, token, MAC or LLC, priority frame, and so on.
- The intended recipient's six-octet MAC address.
- The originator's six-octet MAC address.
- A variable length data field that contains up to 4478 octets.
- A four-octet Frame Check Sequence used to check the integrity of the frame.
- A half-octet (four bits) Ending Delimiter.
- A three-octet Frame Status field that contains three one-octet subfields: Error, Address-match, and Copied. Each subfield is set to either "S" for Set or "R" for Reset.

The IEEE's 802.8 FDDI frame is a maximum of 4500 octets in length, including data and all frame components.

Figure 3.12 illustrates the basic FDDI frame. It is usually implemented in one of two subformats: LLC or SNAP. Neither one, excluding the preamble, can be more than 4500 octets in length.

FIGURE 3.12.

The IEEE 802.8 FDDI frame.

Eight octet preamble	One octet starting delimiter"	One octet "frame control" field	Six octets destination address	Six octets source address	Variable length data field up to 4478 octets	Four octets frame check sequence	One octet ending delimiter	Three octets frame status

FDDI LLC Frame Structure

FDDI also supports LLC by building upon the 802.2 LLC layer (see Figure 3.13). The LLC frame is constructed by adding three fields to the 802.8 FDDI frame. These fields are the DSAP, SSAP, and Control fields.

FIGURE 3.13.

The FDDI LLC frame.

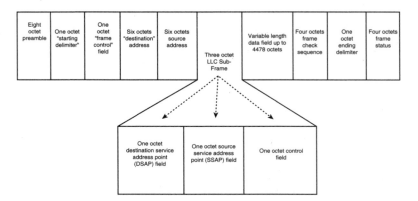

An FDDI LLC frame has the following structure:

- An eight-octet preamble that signals the start of the frame.
- A one-octet Start-of-Frame delimiter that signals the start of the frame's contents.
- A one-octet Frame Control field that signals the type of frame, such as token, MAC or LLC, priority frame, and so on.
- The intended recipient's six-octet MAC address.
- The originator's six-octet MAC address.
- A variable length data field that contains up to 4478 octets.
- A four-octet Frame Check Sequence that is used to check the integrity of the frame.
- A half-octet (four bits) Ending Delimiter.
- A three-octet Frame Status field that contains three one-octet subfields: Error, Address-match, and Copied. Each subfield is set to either "S" for Set or "R" for Reset.

The IEEE's 802.8 FDDI frame can be supplemented with the 802.2 LLC subframe structures. This prepends the DSAP, SSAP, and Control fields onto the Data field.

FDDI SNAP Frame Structure

FDDI also supports SNAP by building upon the 802.2 LLC layer of the FDDI 802.2 frame. The SNAP frame adds a three-octet Protocol Identification field and a two-octet Type field to the 802.2 LLC subframe structure (see Figure 3.14).

FIGURE 3.14.

The FDDI SNAP frame.

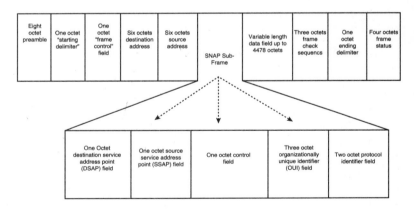

An FDDI SNAP frame contains the following fields:

- An eight-octet preamble that signals the start of the frame.
- A one-octet Start-of-Frame delimiter that signals the start of the frame's contents.

- A one-octet Frame Control field that signals the type of frame, such as token, MAC or LLC, priority frame, and so on.
- The intended recipient's six-octet MAC address.
- The originator's six-octet MAC address.
- A five-octet SNAP subframe, including a three-octet Organizationally Unique Identifier field and a two-octet Protocol Type field that identify the upper-level protocol being carried.
- A variable length data field that contains up to 4473 octets.
- A four-octet Frame Check Sequence that is used to check the integrity of the frame.
- A half-octet (four bits) Ending Delimiter.
- A three-octet Frame Status field that contains three one-octet subfields: Error, Address-match, and Copied. Each subfield is set to either "S" for Set or "R" for Reset.

The IEEE's 802.8 FDDI SNAP frame adds a three-octet Organizationally Unique Identifier and a two-octet Type field to the FDDI LLC frame immediately after the LLC header and before the data. These fields are included in the overall length of the data field.

IEEE 802.12 VG-AnyLAN

The IEEE 802.12 standard specifies a 100Mbps network that uses the demand priority access method (DPAM), an Ethernet or Token Ring frame format (but not both simultaneously), and a star topology. It operates over four pairs of Category 3 UTP, STP, Category 5, and fiber. There can be up to three levels of cascaded repeaters with up to 100 meters between the repeaters and the stations. The network may be up to 4,000 feet in diameter.

This specification provides SNMP compliance by using Management Information Base (MIB) variables that *look* like Ethernet MIBs and Token Ring MIBs. The 802.12 MIB is a superset of both Ethernet and Token Ring MIBs.

The access method is a demand priority scheme that is a round-robin arbitration method in which a central repeater regularly polls ports connected to it. This polling is in port order and is conducted to identify ports that have transmission requests. Once the need to transmit is established, the repeater determines the priority: high or normal. These priorities are designed to service time-sensitive requests before servicing "normal" requests for bandwidth. Any ports that are either not transmitting or have a pending transmission request generate an "idle" signal.

This signal is cleared by the repeater if that station is selected as the next in the priority sequence to transmit. When the port senses the silence, that is, the idle signal ceases, the port begins to transmit.

When this happens, the repeater alerts the other stations that they may receive an incoming message. The repeater then reads the incoming packet's destination address, looks in its link configuration table, and switches it to that destination address as well as any promiscuous ports.

The central, or "root," repeater controls the operation of the priority domain. This can include up to three levels of cascaded hubs, and allows interconnected repeaters to function as a single large repeater. The central repeater sends all traffic to each lower-level repeater. Each lower-level repeater, in turn, polls its active ports for requests after packet transmission.

No station is permitted to transmit twice in a row if other stations have same-priority requests pending. Also, at the central repeater, a high-priority request is not allowed to interrupt a normal-priority request if that request is already in progress. In a lower-level repeater, the normal-priority request is preempted, so that the high-priority request can be accommodated. To ensure that a request isn't completely ignored, any normal-priority requests that have been waiting longer than 250ms are automatically elevated to high-priority status.

Comparison of IEEE Frame Types

Each of the frame types described in this chapter, and their supporting protocols, offer different combinations of performance parameters. Understanding the benefits and limitations of each frame type will help you better unleash the power of high-performance networks.

802.3 CSMA/CD (Ethernet)

Ethernet, Fast Ethernet, and Gigabit Ethernet offer 10Mbps, 100Mbps, or up to 1Gbps transmission rate. This family of specifications uses different physical layers with an almost perfectly interchangeable media access layer. Some minor changes were necessary at this layer to account for the significant differences in the various media types that are supported.

Media access for these three specifications is through a chaotic contention method that does not scale very well. Performance may be boosted significantly by implementing these protocols through a switch. Switches decrease the size of the collision domains without affecting the size of the broadcast domain. In a per-port switched 802.3 LAN, the collision domain is reduced to just two devices: the end device and the hub port it connects to. This greatly relieves the scalability issues that plague "shared" versions of these specifications.

802.5 Token Ring

Token Ring offers 4 and 16Mbps transmission rates with somewhat predictable delays, due to its deterministic access method. Additionally, the token has priority bits that can be set higher to satisfy the more stringent network performance criteria of critical frames.

802.8 FDDI

FDDI offers a 100Mbps transmission rate, and a self-healing dual, counter-rotating ring topology. FDDI can be considered a "Fast Token Ring" as it conducts token-passing in a deterministic fashion. This, and the requisite 802.1 and 802.2 characteristics, are all that these two networks share.

FDDI's clock rate and timed-access methodology distinguish it from Token Ring, and position it for different applications within the LAN environment. Its dual counter-rotating rings can automatically "splice" together logically to heal a broken cable. This provides an innate fault tolerance. The drawback to this is a sudden increase in propagation delay in the event of a cable break.

802.12 VG-AnyLAN

VG-AnyLAN provides for the accommodation of both Ethernet and Token Ring frame formats. The proposal appears to be highly media independent as it can transmit over four pairs of Category 3 UTP wire, Category 5 UTP or STP, or 62.5 micron fiber-optic cabling.

It also attempts to establish a middle ground between true baseband and true broadband communications by implementing a demand-priority media-access method. Essentially, it establishes a priority architecture that lets time-sensitive packets get needed bandwidth on demand. It lacks a native mechanism to actually reserve bandwidth, however.

VG-AnyLAN has two other potentially significant limitations. First, it requires four pair of wire. This may force 10base-T users to rewire their stations prior to migration. Therefore, even though it was intentionally designed for Category 3 wire, users may still find themselves unable to use existing wire if they do not have four pairs of Category 3 wire at each station. The second limitation is that it does not interoperate easily with "real Ethernet" because it uses a different media-access method.

Summary

Each of the LANs in the IEEE 802 family of standards has its own particular framing structure. This structure is based on a minimum level of commonality that can permit bridging of dissimilar network types. The 802 standards are well enough devised that, under normal operating conditions, a superficial understanding of the specifications themselves is sufficient for internetworking.

Details of the different specifications, however, can provide invaluable information about the inner workings of each specification. Though this level of detail isn't for everyone, it is available to anyone who needs them, for a nominal fee. This availability helps maintain the 802 frame types as industry standards, and permits the development of other technologies that need to interface at this level of the protocol stack.

Ordering the IEEE Documentation

To order the complete specifications for any of the Project 802 initiatives or standards, contact the IEEE's Customer Service department using one of the following contact mechanisms:

> PHONE: 1-800-678-IEEE from anywhere in the US and Canada, or 908-981-1393 from outside of the US and Canada.
>
> FAX: 1-908-981-9667
>
> TELEX: 833233

or mail to:

> IEEE Customer Service
>
> 445 Hoes Lane, P.O. Box 1331
>
> Piscataway, NJ 08855-1331.

The IEEE accepts all major credit cards for purchases. They can also accept purchase orders, provided that they are one of the following:

- From IEEE members
- Deposit account customers
- Government and rated commercial organizations
- Organizations with an approved credit application on file

There is a $25 minimum charge, excluding shipping and handling, for such purchases. All payments must be made in US funds and drawn on a US bank. The IEEE reserves the right to change prices without notice and may be required to collect sales tax in certain regions. Thus, you should contact their Customer Service department before placing any order.

Internetworking Protocol Stacks

by Mark Sportack

CHAPTER 4

IN THIS CHAPTER

An internetworking protocol stack is a suite of related communications protocols that offers users the mechanisms and services required to communicate with other network-connected machines. From the users' perspective, the protocol stack is what makes a network usable.

The previous chapters examined the first and second layers of a protocol stack: the physical and data link layers. A protocol stack should offer mechanisms that either provide these two layers' functionality, or interface with existing, standardized network access vehicles. The next layer of the OSI Reference Model is Layer 3, the network layer. This layer provides the mechanisms that enable the transfer of information between source and destination machines across a communications network. This layer is formed by converting Layer 2 frames and addressing into Layer 3 packets with addressing that is recognizable outside the LAN. These packets are then routed to their destination. An example of a Layer 3 routed protocol is the Internet Protocol (IP).

Whereas Layer 3 provides internetwork data transfers, Layer 4 (the transport layer) provides Layer 3 network mechanisms with end-to-end reliability and integrity. The transport layer may be required to guarantee error-free delivery of packets sequencing of delivered packets, and quality of service. An example of a Layer 4 protocol is the Transmission Control Protocol (TCP). TCP is almost always referred to in combination with its Layer 3 counterpart as *TCP/IP*.

The use of Layers 3 and 4 implies that the source and destination computers are not connected to the same LAN, regardless of how close or distant they are. Thus, internetworking two different networks is required to support the requested transmission. Consequently, the communications mechanisms of Layer 2 are inadequate. Conversely, these layers are not always required. For example, if both the source and destination computers are connected to the same LAN, they may communicate satisfactorily using only Layer 2 network frames and protocols.

There are two types of networking protocols that operate at Layer 3: routed protocols and routing protocols. *Routed protocols* are those that encapsulate user information and data into packets, and are responsible for transporting them to their destination. *Routing protocols* are used between routers to determine available routes, communicate what is known about available routes, and forward routed protocol packets along those routes. This chapter focuses on the most common routed protocols. For more information on routing protocols, please see Chapter 9, "Routers."

The Internet Protocol, Version 4 (IPv4)

The Internet Protocol (IP) was developed approximately 20 years ago for the Department of Defense (DoD). The DoD needed a way to interconnect various brands of proprietary computers, and their equally proprietary support networks, across a common internetwork. This was achieved through a layered protocol that insulated applications from networking hardware.

Unlike the OSI Reference Model, the TCP/IP model focuses more on delivering interconnectivity than on rigidly adhering to functional layers. It does this by acknowledging the importance of a hierarchical arrangement of functions but still leaving protocol designers ample flexibility for implementation. Consequently, the OSI Reference Model is significantly better at explaining the mechanics of inter-computer communications, but TCP/IP has become the internetworking protocol of choice in the marketplace.

The flexibility of the TCP/IP Reference Model is shown in Figure 4.1 through a comparison to the OSI Reference Model.

FIGURE 4.1.

Comparison of OSI and TCP/IP Reference Models.

OSI reference model layer description	OSI layer number	TCP/IP equivalent layer description
Application	7	Process/ Application
Presentation	6	
Session	5	Host-to-Host
Transport	4	
Network	3	Internet
Data Link	2	Network access
Physical	1	

The TCP/IP Reference Model, developed long after the protocol it explains, offers significantly more flexibility than its OSI counterpart by emphasizing the hierarchical arrangement of functions, rather than strict functional layering.

Dissecting TCP/IP

The TCP/IP protocol stack includes four functional layers: process/application, host-to-host, Internet, and network access. These four layers, starting at the top and working downward, loosely correlate to the seven layers of the OSI Reference Model without compromising functionality.

The Process/Application Layer

The process/application layer provides protocols for remote access and resource sharing. Familiar applications such as Telnet, FTP, SMTP, HTTP, and many others all reside and operate in this layer and depend upon the functionality of the underlying layers.

The Host-to-Host Layer

The IP host-to-host layer correlates loosely to the OSI Reference Model's session and transport layers. It consists of two protocol entities: Transmission Control Protocol (TCP) and User Datagram Protocol (UDP). A third entity is being defined to accommodate the increasingly transaction-oriented nature of the Internet. This protocol entity is tentatively called Transaction Transmission Control Protocol (T/TCP).

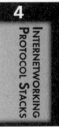

4

INTERNETWORKING
PROTOCOL STACKS

TCP provides a connection-oriented data transmission between two or more hosts, can support multiple data streams, and provides for flow and error control, and even for the reordering of packets that may have been received out of order.

The TCP protocol header is a minimum of 20 octets and contains the following fields:

- TCP Source Port: The 16-bit source port field contains the number of the port making the "call." The source port and source IP address function as the packet's return address.

- TCP Destination Port: The 16-bit destination port field is the address of the "called," or destination, port. The IP address is used to forward the packet to the correct destination machine. At this point, the TCP Destination Port is used to forward the packet to the correct application on that machine.

- TCP Sequence Number: The 32-bit sequence number is used by the receiving computer to reconstruct the fragmented data back into its original form. In a dynamically routed network, it is quite possible for some of the packets to take different routes and, consequently, arrive out of order. This sequencing field compensates for any inconsistency of delivery.

- TCP Acknowledgment Number: TCP uses a 32-bit "piggybacked" acknowledgment (ACK) of the next expected octet. The number used to identify each ACK is the sequence number of the packet being acknowledged.

- Data Offset: This 4-bit field contains the size of the TCP header, measured in 32-bit words.

- Reserved: This 6-bit field is always set to zero.

- Flags: The 6-bit flags field contains six 1-bit flags that enable the control functions of the urgent field, the acknowledgment of significant field, push, reset connection, synchronize sequence numbers, and finished sending data.

- Window Size (16 bits): This field is used by the destination machine to tell the source host how much data it is willing to accept, per TCP segment.

- Checksum (16 bits): The TCP header also contains an error checking field known as a *checksum*. The source host calculates a mathematical value, based upon the segment's contents. The destination host performs the same calculation. If the content remained intact, the result of the two calculations is identical, thereby proving the validity of the data.

- Padding: Extra zeros are added to this field to ensure that the TCP header is always a multiple of 32 bits.

The User Datagram Protocol (UDP) is IP's other host-to-host (or *transport*) layer protocol. UDP provides a basic, low-overhead, data transmission mechanism known as a *datagram*. The simplicity of datagrams makes UDP inappropriate for some applications, but perfect for more sophisticated applications that can provide their own connection-oriented functionality.

Alternatively, UDP can be used for exchanges of data, such as broadcasting NetBIOS names, system messages, and so on, as these exchanges do not require flow control, acknowledgments, reordering, or any of the functionality that TCP provides.

The UDP protocol header has the following structure:

- UDP Source Port Number: The source port is the connection number on the source computer. The source port and source IP address function as the packet's return address.

- UDP Destination Port Number: The destination port is the connection number on the destination computer. The IP address is used to forward the packet to the correct destination machine. At this point, the UDP Destination Port is used to forward the packet to the correct application on that machine.

- UDP Checksum: The checksum is an error-checking field that is calculated based upon the contents of the segment. The destination computer performs the same mathematical function as the originating host. If there is a discrepancy in the two calculated values, an error has occurred during the transmission of the packet.

- UDP Message Length: The message length field informs the destination computer of the size of the message. This provides another mechanism for the destination computer to use in determining the message's validity.

The major functional difference between TCP and UDP is reliability. TCP is highly reliable and UDP is a simple, "best effort" datagram delivery mechanism. This fundamental difference results in vastly different uses of the two host-to-host layer protocols.

The Internet Layer

The Internet, or network, layer of IPv4 consists of all the protocols and procedures necessary to allow data communications between hosts to traverse multiple networks. This means that the data-bearing packets must be routable. The Internet Protocol (IP) is responsible for making data packets routable.

The IP header is a minimum of 20 octets long, and has the following structure:

- Version: The first four bits of the IP header identify the operating version of IP, such as version 4.

- Internet Header Length: The next four bits of the header contain the length of the header, expressed in multiples of 32.

- Type of Service: The next eight bits contain 1-bit "flags" that can be used to specify precedence, delay, throughput, and reliability parameters for that packet of data.

- Total Length: This 16-bit field contains the total length of the IP datagram measured in octets. Valid values can range from 576 to 65,535 octets.

- Identifier: Each IP packet is given a unique, 16-bit identifier.

■ Flags: The next field contains three 1-bit flags that indicate whether fragmentation of the packet is permitted and if it is used.

■ Fragment Offset: This 8-bit field measures the "offset" of the fragmented contents relative to the beginning of the entire datagram. This value is measured in 64-bit increments.

■ Time to Live (TTL): The IP packet cannot be permitted to roam the wide area network in perpetuity. It must be limited to a finite number of "hops." The 8-bit TTL field is incremented by 1 for each "hop" it makes. After reaching its maximum limit, the packet is destroyed.

> **NOTE**
>
> IP packets are forwarded across different networks by devices known as *routers*. Each router that a packet passes through is considered a *hop*. Establishing a maximum hop count ensures that packets do not loop continuously in a dynamically routed network.

■ Protocol: This 8-bit field identifies the protocol that follows the IP header, for example, VINES, TCP, UDP, and so on.

■ Checksum: The checksum field is a 16-bit error-checking field. The destination computer, or any gateway nodes in the network, may recompute the mathematical calculation on the packet's contents as the source computer did. If the data survived the trip intact, the results of these two calculations is identical. This field also informs the destination host of the amount of incoming data.

■ Source IP Address: The source address is the Internet address of the source computer.

■ Destination IP Address: The destination address is the Internet address of the destination computer.

■ Padding: Extra zeros are added to this field to ensure that the IP header is always a multiple of 32 bits.

The IP header is illustrated in Figure 4.2.

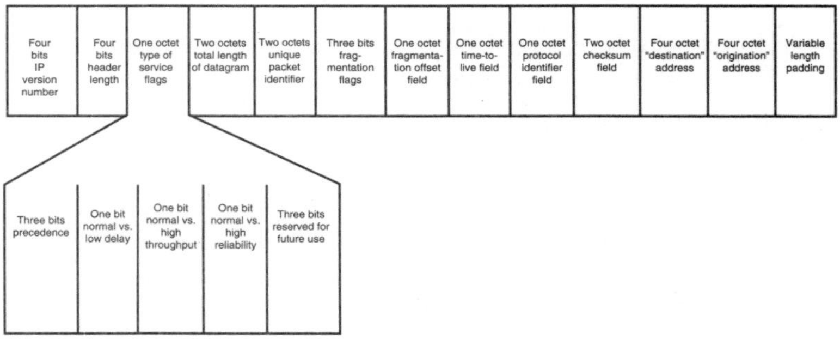

FIGURE 4.2.

The IP header structure.

These header fields reveal that IPv4's Internet layer is inherently connectionless: It lets packets "find" their own way through the networks. It also doesn't provide any of the acknowledgements, flow control, or sequencing functions of higher-level protocols such as TCP. It leaves such functions to those higher-level protocols.

The Internet layer must also support other route-management functions beyond just packet formatting. It must provide mechanisms for resolving Layer 2 addresses into Layer 3 addresses, Layer 3 addresses into Layer 2 addresses, and so on. These functions are provided by peer protocols to IP. These protocols include Interior Gateway Protocols (IGP), Exterior Gateway Protocols (EGP), Address Resolution Protocol (ARP), Reverse Address Resolution Protocol (RARP), and Internet Control Message Protocol (ICMP).

Typical IPv4 Operation

The application layer places a header on to the data packet, identifying the destination host and port. The host-to-host layer protocol (either TCP or UDP, depending on the application) breaks that block of data into smaller, more manageable pieces. Each piece has a TCP header prepended to it. This structure is known as a TCP *segment*.

The segment's header fields are populated appropriately, and the segment is passed to the Internet layer. The Internet layer adds the addressing, protocol type (TCP or UDP), and checksum information. If the segment is fragmented, this layer populates that field as well. Figure 4.3 depicts a TCP/IP packet in this state, just prior to being passed to the data link layer.

FIGURE 4.3.
Structure of an 802.3 Ethernet frame with a TCP/IP payload.

Seven octet "preamble"	One octet "start of frame delimiter"	Six octet "destination" address	Six octet "origination" address	Two octet "length" field	Twenty + octets IP header	Twenty + octets TCP header	Variable length "data" field (> 46 octets < 1482)	Four octet frame check sequence

This illustration shows the positioning of the TCP and IP headers within an 802.3 Ethernet frame. This is the structure used to pass data between the network access and Internet layers.

The destination machine performs the reverse of the operation just described. It receives the packets and passes them to its host-to-host layer protocol for reassembly. If necessary, the packets are reordered into data segments that are passed up to the appropriate application.

IP Addressing Scheme

IPv4 uses a 32-bit binary addressing scheme to identify networks, network devices, and network-connected machines. These addresses, known as IP addresses, are strictly regulated by the Internet Network Information Center (InterNIC). It is entirely possible for a network administrator to arbitrarily select unregistered IP addresses; this practice should not be condoned. Computers having such spurious IP addresses will function properly only within the confines of their domain. Attempts to access the Internet will demonstrate the ramifications of this short-sighted act.

There are five classes of IP addresses, identified by a single alphabetic character—that is, Class A, Class B, Class C, and so on. Each address consists of two parts: a network address and a host address. The five classes represent different compromises between the number of supportable networks and hosts. Although these addresses are binary, they are normally identified with a dotted decimal format, for example, `135.65.121.6`, to facilitate human usage. The dots are used to separate the address's four octets.

- Class A IP Address: The first bit of a Class A address is always a 0. The next seven bits identify the network number. The last 24 bits (that is, three dotted decimal numbers) of a Class A address represent possible host addresses. The range of possible Class A addresses is from `1.0.0.0` to `126.0.0.0`. Each Class A address can support 16,774,214 unique host addresses.

- Class B IP Address: The first two bits of a Class B address are 10. The next 16 bits identify the network number, and the last 16 bits identify potential host addresses. The range of possible Class B addresses is from `128.1.0.0` to `191.254.0.0`. Each Class B address can support 65,534 unique host addresses.

- Class C IP Address: The first three bits of a Class C address are 110. The next 21 bits are used to identify the network's number. The last octet is used for host addressing. The range of possible Class C addresses is from `192.0.1.0` to `223.255.254.0`. Each Class C address can support 254 unique host addresses.

- Class D IP Address: The first four bits of a Class D address are 1110. These addresses are used for multicasting, but have seen only limited usage. A multicast address is a unique network address that results in packets with that destination address being sent to predefined groups of IP addresses. Class D addresses range from `224.0.0.0` to `239.255.255.254`.

- Class E IP Address: A Class E address has been defined but is reserved by the InterNIC for its own research. Thus, no Class E addresses have been released for use on the Internet.

The large gaps between these address classes resulted in the wasting of potential addresses. For example, a medium-sized company might require 300 IP addresses. This means that a Class C address would be inadequate. Using two Class C addresses would provide more than enough addresses, but result in two separate domains within the company.

NOTE

Please note, this is no longer the case. A new inter-domain routing protocol known as Classless Interdomain Routing (CIDR) has been developed to enable multiple smaller address classes to function as a single routing domain.

Stepping up to a Class B address would provide all the needed addresses within a single domain, but would waste 65,234 addresses.

IP addressing requires each machine to have its own unique address. Subnet masks may optionally be used to compensate for the tremendous gaps between address classes by customizing the length of the host and/or network addresses. These two numbers are used to route any given IP datagram to its destination.

As TCP/IP is capable of supporting multiple sessions from a single host, it must then provide a way of addressing specific communications programs that may operate on each host. This is done through *port numbers*. Some of the more common applications are assigned their own "well-known" port numbers. These numbers are reliably constant, per application, from host to host. Other applications are simply assigned an available port number.

IPv4 Conclusion

IPv4 is almost 20 years old. Since its inception, the Internet has experienced several significant changes that have diminished IP's effectiveness as a universal interconnectivity protocol. Perhaps the most significant of these changes has been the commercialization of the Internet. This has brought with it an unprecedented growth in the Internet's user population and a shift in its demographics. This, in turn, has created the tandem need for more addresses and network layer support for new types of service. IPv4's limitations have been driving the development of a completely new version of the protocol. This new version is called IP version 6 (IPv6) but was also commonly referred to as the "next generation" of Internet Protocol (IPng).

The Internet Protocol, Version 6 (IPv6)

IPv6 is designed to be a simple, forward-compatible upgrade to the existing version of IP. This upgrade is also intended to resolve all of the weaknesses that IPv4 is currently manifesting, including the shortage of available IP addresses, the inability to accommodate time-sensitive traffic, and its lack of network layer security.

In addition to these issues, routing is also driving the development and deployment of the new IP protocol. IPv4 is hampered by its 32-bit address, its two-level addressing hierarchy, and its address classes. This two-level addressing hierarchy (host and domain name) simply does not allow construction of efficient address hierarchies that can be aggregated by routers on the scale that today's global Internet requires.

The next generation of IP, commonly known as IPng but more correctly identified as IPv6, resolves all of these issues. It offers a vastly expanded addressing scheme to support the continued expansion of the Internet, and an improved ability to aggregate routes on a large scale.

IPv6 also supports numerous other features, such as real-time audio or video transmissions, host mobility, end-to-end security through network layer encryption and authentication, as well as auto-configuration and auto-reconfiguration. It is expected that these services will provide ample incentive for migration as soon as IPv6-capable products become available. Many of these features still require additional standardization. Therefore, it would be premature to expound upon them at any great length.

The one aspect of IPv6 that can, and should, be expounded upon is its addressing. IPv4's 32-bit address length gave the protocol a theoretical capability to address 2 to the 32nd power, or about 4 billion devices. Inefficient subnet masking techniques, among other wasteful practices, has squandered this resource.

IPv6 uses a 128-bit address and is theoretically capable of 2 to the 96th power times the size of the IPv4 address space. This equals 340,282,366,920,938,463,463,374,607,431,768,211,456 mathematically possible addresses. Only about 15 percent of this potential address space is currently allocated. The remainder is reserved for unspecified future use.

In reality, the assignment and routing of addresses requires the creation of hierarchies. This reduces the number of potential addresses, but increases the efficiency of IPv6-capable routing protocols. One practical implication of the IPv6 address length is that DNS becomes an absolute necessity and not the luxury that it had been in the IPv4 network environment.

As significant as the increased potential address space is, even greater flexibility is afforded through IPv6's new address structures. IPv6 dispenses with the previous class-based addressing. Instead, it recognizes three kinds of unicast address, replaces the former Class D address with a new multicast address format, and introduces a new "anycast" address. These new addressing structures *must* be understood prior to undertaking an IPv6 migration.

IPv6 Unicast Address Structures

Unicast addressing provides connectivity from one endpoint to one endpoint. IPv6 supports several forms of unicasting addresses. They are described in the following sections.

Internet Service Provider Unicast Address

Whereas IPv4 pre-assumed clusters of users requiring connectivity, IPv6 provides a unicast address format designed specifically for use by Internet service providers (ISPs) to connect *individual* users to the Internet. These provider-based unicast addresses offer unique addresses for individuals or small groups that access the Internet via a provider. The architecture of the address provides for efficient aggregation of routes in an environment characterized by individual users, as opposed to large concentrations of users.

The ISP unicast address format is:

3 bits	n bits	m bits	o bits	p bits	125 − (n+m+o+p) bits
010	Registry ID	Provider ID	Subscriber ID	Subnet ID	Interface ID

An example of this address would be 010:0:0:0:0:x, where x can be any number. Given that much of the new address space has yet to be allocated, these addresses will contain lots of 0s. Therefore, groups of 0s may be shortened with a double "::". This shorthand notation would be 010::x.

The other unicast address types are designed for local use. These addresses can be assigned to networked devices within a standalone intranet or to devices on an intranet that access the Internet.

Link-Local Use

The Link-local is for use on a single link, for purposes such as auto-address configuration, neighbor discovery, or when no routers are present. Link-local addresses have the following format:

10 bits	n bits	118 – n bits
1111111011	0	interface ID

The interface ID can be the MAC address of an Ethernet Network Interface Card. MAC addresses, being theoretically unique addresses, can be concatenated with standard IP address prefixes to form unique addresses for mobile or transitory users. An example of a Link-local Use address with a MAC address would be: `1111111011:0:mac_address`.

Site-Local Unicast Address

Site-local addresses are designed for use in a single site. They may be used for sites or organizations that are not connected to the global Internet. They do not need to request or "steal" an address prefix from the global Internet address space. IPv6 Site-local addresses can be used instead. When the organization connects to the global Internet, it can then form unique global addresses by replacing the Site-local prefix with a subscriber prefix that contains a Registry, Provider, and Subscriber Identification.

Site-local addresses have the following format:

10 bits	n bits	m bits	118 – (n + m) bits
1111111011	0	subnet ID	interface ID

An example of a Site-local address is `1111111011:0:subnet:interface`.

IPv6 Transitional Unicast Address Structures

Two special IPv6 unicast addresses have been defined as transition mechanisms to allow hosts and routers to dynamically route IPv6 packets over an IPv4 network infrastructure and vice versa.

IPv4-Compatible IPv6 Unicast Address

The first is called an *IPv4-compatible IPv6 address*. This transitional unicast address can be assigned to IPv6 nodes and contain an IPv4 address in the last 32 bits. These addresses have the following format:

80 bits	16 bits	32 bits
000...0000	00............00	IPv4 address

IPv4-Mapped IPv6 Unicast Address

A second, similar, type of IPv6 address that also contains an IPv4 address in its last 32 bits is known as an *IPv4-mapped IPv6 address*. This address is constructed by a dual protocol router and permits IPv4-only nodes to tunnel through IPv6 network infrastructure. The only difference between IPv4-mapped IPv6 addresses and IPv4-compatible IPv6 addresses is that IPv4-mapped addresses are constructs only. They are built automatically by dual protocol routers and cannot be assigned to any nodes! This address is formatted as follows:

80 bits	16 bits	32 bits
000.......................................0000	FF.........FF	IPv4 address

Both the IPv4-mapped and the IPv4-compatible unicast addresses are essential to *tunneling*. Tunneling enables the transport of packets through an otherwise incompatible network region by wrapping those packets in an externally acceptable framework.

IPv6 Anycast Address Structures

The anycast address, introduced in IPv6, is a single value assigned to more than one interface. Typically, these interfaces belong to different devices. A packet sent to an anycast address is routed to only *one* device. It is sent to the "nearest" interface having that address, as defined by the routing protocols' measure of distance. For example, a World Wide Web (WWW) site may be mirrored on several servers. By assigning an anycast address to these servers, requests for connectivity to that WWW site are automatically routed to only one server: the server nearest the user.

Anycast addresses are formed from the unicast address space and may take the form of any unicast address type. Anycast addresses are formed simply by assigning the same unicast address to more than one interface.

IPv6 Multicast Address Structures

Multicasting was previously supported in IPv4, but required the use of obscure Class D addressing. IPv6 eliminates Class D addresses in favor of a new address format that permits trillions of possible multicast group codes. Each group code identifies two or more packet recipients. The scope of a particular multicast address is flexible. Each address can be confined to a single system, restricted within a specific site, associated with a particular network link, or distributed globally.

It should be noted that IP broadcasts, too, have been eliminated in favor of the new multicasting address format.

IPv6 Conclusion

Despite the potential benefits of IPv6, the migration from IPv4 is not risk free. The extension of the address length from 32 to 128 bits automatically limits interoperability between IPv4 and IPv6. *IPv4-only nodes cannot interoperate with IPv6-only nodes as the address architectures are not forward compatible.* This business risk, in combination with the ongoing evolution of IPv4, will likely forestall the acceptance of IPv6 in the marketplace.

Novell's IPX/SPX

The Novell protocol suite is named after its two primary protocols: Internet Packet Exchange (IPX) and Sequenced Packet Exchange (SPX). This proprietary protocol stack is based on Xerox's Network Systems (XNS) protocol, used with first generation Ethernets. IPX/SPX became prominent during the early 1980s as an integral part of Novell, Inc.'s NetWare. NetWare became the *de facto* standard network operating system (NOS) of first generation LANs. Novell complemented its NOS with a business-oriented application suite and client-side connection utilities.

IPX is much like IP. It is a connectionless datagram protocol that does not require, nor provide, an acknowledgment for each packet transmitted. IPX also relies upon SPX in the same way that IP relies upon TCP for sequencing and other Layer 4 connection-oriented services. The relationship between the OSI Reference Model and the IPX/SPX protocol suite is illustrated in Figure 4.4.

FIGURE 4.4.
Comparison of the OSI Reference Model and IPX/SPX.

OSI reference model layer description	OSI layer number	IPX/SPX equivalent layer description				
Application	7	R I P	S A P	N C P	N L S P	Misc. Protocols
Presentation	6					
Session	5					
Transport	4				SPX	
Network	3	Internet Packet Exchange				
Data Link	2	Open data link interface				
Physical	1	Medium access				

Novell's IPX and SPX protocols provide functionality equivalent to the OSI Layers 3 and 4, respectively. The full suite of IPX/SPX protocols provides the functionality of the other OSI layers in four layers.

Dissecting IPX/SPX

The IPX/SPX protocol stack includes four functional layers: application, internet, data link, and medium access. These four layers are presented from the highest to the lowest, and loosely correlate to the seven layers of the OSI Reference Model without compromising functionality.

4
INTERNETWORKING PROTOCOL STACKS

Application Layer

Novell's application layer encompasses the application, presentation, and session layers of the OSI model, although some of its application protocols extend as far down the stack as the OSI network layer. The primary application layer protocol in this stack is the NetWare Core Protocol (NCP). NCP can interface directly with both SPX and IPX. NCP is used for printing, file sharing, e-mail, and directory access.

Other application layer protocols include Routing Information Protocol (RIP), a proprietary Service Advertisement Protocol (SAP), and NetWare Link Services Protocol (NLSP), among others.

RIP is the default routing protocol for NetWare. It is a distance-vector routing protocol that uses only two metrics: ticks and hops. A *tick* is a measure of time, and a hop, as explained earlier in this chapter, is the running tally of routers that have handled the routed packet. These two metrics are the basis for IPX routing path decisions. Ticks are the primary metric for determining paths. Hops are used only as "tie breakers" in the event of two or more paths having the same tick value.

RIP is a very simple and mature routing protocol. In addition to its limited number of distance-vector metrics, it suffers from a high level of network overhead incurred because RIP routing table updates are broadcast every 60 seconds. This can have adverse effects on large or very busy networks.

SAP is a unique and proprietary protocol that Novell has successfully used to enhance the client/server relationship. Servers use SAP to automatically broadcast their available services throughout the network immediately after becoming active on the network. They periodically broadcast SAPs to keep clients and other servers informed of their status and services.

SAP broadcasts include the server's name and type, operational status, and network, node, and socket numbers. Routers can store information from an SAP broadcast and propagate it to other network segments. Clients can also initiate SAP requests when they need a specific service. Their request is broadcast throughout the network segment. Hosts can then respond and provide the client with enough SAP information to determine whether or not the service is available within a reasonable distance.

Unfortunately, SAP is an extremely mature protocol that is becoming increasingly ill-suited to functioning in contemporary networks. As with RIP, service advertisements occur every 60 seconds. On today's large, flat, switched LANs, this degree of broadcasting can be problematic.

The newest application layer protocol is NetWare Link Services Protocol (NLSP). NLSP is a link-state routing protocol that Novell intends to use as a replacement for the aging RIP and SAP protocols. NLSP updates routes only when changes have been made.

Internet Layer Protocols

The Internet layer of IPX/SPX maps loosely to both the network and transport layers of the OSI Reference Model. IPX is predominantly a Layer 3, or network layer, protocol although it is capable of directly interfacing with the application layer. SPX is distinctly a Layer 4, or transport layer, protocol and cannot directly interface with the data link layer's ODI. It must pass data through IPX and let IPX interface with the ODI. IPX and SPX function as sublayer protocols within a common Internet layer.

SPX is connection-oriented and can be used to transmit data between a client and server, two servers, or even two clients. As with TCP, SPX provides reliability to IPX transmissions by managing the connection, providing flow control, error checking, and packet sequencing.

The SPX header has the following size and structure:

- Connection Control: The first octet (eight bits) of the SPX header provides four 2-bit flags that control the bi-directional flow of data across an SPX connection.
- Datastream Type: The next eight bits of the header define the type of datastream.
- Source Connection Identification: The 16-bit Source Connection Identification field is used to identify the process responsible for initiating the connection.
- Destination Connection Identification: The 16-bit Destination Connection Identification field is used to identify the process that accepted the inbound SPX connection request.
- Sequence Number: The 16-bit Sequence Number field provides the destination host's SPX protocol with a count of packets transmitted. This sequential numbering can be used to reorder the received packets, should they arrive out of sequence.
- Acknowledgment Number: The Acknowledgment Number field is a 16-bit field that indicates the next expected packet.
- Allocation Number: The Allocation Number field is 16 bits in length and is used to track the number of packets sent, but not yet acknowledged, by the intended recipient.
- Data: The last field in the SPX header contains the data. Up to 534 octets of data may be transmitted, per SPX packet.

Novell's other Internet layer protocol is IPX. IPX provides a connectionless, best-effort, datagram delivery service. It prepares SPX, or other protocols', packets for delivery across multiple networks by prepending an IPX header to them. This new structure is called an IPX datagram. This datagram's header contains all the information necessary to route the packets to their destination, regardless of where that might be.

The IPX header is 11 octets long and has the following structure:

- Checksum Field: The IPX header begins with a 16-bit legacy field that exists solely to provide backward compatibility with its ancestral XNS protocol. XNS used this field for error checking. IPX defaults this field to "FFFFH" and trusts higher-level protocols to detect (and correct) any transmission errors.

- Packet Length Field: This 16-bit field defines the length of the IPX datagram, including the header and data. Packet Length is checked to verify packet integrity.

- Transport Control: This 8-bit field is used by routers during the forwarding of the datagram. IPX sets it to 0 prior to transmission. Each router that receives and forwards the datagram increments this field by 1.

- Packet Type: This 8-bit field identifies the type of packet that is embedded in the IPX datagram. This field allows the destination host to pass the contents to the next appropriate protocol layer. Types can include RIP, NCP, SPX, error, and so on.

- Destination Network Number: This 32-bit field identifies the network number of the destination node.

- Destination Node: This 48-bit field contains the node number of the destination machine.

- Destination Socket Number: As IPX allows for multiple simultaneous connections to one system, it is essential to identify the socket number of the process or program receiving the packets. This 16-bit field provides this information.

- Source Network Number: This 32-bit field identifies the network number of the source node.

- Source Node Address: This 48-bit field contains the node number of the source machine.

- Source Socket Number: This 16-bit field identifies the socket number of the process or program sending the packets.

Typical IPX/SPX Operation

SPX creates and maintains a connection-oriented bit stream between two networked devices. The protocol accepts large blocks of data from higher-level protocols and breaks them into more manageable pieces that are up to 534 octets long. The header just described is prepended to the data to create SPX packets. These packets are passed to the Internet sublayer protocol IPX.

The segment's header fields are populated appropriately, and the segment is passed to IPX. IPX adds the network addressing, length, checksum, and other header information before passing the packet on to the data link layer. Figure 4.5 depicts an IPX/SPX packet in this state, just prior to being passed to the data link layer.

FIGURE 4.5.

Structure of an 802.3 Ethernet frame encapsulating an IPX/SPX payload.

Seven octet "preamble"	One octet "start of frame delimiter"	Six octet "destination" address	Six octet "origination" address	Two octet "length" field	Thirty octet IPX header	Variable length SPX header	Variable length "data" field (> 46 octets < 1482)	Four octet frame check sequence

This illustration shows the positioning of the IPX and SPX headers within an 802.3 Ethernet frame. This is the structure used to pass data between the two sublayers of Novell's Internet layer.

The destination machine performs the reverse of the operation just described. It receives the packets and passes them to its SPX protocol for reassembly. If necessary, the packets are reordered into data segments that are passed up to the appropriate application.

Data Link and Medium Access Layers

NetWare's equivalents of the OSI physical and data link layers are the medium access and data link layers. The data link layer is directly compatible with the Open Data-Link Interface (ODI) standard. Similarly, the medium access layer is directly compatible with all common, standardized media access protocols.

This low-level adherence to open industry standards enables NetWare and the IPX/SPX protocol stack to be implemented almost universally.

IPX Addressing

IPX addresses are 10 octets (80 bits) long. This is significantly larger than IPv4's 32-bit address, but less than IPv6's 128-bit address. Each address is comprised of two components: a network number up to 32 bits in length and a 48-bit node number. These numbers are expressed in dotted hexadecimal notation. For example, 1a2b.0000.3c4d.5e6d could be a valid IPX address where the 1a2b represented the network number and 0000.3c4d.5e6d was the node number.

IPX addresses, too, can be "invented" by a network administrator. However, this runs the risk of address conflicts when internetworking. Invention of network numbers also places the burden of maintaining and managing all such fabricated numbers on the network administrator. The better approach is to obtain registered IPX network numbers from Novell.

The universally assigned address (MAC address) on the network interface card (NIC) is usually used as the IPX host number. Given that these addresses are, at least in theory, unique, this provides a convenient, unique host numbering.

As with IP, IPX is capable of supporting multiple simultaneous sessions. This creates the need for identifying the specific process or program that is communicating on any given session. This identification is achieved through the use of a 16-bit socket number in the IPX header. This socket number is analogous to TCP/IP's port number.

IPX/SPX Conclusion

Novell, Inc. has watched the market share of its proprietary IPX/SPX protocol stack plummet under competitive pressure. As "open" protocol stacks such as OSI, IP, and others became available, IPX/SPX suffered. Commercially available office automation software bundles also cut into Novell's sales. Having a proprietary, tightly coupled series of products became viewed as a liability in a marketplace that valued openness and interoperability.

Novell has demonstrated its commitment to regaining its lost prominence by making IPv6 its default protocol for future versions of NetWare. To successfully implement this change of strategy, Novell must ensure backward compatibility of IPv6 and IPX/SPX. To achieve this goal, Novell has worked closely with the Internet Engineering Task Force (IETF) during the design of IPv6. This has resulted in numerous IPX services becoming integral to IPv6.

Having set the stage for its future, Novell now must ensure a seamless migration of its current protocol stack and application suite to this new environment. More importantly, it needs to provide value-adding products and services using an open network platform. Novell's vision for the future is to provide Network Directory Services (NDS) and related products for two customer bases: the Internet community and corporate intranet communities.

NDS provides a single, global, logical view of all network services and resources. This allows users to access network services and resources with a single login, regardless of the user's location or the location of the resources.

Apple Corporation's AppleTalk Protocol Suite

As Apple computers increased in popularity, and their users became increasingly sophisticated in their use, the need to network them became inescapable. It is no surprise that the network Apple developed is as user friendly as their computers. AppleTalk, the name for Apple's networking protocol stack, and its necessary hardware are included with every computer Apple sells.

Connecting to the network can be as simple as plugging in the network connection and powering up the Apple computer. The AppleTalk network is a peer-to-peer network that provides basic functionality such as file and printer sharing. Unlike client/server networks, there are no hardened definitions constraining the functionality of a peer-to-peer network. Each machine can act simultaneously as both a client and a server.

AppleTalk has also been embraced by many other operating system (OS) manufacturers. It is not uncommon to find support for the AppleTalk protocol stack available on non-Apple computers. This enables customers to use AppleTalk and Apple computers to create, or join existing, non-Apple client/server networks.

Dissecting AppleTalk

The AppleTalk protocol stack contains five functional layers: network access, datagram delivery, network, zone information, and application. Apple's AppleTalk protocol stack closely follows the functionality of the OSI Reference Model on its network transport and session layers. The physical and data link layers are collapsed into numerous, frame-specific, individual layers. Similarly, AppleTalk integrates the application and presentation layers into a single application layer. Figure 4.6 illustrates this functional relationship.

FIGURE 4.6.
Comparison of the OSI Reference Model and AppleTalk.

OSI reference model layer description	OSI layer number	AppleTalk equivalent layer description
Application	7	Application
Presentation	6	Application
Session	5	Session
Transport	4	Transport
Network	3	Datagram delivery
Data Link	2	Network access
Physical	1	Network access

The AppleTalk Application Layer

As mentioned, AppleTalk combines the functionality of the OSI Reference Model's application and presentation layers into a single application layer. Because AppleTalk is a fairly simple protocol stack, there is only a single protocol occupying this layer. It is the AppleTalk Filing Protocol (AFP). AFP provides network file services to applications that exist separate from the protocol stack, for example, electronic mail, print queuing, and so on. Any application running on an Apple computer must pass through AFP if it needs to send or receive information across the network.

The AppleTalk Session Layer

AppleTalk's version of the OSI session layer contains five primary protocols that provide such services as full-duplex transmission, logical name-to-address resolution, printer access, packet sequencing, and so on.

The first session layer protocol is the AppleTalk Data Stream Protocol (ADSP). ADSP provides full-duplex connection-oriented services in a highly reliable manner by establishing a logical connection (session) between the two communicating processes on client machines. ADSP also manages this connection by providing flow control services, sequence management, and acknowledgment of transmitted packets. ADSP uses socket addresses to establish this process-to-process logical connection. Once the connection is established, the two systems can exchange data.

Another AppleTalk session layer protocol is AppleTalk Session Protocol (ASP). This protocol provides reliable data delivery using sequence-oriented session management and the transport services of AppleTalk Transport Protocol (ATP), a transport layer protocol.

The AppleTalk Update-Based Routing Protocol (AURP) is used in larger AppleTalk networks. AURP is used primarily for route management and information exchange between routing devices, particularly Exterior Gateway routers.

AppleTalk's session layer also includes a Printer Access Protocol (PAP). Although PAP was originally developed for managing access to networked printers, it can be used for a variety of data exchanges. It provides a bi-directional session between two devices, complete with flow control and sequence management.

The last of the AppleTalk session layer protocols is the Zone Information Protocol (ZIP). ZIP provides a mechanism for logically grouping individual networked devices using "friendly" names. These logical groups are called *zones*. In an extended network, computers can span multiple networks, but still be logically grouped into a zone. However, in small, non-extended networks only one zone can be defined.

ZIP uses the Name Binding Protocol (NBP), a transport layer protocol, to translate these names to network and node numbers, and the ATP protocol for delivery of zone information updates.

These five session layer protocols provide AppleTalk clients with logical connections and data transfers between computers, regardless of how near or far apart they are.

The AppleTalk Transport Layer

The AppleTalk transport layer offers transport services to the layers above it. There are four distinct protocols in this layer. The most frequently used protocol in this layer is the AppleTalk Transport Protocol (ATP).

ATP provides a reliable, loss-free mechanism for packet delivery between two computers. ATP uses the sequence and acknowledgment fields in the packet header to ensure packets are not lost on their way to their destination.

Another significant AppleTalk transport layer protocol is the Name Binding Protocol (NBP). As previously indicated, NBP enables ZIP to translate friendly names into actual addresses.

NBP performs the actual translation of zone names to network and node addresses. NBP contains four basic functions: registration, lookup, confirmation, and deletion of names.

- Name Registration: Name registration registers a unique logical name in an NBP Registry database.

- Name Lookup: Name lookup is provided to a computer that requests another computer's address using an object name. NBP always attempts to resolve such requests by looking at local node numbers. If no match is found, it broadcasts a request to other internetworked AppleTalk networks. If a match still cannot be found, the request times out and the requestor receives an error message.

- Name Confirmation: Confirmation requests are used to verify object-address relationships.

- Name Deletion: Devices on the network are periodically shutdown or removed. When this happens, a name deletion request is sent and object-name-to-addressing tables are automatically updated.

AppleTalk Echo Protocol (AEP) is another transport layer protocol. It is used to determine the accessibility of a system and to compute the Round Trip Transmit time (RTT).

The last transport layer protocol is AppleTalk's Routing Table Maintenance Protocol (RTMP). As AppleTalk uses routed protocols in its network layer, it must provide for management of routing tables. RTMP provides routers with content for its routing tables.

AppleTalk's Datagram Delivery Layer

AppleTalk's datagram delivery layer, directly analogous to OSI's Layer 3 (network layer), provides connectionless, packet-sized datagram delivery. This is the basis for establishing communications and delivering data over an AppleTalk network. This layer is also responsible for providing the dynamic addressing of networked nodes, as well as MAC address resolution for IEEE 802 networks.

The primary protocol in this layer is the Datagram Delivery Protocol (DDP). DDP provides best-effort data transmission in a connectionless fashion across multiple networks. It adapts its header types depending upon the intended destination. The basic components remain constant; additional fields are added, as needed.

Datagrams that will be delivered locally, that is, on the same subnetwork, use the *short header* format. Datagrams that require routing to other subnetworks use the *extended header* format. The extended header format contains network addresses and a hop counter field.

The DDP header contains the following fields:

- Hop Count: This field contains a counter that is incremented by 1 for each router device it travels across. Hop count is only used in the extended header.

- Datagram Length: This field contains the length of the datagram and can be used to determine whether it was damaged in transit.

4

INTERNETWORKING PROTOCOL STACKS

■ DDP Checksum: This is an optional field. When used, it provides a more robust form of error detection than simply checking the length of a datagram. Checksum verification detects whether the contents were changed even slightly, regardless of whether or not the length of the datagram changed.

■ Source Socket Number: This field identifies the communicating process on the machine that initiated the connection.

■ Destination Socket Number: This field identifies the communicating process on the machine that responded to the connection request.

■ Source Address: This field contains the network and node numbers of the originating computer. This field is used only in the extended header format and enables routers to forward datagrams across multiple subnetworks.

■ Destination Address: This field contains the network and node numbers of the destination computer. This field is used only in the extended header format and enables routers to forward datagrams across multiple subnetworks.

■ DDP Type: This field identifies the upper-layer protocol that is encapsulated in the datagram. It is used by the destination computer's transport layer to identify the appropriate protocol to pass the contents to.

■ Data: This field contains the data that is being transmitted. It can vary in size from 0 to 586 octets.

The datagram delivery layer also contains a protocol that is used to resolve node addresses into MAC addresses for machines connected to IEEE 802 networks. This protocol is the AppleTalk Address Resolution Protocol (AARP). AARP can also be used to determine the node address for any given station. AARP stores its information in the Address Mapping Table (AMT). Because of the dynamic assignment of node numbers, the table used by AARP is constantly and automatically updated.

AppleTalk Data Link Layer

AppleTalk's data link layer provides the functionality of the OSI Reference Model's physical and data link layers. This functionality is integrated into frame-specific sublayers. For example, EtherTalk is a data link layer protocol that provides all the OSI physical and data link layer functionality in a single sublayer. This sublayer enables AppleTalk to be encapsulated in an 802.3-compliant Ethernet framing structure.

There are similar AppleTalk sublayers for Token Ring (known as TokenTalk) and for FDDI (FDDITalk). These protocols are called *access protocols* because of the physical network access services they offer.

EtherTalk uses a line access protocol known as EtherTalk Link Access Protocol (ELAP) to package data and place the 802.3-compliant frames onto the physical medium. This line access protocol naming convention and functionality holds true for the remainder of the access protocols, for example, TokenTalk relies upon TokenTalk Link Access Protocol (TLAP).

In addition to access protocols that conform to industry standards, Apple offers a proprietary local area network protocol in its data link layer. This protocol is known as LocalTalk. LocalTalk operates at 230Kbps over twisted pair wiring. It uses, predictably, the LocalTalk Link Access Protocols (LLAP) to assemble frames and place them onto the network. LLAP also includes mechanisms for medium access management, data link–level addressing, data encapsulation, and bit representation for frame transmission.

AppleTalk's Addressing Scheme

The AppleTalk addressing scheme is composed of two parts: the network number and the node number.

Network numbers are usually 16 bits long, although unary numbering may be used for non-extended or very small extended networks. These numbers must be defined by the network administrator and used by AppleTalk to route packets between the different networks. The network number 0 is reserved by the protocol for use in connecting new network nodes for the first time. The network number must have a value between 00000001 and FFFFFFFF.

Node numbers are 8-bit addresses consisting of four hexadecimal numbers. The valid range of addresses for hosts, printers, routers, and other devices is from 1 to 253. Node numbers 0, 254, and 255, although mathematically possible within an 8-bit binary address, are reserved by AppleTalk for use on extended networks. All node numbering is done dynamically by AppleTalk's data link layer.

AppleTalk addresses are expressed in dotted decimal notation. That is, the binary address is converted to the decimal (Base 10) number system and a dot (.) is used to separate the node and network numbers. For example, 100.99 refers to device 99 on network 100. The leading zeroes are suppressed.

AppleTalk Conclusion

AppleTalk is a proprietary protocol stack designed expressly for networking Apple's Personal Computers (PCs). Its future is directly tied to the fortunes of Apple Corporation and the trajectories of its technologies. As with Novell's proprietary stack, the physical and data link layers are used to provide compatibility with established standards, although a proprietary LocalTalk physical layer can be used to interconnect Apple computers using twisted pair wiring at up to 230Kbps.

Summary

The selection of a protocol stack can be one of the more important decisions in developing a high-performance network. This is the mechanism that provides the interface between the network's hardware and the applications that rely upon the network for connectivity.

Once a protocol has been selected, the next decision must be *whose* stack should be purchased. OS vendors and application suite vendors are all competing in this arena. It is imperative that, before you place a purchase order for any given stack, you understand exactly what that stack can do and what makes it different from the same protocol's stacks available from other vendors.

II

PART

IN THIS PART

Bringing Your Lines Together

LAN Topologies

by Mark Sportack

IN THIS CHAPTER

Local area network topologies can be described using either a physical or a logical perspective. A *physical topology* describes the geometric arrangement of components that comprise the LAN. The topology is not a map of the network. It is a theoretical construct that graphically conveys the shape and structure of the LAN.

A *logical topology* describes the possible connections between pairs of networked endpoints that can communicate. This is useful in describing which endpoints can communicate with which other endpoints, and whether those pairs capable of communicating have a direct physical connection to each other. This chapter focuses only on physical topological descriptions.

Basic Topologies

There are three basic physical topologies: bus, ring, and star. Each basic topology is dictated by the LAN frame technology. For example, Ethernet networks, by definition, have historically used star topologies. The introduction of frame-level switching in LANs is changing this. Frame-switched LANs, regardless of frame type or access method, are topologically similar. Switched can now be added to the long-standing triad of basic LAN topologies as a distinct, fourth topology.

Bus Topology

A *bus topology*, shown in Figure 5.1, features all networked nodes interconnected peer-to-peer using a single, open-ended cable. These ends must be terminated with a resistive load—that is, *terminating resistors*. This singe cable can support only a single channel. The cable is called the *bus*.

FIGURE 5.1.
Typical bus topology.

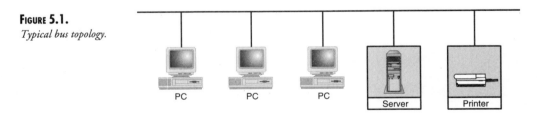

The typical bus topology features a single cable, supported by no external electronics, that interconnects all networked nodes peer to peer. All connected devices listen to the bussed transmissions and accept those packets addressed to them. The lack of any external electronics, such as repeaters, makes bus LANs simple and inexpensive. The downside is that it also imposes severe limitations on distances, functionality, and scaleability.

This topology is impractical for all but the smallest of LANs. Consequently, today's commercially available LAN products that use a bus topology are inexpensive peer-to-peer networks that provide basic connectivity. These products are targeted at home and small office environments.

One exception to this was the IEEE's 802.4 Token Bus LAN specification. This technology was fairly robust and deterministic, and bore many similarities to a Token Ring LAN. The primary difference, obviously, was that Token Bus was implemented on a bus topology.

Token Bus found extremely limited market support. Its implementation tended to be limited to factory production lines. Technological refinement of other LAN technologies and topologies has made this sophisticated bus LAN obsolete.

Ring Topology

The *ring topology* started out as a simple peer-to-peer LAN topology. Each networked workstation had two connections: one to each of its nearest neighbors (see Figure 5.2). The interconnection had to form a physical loop, or ring. Data was transmitted unidirectionally around the ring. Each workstation acted as a repeater, accepting and responding to packets addressed to it, and forwarding on the other packets to the next workstation "downstream."

FIGURE 5.2.

Peer-to-peer ring topology.

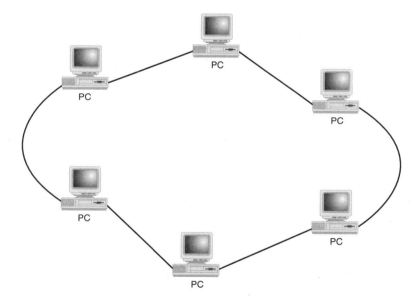

The original LAN ring topology featured peer-to-peer connections between workstations. These connections had to be *closed*—that is, they had to form a ring. The benefit of such LANs was that response time was fairly predictable. The more devices there were in the ring, the longer the network delays. The drawback was that early ring networks could be completely disabled if one of the workstations failed.

These primitive rings were made obsolete by IBM's Token Ring, which was later standardized by the IEEE's 802.5 specification. Token Ring departed from the peer-to-peer interconnection in favor of a repeating hub. This eliminated the vulnerability of ring networks due to workstation failure by eliminating the peer-to-peer ring construction. Token Ring networks, despite their name, are implemented with a star topology and a circular access method, as shown in Figure 5.3.

FIGURE 5.3.

Star-shaped ring topology.

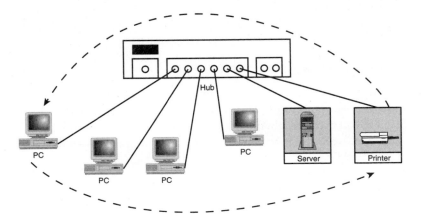

LANs can be implemented in a star topology yet retain a circular access method. The Token Ring network illustrated in this figure demonstrates the virtual ring that is formed by the round-robin access method. The solid lines represent physical connections, and the dashed line represents the logical flow of regulated media access.

Functionally, the access token passes in a round-robin fashion among the networked endpoints. Thus, many people succumb to the temptation of describing Token Ring networks as having a logical ring topology, even though it is no longer a ring.

Star Topology

Star topology LANs have connections to networked devices that radiate out from a common point—that is, the *hub*, as shown in Figure 5.4. Unlike ring topologies, physical or virtual, each networked device in a star topology can access the media independently. These devices have to share the hub's available bandwidth. An example of a LAN with a star topology is Ethernet.

FIGURE 5.4.

Star topology.

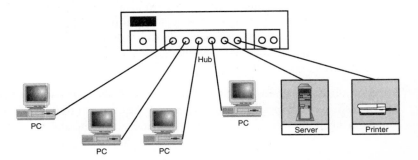

A small LAN with a star topology features connections that radiate out from a common point. Each connected device can initiate media access independent of the other connected devices.

Star topologies have become the dominant topology type in contemporary LANs. They are flexible, scaleable, and relatively inexpensive compared to more sophisticated LANs with strictly regulated access methods. Stars have all but made buses and rings obsolete in LAN topologies and have formed the basis for the final LAN topology: switched.

Switched Topology

A *switch* is a multiport data link layer (OSI Reference Model Layer 2) device. A switch "learns" MAC addresses and stores them in an internal lookup table. Temporary, switched paths are created between the frame's originator and its intended recipient, and the frames are forwarded along that temporary path.

The typical LAN with a switched topology features multiple connections to a switching hub. (See Figure 5.5.) Each port, and the device it connects to, has its own dedicated bandwidth. Although originally switches forwarded frames, based upon the MAC address, technological advances are rapidly changing this. Switches are available today that can switch cells (a fixed-length, Layer 2 data-bearing structure). Switches can also be triggered by Layer 3 protocols, IP addresses, or even physical ports on the switching hub.

Switches can improve the performance of a LAN in two important ways. First, they increase

FIGURE 5.5.

Switched topology.

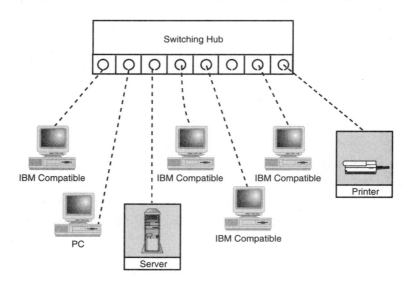

the aggregate bandwidth available throughout that network. For example, a switched Ethernet hub with 8 ports contains 8 separate collision domains of 10Mbps each, for an aggregate of 80Mbps of bandwidth.

The second way that switches improve LAN performance is by reducing the number of devices that are forced to share each segment of bandwidth. Each switch-delineated collision domain is inhabited by only two devices: the networked device and the port on the switching hub to which it connects. These are the only two devices that can compete for the 10Mbps of bandwidth on their segment. In networks that do not utilize a contention-based media access method, such as Token Ring or FDDI, the tokens circulate among a much smaller number of networked machines.

One area for concern with large switched implementations is that switches do not isolate broadcasts. They bolster performance solely by segmenting collision, not broadcast, domains. Excessive broadcast traffic can significantly and adversely impact LAN performance.

What is the Right Topology for You?

These four basic topologies are the building blocks of local area networking. They can be combined, extended, and implemented in a kaleidoscopic array of ways. The right topology for your LAN is the one that is best suited to your clients' particular network performance requirements. More likely than not, this ideal topology will be some combination of the basic topologies.

Complex Topologies

Complex topologies are extensions and/or combinations of basic physical topologies. Basic topologies, by themselves, are adequate for only very small LANs. The scaleability of the basic topologies is extremely limited. Complex topologies are formed from these building blocks to achieve a custom-fitted, scaleable topology.

Daisy Chains

The simplest of the complex topologies is developed by serially interconnecting all the hubs of a network, as shown in Figure 5.6. This is known as *daisy chaining*. This simple approach uses ports on existing hubs for interconnecting the hubs. Thus, no incremental cost is incurred during the development of such a backbone.

Small LANs can be scaled upward by daisy-chaining hubs together. Daisy chains are easily built and don't require any special administrator skills. Daisy chains were, historically, the interconnection method of choice for emerging, first-generation LANs.

The limits of daisy chaining can be discovered in a number of ways. LAN technology specifications, such as 802.3 Ethernet, dictate the maximum size of the LAN in terms of the number of hubs and/or repeaters that may be strung together in sequence. The distance limitations imposed by the physical layer, multiplied by the number of devices, dictate the maximum size of a LAN. This size is referred to as a *maximum network diameter*. Scaling beyond this diameter will adversely affect the normal functioning of that LAN. Maximum network diameters frequently limit the number of hubs that can be interconnected in this fashion. This is particularly true of contemporary high-performance LANs, such as Fast Ethernet, that place strict limitations on network diameter and the number of repeaters that can be strung together.

Figure 5.6.
Daisy-chaining hubs.

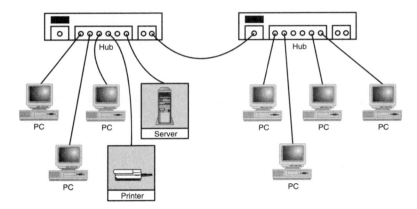

Daisy-chaining networks that use a contention-based media access method can become problematic long before network diameter is compromised, however. Daisy chaining increases the number of connections, and therefore the number of devices, on a LAN. It does not increase aggregate bandwidth or segment collision domains. Daisy chaining simply increases the number of machines sharing the network's available bandwidth. Too many devices competing for the same amount of bandwidth can create collisions and quickly bring a LAN to its knees.

This topology is best left to LANs with less than a handful of hubs and little, if any, wide area networking.

Hierarchies

Hierarchical topologies consist of more than one layer of hubs. Each layer serves a different network function. The bottom tier would be reserved for user station and server connectivity. Higher-level tiers provide aggregation of the user-level tier. A hierarchical arrangement is best suited for medium- to large-sized LANs that must be concerned with scaleability of the network and traffic aggregation.

Hierarchical Rings

Ring networks can be scaled up by interconnecting multiple rings in a hierarchical fashion, as shown in Figure 5.7. User station and server connectivity can be provided by as many limited size rings as is necessary to provide the required level of performance. A second-tier ring, either Token Ring or FDDI, can be used to interconnect all the user-level rings and to provide aggregated access to the WAN.

FIGURE 5.7.

Hierarchical ring topology.

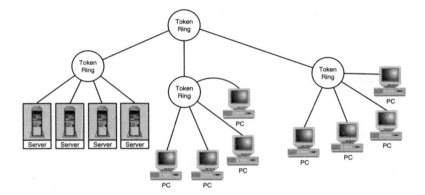

Small ring LANs can be scaled by interconnecting multiple rings hierarchically. In this figure, 16Mbps Token Ring (shown logically as a loop, rather than in its topologically correct star) is used to interconnect the user stations and FDDI loops are used for the servers and backbone tier.

Hierarchical Stars

Star topologies, too, can be implemented in hierarchical arrangements of multiple stars, as shown in Figure 5.8. Hierarchical stars can be implemented as a single collision domain or segmented into multiple collision domains using either switches or bridges.

FIGURE 5.8.

Hierarchical star topology.

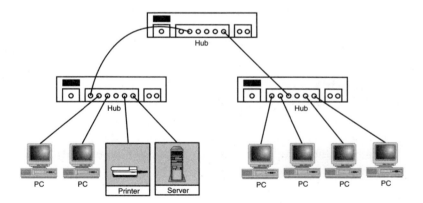

A hierarchical star topology uses one tier for user and server connectivity and the second tier as a backbone.

Hierarchical Combinations

Overall network performance can be enhanced by not force-fitting all the functional requirements of the LAN into a single solution. Mixing multiple technologies is enabled by today's high-end switching hubs. New topologies can be introduced by inserting the appropriate circuit board into the high-bandwidth backplane. A hierarchical topology lends itself to such combination of topologies, as shown in Figure 5.9.

FIGURE 5.9.
A hierarchical combination topology.

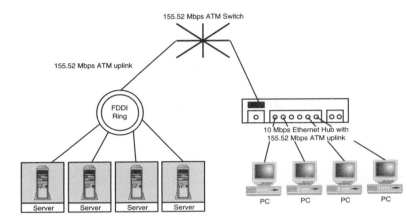

In this example of a hierarchical combination topology, an Asynchronous Transfer Mode (ATM) backbone is used to interconnect the user-level hubs. FDDI interconnects the "server farm" while Ethernet interconnects the user stations.

LAN Functional Areas

Topological variation can be an important way to optimize network performance for each of the various functional areas of a LAN. LANs contain four distinct functional areas: station connectivity, server connectivity, WAN connectivity, and backbone. Each may be best served by a different basic or complex topology.

Station Connectivity

The primary function of most LANs is station connectivity. Station connectivity tends to have the least stringent performance requirements of the LAN's functional areas. There are obvious exceptions to this, such as CAD/CAM workstations, desktop videoconferencing, and so on. In general, compromises in the cost and performance of this part of a LAN's technology and topology are less likely to adversely affect the network's performance.

Providing connectivity to machines that have divergent network performance requirements may require the use of multiple LAN technologies, as shown in Figure 5.10. Fortunately, many of today's hub manufacturers can support multiple technologies from the same hub chassis.

LANs provide basic connectivity to user stations and the peripherals that inhabit them. Differences in the network performance requirements of user station equipment can necessitate a mixed topology/technology solution.

5

LAN TOPOLOGIES

FIGURE 5.10.
Station connectivity LAN.

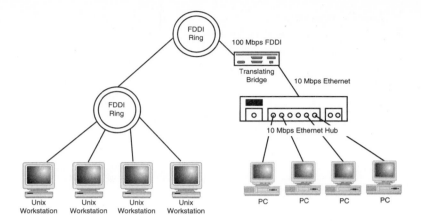

Server Connectivity

Servers tend to be much more robust than user workstations. Servers tend to be a point of traffic aggregation and must serve many clients and/or other servers. In the case of high-volume servers, this aggregation must be designed into a LAN's topology; otherwise, clients and servers suffer degraded network performance. Network connectivity to servers, typically, should also be more robust than station connectivity in terms of available bandwidth and robustness of access method.

LAN topologies can also be manipulated to accommodate the robust network performance requirements of servers and server clusters. In Figure 5.11, for example, a hierarchical combination topology is employed. The "server farm" is interconnected with a small FDDI loop, while the less-robust user stations are interconnected with Ethernet.

FIGURE 5.11.
Server connectivity LAN.

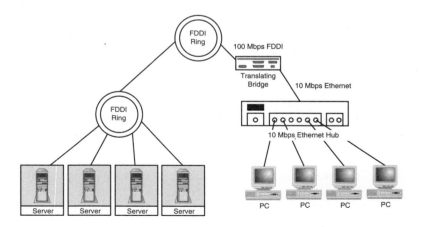

WAN Connectivity

A frequently overlooked aspect of a LAN's topology is its connection to the wide area network. In many cases, WAN connectivity is provided by a single connection from the backbone to a router, as shown in Figure 5.12.

FIGURE 5.12.
WAN connectivity of the LAN.

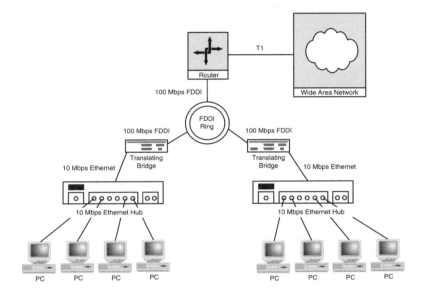

The LAN's connection to the router that provides WAN connectivity is a crucial link in a building's overall LAN topology. Improper technology selection at this critical point can result in unacceptably deteriorated levels of performance for all traffic entering or exiting the building. LAN technologies that use a contention-based access method are highly inappropriate for this function.

Networks that support a high degree of WAN-to-LAN and LAN-to-WAN traffic benefit greatly from having the most robust connection possible in this aspect of their overall topology. The technology selected should be robust in terms of its nominal transmission rate and its access method. Contention-based technologies should be avoided at all costs. The use of a contention-based media, even on a dedicated switched port, may become problematic in high-usage networks. This is the bottleneck for all traffic coming into, and trying to get out of, the building.

Backbone Connectivity

A LAN's *backbone* is the portion of its facilities used to interconnect all the hubs. A backbone can be implemented in several topologies and with several different network components, as shown in Figure 5.13.

FIGURE 5.13.

LAN backbone.

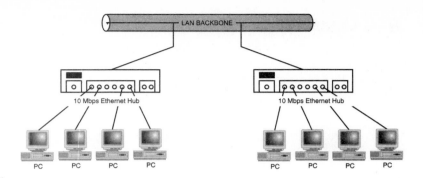

The LAN's backbone provides a critical function. It interconnects all the locally networked resources and, if applicable, the WAN. This logical depiction of a backbone can be implemented in a wide variety of ways.

Determining which backbone topology is correct for your LAN is not easy. Some options are easier to implement, very affordable, and easy to manage. Others can be more costly to acquire and operate. Another important difference lies in the scaleability of the various backbone topologies. Some are easy to scale, up to a point, and then require reinvestment to maintain acceptable levels of performance.

Each option must be examined individually, relative to your particular situation and requirements.

Serial Backbone

A *serial backbone*, shown in Figure 5.14, is nothing more than a series of hubs daisy-chained together. As described in the preceding section, this topology is inappropriate for all but the smallest of networks.

FIGURE 5.14.

Serial backbone, also known as daisy chaining.

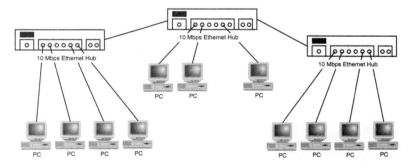

The hubs interconnecting users and servers may be serially connected to each other to form a primitive backbone. This, as previously mentioned, is what is known as *daisy chaining*.

Distributed Backbone

A *distributed backbone* is a form of hierarchical topology that can be built by installing a backbone hub in a central location. A building's PBX room usually serves as the center of its wiring topology. Consequently, it is the ideal location for a distributed backbone hub. Connections from this hub are distributed to other hubs throughout the building, as shown in Figure 5.15.

FIGURE 5.15.
A distributed backbone.

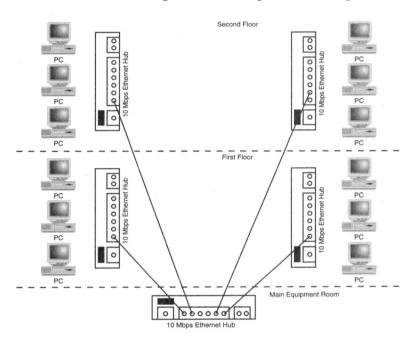

A distributed backbone can be developed by centrally locating the backbone hub. Connections are distributed from this hub to other hubs throughout the building. Unlike the serial backbone, this topology enables LANs to span large buildings without compromising maximum network diameters.

Distributing the backbone in this fashion requires an understanding of the building's wire topology and distance limitations of the various LAN media choices. In medium to large locations, the only viable option for implementing a distributed backbone will likely be fiber-optic cabling.

Collapsed Backbone

A *collapsed backbone* topology features a centralized router that interconnects all the LAN segments in a given building. The router effectively creates multiple collision and broadcast domains, thereby increasing the performance of each of the LAN segments.

5

LAN
TOPOLOGIES

Routers operate at Layer 3 of the OSI Reference Model. They are incapable of operating as quickly as hubs. Consequently, they can limit effective throughputs for any LAN traffic that originates on one LAN segment but terminates on another.

Collapsed backbones, like the one shown in Figure 5.16, also introduce a single point of failure in the LAN. This is not a fatal flaw. In fact, many of the other topologies also introduce a single point of failure into the LAN. Nevertheless, it must be considered when planning a network topology.

FIGURE 5.16.

Collapsed backbone.

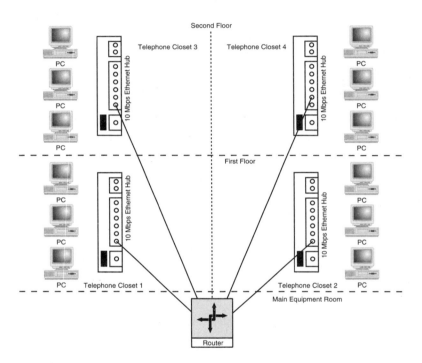

LAN segments can be interconnected by a router that functions as a collapsed backbone. This topology offers centralized control over the network, but introduces delays and a single point of failure.

An important consideration in collapsed backbone topologies is that user communities are seldom conveniently distributed throughout a building. It is more probable that multiple LAN segments will be needed for any given community. It is equally probable that multiple segments will exist in close proximity. Collapsed backbone topologies need to be carefully planned. Hastily or poorly constructed topologies will have adverse effects on network performance.

Parallel Backbone

In some of the cases where collapsed backbones are untenable solutions, a modified version may prove ideal. This modification is known as the *parallel backbone*. The reasons for installing a parallel backbone are many. User communities may be widely dispersed throughout a building, some groups and/or applications may have stringent network security requirements, or high network availability may be required. Regardless of the reason, running parallel connections from a building's collapsed backbone router to the same telephone closet enables supporting multiple segments from each closet, as shown in Figure 5.17.

FIGURE 5.17.

Parallel backbone topology.

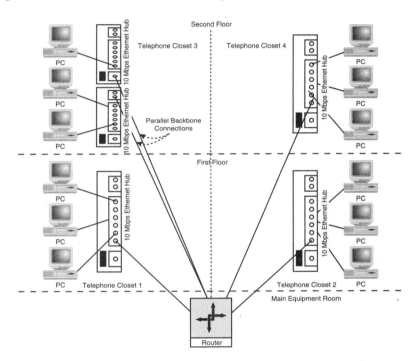

The parallel backbone topology is a modification of the collapsed backbone. Multiple segments can be supported in the same telephone closet or equipment room. This marginally increases the cost of the network, but can increase the performance of each segment, and satisfy additional network criteria, like security.

LAN Functional Areas Conclusion

Careful understanding of the performance requirements imposed by customers, stratified by LAN functional area, is the key to developing the ideal topology for any given set of user requirements. The potential combinations are limited only by one's imagination. Continued technological innovation will only increase the topological variety available to network designers.

Miscellaneous Criteria

Numerous other criteria, both technical and financial, are also factors in the selection of a LAN topology. The overall topology should be determined by customer performance requirements. These options should be used to refine and/or temper topological design decisions.

Cost

It doesn't take too much of an imagination to conjure up a network topology that can't be cost justified. Even large, well-funded network implementations have finite budgets. The implemented topology must balance cost against satisfaction of existing user requirements.

Legacy Drag

The ideal topology may prove impossible to implement for a number of reasons. The physical wire and distribution throughout a building may be inappropriate for the planned network. Rewiring might be cost prohibitive. Similarly, if your company has an extensive financial commitment to legacy technologies, it might not be feasible to implement an "ideal" network and topology. Lastly, the lack of adequate budgeting can quickly scale back network plans.

These are valid reasons for tempering an idealistic topology. Therefore, they should be examined and factored in *before* hardware is purchased.

Future Expectations

It is foolish to design a network without first considering what is likely to occur in the foreseeable future. Innovations in network and computing technologies, changes in traffic volume and/or patterns, and a myriad of other factors could greatly alter the users' expectations for network performance in the future. The network and its topology must be flexible enough to accommodate expected future changes.

Summary

LAN topology is one of the most critical components of aggregate LAN performance. The four basic topologies—switched, star, ring, and bus—can be implemented in a dizzying array of variations and combinations. These combinations are not limited to just those that were presented in this chapter. Many of today's LAN technologies lend themselves quite readily to creative arrangement and combinations. It is important to understand the strengths and weaknesses of each topology relative to the LAN's desired performance and underlying technologies. These must be balanced against the realities of a building's physical layout, cable availability, cable paths, and even cable and wire types.

Ultimately, however, the successful topology is driven by the users' required performance levels and tempered with other considerations like cost, expected future growth, and technology limitations. The biggest challenge is translating the users' requirements into megabits per second (Mbps) and other network performance metrics.

Hubs

*by Frank C. Pappas
and Emil Rensing*

IN THIS CHAPTER

CHAPTER 6

As you continue in your quest to build the perfect networking environment for your organization, you will be faced with many decisions. One of the most basic yet most important is the topology of your network. That decision sets the stage for everything that is yet to come: what levels of performance and reliability you can expect, what kind of administrative and support issues you will have to face, how you can scale or expand your network, and how large a dent the network will make in your operating budget.

In many cases, the thought of having to purchase hubs prevents most people from building 10base-T networks. While a fear of the unknown is natural, the fear of hubs is sometimes more like an uncontrollable phobia. If you are in the position of having to upgrade an existing 10base-2 LAN, you should not let the additional cost of hubs stop you from enjoying the increased performance and flexibility of your infrastructure that hubs can offer. In fact, the cost of a hub will probably be somewhere in the neighborhood of 20 to 150 dollars more per workstation, depending on the type of hub you decide to purchase. Later on, we will discuss why there is such a price difference—which we hope will help you to determine the right hub for your needs. In all probability, you will spend more on wiring than you will on any other component—especially if you have to wire an entire building and want things to look neat.

What Is a Hub?

As its name implies, a *hub* is a center of activity. In more specific network terms, a hub, or concentrator, is a common wiring point for networks that are based around a star topology. Arcnet, 10base-T, and 10base-F, as well as many other proprietary network topologies, all rely on the use of hubs to connect different cable runs and to distribute data across the various segments of a network. Hubs basically act as a signal splitter. They take all of the signals they receive in through one port and redistribute it out through all ports. Some hubs actually regenerate weak signals before re-transmitting them. Other hubs retime the signal to provide true synchronous data communication between all ports. Hubs with multiple 10base-F connectors actually use mirrors to split the beam of light among the various ports.

Figure 6.1 shows what a basic 10base-2 network might look like. Notice the way the machines are connected to each other. Remember that data being sent from the first system in the chain must be handled by each system between the originating and destination systems.

FIGURE 6.1.

A basic diagram of a 10base-2 network. Notice how data must travel through each device between the source and target device.

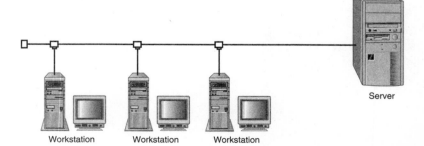

Figure 6.2 shows the same network as Figure 6.1 if it were built using 10base-T. You can see how the topology is different and how a hub fits into the network topology.

FIGURE 6.2.

A basic diagram of a 10base-T network. Notice the hub, which is the device to which all systems initially connect.

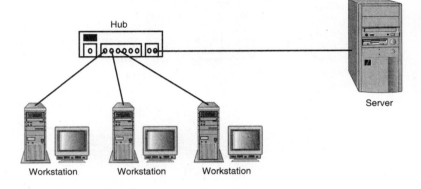

For example, on a 10base-T network, all of your devices will be physically wired to one or more hubs using unshielded, twisted-pair cabling. Your hub will have multiple ports and possible multiple types of ports so that you can connect many devices to it. You may need to connect multiple hubs together. If that is the case, you may want to use one of the other higher-speed ports on your hubs to build a backbone to your network. Each hub—and possibly your network servers—should connect directly to your high-speed backbone. Because the majority of communication on most LANs is between workstations and the primary servers, your back-bone of network wire or segment will play a very important part in the overall performance of your network.

Notice in Figure 6.3 how the backbone connects the multiple hubs and servers directly over a dedicated connection. That dedicated connection ideally should be high-speed Ethernet or some other kind of high-speed connection, possibly fiber-optic.

Token-Ring networks also have devices on them that can be referred to as hubs. A Multi-Station Access Unit or MSAU can also be considered a type of hub, because it serves a similar purpose to an Ethernet hub. However, MSAUs use mechanical switches and relays to reroute packets to each active device in serially—not in parallel like Ethernet hubs. To reduce confusion between types of networks, Token-Ring MSAUs will not be discussed as hubs.

FIGURE 6.3.

A diagram of a more complex 10base-T network. Notice the way that this 10base-T network connects each hub using a backbone. Typically, a backbone can be a higher-speed type of connection such as FDDI, and your server can be connected directly to the backbone.

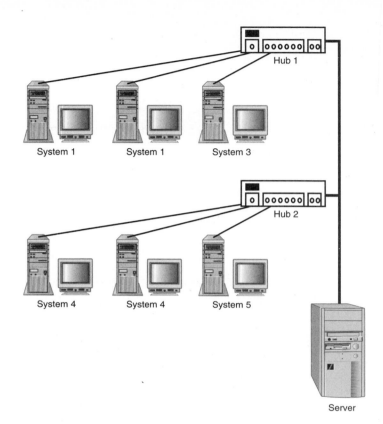

Who Needs Hubs?

There is a simple way to determine whether you need a hub on your LAN. If you are building a network with a star topology and you have two or more machines, you need a hub. There is, however an exception to this rule. If you are building a 10base-T network and you have only two machines, you can connect them to each other without using a hub. You do, however, need to have a special jumper cable to match the transmitter leads of one system with the receiver leads of the other system and vice-versa. These kinds of cables are becoming more and more common. If you cannot find one, however, you can easily make one. It is also important to point out that the parts required to assemble them are relatively inexpensive. If you have a small length of twisted-pair cable, two RJ-45 connectors, and a crimping tool, you can build one yourself using Table 6.1 as a guide. It shows how the pins must be connected on a section of Ethernet cable to allow connections between two systems without the use of a hub. This type of Ethernet jumper is commonly referred to as a *cross-over cable*.

Table 6.1. Connecting the pins on a section of Ethernet cable to allow connections between two systems without the use of a hub.

RJ-45 Connector 1			RJ-45 Connector 2	
Pin Number	Function		Pin Number	Function
1	Transmit +	← →	3	Receive +
2	Transmit -	← →	6	Receive -
3	Receive +	← →	1	Transmit +
6	Receive -	← →	2	Transmit -

The preceding table shows how the pins must be connected on a section of Ethernet cable to allow it to be used to connect two systems together without the use of a hub. When you add a third machine to your mix, you will need a hub and two additional lengths of 10base-T. Remember to save your dual system 10base-T jumper. You never know when you may need it.

Types of Hubs

As you may have already guessed, hubs provide a crucial function on networks with a star topology. There are many different types of hubs, each offering specific features that allow you to provide varying levels of service. In the next section, we talk about some of the standard features of most hubs, the differences between passive, active, and intelligent hubs, as well as some of the additional features found in today's more high-performance hubs.

Basic Specifications

All hubs have a basic set of features that is determined in part by the types of cabling that run to the hub. In many respects, a hub is simply another network device that must perform within the standard parameters of the particular type of network to which the hub is connected. Despite the fact that hubs provide additional services to a network than simply an interface, they must still follow the restrictions placed on the medium by the IEEE.

The majority of connections to most hubs are through RJ-45 jacks. RJ-45 jacks are the standard connector type for many types of Ethernet that rely on twisted-pair cabling. From 10base-T to 100base-T, the cabling that runs from most workstations, printers, and other devices on your LAN to the hub is more than likely some type of twisted-pair cable, depending on the speed of the network. At either end of that cable is an RJ-45 connector.

> **NOTE**
>
> An RJ-45 connector looks similar to the connector that comes out of most North-American telephones except it is just a little bit wider. Although primarily used to connect devices that rely on twisted-pair Ethernet, RJ-45 connectors can also be used to connect Token Ring devices.

The length of each cable run to a hub is limited by the medium in use. (See Table 6.2.) For example, any length of 10base-T cabling cannot exceed 100 meters or roughly 330 feet in length. This is a limitation in the specification of 10base-T from the IEEE, not a limitation of any particular hub. For example, if your hub has a 10base-F connector to connect the hub to a high-speed backbone, the maximum run of that connection may be as far as 2 kilometers—as defined by the IEEE specification for 10base-F.

Table 6.2. The maximum distances of cable runs for different types of Ethernet, as determined by the IEEE.

Ethernet Type	Distance
10base-2	185 meters/607 feet
10base-5	500 meters/1,640 feet
10base-T	100 meters/330 feet
10base-F	2 kilometers
10broad-36	3,600 meters/2.25 miles

Table 6.2 lists Ethernet specifications and the maximum length that a single run of each type can be. Remember that most of these runs can be extended with the use of Ethernet repeaters.

Of course, there are other standard requirements. Since hubs are electronic devices that take a single signal and broadcast it to multiple ports, hubs need a power source. Most hubs have LEDs that can be used to monitor various conditions. The two most common are LEDs to monitor power and active connections at particular ports. Other hubs have additional LEDs to monitor traffic on a particular port, as well as packet collisions on the LAN in general.

> **NOTE**
>
> One way to get in trouble with the FAA is to setup a LAN on an airplane using a battery-powered hub. While the promise of six-hours of multi-player Quake or Interstate '76 on a trip from New York to Los Angeles may seem like an acceptable risk, believe me when I say, "It is not!" Apparently, connecting electronic devices (such as computers and hubs) using external cables (such as unshielded twisted pair) is against FAA regulations.

Passive Hubs

Passive hubs, as the name suggests, are rather quiescent creatures. They do not do very much to enhance the performance of your LAN, nor do they do anything to assist you in troubleshooting faulty hardware or finding performance bottlenecks. They simply take all of the packets they receive on a single port and rebroadcast them across all ports—the simplest thing that a hub can do.

Passive hubs commonly have one 10base-2 port in addition to the RJ-45 connectors that connect each LAN device. As you have already read, 10base-5 is 10Mbps Ethernet that is run over thick-coax. This 10base-2 connector can be used as your network backbone. Other, more advanced passive hubs have AUI ports that can be connected to the transceiver of your choice to form a backbone that you may find more advantageous.

Most passive hubs are excellent entry-level devices that you can use as your starting points in the world of star topology Ethernet. Most eight-port passive hubs cost less than $200, and if you are upgrading from 10base-2, even the most inexpensive 10base-T setup will deliver a whole new world of performance.

Active Hubs

Active hubs actually do *something* other than simply rebroadcasting data. Generally, they have all of the features of passive hubs, with the added bonus of actually watching the data being sent out. Active hubs take a larger role in Ethernet communications by implementing a technology called *store & forward* where the hubs actually look at the data they are transmitting before sending it. This is not to say that the hub prioritizes certain packets of data; it does, however, repair certain "damaged" packets and will retime the distribution of other packets.

If a signal received by an active hub is weak but still readable, the active hub restores the signal to a stronger state before rebroadcasting it. This feature allows certain devices that are not operating within optimal parameters to still be used on your network. If a device is not broadcasting a signal strong enough to be seen by other devices on a network that uses passive hubs, the signal amplification provided by an active hub may allow that device to continue to function on your LAN. Additionally, some active hubs will report devices on your network that are not fully functional. In this way, active hubs also provide certain diagnostic capabilities for your network.

Active hubs will also retime and resynchronize certain packets when they are being transmitted. Certain cable runs may experience electromagnetic (EM) disturbances that prevent packets from reaching the hub or the device at the end of the cable run in timely fashion. In other situations, the packets may not reach the destination at all. Active hubs can compensate for packet loss by retransmitting packets on individual ports as they are called for and retiming packet delivery for slower, more error-prone connections. Of course, retiming packet delivery slows down overall network performance for all devices connected to that particular hub, but sometimes that is preferable to data loss—especially since the retiming can actually lower the number of collisions seen on your LAN. If data does not have to be broadcast over and over again, the LAN is available for use for new requests more frequently. Again, it is important to point out that active hubs can help you diagnose bad cable runs by showing which port on your hub warrants the retransmission or retiming.

Active hubs provide certain performance benefits and, sometimes, additional diagnostic capabilities. Active hubs are more expensive than simple, passive hubs and can be purchased in many configurations with various numbers and types of ports.

Intelligent Hubs

Intelligent hubs offer many advantages over passive and active hubs. Organizations looking to expand their networking capabilities so users can share resources more efficiently and function more quickly can benefit greatly from intelligent hubs. The technology behind intelligent hubs has only become available in recent years and many organizations may not have had the chance to benefit from them; nevertheless intelligent hubs are a proven technology that can deliver unparalleled performance for your LAN.

In addition to all of the features found in active hubs, incorporating intelligent hubs into your network infrastructure gives you the ability to manage your network from one central location. If a problem develops with any device on a network that is connected to an intelligent hub, you can easily identify, diagnose, and remedy the problem using the management information provided by each intelligent hub—that is, in the event it is a problem that cannot be remedied by the hub itself. This is a significant improvement over standard active hubs. Troubleshooting a large enterprise-scale network without a centralized management tool that can help you visualize your network infrastructure usually leaves you running from wiring closet to wiring closet trying to find poorly functioning devices.

Another significant and often overlooked feature of intelligent hubs is their ability to offer flexible transmission rates to various devices. Of course, intelligent hubs have additional ports for connecting high-speed backbones—just like other types of hubs. However, the intelligent hubs support standard transmission rates of 10, 16 and 100Mbps to desktop systems using standard topologies such as Ethernet, Token Ring or FDDI. That means that you can gradually upgrade your systems from 10Mbps connections to 100Mbps connections, or simply deliver faster transmission speeds to devices that need faster services.

In addition, to boost the flexibility in configuration and management of networks of mixed media and mixed levels of technology, intelligent hubs have incorporated support for other technologies such as terminal servers, bridges, routers, and switches. Additionally, modern intelligent hubs provide more comprehensive and easier-to-use network management software, which make them a crucial component of most comprehensive network management systems.

Advanced Features

There are many additional features supported by some of the more high-end hubs from various manufacturers. Some hubs feature redundant AC power supplies. If one should fail, the other takes over—and is fully capable of powering the entire unit. Other hubs have built-in DC power supplies to function in the event of a power outage. Redundant fans in some hubs provide cooling of the hub in the event that either fan fails. Other more commonly encountered advanced features in some intelligent hubs include automatic termination for coaxial connections, full hot-swap capabilities for connector modules, as well as the ability to automatically reverse the polarity of improperly wired 10base-T connections. More advanced intelligent hubs have features such as redundant configuration storage and redundant clocks. The redundant clocks allow any hub with an onboard clock on the network to act as a master to help in timing packet delivery. The redundant configuration storage feature available on some intelligent hubs is used when assigning various properties to various ports. Each similar hub on the network stores the configuration of one other hub, allowing configuration information to be restored by way of the intelligent link between hubs. Additionally, some manufacturers deliver modules for routing and bridging services that can live inside of the same chassis as your larger enterprise-level hubs.

Choosing a Hub

One of the most fascinating aspects of the computer industry is the rapid pace at which available products manage to evolve, consistently beating IT professionals in their attempt to maintain cutting-edge networks. Unlike most other industries, where core product lines experience revolutionary growth every five to fifteen (or potentially more) years, even the most conservative projections show networking technology undergoing logarithmic growth every year and a half—sometimes even more frequently. Part of the reason for this explosive growth, other than the obvious demand factors, is the rather large number of software publishers and hardware manufacturers dedicated to improving the speed and performance of computing. Because network computing is such a large component of computing in the business world, it is quite easy to see why there are so many vendors who specialize in networking hardware and software—all dedicated to making your LAN and WAN perform as well as they possibly can.

When it comes time for you to choose a vendor for your networking hardware, not necessarily just your hubs, there are three things you want to consider before making any purchases:

- Breadth of products offered
- Depth of services offered
- Price of product versus operational savings

Breadth of Products Offered

As you begin your search for the perfect hub, you will undoubtedly encounter more vendors than you know what to do with, many of whom will be offering almost identical product lines. If your intent is to network only a few machines together, perhaps fewer than 12, you will more than likely be satisfied by selecting any of the many passive hubs offered on the market. If you have a long-term goal for your workgroup that includes a larger, more high-end network infra- structure, you may wish to make a more educated purchasing decision. Finding a vendor who makes a highly scaleable workgroup- to enterprise-level intelligent hub system and additional products such as routers, bridges, and network interface adapters that all function under the same network management system, might prove to be a bit of a challenge. While there are many vendors that make hubs for specific audiences, and it may be really easy to purchase any old product from your local computer store to get you started, it is important to look at the big picture. This step is critically important if you are on the verge of expansion or are just now implementing a star topology on your LAN as part of your overall upgrade path. Besides, many vendors will argue that their products work best in a brand-homogeneous environment.

Depth of Services Offered

Many larger vendors also provide networking consulting and installation services through lo- cal distributors and certified resellers. If you are in the position of having to build a network or upgrade an existing one, and you really do not want to get involved much further than paying the bills, you may find these services quite beneficial. If you feel that your LAN implementa- tion is going to be a one-time-only type of project and have no immediate plans to upgrade until the technology significantly improves, you really have nothing to lose by picking any product that will fulfill your needs from any vendor. At the same time, there is no telling how any level of assistance from a qualified professional can benefit your implementation. Having someone to bounce an idea off of may change your whole outlook on what you are trying to accomplish with your network. Remember, you know what you need your network to do so that you can get your job done; however, only an experienced network engineer can help you build a network computing environment that will fulfill your needs in the best possible way.

Price of Product Versus Operational Savings

Many of the more high-end manufacturers of intelligent hubs and comprehensive network hardware solutions are significantly more expensive than their nearest competitors with seem- ingly similar product lines. While entry-level passive hubs obviously will be less than entry- level intelligent hubs, the three-digit price difference for the same number of ports and the same overall specified speed may seem like wasted money. However, depending on the scope of your project or the performance that you *need* from your LAN, the additional expense in hardware may save you lots of time, money, and aggravation when it comes down to adding additional nodes, adding routing capabilities, trying to troubleshoot problem connections, increasing operating speed on certain systems, or simply using your network. You should be aware that certain increased costs in hardware can offer substantial savings in operation later, when you need to be more flexible and open.

Summary

You can see how crucial hubs are to even the most basic LAN. All of the communicating you do over a star topology has to be routed through one or more hubs and it is crucial that your center of activity performs in a manner that is most beneficial for you. Basic, passive hubs are great for small networks—even in mixed protocol and/or multiple-operating system environments. 10base-T networks based upon the simplest and least expensive hubs can easily deliver performance and services that can rival even the most advanced 10base-2 networks. As your network grows and your needs increase, you will clearly see how better, more advanced systems will enhance your network performance. If you add active hubs, collisions and retransmissions decrease substantially. You may even see a performance increase in systems that were more problematic under basic, passive hubs. As your organization expands, and your network infrastructure grows, you will most likely take advantage of certain features of active hubs, and want to move as quickly as possible to more intelligent hubs that will become the nucleus of your overall network management system. It is for that very reason that the hub can make or break your network computing environment.

Bridges

by Martin Bligh

IN THIS CHAPTER

CHAPTER 7

This chapter provides an overview of bridges and the way that they work, covering both transparent and source route bridging. The spanning tree algorithm is also explained—this is the basis of the way that transparent bridges are controlled.

What Is a Bridge?

Bridges, which operate at the data link layer, connect two LANs (local area networks) together, and forward frames according to their MAC (media access control) address (see Figure 7.1). Often the concept of a router is more familiar than that of a bridge; it may help to think of a bridge as a "low-level router" (routers operate at the network layer, forwarding by addresses such as an IP address).

FIGURE 7.1.

Where connecting devices fit into the OSI stack.

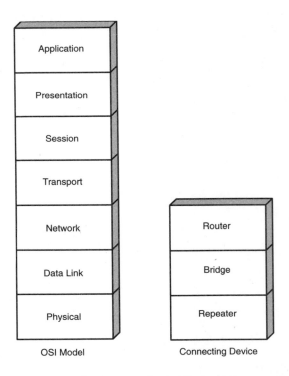

A remote bridge connects two remote LANs (bridge 1 and 2 in Figure 7.2) over a link that is normally slow (for example, a telephone line), while a local bridge connects two locally adjacent LANs together (bridge 3 in Figure 7.2). With a local bridge, performance is an issue, but for a remote bridge, the capability to operate over a long connecting line is often more important.

FIGURE 7.2.

A sample network with local and remote bridges.

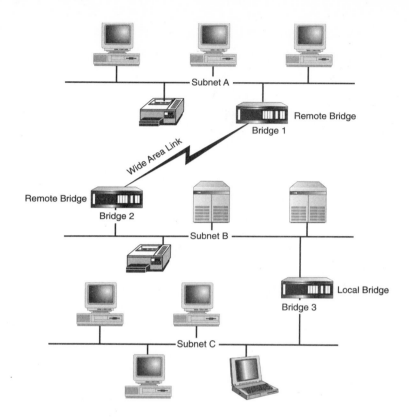

Bridges Versus Routers

Bridges do not know about the higher level protocols inside the frames that they forward. This means that they will deal with IP, IPX, and so on all at the same time (and in a consistent manner) together with any new protocols that come along. Bridges also provide a way to segment networks that are using nonroutable protocols, such as NetBEUI.

The fact that routers deal with data at the network level means that it is much easier for them to interconnect different data-link layers, such as connecting a Token Ring segment to an Ethernet segment.

Bridges are often more difficult to control than routers. Protocols such as IP have highly sophisticated routing protocols associated with them, allowing the network administrator to exercise tight control over routing. Protocols such as IP also provide more information about how networks should be logically segmented (even in the addresses themselves). Bridges are inherently more difficult to control—they only have the MAC address and the physical topology to work with. For this reason, bridges are generally more suitable for smaller, simpler networks.

There are two main types of bridge:

- Transparent: generally used to interconnect Ethernet segments.
- Source route: generally used to interconnect Token Ring segments.

These different types of bridge will now be examined in detail.

Transparent Bridges

Transparent bridges are mostly used to interconnect Ethernet segments. The bridge passes traffic that needs to go between different segments, but isolates traffic that is local to the segment on which it is received. The bridge thus reduces the total amount of traffic on the network.

Bridges have two or more interfaces to the network—each of these is called a port.

Simple Transparent Bridge Operation

This section describes bridge operation when there are no loops in the network and there is only one path between any two given hosts.

The bridge is called transparent because it appears to all hosts on the network as though it is not there. As far as the network layer (IP for example) is concerned, all networks connected by a bridge might as well be physically connected.

How is this transparency maintained? The "default" action for a bridge is to forward any received frame. The only situation where frames will not be forwarded is when the bridge knows that the destination host is connected via the same bridge port as the source host (for example, if a frame is received on port 1 that is also destined to go out only on port 1). Fortunately, the bridge can use this rule to eliminate the forwarding of many frames.

For each of the bridge's ports, a list of MAC addresses connected to that port is maintained. The bridge knows that host G is connected to port 3 if it receives a frame from host G on port 3. In case hosts move their position on the network, each entry in this list has a TTL (time to live) associated with it, and it will expire after a set time. Whenever a frame is received from that MAC address, the TTL for the relevant entry will be reset.

The simplest bridge configuration is one bridge connecting two subnets. In Figure 7.3, the bridge should forward frames from host A to host C, but not from host A to host B.

However, in the initial learning phase, the situation is not quite as simple. Imagine that the bridge has just been turned on. All of its data tables are empty—it does not know where any other hosts are. The bridge's tables through an initial packet sequence might be as follows:

- Bridge tables: Port 1—<empty>; Port 2—<empty>
- Host A sends a frame to host B. The bridge receives the frame on port 1, but does not know where host B is located, so forwards the frame to port 2 as well. The bridge also updates its table for port 1, adding an entry for host A.

- Bridge tables: Port 1—<A>; Port 2—<empty>
- Host B sends a reply back to host A. The bridge receives the frame on port 1, but it is not forwarded to port 2, because the bridge knows that host A is also on port 1. The bridge updates its table for port 1, adding an entry for host B.
- Bridge tables: Port 1—<A, B>; Port 2—<empty>
- Host A sends a frame to host B. The bridge receives the frame on port 1, but this time it knows where host B is located (also on port 1), so it does not forward the frame to port 2. The only change to the bridge's tables is to reset the TTL on the entry for host A.
- Bridge tables: Port 1—<A, B>; Port 2—<empty>

FIGURE 7.3.

The simplest bridged network.

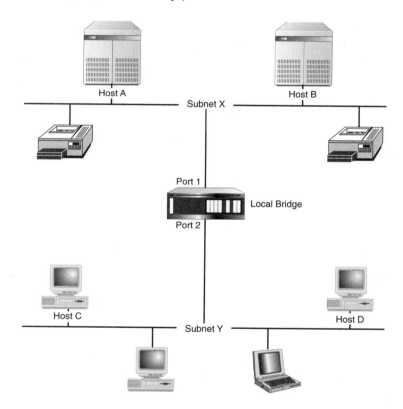

IEEE 802.1d Spanning Tree Algorithm

The simple transparent bridge described in the previous section will function well, even with a much more complex network with many bridges. However, when loops in the network or multiple paths between any two points are created, the model breaks down. In Figure 7.4, a network is shown with two bridges, both connecting two subnets together, and thereby creating a loop. This type of design would be useful to create redundancy, in case one of the bridges fails.

FIGURE 7.4.

A small bridged network with a loop.

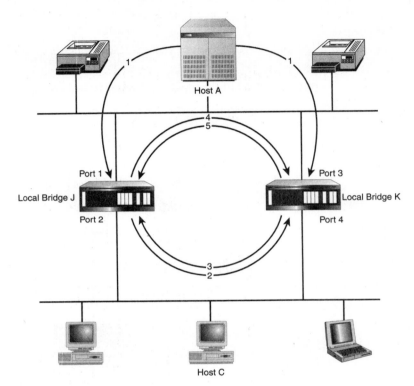

Now imagine the following situation: All bridge tables are empty to start with, and host A sends a frame to host B (transmission 1 on the diagram).

- Bridge J tables: Port 1—<empty>; Port 2—<empty>
- Bridge K tables: Port 3—<empty>; Port 4—<empty>
- Bridge J receives transmission 1 on port 1—not knowing where B is, it forwards the frame to port 2 (transmission 2 on the diagram). It adds host A to its table for port 1. Bridge K also receives transmission 1 on port 3; not knowing where B is, it forwards the frame to port 4 (transmission 3 on the diagram). It adds host A to its table for port 3.
- Bridge J tables: Port 1—<A>; Port 2—<empty>
- Bridge K tables: Port 3—<A>; Port 4—<empty>
- Bridge J receives transmission 3 on port 2—not knowing where B is, it forwards the frame to port 1 (transmission 4 on the diagram). It has received a frame from host A

on port 2, so it must update its tables. Bridge K receives transmission 2 on port 4; not knowing where B is, it forwards the frame to port 3 (transmission 5 on the diagram). It has received a frame from host A on port 4, so it must update its tables.

- Bridge J tables: Port 1—<empty>; Port 2—<A>
- Bridge K tables: Port 3—<empty>; Port 4—<A>

It is clear that a loop has been created, along with a large amount of unnecessary traffic. Worse still, there are *two* packets going around in circles for each packet sent, and the bridges tables are being continuously updated.

The problem is caused by the presence of more than one bridge forwarding traffic between the same two subnets, and this is clearly an unacceptable situation. The chosen way to resolve this problem is the "Spanning Tree Algorithm" defined by IEEE 802.1d.

Spanning Trees

Figure 7.5 shows a complex network with many bridges—each network is represented as a cloud marked *LAN*, and each bridge link is represented by an arrow.

FIGURE 7.5.

A complex network with several loops, showing a spanning tree.

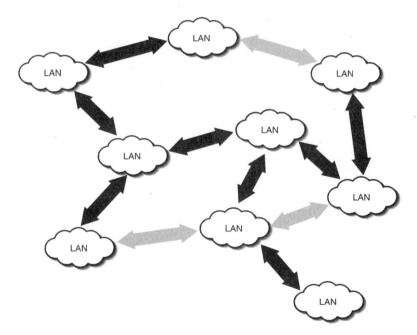

When all the arrows are used, loops can be seen. The black arrows form a spanning tree by using a subset of the links. Notice that all nodes are directly or indirectly connected to each other, but there are no loops. This is the definition of a spanning tree.

Spanning trees are not always unique. Given sufficient redundancy in the network, it is normally possible to draw a different spanning tree. A resilient network design will ensure that it is possible to draw a spanning tree in the absence of any given link. The paranoid (or the military) may try to achieve a network that contains a spanning tree despite the absence of any two links (or more!). Figure 7.6 shows an alternative spanning tree.

FIGURE 7.6.

The complex network, showing an alternative spanning tree.

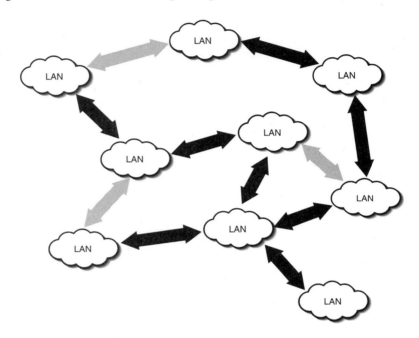

Compare Figures 7.5 and 7.6, noting the similarities and the differences. Both have eight black arrows to link their nine networks. It turns out that it is fairly easy to prove mathematically (graph theory) that a spanning tree always requires one fewer link than the number of networks it is connecting.

It is also easy to see that a completely different set of three links are gray between the two diagrams. In fact, there is no single link in the diagram that could be turned gray (that is, broken), which would prevent us from drawing a spanning tree (or in other words, interconnecting the networks).

It can be proven mathematically that given any set of networks that are connected to one another, it is possible to find a subset of the links that form a spanning tree (that is, a set that still connects all the networks, but with no loops).

Implementing the Spanning Tree Algorithm

Now that you know a subset of the bridged links exists that will allow any network to operate without loops (a spanning tree), how do the bridges determine a spanning tree and decide which spanning tree to use?

Bridges communicate via messages called *Bridge Protocol Data Units (BPDUs)*. Before the bridges in the network can make sensible decisions about how to configure themselves, each bridge and each port need some configuration data:

- Bridge: Unique identifier (Bridge ID)
- Port: Unique identifier (Port ID)
- Port: Relative port priority
- Port: Cost for each port (higher bandwidth link = lower cost)

Having configured each bridge, the bridges will automatically determine a spanning tree to use. The configuration parameters that you have set will determine which spanning tree is chosen.

There are three stages in determining the spanning tree:

1. Select the root bridge.

   The bridge with the lowest bridge ID is selected as the root bridge. Bridge IDs are supposed to be unique, but if there two bridges with the lowest ID, the one with the lowest MAC address is used as a tie-breaker. In Figure 7.7, bridge 1 is selected as the root bridge.

2. Select a root port on all the other bridges.

   On every bridge except for the root bridge, a root port must be selected. This is supposed to be the best port for the bridge to communicate with the root bridge. The lowest cost path from each of the bridge's ports to the root bridge is calculated. On each bridge, the port with the lowest cost path to the root bridge is selected—marked as *(Root)* in Figure 7.7.

3. Select a designated bridge and port for each LAN.

   If there is only one bridge connecting to a given LAN, it must be the designated bridge for that LAN (for example, bridge 3 is the designated bridge for LAN G in Figure 7.7). If there is more than one bridge connected to a given LAN, the bridge with the lowest cost path to the root bridge is chosen (for example, bridge 4 is chosen over bridge 3 for LAN F in Figure 7.7). The designated port connects the designated bridge to the relevant LAN (if there are multiple ports, the one with the lowest priority is chosen).

FIGURE 7.7.

A bridged network showing root and designated ports.

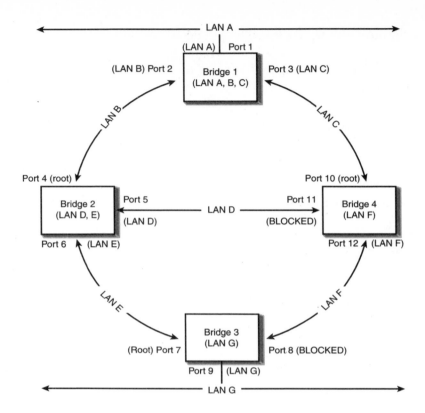

Note that a port must be one (and only one) of the following:

- Root port
- Designated port for a LAN
- Blocked

Note that a root port is never a designated port for a LAN (in Figure 7.7, port 7 on bridge 3 is not the designated port for LAN E, for example). The root port is a path to the root bridge, so there must be another bridge closer to the root bridge attached to this LAN (in this case, bridge 2). This other bridge would therefore be the designated bridge for the LAN, and would hold the designated port (port 6).

When a bridge is switched on, it assumes that it is the root bridge. The bridge transmits a configuration bridge protocol data unit (CBPDU), stating the bridge ID of the bridge it perceives to be the root bridge.

A bridge receiving a CBPDU frame with a lower bridge ID than its known root bridge will update its tables. If the frame was received upon the bridge's root port (upstream), the information is disseminated to all designated ports (downstream).

If the given bridge ID is higher that its known root bridge, the information will be discarded. If the frame was received on a designated port (downstream), a reply is sent, containing the lower bridge ID of the real root bridge.

If the network is reconfigured, either deliberately or due to a link failure, the process will be repeated, and a new spanning tree decided upon.

Source Routing Bridges

Source routing bridges operate on a different principle than transparent bridges. Transparent bridges present the illusion of one continuous network segment to the connected hosts. Source route bridges do not make any decisions about where to forward packets, and do not build up lists of host MAC addresses.

Though the principle of routing is different, source route bridges must still be configured with identification information. Each bridge is given a unique number (the bridge ID). Each LAN (Token Ring) is also given a unique identifier (the ring ID). This can be seen clearly in Figure 7.8. Note that some bridges use different bases for identifiers (that is, some are in hexadecimal, and some are in decimal).

Any station wishing to send a frame to a station on a remote network must specify which bridges the frame should traverse. For instance in Figure 7.8, if host A wishes to send a frame to host D, it could specify:

```
A -> TR1 -> B2 -> TR3 -> B7 -> TR5 -> D
```

or ...

```
A -> TR1 -> B4 -> TR4 -> B8 -> TR5 -> D
```

or any of a number of other possible routes.

There is not always such a large choice of routes—the network in Figure 7.8 is highly robust, providing a large number of alternative routes. In a simpler network, there might only be one available route. The choice of which route to use is strictly the responsibility of the sending host.

What would transparent bridging do with this network? The spanning tree algorithm would force some of the bridge ports to be blocked. You might well end up with a spanning tree where bridges 1, 4, 5, and 8 are totally redundant (until a failure occurs). However, this would put a massive load on Token Ring 3. With source route bridging, a more flexible routing scheme can be achieved at the cost of the hosts managing all the routing information.

The IEEE 802.5 standard for Token Ring defines several fields of interest in the frame header. The I/G bit at the head of the source address is set if routing information is present in the frame. The route itself is defined in the routing information section as a list of 2-byte route designators.

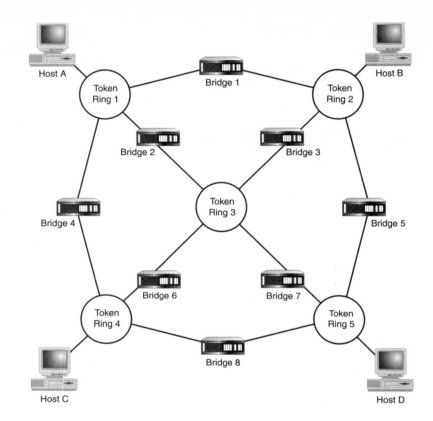

FIGURE 7.8.
A bridged network showing root and designated ports.

Path Discovery

If the stations are to specify the path to be taken to the remote host, they must have a way of finding the path. This function is performed by sending out path discovery messages. Path discovery need not be performed for each packet sent, but rather the path information is cached and reused.

All Routes Explorer

The transmitting host sends out an All Routes Explorer (ARE) frame with a blank list of route designators. Each bridge receiving the frame adds the bridge ID and the network ID to the list of route designators, and forwards the frame to all ports other than the port on which it was received.

The receiving host will receive one ARE frame for each possible route, from the transmitter to the receiver. For each ARE frame arriving at its destination, an SRF (specified route frame) is sent in reply to the original host. A path to the destination is then chosen by the original host.

Spanning Tree Explorer

The Spanning Tree Explorer (STE) frame relies upon a spanning tree being defined. An STE frame is broadcast from the originating host, which is passed across a spanning tree by the bridge network (see the previous section on spanning trees). This means that exactly one copy of the STE frame will arrive at each LAN on the network. The destination host will therefore receive only one copy of the STE frame, with a copy of the route taken in it. The destination host responds with an ARE frame to the originating host.

Source Route Bridges Versus Transparent Bridges

Source route bridges put the requirement on the host to determine all the routing information and route discovery. This means that more traffic is generated by routing information—assuming there are more hosts than bridges on the network!

Transparent bridges require no input from the host, and therefore no modifications to the network stack. However, the set of paths used are often suboptimal. The method used to avoid loops is simply to disable some ports!

Summary

Bridges operate at the data link layer, allowing them to be independent of the network layer protocols being used. There are two main types of bridges: transparent bridges and source routing bridges. Transparent bridges make decisions about frame routing for themselves and are most commonly found on Ethernet networks. Source route bridges rely on the host for routing decisions, and are most commonly found on Token Ring networks.

Switches

by Frank C. Pappas
and Emil Rensing

IN THIS CHAPTER

One of the most amazing, and most aggravating, aspects of networking in the late 1990s is the rapid pace at which the underlying technologies consistently manage to evolve. In other industries, core technologies experience revolutionary growth every 5 to 15 years (or more), but even the most conservative projections show the underpinnings of the information technology industry growing by leaps and bounds every 18 months, sometimes even more frequently! Most recently, companies have become locked in a number of heated battles over which vendors will provide the hardware and software that will lead the industry into the twenty-first century. These companies have been releasing at breakneck speeds attractive yet bloated browsers, plug-and-play desktop operating systems, and proprietary high-speed modem designs, in addition to wiring various cities with cutting-edge communications media, including ATM (Asynchronous Transfer Mode), ADSL (Asynchronous Digital Subscriber Line), and more. The race to provide fast, robust, and cost-effective data-sharing solutions is on, and everyone—from vendors to corporate clientele—is playing for keeps.

The one disheartening factor associated with this tremendous growth is that the budgets of most corporate IT managers and network engineers continue to shrink. If you think about it from the technologically illiterate standpoint of most executives, unless system problems become chronic and network reliability begins to suffer noticeably, there's obviously no need to invest tens of thousands of additional dollars for infrastructure build-outs. After all, if it ain't broke, why fix it? Rarely, if ever, are any long-term plans or proactive procedures developed for identifying upcoming network issues and resolving them in a timely and low-cost manner.

Unfortunately, this hands-off attitude leaves the network engineer in a rather precarious position. Financially, your hands are tied: You'll be lucky to get even enough funding to maintain your current network infrastructure, let alone make the serious improvements to cabling, hardware, and software necessary to support your ever-growing user community. So how do you stave off latency, device time-outs, intermittent connections, and crotchety users, all while not spending thousands of dollars to physically increase bandwidth, add new servers, or hire a staff of thousands? The solution can be described in two words: Ethernet switching.

Why Switch to Switching?

As executive management becomes increasingly tight-fisted when it comes to providing financial assistance for the support, maintenance, and expansion of network resources, you'll frequently be confronted by a number of different problems that will require innovative or unorthodox solutions—often your only route when funding is scarce. Two factors will significantly affect your network. You'll need to pay special attention to both of them, or you're liable to suddenly find yourself between a rock and a hard place.

First, computers, workstations and servers alike, simply aren't what they used to be. No longer are desktop machines simply dumb terminals or systems that are only slightly more intelligent than the average toaster. Today's class of desktops, workstations, and network servers have been rebuilt bigger, faster, and stronger than their predecessors, with the memory and processing capacity to crush many of the server-class machines that were in wide use only five years ago. This has resulted in newer, more demanding roles for these machines, roles that require the systems to be constantly transmitting across your network to access remote files, surf the Internet, use shared devices, and so on.

As if this weren't enough of a challenge all by itself, overall network growth will, if left unchecked, work to cripple your network infrastructure. As your network grows in terms of nodes, users, and services provided, sooner or later you'll be faced with the mother of all network problems: insufficient bandwidth. Performance will undoubtedly degrade, users will gripe about slow network response times, client/server applications will grind to a halt, and cross-network connections will be few and far between. This is not good for your network or for your hopes for a promotion. You've got two options at this point—work for a company that doesn't care how much money you spend and can afford long spans of network downtime, or adopt Ethernet switching.

To Bridge or Not to Bridge

Using bridges to separate multiple network segments has long been seen as an excellent method of reducing cross-segment traffic and realizing modest performance increases in growing or mature networks. Although bridging allows network engineers to subdivide saturated networks into more manageable mini-networks, the gains achieved through bridge solutions are only effective to a certain point, when the initial saturation problems recur. This generally happens when large numbers of users, on any of your segments, begin to demand significant numbers of intersegment connections. This is when the bridge's incapability to provide simultaneous cross-segment connections starts to hobble the effectiveness of the bridge solution. Thankfully, one of the strengths of switches revolves around multiple cross-segment communications, so there is a route out of your misery. Despite all this, it is important to recognize that in certain situations, bridges offer a better solution than switches—don't reject bridges out of hand. If your subnets will require little, if any, cross-segment contact, a bridge may just do the trick.

In an Ideal World

In an ideal world, you'd never be faced with critical network congestion. You'd always have plenty of time, staff, and financial support to isolate and neutralize even the most nascent of problems. You say that your company has just acquired your major competitor and that you have to integrate an additional 12,000 nodes into your currently overburdened token ring network? Just scrap the damn thing and install FDDI. You've just taken over three new floors in your building and are hiring a bunch of new employees? Heck, why not just rip out your old wiring, run some CAT5, and sing the praises of Fast Ethernet? Pardon the sarcasm, but on what planet are you currently living?

Alas, we operate in anything but an ideal world. Fast Ethernet, ATM, FDDI, and ADSL solutions (among others) are simply too expensive and resource-intensive to be used as fast-response weapons in your fight against network congestion. Although your IS team is probably quite versatile, the task of designing, implementing, and supporting a network based on these new technologies requires a good deal of time and effort, is anything but a straightforward procedure, and no doubt will require significant outlays of cash for staff training. Not to mention, of course, transition downtime, the inevitable glitches associated with large-scale installations of new technology, as well as any of a host of unanticipated issues that will need immediate attention. Maybe, just maybe, you can pull it off successfully. But if this is your only contingency plan, you can start looking for a new job soon.

Another avenue that is frequently explored when trying to alleviate network congestion centers on the installation of bridges and routers to segregate intersegment traffic. Although this is a valid solution that can often yield at least marginal results, configuring bridges and routers to provide optimal performance takes high degrees of skill, patience, and lots of network traffic analysis. Again, this option should be exercised only if time and money are on your side.

Switching to the Rescue

In reality, you can't simply dump your entire infrastructure every time problems begin to crop up with the current iteration of your network. Your boss won't stand for it, most likely won't (or can't) pay for new hardware and software. Your company certainly can't afford the hassle of one transition after another, along with the downtime and other hassles, every time you want to take the easy way out of a networking fiasco. In many instances, Ethernet switching has emerged as the de facto solution for dealing with these types of network congestion issues, often saving network administrators time, money, and frustration in the process.

The redesign of networking infrastructure to integrate Ethernet segment switches into a traditional, nonswitched networking environment can yield surprising results, not only in terms of increased overall network performance but also in light of the low price/performance trade-offs that will be required to implement switching solutions, as opposed to FDDI, Fast Ethernet, or other high-speed networking technologies. The benefits of Ethernet switching are many: It is relatively inexpensive compared to other options; it can reap tangible improvements in network performance, regaining lost bandwidth and allowing for full duplex (20Mbps) networking; it can be implemented in a proportionately shorter period of time than FDDI, Fast Ethernet, or other technologies; and it allows you to retain your investments in current network infrastructure. All in all, this sounds like a pretty good option when the demon of clogged networks is staring you in the face.

How do switches work? In a very broad sense, Ethernet switches function by helping you break down greater, traffic-intensive networks into smaller, more controllable subnetworks. Instead of each device constantly vying for attention on a single saturated segment of 10Mbps Ethernet, switches allow single devices (or groups of devices) to "own" their own dedicated 10Mbps segments connected directly to the high-speed switch, which then facilitates intersegment communication. Although this sounds a lot like a bridge, there are some important distinctions that make switches much more dynamic and useful pieces of hardware.

Switches themselves are hardware devices not entirely different in appearance from routers, hubs, and bridges. However, three important factors separate switches from their networking brethren: overall speed (switches are much faster); forwarding methodology or electronic logic (smarter); and higher port counts. In contrast to the functionality of bridges and routers, which traditionally utilize the less effective and more expensive microprocessor and software methods, switches direct data frames across the various segments in a faster and more efficient manner through an extensive reliance upon on-board logic, through Application-Specific Integrated Circuits (ASICs).

Like bridges, switches subdivide larger networks and prevent the unnecessary flow of network traffic from one segment to another, or in the case of cross-segment traffic, switches direct the frames only across the segments containing the source and destination hosts. In a traditional nonswitched Ethernet situation, each time a particular device broadcasts, or "talks," on the network, other devices become incapable of accessing the network, thus preventing collisions (as defined in the IEEE's 802.3 specification). Although this ensures the integrity of your data, it does nothing to increase overall network speed. Switches help to ensure additional network access opportunities for attached devices (increasing speed and reducing latency) by restricting data flows to local segments unless frames are destined for a host located on another segment. In such a case, the switch would examine the destination address and forward the requisite frames only across the destination segment, leaving all additional segments attached to that switch free from that particular broadcast and (theoretically) able to facilitate local-segment traffic. Rather than being a passive connection between multiple segments, the switch works to ensure that network traffic burdens the fewest number of segments possible.

Switch Properties

By now you should be convinced of the important role that switches can play as part of your Ethernet network. If not, you may want to reread the chapter up to this point. Switches may save your job when your network starts down the inevitable road toward total collapse.

If you've whole-heartedly embraced this chapter's recommendations and are ready to go switch-shopping, a question presents itself: How do you pick a switch that will suit your needs? You'll need to spend a little time getting to know switches, some of their more important features, and how they do that which they do so well. Once you've got that information under your belt, you should be in a fairly good position to make authoritative choices about switch purchases.

Static Switching Versus Dynamic Switching

If you've gotten to the point where your network is extremely congested and you've called vendors in for demonstrations and quotes, be extraordinarily wary if their solutions depend on *static switches*. Although the devices that you evaluate during the course of re-engineering your network may or may not be explicitly referred to as static switches, take a good look at the functionality of the particular piece or pieces of hardware. If the products perform in a fashion that appears to make them nothing more than glorified hubs, chances are that you really don't want to invest in that type of switch. After all, the point of this whole operation is to segment and intelligently control intersegment traffic, thus reducing congestion. Static switches just don't hit the mark.

On the other end of the spectrum are the products that you do want to consider seriously: *dynamic switches*. Dynamic switches not only pay special attention to the forwarding of packets to their proper destination, but also maintain a table that associates individual nodes with the specific ports to which they are connected. This information, updated each time a particular machine transmits across the network, or perhaps at operator-defined intervals, keeps the switch's information as to node/port combinations up to date, allowing the switch to quickly direct frames across the proper segments, rather than across all segments on the switch.

> **NOTE**
>
> Dynamic switches will continue to save you huge amounts of time and energy long after you first integrate them into your network. Because dynamic switches update their forwarding tables every time devices broadcast across the network, you can rearrange your network, switching workstations from port to port to port, until your network is configured in the manner that suits you best, or you're blue in the face, whichever comes first! The tables will be updated automatically and your network won't go down!

Segment Switching Versus Port Switching

There's a great ongoing debate about whether segment switching or port switching provides the optimum solution for resolving network congestion crises. It all boils down to a question of cash on hand: If you've got the cash, go with port switching; if not, then segment switching will be the order of the day. What's great about the segment-versus-port debate is that, for a change, you win either way.

Segment switches are able to handle the traffic from an entire network segment on each port, allowing you to connect a higher number of workstations or segments with fewer switches/physical ports. The great aspect of segment switches is that they are also capable of handling a single workstation on each port (in essence, a segment with one node). This will allow the network engineer to prearrange machines requiring only intermittent network access along the same segment, sharing one (relatively) low-traffic 10Mbps pipe. At the same time, high-end machines, such as network and database servers, optical drives, and other devices can be connected with a one device/one port scheme, allowing these high-bandwidth and critical devices their own dedicated path to the greater network without having to compete with someone's Internet game for network access. Because of the inevitable cost controls that you encounter on a daily basis, segment switching is the preferred and most readily implemented solution because it requires little in the way of additional expenditures for hardware, additional cabling, and so on.

Port switches (also referred to as *switching hubs*) are designed to accommodate a single device on each physical port. This is a network manager's dream—each workstation, server, and random device would have its own dedicated, 10Mbps path to the rest of the network. However, implementing a port-switching solution demands a good deal of capital for additional wiring (cable runs are needed from each device directly to the switch) and enough switches to provide the requisite number of physical ports. Additionally, as your network grows, you'll be faced with significantly increased expansion costs because you'll need new cable runs and possibly entirely new switches every few months. Again, if you've got lots of cash, this is a great option; you'll have quite the impressive network. However, whatever route you choose, you'll certainly end up with a much better network than you had prior to implementing switching.

Cut-Through Switching

Although switches by themselves will provide impressive gains in your overall network performance, there will occasionally be certain situations in which you will want (or need) to squeeze just a little more juice out of the system. Instead of looking at your boss and screaming in despair, an excellent alternative is to implement a *cut-through switching* solution.

Cut-through switching helps speed network communication by forwarding packets much sooner than traditional switching configurations will allow. This is achieved by forwarding packets to their destination machine prior to receiving them in their entirety, sending them on as soon as the switch is able to determine the destination address. Although this generally reduces network latency, cut-through switching can often allow many bad packets to eat up available bandwidth. To prevent this, reconfigure your switch to allow for a marginally longer delay between the receipt and forwarding of packets. Ideally, as soon as the switch receives the packet, it should buffer 64 bytes to ensure that the possibility of packet errors has been eliminated. After the possibility of these errors has passed, the switch can then forward the packets across the appropriate segment to the destination host. This slightly increases network latency, though it will provide for faster speeds than floor-model switching. Unfortunately, if yours is an extraordinarily busy network, the benefits of cut-through switching will be less noticeable, and will reach their limits much sooner than in a less intensive environment.

Store and Forward

Store-and-forward switching devices, as the archnemesis of cut-through switches, take an entirely different approach. It's very much like the tortoise and the hare, with store-and-forward devices playing the slower, yet more dependable, role of the two.

Instead of the faster send-it-as-soon-as-you-can rule used by cut-through devices, store-and-forward devices wait until the entire packet is received by the switch, only then sending it on to

8

SWITCHES

its destination. This lets the switch verify the packet's CRC and eliminate the possibility of other transmission errors, allowing for highly reliable data transmission across your network. Although this doesn't strictly increase network performance, it *does* eliminate the additional transmissions that must occur as a result of packet errors that otherwise would have occupied network resources, thus providing an associated speed increase.

Other Switching Issues

As with just about any area of networking technology, there are a number of additional issues that must be considered when implementing a switching solution for your network. These topics go above and beyond the simple selection of a basic switch and instead take a holistic view of networking in order to create a more powerful and more efficient finished package. The following section briefly covers high-speed network interfaces, competing solutions for high-speed Ethernet, network management issues, and virtual network options that can work in concert to make your network perform well above your expectations.

High-Speed Interfaces

When building (or rebuilding) a network with high-speed switching as the centerpiece of the endeavor, it's important to upgrade and to standardize as many of your network connections as you can, based on your particular hardware and financial constraints. In addition to the host adapters in each of these instances, it is also important to provide the associated high-speed connection, such as CAT5. Three areas need to be addressed: servers, workstations and attached devices, and interswitch connections.

Network Servers

Because the NIC on a server is one of the prime areas where bottlenecks occur, it's important to install a high-speed interface on the server to alleviate NIC congestion. Because your network is only as fast as its slowest part, it's up to you to ensure that easily upgraded items, such as host adapters, do not pose significant performance barriers in and of themselves. This will allow for fast data transfers to and from the server.

Workstations (and Other Network Devices)

As the second factor in the network equation, workstations and other devices that are attached to your network can also make or break a network's performance based on the type and speed of network adapters that are installed throughout your workstation community. High-speed interfaces are important because they allow for faster connections and data transfers with switches and servers, and will free up the network for other devices in a much shorter time frame. Additionally, your network, switches notwithstanding, will experience degraded performance if there is a significant differential among the interface speeds of your various network devices. The reason for this is that fast ports usually can't transmit prior to receiving the whole transmission from a slow port, and slow ports cannot even begin to utilize the full bandwidth provided by a fast port. In either case, bandwidth is wasted because the faster port is at the mercy of the slower port, with the associated bandwidth going to waste.

Interswitch Connections

Just as it is important to provide high-speed interfaces to servers and workstations, it is equally important to ensure that your switches, when interconnected, can communicate with one another at similarly fast rates. After all, your network redesign is for naught if your switches themselves become the very bottleneck that you have been trying to avoid!

Streamlining interswitch connections is generally not the most urgent issue that you'll encounter when integrating switches into your network, simply because the majority of installations will require only a single switch, or will have switches that themselves are supporting completely isolated segments. However, when switches need to be interconnected, in effect creating a miniature high-speed backbone between each other, it's important to provide the fastest interfaces and cabling possible to ensure plentiful bandwidth and low-latency network access.

High-Speed Ethernet Options

Two of the more recent developments in Ethernet networking deserve a paragraph or two when discussing switched Ethernetworks. Both technologies can afford significant increases in overall network performance with only modest expenditures in labor and hardware necessary to implement them.

Full Duplex (20Mbps) Ethernet

Designing a switched Ethernet network that combines port and segment switching, coupled with full duplex (20Mbps) Ethernet operation will increase overall network throughput and will greatly decrease network latency, providing a much more responsive network for your user community. Full duplex Ethernetworks are implemented by disabling the collision detection procedures involved with the traditional (half duplex) Ethernet CSMA/CD schema. Full duplex Ethernetworks function across existing cable infrastructure, allowing you to retain a good portion of your current investment in network technology. Of course, there's always a catch. Although you can use your current wiring, you will need to purchase newer, high-speed network interface cards (NICs) for PCs, network and other servers, and any other devices attached to your network.

100Mbps Fast Ethernet

Another of the amazing technologies that have been increasing the speed at which network communications are taking place is Fast Ethernet, which is a new system that allows Ethernet-based traffic to cross your network at speeds at or near 100Mbps, well beyond the speed of traditional Ethernet (10Mbps) or Token Ring (4 or 16Mbps) networks. The 100base-TX implementation of Fast Ethernet will operate across existing CAT3 or CAT5 cable, although CAT5 is preferred because its lower signal-to-noise ratio ensures a more reliable level of communication.

As we've already discussed, one of the most frequent areas that suffer from network congestion occurs at the network server. Although switched networks are the first step in lessening this bottleneck, supplementing your switch with high-speed Ethernet can provide greater performance gains than can be realized by either technology by itself. If you're up to the task of rewiring your entire office building, Fast Ethernet is the least expensive and most easily implemented solution available for providing 100Mbps networking throughout your organization. ATM, FDDI, and ADSL are nice, but without a lot of time for training, a large budget, and a whole lot of patience, they're not likely to be deployed in your company any time soon!

Network Management

When evaluating your switching solutions, be sure that your manufacturer supports (or hopefully provides) some type of SNMP-compliant management tools so that you can easily and effectively monitor and troubleshoot your switches. Although network management resources will vary to some degree from vendor to vendor, make sure that your particular switch can readily supply you with performance, error, and other related information so that you can easily spot and address network trouble.

Virtual Networks

If proactively monitoring your network, designing speed-saving cut-through switches, and installing high-speed interfaces throughout your network still hasn't delivered the fantasy performance levels that you've been pining for, you're not out of options just yet. Another step you can take will require a lot more time and effort, but if you're working in a particularly large and unwieldy switched environment, then perhaps *virtual networking* is the right solution for your particular needs.

The reality of virtual networking is not far off from what you're probably envisioning right now. Virtual networking is the creation of multiple *logical* networks out of a single *physical* network or grouping of segments connected to a single switching device. This can be accomplished by configuring the switch to allow certain workstations or segments access only to specifically delineated segments, thereby denying access to all other segments connected to that particular switch.

Virtual networking can also be used as a management and security tool, enabling an administrator to group segments together into logical networks based on department (legal, production, customer service, and so on), physical location in the building, or simply to further filter excess traffic from busier parts of the network. What's more, virtual networking can be implemented in such a way as to allow only packets from certain predefined hosts access to restricted segments. In this way, the flow of data from potentially hostile machines can be eliminated long before those machines pose a threat to corporate data or the performance of your network.

Summary

As local area networks become increasingly more complex and crowded beasts, the limits, financial and otherwise, that are imposed on technology support teams require that these troubleshooters approach network problems in new and often unconventional ways. Rather than scrapping your current network in favor of the revolutionary and often enticing technologies that are constantly flooding the market from a variety of vendors, one of the best ways to address network performance issues is to redesign your current network to include Ethernet switches.

By including Ethernet switches as part of your greater network, you'll gain a wide variety of benefits, including decreased latency, faster file transfers, fewer collisions and other transmission errors, and significantly easier management of the greater network. Your users will love you for providing a much more user-friendly network environment, you bosses will be thrilled with the fact that you've managed to keep the network together and responsive with a minimum of cash, threats, and ultimatums, and you'll be happy to avoid the gripes, groans, and midnight pages from the network operations center that tend to go hand in hand with slow-performing networks.

Routers

by Martin Bligh

IN THIS CHAPTER

The simplest of networks can be imagined as a one-wire bus (see Figure 9.1), where each computer can talk to any other by sending a packet out onto that bus.

FIGURE 9.1.
The simplest of networks.

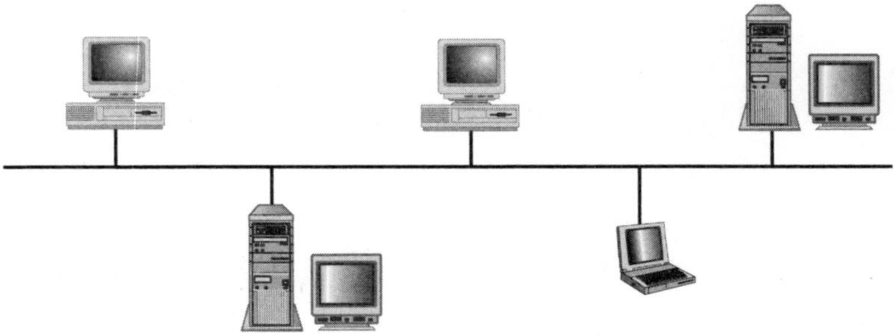

But as you increase the number of computers on the network, this becomes impractical. There are several main problems:

1. You run out of bandwidth on the network.
2. Each computer wastes more time processing unnecessary broadcast traffic.
3. The network becomes unmanageable. Any fault can bring the whole network down.
4. Each computer can listen to any other computer's conversation.

Segmenting the network helps solve all of these problems. But if you break the network into separate segments, you must provide a mechanism for the different segment hosts to communicate. This normally involves selectively passing data between segments at some layer of the ISO network stack. Let's look again at the network stack (see Figure 9.2) to see where routers fit in.

Routers operate at the network layer. This chapter assumes that the network layer is IP (version 4), as this is by far the most popular protocol. The concepts involved are similar to those behind other network layer protocols.

Routing Versus Bridging

Routing is a higher-level concept than layer 2 switching/bridging—you are further removed from the physical details of the network. Any machine on a routed network has the same network layer address format (for example, an IP address) whether it is communicating over an Ethernet, Token Ring, FDDI, or WAN link.

Data link layer addresses (for example, MAC addresses) are just unique identifying tags for a particular network interface *within* a particular layer 3 network (they may also be globally unique—for example, Ethernet addresses). Network layer addresses usually hold more information than this—they consist of two parts: a network address and a host address. (For example, the IP address of my network interface card is 158.84.81.39, the network address is 158.84.81, and the host address is 39).

FIGURE 9.2.
Where connecting devices fit into the OSI stack.

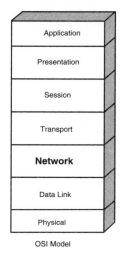

OSI Model

| Application |
| Presentation |
| Session |
| Transport |
| **Network** |
| Data Link |
| Physical |

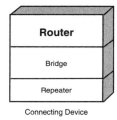

Connecting Device

| **Router** |
| Bridge |
| Repeater |

> **NOTE**
>
> Here the network address is taken to mean the whole of the number specifying the network (that is, including any subnet address).

A bridge can only connect networks with the same (or very similar) data link layer protocols. A router transcends this problem. It can connect any two networks, provided that the hosts use the same network layer protocol.

Connecting the Network Layer to the Data Link Layer

Underlying the network layer is the data link layer. For the layers to interoperate, they need some "glue" protocols. ARP (*Address Resolution Protocol*) is used to map network layer (layer 3) addresses to data link layer (layer 2) addresses (see the description in the following section). RARP (*Reverse Address Resolution Protocol*) is used to map layer 2 addresses to layer 3 addresses.

The most common use of ARP is to resolve IP addresses, though the protocol is defined in such a way that it is independent of the network layer protocol. The most common data link layer is Ethernet. Accordingly, the examples in the ARP and RARP sections are based on IP and Ethernet, though the concepts are identical for use with other protocols.

9

ROUTERS

Address Resolution Protocol

Network layer addresses are an abstract mapping defined by the network administrator—the network layer doesn't have to worry which data link layer it is running over. However, network interfaces can only communicate with each other according to the layer 2 address, which is dependent on the network type. These layer 2 (hardware) addresses are derived from the layer 3 address by the Address Resolution Protocol (ARP).

An ARP request is not necessary for every datagram sent—the responses are cached in the local ARP table, which keeps a list of `<IP address, hardware address>` pairs. This keeps the number of ARP packets on the network very low. ARP is generally a low maintenance protocol that raises few problems; it is normally seen only when there are conflicting layer 3 addresses on the network. ARP is a simple protocol, presenting few complications.

Overview

If interface A wants to send a datagram to interface B, and it only has the IP address for B (`B-IP`), it must first find the hardware address for B (`B-hard`). Interface A sends an ARP broadcast specifying `B-IP` and requesting `B-hard`. Interface B receives the broadcast, and replies with a unicast to A, giving the correct `B-hard` for `B-IP` (see Figure 9.3).

FIGURE 9.3.
An ARP exchange.

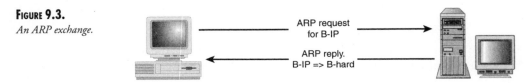

ARP request
for B-IP

ARP reply.
B-IP => B-hard

Note that only interface B responds to the request, even though other interfaces on the network may have the relevant information. This ensures that responses are correct and do not provide out-of-date information.

It is important to understand that ARP requests are sent out only for the next-hop gateway, not always for the destination IP address. Thus, if interface A wants to send a datagram to interface B, but its routing table tells it that traffic must pass through router C, it sends out an ARP request for router C's address, not for interface B's address (see Figure 9.4).

What Happens When an ARP Packet Is Received?

The flowchart in Figure 9.5 details the process followed when an ARP packet is received. Note that the `<IP address, hardware address>` pair of the sender is inserted into the local ARP table in addition to a reply being sent; if A wishes to talk to B, then it is very likely that B also needs to talk to A.

FIGURE 9.4.

An ARP exchange through a router.

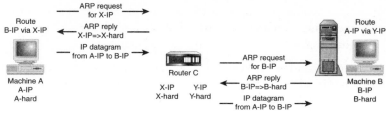

FIGURE 9.5.

Receipt of an ARP packet (constructed from information in RFC826).

IP Address Conflicts

The most commonly seen error produced by ARP is caused by a conflicting IP address. This is where two different stations claim to own the same IP address—IP addresses *must* be unique on any connected set of networks.

IP address conflicts are apparent when two replies come in answer to an ARP request—each reply specifying a different hardware address. This is a serious error, with no easy solution—which hardware address do you send the datagrams to?

To avoid IP address conflicts, when interface A is first initialized it sends out an ARP request for *its own* IP address. If no response is sent back, interface A can assume that the IP address is not in use. However, suppose interface B is already using the IP address in question: B sends an ARP reply with the hardware address *B-hard*. Interface A now knows that the IP address is already in use—it must not use the address and must flag an error.

There is still a problem though. Suppose that host C had an entry for the disputed IP address, mapping it to *B-hard*. Looking at Figure 9.3, you see that on receipt of the ARP broadcast from interface A, host C updates its ARP table to map the address to *A-hard*. To correct such errors, interface B (the "defending" system) sends out an ARP request broadcast for the IP address again. Host C now updates its ARP entry for the disputed IP address to *B-hard* again. The network state is now back as before, but host C may have sent IP datagrams intended for host B to host A by mistake while the ARP table was (briefly) incorrect. This is unfortunate, but as IP does not guarantee delivery, this situation does not cause major problems.

Managing the ARP Cache Table

The ARP cache table is a list of `<IP address, hardware address>` pairs, indexed by IP address. The table can often be managed with the `arp` command. Common syntax for this command includes

- Add a static entry to the cache table—`arp -s <IP address> <hardware address>`
- Delete an entry from the cache table—`arp -d <IP address>`
- Displaying all entries in cache table—`arp -a`

Dynamic entries in the ARP cache table (that is, those that have not been manually added with `arp -s`) are normally deleted after a period of time. This period is determined by the specific TCP/IP implementation, but an entry would commonly be destroyed if unused for a fixed time period (for example, five minutes).

Use of a Static ARP Address

One typical use of a static ARP entry is to set up a standalone printer server. These small units can normally be configured by way of Telnet, but first they need an IP address. There is no obvious way to feed them this initial information, except by using the built-in serial port. However, it is often inconvenient to find an appropriate terminal and serial cable, set up baud rates, parity settings, and so on.

Suppose we wish to set up a print server, P, with an IP address of *P-IP*, and that we know the print server's hardware address to be *P-hard*. A static ARP entry is created on workstation A to map *P-IP* to *P-hard*. Any IP traffic from workstation A to *P-IP* is now sent to *P-hard*, though the print server does not yet know its IP address. We can now telnet to *P-IP*, which connects to the print server, and configure its IP address. Then we can tidy up by deleting the static ARP entry. (See Figure 9.6.)

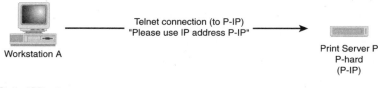

Workstation A

Telnet connection (to P-IP)
"Please use IP address P-IP"

Print Server P
P-hard
(P-IP)

Static ARP entry
P-IP=>P-hard

It is often useful to configure the print server on one subnet, but use it on another. This is easy to achieve by a very similar process to that illustrated in the preceding figure. The IP address of the print server on the subnet it uses is *P-IP*. Allocate a temporary IP address, *T-IP*, on the subnet that you wish to configure the print server on, and attach the print server to that subnet. On a workstation (A) connected to the configuring subnet, create the static ARP entry mapping *T-IP* onto *P-hard*, and telnet to *T-IP*. Configure the print server to use IP address *P-IP*. Move the print server to the subnet it will be used on, and tidy up by deleting the static ARP entry. (See Figure 9.7.)

Workstation A

Telnet connection (to T-IP)
"Please use IP address P-IP"

Print Server P
P-hard
(P-IP)

Static ARP entry
T-IP=>P-hard

Proxy ARP

It is possible to avoid configuring the routing tables on every host by using *proxy ARP*. This is particularly useful where subnetting is being used, but not all hosts are capable of understanding subnetting (see the section on subnetting later on in this chapter).

The basic idea is that a workstation sends out ARP requests even for machines that are not on its own subnet. The ARP proxy server (often the gateway) responds with the hardware address of the gateway. See Figure 9.8, where proxy ARP is used, and compare it to Figure 9.4, where routing tables are used.

Proxy ARP makes the management of host configurations much simpler. However, it increases network traffic (though not significantly) and potentially requires a much larger ARP cache. An entry for each IP address off the local subnet is created, all mapping to the gateway's hardware address.

9

ROUTERS

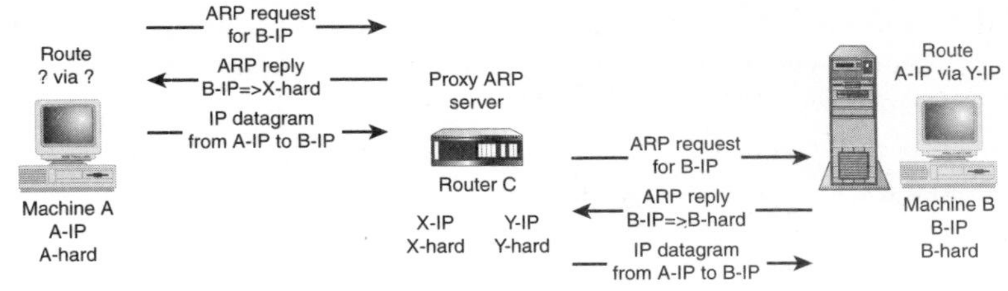

FIGURE 9.8.

A workstation using proxy ARP.

In the eyes of a workstation using proxy ARP, the world is just one large physical network, with no routers in sight!

IP Addressing

In routable network layer protocol, the protocol address must hold two pieces of information: the network address and the host address. The most obvious way to store this information is in two separate fields. We must cope with the largest possible case in both fields, perhaps allocating 16 bits for each field. Some protocols (such as IPX) behave like this, and it works well for small- to medium-sized networks.

Another solution would be to keep the host address field small, perhaps allocating 24 bits for the network address and just 8 for the host address. This would allow plenty of networks, but not many hosts on each network. However, for networks with more than 256 (2^8) hosts, you could allocate multiple addresses. The problem with this scheme is that the large number of networks created tends to place an intolerable load on the network's routers.

IP packs the network address and host address together into one 32-bit field. Sometimes the host address portion is short, sometimes it is long. This allows very efficient use of the address space, keeping IP addresses short, and the total number of networks fairly low. There are two different ways of splitting the address back into its two parts—class-based addressing and classless addressing. These are discussed in the following section.

Hosts Versus Gateways

The distinction between hosts and gateways often causes some confusion. This is because of a shift in the meaning of the term "host." As defined by the original RFCs (1122/3 and 1009):

■ A *host* is a device connected to one or more networks. It can send and receive traffic on any of these networks, but it *never* passes traffic from one network to another.

■ A *gateway* is a device connected to more than one network. It selectively forwards traffic from one network to another.

In other words, the terms *host* and *gateway* used to be mutually exclusive—computers were not generally powerful enough to act as both a host and a gateway. The host was a computer that a user did some work on, or that perhaps acted as a file server. Modern computers are powerful enough to both act as a gateway and do useful work for a user; therefore, a more modern definition of a host might be the following:

■ A *host* is a device connected to one or more networks. It can send and receive traffic on any of these networks. It may function as a gateway, but this is not its sole purpose.

A *router* is a dedicated gateway. The hardware is specially designed to allow the router to pass high volumes of traffic, and with little delay for each packet (latency). However, a gateway can also be a standard computer with multiple network interfaces, where the operating system's network layer allows it to forward packets. Now that dedicated routing hardware is becoming less expensive, the use of computers as gateways is becoming much less common. At a very small site with a only a cheap dial-up connection, a user's computer might be used as a nondedicated gateway.

Class-Based Addressing

When IP first designed, the address was split into its composite parts according to the first byte of the address:

`0:`	Reserved (for the network address)
`1–126:`	Class A (network: 1 byte, host: 3 bytes)
`127:`	Reserved (for the loopback address)
`128–191:`	Class B (network: 2 bytes, host: 2 bytes)
`192–223:`	Class C (network: 3 bytes, host: 1 byte)
`224–255:`	Reserved (see the note that follows)

> **NOTE**
>
> Part of this range is for multicast addresses, sometimes referred to as *class D* addresses. For the sake of simplicity, these are not discussed here.

If you needed a large network you were given a class A address, but if you only had a few hosts, you were given a class C address. A few examples:

IP address	Network address	Host address
56.81.38.28	56	81.38.28
137.89.15.88	137.89	15.88
200.77.32.61	200.77.32	61

Subnetting

Although the class-based addressing system worked well for the Internet service provider, it was impossible to do any routing inside a network. The intention was that a network would use layer 2 (bridging/switching) to direct packets within a network. The lack of routing was a particular problem if you had a large class A network, as bridging/switching on a large network becomes very difficult to manage.

The logical solution is to break down some larger networks into smaller segments, but this was not possible within the original confines of the class-based addressing system. In the previous example, the network address 137.89 is treated as a class B address, so it is not possible to route different parts of this network to different sites.

To solve this problem, a new field called a *subnet mask* was introduced and associated with every address. The subnet mask indicated which portion of the address was the network address, and which was the host address (instead of deciding by the first byte).

In the subnet mask, binary 1 indicates a network address bit, and binary 0 indicates a host address bit. Thus for the 137.89.15.88 example given earlier, the format would be:

```
Address:       10001001 . 01011001 . 00001111 . 01011000 (137. 89. 15. 88)
Subnet mask:   11111111 . 11111111 . 00000000 . 00000000 (255.255.  0.  0)
```

The subnet mask given indicates that the first two bytes are the network address, the second two bytes are the host address. Thus your traditional class addresses have subnet masks:

- Class A (network: 8 bits, host: 24 bits): 255.0.0.0
- Class B (network: 16 bits, host: 16 bits): 255.255.0.0
- Class C (network: 24 bits, host: 8 bits): 255.255.255.0

If you wish to use the 137.89.0.0 network address as a set of distinct class C-sized networks, the following address would be used:

```
Address:       10001001 . 01011001 . 00001111 . 01011000 (137. 89. 15. 88)
Subnet mask:   11111111 . 11111111 . 11111111 . 00000000 (255.255.255.  0)
```

Breaking a network into *subnetworks* using a longer subnet mask (for example, 255.255.255.0 instead of 255.255.0.0) is called *subnetting*. Be aware that some very old software won't support subnetting, as it doesn't understand subnet masks. For instance UNIX's routed routing daemon normally uses a routing protocol called RIP version 1, which was designed before subnet masks.

Non-Byte-Aligned Subnetting

So far, I have only discussed subnet masks of 255.0.0.0, 255.255.0.0, and 255.255.255.0. These are referred to as *byte-aligned subnet masks*, because they split the network and host portions on a byte boundary. However, it is also possible (though slightly more difficult to work with) to split the address inside a byte (using non-byte-aligned subnet masks), for instance:

```
Address:        10001001 . 01011001 . 00001111 . 01011000 (137. 89. 15. 88)
Subnet mask:    11111111 . 11111111 . 11111111 . 11110000 (255.255.255.240)
```

Now you have only 4 bytes for the host address, giving 16 possible addresses within the network. One address is reserved for the network itself, and one for the broadcast address, leaving a possible 14 hosts.

```
Address:        10001001 . 01011001 . 00001111 . 01011000 (137. 89. 15. 88)
Subnet mask:    11111111 . 11111111 . 11111111 . 11110000 (255.255.255.240)
Network addr:   10001001 . 01011001 . 00001111 . 01010000 (137. 89. 15. 80)
Broadcast addr: 10001001 . 01011001 . 00001111 . 01011111 (137. 89. 15. 95)
```

Note that the network address (137.89.15.80) no longer ends in the familiar 0 and the broadcast address (137.89.15.95) no longer ends in the familiar 255. Although they don't look like the familiar network and broadcast addresses, they are formed in exactly the same way (setting the host portion of the address to all 1s or all 0s, respectively). The subnet mask also looks unfamiliar, but it, too, is formed in exactly the same way.

This extension of the subnetting technique makes new sizes of network possible, including tiny networks for point-to-point links (mask 255.255.255.252, giving 30 bits network, and 2 bits host), or medium-sized networks (for example, mask 255.255.240.0, giving 20 bits network, and 12 bits hosts—4,096 possible hosts).

Humans would find the subnet mask system a lot easier to understand (and to read on a day-to-day basis) if the mask was just represented as the number of bits that were allocated to the host portion of the address (for instance, in the preceding example the mask 255.255.240.0 would be 12). Unfortunately, history has handed us a system where the representation makes it easy for computers to do an AND operation, not for us to read. You can soon learn to think in binary though!

Writing subnet masks in hexadecimal (base 16) rather than decimal (base 10) can also help greatly—a subnet mask of FF.FF.F0.00 is easier to work with than 255.255.240.0, as it is easier to convert between hexadecimal and binary than between decimal and binary.

If you are using DNS (domain name system) to map between host names and IP addresses, be slightly wary of non-byte-aligned subnet masks. They may prevent you from delegating control of the reverse lookup records, used to map from IP addresses to host names. DNS is designed to allow only a delegation split on an IP address byte boundary (inside the in-addr.arpa. domain).

Supernetting

Supernetting is a very similar concept to subnetting—the IP address is split into separate network address and host address portions according to the subnet mask. However, instead of breaking down larger networks into several smaller subnets, you group smaller networks together to make one larger *supernet*.

Imagine that I am given a bank of 16 class C networks, ranging from 201.66.32.0 to 201.66.47.0—my whole network can be addressed as 201.66.32.0 with a subnet mask of 255.255.240.0 (any address on the network has the same initial 20 bits as 201.66.32.0—to address the network, set the host address to 0).

Unfortunately it's not possible to allocate totally arbitrary groups of addresses—a range of 16 class C networks from 201.66.71.0 to 201.66.86.0 doesn't have a single network address (try to find one!). Why is this? Given the required subnet mask of 255.255.240.0, the host portion of the beginning of the address range is not 0:

Address	Subnet mask	Network address	Host address
201.66.32.0	255.255.240.0	201.66.32	0.0
201.66.84.0	255.255.240.0	201.66.64	3.0

Fortunately this isn't a real problem—given a sensible address allocation strategy, you can find suitable blocks of addresses.

Variable Length Subnet Masks (VLSM)

If you want to split your network into multiple subnetworks of unequal size, you can use a *variable length subnet mask* (VLSM). This slightly intimidating acronym just means that each of your subnetworks can have a different length subnet mask. If you were splitting a company's network by department, some networks might have 255.255.255.0 (for most departments), while others might have 255.255.252.0 (for a particularly large department).

Classless Addressing (CIDR)

As the Internet has taken off, the number of hosts attached to the network has grown beyond all expectations. Although there are still far fewer than 2^{32} hosts connected directly to the Internet, there is a shortage of addresses. RFC 1519, *Classless Inter-Domain Routing* (*CIDR*), was published in 1993 in an attempt to address inefficiencies in the allocation of the address space.

CIDR is an attempt to extend the life span of IP v4; it does not address the eventual exhaustion of the whole address space. IP v6 addresses the eventual exhaustion of the address space by using a 128-bit address rather than a 32-bit address. However, implementing IP v6 is a mammoth task, which the Internet is not yet ready for. CIDR gives us time to implement IP v6.

The class-based address system worked well. It provided a reasonable compromise between efficient address usage and a low number of networks for routers to cope with. However, two major problems were caused by the unexpected growth of the Internet:

- The increased number of allocated networks meant that the number of entries in routing tables became unmanageably large, and slowed down routers considerably.

■ Much of the address space was being wasted by the allocation policy—allocating inflexible blocks of 256 = 2^8 (class C), 65536 = 2^{16} (class B), or 16777216 = 2^{24} (class A) resulted in many wasted addresses. This has resulted particularly in a shortage of class B addresses.

To solve the second problem, it is possible to allocate multiple smaller networks instead of one larger network: for instance, multiple class C networks instead of one class B. Although this results in much more efficient address allocation, it exacerbates the growth of routing tables (the first problem).

Under CIDR, addresses are assigned according to the topology of the network. This means that a consecutive group of network addresses would be allocated to a particular service provider, allowing the whole group to be covered by one (probably supernetted) network address.

For example, a service provider is given a bank of 256 class C networks, ranging from 213.79.0.0 to 213.79.255.0. The service provider allocates one class C address to each customer, but routing tables external to the service provider know all of these routes by just one entry in the routing table—213.79.0.0 with a network mask of 255.255.0.0.

This method obviously greatly reduces the growth of routing tables for each new address that is allocated. Estimates given by the authors of the CIDR RFC (1519) indicate that if 90% of service providers used CIDR, routing tables might grow by 54% over a 3-year period, as opposed to 776% growth without CIDR (these figures assume CIDR is not in place at the start of the period).

If renumbering the existing address space were possible, the number of advertised routes that the Internet backbone routers had to deal with could be *massively* reduced. Unfortunately, this is unlikely to be practical, due to the huge amount of administrative effort involved.

Routing Tables

If a host has several network interfaces, how does it decide which interface to use for packets to a particular IP address? The answer lies in the routing table. Consider the following routing table:

Destination	Subnet mask	Gateway	Flags	Interface
201.66.37.0	255.255.255.0	201.66.37.74	U	eth0
201.66.39.0	255.255.255.0	201.66.39.21	U	eth1

The host sends all traffic for hosts on network 201.66.37.0 (for example, host addresses 201.66.37.1–201.66.37.254) out through interface eth0 (which has IP address 201.37.37.74), and all traffic for hosts on network 201.66.39.0 out through interface eth1 (which has IP address 201.37.39.21). The flag U just means that the route is "up" (that is, active).

Note that, for directly attached networks, some software doesn't give the IP address of the interface in the gateway field as shown. The name of the interface alone is listed.

This example only covers hosts that are connected directly to you—what if the host in question is on a remote network? If you are connected to network 73.0.0.0 by way of a router with an IP address of 201.66.37.254, you can add an entry to the routing table:

Destination	Subnet mask	Gateway	Flags	Interface
73.0.0.0	255.0.0.0	201.66.37.254	UG	eth0

This tells the machine to route packets for any hosts on the 73.0.0.0 network through 201.66.37.254—note that there must be another entry in the table, telling the host how to send packets to 201.66.37.254! The G (gateway) flag just means that this routing entry directs traffic through an external gateway. Similarly, a route to a specific host through a gateway can be added, and it receives the H (host) flag:

Destination	Subnet mask	Gateway	Flags	Interface
91.32.74.21	255.255.255.255	201.66.37.254	UGH	eth0

This example covers all the basics of the routing table, apart from a few special entries:

Destination	Subnet mask	Gateway	Flags	Interface
127.0.0.1	255.255.255.255	127.0.0.1	UH	lo0
default	0.0.0.0	201.66.39.254	UG	eth1

The first of these is the *loopback interface*, for traffic from the host to itself. This is used for testing, and for communications for applications that are designed to operate over IP but that happen to be communicating locally. It is a host route to the special address 127.0.0.1 (the interface lo0 refers to a "fake" network card internal to the IP stack).

The second entry is more interesting. To save having a route defined on the host to every possible network on the Internet, a *default route* can be defined. If no other entry in the routing table matches the destination address, the packet is sent to the *default gateway* (given in the default route).

Most hosts in a simple setup are connected by way of one interface card to a LAN, which has only one router to other networks. This results in just three entries in the routing table: the loopback entry, the entry for the local subnet, and the default entry (pointing to the router).

Overlapping Routes

Suppose you have entries in the routing table that overlap:

Destination	Subnet mask	Gateway	Flags	Interface
1.2.3.4	255.255.255.255	201.66.37.253	UGH	eth0
1.2.3.0	255.255.255.0	201.66.37.254	UG	eth0

Destination	Subnet mask	Gateway	Flags	Interface
1.2.0.0	255.255.0.0	201.66.39.253	UG	eth1
default	0.0.0.0	201.66.39.254	UG	eth1

The routes are said to be *overlapping* because all four include the address 1.2.3.4. So if I send a packet to 1.2.3.4, which route is chosen? In this case, it is the first route, through gateway 201.66.37.253; the route with the longest (most specific) subnet mask is always chosen. Similarly, packets to 1.2.3.5 are sent by the second route in preference to the third.

IMPORTANT: This rule applies only to indirect routes (those routing packets through gateways). Having two interfaces defined on the same subnet is not legal in many implementations of software. The following setup is normally *illegal* (though some software will attempt to load-balance over the two interfaces):

Interface	IP address	Subnet mask
eth0	201.66.37.1	255.255.255.0
eth1	201.66.37.2	255.255.255.0

The policy on overlapping routes is extremely useful; it allows the default route to work as just a route with a destination of 0.0.0.0, and a subnet mask of 0.0.0.0, rather than having to implement it as a special case for the routing software.

Looking back at CIDR, let's take the preceding example where a service provider is given a bank of 256 class C networks, ranging from 213.79.0.0 to 213.79.255.0. Routing tables that are external to the service provider know all of these routes by just one entry in the routing table—213.79.0.0, with a network mask of 255.255.0.0.

But suppose that one customer moves to a different service provider. The customer had the network address 213.79.61.0, but must he now get a new network address from the new service provider's range of addresses? That would mean renumbering every machine in the organization, changing every DNS entry, and so on, and so on.

Fortunately, there is an easy solution. The old service provider keeps the route 213.79.0.0 (with subnet mask 255.255.0.0), while the new service provider advertises the route 213.79.61.0 (with subnet mask 255.255.255.0). As the new route has a longer subnet mask than the old service provider's route, it overrides the old route.

Static Routing

Looking back at the routing table that you have been building up, there are now six entries in it. These are listed next, and a diagram of the network is given in Figure 9.9:

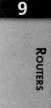

Destination	Subnet mask	Gateway	Flags	Interface
127.0.0.1	255.255.255.255	127.0.0.1	UH	lo0
201.66.37.0	255.255.255.0	201.66.37.74	U	eth0
201.66.39.0	255.255.255.0	201.66.39.21	U	eth1
default	0.0.0.0	201.66.39.254	UG	eth1
73.0.0.0	255.0.0.0	201.66.37.254	UG	eth0
91.32.74.21	255.255.255.255	201.66.37.254	UGH	eth0

> **NOTE**
>
> A routing table can usually be listed like this by using the command netstat -Rn. See your vendor's documentation for netstat.

How did these entries get there? The first one is added by the network software when the routing table is initialized. The second and third are created automatically when the network interface cards are bound to their IP addresses. However, the last three must be added specifically. On a UNIX system, this is done by issuing the route command, either manually by a user, or by the rc scripts upon bootup.

All these methods involve *static routing*. Routes are generally added on bootup, and the routing table remains unchanged, unless manual intervention occurs.

Routing Protocols

Both hosts and gateways can use a technique called *dynamic routing*. This allows the routing table to be automatically altered if, for instance, a router fails. Another router could be used instead, without user intervention, providing a much more resilient system.

Dynamic routing requires a routing protocol, which adds and deletes entries from the routing table. The routing table still works the same way as in static routing, but entries are added and removed automatically rather than manually.

There are two types of routing protocols: interior and exterior. *Interior protocols* route *inside* an autonomous system (AS), while *exterior protocols* route *between* autonomous systems. An *autonomous system* is a network normally under one administrative control, perhaps by a large company or a university. Small sites tend to be part of their Internet service provider's AS.

Only interior protocols are discussed here; few people ever have to deal with (or have even heard of!) exterior protocols. The most common exterior protocols are EGP (*Exterior Gateway Protocol*) and BGP (*Border Gateway Protocol*). BGP is the newer protocol, and it is slowly replacing EGP.

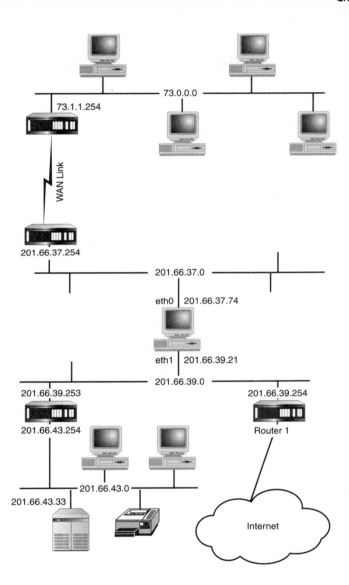

FIGURE 9.9.
*A more complex
network.*

ICMP Redirects

ICMP is not normally considered to be a routing protocol, but ICMP redirects act in much the same way as a routing protocol, so I'll discuss them here. Suppose that you have a routing table with the six entries given earlier. A packet is sent to the host 201.66.43.33. Looking through the table, this does not match any route except the default route, which sends traffic by way of the router 201.66.39.254 (see trip 1 in Figure 9.10). However, this router has full knowledge of the network, and knows that all packets for the 201.66.43.0 subnet should go through

`201.66.39.254`. Accordingly, it forwards the packet to the appropriate router (trip 2 in Figure 9.10). But it would have been much more efficient if the host had sent the packet straight to `201.66.39.254` (trip 3 in Figure 9.10).

FIGURE 9.10.
An ICMP redirect.

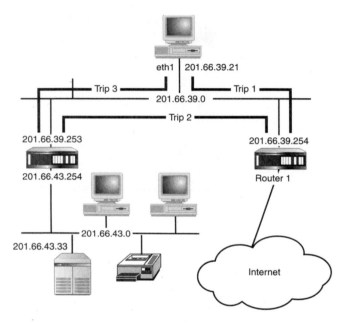

The router can instruct the host to use a different route by sending an ICMP redirect. The router knows that there is a better route, because it is sending the packet back out on the same interface it came in on. Though the router knows that the whole of the `201.66.43.0` subnet should go by way of `201.66.39.254`, it normally only sends an ICMP redirect for a particular host (in this case `201.66.43.33`). The host creates a new entry in the routing table:

Destination	Subnet mask	Gateway	Flags	Interface
`201.66.43.33`	`255.255.255.255`	`201.66.39.253`	UGHD	eth1

Notice the D (redirect) flag—this is set on all routes created by an ICMP redirect. In the future, all packets will be sent by the new route (trip 3 in Figure 9.10).

Routing Information Protocol (RIP)

RIP is a simple interior routing protocol, which has been around for many years, and is widely implemented (UNIX `routed` uses RIP). It is a distance-vector algorithm, which means that its routing decisions are based purely upon the number of "hops" between two points. Traversing a router is considered to be one hop.

Both hosts and gateways can run RIP, although hosts only receive information; they do not send it. Information can be specifically requested from a gateway, but is also broadcasted every 30 seconds in order to keep routing tables current. RIP uses UDP to intercommunicate between hosts and gateways through port 520.

The information passed between gateways is used to build up a routing table. The route chosen by RIP is always the one with the shortest number of hops to the destination.

RIP version 1 works reasonably well on simple, fairly small networks. However, it shows several problems working on larger networks, some of which are rectified in RIP v2, but some of the limitations are inherent in its design. In the following discussion, points applicable to v1 *and* v2 are referred to simply as RIP, while RIP v1 or RIP v2 refer to the specific versions.

RIP doesn't have any concept of quality for links; all links are considered to be the same. Thus a low-speed serial line is considered to be as good as a high-speed fiber-optic link. RIP gives preference to the route with the least number of hops; thus, when given a choice between going across:

- A 100Mbps fiber-optic link, then a router to a 10Mbit Ethernet, or
- A 9600bps serial link

RIP will choose the latter. RIP also has no concept of the traffic levels on a link; given a choice between two Ethernet links, one of which is very busy, and one of which has no traffic at all, RIP will quite happily use the busier link.

The maximum number of hops interpreted by RIP is 15, any more than this is considered to be unreachable. Thus on very large autonomous systems, where the number of hops on any useful route may exceed 15, use of RIP is impractical.

RIP v1 does not support subnetting; the subnet mask is not transmitted with each route. The method for determining the subnet mask for each given route varies from implementation to implementation. RIP v2 corrects this shortcoming.

RIP updates are only sent every 30 seconds, so information about the failure of a link can take some time to propagate through a large network. The time for routing information to settle down to a stable state can be even longer, and routing loops can occur during this period of change.

We can conclude that RIP is a simple routing protocol, with some restrictive limitations, especially in version 1. However, it is often the only choice for particular operating systems.

Summary

ARP (Address Resolution Protocol) is used to map IP addresses to hardware addresses (MAC addresses). It is a transparent protocol that is normally only seen by the user when an IP address conflict occurs. In special situations, the ARP cache table can be controlled manually via the `arp` command.

9

ROUTERS

An IP address splits into two parts: the network part and the host part. How the address is split used to depend on the network class, given by the first byte of the address. Modern implementations of IP hold an extra field called the subnet mask, which is used to determine how the address is split. This greatly enhances the functionality of IP routing, but also adds a lot of complexity.

Routing tables can be static or dynamic. Static routes are controlled manually, or by a sequence of commands in a bootup script. Dynamic routes are controlled by a daemon running a routing protocol, such as RIP or OSPF. Though, strictly speaking, ICMP isn't a routing protocol, it can still alter the routing tables in response to a redirect message.

Gateways

by Mark A. Sportack

IN THIS CHAPTER

CHAPTER 10

Gateways were once a readily understood part of the network. In the original Internet, the term gateway referred to a router. The router was the only tangible sign of the cyberworld beyond the local domain. This "gateway" to the unknown was (and still is) capable of calculating routes and forwarding packetized data across networks spanning far beyond the visible horizon of the originating local area network (LAN). Thus, it was regarded as the gateway to the Internet.

Over time, routers became less of a mystery. The emergence and maturation of corporate IP-based wide area networks (WANs) witnessed the proliferation of routers. Technological innovation, too, bred even more familiarity. The routing function can now reside in servers and even in network switching hubs. The original "gateway" no longer held the same mystique. Instead, the router grew into a multipurpose network device that did everything from segmenting LANs into smaller segments, to interconnecting related LANs in private WANs, to interconnecting private WANs with the Internet. Thus the router lost its synonymity with the term *gateway*.

The term *gateway*, however, has lived on. It has been applied and reapplied so frequently, and to so many different functions, that defining a gateway is no longer a simple task. Currently, there are three main categories of gateways:

- Protocol gateways
- Application gateways
- Security gateways

The only commonality remaining is that a gateway functions as an intermediary between two dissimilar domains, regions, or systems. The nature of the dissimilarity you are attempting to overcome dictates the type of gateway that is required.

Protocol Gateways

Protocol gateways usually convert protocols between network regions that use dissimilar protocols. This physical conversion can occur at Layer 2 of the OSI Reference Model (the Network Layer), Layer 3 (the Internetwork Layer), or between Layers 2 and 3. Two types of protocol gateways do not provide a conversion function: security gateways and tunnels.

Security gateways that interconnect technically similar network regions are a necessary intermediary because of logical dissimilarities between the two interconnected network regions. For example, one might be a private WAN and the other a public one, like the Internet. This exception is discussed later in this chapter, under the heading "Combination Filtration Gateways." The remainder of this section focuses on protocol gateways that perform a physical protocol conversion.

Tunneling Gateways

Tunneling is a relatively common technique for passing data through an otherwise incompatible network region. Data packets are encapsulated with framing that is recognized by the network that will be transporting it. The original framing and formatting are retained, but are treated as data. Upon reaching its destination, the recipient host unwraps the packet and discards the wrapper. This results in the packet being restored to its original format. In Figure 10.1, IPv4 packets are wrapped in IPv6 by Router A for transmission through an IPv6 WAN for delivery to an IPv4 host. Router B removes the IPv6 wrapper and presents the restored IPv4 packet to the destination host.

FIGURE 10.1.

Passing data by tunneling techniques.

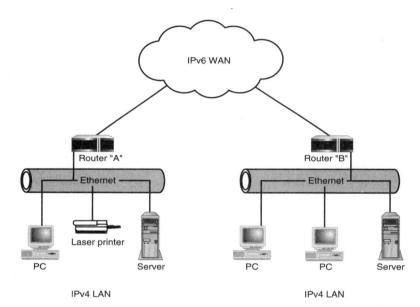

Tunneling techniques may be used for just about every Layer 3 protocol, from SNA to IPv6, as well as many individual protocols within those aforementioned suites. As beneficial as tunneling can be to overcoming the limitations of any given network topology, it has its dark side. The very nature of tunneling consists of hiding unacceptable packets by disguising them in an acceptable format. Quite simply, tunneling can be used to defeat firewalls by encapsulating protocols that would otherwise be blocked from entry to a private network region.

Proprietary Gateways

A myriad of proprietary gateway products have been available to bridge the gap between legacy mainframe systems and the emerging distributed computing environment. The typical proprietary gateway connected PC-based clients to a protocol converter at the edge of the LAN. This converter then provided access to mainframe systems using an X.25 network. The gateway in Figure 10.2 demonstrates tn3270 emulation sessions from client PCs to the gateway. The gateway dumps the IP sessions onto an X.25 WAN for transport to the mainframe.

These gateways were usually inexpensive, single-function circuit boards that needed to be installed in a LAN-attached computer. This kept the cost of the gateway to a minimum, and

10

GATEWAYS

facilitated technology migrations. In the example illustrated in Figure 10.2, the single-function gateway facilitated the migration from the mainframe era's hard-wired terminals and terminal servers to PCs and LANs.

FIGURE 10.2.

A primitive, proprietary, single-function gateway.

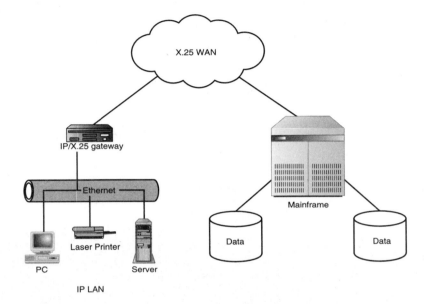

Layer 2 Protocol Gateways

Layer 2 protocol gateways provide a LAN-to-LAN protocol conversion. They are usually referred to as *translating bridges* rather than protocol gateways. This type of conversion may be required to permit interconnection of LANs with different frame types or clock rates.

Frame Mismatches

Local area networks that are IEEE 802–compliant share a common media access layer. However, their frame structures and media access mechanisms make them unable to interoperate directly. A translating bridge takes advantage of the Layer 2 commonalties, such as the MAC address, and enables interoperability by providing on-the-fly translation of the dissimilar portions of the frame structures.

First-generation LANs required a separate device to provide translating bridges. The current generation of multiprotocol switching hubs usually provides a high-bandwidth backplane that functions as a translating bridge between dissimilar frame types, as shown in Figure 10.4.

The automated behind-the-scenes nature of modern-day translation bridging has all but obscured this aspect of protocol conversion. Discrete translation devices are no longer required. Instead, the multitopology switching hub functions innately as a Layer 2 protocol converting gateway.

FIGURE 10.3.

The common media access mechanisms of 802-compliant frames.

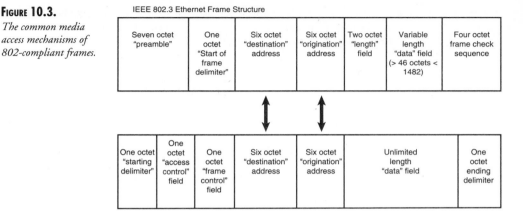

FIGURE 10.4.

Contemporary multi-topology switching hubs automatically provide MAC-layer translation between dissimilar LANs.

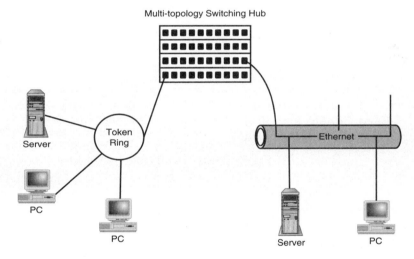

An alternative to using a Layer 2–only device like a translating bridge or multitopology switching hub would be to use a Layer 3 device: a router. Routers have long established themselves as a viable collapsed LAN backbone (see Figure 10.5). Given that routers interconnect LANs to the WAN, they typically support standard LAN interfaces. Configured properly, a router can easily provide the translation between mismatched frame types.

The drawback to this approach is that using a Layer 3 device, a router, requires table look-ups. This is a software function. Layer 2–only devices like switches and hubs operate in the silicon of the device's hardware, and are able to operate significantly faster.

Transmission Rate Mismatches

Many of the older LAN technologies have been treated to an upgraded transmission rate. For example, IEEE 802.3 Ethernet is now available in 10Mbps and 100Mbps versions, and soon

10

GATEWAYS

will be supported in a 1Gbps version, too. The frame structures and interframe gaps are identical. The primary differences lie in their physical layer and, consequently, in their media-access mechanisms. Of these differences, the transmission rate is the most obvious difference.

FIGURE 10.5.

Routers can be used to translate dissimilar LAN frames and provide a neutral gateway between LANs.

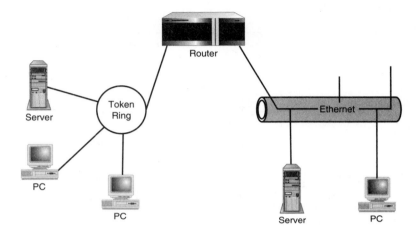

Token Ring, too, has been upgraded to operate at higher transmission rates. The original Token Ring specification operated at 4Mbps. Contemporary versions transmit at 16Mbps. FDDI, a 100Mbps LAN, descended directly from Token Ring and is frequently used as a backbone transport for Token Ring LANs.

These disparities in clock rates of otherwise identical LAN technologies require a mechanism to provide a speed-buffering interface between two otherwise compatible LANs. Many of today's multitopology, high-bandwidth switching hubs provide a robust backplane that can buffer speed mismatches, as shown in Figure 10.6.

FIGURE 10.6.

Speed buffering with a multitopology, high-bandwidth switching hub.

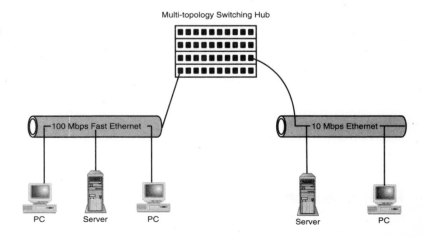

The current generation of multitopology LAN switching hubs can provide internal speed buffering for different transmission rate versions of the same LAN technology. They can also provide Layer 2 frame conversion for different 802-compliant LANs.

Routers, too, can buffer transmission rate differences. They offer an advantage over switching hubs in that their memory is expandable. This memory buffers incoming and outgoing packets long enough for the router to determine which, if any, of the router's access list permissions apply, and to determine the next hop. This memory can also be used to buffer the speed mismatches (see Figure 10.7) that may exist between the various network technologies that are internetworked by the router.

FIGURE 10.7.
Routers can be used as speed buffers.

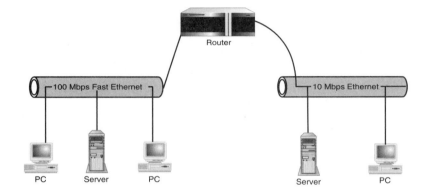

Application Gateways

Application gateways are systems that translate data between two dissimilar formats. Typically, these gateways are intermediate points between an otherwise incompatible source and destination. The typical application gateway accepts inputs in one format, translates it, and ships the outputs in a new format, as shown in Figure 10.8. The input and output interfaces can either be separate or use the same network connection.

FIGURE 10.8.
A highly simplified, logical perspective of an application gateway.

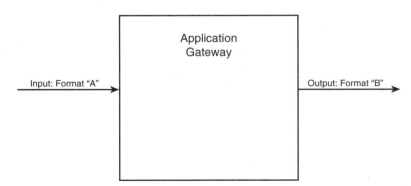

A single application can have multiple application gateways. For example, electronic mail can be implemented in a wide variety of formats. Servers that provide electronic mail may be required to interact with other mail servers, regardless of their format. The only way to do this is to support multiple gateway interfaces. Figure 10.9 demonstrates some of the many gateway interfaces available for an e-mail server.

FIGURE 10.9.

One application may be required to support interaction with multiple external formats.

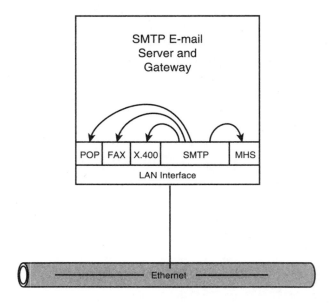

Application gateways can also be used to connect LAN clients to external data sources. This type of gateway provides for local connectivity to an interactive application. Keeping the application's logic and executable code on the same LAN as the client base avoids lower bandwidth, higher-latency WANs. This, in turn, enables better response time to clients. The application gateway would then ship an I/O request to the appropriate networked computer that housed the data requested by the client. The data is fetched and reformatted as needed for presentation to the client.

This chapter does not conduct an exhaustive review of all the potential application gateway configurations, but these few examples should adequately convey the network ramifications of application gateways. They usually represent a point in the network at which traffic aggregates. To adequately support such traffic points, an appropriate combination of network technologies and LAN and/or WAN topologies is required.

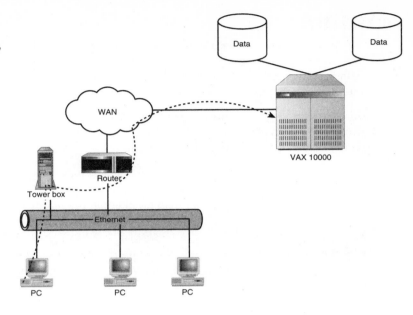

FIGURE 10.10.
Application gateways can also be used to fetch remote data for users.

Security Gateways

Security gateways are an interesting mix of technologies that are important, and distinct, enough to warrant their own category. They range from protocol-level filtration to fairly sophisticated application-level filtration.

Firewalls come in three flavors:

- Packet filters
- Circuit gateways
- Application gateways

> **NOTE**
>
> Only one of these firewalls is a filter. The remainder are gateways.

These three mechanisms are frequently used in combination. A *filter* is the screening mechanism(s) used to discriminate between packets that have legitimate need to access the specified destination port, and spurious packets that represent an unacceptable level of risk. Each has its own capabilities and limitations that must be carefully evaluated against the security requirements.

Packet Filters

Packet filtration is the most basic form of security screening. Routing software enables the establishment of permissions, per packet, based on the packet's source address, destination address, or port number. Filtering on well-known port numbers provides the ability to block or enable internetworking protocols, such as FTP, rlogin, and so on.

Filtration can be performed on incoming and/or outgoing packets. Implementing filtering at the network layer means that a preexisting, general-purpose machine (the router) can provide some security screening function for all applications traversing the network.

As a resident component of the router, this filter is available for use free of charge in any routed network. This should not be misconstrued as a preexisting panacea! Packet filtration suffers from multiple vulnerabilities. It is better than no filtering, but not by much.

> **NOTE**
>
> The term *router* is used logically to describe a network function. The actual device performing that function may be a router or a host.

Packet filters can be deceptively difficult to implement well, particularly if your security requirements are poorly defined and lack critical detail.

This filter is also defeated remarkably easily. A packet filter evaluates each packet and makes a "go/no go" determination based solely on the packet's header information relative to the router's programmed access lists. This technique suffers from several potential vulnerabilities.

First and foremost, it is directly dependent on the router administrator to correctly program the desired set of permissions. Typographical errors, in this situation, are hardly benign. They create holes in one's perimeter defenses that require few, if any, special skills to exploit.

Even if the administrator programmed the set of permissions accurately, the logic behind those permissions must be flawless. Though it may seem trivially easy to program a router, developing and maintaining a complex, lengthy set of permissions can be quite cumbersome. The day-to-day change in a networked computing environment must be understood and assessed relative to the firewall's set of permissions. New servers that were not explicitly protected at the firewall may find themselves vulnerable to attack.

Over time, access look-ups can degrade the rapidity with which routers forward packets. As soon as a router receives a packet, it must identify the next hop for that packet to reach its specified destination. This must be accompanied by another CPU-intensive task: checking the access list to determine if it is permitted to access its destination. The longer the access list, the more time this process will take.

The second vulnerability of packet filtration is that it accepts the packet header information as valid, and has no way of authenticating the packet's origin. Header information is easily falsified by network-savvy hackers. This falsification is commonly known as *spoofing*.

The myriad weaknesses of packet filtration leave it ill-prepared to adequately defend your networked computing resources. It is best used in combination with other, more sophisticated filtering mechanisms, rather than used to the exclusion of other mechanisms.

Circuit Gateways

Circuit-level gateways are ideal for protecting outbound requests that originate in a private, secured network environment. The gateway intercepts the TCP request, or even certain UDP requests. It then retrieves the requested information on behalf of the originator. This proxy server accepts requests for information stored on the World Wide Web and fulfills those requests on behalf of the originator. In Figure 10.11, the dashed line demonstrates the logical path of the request, and the dotted line represents the actual path. In effect, the gateway acts like a wire that links the originator with the destination, without exposing the originator to the risks associated with traversing an unsecured network region.

FIGURE 10.11.

The proxy server.

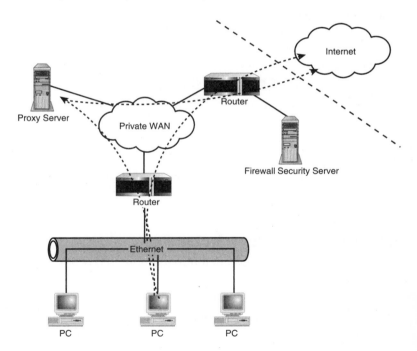

Proxitizing requests in this manner simplifies the management of border gateway security. If access lists are implemented, all outgoing traffic can be blocked, except for the proxy server.

Ideally, this server would have a unique address and not be a part of any other internally used network address range. This would absolutely minimize the amount of information that would otherwise be inadvertently, and subtly, advertised throughout the unsecured region. Specifically, only the network address of the proxy server would become known, and not the network addresses of each network-connected computer in the secured domain.

Firewall Application Gateways

Application gateways are almost the polar opposite of packet filtration. Packet filtration uses general-purpose protection of all traffic that crosses the network-level packet-filtering device. Application gateways place highly specialized application software at each host to be protected. This avoids the traps of packet filtration and enables tighter security per host.

One example of an application gateway is the virus scanner. This specialized software has become a staple of desktop computing. It is loaded into memory at boot time and stays resident in the background. It continuously monitors files for known viruses, or even altered system files. Virus scanners are designed to shield the user from the potential damage of a virus *before* damage can be inflicted.

This level of protection would be virtually impossible to implement at the network layer. It would require examining the contents of each and every packet, authenticating its source, determining the appropriate network path, *and* determining whether the contents were as purported or spurious. This process would incur an unsupportable level of overhead that would severely compromise network performance.

Application gateways offer the ability to create copious logs of all inbound and outbound traffic. Residing in a host also affords access to CPU, disk, RAM, and other useful resources that can be applied.

The principal limitation of application gateways is that they are applied on a per-host or per-application basis. In a host and/or application-rich environment, this can become quite expensive. Economics should dictate, however, that the most important applications are protected. Network-level security gateways, conversely, apply protection almost equally with a broad brush.

Combination Filtration Gateways

Gateways that utilize a combination filtration approach typically provide a fairly tight set of access controls by implementing redundant, overlapping filters. These can include any combination of packet-, circuit-, and application-level mechanisms.

One of the more common implementations of such a security gateway is as a network sentry that guards the point(s) of ingress and egress along the edges of a private network domain. Such gateways are more commonly referred to as *border gateways* or *firewalls*. This critical function often requires multiple filtration techniques to develop an adequate defense. Figure 10.12 demonstrates a two-component security gateway: a router and a processor. In combination, they can provide protocol-, circuit-, and application-level protection.

FIGURE 10.12.

A two-component security gateway.

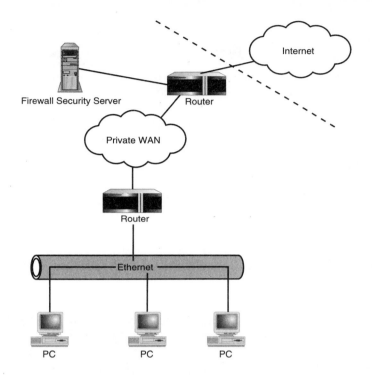

This specialized form of gateway does not necessarily provide a conversion function, as do the other types of protocol gateways. Given that border gateways are used at the borders of one's network, they are responsible for regulating both ingress and egress traffic. Ostensibly, both the internal and external WANs linked by the gateway will be using the Internet Protocol (IP). Thus, no conversion should be necessary: the two are directly compatible. Filtration, however, becomes critical.

The reasons for protecting a network from unauthorized, external access are obvious. It's done for the same reason that corporate employees are frequently issued identification badges and/or access cards. It provides a mechanism for differentiating between legitimate members of the corporation who require access to its facilities, and pretenders whose motives are assumed to be suspicious. Any inbound attempts to access networked computing resources *must* be evaluated to determine the authenticity of the request.

The reasons for regulating outbound access may not be quite as obvious. Under some circumstances, it may be necessary to provide a filtration of outbound packets. For example, the proliferation of browsers among the user base may result in a significant increase in WAN traffic. If left unregulated, browsing, newscasting, or any other Web-based traffic could easily compromise the WAN's ability to transport other applications. Thus, it may be necessary to block this form of traffic, either in whole or in part.

IP (the dominant internetworking protocol) is an open protocol. It was designed to facilitate communication across network domains. This is both its primary strength and its greatest weakness. Providing any interconnectivity between two IP WANs, in essence, creates one big IP WAN. The sentry left to guard one's network borders, the firewall, is tasked with discriminating between legitimate internetworking traffic and spurious traffic that can't be trusted.

Implementation Considerations

Implementing a security gateway is not a task that can be taken trivially. Success absolutely depends upon definition of requirements, careful planning, and flawless implementation. The first task must be establishing a comprehensive set of rules that define an understood and accepted compromise between security and cost. These rules constitute the security policy.

This policy can be lax, severe, or anything in between. On one extreme, a security policy can start with the basic premise that everything is allowable. Exceptions are expected to be few and manageable. These exceptions are explicitly added to the security infrastructure. This policy is easy to implement, requires almost no forethought, and guarantees that even the amateurs will find a way around the minimal protection.

The other extreme is almost draconian. This policy requires that all connectivity across the network is explicitly denied. This is relaxed, carefully and intentionally, to accommodate the user community's access requirements. Only these requirements are permitted. This approach is difficult to implement, won't win any popularity contests with the users, and can be extremely expensive to maintain. It will, however, provide the intangible benefit of a secured network. From the "net.police" perspective, this is the only acceptable security policy.

In between these extremes are an infinite series of compromises between ease of implementation and use, and cost of maintenance. Most implementations will fall into this broad category of compromise, either intentionally or by accident. The right balance requires careful evaluation of the risks and costs.

Summary

As networked computing continues to evolve, it is likely that more and more mission-critical applications will find themselves internetworked in an open network environment. To the extent that such applications may continue to rely upon disparate protocols, protocol conversion gateways will be essential.

The increased reliance on an open internetworking protocol for support of distributed computing also directly increases the need for security gateways. All forms of security gateways, application, packet, and circuit level, can provide much needed protection.

Regardless of their form and implementation, gateways are indispensable adjuncts to any network. Properly selected and implemented, gateways are one of the keys to unleashing the potential of high-performance networks.

IN THIS PART

Selecting the Right WAN

CHAPTER 11

Selecting the Right WAN

by Mark Sportack

IN THIS CHAPTER

Wide Area Networks (WAN) are frequently taken for granted. Most users, and even some LAN administrators, don't know what's on the other side of the router connecting them to the WAN. If the WAN was properly designed, implemented, and operated, it is extremely easy to take for granted. It's always there and it always works.

Unfortunately, WANs are rather more complicated than they might appear. Proper WAN design requires an understanding of the various transmission facilities, routers, routing protocols, and the topological arrangement of these technologies. This chapter examines each aspect of WAN design and provides the reader with an understanding of the abilities and limitations of each potential WAN technology and topology.

Internetworking Requirements

Selecting the "right" wide area network (WAN) assumes that some set of criteria exists that the completed WAN's performance will be measured against. If the WAN fails to perform as expected, it obviously isn't the "right" WAN. Therefore, the very first step in selecting the right WAN must be to develop the right selection criteria. Properly chosen, these criteria will guide selection of network technologies, determine the proper size of transmission facilities, and drive the topographical arrangement of the WAN.

Criteria Development

The key issue is developing specific and appropriate criteria. This is a task that is easy to define, yet almost impossible to execute. For example, the potential users of the WAN must be located and identified. A fairly accurate count of them must be made, and correlated to their physical location. So far, so good. The difficult part is estimating their propensity to consume bandwidth. If history can be used to predict future events, users will demand top-of-the-line everything in unlimited quantities—until they get the bill for it. Network planners, contrarily, believe in an obscure law of physics that dictates all available bandwidth will immediately be consumed, regardless of the quantity supplied.

One way to estimate the bandwidth requirements is to identify how the users are currently performing their work. If there are existing networks being used, such as X.25, asynchronous networks, or even modems, they can be invaluable sources of information. They should be monitored to determine

- Type of communications session (for example, bulk data transfer, online transaction processing, Web access, videoconferencing, and so on)
- Frequency of use
- Peak utilization times
- Peak utilization traffic volumes
- Average duration of each session
- Average number of bytes transmitted per session
- Each user groups' frequently accessed destinations

> **NOTE**
>
> Ordinarily, the term bytes should be shunned as imprecise in network planning exercises. In this particular case, bytes is the appropriate term. The average information worker is trained to think in bytes, not octets, so using familiar language will facilitate the data collection effort.

These are vital pieces of information that should form the core of your success criteria as the right WAN will be able to accommodate the projected traffic loads. In combination, these data reveal how much traffic will be put on the WAN and when it will be on the LAN. This is crucial to estimating the bandwidth required across every link of the network.

Other important data that should be determined during this data collection phase is the type of network performance needed. For example, will bulk data transfer constitute the majority of the traffic, or will interactive videoconferencing be the primary application? Is this situation likely to change in the near future? These two particular applications have opposite network performance requirements. Bulk data transfer requires guaranteeing the integrity of the data delivered to its destination, regardless of the time it takes to get it there. Videoconferencing requires the network to deliver packets on time. Damaged packets are as worthless as late packets: They are both discarded. Therefore, it is essential that the performance requirements of the applications be factored into the WAN design.

Another important piece of data that should be determined is the projected aggregate traffic flow. These selection criteria are neither perfect nor complete, but they are an excellent start. Unfortunately, collecting this data won't be quick or easy. In real life, "guesstimates" will likely be substituted for hard facts.

Additionally, if there are existing LANs in use, they must be carefully examined as they will need to be interconnected by the proposed WAN. Important details are

- The type and transmission rate of each LAN
- The number of users connected to it
- The number of hosts connected to it
- Unsecured means of ingress
- Routed protocols (such as IP, IPX, and so on)
- The number of routers connected and the routing protocols used (such as RIP, OSPF, IGRP, and so on)
- Internet addressing schemes

Again, these details should be collected for each and every group of users that will be using the new WAN. Armed with this knowledge, the network planner charged with selecting the right WAN can then consider the two primary aspects of wide area networking: *technology* and *topology.* Each of these aspects offers a multitude of options for custom designing the right wide area network for your client base, if you understand their requirements.

Technology

The wide area network's technology base includes

- Transmission facilities
- Channel Service Units and Digital Service Units
- Premise edge vehicles, such as routers and switches
- Internet addressing
- Routing protocols

Each of these technologies must be examined for their performance capabilities relative to the expected WAN traffic load and performance requirements.

Transmission Facilities

Transmission facilities that will be used to construct the WAN present the richest array of options for the network planner. These facilities come in a variety of sizes and "flavors." For example, point-to-point private lines can range in size from 9.6 kilobits per second (Kbps) to 44.476 megabits per second (Mbps) and beyond. These transmission facilities support a digital stream of data at a fixed and predetermined transmission rate. They can be implemented over a variety of physical media, for example, twisted pair or fiber-optic cabling, and can even support numerous framing formats.

These facilities also vary greatly in the manner that they provide connections. There are two primary types of facilities: circuit switched and packet switched. These two encompass all types of facilities, although technological innovation may be blurring their boundaries somewhat. These technologies are briefly described in this chapter to provide a context for selecting the right WAN.

Circuit-Switched Facilities

Circuit switching is a communications method that creates a switched, dedicated path between two end stations. A good example of a circuit-switched network is the telephone system. Any station can make a dedicated connection to any other station through the central office switches.

Private Lines

The basic circuit-switched transmission facility is a dedicated point-to-point private line. These facilities are leased from a Local Exchange Carrier (LEC) and can be obtained in a variety of forms. They can be either analog or digital, either 1.544Mbps (DS-1) or 44.476Mbps (DS-3) and can deliver service either electrically or optically. They can be also subrated into fractional components, such as 9.6Kbps.

> **NOTE**
>
> The terms DS-1 and DS-3 refer specifically to the CCITT specifications for transmission formats. These terms are often confused and incorrectly used interchangeably with the more familiar T-1 and T-3 terms. The "T" prefix denotes a physical transmission facility, and should only be used to describe the physical facilities.

These circuits provide basic, dedicated bandwidth between two points.

Integrated Services Digital Network (ISDN)

ISDN is a dial-on-demand form of digital circuit-switched technology that can transport voice and data simultaneously over the same physical connection. ISDN can be ordered in either Basic Rate (BRI) or Primary Rate (PRI) interfaces.

The BRI offers 144Kbps in a format known as 2B+D. The 2B refers to two 64Kbps "B" channels that can be bonded together to form one logical connection at 128Kbps. The "D" channel is a 16Kbps control channel used for call setup, take-down, and other control functions.

The PRI is typically delivered over a DS-1 facility at a gross transmission rate of 1.544Mbps. This is usually channeled into twenty-three 64Kbps "B" channels and one 64Kbps "D" channel. Alternatively, higher rate "H" channels of either 384, 1536, and 1920Kbps can be used instead of, or in combination with, the "B" and "D" channels.

> **NOTE**
>
> The 1920Kbps H3 channel is only useable in Europe where the standard transmission rate is 2.048Mbps, instead of the 1.544Mbps that is standard in the US, Canada, and Japan. Attempts to use an H3 channel over a 1.544Mbps transmission facility will result in unuseable channels.

Although ISDN is technically a circuit-switched facility, it can support circuit-switched, packet-switched, and even semi-permanent connections.

Packet-Switched Facilities

Packet-switching facilities feature an internal packet format that is used to encapsulate data to be transported. These packets are then forwarded in a connectionless manner through the commercial packet-switched network (PSN). An example of an old but familiar packet-switched network is X.25.

Frame Relay

Frame Relay, shown in Figure 11.1, is a faster version of X.25 packet switching that features smaller packet sizes and fewer error-checking mechanisms. Frame Relay currently supports only transfer of packets through permanent virtual circuits (PVCs) between the network's endpoint routers. The PVC's endpoints are defined by Data Link Connection Identifiers (DLCIs) and are given a committed information rate (CIR) through the Frame Relay network.

FIGURE 11.1.

Frame Relay uses virtual circuits.

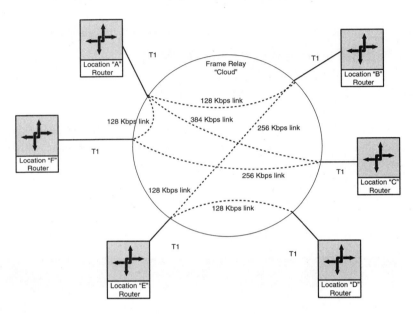

Frame Relay requires the establishment of logical pairs of data link connections. These pairs are also given a minimum available quantity of bandwidth, with the option to temporarily "burst" beyond that limit under certain circumstances.

Frame Relay WANs are built by provisioning a point-to-point private line to the nearest central office that provides this service. Much like the central office voice switches that comprise the Public Switched Telephone Network, the Frame Relay switches remain invisible to the user community and their applications.

Frame Relay's primary benefit is that it can reduce the cost of networking locations that are geographically dispersed by minimizing the length of premise-access facilities. These circuits are commercially available at 1.544Mbps, with CIRs used to create logical subrate connections to multiple locations.

Asynchronous Transfer Mode (ATM)

ATM was originally designed as an asynchronous transport mechanism for broadband ISDN. Its low latency and high bit rate, it was speculated, would make it equally ideal for use in local area networks. The subsequent market hype has almost completely cemented its reputation as a LAN technology, to the exclusion of its abilities as a WAN technology.

As a cell-switched WAN technology, ATM is commercially available at either 1.544Mbps (DS-1) or 44.476Mbps (DS-3), although this availability will likely vary geographically.

Customer Premise Equipment (CPE)

Customer Premise Equipment is the physical layer telephony hardware that is required at each customer's premises to terminate the incoming transmission facilities' circuits. Depending upon the type of circuit, CPE can encompass several different devices.

Circuit-switched facilities require the use of Channel Service Units and/or Digital Service Units (CSU/DSU). Customer premise data communications equipment (DCE) are devices that terminate channelized and digital transmission facilities.

Packet-switched facilities require the use of an equivalent device that can assemble and disassemble packets. Such devices are known as *PADs*.

Premise Edge Vehicles

Routers are typically used to connect LANs to long-haul transmission facilities to create WANs. Although they can also be used as a LAN segmentation device, they are primarily the boundary mechanism that interconnects LANs and WANs.

Internet Addressing

An aspect of the WAN that must be carefully considered is the Internet (that is, Layer 3 of the OSI Reference Model) addressing that will be used. These addresses are used to access and exchange data with hosts on other subnetworks within the WAN. As such, they are a critical component to consider as you select the right WAN for your users.

Theoretically, if your WAN will not be interconnected with the Internet, these addresses could be arbitrarily selected and function perfectly. *This should not be done!* Use only official, registered addresses in your WAN. This will reduce the workload required to manage the Internet addresses within the WAN, and will prevent duplicate addresses from being assigned.

These addresses will be determined by the routable protocol selected for use within the WAN. Some of the possibilities are: IPv4, IPv6, IPX, and AppleTalk. Each has its own unique addressing scheme. Thus, the choice of protocol determines the possible address hierarchies than can be implemented.

If your WAN requires the interconnection of networks with dissimilar routed protocols, you must have a *gateway* router at the border of the dissimilar regions. This router must be capable of calculating routes, forwarding route information, and forwarding packets in both protocols.

For more information on the Internet addressing of routable protocols, please refer to Chapter 4, "Internetworking Protocol Stacks."

Routing Protocols

Dynamic routing protocols are used by routers to perform three basic functions:

- Discover new routes
- Communicate the discovered route information to other routers
- Forward packets using those routes

There are three broad categories of dynamic routing protocols: distance-vector, link-state, and hybrids. Their primary differences lie in the way that they perform the first two of the three aforementioned functions. The only alternative to dynamic routing is static routing.

Distance-Vector Routing

Routing based on distance-vector algorithms, also sometimes called Bellman-Ford algorithms, periodically pass copies of their routing tables to their immediate network neighbors. Each recipient adds a distance vector, that is, their own distance "value," to the table and forwards it on to their immediate neighbors. This process occurs omnidirectionally between immediately neighboring routers.

This step-by-step process results in each router's learning about other routers, and developing a cumulative perspective of network distances. For example, an early distance-vector routing protocol is Routing Information Protocol or RIP. RIP uses two distance metrics for determining the best next path to take for any given packet. These are time, as measured by "ticks" and hop count.

> **NOTE**
>
> Network distances are somewhat euphemistic. They may actually be any of a variety of metrics, and are not limited to physical distances.

The cumulative table is then used to update each router's routing tables. When completed, each router has learned vague information about the distances to networked resources. It does not learn anything specific about other routers, or the network's actual topology.

This approach can, under certain circumstances, actually create routing problems for distance-vector protocols. For example, a failure in the network requires some time for the routers to converge on a new understanding of the network's topology. During the convergence process, the network may be vulnerable to inconsistent routing, and even infinite loops. There are safeguards to contain many of these risks, but the fact remains that the network's performance is at risk during the convergence process. Therefore, older protocols that are slow to converge may not be appropriate for large, complex WANs.

Link-State Routing

Link-state routing algorithms, known cumulatively as Shortest Path First or SPF protocols, maintain a complex database of the network's topology. Unlike distance-vector protocols, link-state protocols develop and maintain a full knowledge of the network's routers, as well as how they interconnect.

This is achieved through the exchange of Link-state Packets (LSPs) with other directly connected routers. Each router that has exchanged LSPs then constructs a topological database using all received LSPs. A Shortest Path First algorithm is used to compute reachability to networked destinations. This information is used to update the routing table. This process is capable of discovering changes in the network topology caused by component failure or network growth. In fact, the LSP exchange is triggered by an event in the network, rather than just running periodically.

Link-state routing has two potential areas for concern. First, during the initial discovery process, it can flood the network's transmission facilities, thereby significantly decreasing the network's ability to transport data. This performance degradation is temporary, but very noticeable.

The second area for concern is that link-state routing is both memory and processor intensive. Routers configured for link-state routing tend to be more expensive because of this.

Hybridized Routing

The last form of routing discipline is hybridization. Although "open," balanced hybrid protocols exist, this form is almost exclusively associated with the proprietary creation of a single company, Cisco Systems, Inc. Hybrid protocols attempt to combine the best aspects of distance-vector and link-state routing protocols, without incurring any of their performance limitations or penalties.

The balanced hybrid routing protocols use distance-vector metrics, but emphasize more accurate metrics than conventional distance-vector protocols. They also converge more rapidly than distance-vector protocols, but avoid the overheads of link-state updates. Balanced hybrids are event driven, rather than periodic, thereby conserving bandwidth for real applications.

Static Routing

A router that is programmed for static routing forwards packets out of predetermined ports. Once this is configured, there is no longer any need for routers to attempt route discovery or even communicate information about routes. Their role is reduced to just forwarding packets.

Static routing is good only for very small networks that have only a single path to any given destination. In such cases, static routing can be the most efficient routing mechanism because it doesn't consume bandwidth trying to discover routes or communicate with other routers.

As networks grow larger, and add redundant paths to destinations, static routing becomes a labor-intensive liability. Any changes in the availability of routers or transmission facilities in the WAN must be manually discovered and programmed in. WANs that feature more complex topologies that offer multiple potential paths, absolutely require dynamic routing. Attempts to use static routing in complex, multipath WANs defeat the purpose of having that route redundancy.

Topology

The topology describes the way the transmission facilities are arranged. Numerous topologies are possible, each one offering a slightly different mix of cost, performance, and scalability.

Peer-to-Peer Network Topology

A peer-to-peer network (as shown in Figure 11.2) can be developed using dedicated private lines, or any other transmission facility.

FIGURE 11.2.
Peer-to-peer WAN topology.

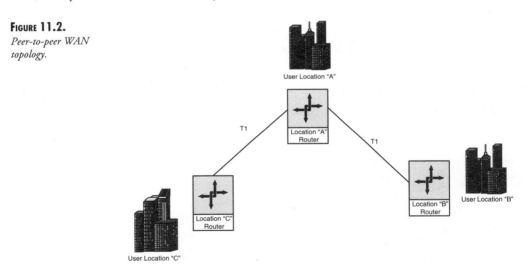

A peer-to-peer WAN constructed with point-to-point transmission facilities can be a simple way to interconnect a small number of sites.

This topology is often the only feasible solution for WANs that contain a small number of internetworked locations. As each location contains only a single link to the rest of the network, static routing can be used.

Unfortunately, peer-to-peer WANs suffer from two basic limitations. First, they do not scale very well. As additional locations are introduced to the WAN, the number of hops between any given pair of locations is likely to increase. The second limitation of this approach is its inherent vulnerability to component failure. An equipment or facility failure anywhere in a peer-to-peer WAN can split the WAN. Depending upon the actual traffic flows and the type of routing implemented, this can severely disrupt communications in the entire WAN.

Ring Network Topology

A ring topology, shown in Figure 11.3, can be developed fairly easily from a peer-to-peer network by adding one transmission facility and an extra port on two routers. This minor increment in cost provides route redundancy that can offer small networks the opportunity to implement dynamic routing protocols. Dynamic routing can automatically detect and recover from adverse changes in the WAN's operating condition.

FIGURE 11.3.

Ring WAN topology.

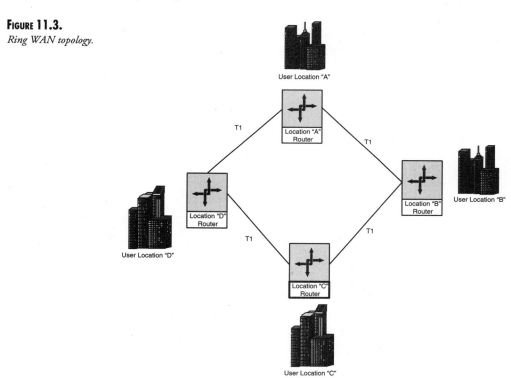

A ring WAN constructed with point-to-point transmission facilities can be used to interconnect a small number of sites and provide route redundancy at minimal additional cost.

Rings, too, have some basic limitations. First, depending upon the geographic dispersion of the locations, adding an extra transmission facility to complete the ring may be cost prohibitive. In such cases, Frame Relay may be a viable alternative to dedicated leased lines.

A second limitation of rings is that they are not very scalable. Adding new locations to the WAN directly increases the number of hops required to access other locations in the ring. This additive process may also result in having to order new circuits. For example, in Figure 11.3, adding a new location, X, that is in geographical proximity to sites C and D, requires terminating the circuit from C to D. Two new circuits would have to be ordered to preserve the integrity of the ring: one running from C to X, and the other from D to X.

The ring topology, given its limitations, is likely to be of value only in interconnecting very small numbers of locations.

Star Network Topology

A variant of the peer-to-peer topology is the star topology, so named for its shape (see Figure 11.4). This topology can also be constructed using almost any dedicated transmission facility, including Frame Relay and point-to-point private lines.

FIGURE 11.4.

Star WAN topology.

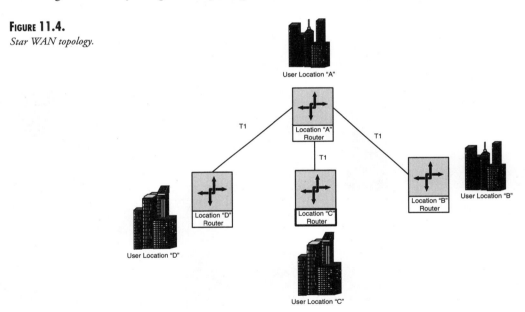

A star topology WAN with point-to-point transmission facilities is much more scalable than a peer-to-peer or ring network. Network-connected devices are a maximum of two hops away from each other.

The star topology rectifies the scalability problems of peer-to-peer networks by using a *concentrator router* to interconnect all the other networked routers. This scalability is available with only a modest increase in the number of routers, router ports, and transmission facilities, compared to a comparably sized peer-to-peer topology. Star topologies may actually be developed with *fewer* facilities than ring topologies, as Figures 11.3 and 11.4 demonstrate.

The one drawback to this approach is that it creates a single point of failure that can effectively stop all WAN communications. This point of failure, as illustrated in Figure 11.3, is the concentrator node at the center of the star.

Full Mesh

At the opposite end of the reliability spectrum, is the full mesh topology (see Figure 11.5). This topology features the ultimate reliability and fault tolerance. Every networked node is directly connected to every other networked node. Full mesh networks can be built with almost any dedicated transmission facility.

Figure 11.5.

*Full Mesh WAN
topology.*

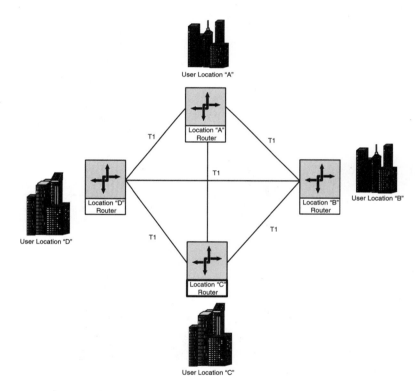

A fully meshed WAN topology is readily identified by the complete interconnection of every node with every other node in the network. This approach absolutely minimizes the number of hops between any two network-connected machines, but can be fairly expensive to build and has a finite limit on its scalability.

The reliability of a full mesh network does not come cheaply. To interconnect any given number of nodes requires substantially more transmission facilities and router ports than any other topology. It also has the unfortunate effect of reducing the extensibility of the WAN. Thus, full mesh topologies are more of a utopian ideal with limited practical application.

One application would be to provide interconnectivity for a limited number of routers that require high network availability. Another potential application is to fully mesh just parts of the WAN, like the "backbone" of a multi-tiered WAN, or tightly coupled work centers.

Partial Mesh

A WAN could also be developed with a partial mesh topology. Partial meshes, shown in Figure 11.6, are highly flexible topologies that can take a variety of very different configurations. The best way to describe a partial mesh topology is that the routers are much more tightly coupled than in any of the basic topologies, but are not fully interconnected, as would be the case in a fully meshed network.

FIGURE 11.6.

Partial Mesh WAN topology.

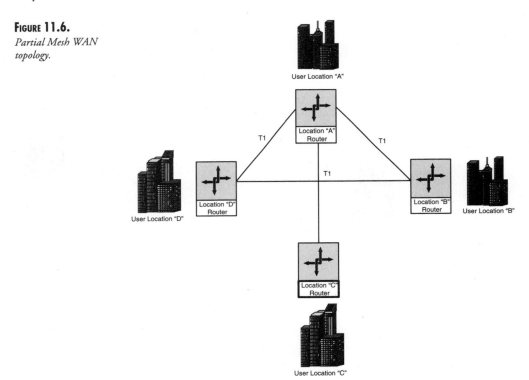

A partially meshed WAN topology is readily identified by the almost complete interconnection of every node with every other node in the network.

Partial meshes offer the ability to minimize hops for the bulk of the WAN's users. Unlike fully meshed networks, a partial mesh can reduce the startup and operational expenses by not interconnecting low traffic segments of the WAN. This enables the partial mesh network to be somewhat more scaleable and affordable than a full mesh topology.

Two-Tiered Topology

A two-tiered topology is a modified version of the basic star topology. Rather than a single concentrator router, two or more routers are used. This rectifies the basic vulnerability of the star topology without compromising its efficiency or scalability.

Figure 11.7 presents a WAN with a typical two-tiered topology. The worst-case hop count does increase by one, as a result of the extra concentrator (or backbone) router. However, unlike with the peer-to-peer network presented in Figure 11.3, the hop count is not adversely affected every time a new location is added to the WAN.

Figure 11.7.

Two-tiered WAN topology.

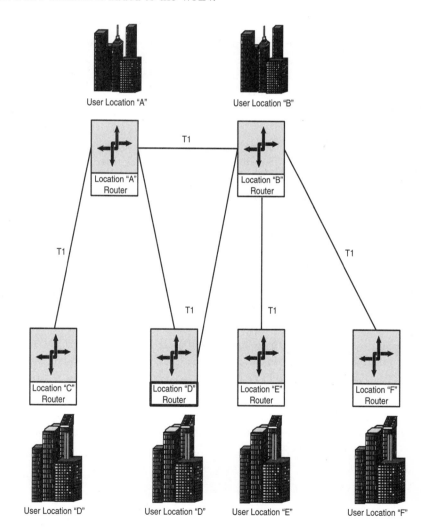

A two-tiered WAN constructed with dedicated facilities offers improved fault tolerance over the simple star topology without compromising scalability.

This topology can be implemented in a number of minor variations, primarily by manipulating the number of concentrator routers and the manner with which they are interconnected. Having three or more concentrator routers introduced requires the network designer to select a sub-topology for the concentrator tier. These routers can be either fully or partially meshed, or strung together peer to peer.

Regardless of the sub-topology selected, hierarchical, multi-tiered topologies function best when some basic implementation principles are adhered to. First, the concentration layer of routers should be dedicated to their task. That is, they are not used to directly connect user communities. Second, the user premises routers should only internetwork with concentrator nodes and not with each other in a peer-to-peer fashion. Third, the interconnection of user premises routers to concentrator routers should not be made randomly. Some logic should be applied in determining their placement. Depending upon the geographic distribution of the users and the transmission facilities used, it may be prudent to place the concentrator nodes so as to minimize the distances from the user premises.

Given that one or more routers will be dedicated to route aggregation, this topology can be an expensive undertaking. This tends to limit the use of these topologies to larger companies.

Three-Tiered Topology

WANs that need to interconnect a very large number of sites, or are built using smaller routers that can support only a few serial connections, may find the two-tiered architecture insufficiently scaleable. Thus, adding a third tier may well provide the additional scalability they require (see Figure 11.8).

A three-tiered WAN constructed with dedicated facilities offers even greater fault tolerance and scalability than the two-tiered topology.

Three-tiered networks are expensive to build, operate, and maintain. They should be used only for interconnecting very large numbers of locations. Given this, it is foolish to develop a WAN of this magnitude and not fully mesh the uppermost, or backbone, tier of routers.

Hybridized Topology

Hybridization of multiple topologies is useful in larger, more complex networks. It allows you to tailor the WAN to actual traffic patterns, rather than trying to force-fit those patterns into a rigid topological model.

FIGURE 11.8.

*Three-tiered WAN
topology.*

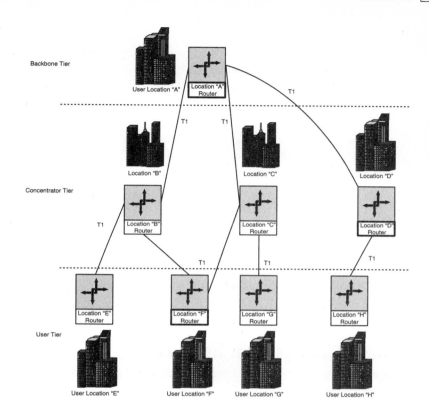

Multi-tiered networks, in particular, lend themselves to hybridization. As previously discussed, multi-tiered WAN can be hybridized by fully meshing the backbone tier of routers, as shown in Figure 11.9.

An effective hybrid topology may be developed in a multi-tiered WAN by using a fully meshed topology for the backbone nodes only. This affords a fault-tolerance to the network's backbone and can provide some of the hop-minimization of a full mesh network without experiencing all of its costs or incurring its limitations on scalability.

Fully meshing the backbone of a multi-tiered WAN is just one form of hybridized topology. Other hybrids, too, can be also highly effective. The key is to look for topologies, and subtopologies, that can be used in combination to satisfy your particular networking requirements.

FIGURE 11.9.
Multi-tiered hybrid WAN topology.

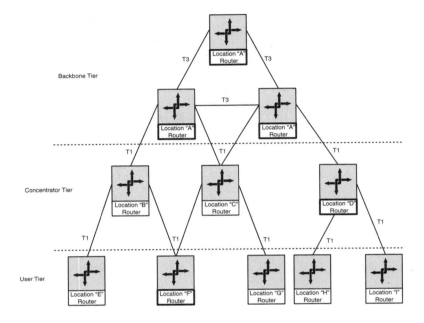

Issues with Large Multi-Tiered WANs

Medium and large sized multi-tiered WANs may fall into a common trap: lost focus. Though most common in larger networks, this can strike any company whose network management personnel are evaluated and compensated based on the network's efficiency. Efficiency is a tempting metric because it can be easily measured using superficial techniques. Unfortunately, it is an inappropriate metric that can actually induce inefficiency and increased costs.

Typically, this metric motivates network managers to strive to minimize operational expenses. In a multi-tiered WAN, this can mean using the least expensive method for interconnecting all the user-level nodes to the backbone. Given that most of the transmission facilities available for use in a WAN are priced in a mileage- and bandwidth-sensitive manner, minimizing the mileage of each facility minimizes the cost. Thus, a tiered topology that connects user premises to the geographically closest backbone router represents the most efficient solution.

Wide area networks must be designed to carefully balance costs against performance for *all* traffic, not just one particular session or location. Since geography seldom, if ever, corresponds to actual traffic patterns, this approach drives systemic inefficiencies. These inefficiencies will be manifested in an increase in the number of hops for the majority of the traffic on the WAN. Consequently, aggregate traffic volumes will be artificially inflated.

Figure 11.10, which shows an example of a three-tiered, point-to-point WAN with actual traffic patterns superimposed, demonstrates the potential inefficiencies of this approach. Access to the concentrator layer is based solely on geography. This minimizes the operational expenses of the network, but results in greater network intensity for any given session.

FIGURE 11.10.
Three-tiered, point-to-point WAN.

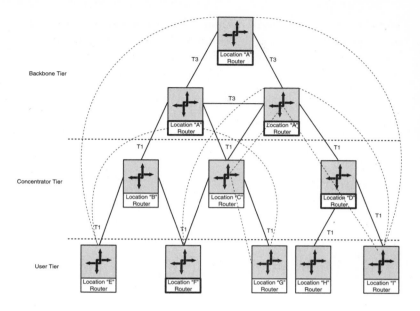

Thus, the efficient solution from the network management's perspective results in performance penalties for all the traffic on the WAN. The irony is that this inefficiency actually results in a more costly network to operate. Despite this, continued use of the wrong metrics will fail to demonstrate this. In fact, a cost minimization philosophy will continue to demonstrate that the geographically distributed network is the least expensive model, despite its increasing costs.

This is in direct conflict with the original purpose of the WAN! They are not built to provide minimal functionality at the lowest possible cost. Rather, these networks are built to support a company's business processes. As such, the primary metric for evaluating the effectiveness of a WAN should be the degree to which it supports the company's applications and information workers. Therefore, they should be designed to maximize the company's revenue stream, rather than to minimize its expenses.

Once the appropriate network performance metrics are implemented, more effective topologies may be pursued. One such topology is the multi-tiered traffic flow model.

Multi-Tiered Traffic Flow Topology

The solution to the quandary depicted in Figure 11.10 is a multi-tiered topology that is based on actual, aggregate traffic flows. Each router in the concentration layer would be dedicated to one or more groups of users, based on their aggregate traffic patterns. Thus, the topology mirrors the way that traffic flows through the network.

Given that the cost of the vast majority of wide area networking transmission facilities are mileage sensitive, this may be counter-intuitive as it increases the costs of interconnecting user premises to the concentration layer. This sub-optimizes the cost of the premise access facilities.

However, the overall cost of running the network will likely decrease because the traffic flow topology, shown in Figure 11.11, minimizes the network intensity of any given session. Please note that this approach is viable only for very large networks that require a tiered topology. It may be possible to implement this topology in a two-tiered WAN, but it really demonstrates the most value in large, three-tiered networks.

FIGURE 11.11.
Traffic flow-based WAN.

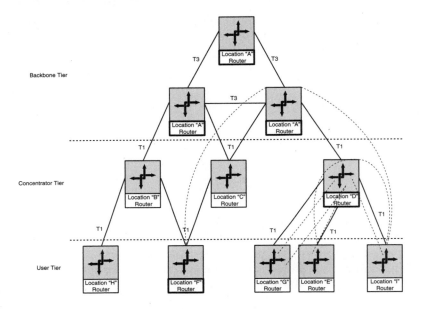

Figure 11.11 demonstrates a traffic flow approach to WAN design. This approach sub-optimizes access facility costs in favor of maximizing aggregate network performance. A multi-tiered community of interest WAN is built by distributing the premise access facilities based upon traffic flows, not geography.

Proper implementation of this topology will benefit all the WAN's users, not just the ones in well-defined communities. This is because the amount of traffic placed on the backbone is kept to an absolute minimum.

Summary

The topologies presented in this chapter can be implemented using almost any combination of networking technologies. Additional complexity can be introduced by examining the subtle differences between vendor brands of each technology product. Selecting the "right" WAN is much more complicated than just picking technologies and a topology. It absolutely must begin with an understanding of the users' collective performance requirements. This is the baseline against which potential technologies and topologies must be evaluated.

The next step in selecting the right WAN requires an understanding of the benefits and limitations of each topology and technology. This must be tempered with an assessment of each one's compatibility with other potential technologies. Other factors, too, must be considered during this process. Embedded base, budget constraints, skill sets, training costs, and even the scalability and expected lifespan of each technology may all affect the selection process.

Last, each technology component must be carefully fitted to the network's topology. For example, using RIP on large, heavily trafficked, multi-tiered WANs would probably be a mismatch noticed by the user community.

Each decision made in the design phase has direct consequences on the functionality of the WAN. *These consequences should be evaluated as carefully as the user requirements themselves.* For example, an important consideration is how much bandwidth should each physical link in the WAN provide? The consequences of this type of decision are easy to extrapolate. Transmission facilities incur monthly recurring charges that are mileage and/or bandwidth sensitive. Selecting too small a facility may save some money in the short run, but can cripple a company's ability to function. The consequences of selecting an inordinately large facility are usually limited to budget overruns for that expense category. In this case, erring on the side of conservatism dictates rounding bandwidth consumption estimates upward.

The last item to consider as you plan the WAN is the future. A well-designed WAN will not only satisfy its clients on its first day of operation, it will continue to satisfy them long into the future. This requires the network to be robust and flexible enough to accommodate technological change, shifts in aggregate traffic patterns, and growth.

Remember, the WAN exists to facilitate the company's ability to conduct its business. Thus, its success should be measured more by the earnings potential it has created than by the costs it has incurred. With this in mind, study the technological and topological options. Be creative. See what, if any, combinations may be more effective than any homogeneous solution. The right WAN is the one that delivers the performance your user base requires.

POTS

by Arthur Cooper

IN THIS CHAPTER

How does the Plain Old Telephone System (POTS) tie in with wide area networking or local area networking? The answer is not that simple anymore. This chapter discusses the POTS issue as it relates to LAN/WAN internetworking. First, following a brief history of POTS, we look at the function and workings of a single dial-up POTS line. Then, we explore the various uses of dedicated, singular POTS lines between network locations. Following that, we look at aggregate arrangements on POTS connections between nodes and/or network locations.

POTS–A Brief History

One of the most misunderstood technologies in use throughout the world is the POTS circuit. Almost anyone on earth who can speak has used a telephone in the last year. In the process of talking on the phone, the signal being transmitted from one end to the other undergoes many transformations. Sixty years ago, the signal being transmitted would remain in analog form from one end to the other. The only signal regeneration that occurred would have been, perhaps, an amplification or two along the signal's path and between switching points. The term *Via Net Loss* (*VNL*) was used in those days to calculate the total loss in decibels on a POTS path. Test tones and decibel (dB) or volume unit (VU) meters were the only pieces of test equipment needed to keep POTS lines running efficiently. These meters simply show the amount of gain or loss inherent on a POTS circuit. The decibel is a measurement that is related to the ratio of input to output. The volume unit was similar to the decibel, but it was used to measure complex signals such as the human voice.

In the 1940s and 1950s, POTS circuits would have been far too noisy to be put to any use other than what they were originally intended for: two humans conversing on a telephone. However, since the 1960s, there has been a marked improvement in the way POTS circuits are connected, switched, and transmitted. These changes were due to the advent and proliferation of Bell T-1 transmission systems. As the Bell System began to incorporate T-1 systems throughout the Public Switched Network, the quality and quantity of POTS circuits increased steadily.

During the late 1970s and early 1980s, the Bell System made great efforts to improve the quality of the Digital Access Cross-Connect System (DACCS), which all of the T-1 and T-3 digital carriers traversed. The DACCS system was notorious in the 1980s for minor bursts, frame slips, timing lags, and other similar transmission problems. However, POTS service benefited greatly from the many upgrades made to the DACCS and other digital services of the Bell System. In fact, as digital subscriber service improved, POTS lines were looked at as an alternative to expensive, dedicated, point-to-point data connections. Although the Bell System was aggressively marketing 56Kbps (DS0) and 1.544Mbps (T-1/DS1) circuits to customers, the POTS circuit was just "tagging along for the ride."

After all, on most of these early DS1 systems, the major use for the T-1 stream (1.544Mbps) was to terminate on a D3 or D4 channel bank. These channel banks would in turn deliver wonderful, clear, crisp POTS service from one end to the other of the DS1 stream. What a waste of bandwidth these systems incorporated in those days! An entire 64Kbps slot of a DS1 was being used for Grandma and Grandpa to speak to each other. It was at this point POTS lines were looked at as an alternative to expensive, dedicated, point-to-point data connections. Many of the networks in existence at that time were actually collections of dedicated circuits. There really was no structure or flexibility on these "networks." If the line to Peoria was down, Peoria was out of luck.

These dedicated circuits seemed to be marvels to information systems (IS) professionals. Generally Ma Bell would install the circuit and the related modem. What the IS professionals of that day did not understand was that the modem in use on any particular data circuit was being routed to an interface card. This interface card, in most cases, existed in a channel bank somewhere. If the IS professionals had any inclination or ability to realize this fact, they probably would have immediately reviewed the way they were doing their internetworking and connectivity. These point-to-point circuits were outrageously priced in the 1970s and early 1980s. With the costs of dedicated data circuits reaching levels of thousands and thousands of dollars, many IS professionals began to look at POTS as a cheap, reliable backup.

Dedicated 9600bps and slower circuits were, for the most part, extremely reliable. Once IS professionals realized these circuits were traversing the same path as their telephone conversations, the POTS world became extremely important to the data communications world. Companies such as RACAL-MILGO, PENRIL, MOTOROLA, and many others began to sell dial-up and dedicated modems at a rapid rate. As we moved into the 1980s, POTS became more than just a dial-up backup to dedicated circuits. Network computer systems and nodes began to incorporate POTS dial-up support within the major routines of their operating systems and functions. POTS circuits were finally accepted as legitimate members of the data communications family.

How a POTS Line Works

The most important thing to keep in mind when looking at the function of POTS lines is the fact that these lines, or circuits, were originally intended to be used by human beings. Also, the original concept of the Bell System was a series of POTS trunks interconnecting the major cities of the United States. Within these major cities, telephone operators would manually connect the calls coming in over the trunks and local lines. The term *local loop* has often been used to describe local POTS circuits, and it is a fairly accurate assessment of what is happening when one uses the circuit. With that in mind, let us now look at how these lines operate.

Each POTS circuit uses two wires to complete the path between an end user device (telephone, modem, and so on) and the local exchange switch. These wires are referred to as TIP and RING. Believe it or not, these terms go back to the days of cord patch boards manned by human operators—the TIP and the RING of the patchcord were wired out to each local subscriber; hence, these two terms.

Refer to Figure 12.1 for an illustration of how a POTS circuit functions.

FIGURE 12.1.
Basic POTS circuit.

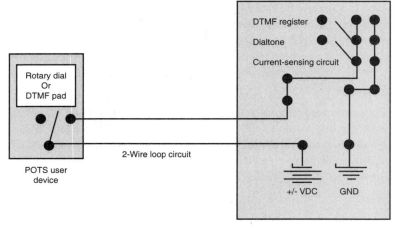

Notice that there is a switch on the user end of the POTS circuit. This switch refers to the electronic portion of your user device (telephone, modem, and so on) that closes the two-wire loop when you are demanding service from the local exchange carrier (or LEC). The other end of the circuit terminates somewhere in the LEC's local switching facilities. The point must be made here that there may or may not be actual metallic, copper connectivity between the end user and the LEC.

On the contrary, there may be a series of channel banks and/or multiplex units between these two endpoints of the POTS circuit. For the purposes of this discussion, let us assume there is two-wire copper connectivity of some sort between the user and the local switch providing dial tone. When the user picks up the phone and closes the two-wire loop, the local switching equipment senses a return of current on the loop. This is accomplished through completion of the DC circuit between the switch and the user device. In other words, when the user device goes "off-hook," a DC signal applied to one side of the circuit by the switch then returns on the other side of the circuit. The switch sees DC current flowing through the entire loop.

This is what causes the switch to recognize there is a request for service from the user. At that point, the switch connects a dial-tone generator to the loop. Remember, dial tone is in an analog format. When dial tone is sent over the loop and reaches the user device, either a human hears the tone, or a modem or some other device "senses" the tone and dialing commences. If the user device is incapable of producing Dual-Tone Multifrequency (DTMF) signals, sometimes referred to as *touch tone*, then dial pulse is used.

Dial pulse works quite simply. When the user device sends out dial pulses—that is, a person or a modem dials—the loop is simply opened for a short interval of time that directly corresponds with the number being dialed. In other words, if a 1 is dialed, the loop momentarily opens for one short interval. If a 5 is dialed, the loop momentarily opens and closes for five short intervals. When the digit has been sent, the loop is again closed. This series of openings and closings of the loop activates a relay in the switching equipment, and that relay provides the switch with the numbers actually being dialed by the user device. Also, the dial-tone generator is disconnected at the first sign of an incoming dial pulse.

Since the early 1970s, most telephone switches began the conversion to DTMF, touch-tone signaling. When a user device is using DTMF instead of dial pulse, the sequence is somewhat different. After the loop has been closed, the switch simultaneously connects a DTMF register/receiver and a dial-tone generator to the loop. After the user device "senses" the dial tone, or a human ear hears it, DTMF signals are sent to the switch by a user pushing the buttons on a phone or a modem transmitting the DTMF signals. Once again, the dial-tone generator is disconnected at the first sign of an incoming DTMF signal. All of the DTMF signal frequencies are within the audible spectrum, hence the "beep, beep, beep" sounds in your ear when using a touch-tone phone or listening to the dialing sounds a modem makes.

Now that we have seen how the switch senses a closing of the loop, provides dial tone, and then receives digits, it is easy to see how a POTS line functions. It is important to note, once again, that the example we have been using assumes a copper two-wire connection between the switching facility and the user device. In reality, however, most POTS circuits are not wired as straight copper to all user locations. For user locations located far from the switching facility, fiber and digital carrier systems are used between the switch and collocated wire plants in various parts of a city or town.

All of us have seen the green boxes at the side of the road with the Bell System logo on them. Most of these are covering up repeaters and subscriber loop equipment of some type. These repeaters and line interface units are what allow a local loop to be located far away from the actual switch providing dial tone on the circuit. Today, with the advent of microelectronics, the local telephone companies are using very small units connected to fiber runs underneath the streets. These units then break out into interface boxes with copper wire in them. Why doesn't the telephone company run straight fiber into the home? The answer is simple. Almost all user devices still use copper wire to connect to a POTS circuit. Also, until the cost of ripping up the streets of a city to run fiber connectivity into all buildings and houses comes into an acceptable range, the telephone company will no doubt continue to use the old tried-and-true copper wire that has been buried under the street for many, many years.

Interfacing POTS Circuits with Data Networks

When interfacing POTS circuits, it is important to consider that a single POTS circuit consists of a TIP wire and a RING wire, as mentioned earlier in this chapter. The TIP and RING of the POTS circuit are generally wired to some sort of jack or interface. In the United States, the typical termination for a single line is wired according to USOC standard RJ-11. If there are two POTS circuits present in one spot, typically they are wired into one jack according to USOC standard RJ-14. If there are between three and twenty-five POTS lines in one location, typically they are all terminated on the left side of a 66-type demarcation block. This arrangement and the associated wiring is in accordance with USOC standard RJ-21X.

These standards may seem confusing, but they are actually simple. Think of the RJ-11 and RJ-14 as being standard, modular phone jacks. The RJ-21X is simply a 66-type termination block that utilizes a "quick-disconnect" on one side in order for the local exchange carrier's technicians to disconnect the network side from your equipment side should there be a difficulty or failure of some sort.

> **NOTE**
>
> The 66-type block is simply a square piece of plastic, usually white, with rows of metal pins sticking through it. The block allows you to connect wires to it by "punching" them down onto the pins. Each pin has a y-shaped opening on the end, and as you punch the wire into this y shape, the wire is "squished" between the sides of the y shape. This forms a strong mechanical and electrical connection to whatever is hooked up to the pin on the other side of the 66-type block. Typically, the other side of the pin is factory wired to a connector on the side of the block. In other instances, the rows of pins on the block are connected together horizontally. If this is the case, you will have to "punch down" something on either side of the pins to make a connection.

Having the disconnect also facilitates troubleshooting at your location should it be required. On the right side of this block, you would need to punch down any connections you need to make. The wiring you punch down, or connect, to this side could then be extended out to standard, modular phone jacks. Or in some cases, there may be a need to wire the right side through a series of patch panels or frame blocks. The truth of the matter is, after 1982 when the divestiture of the Bell System occurred, most local telephone companies do not really care what you do with your internal wiring.

For that reason, IS professionals have a wide range of options when it comes to deciding how their network will interface with the outside POTS world. It is with great apologies to all other configurations that I now suggest what I feel is an ideal connection situation. Let us assume that the LAN we are using for our discussion consists of approximately 50 workstations and one large server. The server has need to do dial-up connectivity with other LANs within the organization that are not located in the same city, so there are six POTS circuits connected to the server. Let us also assume that these POTS circuits are strictly dial-up, therefore they will be using 33.6Kbps dial-up modems of some type. (We discuss POTS modems later in this chapter.) Let us also assume that these dial-up lines are going to be used for local access to the LAN by the organization's employees.

In order to follow along with this discussion, please refer to Figure 12.2.

FIGURE 12.2.
Basic connection diagram.

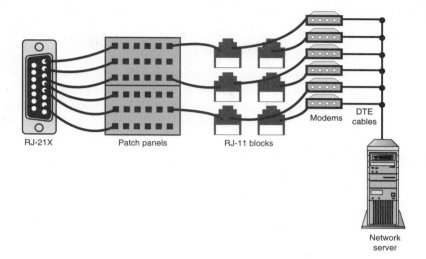

RJ-21X   Patch panels   RJ-11 blocks   Modems   DTE cables   Network server

Notice that there is a block labeled RJ-21X. This is a 66-type block as mentioned earlier in this chapter. Also, notice that the premise, or local in-house, wiring is on the right side of this block as also mentioned earlier. This may vary according to the practices of the local exchange carrier. The next item on the circuit diagram (following it backward into the LAN) is a patch panel of some sort. Many people say this is an unnecessary step. I have heard people say for years that patch panels are wasted pieces of equipment. Further, people have told me that patch panels only add to the problems a circuit may develop. These statements are both false, in my opinion.

In the nearly 19 years I have been involved in networking, the ability to patch around failed equipment and circuits, coupled with the excellent monitoring and troubleshooting capabilities of patch panels, have convinced me of their necessity. In our dream configuration, patch panels will be a part of the circuit. These patch panels allow you to monitor and access your POTS circuits with ease and efficiency. These panels pay for themselves the first time you patch rapidly around a failed modem in a hunt sequence.

> **NOTE**
>
> A *hunt-sequence* refers to a group of POTS lines in which, typically, one telephone number is assigned to the entire group of lines. If the number is dialed, the local exchange carrier rings in on the first available line that is not in use. Likewise, if the lines are used for outward calls, the user's system uses the first available line to place the call on.

This ability to patch around a failed modem ensures that both inward and outward calls are completed on properly operating circuits only. The failed modem is removed from the configuration by the use of the patchcord in the patch panel.

Why not just swap out the bad modem with a good one? There may be a lot of reasons why this would have been the wrong approach. First, the modems may be rack mounted, and pulling modem cards from a "live" rack can damage them. Second, what if the modems are not collocated with the interfaces or the server? Rather than running back and forth and getting upset over the fact that you have wasted time and still not solved the problem, why not simply make the patch, perform the simple deactivation and activation mentioned, and return a high level of service to the system users? You can always go back at your leisure and repair or replace the modem. The good thing about having followed the patching procedure is the fact your users will have a lot less interruption of service when you do it this way.

Let us refer once again to Figure 12.2 and continue following the connectivity diagram. Now, from the patch panel backward, there is an interface of some type between the panel and the actual modems being used. This too can vary greatly, but the best configuration, in my opinion, is to have a modular connection cord between the patch panel and the modems themselves. Many companies, such as ADC, Inc., offer excellent modular patch panels to be used with POTS lines and modems. The great thing about using modular connections is the relative ease of use and cost associated with this type of connection. Ideally, the patch panel equipment and the modem equipment should be located together. In a single rack, on a single backboard mounted on a wall, or even inside a single cabinet or set of cabinets, is the best configuration to have when using POTS circuits.

Once again, looking at Figure 12.2 and following backward from the modems, you can see that the next connection is on the data terminal equipment (DTE) side of the modem. This connection goes back to the data communications equipment (DCE) portion of the server. This connection can vary greatly, but today, most people are using either Winchester-Type connections, or they are using standard cables with serial RS-232/DB-25 pin configurations.

> **NOTE**
>
> Winchester-Type connections do *not* necessarily have to be associated with V.35 interfaces; however, they usually are used for V.35 interfaces only. Also, a DB-25 connector, which is a standard 25-pin connection, may be used with V.35 interfaces.

Once again, the interfaces and cables are not important here. We are only trying to show the location of their placement within the circuit flow of a typical POTS connection to a network.

To sum this discussion up, let us review what we have learned in this section. Typically the local exchange carrier brings POTS lines in on an RJ-21X/66-block arrangement when there are three or more POTS lines. Typically, the user (you) connects on the right side of these blocks with some type of approved cabling. This cabling then completes the circuit to the output/input line connections of the modem(s). In between this connection, I am recommending patch panels be installed. The next step is the actual data cabling between the modem(s) and the network server or termination (router, bridge, and so on) equipment.

NOTE

The only exception to this would be for modems that are internal to the server or termination (router, bridge, and so on) equipment. In these cases, there would be no cabling between the DTE of the modem and the DCE of the server. With internal modems, the DTE/DCE connection is handled internally between the "slot" in the system and the printed circuit board of the modem.

This completes the interface between a POTS line and a network server. The only variation to this typical connection design would be if the network or LAN servers were connected to termination equipment such as routers or bridges. In that case, the modems for the POTS circuits would be between the routers or bridges and the patch panels mentioned earlier. The DCE connections would be on the routers or bridges and not on the server itself. Also, if the router or bridge is going to control the dialing of the POTS modem, it must be equipped with software capable of doing so. CISCO, Bay Networks, 3COMM, and most other intelligent bridges and routers are quite capable of handling modems and "modem-pools."

NOTE

A *modem-pool* refers to a collection of POTS lines and modems that are connected to a server, router, or bridge and that can be accessed by all of the users on the LAN via the server.

Type of POTS Modems Used on Networks

It would be difficult to cover every type of POTS modem that exists, so for the purposes of this discussion, I will introduce three basic classifications of POTS modems that are currently popular and in widespread use. The first type of POTS modem is the single-line, dial-up, external standalone type. The second type is the single-line, dial-up, internal standalone type. The third type is the multiline, dial-up, rack-mounted or shelf-mounted type.

> **NOTE**
>
> Chapter 13 of this book covers ISDN, so I mention here only the fact that ISDN modems are being considered POTS modems in many circles. There is a debate over whether a POTS line can only be the standard analog TIP and RING circuit. However, ISDN 128Kbps circuits are being made available for home and business use and are sometimes referred to as POTS ISDN lines.

Let us now look at these three basic classifications of POTS modems.

Single-Line, Dial-Up, External Standalone Modems

This type of modem is the most common one in use today. Many Internet Service Providers (ISPs) use external standalone POTS modems to comprise their local modem pools. A common brand of modem in use at ISP locations is the U.S. Robotics Dual-Standard/33.6 dial-up modem. ISP organizations simply use shelves or wall mounting to place all of these modems in close proximity to each other. If the RJ-21X connection for these modems is physically close to them, it makes no sense to wire patch panels in line with the modems as shown earlier in this chapter. In these cases, the right side of the RJ-21X block is wired to individual modular RJ-11 jacks. The modems are then connected to these RJ-11 jacks with common modular line cords.

In the case of a network using standalone modems, it is a good idea to try to locate the server or terminating equipment (router or bridge), the modems, and the RJ-11/14/21X interface points in close proximity to each other. Another factor to consider with these modems is the amount of heat they give off and/or can tolerate. If the closet or room where your interfaces are located is not cool or equipment-friendly, these standalone modems may overheat or malfunction. The newer modems are pretty reliable, but there is always the chance one may fail due to excessive heat.

Single-Line, Dial-Up, Internal Standalone Modems

This type of modem is basically identical to the first type with one exception, which concerns the placement of the modem. Since these modems are internal, they become an integral part of the circuit boards making up your server, router, or bridge. Most companies make internal POTS dial-up modems to fit their equipment. For example, CISCO Systems, Inc. makes modem cards that fit into their router products. These can use POTS or ISDN trunks for dial-up networking. If we are talking about a small network using a PC as the server, a standard internal modem operating at speeds between 300bps and 33.6Kbps can be used. The cost of these modems has come way down in the last two years. There are also companies that produce a single board holding more than one POTS modem and that can be plugged into a single slot on a PC's motherboard. This is an outstanding solution for a small LAN that uses POTS circuits as its main LAN/WAN interconnection method.

One point needs to be made again for patch panel configuration. With internal POTS modems, there are going to be no LEDs or lamps on the face of the modem that can be observed during the modem's operation. Many people call these idiot-lamps, but they can prove invaluable to someone who is troubleshooting a problem with a POTS modem or circuit. With an internal modem, there needs to be some sort of routine in the server, router, or bridge's internal operating system that extends this information out to the user or network administrator. If there are no software means of getting this information to the outside world, it can be very difficult to tell just what a modem is "doing" at different times during its normal operating cycle, hence, the necessity of good patch panel facilities between the modem(s) and the outside POTS circuit(s).

With only a speaker or a telephone butt set, a technician can patch into the monitoring portion of the patch panel and ascertain what the status of the modem is. I have seen many network administrators forced to reboot their servers when their POTS circuits and/or modems failed. Not only does this inconvenience users and cause data loss, but it also does not tell the administrator what the real cause of the problem was. In the case of a network using three or more internal POTS modems, a patch panel becomes an absolute necessity.

Multiline, Dial-Up, Rack- or Shelf-Mounted Modems

These types of modems are becoming extremely popular. There are many companies offering modem solutions in many different forms for LAN/WAN interconnection. A typical arrangement is a rack of modem cards in individual slots. From this rack are individual modular connections out to the POTS circuit interface equipment. The other side of this arrangement has an interface box or widget of some sort that interfaces the modem rack to the server, router, or bridge. The obvious benefit of these systems is that more than one connection can be made at a time, and therefore many POTS calls can be up at a time.

One of the best variations I have seen of this technology is used by CISCO Systems, Inc. They provide multiline POTS interface capabilities on their router systems to place on-demand calls between routers of different LAN systems. By using this type of interconnection, these so-called modem racks, or nests, can provide excellent, on-demand bandwidth between the routers of an organization's LANs.

There are also vendors that can provide racks capable of holding several of the internal modems mentioned in the last section. These racks of internal modems can be controlled by an interface widget that connects to serial ports on the server, router, or bridge, or directly to the LAN. In fact, some vendors are designing standalone racks of dial-up POTS modems that can interface directly with the internal structure of a LAN. For example, there could be a connection made by coaxial Ethernet to this nest of modems. A software package would allow all servers on the LAN to get to the modem nest and use one of the modems if one is indeed available.

12

POTS

Once again, there are simply too many variations of interfaces, racks, shelves, and electrical characteristics to attempt to list them here. However, IS professionals should be aware of the virtually limitless types of POTS modem racks, nests, or pools available for LAN/WAN interconnection.

Aggregate POTS Systems

If an organization needs more bandwidth than a single POTS line can provide at any given time, it makes sense to use more than one, right? Well, the simple truth of the matter is that there is currently a limit of 33.6Kbps on most singular POTS circuits. Since most servers on LANs are incapable themselves of using the bandwidth of a combination of two or more POTS lines at the same time, the highest amount of bandwidth most servers can gain from a POTS circuit at any given time is 33.6Kbps. In other words, if an organization's server in Maine is connected to another of its servers in Colorado through a POTS circuit, the two servers can only hope to have a bandwidth of 33.6Kbps available for their use, right? Wrong. There has been a recent rise in the number of vendors willing to provide the termination equipment capable of combining POTS circuits to provide higher aggregate bandwidths.

This started with the voice communications world back in the 1970s. In those days, Northern Telecom, Inc. came up with a system called Comm-II (or Comm-Two) equipment. This equipment was able to take 10 POTS circuits, and provide dial tone for maybe 12 to 18 circuits using only the path of the original 10. It is obvious how this equipment worked. It simply stole free time from circuits where no human voice was present and crammed data from other circuits with voice present into this stolen time.

Many would argue that T-1 was doing this job in the 1960s. Why did we need Comm-II equipment? You are comparing apples and oranges. A T-1 circuit is a digital stream that facilitates the transmission of 24 analog POTS circuits using two pairs of wires. The main reason the Bell System created T-1 was to maximize the use of its copper wire facilities and transmit more than one circuit over two pairs of wires. When Northern Telecom was creating their Comm-II equipment, T-1 was not readily available for use by private industry. Further, LANs were not nearly as prevalent in business as they are today. Rather, Northern Telecom was providing a business customer a means to connect more people than they were paying for.

Since the invention of this equipment, many other vendors have come up with ways to provide increased bandwidth using more than one POTS circuit simultaneously. However, today the most common use of combining POTS circuits is done within a router or an intelligent bridge. When a LAN/WAN interconnect design is put together with routers on the controlling end of the interconnection, it is possible to take POTS lines and combine them into aggregate connections. See Figure 12.3.

FIGURE 12.3.
Aggregate POTS connectivity.

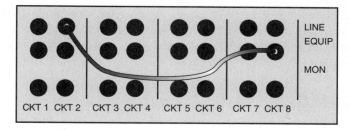

NOTE: As you can see, the bad modem was in circuit 2. The patch made from the circuit 2 line jack over to the spare circuit 8 is completed by patching into the equipment jack. By doing so, the modem on spare circuit 8 is now connected to the good POTS line that makes up circuit 2.

By using a router intelligent enough to put up two or more POTS calls to the other LAN's router, there can be an aggregate connection at speeds beyond the 33.6Kbps barrier of most POTS singular lines. This reduces the need for long connect times between LANs, and it speeds up the transfer of large files and/or e-mail between the LANs comprising an organization's WAN. Also, many of these new router systems are able to break out telephone and fax capabilities to be used when the server is not using the POTS circuits for data transmission.

It is interesting to note that at the time of this writing, many vendors are looking to increase POTS speeds to 56Kbps. One of the foremost vendors in this area is U.S. Robotics, Inc. (USR). It has devised a standard called X2 Technology. Their position is a very valid one: Because most of the Public Switched Telephone Network (PSTN) is now in a digital state and capable of passing higher bandwidths, USR feels the time has come to produce a system capable of passing 56Kbps over a standard POTS line. I am not talking about an ISDN line; most ISDN lines in use today are of the 128Kbps variety. No, rather, what I am talking about here is a chance to push the envelope of what was previously held as the limit for an analog POTS circuit's bandwidth.

If USR is effective in developing and marketing the X2 standard, we may see POTS circuits operating routinely at speeds up to 56Kbps. If we take this a step further and look at the intelligent capabilities being designed into routers in order to combine POTS circuits and increase bandwidth, many IS professionals will have to rethink the way they have been designing their LAN/WAN interconnections. A combination of X2-capable modems and intelligent routers will provide organizations with outstanding POTS aggregate bandwidth capabilities.

Assembling LAN/WAN Interconnection with POTS

When using POTS lines in a data network, generally it is for the purpose of bringing connectivity in from a location far-removed from your local area network (LAN). In other words, the

POTS line is being used to facilitate a connection to another LAN, which may be a part of your organization but is located across town, across the country, or across the world. The second reason POTS circuits are typically used is to facilitate the local or traveling corporate employee who needs access to the services of the corporate LAN when he or she is at home or away on company business.

There has been much discussion over the years as to just what constitutes a LAN or a WAN. In my opinion, any time you are networking individuals together who reside in the same office, room, or building within a corporation, you are involved in a LAN situation. When you start connecting these LANs to other LANs that may be across town, or in another country, then you are taking the step into Wide Area Networking (WAN). The connections made between LANs and WANs are the most misunderstood.

There are many schools of thought concerning what technology to use on LAN/WAN interconnections. For the purposes of this chapter, I shall make no attempt to pick a certain technology and declare it as the *only* one to use. Rather, I will highlight situations when POTS lines themselves would be the best candidates for LAN/WAN interconnections. There are basically three situations which I see as being correct for the use of POTS circuits as the means to connect LANs together, hence creating a WAN.

The first situation would be when only e-mail and a small amount of file sharing is needed between LANs in an organization. The second situation would be where the geographical separation of the LANs in an organization is far-flung. For example, a company with offices in Paris, France, and Los Angeles, California. The third and final situation would be where the organization has only one LAN and does business with other organizations only on an as-needed basis. As you can see, in all of these situations, it would make no sense to make LAN/WAN interconnections using expensive, leased connections between locations on the network. Further, in the last example, POTS lines are the *only* way the two LANs could make connections, unless they decide to use the Internet for connectivity and their Internet connection is by some other means. However, even in that scenario, there would most likely be a POTS connection to the Internet at one or both organization's networks. Let us explore these three situations individually.

Networks Using E-Mail and Small Transfers Only

In this situation, the best way to gain connectivity between two or more LANs in the organization would be to use a few POTS lines in a modem pool on each of the servers within the LAN structure. Whenever there is a situation requiring the LAN to connect with one of the other LANs in the organization, the server would be programmed and setup to automatically dial the other LAN's modem pool and make a connection. This seems to work really well when the organization's LANs need only small amounts of interaction between themselves. I have seen many organizations waste money and bandwidth by installing T-1s and even T-3s between themselves in an effort to provide a WAN interconnection between their LANs.

If they had only taken the time to do an effective network traffic analysis, they would have seen where a few POTS lines would have sufficed. It makes no sense to pay for bandwidth that is *not* being used. An on-demand modem pool can pass data between LANs extremely efficiently. Also, if the time factor is not as crucial, the servers can be programmed to make connectivity only with other LANs in the organization when the rates on the POTS lines are cheaper. If e-mail is the only thing being passed between LANs, it may also make sense to purchase POTS service from a local Internet service provider (ISP) and simply do a dial-up Internet connection at the organization's LAN locations.

The only benefit from using an ISP to pass e-mail is that most ISPs provide e-mail software of some sort for you to use. Either way, whether you use direct dial-up between LANs, or an ISP/ Internet connection to pass e-mail, a modem pool using POTS service is the only way for these organizations to go.

Networks with Large Geographic Space Between LANs

This situation is very prevalent today with the advent of international business relations and the so-called "global village." There are many organizations with offices all over the world, and to try and maintain fixed, leased, or owned connections between these LANs would be expensive and unnecessary. For this reason, it only makes sense to use POTS connectivity between LANs. If an organization's LANs are sharing large amounts of file transfers, e-mail, or on-line data, it may become necessary to put in fixed, leased, or owned connections between the LANs. However, most situations involving LAN/WAN interconnect with organizations that are spread out can be facilitated through the use of POTS circuits.

Once again, as in the situation above, a modem pool connected to the server(s) on the LANs is the best method to use. Most LAN application software available today can be configured specifically to an organization's desires. If there is only a small amount of e-mail going back and forth, and it is possible to tie in with local ISPs at each LAN location, the modem pools would only be used to connect with the ISP. The mail would travel the Internet to reach its destination.

However, if security is a consideration, or if there is time-critical e-mail and file sharing that must occur, then an ISP would not be used, and the modems would be configured to direct dial each other and make a LAN-to-LAN connection. If the LANs begin to use longer and more costly connect times, the organization may decide to go with Frame Relay connectivity between LANs. This is covered in Chapter 17, "Frame Relay." Without going into a long discussion concerning Frame Relay, it too may use POTS circuits in modem-pools, or it may consist of routers and leased loops to the frame relay network provider.

The main thing to understand, once again, is the traffic of the organization's network. If the traffic is somewhat normal or moderate, POTS lines are the only way to go. The LAN administrators at all of the organization's locations would then need to purchase the cheapest long-distance service available and configure the network servers to dial only when needed and hopefully at the cheapest times. If a little common sense is used, POTS lines can provide the users at all of the organization's LAN locations with a decent level of service.

Organizations with Only One LAN

If an organization is small, and it has only one LAN in use, POTS is really the *only* sensible way to connect this LAN with the outside world. Typically, POTS lines would be used to gain access to an ISP in the organization's locale. If the LAN has need only for e-mail services and nothing else, a single POTS line to connect to a local ISP is the best way to go. It is amazing the amount of e-mail that can pass on a 33.6Kbps modem over a POTS line. It is just as amazing how many small organizations I have seen purchase too many POTS lines for their LAN. The typical ratio is 10 users per modem. That seems to work really well. With the cost of modems going down, and the cost of monthly Internet access through an ISP going down, using the Internet to pass corporate e-mail has become the best way to go. If security is a concern, there are many software-based encryption programs that can provide organizations with secure mail on the Internet.

Now that we have looked at the three situations involving POTS lines as the best candidates for LAN-to-WAN interconnection, I am sure there are a million exceptions to these three situations. However, if you look at the general points made in the earlier discussion concerning these three situations, I am sure you will agree POTS lines *are* a viable technology to be used when connecting LANs together. The only reason many network people still look at POTS interconnectivity as being a backup to a real LAN/WAN network connection is the fact they have fallen into the same trap as many IS professionals over the past 10 years.

Many network companies such as MCI and Wiltel offer cheap, fast interconnection between LANs. To many IS professionals, these types of connections are the only way to go. However, if they really knew how little of the bandwidth of those T-1s they purchased was actually being used, they might think twice about continuing to pay for them. Also, time-sharing has become a somewhat anachronistic way of doing business in the IS world. There are very few situations where people are using their PCs or terminals and interacting directly with a server over long distances.

Rather, this direct interaction most likely is occurring on a local level between the user terminal, or PC, and the LAN server the PC is connected to. If an organization has terminals and employees all over the world and these employees are interacting live, online, with a server that is located many, many miles away, it is time for that organization to give up the central control mindset that must rule in their network design ideology. Now I am not saying there are no situations in which this design might be correct. However, I am confident that when the analysis of an organization's business is thoroughly reviewed, it will make sense to provide modern, high-speed LAN functions at user locations. The next step is the connection of these LANs as the means to pass data between all the members of the organization. It is this connection, this LAN/WAN tie-in, that will be the most crucial part of any network. Most LANs in an organization do not need to interact with each other's servers on a constant basis. For that reason, POTS circuits may be the best choice in making this all-important LAN-to-WAN interconnection.

POTS and the Use of SLIP or PPP

In any discussion of POTS, it is necessary to talk about the Serial Line Internet Protocol (SLIP) and the Point-to-Point Protocol (PPP). These two protocols are probably the ones most widely used on POTS lines connecting home/business users and the Internet. Also, as more and more enterprise networks are being built on TCP/IP-based platforms, SLIP and PPP protocols will provide the capabilities of POTS interconnection between LANs on these types of networks. Let us look briefly at both.

SLIP

This is an older protocol that was developed to pass TCP/IP data transmission over serial lines. Because TCP/IP networks have become more important in recent years, it is important to know about this protocol. It was originally developed to be used over serial lines, and it provides a TCP/IP connection over POTS circuits. The SLIP protocol is *not* an Internet standard, and there are many different versions of SLIP floating around. However, it is capable of framing and transmitting IP datagrams on serial connections. Because it is not a standard protocol, SLIP has no maximum packet size specified. Therefore, any size can be used as long as both ends of the connection are using compatible packet sizes.

PPP

The PPP protocol is a standard protocol for use over serial line connections. The difference between PPP and SLIP is the fact that PPP is based on a standard developed by the ISO called High-Level Data Link Control (HDLC). HDLC is very common and has been incorporated into X.25, Frame Relay, and ISDN. Hence, PPP is more common and more widely accepted than SLIP. Once again, PPP provides a TCP/IP connection over POTS circuits just as SLIP does. The difference is the fact that PPP is a standard protocol and therefore more likely to be used.

Dial-Up SLIP and PPP

There are many popular software packages that create a TCP/IP stack in the Windows or UNIX environment and that are capable of dialing into either ISP networks or into an organization's server. Once this dial-up connection is made through a POTS circuit, the system using the connection is capable of running most TCP/IP-based protocols and functions over the connection. As more and more enterprise networks go in the direction of the Internet and use TCP/IP as the backbone of their LAN/WAN interconnection services, there will still be a need to pass TCP/IP services over POTS circuits. SLIP and PPP are currently the only methods of doing so that are in common use today.

Remote Access and Other POTS Uses

No matter how much one wants to get away from work when the day is over, there will always be a need for remote access into an organization's network by its members. In order to facilitate easy remote access to an organization's network, there is only one accepted method: POTS circuits. There are many different ways to provide remote access, however, typically it is done by simply dialing in on one of the POTS circuits assigned to your modem pool or nest and creating a data connection between your home or laptop PC and the network's server.

Today, most remote access users are employees on the go or those authorized to telecommute from their homes. These are the people who are most likely to need remote access to the organization's network and its resources. There are many ways to make these connections, but the simplest method is through the use of a dial-up modem on the remote user's PC or laptop. The other end of the picture is a modem, modem pool, or modem nest located as an integral part of the organization's network. The user simply dials into the network's equipment and the connection is made, after some sort of security check for the authenticity of the user.

> **NOTE**
>
> Telecommuting is a term given to those who work at home, yet are connected somehow into the organization's network and computer resources.

Organizations today are apt to use security checkpoints and other software tools to ensure that only authorized users are able to gain access to their networks. Once the user has connected to the organization's network, the server determines what type of connection in terms of use and appearance is afforded to the user. There are many client/server software application packages around today that allow a remote access connection to look and act nearly the same if not identically to the connection users receive when logged into the LAN on a locally connected workstation.

However, remote access is but one use of POTS other than network LAN/WAN interconnection. Another common use of POTS circuits is on Point-of-Sale (POS) transaction machines, such as credit card readers, cash registers, and Automated Teller Machine (ATM) equipment. In many ATM networks, banks have taken it upon themselves to use leased, fixed lines between terminals and banks. However, the smarter banks are using on-demand POTS circuits and modems to connect ATM machines, banks, and credit-approving networks. Whenever a credit card check is made on a small POTS-oriented credit card reader, an on-demand connection to a credit-approving network is made.

Still another use for POTS circuits that is becoming extremely common is the connection used by various state-run lotteries. In states where there is a lottery, there seems to be a store on every corner where lottery tickets can be purchased. However, what do you think is the glue holding these lottery ticket vendors to the main or central lottery network in the state's capital? A simple POTS circuit, of course. Whenever these vendors are involved in small numbers of ticket sales, an on-demand POTS circuit is used. Only when vendors consistently generate an extremely large number of ticket sales do states tend to install leased, fixed lines between themselves and the vendors. Even then, the leased line may actually be a POTS connection that is dialed and left up all day long.

Summary

As you can see, the many uses for connecting various networks together by way of POTS are astounding. It would be foolish to try cover all of them in this chapter. What we have tried to do is provide a general outline of what POTS lines are all about and how they can be used in the business of networking. It always amazes me when I see new uses for POTS lines. Over the years, I have dealt with many creative IS professionals who have come up with some pretty far-fetched uses for POTS circuits.

I even met a man once who used a POTS circuit to connect his LAN to the electric fence holding his horses. This was how he was able to know immediately if the electric fence on his property had been breached. The fence's alarm system had a POTS line terminated in its cabinet, and when a breach occurred, the system would dial the man's LAN and send a prearranged login sequence to the server. The server had been instructed to notify the man whenever this login name was used. Does it seem far fetched? Maybe. But to my friend, it was a means to continue working at his office and know that his horses and their fence were probably still intact.

Literally, we are moving to a time when the only analog portion of a telephone line will be at the user's handset. Until human beings are able to hear and speak in digital signals, that analog portion will remain intact. However foolish the preceding statement may seem, it illustrates dramatically the main reason why POTS lines have always been considered analog in nature and somehow less important than digital circuits and systems. While most of the public networks these POTS circuits traverse are digital, there is still a lot of copper wire buried under the streets of the world's cities. While some of this copper wire can be used for digital transmission, a lot of it is old and not in the best condition.

For these reasons, there will always be a certain stigma applied to POTS circuits by IS professionals. Even when I have not been involved in the conversation, I have overheard IS people talking about their nice, new fiber connections and their old, rotten copper connections. There is one fact that still remains true. The public switched network is the most rapid means of gaining connectivity into any area at any time. There will always be a need for this network, as people will always want to have telephones in their homes and businesses.

The telephone is still the most important device in any office. Do not let anyone tell you differently. As long as we continue to tie high-speed data technology to the technology of the public telephone network, there will be continued use of POTS circuits in LAN/WAN interconnections. With the advent of new technologies such as USR's X2 modem technology, the

POTS circuit will continue to redefine its rightful place in the world of data networking. ISDN is the technology a lot of people are looking at now for dial-up network access. There is a lot of spirited talk of how ISDN will replace POTS. What I say to you is this: POTS will never go away. It will simply transform itself.

The term POTS will simply be applied to newer, different technologies that emerge in the public switched network. Perhaps all of us "old-timers," those who came to know and understand the fact that POTS meant wires and the ability to converse over them, will never be able to fully let go of POTS as we knew it. However, there will be a new generation of laptops, hand-held assistants, fax machines combined with cellular telephones, and other such innovations that will all simply reinvent the term POTS. The Plain Old Telephone System, POTS, may come to mean digital-switched circuits that run at speeds in excess of 1Mbps or better. I am confident the term POTS and the circuits denoted by the term POTS will be with us for many years to come.

ISDN

by Michael Starkenburg

IN THIS CHAPTER

CHAPTER 13

Thanks to recent massive advertising by the Regional Bell Operating Companies, Integrated Services Digital Network (ISDN) is quickly gaining acceptance among consumers as the up-and-coming digital communication system. Most people, however, aren't aware that ISDN has been around for over ten years.

The vision of ISDN is to provide digital clarity and reliability in every home and office. ISDN data connections are many times faster than today's analog modems. ISDN can provide both voice and data service simultaneously over existing wiring.

Besides the speed benefits of the data ISDN service, ISDN provides many voice features to the residential and small office user that were previously only found on large scale PBX systems. Call forwarding, call hold, and caller ID are just a few of the features commonly found in ISDN service.

Finally, ISDN is expandable. The service is designed to support applications like a simple home office, and can also replace T-1 connectivity for large installations. As ISDN becomes widely available, it may make video conferencing and other high-bandwidth applications a reality.

The multitude of ISDN acronyms can be daunting to the end user. In this chapter, we will explain some of the basics behind ISDN, and help you understand the technology behind the alphabet soup.

> **TIP**
>
> This chapter provides a good overview, but if you want to drill down on any specific area, there is a wealth of information available on the Internet. In particular, an excellent place to start is Dan Kegel's ISDN page: www.alumni.caltech.edu/~dank/isdn/.

ISDN—A Brief History

The earliest phone systems relied on human operators to make connections between customers as each call was made. This system was quickly replaced by automated *switches*, which allowed the end user to "dial" their desired party. Besides being less labor-intensive, these switches allowed the phone companies to more quickly scale the phone network to meet the surging demand.

In the 1950s, telephone companies began looking for ways to make the phone network more efficient. How could they put more calls on a switch or a wire? They began to explore how digital technology in the central offices could increase the flexibility and expandability of the existing analog phone network.

From Analog to Digital

Through the 1960s, telephone companies began to deploy digital switches into their central offices. Human voices traveled from offices and residences to these central office switches as an analog signal. At the switch, they were digitized, and sent digitally on to another central office, where they were converted back to an analog signal and sent to their final destination.

The Analog-to-Digital Conversion

To carry a voice signal on a digital carrier, the telephone companies had to develop equipment that could convert the voice signal. They did this by *sampling* the signal, or taking a measurement many times per second and converting that measurement into a number. That numerical data was then transmitted over the digital link, and converted back into analog at the receiving switch.

While the human voice can produce sounds in the range between 50 and 1500Hz, engineers found that most of what we hear could travel in the range between 300 and 3400Hz. In effect, they cut off the very highest sounds, and the very lowest sounds but still had an acceptable quality signal.

So, the phone companies needed to provide 3Khz of bandwidth for each voice signal, plus 1Khz for separation between calls, for a total of 4Khz. They determined that for an accurate digital signal, they needed to sample at twice that rate, or 8,000 times per second.

Each sample resulted in a number that was represented in an 8-bit digital "word". So, to transmit the human voice digitally, the company needed to provide enough bandwidth to send 8 bits of data, 8 thousand times per second, or 64Kbps. As you'll see later in this chapter, this became the foundation for the architecture of ISDN.

13

ISDN

> **TIP**
>
> Standard analog modems work by converting the digital signal into an audible tone. This audible tone travels from your computer to the phone company's central office, where it is converted *back* to digital as described here. Because of the limitations of all that conversion, analog modems can't effectively transfer any faster than 28.8Kbps. Modem manufacturers use compression techniques to effectively get higher rates (hence 33.6Kbps and 56Kbps modems). ISDN never has to convert the signal from digital to analog and back again, which is why you can transmit so much more data across the same line.

These central office digital switches were connected together by a new type of digital communications link: the T-1 carrier. The T-1 carrier could carry twenty-four of these 64Kbps voice channels, and it used the same amount of copper wire as only two analog voice calls. The T-1 circuit is explained in greater detail in Chapter 16, "T-1 and Fractional T-1."

From IDN to ISDN

In an effort to find the most cost-effective solution, engineers developed several different types of digital conversion and switching hardware. Not all of these types of hardware could talk to each other. The phone companies recognized that they needed a digital standard.

In the late 1960s, the Consultative Committee for International Telephony and Telegraph (CCITT) began working on the Integrated Digital Network (IDN). Besides trying to standardize digital hardware, the IDN would combine the functions of switching and transmission into one piece of hardware, further raising the efficiency of the network.

In the IDN, however, the last segment between the central office and the customer premises remained an analog connection. The phone companies would still have to perform expensive analog-digital conversion within their central switch.

The concept of ISDN was introduced in 1972 as a possible solution. By moving the analog-digital conversion equipment into the customer premises, the phone company could provide both data and voice services over a single line. The voice service would be digitized at the customer premises, combined with any data services, and then these Integrated Services would be transmitted to the phone companies central office.

ISDN Evolves

Throughout the 1970s, the telephone network was slowly upgraded to better switching hardware and higher volume connectivity. The phone companies explored digital technology further, and began providing T-1 service directly to customer premises.

The majority of this research was funded and executed by AT&T Bell Labs. In 1984, the Department of Justice broke AT&T up into our existing phone companies, known collectively as the Regional Bell Operating Companies (RBOCs). Each of the seven companies became responsible for their own product development, with help from a new research consortium called Bellcore. Before long, there were seven widely divergent research efforts into ISDN, each with its own requirements. This is a primary reason why, even today, ISDN offerings and prices are different from region to region.

To further complicate this, the Department of Justice ruling forbid the RBOCs from manufacturing customer equipment. Hardware developers were frustrated by the major differences between the RBOCs ISDN implementations, and progress was slow.

In the early 1990s, ISDN began to roll out in major metropolitan markets. Driven by demand from computer and network technology users, the RBOCs began to offer businesses and finally residential customers the opportunity to try the new technology.

Today, ISDN hardware and service is widely available to both businesses and residences. Prices are dropping, and service is reaching an acceptable level. A large number of Internet providers allow ISDN access to their services. It is clear that ISDN is quickly becoming a standard telecommunication offering for the US market.

How ISDN Works

The existing digital network is incredibly complex. It contains literally thousands of switches and trunk connections, each capable of handling hundreds of calls simultaneously. Describing the network in detail would require its own book, but we can get the general idea by looking at what components make up a connection.

In Figure 13.1, you can see the components of a local call. In this example, the call goes from Subscriber A's local loop to his central office. From there, the call is routed to a Tandem office, and on to a second central office. The second central office routes the call to Subscriber B's local loop. This process causes the clicks and delays you hear in an analog system, but is noiseless and instantaneous in a digital system.

FIGURE 13.1.
Local call components.

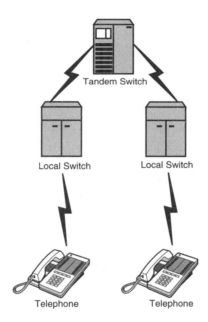

In Figure 13.2, you see an example of a long distance call. A long distance call travels the local loop-central office-tandem office path like a local call, but is then routed to one of hundreds of long-distance tandem switches.

The Local Loop

The local loop, or as it is often called, the last hundred feet, is the piece of the phone system that you are most familiar with. In a traditional phone system, this is the only piece of the network that remains analog. In an ISDN network, the local loop itself is digital.

The first piece of the local loop is commonly referred to as CPE, or customer premises equipment. The telephone company provides service up to a junction box somewhere on your property, called a demarcation point, or *demarc*. From the demarc, all the hardware and cabling is considered CPE. In an analog system, this would include your telephone equipment and any cabling installed in your residence or office.

FIGURE 13.2.
Long distance call components.

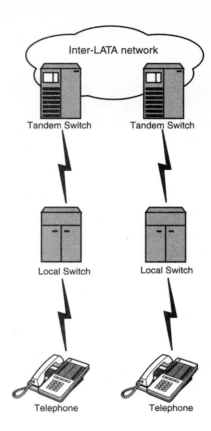

In an ISDN system, the local loop is significantly more complex. The cabling is identical in most cases, but the CPE is far different. Since the phone company is sending the full digital signal to the demarc, you need to provide the equipment to handle the physical and electrical termination for this signal, and the equipment to interface it to your telephone or data equipment. These devices, called Network Terminators and Terminal Adapters, are explained later in this chapter.

The Central Office

From the demarc on your property, the phone company runs wire to its local Central Office. Because of the limitations of the copper wire, your Central Office will usually be within 18,000 feet of your premises.

The central office is the core of all the local loops in the area. The copper wire from each residence and business terminates in the central office switch.

A phone company switch is actually a complex computer with hundreds or thousands of input/output ports. Central office switches, also called Class Five switches, handle call-setup, teardown, and monitoring. They manage features like call waiting and call forwarding, and communicate with other switches in other central offices.

> **NOTE**
>
> There are a number of different models of switches in service today. Because each switch has different features and capabilities, you may need to know which switch your local phone company office uses to properly install your ISDN equipment. Common switch models in the United States include the AT&T 5ESS, the Northern Telecom DMS100, and the Siemens EWSD.

The phone companies have been upgrading these switches to be ISDN compatible, and between 75 and 90 percent of North America is now able to get ISDN connectivity. If your local switch is not capable of servicing ISDN subscribers, you may still be able to get ISDN by using a BRITE (basic rate ISDN terminal extension) device. Your local phone company will be able to give you more details about ISDN availability.

The Telephone Company Network

Beyond the local central office, the complexity of the network grows exponentially. To help engineers understand this complexity, the network was originally designed with five tiers. These tiers are described in the following sections.

The Network Hierarchy

The fifth tier was called the end office, and is what we now call the central office. The central switch is known as a Class Five switch to fit in this hierarchy.

The fourth tier provides interoffice communication, through what is known as a tandem (or Class Four) switch. The tandem switch routes traffic between Class Five switches so that all switches do not need direct trunk connections. Figure 13.3 shows how the network looks with and without tandem switches.

FIGURE 13.3.
Networks with and without a Tandem Switch.

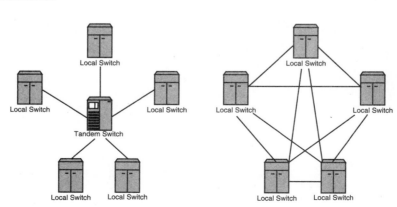

The remaining tiers, which handled long distance routing between tandem (Class Four) switches, lost their identity with the breakup of AT&T. Now, all the Class Four and Five switches are grouped into over a hundred geographic areas called Local Access and Transport Areas (LATA). When a call goes from one Class Five switch to another in the same LATA, it is generally handled by the local RBOC. When a call originates in a different LATA from its destination, it is then handled by an Inter Exchange Carrier.

Signaling System Number 7 (SS7)

The phone company switches communicate using a language called Signaling System Number 7 (SS7). SS7 is an *out of band* signaling protocol, which means it does not share bandwidth with the actual signal. Analog systems commonly used in-band systems for call setup and teardown. This resulted in user perceivable delays while the voice channel was used for setting up the call. By using SS7, the ISDN network can set up calls almost instantly.

Besides providing basic call setup communication between switches, SS7 also enables services like caller ID (formally known as Automatic Number Identification, or ANI). Other supported services, such as automatic callback and call forwarding, are starting to be offered in almost all residential markets, even to analog customers.

ISDN Terminology

ISDN was designed by engineers in large, bureaucratic phone companies. Accordingly, every element of the ISDN standards has an acronym. It's hard to hold a discussion about ISDN that doesn't sound like secret code. Hopefully, this section will help you decipher this code. Most of the information in this section comes directly from the ISDN standards developed by the International Telecommunications Union. For more information on any specific term, device, or protocol, you may want to refer to their website at www.itu.ch.

ISDN Channels

An ISDN transmission circuit is merely a logical grouping of data channels. Each of these channels have a specific purpose and handle a specific amount of bandwidth. By grouping these channels in different configurations, ISDN can be used for almost any digital transmission application, no matter how much bandwidth is required.

The B-Channel

The core of any ISDN channel is the bearer channel, or B-channel. A single B-channel carries 64Kbps of digital traffic. This traffic can be a digitized voice signal, digitized video, or raw data. The 64Kbps throughput, as we discussed earlier, is the perfect amount of bandwidth to sample a voice signal.

> **NOTE**
>
> In some areas, the phone companies only provide 56Kbps B-channels. This is for backward compatibility with older phone systems that use that 8K for in-band signaling.

B-channels are usually used in groups of 2, 23, or even more, to provide additional bandwidth or voice lines. To control the transmission of this data, they are always combined with a D-channel.

The D-Channel

The D-channel is primarily used for out-of-band messaging. This allows the call setup and tear-down signals to have their own dedicated channel, while the entire bandwidth of the B-channel is left for the actual data.

D-channels can be different sizes, depending on how many B-channels they are controlling. Naturally, as more B-channels are in use, there will be more signaling bandwidth needed. For a Basic Rate Interface (with two B-channels), the D-channel is a 16Kbps pipe, which a Primary Rate Interface (with 23 B-channels) requires a 64Kbps Pipe.

Earlier in the chapter we mentioned SS7, the language used to communicate between phone company switches. The language that travels on a D-channel is the little brother to SS7, and is known as DSS1. DSS1 communicates between your customer premises equipment and the telephone companies switch, and handles the setup and tear-down of calls.

> **NOTE**
>
> For applications that required large amounts of bandwidth, standard configurations of many B-channels were set up. The H-channels, which are described in greater detail later in this chapter, provide bandwidth between 384Kbps and 135Mbps.

Access Interfaces

Although B-channels and D-channels can be combined in any number of ways, the phone companies wanted to support a manageable number of standard configurations. Two standard access interfaces were developed, the Basic Rate Interface and the Primary Rate Interface.

Basic Rate Interface

The Basic Rate Interface (BRI) is a logical grouping of two 64Kbps B-channels and one 16Kbps D-channel.

13

ISDN

> **NOTE**
>
> While some people will promote the BRI as being a 144Kbps data channel (64 + 64 + 16 = 144), remember that only the 128Kbps B-channel bandwidth (64 +64 = 128) is commonly available to the user. The 16Kbps data channel is reserved for signaling in most circumstances.

The BRI was intended for residential or home-office use. It was designed as the maximum amount of data that could use existing wiring. A BRI will allow users to access both voice and data services simultaneously.

Depending on your hardware, you can connect up to eight distinct devices to your BRI. This allows you to build a network of devices, both phone, data, and video, and use any three of them at the same time.

Primary Rate Interface

While the BRI was designed as the maximum amount of data that could flow over normal wiring, the Primary Rate Interface (PRI) was designed as the maximum amount of data that could flow over a T-1 carrier. A PRI consists of 23 64Kbps B-channels, and a single 64Kbps D-channel, for a total of 1.472Mbps available to the user. If you add the D-channel, you'll find that the total bandwidth of a PRI is 1.536Mbps, almost the same as a T-1 Carrier. An additional 8K of bandwidth is used by the T-1 Carrier for framing.

> **NOTE**
>
> The 1.544Mbps T-1 is available in North America only. In Europe, the corresponding circuit is called an E1, and carries 2.044Mbps. Euro-ISDN will makes use of this additional bandwidth by assigning thirty B-channels to each PRI instead of the North American standard of 23.

The primary use of the PRI today is for large scale voice services. Many Private Branch Exchange (PBX) units include their own ISDN hardware, and will accept a PRI directly from the telephone company. The ability to easily reallocate trunk lines in the PRI makes it a natural for this function.

The User-Network Interface

ISDN standards clearly identify the various devices that connect the end user to the telephone network. Each specific function was defined in the standards as a separate device, although today many ISDN vendors will combine several functions into a single piece of hardware. We'll explain this in greater detail later in the chapter.

After defining the functional devices, the standards went on to define the protocol that each device used to speak with the devices on either side of it. These protocols were assigned the letters R, S, T, and U as identifiers, and were termed *reference points*.

Figure 13.4 shows the order of functional devices, and the locations of the different reference points. The alphabet soup of the user-network standards gets confusing, so refer back to this figure often.

FIGURE 13.4.

Functional devices and reference points.

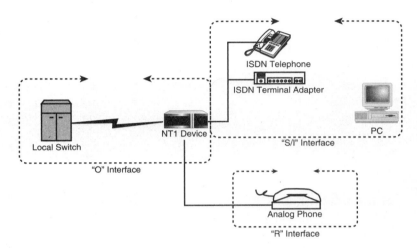

NOTE

Because vendors can combine several functional devices in a single piece of hardware, you may not see all reference points in your installation. For example, a device that is called an NT1 by the vendor will often provide the functionality of an NT2 device as well. In this case, the vendor will usually label the customer-side interface and "S/T" interface. This interface will then connect to the terminal equipment or terminal adapter. You never see a pure "T" reference point in this configuration.

The ISDN standards define five groups of functional devices: The NT1, NT2, TE1, TE2, and the TA.

Network Terminator 1

The Network Terminator 1 (NT1) is the device that communicates directly with the Central Office switch. The NT1 receives a "U" interface connection from the phone company, and puts out a "T" interface connection for the NT2, which is often in the same piece of physical hardware.

The NT1 handles the physical layer responsibilities of the connection, including physical and electrical termination, line monitoring and diagnostics, and multiplexing of D- and B-channels.

> **CAUTION**
>
> In an analog system, the phone company provides the power to the phone line. This explains why, in a blackout, you can still call the power company to complain. The ISDN system, however, relies on power at your site, generally provided by the NT1 device. In the event of a power failure at the NT1, you will lose the ability to make *any* ISDN calls, either voice or data. For this reason, it may be wise to keep an analog backup line.

Network Terminator 2

The Network Terminator 2 (NT2) sits between an NT1 device and any terminal equipment or adapters. An NT2 accepts a "T" interface from the NT1, and provides an "S" interface In most small installations, the NT1 and NT2 functions reside in the same piece of hardware. In larger installations, including all PRI installations, a separate NT2 may be used. ISDN Network routers and digital PBX's are examples of common NT2 devices.

The NT2 handles data-link and network layer responsibilities in ISDN installations with many devices, including routing and contention monitoring.

Terminal Equipment 1

A Terminal Equipment 1 (TE1) device is a piece of user equipment that speaks the "S" interface language natively, and can connect directly to the NT devices. Examples of a TE1 device would be an ISDN workstation (such as the SGI Indy), an ISDN fax, or an ISDN-ready telephone.

Terminal Equipment 2

Terminal Equipment 2 (TE2) devices are far more common—in fact, every telecommunications device that isn't in the TE1 category is a TE2 device. An analog phone, a PC, and a FAX are all examples of TE2 devices. To attach a TE2 device to the ISDN network, you need the appropriate Terminal Adapter. A TE2 device attaches to the Terminal Adapter through the "R" interface.

Terminal Adapters

These devices connect a TE2 device to the ISDN network. The Terminal Adapter (TA) connects to the NT device using the "S" interface and connects to a TE2 device using the "R" interface.

Terminal adapters are often combined with an NT1 for use with personal computers. Because of this, they are often referred to as ISDN modems. This is actually not accurate, because TA's do not perform analog-digital conversion like modems.

Identifiers

When you order an analog telephone line from the company, you are assigned a simple ten digit number that permanently identifies your connection. Unfortunately, ISDN service isn't that simple. There are five separate identifiers involved in each connection. Two of these, the Directory number and the Service Profile Identifier, are assigned by the phone company when service is ordered. These are probably the only two identifiers you will ever have contact with.

The other three identifiers are dynamically assigned, and are normally transparent to the end user. The important difference between the identifiers is when they are assigned: the SPID is assigned once, when service is set up. The TEI, SAPI, and BC are assigned every time a device is connected to the system.

Directory Number

The directory number (DN) is simply the normal ten-digit phone number the phone company would assign any analog service. In an ISDN service, however, there is much more flexibility in the use of the directory number. The directory number is only a logical mapping, and doesn't have the one-to-one relationship with your line that analog service would have.

A single device can have up to eight directory numbers. Since an ISDN BRI can support up to eight devices, this means that a single BRI can support up to 64 directory numbers. This might allow you to have eight extensions in an office, each with its own directory number. In most BRI installations, you are assigned two directory numbers.

The opposite is also true. You can have several ISDN channels or devices share a single directory number. This is helpful when you want the ability to receive more than one call at a time, without using call-waiting or having the caller hear a busy signal.

Service Profile Identifier

The Service Profile Identifier (SPID) is the most important identifier to the ISDN system. Like the directory number, it is assigned by the phone company when service is set up. In fact, most SPIDs consist of the Directory number for that device, plus some extra digits.

The format of the SPID varies widely from region to region. The SPID is usually between 10 and 14 digits long, depending on the policy of your phone company. You may receive one SPID per B-channel, one per ISDN device, or one for your entire line.

Generally, the phone company will issue one SPID for each application. So, for example, you may receive two SPIDs for your BRI:

> aaa-ppp-nnnn-01, and
>
> aaa-ppp-nnnn-11,
>
> where aaa is the area code, ppp-nnnn is the directory number, and the last two digits identify each B-channel.

Your SPID is unique across the switch, and must be properly entered into your terminal equipment before your ISDN devices can be recognized by the switch.

When an ISDN device or Terminal Adapter is connected to the line, it follows a hard coded procedure to set up the physical communication with the phone company switch. During the procedure, it sends the SPID to the switch. If the SPID is correct, the switch uses the information it has stored about your service profile to set up the data link. The SPID is not sent again unless the device is disconnected from the network.

> **TIP**
>
> A SPID never seems to be around when you need it. Some phone companies do not include it on the bill, and SPIDs are not published like Directory Numbers. When your service is installed, it would be wise to label your ISDN devices with the SPIDs they will be using. If you have an internal device, you may want to label the wall jack.

Terminal Endpoint Identifier

A Terminal Endpoint Identifier (TEI) is allocated dynamically for each SPID as the switch recognizes it. The TEI changes every time a device is connected to the network, while the SPID remains the same. The TEI identifies the particular ISDN device to the switch. Because it doesn't have to be manually entered like the SPID, the TEI is usually transparent to the end user.

Service Address Point Identifier

The Service Address Point Identifier (SAPI) identifies the particular interface on the switch that your devices are connected to. The SAPI is switch-specific, and is never seen by the user.

Bearer Code

The TEI and SAPI, when taken together, uniquely identify the link between your equipment and the phone company switch. This identifier, called the bearer code (BC) or call reference, changes every time a new connection is set up.

ISDN Standards

As ISDN evolved, several different versions of ISDN were developed and tested. Each version had its own protocols, features, and identifiers.

Some feature sets were standardized early on by market forces: everyone wanted to have call forwarding and caller ID. Other features were standardized through technical necessity—the BRI became a standard partially because it was the most bandwidth that could reliably travel over existing wiring.

But a large number of issues remained—services and tariffs varied widely from region to region. The phone companies have been working diligently to produce a set of standards that will allow all ISDN implementations to interact.

Who Sets the Standards?

A network of governmental and non-profit organizations has been built to create telecommunications standards, including those used in the ISDN. These organizations generally represent a geographic region or group of companies.

Global Standards: ITU

The International Telecommunications Union (formerly known as the Consultative Committee for International Telephone and Telegraph or CCITT) has been the primary global force in telecommunications standards since 1865. As a part of the United Nations, the ITU is comprised of governments from around the world, who represent their constituent companies and organizations.

North American Standards: TIA/ATIS

Two industry associations provide the US government with the majority of standards recommendations. The Telecommunications Industry Association (TIA) handles the terminal equipment and the Alliance for Telecommunications Industry Solutions (ATIS) handles the network standards.

European Standards: ETSI

In Europe, the European Telecommunications Standards Institute (ETSI) provides recommendations for both equipment and network technology. ISDN is much more common in Europe than in the United States, in part because of the strength of the ETSI. In 1989, 26 European network providers agreed on a standard for Euro-ISDN and implemented it by 1993.

ISDN and OSI

The Open Systems Interconnect model is a description of how telecommunications devices communicate at different levels. The OSI model consists of seven layers, with each subsequent layer being one step closer to the users.

An ISDN addresses the first three layers (physical, data-link, and network) of the OSI model. The higher layers are addressed by the hardware and software in the terminal equipment (such as a PC).

The Physical Layer

The physical layer of the OSI model defines the hardware, wiring, connectors, and other electrical and physical characteristics of a network connection. In the ISDN standard, the physical layer is represented by the user-network interface discussed earlier in this chapter, including the functional device and reference point specifications. The ISDN standards also address cabling and hardware issues we will discuss later in the chapter.

The Data-Link Layer

The OSI Data-link layer handles connection maintenance and error correction. In the ISDN standards, a protocol called Link Access Procedures-D Channel (LAP-D) handles flow control, error retransmission, and packet framing.

The Network Layer

In the OSI model, the Network layer defines signaling procedures between the network and users. The ISDN standards for this layer describe the signaling protocols DSS1 and SS7, which we discussed earlier in this chapter.

National ISDN

In the United States, the most widely used and important ISDN standard is called National ISDN. Created by Bellcore in 1991, National ISDN provided standardization on features, protocols, and hardware specifications for the BRI. Since the original release of the National ISDN standard, a group at Bellcore called the National ISDN Council has been proposing improvements to the standard. Today, there are several levels of the National ISDN standard.

National ISDN-1

The first set of National ISDN (NI-1) proposals called for a set of core services to be offered with all Basic Rate interfaces, including

- Voice call service
- Data call service
- Call forwarding
- Call conferencing
- Call holding

Today, the NI-1 standard is almost fully deployed. Most terminal hardware and all major switches conform to NI-1.

National ISDN-2

Released in 1992, the first major goal of National ISDN-2 (NIS) was to standardize the service features for the Primary Rate Interface, as NI-1 did for the Basic Rate Interface. That effort was only partially successful. Many companies felt that the standard didn't offer enough features, so there are still several proprietary PRI products on the market.

A secondary goal of NI-2 was to standardize and simplify the identification process. Bellcore proposed that ISDN vendors implement a series of standards that would allow automatic setup of hardware and easy connection to the ISDN network. The Automatic Terminal Setup system, along with efforts to standardize the format and use of the SPID, should reduce the technical difficulty that has caused ISDN to be such a mystery to end users.

Finally, NI-2 calls for several enhanced features to the existing services, including better billing support and more consistency of features between switch types.

NI-2 support is available in many brands of terminal hardware today, but has not been extensively rolled out in the central office switches. If your terminal equipment supports NI-2, you will be ready to use these features when the local switch in your area is upgraded. Current expectations are that NI-2 will fully roll out in late 1997.

National ISDN-3

National ISDN-3 (NI-3) is a huge leap forward in terms of ease of use and features, but won't widely be available in the near future.

Some of the features in the NI-3 standard include

- Music on Hold
- Enhanced caller ID, which will include caller name
- ISDN inspect, which allows you to query the switch for service information
- Multiple party video conferencing
- Interfaces to PCS and Frame Relay services
- Basic services (such as 911 emergency service) for uninitialized terminals

Non-Standard ISDN Implementations

By the time the National ISDN-1 specification had been released, several phone companies had already rolled out ISDN services. Most of these services had features which the subscribers (primarily businesses) found useful, but that weren't included in the NI-1 spec.

So, the as these phone companies started to adopt the NI-1 spec, they kept some of the additional features in their services. Services with these additional features are called Custom ISDN services. Services that conform strictly to the NI-1 guidelines are called Standard ISDN.

Generally, if you have NI-1 compliant hardware and software, you can still connect to a custom service, but you cannot make use of the extended features. If you want to use custom features, ask your terminal hardware vendor and phone company for information about their Custom ISDN support.

ISDN Hardware

One of the fundamental differences between the POTS analog system and the ISDN system is the complexity of the hardware installed in customer premises. Luckily, vendors are aware of this barrier to consumer acceptance of their products, and there are a number of resources available to assist you in choosing and installing the right hardware for the job. Some ISDN user groups are listed below:

> Bellcore
> www.bellcore.com
>
> California ISDN Users Group
> www.ciug.org
>
> Florida ISDN Users Group
> www.ccg4isdn.com/isdn/fiug.html
>
> New York ISDN Users Group
> www.interport.net/~digital/index.html
>
> North American ISDN User's Forum
> www.niuf.nist.gov/misc/niuf.html

In a typical ISDN installation, you are responsible for three major categories of hardware: cabling within your premises, the network terminator, and the terminal equipment or adapter.

> **NOTE**
>
> The information in this section is heavily focused towards the US ISDN subscriber. European ISDN standards are significantly different: for example, in Europe, your ISDN service provider will be responsible for network termination equipment. Also, it is unlikely that any ISDN equipment purchased in Europe will work in the US without a hassle. If you are planning an ISDN network that includes a European installation, you may want to consult with an ISDN professional in that country.

Cabling

The first piece of hardware you will be responsible for is the cabling at your premises. The phone company will provide and maintain the cable for your service up to the demarcation point. From that point, you need to ensure that you are using the right type of wire and connectors, and that you have enough to support your application.

People generally take wiring for granted in office and residential installations, but there are a few things you should know about your phone wiring.

Wiring Types

Throughout the phone system, copper wiring is run in twisted pairs. The twists in the wire assist in keeping noise levels down, which increases the effectiveness of the wire as a signal carrier. The twisting has to remain constant throughout all the wire, connectors, and jacks in the cabling system.

The Telecommunications Industry Association released standards for wiring that specified three common categories of wire:

- Category 3: The most common type of wire installed for voice purposes in office and residences. Cat 3 cable can be used up to 10Mbps over short runs.

- Category 4: A less common category capable of carrying voice or data up to 16Mbps.

- Category 5: The highest standard for data communication. Handles voice or data up to 100Mbps.

Generally speaking, if you need to install new wiring to support your ISDN installation, you should use Category 5 cable. While Category 3 cable is acceptable for ISDN use (and is the minimum installed in most residences), Category 5 cable is capable of handling future enhancements to your data network.

How Many Pairs?

For a residential installation, you should check to ensure that you have at least one pair for each BRI you plan to install, plus one pair for each analog line you plan to keep.

For an office installation, your wiring will depend on the specific terminal equipment you plan on using. An ISDN line will enter your facility on one pair (for a BRI) or two pair (for a PRI carried on a T-1). At the network terminator, which may be your PBX or ISDN router, the number of pairs required may change. In general, you will want at least two pair available to each ISDN device in an office setting.

Network Terminators

The Network Terminator, as we described earlier in the chapter, is the electrical and physical termination of the connection between your premises and the telephone company. The NT1 is a relatively simple device—so simple, in fact, that is in often integrated into a piece of terminal equipment.

Standalone or Integrated?

If you are using only a single ISDN device on a BRI, you might want to consider getting a terminal adapter with an integrated NT1. An integrated device is easier to install and is guaranteed to be compatible with the attached terminal equipment. There are a few reasons why you may still want to consider a standalone NT1 with a single device:

- Some standalone NT devices have POTS jacks, which allow the use of an analog phone even if the ISDN terminal equipment is disconnected or switched off.

- Some standalone NT devices provide backup batteries to keep your ISDN line up for a period of time after a power loss.

- Some standalone NT devices have multiple ISDN device connections, which allow you to grow your ISDN system flexibly.

If you are using more than one ISDN device on a BRI, you will probably want to use a standalone device. While you can find integrated NT1/TA's with more than one ISDN device connection, they are generally not available in many configurations. In addition, power and connectivity to all devices on the entire ISDN circuit will be provided by the integrated unit, which may not be desirable. If you need to disconnect or turn off the integrated unit, your other devices will not function.

If you are installing a PRI circuit, the Network Terminator device will probably be integrated into your PBX or ISDN router. If you have an existing PBX that doesn't support ISDN, you can get an intermediate device commonly called a *drop and insert* unit. The drop and insert unit will manage the ISDN power, call handling and signaling functions, and will deliver the PRI channels into the PBX as standard analog trunk lines. If you are considering replacing existing trunk lines with an ISDN PRI, you should retain an ISDN consultant to help you look at all the possibilities.

Connections

The most important function of a Network Terminating device, be it standalone or integrated, is to take a long-run ISDN connection from the phone company and provide a short-run connection to the terminal equipment. An NT device should include one or more of each of the following connections:

- From the phone company: For a BRI, the NT should accept the one-pair U interface connection from the phone company. This connection should use an RJ-11 connector.

- To your equipment: The NT should provide the two-pair S/T interface to your terminal equipment. If you plan to use multiple ISDN devices in your system, you will want an NT device that provides one "S/T" interface for each ISDN terminal device (up to the maximum of eight).

- To your analog phone: Optionally, the NT may provide a one pair "R" interface POTS jack for your analog phone. Some advanced NT devices will allow your analog phone to use key features (such as call forwarding or hold) through this interface.

> **TIP**
>
> If your NT1 provides an analog POTS jack, that doesn't necessarily mean you can get rid of your POTS service entirely. First, most NT devices do not provide the additional voltage to the POTS jack that tells the analog phone to ring. Second, in the event of a power loss to the NT device, the analog POTS jack will be unusable, along with the ISDN devices. If you are set on getting rid of all your analog lines, you'll want to be sure to get an NT1 that provides a ring generator and a backup power supply—but I don't recommend it.

Power Supply

The second important function of the NT device is to provide power to the ISDN circuit. Depending on the criticality of your ISDN application, you may want some sort of battery backup on your NT. There are three different ways to get this kind of battery backup:

- Some NT devices have internal capacitors, which provide a short life (10–30 seconds) power reserve. This allows the ISDN line to survive momentary power loss, spikes, and brownouts uninterrupted.

- Some NT devices have an internal battery backup to protect against longer power outages. These units can generally provide between 30 minutes and 3 hours of battery power. In some of these units, only the analog POST jack is backed up to conserve power.

- Finally, an off-the-shelf external UPS can provide hours of backup. A "smart UPS" can be programmed to notify an operator or activate a shutdown program on a PC.

> **NOTE**
>
> If you get an integrated NT/TA, especially one that is designed to live inside a PC, that piece of hardware may need to remain on all the time to provide service to your ISDN devices and analog devices attaches to the NT/TA.

Data Terminal Equipment

The last, and most important, piece of equipment you will need to choose is the terminal equipment or terminal adapter. The Terminal adapter provides the connectivity between the NT device and your end-user hardware, be it a PC, a LAN, or an analog device.

If you want to connect more than one PC to your ISDN BRI, or if you have an existing LAN, you may want to consider an ISDN router. Most home or small office installations require connectivity for only one PC and possibly an analog phone or fax and will use an ISDN terminal adapter.

External TA Features

The most important decision you will make when choosing your Terminal Adapter is whether to use an external or internal TA.

The external terminal adapter is often referred to as an "ISDN modem" because it looks like a standard modem, and connects to a serial port like a modem. Of course, the word "modem" is a misnomer: ISDN TAs do not MOdulate or DEModulate the data at all. But because they function just like a modem, the external TA is often the simplest choice. You merely connect the TA to the ISDN line and to a serial port on the computer. You can access the ISDN line through your serial port like a modem.

The drawback of an external TA is speed—or lack thereof. With an external TA, you can rarely take advantage of the full 128Kbps of an ISDN BRI. External TAs are generally slower than their internal counterparts for two reasons.

- The serial port on your computer will probably be a bottleneck. On a PC, the fastest serial ports available max out at a theoretical 115Kbps. After subtracting the overhead for error correcting, the effective maximum transmission rate on these serial ports is about 92Kbps. Even worse, some Mac serial ports are limited to 56Kbps!

- Many external TAs do not support BONDING or MLPPP, which allow you to aggregate the two B-channels for speeds faster than 64Kbps. Of course, you can still use one B-channel for data (at more than twice the speed of a 28.8Kbps modem) and use the other for voice and fax.

> **CAUTION**
>
> Before committing to an external ISDN TA, be sure you have an available serial port. On a PC, there are only four serial ports available, and two of them are not addressable by all software programs. On most Macs, there are only two serial ports. If you have maxed out your serial ports with other devices, you may want to consider an internal adapter—although it may still be tricky to configure around all those other peripherals.

Enternal TAs need to be configured with your SPID before they can initialize. There are three ways this can be done, depending on your specific TA:

- You can dial in your SPID on an analog phone plugged into a POTS jack on the device.
- You can supply your SPID to the TA through a standard modem init string.
- You can send your SPID to the TA using a proprietary program provided by the manufacturer.

Internal TA Features

Internal Terminal Adapters fit inside your PC, and connect directly to the PC bus. Because they don't need to use a serial port, they avoid the speed drawbacks of the external Terminal Adapter. You can expect to get the full 128Kbps performance out of your ISDN line using an internal adapter.

Internal cards generally offer POTS jacks and integrated NT devices, and cost less than a comparable external device. They usually support BONDING and MLPPP, and don't have several different pieces to clutter up a work area.

In many ways, an Internal TA is like a network card—it is configured in a similar way, and performs similar functions. Of course, this means that your internal TA may be as difficult to configure as a network card. If you are using an operating system that doesn't support Plug and Play devices, you should prepare yourself for a struggle configuring the device.

> **TIP**
>
> With an internal adapter, if your PC locks up or fails, an attached analog fax or phone may stop working. If you plan on using the analog port for mission critical applications, you may be happier with an external NT device running your analog service, and an internal TA for your data applications.

You should only consider an Internal TA if you have no plans to expand your ISDN network to include another PC or ISDN device. Internal TAs rarely offer the option to connect other ISDN units, although it is common for them to include one or more POTS jacks.

ISDN Bridging/Routing Hardware

The next category of terminal equipment is more complex. Instead of just interfacing a single device to the ISDN network, ISDN routers perform a "bridging" function. A *network bridge* connects two dissimilar networks, providing the necessary protocol translation between them. The most common ISDN bridge connects an ISDN BRI to an Ethernet Local Area Network.

Most ISDN-to-Ethernet bridges provide some sort of routing ability. Routing is a more complex version of bridging, where each packet is analyzed to determine if its destination is on the LAN or across the ISDN line. Depending on your specific hardware choice, you can find ISDN-to-Ethernet bridges that route several different protocols.

Which protocol your hardware supports depends on your installation. If you are linking two appletalk LANs in different locations, you'll need an ISDN router which supports this protocol. Similarly, if you want to connect two Novell networks, you'll need a router that supports the IPX protocol. To connect your LAN to the internet, you need to route TCP/IP.

ISDN-to-Ethernet routers generally have an integrated NT device. They provide one RJ11 connection for a BRI "U"-interface from the phone company, and an RJ45 connection for your Ethernet LAN. If your application needs more than 128Kbps bandwidth, you'll want to look for an ISDN router that can accept a PRI interface.

Other important features to look for in your ISDN router include

- Compression support
- Dial-on-demand, MLPPP+, or BONDING support
- SNMP network monitoring
- Remote Configuration

Aggregating Bandwidth with ISDN

One of the most useful features of the ISDN network design is the ability to combine 64Kbps B-channels for applications that require larger amounts of bandwidth. While many of today's data applications will be well serviced by a BRI or PRI, you can imagine that future applications will need different solutions.

As you add more B-channels to an ISDN installation, you need to choose a method of controlling and combining the channels into one connection. Each B-channel may travel a different path through the phone network to reach its destination. These different paths may introduce timing differences between data passed over different B-channels. ISDN aggregation techniques can both control multiple B-channel connections, and compensate for timing delays between channels.

The H-Channel

When the ITU originally developed the ISDN standards, they included several common B-channel aggregations, called H-channels. H-channels can be set up by sending a special signal to the switch, which will handle opening the lines and controlling the connection. Table 13.1 shows the common H-channel connection types.

Because the local switch recognizes the H-channel standard, it is the easiest method of aggregating bandwidth. No additional hardware is needed, and the call is handled just like any other ISDN call.

Table 13.1. Common H-Channel Connection Types

Name	*Bandwidth*	*B-Ch.*	*Applications*
H0	384Kbps	6	Video conferencing, broadcast audio.
H11	1.563Mbps	23	Replaces the T-1.
H12	1.920Mbps	30	Replaces the E-1.
H21	32.8Mbps	512	High speed data.
H22	44.2Mbps	690	High speed data.
H3	60/70Mbps	1050	Broadcast video.
H4	135Mbps	2112	Broadcast video, data trunks.

Another option for applications that need a specific bandwidth allocation that isn't addressed by an H-channel is to use special ISDN router hardware that dials a groups of B-channels individually.

The drawback of using an H-channel is that you might waste bandwidth if your application has dynamic needs. The H-channel connection keeps all B-channels open for the entire length of the call, regardless of the demand for bandwidth. To solve this, the industry has developed several methods of dynamically allocating bandwidth.

Inverse Multiplexing

Inverse multiplexing is the process of taking one signal and distributing it over several B-channels. The inverse multiplexers are hardware devices that sit on either side of the ISDN connection. These devices are capable of picking up and dropping additional B-channels as bandwidth needs change during the call.

Because ISDN is priced per B-channel per second, you can save a significant amount by using an inverse multiplexer. On the other hand, the expense of the device, and the additional complexity it causes your installation, may not be worth the line charge savings.

Each inverse multiplexer has its own method of determining when to pick up or drop a line. Because there is little standardization, it is unlikely that two different inverse multiplexers will be able to talk to each other reliably.

BONDING

Many manufacturers have started adding support for the BONDING protocol to their hardware devices. The BONDING protocol, short for Bandwidth ON Demand Interoperability Group, was developed in an effort to standardize on a single inverse multiplexing design. Many ISDN BRI terminal adapters include BONDING support to allow the end-user to access the full 128Kbps. Because BONDING is a hardware feature, it is fast and efficient, but you need to ensure that both ISDN devices on the connection support it.

MultiLink PPP

The most common method of B-channel aggregation is MultiLink PPP. MLPPP is a software solution that functions very similarly to BONDING. The only major difference is that standard MLPPP connections cannot dynamically allocate additional B-channels during the call. With standard MLPPP, you choose one or two B-channels at the beginning of the call, and you keep that number of B channels open for the entire duration of the call.

A newer standard, developed by ASCEND, fixes this problem. Calls using MLPPP+ can begin with only one B-channel. When a certain percentage of that B-channel is used, the second B-channel is opened up. When the second B-channel is not needed, it is dropped. MLPPP+ is being widely implemented, and is supported now by several manufacturers.

ISDN and the T-1

Once you go beyond the 2B+D BRI, ISDN starts to compete with a T-1. Because both services are digital, and they can both carry the same amount of data, which should you use?

13

ISDN

The answer is a financial one: which will cost less in your application? T-1 lines are priced on a flat-rate monthly scale. If you use a fairly constant amount of bandwidth, you will probably find that a T-1 or fractional T-1 is more cost effective.

If your application has widely variable bandwidth needs, you may want to use ISDN aggregation. With ISDN, you only pay for the B-channels you have open at a given time.

Getting ISDN Data Service

Once you've decided that ISDN is the correct choice for your data networking application, and chosen the appropriate hardware, you need to get ISDN service from your local carrier.

Until very recently, ordering ISDN was a lengthy and painful process. RBOC's had little standardization, and quite frankly, seemed uninterested in providing acceptable ISDN customer service. Today, however, ordering your ISDN line is fairly simple, depending in large part on which RBOC services your locality.

ISDN Carriers

Each RBOC handles the ISDN service in its local area. The following list of ISDN carriers provides you with a list of contact information for these companies.

Ameritech ISDN
National ISDN Hotline: 1-800-832-6328
www.ameritech.com/products/data/teamdata/isdn/index.html

Bell Atlantic ISDN
ISDN Sales & Tech Center: 1-800-570-4736
Residential ISDN Sales & Service Center: 1-800-204-7332
www.bell-atl.com/html/hot/

BellSouth ISDN
ISDN HotLine: 1-800-428-4736
bsonline.bellsouth.net/cgi-bin/WebObjects/ISDN

Cincinnati Bell ISDN
ISDN Service Center: 513-566-3282
www.cinbelltel.com/business/isdninfo.html

NYNEX ISDN
ISDN Hotline: 1-800-438-4736
www.nynex.com/isdn/isdn.html

Pacific Bell ISDN
ISDN Service Center: 1-800-472-4736
24-Hr. ISDN/Availability Hotline: 1-800-995-0346
www.pacbell.com/products/business/fastrak/networking/isdn/info/index.html

SNET ISDN
ISDN Sales & Technical Support Center: 1-800-430-4736
`www.snet.com`

SBC ISDN
ISDN Information: 1-800-792-4736
`www.sbc.com/swbell/shortsub/isdn_services.html`

Stentor ISDN
ISDN "Facts by Fax": 1-800-578-4736
`www.stentor.ca`

U S WEST
ISDN Fax File Server: 1-800-728-4929
`www.uswest.com/isdn/index.html`

> **TIP**
>
> If you don't know which RBOC you are serviced by, or have questions about the level of service in your area, you can refer to the National ISDN Hotline, provided by Bellcore. They can be reached at 1-800-992-ISDN, or by sending e-mail to `isdn@cc.bellcore.com`.

Tariffs

ISDN charges, like all telecommunications fees, are heavily regulated. While these tariffs are different for each RBOC, all RBOCS offer a measured rate. In a measured system, you pay a flat monthly fee, plus a second fee per second. Generally, the fee per second is charged for each B-channel, so if you have established a 128Kbps connection, you will pay twice the tariff of a single B-channel 64Kbps connection. In some areas, there is an option for a monthly flat rate instead of measured. If you are a heavy user, this option may appeal to you.

Tariffs are generally set per capability package (which is a set of features, described later in this section). If you don't need all the features of an advanced capability package, you may be able to save money by choosing a simpler one.

ISDN Features

ISDN voice features rival the most complicated of PBX systems, but it's unlikely that you will need all of those capabilities. The exact features you can get in your area will vary. Table 13.2 details some of the most common features.

Table 13.2. Common ISDN Service Features.

Category	Features
Voice	Caller ID
	Call Hold
	Call Conferencing
	Call Forwarding
	Call Transfer
	Message Waiting Indicator
Data	Caller ID
	Multi-Line Hunt Group
	Basic Business Group

Capability Packages/Ordering Codes

As you can imagine, there are thousands of combinations of the ISDN voice and data features. In an effort to make the ordering process a little less cumbersome, the North American ISDN User's Forum created a standard set of functionality called "capability packages." Now, instead of having to specify every last detail of your connection, you can simply provide the carrier with the correct order code for the feature set you need. A list of the order codes is provided in Table 13.3.

Table 13.3. Capability Package Definitions.

Package Title	Included Services
Capability Package A	Basic D-channel Packet services. No voice capabilities are provided.
Capability Package B	Circuit switched Data on one B-channel. No voice capabilities are provided, basic voice capabilities (no features) are supported.
Capability Package C	Alternate Voice/Circuit Mode Data on one B-channel. Only basic voice capabilities (no features) are supported.
Capability Package D	Voice on one B-channel and basic D-channel Packet services. Only basic voice capabilities (no features) are supported.
Capability Package E	Voice on one B-channel and basic D-channel Packet services. Voice capabilities include Three-way (Conference) Calling, Call Hold, Call Drop, and Call Transfer.

Package Title	Included Services
Capability Package F	Voice on one B-channel and basic D-channel Packet services. Voice capabilities include Three-way (Conference) Calling, Call Hold, Call Drop, and Call Transfer, and uses CACH EKTS.
Capability Package G	Voice on one B-channel and Circuit Mode Data on the other B-channel. Voice capabilities include Three-way (Conference) Calling, Call Hold, Call Drop, and Call Transfer.
Capability Package H	Voice on one B-channel and Circuit Mode Data on the other B-channel. Voice capabilities include Three-way (Conference) Calling, Call Hold, Call Drop, and Call Transfer, and uses CACH EKTS.
Capability Package I	Circuit Mode Data on both B-channels. No Voice or Packet capabilities are provided.
Capability Package J	Alternate Voice/Circuit Mode Data on one B-channel, and Circuit Mode Data on the other B-channel. Only basic voice capabilities (no features) are provided.
Capability Package K	Alternate Voice/Circuit Mode Data on one B-channel, and Circuit Mode Data on the other B-channel. Voice capabilities include Three-way (Conference) Calling, Call Hold, Call Drop, and Call Transfer.
Capability Package L	Alternate Voice/Circuit Mode Data on one B-channel, and Circuit Mode Data on the other B-channel. Voice capabilities include Three-way (Conference) Calling, Call Hold, Call Drop, and Call Transfer, and uses CACH EKTS.
Capability Package M	Alternate Voice/Circuit Mode Data on both B-channels. Only basic voice capabilities (no features) are provided.
Capability Package N	Alternate Voice/Circuit Mode Data on one B-channel, Circuit Mode Data on the other B-channel, and D-channel Packet. Voice capabilities include Three-way (Conference) Calling, Call Hold, Call Drop, and Call Transfer.
Capability Package O	Alternate Voice/Circuit Mode Data on one B-channel, Circuit Mode Data on the other B-channel, and D-channel Packet. Voice capabilities include Three-way (Conference) Calling, Call Hold, Call Drop, and Call Transfer, and uses CACH EKTS.

13

ISDN

continues

Table 13.3. continued

Package Title	Included Services
Capability Package P	Alternate Voice/Circuit Mode Data on both B-channels, and D-channel Packet. Voice capabilities include Three-way (Conference) Calling, Call Hold, Call Drop, and Call Transfer.
Capability Package Q	Alternate Voice/Circuit Mode Data on both B-channels, and D-channel Packet. Voice capabilities include Three-way (Conference) Calling, Call Hold, Call Drop, and Call Transfer, and uses CACH EKTS.
Capability Package R	Circuit-Switched Data on two B-channels. Data capabilities include Calling Number Identification. No voice capabilities are provided.
Capability Package S	Alternate Voice/Circuit-Switched Data on two B-channels. Data and voice capabilities include Calling Number Identification.
Capability Package T	Voice on two B-channels and basic D-channel packet. Only basic voice capabilities are provided, with no features.
Capability Package U	Alternate Voice/Circuit-Switched Data on both B-channels. Voice capabilities include non-EKTS voice features including Flexible Calling, Call Forwarding Variable, Additional Call Offering, and Calling Number Identification (which includes Redirecting Number Delivery). Data capabilities include Calling Number Identification (which includes Redirecting Number Delivery).
Capability Package V	Alternate Voice/Circuit-Switched Data on two B-channels. Voice capabilities include non-EKTS voice features including Flexible Calling, Advanced Call Forwarding (such as Call Forwarding Variable, Call Forwarding Interface Busy, Call Forwarding Don't Answer, and Message Waiting Indicator), Additional Call Offering, and Calling Number Identification (which includes Redirecting Number Delivery). Data capabilities include Calling Number Identification (which includes Redirecting Number Delivery).

> **TIP**
>
> In the manual for your Terminal Equipment, the manufacturer of your equipment may suggest which capability packages will work best with your specific piece of hardware. If not, you can call the vendor or ask your retailer for advice.

The Future of ISDN

ISDN is just now coming into its own, with advances in hardware, wider availability, and stronger consumer acceptance. The next section explains what you can expect from ISDN in the near future.

National ISDN 19XX

Since 1994, Bellcore has accepted enhancements to the National ISDN standards from the switch manufacturers. Enhancement features are included in the NI for a given year (NI-XX) when at least two participating switch suppliers have the capability available in the first quarter of that year. NI-1995, for example, provided more standardization for SPID format and call control.

We will see more standardization on services between the regional telephone companies. Also, ISDN hardware and software will become easier to install and use.

Broadband ISDN

As bandwidth needs rise, the standard aggregation techniques for ISDN will not be adequate. Applications which require large amounts of bandwidth for short periods of time are inefficiently served by today's ISDN implementation.

Enter Broadband ISDN, which does away with the idea of "channels" of ISDN. With B-ISDN, the end-user gets true bandwidth on demand, only paying for the bandwidth used.

B-ISDN supplies bandwidth in excess of 1.544Mbps, or faster than a T-1. B-ISDN will be found in three common forms:

- Frame Relay: Available today in 56Kbps and 1.5Mbps lines, frame relay service is an example of a B-ISDN solution. Frame Relay uses packet switching instead of the circuit switching protocols commonly used in BRIs.

- SMDS: The Switched Multimegabit Digital Service provides packet switched connectivity from 1.5Mbps to 45Mbps.

- ATM: Asynchronous Transfer Mode communication uses small, 53byte "cells" to transfer data at up to 155Mbps and 622Mbps. ATM is commonly held as the future direction of B-ISDN services.

13

ISDN

DSL Systems

The Digital Subscriber Line is the basic underlying technology behind the T-I and the Switched 56 services in common use today. DSL systems come in three basic types:

- HDSL: The High-bit-rate Digital Subscriber Line is the core DSL technology, and provides bandwidth up to 768Kbps in both directions. HDSL is similar in many respects to a T-1: it requires expensive terminating hardware, a special line from the phone company, and travels on two pairs of wire.

- ADSL: Asymmetrical DSL provides up to 6 megabits/second downstream and 576 kilobits/second upstream, all over the existing telephone line. Pricey and not widely available, this technology is looked at as the telephone industry's answer to cable modems.

- VDSL: Still in the definition stages, Very-high-bit-rate DSL is supposed to replace both ADSL and HDSL. Depending on line length, VDSL will support speeds between 13Mbps and 52Mbps.

Industry observers are questioning if the DSL technologies might make ISDN obsolete over the next few years. The answer depends on the speed with which the telephone companies can deploy DSL switches and hardware, and the growth of high-bandwidth consumer markets.

Summary

As a WAN technology, ISDN is becoming more affordable, easier to use, and widespread. A wide range of vendors now make interoperable ISDN equipment, which has driven hardware prices down. Most local carriers are offering both residential and office ISDN at prices that make the technology a viable competitor for T-1, 56K, and even POTS connectivity.

The metered nature of ISDN and the wide variety of equipment now available makes it best suited for WAN applications that

- require a widely variable amount of bandwidth
- expect fast growth in bandwidth needs, or
- have a mixture of analog and digital requirements.

After reading this chapter, and the other chapters in this book, you should be able to determine if ISDN is the right WAN technology for you.

xDSL

by Louis Masters

IN THIS CHAPTER

CHAPTER 14

This chapter introduces Digital Subscriber Line, or DSL, along with a brief history and background information on why is was invented. It explains the many derivatives of DSL (ADSL, SDSL, HDSL, VDSL), their advantages and disadvantages, and possible uses and capabilities. Several tables are provided to summarize speed/distance relationships and specific technological advantages. The chapter ends with a DSL cross reference table, contact information, and a few Internet resources.

Introduction to xDSL Technology

Current copper telephone lines carry voice-grade communications at speeds up to 28.8Kbps (53.3Kbps with software help). These lines use the existing telephone network and require no additional hardware or software to access almost any existing network location. This is copper's main advantage: instantaneous access to anywhere that the telephone network is. But, this is also a disadvantage: the entire network is wired for yesterday's speeds.

In a perfect environment, copper speeds would be limited only by the cable attenuation. But, in the existing telephone network, the bandwidth is largely limited by the filters in the network and the networks themselves. The upgrade of existing twisted copper wires would serve to enhance the entire network and allow for speeds virtually unheard of several years ago. But, the costs associated with this are extreme; another method would be needed.

This method would have to use existing cables and give notably increased performance. Bellcore, the research entity of several Bell operating companies, created the first Digital Subscriber technology and coined the term DSL (Digital Subscriber Line). Bellcore had two main reasons for creating this technology: increased performance and low cost. They aimed for a bandwidth of at least 2Mbps, but over the current copper network. This would make it both an easy and quick installation, but also a cheap alternative to other network upgrades.

The main reason DSL was invented was to provide high-speed digital access to local corporate and residential customers. DSL's main concept is to use older copper cables as high-speed digital pipelines. It does this entirely with electronics and software at each endpoint. DSL interfaces are installed at endpoints on the network, while the existing cabling is left untouched.

In a nutshell, DSL compensates for the copper wire's imperfections. As mentioned previously, attenuation by the cable is a major impedance to network bandwidth. DSL uses software and electronics to "fix" the problems with copper wire, creating an overall higher bandwidth data pipe.

What does DSL give us?

- An almost instantaneous network upgrade. DSL uses the existing copper network to give a marked increase in efficiency.
- A cheaper alternative to fiber or coaxial cable.
- DSL's algorithms make the data transmission more dependable.

DSL provides for several more upgrades to the existing network infrastructure, including increased distances, decreased installation time, immunity to normal cable problems, and the like.

DSL can be used in a variety of environments. The local phone companies could use it for delivering video, audio, and increased bandwidth to both local residential and business customers. Businesses could also use it in a multiple building or even multiple floor setting, to provide increased network bandwidth or allow for newer interoffice network technologies (video on demand, conferencing, and more). The possibilities for this cheap network upgrade are as endless as the networks it can be applied to.

The Different Flavors of DSL

Several acronyms/technologies exist when speaking of the Digital Subscriber Line: DSL, SDSL, ADSL, HDSL, VDSL, VADSL, and BDSL. Table 14.1 summarizes the acronyms and their meanings. The two most common are ADSL and VDSL.

Table 14.1. DSL acronym table.

Type	Definition
DSL	Digital Subscriber Line (generic)
SDSL	Single line/Symmetric Digital Subscriber Line
ADSL	Asymmetric Digital Subscriber Line
HDSL	High bit (data) rate Digital Subscriber Line
VDSL	Very high data rate Digital Subscriber Line
VADSL	Very high speed Digital Subscriber Line (another term for VDSL)

What Is ADSL?

ADSL, or Asymmetric Digital Subscriber Line, is an asymmetric version of DSL. The speed of this technology for use over existing mediums (phone lines) is astounding: up to 8.448Mbps to the customer and up to 800Kbps to the "network" (see Figure 14.1).

FIGURE 14.1.

A basic ADSL.

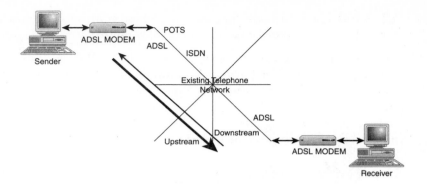

The overall downstream rate depends on, among other things, the distance covered, the size of the wire, and interference. Upstream speeds range from 16Kbps to 64Kbps to 640Kbps. Table 14.2 gives the standard downstream speeds at certain distances.

Table 14.2. ADSL speed/distance.

Speed (feet)	Distance (Mbps)
<=9000	8.448
>9000 to <= 12000	6.312
>12000 to <= 16000	2.048
>16000 to <= 18000	1.544

ADSL was designed for two major functions: high speed data communications and interactive video. Data communication functions can be Internet access, corporate telecommuting, or other specialized network applications. Interactive video covers things such as video on demand, movies, games, or any other application that requires high-speed networked video. Presently, ADSL only supports interfaces to T-1/E-1; future enhancements are planned for ADSL to the desktop.

The biggest strength in ADSL lies in the fact that it uses existing telephone lines over which to communicate. This means that more than 700 million (existing) phone customers are already cabled for ADSL and require little or no upgrade. Technologies such as ISDN or cable modems can require expensive hardware and software upgrades in both the network and in the client site. But, ADSL is still in testing around most of the world, with an anticipated niche release slated for late 1997. This release will be available mainly for Internet access and other packet-based communication applications.

What Are CAP and DMT?

CAP and DMT are the two prevalent ADSL modulation systems out today. CAP was engineered by AT&T Paradyne, and DMT was developed by Amati Communications Corporation. The difference between the two is the way they send data down the pipe. Also, ANSI standard T1.413 is based on DMT.

Carrierless Amplitude/Phase Modulation CAP

Carrierless amplitude/phase modulation CAP is a proprietary modulation (line code) of AT&T Paradyne. Incoming data modulates a single carrier channel that is then sent down a telephone line. The carrier is suppressed before transmission and reconstructed at the receiving end.

Discrete Multi-Tone

It separates incoming data into many sub-carrier channels. Each channel is measured for quality, and then the channel is assigned a certain number of bits based on quality of the channel. DMT creates these channels using the technique of Discrete Fast-Fourier Transform.

DMT uses a mechanism we are familiar with to create a modem connection. When two DMT modems connect, they try the highest speed possible. Depending on line noise and attenuation, the modems will successfully connect at the highest rate or decrease the rate until a satisfactory connection speed can be reached.

How ADSL Works

ADSL uses its own proprietary modem hardware to connect each end of an existing twisted-pair connection. It creates a three-channel pipe (see Figure 14.2).

FIGURE 14.2.
An ADSL three-channel pipe.

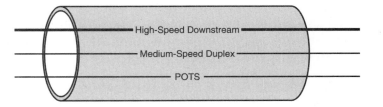

High-Speed Downstream
Medium-Speed Duplex
POTS

14

xDSL

This pipe consists of one high-speed downstream channel (to the client), one medium-speed duplex channel, and one Plain Old Telephone Service (POTS) channel (4KHz) to ensure POTS, even if ADSL fails. Both the high-speed and medium-speed channels can be multiplexed to create multiple lower-rate pipes. Consult Table 14.3 for more speed information.

Table 14.3. ADSL average, minimum, and maximum speed.

Channel	Average	Minimum	Maximum
High-speed downstream	6Mbps	1.5Mbps	9Mbps
Medium-speed duplex	64Kbps	16Kbps	640Kbps

Again, line speed is also affected by the length of the physical pipeline (as seen in Table 14.3), the thickness of the wire, and cross-coupled interference, just to name a few. The numbers in the Table 14.3 are estimates that can be used as a simple reference.

Technical ADSL

During the past several years, there have been numerous advances in telephone hardware technologies that permit ADSL to work. Yet, ADSL uses a very simple method to achieve its amazing speed results: squeezing. It uses very advanced DSP and algorithms to squeeze as much information as possible through the existing twisted-pair telephone lines.

ADSL creates a multiple-channel telephone line in one of two ways. It either uses Frequency Division Multiplexing (FDM) or echo cancellation. FDM uses one band of downstream data and one band of upstream data. It splits the downstream path by using a technique called *time division multiplexing*. The upstream pipe is also split into multiple low-speed channels. Echo cancellation overlaps the downstream pipe with the upstream and separates them by means of local echo cancellation (such as the V.34 line specification). Echo cancellation, while being more efficient, suffers from increased complexity and higher costs.

ADSL multiplexes the downstream, duplex, and maintenance channels into blocks; attaches an error code to that block; and sends the data. The receiver then corrects errors up to the limit implied by the code and the block length. Typically, 20ms of data is buffered, allowing for suitable error correction over ADSL's high-speed pipe. Initial tests indicate that ADSL modems can tolerate error rates suitable for MPEG2 and several other digital video schemes.

What Standards Are in Place for ADSL?

The American National Standards Institute (ANSI) has an approved ADSL standard with rates up to 6.1Mbps. This is denoted as ANSI Standard T1.413. The European Technical Standards Institute (ETSI) added an Annex to T1.413 that describes the European requirements. Issue II, now under study by T1E1.4, will expand the standard to include a multiplexed interface at the premise end, protocols for configuration and network management, and other improvements.

ADSL is a recognized physical layer transmission protocol by both the ATM forum and DAVIC.

What Is the Future of ADSL, Technically Speaking?

What ADSL will become may not be radically different from what it is today. ADSL is currently implemented in two ways: CAP and DMT, the latter being the standard. Although CAP is not the standard, it was developed by AT&T Paradyne and has been widely implemented by the telecommunications industry. It is difficult to say with any certainty what will happen to ADSL. However, we do know that there is a bottleneck that the vendors and telephone companies need to overcome to develop networks that can be used quickly today, and still used tomorrow.

What Is VDSL?

Simply put, VDSL is a very fast version of ADSL. With VDSL, the maximum downstream rate for short lengths of cable can reach almost 55Mbps (see Table 14.4). Upstream rates can reach speeds of up to 2.3Mbps (future projections reach 19.2Mbps or higher). Both the upstream and downstream data channels can be separated (by frequency) and overlaid on existing POTS or ISDN services, making VDSL a very appetizing solution to high-speed, cheap networking. Later upgrades may need to switch to echo cancellation or some other method to manage the pipeline. Like ADSL, VDSL will be used mainly for real-time video transmissions and high-speed data access.

Table 14.4. VDSL speed/distance (estimates).

Speed (Feet)	Distance (Mbps)
>1000	51.84
>1000 to <= 3000	25.82
>3000 to <= 4500	12.96

Technical VDSL

Architecturally, VDSL is like a high-speed ADSL. VDSL uses both upstream and downstream multiplexing to achieve the very fast transfer rates. It also uses inline error correcting to compensate for line noise and other interference. VDSL is meant for shorter reaches of line, with far less transmission restrictions (see Figure 14.3).

Figure 14.3.
A basic VDSL.

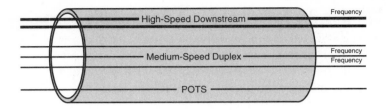

To date, four line codes have been proposed for VDSL: CAP, DMT (both are discussed in the section "What Is ADSL?"), DWMT, and SLC.

What Is DWMT?

DWMT, or Discrete Wavelet Multitone, is a multiple carrier modulation system that uses wavelet transforms for the individual carriers.

What Is SLC?

SLC, or Simple Line Code, is a version of baseband signaling that filters the base band and restores it on the receiver.

VDSL separates its channels using frequency division multiplexing. In the future, if VDSL supports symmetric data rates, this may have to change to echo cancellation. The normal configuration is to have the downstream channel above the upstream, but the DAVIC specification reverses this to enable the distribution of VDSL signals over coaxial cable.

Forward error control is another characteristic of VDSL. Very similar to ADSL (T1.413), it uses a form of Reed Solomon encoding coupled with interleaving to correct for line noise.

The Current Condition of VDSL

VDSL is still in the embryonic stage. It has yet to be tested over long distances at all of its data rates. Most data about line characteristics are speculative at best, and this may be detrimental to VDSL performance on the whole. Also, VDSL signals are in the range of amateur radio and may be impacted severely by this over both long and short line reaches. Equipment costs at each point (customer and premises) may also be substantial and interfere with a widespread rollout.

ADSL, unlike VDSL, has the advantage of having a better established product base. A strategy of coupling VDSL with ADSL might be wiser—use ADSL for the longer stretches and a combination of ADSL and VDSL for the short stretches of pipeline. Both ADSL and VDSL offer more "pipe for the buck" and may better serve to meet the future's data needs today.

What Is HDSL?

HDSL is mainly aimed at a better and more efficient way of transmitting T-1/E-1 over traditional copper lines (using no repeaters and being more efficient). While ADSL uses one wire to transmit both upstream and downstream, HDSL implements a second wire to transmit data in both directions (see Figure 14.4). HDSL transmits at speeds of 1.544Mbps to more than 2Mbps. Typical applications inlcude, but are not limited to, Internet service providers, private networks, PBX networks, and more.

FIGURE 14.4.
A basic HDSL.

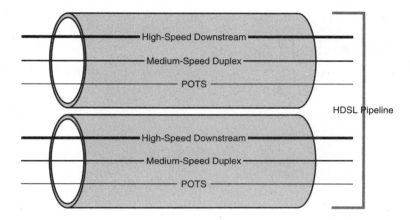

What Is SDSL?

SDSL is a single line version of HDSL. It is, however, limited to shorter distances, but at speeds up to 6Mbps (in the future). Current speeds range from 160Kbps to 400Kbps to 2.048Mbps at distances up to 9,000 feet. Common applications are users with limited access to only a single communication line and who require only symmetric access.

DSL Cross Reference Table

Table 14.4 shows the more common DSL technologies, their standard mode of operation, and the relative speeds of each.

Table 14.4. DSL cross reference.

Name	Description	Rate	Mode
DSL	Digital Subscriber Line	192Kbps	Duplex
HDSL	High Data/Bit Rate Digital Subscriber Line	1.544Mbps 2.048Mbps	Duplex Duplex
SDSL	Single Data Line Digital Subscriber Line	1.544Mbps 2.048Mbps	Duplex Duplex
ADSL	Asymmetric Digital Subscriber Line	1.5 to 9Mbps 16 to 640Kbps	Down Up
VDSL	Very High Data Rate Digital Subscriber Line	13 to 52Mbps 1.5 to 2.3Mbps	Down Up

14

xDSL

Where to Find Information on ADSL?

The following sections provide a list of ADSL resources on the Web. Keep in mind that xDSL as a technology is growing in popularity every day. Therfore this list is but a sampling of some of the companies and links involved with xDSL development.

ADSL Involved Companies

For more information on xDSL products, contact the following companies:

3M	ADC Telecommunications
Advanced Micro Devices	AG Communication Systems
Alcatel Telecom	Amati
Ameritech	Analog Devices
Aptis Communications	Atlantech Technologies
Aware	BellSouth Telecommunications
British Telecom	Broadcom Corporation
Burr-Brown Ltd.	Cabletron Systems
Cellware GmbH	Cincinnati Bell
Compaq Computer	Digital Technology MA
DSC Communications	DSL Networks
ECI Telecom	EPL Ltd.
Ericsson	Fluke Corporation
Global Village Communication	GlopeSpan Technologies
Harris Semiconductor	Hi/fn
Integrated Device Technology	Integrated Network Systems
Integrated Technology Express	Intel
Interphase	Kingston Communications
Metalink	Motorola Semiconductor
NEC Australia	NEC Electronics
Orckit Communications	Paradyne
Performance Telecom	Promatory Communications
Promptus Communications	RNS
Rockwell Semiconductor Systems	SGS-Thomson Microelectronics
SpellCaster Telecommunications	Sprint

Telecom Finland	Teltrend
TERACOM Svensk Rundradio AB	TTC
U.S. Robotics	US West
Westell Inc.	Westell INternational

A Few ADSL Internet Resources

The following is a sampling of several of the best Web sites for xDSL information. Please be aware that most are companies involved in not only promoting the technology, but also in selling it. For more links, simply use your favorite search engine. New sites are being added all the time.

```
http://www.adsl.com/

http://www.mot.com/SPS/MCTG/MDAD/adsl/index.html

http://poseidon.aware.com/product_info/adsl

http://www.zdnet.com/intweek/print/960408/infra/doc5.html

http://www.gte.com/Adsl/

http://www.westell.com/

http://www.telechoice.com/

http://www.pairgain.com/
```

Summary

This chapter should have given you a thorough introduction into the realm of DSL. You should be able to differentiate between the different styles of DSL, which to use for specific instances, and how to implement them in a network. The tables provided can and should be used for a reference into DSL.

DSL is a relatively young technology that is based on a relatively old infrastructure. Yet, this should not be looked upon as only a hindrance. DSL can be implemented with relatively lower startup costs and in a very short period of time. Smaller companies or organizations that do not wish to spend a great deal of money, or don't have the time to implement a full-scale network redesign (both hardware and software), should look to DSL as a viable solution.

Switched 56Kbps

*by Arthur Cooper
and David Welk*

IN THIS CHAPTER

Switched 56 is another neat little name used to denote the use of 56Kbps circuits as a Wide Area Net (WAN) technology or strategy. It is really just a souped-up version of plain old telephone system (POTS) service. The main differences between POTS service and switched 56 service are the speeds that can be obtained. Most POTS circuits are still only capable of providing between 28.8Kbps and 33.6Kbps. Granted, there are new technology modems such as USR's X2 technology modem that claim to provide 56Kbps on a standard POTS line, but the fact remains, the speed of 56Kbps is not a guaranteed thing. If the POTS system in your area still has old copper wire or carrier facilities, you may not obtain the higher speeds capable with these types of modems. For that reason, it is sometimes necessary for network managers to avoid the use of POTS lines and make the jump to a switched line capable of providing a clean, consistent rate of 56Kbps. When this occurs, we are then entering the world of switched 56 technology.

Why Select Switched 56?

What exactly is switched 56 technology? Is it just an alternative leased line service or is it more? Switched 56 *service* is a digitally switched or "dial-up" technology that has the capacity to provide a single channel for dependable data connectivity. This single channel has a clock speed of 56,000 bits per second, which means that theoretically, it can pass about two pages of documentation per second.

To get an idea of where switched 56 service fits in the big picture of carrier speeds and services, let's look at a brief description of T-1 service and where switched 56 fits into the picture.

A T-1 circuit is divided into 24 channels of 64Kbps. Control signaling typically requires the isolation of the upper 8K bits of the channel from the data transport section of the bandwidth. Hence, you are left with 56Kbps of useable data on each channel. This 56Kbps of useable data is typically used on a per channel basis to move data from one point to another. Now remember, a T-1 circuit refers to a carrier mechanism. In other words, there does not necessarily have to be a switch or switching device associated with T-1 carrier systems. Many times, there may be Point-to-Point T-1 circuits used, and it is not necessary that any switching be performed on the terminating ends of these carrier circuits. It is when the individual channels are pulled out of a T-1 and route these signals to other channels in another T-1, or over to a user location, that some type of switching must be performed. When this 56Kbps of data has been *switched* out of a T-1 and is sent to a specific user location, the resulting circuit is referred to as a switched 56 circuit. Some people refer to the process of allocating the bandwidth of a T-1 channel as *dropping-and-inserting*. When a 56Kbps circuit is *dropped* into a customer or user location and the circuit is terminated, that customer or user must be provided with a switched 56 circuit. The term *switched* means that the other end of the 56Kbps circuit will generally ride a T-1 circuit into the *cloud* of the Public Switched Telephone Network (PSTN). Within the PSTN, the individual switched 56 circuits can be routed or switched to any other termination point connected to the PSTN.

NOTE

The term *cloud* is a general term that network people will sometimes use to refer to the entire network. The network would of course be comprised of network switches, wire, carrier systems, and anything else needed to move signals from one place to another.

Switched 56 access lines were some of the original digital circuits installed by the telecommunication carriers. The low cost of switched 56 relative to digital leased lines makes it ideal even today for supporting sporadic high-speed applications that are extending into new or existing locations. The fast data transmission capabilities and low error rates, relative to analog dial-up, which is just now gaining this quantity of throughput, make switched 56 access an ideal solution for today's wide area environments.

A savvy network manager must know when it is right to choose this solution versus direct T-1 lines or other methods of WAN interconnectivity. Cost is always a factor when deciding on a specific technology, and switched 56 is a very cost-effective solution. Because the connections are only made when actual data must be transmitted, this is a cost-effective means of transferring data. Further, because switched 56 has been around a lot longer than other newer technologies, such as frame relay or ATM, the costs for terminating equipment, circuit turn/up and installation fees, and the monthly access charges are much lower for switched 56.

If T-1 lines are used to interconnect sites, there will be high flat-rate charges each month, whether any data is transmitted over the lines or not. With a switched 56 solution, the costs for termination equipment are cheaper than those of T-1 terminating equipment. Also, because it is an on-demand connection, there is less wasted bandwidth than there would be if you were using T-1 connectivity. There are many vendors who are doing on-demand switched frame relay connectivity over T-1 circuits, but once again the cost for this type of service far exceeds the cost of a switched 56 connection.

Although very widespread, especially in populous areas, switched 56 circuits are quickly becoming outdated with the acceptance and propagation of ISDN. The type of connectivity provided by a switched 56 service is ISDN-compatible and versatile, with the ability to carry switched digital signals such as video, voice, and data. The main difference between switched 56 technology and ISDN technology is the dependence of ISDN on D-channel signaling. This difference creates the absolute limitation of 56Kbps in switched 56 as opposed to ISDN, which is capable of utilizing the entire channel of 64Kbps. The technical explanation for the limitation of switched 56 service is that the communication control signaling protocol uses only 7 of the 8 frame bits that are available in a 64Kbps channel. See Figure 15.1 for an illustration of a frame.

ISDN services tend to have higher capabilities as far as aggregating circuits when compared to switched 56. Aggregating circuits or *inverse multiplexing* is a technology that consolidates various telecommunications circuits for extremely high-speed applications such as video-conferencing or bulk data transfers. One example might be CAD/CAM/CAE (high-end drafting) applications. A CAD system dials through the telco cloud, as shown in Figure 15.2.

FIGURE 15.1.
A graphical display of the signaling bits that compose character framing.

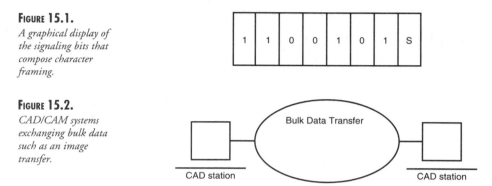

FIGURE 15.2.
CAD/CAM systems exchanging bulk data such as an image transfer.

One of the uses of inverse multiplexing technology can even be to aggregate both ISDN services and switched 56 services to create a single communication link. This is an excellent way of utilizing existing equipment and services in conjunction with the new capabilities and equipment requirements of ISDN.

What Is the Essence of Switched 56?

Information that does not require data speeds greater than 56Kbps through the enterprise network can utilize a switched 56 service. The ability of the carrier's equipment to support leased digital lines and provide dial-up capable digital lines requires extra processing power. This additional processing feature, added to CSU/DSUs for support of switched 56 dial service, tends to make the equipment more expensive.

NOTE

A CSU/DSU is an acronym that was created by combining the two terms *Channel Service Unit* (CSU) and *Data Service Unit* (DSU). A channel service unit is a device that can take the quasi-analog signal coming in on a data circuit and derive intelligence from it that will be passed to the user. Likewise, in the opposite direction, the data coming from the user is converted into a quasi-analog signal by the channel service unit in order to enable it to be transmitted out on the data circuit. The data service unit is between the channel service unit and the user. This unit provides for things such as proper termination specifications, data isolation, and proper mechanical connection specifications. In other words, the data service unit would be the actual physical connection between a user and the data circuit's channel service unit. In the past ten years, these two devices have been combined into one small appliance that looks similar to a modem. This new combined channel service unit and data service unit is almost always referred to as a CSU/DSU. Old-timers will sometimes call them a CSU, but in most cases there is a DSU attached as well.

Telecommunications equipment that provides solutions used in a backup and restoration situation or in a dial-on-demand situation usually deploys switched 56 circuits and equipment. As a wide area technology with most of the pricing based on usage, switched 56 service is also a viable solution for digital audio and video desktop-conferencing applications. In fact, for many years this was the only technology available for wide area video conferencing. Most systems utilize one channel for transmitting data and one channel for receiving data (see Figure 15.3).

FIGURE 15.3.
Audio and video conferencing utilizing switched 56 for connectivity.

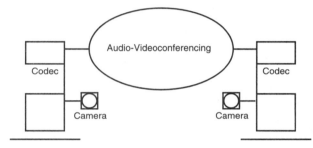

Other sporadic high-speed applications, such as image transfer and viewing, datafax transfers, and disaster recovery situations, require the accommodation of varying network traffic patterns.

Switched 56 service handles these requirements adequately.

CAUTION

Determine the availability and interoperability of technologies before settling on any disaster recovery or dial-on-demand applications. Most of the regional Bell operating companies interoperate well, but there are differences going across national borders such as into Canada.

What Should You Expect from the Telcos?

After the application processing, the binary information traverses the enterprise network through the telco-provided, wide area "cloud." It is by way of these digital service access points, sometimes called *switch points*, that information flows through digital facilities from end to end.

This quality of service ensures the highest level of data accuracy and throughput that most corporate networks, as well as Internet access, require. In looking at the following five carriers, which provide a good cross section of capabilities and operating domains, you can start to get a feel for their level of deployment of switched 56 technology. You can also start to understand the level of ISDN implementations and how that service offering is affecting the market for switched 56 services.

Services Range

Overall, a dramatic price drop has occurred in switched 56 service offerings during the last two years. ISDN technology is growing in popularity, but a new analog technology that is promising 56Kbps throughput on file downloads is gaining acceptance.

AT&T

Switched 56 service is part of AT&T's ACCUNET Global Switched Digital Services (GSDS) service offering. AT&T is the largest domestic long-distance carrier and a formidable competitor in the global arena. The model 4ESSTM nodal switching machines offer a four-wire configuration that uses the well-known 700 56X XXXX number for switched 56 addressing. AT&T also uses a standard dialing capability known as RS-366 and a *terminal interface unit*, which converts V.35 signaling to the DDLC format for digital data. The global network makes use of fiber optic cabling and satellite technology to connect distant "phone calls." The installation of a Northern Telecomm (Nortel) data unit at the customer's premises is all that is required to support two-wire switched 56. Using audio and video bridges allows AT&T to offer Desktop Visual Collaborative Conferencing. Additionally, using multiport audio bridging enables audio broadcast conferencing.

Table 15.1 is compiled from information on AT&T's Web page (www.ATT.com).

Table 15.1. The switched 56 naming conventions of various telcos.

Company	Naming Convention
Ameritech	PGSDS
Bell Atlantic	Switched 56
Bell South	Accupulse 56
GTE	Switched Data
Nynex	Switchway 56
Pacific Bell	CenPath or Centrex
Southwest Bell	MicroLink 1
US West	Switchnet 56

Pacific Bell

After completing searches of various telcos on the Web, I was only able to find that California-based telco, Pacific Bell, posted the most straightforward pricing information. Pacific Bell's claim, "to have switched 56 capabilities available to 90% of their business and residential customers," is impressive. Pacific Bell also touts the flexibility of serving two-wire and four-wire configurations, which "enables installation to locations that are farther in distance from the Central Office."

> **NOTE**
>
> The preceding quotations are from Pacific Bell's WWW page:
>
> www.pacbell.com
>
> The following pricing is outdated and almost certainly will have been changed:
>
> SDS 56 = $500 one time installation (waived if service contracted for two years) + $45 per month + usage (voice rates with time-of-day discounts)
>
> (800)PAC-BELL

Ameritech

Ameritech serves seven major metropolitan areas and has advertised very limited switched 56 capabilities. Pushing to implement ISDN throughout their five-state region has been an ongoing effort.

> **NOTE**
>
> The URL for Ameritech's Web page is
>
> www.ameritech.com

MCI

MCI provides Digital Gateway T-1 service and bases their pricing on usage. As an interexchange carrier (IXC), MCI requires access from the local exchange carrier (LEC) for the DDS loop and switched digital access. Their network uses 64Kb bandwidth and rate adaptation to conform to switched 56 standards.

> **NOTE**
>
> MCI's Web page can be found at
>
> www.mci.com

Sprint

The SprintNet Global Data Network provides Switched Data Services (SDS).

> **NOTE**
>
> Sprint's Web page is located at
>
> `www.sprint.com`

Summary

Switched 56 is an important WAN technology. Because the traffic of a network is often localized on a Local Area Network (LAN), it is not necessary to pass data from one LAN location to another. When it does become necessary to pass data from one location to another, the amount of data is usually sporadic and relatively small. If the amount of data to be passed is not a particularly large amount, it makes no sense for a network manager to purchase and maintain leased connections between the LANs, thus comprising the entire network.

When this is the case, the network manager must come up with a wide area networking topology that will be cost-effective and able to handle the sporadic data needs of the network. For some networks, this may mean only a few POTS lines would be needed between network LANs. However, when a POTS line alone will not suffice, switched 56 is the technology of choice. It will handle a fairly large amount of data quickly and keep costs down, because the only time the connection will be up is when it is actually needed.

The switched 56 line is the best dial-up data circuit available today. ISDN lines, it may be argued, can handle higher bandwidths than switched 56, but the cost of ISDN has not come down to match the cheaper rates available on switched 56 circuits in most parts of the United States. There is also an abundance of equipment that will readily interface with switched 56 circuits. ISDN requires costly modems and/or interface equipment. When the cost of doing long-range ISDN comes down, then, and only then, will switched 56 circuits disappear. Until that time, any network manager with sporadic, smaller amounts of inter-LAN data traffic should always consider switched 56 when deciding on a WAN topology for the network.

T-1 and Fractional T-1

by Mike Starkenburg

IN THIS CHAPTER

T-1, fractional T-1, and T-3 services are high bandwidth digital data transmission systems originally designed for carrying voice calls between telephone company central offices. Today, the T-carrier system is used for transfer of voice, data, and video signals in business applications of all sizes.

T-1 lines can connect distributed offices or a corporate office to the Internet, at speeds ranging from 1.5Mbps up to 44Mbps.

Brief History of The T-Carrier

When the telephone system was originally designed, it was built on the premise that a large percentage of calls would be handled locally. Within several thousand feet of every subscriber, there were central offices that handled the connections of calls. Often, the originating party and receiving party were both serviced by the same central office, so the call could be switched locally.

If the two parties were not served by the same central office, the phone company handled the connection between two of their offices. These connections between offices were called *inter-office trunks (IOT)*.

Over time, call patterns became more diverse; people were using the system to make calls farther and farther away. As the number of long distance calls went up, it increased the demand for IOT connections.

The N-Carrier and L-Carrier Systems

The original IOT connections were made over an analog system called the *N-carrier*. The N-carrier system used an analog device that multiplexed calls, allowing 12 voice calls to share the same physical wire. Unfortunately, the system quickly outgrew this capacity. To avoid running more expensive wire between central offices, the phone company looked for ways to increase the number of calls it could squeeze into existing wire.

The *L-carrier system*, which was used in the late 1960s, had a much higher capacity. Using coaxial cable, Bell was able to carry up to 6,000 calls on one wire pair. To run coaxial cable long distances, however, the phone companies had to place amplifiers periodically along the line. These amplifiers were expensive, unreliable, and produced poor quality calls. In addition, running coaxial cable was more difficult and expensive than running the simple copper wire used by the N-carrier. In the early 1970s, the phone companies began using digital systems to solve these problems and increase capacity even further.

The T-Carrier System

The *T-carrier system* was the first widely deployed digital transmission system. The phone companies placed hardware in the central offices that converted the analog voice signal to a digital bit stream. This bit stream could easily be multiplexed onto a single carrier. Using the T-1 version of the T-carrier, 24 calls could be carried on two pairs of inexpensive copper wire. The quality of the digital signal did not degrade over long distances, and the copper wire could use simpler amplification hardware. Over time, the phone companies deployed higher capacity versions of the T-carrier system, such as T-3, to meet increasing demand.

Originally, the T-carrier was used only as an IOT. End-user services were still available only in analog format. In the mid 1970s, the phone companies reluctantly began rolling out T-1 service to large businesses. The primary use of this was for businesses with large call centers and 800 numbers. Digital service was expensive and time-consuming to install, because the line needed to be specially conditioned by the phone company.

> **NOTE**
>
> Another type of digital line was made available to the public before the T-carrier system. Digital Data Service (DDS) was available for data transfer of up to 56Kbps. Because a T-1 was only 4 to 8 times more expensive than DDS but carried over 24 times the bandwidth, it quickly became the data service of choice for businesses.

Today, T-carrier service is affordable and widely available. The rise of the Internet and the growth of e-mail as a communications medium has made the T-1 a household word.

How the T-Carrier Lines Work

The T-carrier system is a bipolar, framed format, full-duplex, channel-based digital communications system. In this section, we'll explain how those technologies work together to produce a reliable digital connection.

Line Coding

A digital signal is made up of ones and zeros. In the T-carrier system, these ones and zeros are represented by changes in voltage along the wire. In the simplest implementation of this, you can imagine that there would be a positive voltage for every one, and no voltage at all for every zero. The problem with this kind of encoding (called *unipolar*) is that there is no "return to zero" between positive pulses. Without some sort of "return to zero," the signal can lose track of how many positive "one" pulses occurred, called loss of synchronization. Figure 16.1 shows an example of a unipolar signal.

FIGURE 16.1.

An example of unipolar line coding.

Bipolar Line Coding

To counter this, the T-carrier system uses a process called *alternate mark inversion (AMI)* or *bipolar encoding*. As Figure 16.2 shows, bipolar encoding still uses no voltage to represent a digital zero, but uses alternative positive and negative voltages to represent digital ones. This system adds redundancy to the timing of the circuit.

FIGURE 16.2.

An example of bipolar line coding.

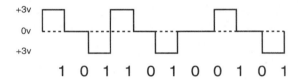

Ones Density

The only remaining danger with the AMI system is that a large number of sequential zeros will cause a loss of synchronization. The ones density rule states that no more that 15 zeros could be transmitted consecutively. Obviously, in a random bit stream, it is easy to imagine that there would be more that 15 zeros in a row.

Originally, the phone companies used a technique called *pulse stuffing* where every eighth bit was taken out of the signal and forced to be a pulse. This reduced the bandwidth of the channel from 64Kbps to 56Kbps.

To get back the use of that additional bandwidth, the pulse stuffing method of synchronization was replaced by the bipolar 8 zero substitution (B8ZS) method. Using this method, the hardware at either end of the signal listens for eight consecutive zeros in the signal. When it finds them, it replaces the entire 8-bit word with a fictional word.

> **NOTE**
>
> A T-3, because it is so much faster, needs more frequent synchronization than a T-1. The B8ZS system is far too slow. A T-3 uses a B3ZS system, which works the same as B8ZS but modifies any group of three zeros instead of eight.

Bipolar Violations

To differentiate between a real word and a fictional one, the hardware creates a bipolar violation. In the AMI system, every consecutive "one" pulse alternates between positive and negative voltage. By sending two consecutive positive pulses, the system signals that there is a fictional word coming. Figure 16.3 shows an example of a bipolar violation.

FIGURE 16.3.

An example of bipolar violation.

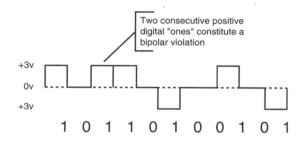

Framing

To assist in synchronizing the devices on the T-carrier line, the phone companies developed a framing system. The early frame standards—called D1, D2, and D3—were used only for analog data and voice over a T-1. Today, there are two primary framing standards for the T-1 circuit, called D4 and extended superframe (ESF). The T-3 circuit uses another protocol called M13.

T-1 Framing

In Figure 16.4, you can see an example of the D4 framing format. One framing bit prefixes 24 bytes of data, each from one of the 24 channels in a T-1. The framing bit follows a special 12-bit pattern, called the *frame alignment signal*. Every 12 frames, the signal repeats, allowing the hardware on either side of the connection to signal changes in line status. This group of 12 D4 frames is called a *superframe*.

> **NOTE**
>
> Why is a T-1 a 1.544Mbps connection if 24 64Kbps channels totals 1.536Mbps? D4 framing adds one bit for every 192 data bits, so it adds 8Kbps to the total T-1 line.

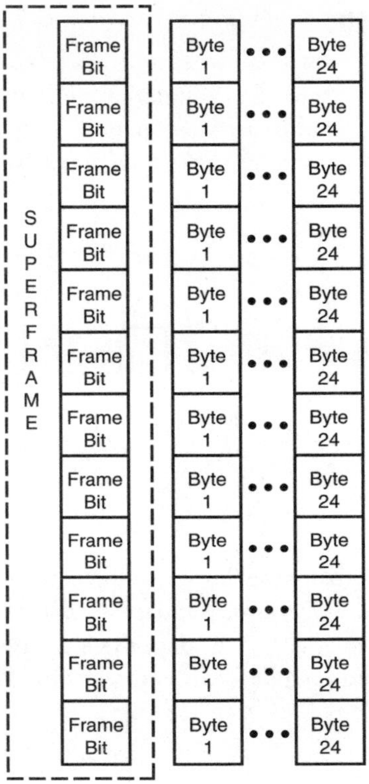

FIGURE 16.4.

The D-4 Framing Format.

Extended Superframe

In the early 1980s, AT&T decided that it could make better use of the 8Kbps frame overhead. By extending the superframe from 12 frames to 24, AT&T found that it could provide sufficient synchronization in only six of the 24 framing bits. Six of the bits were used for error correction, and the remaining 12 were used for network monitoring. Figure 16.5 shows the extended superframe format.

T-3 Framing

A T-3 uses a framing system called M13. Because the T-3 is much faster than a T-1, its frames are much larger. The M13 frame uses a 4,760-bit frame, compared to a 193-bit D4 frame. Of this, 56 bits are used for frame alignment, error correction, and network monitoring.

FIGURE 16.5.
The ESF Frame.

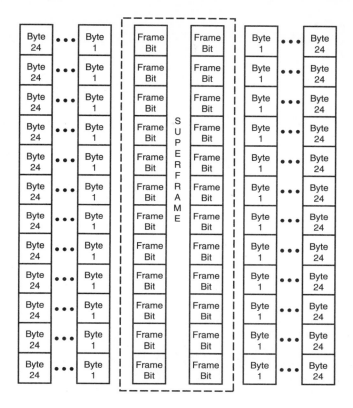

Multiplexing

As the T-1 became available commercially, a large number of companies began producing hardware to maximize the benefits of the carrier system. Because the T-1 is made up of 24 separate channels, configuration of the system is very flexible. Voice, data, video, and other signals can all share the same T-carrier. Allowing all these signals to use the same transmission carrier is called *multiplexing*.

A T-1 multiplexer can simply manage the data input sources, or it can combine channels for high bandwidth applications. Today, for example, it is common for the entire T-1 to be used for a single 1.536Mbps data application.

Figure 16.6 shows a typical multiplexer installation with a T-1. Note that the analog-to-digital conversion of the voice lines can occur in either the PBX or the multiplexer, depending on the exact hardware installed.

FIGURE 16.6.
A typical multiplexer application.

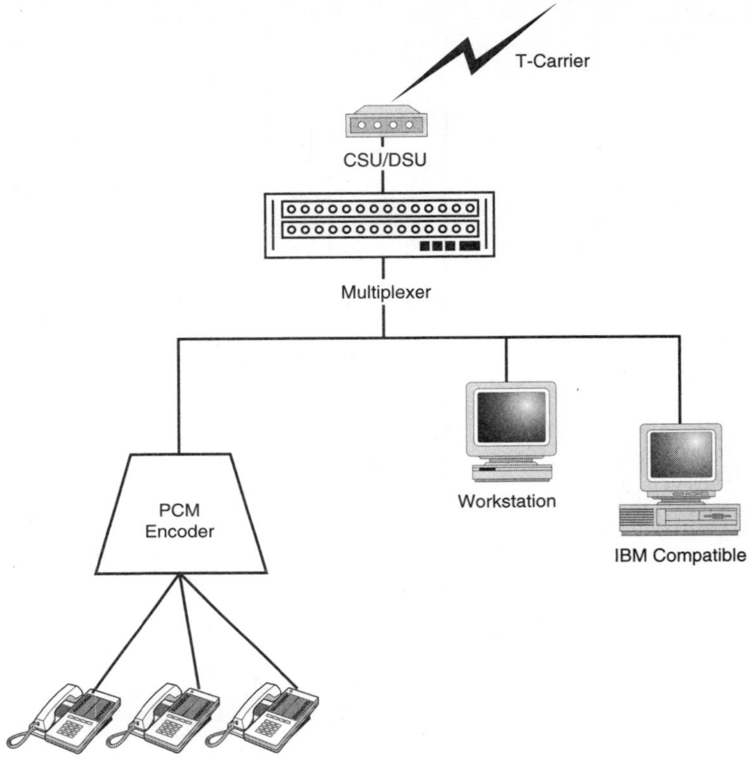

Time Division Multiplexing

The T-carrier system uses *time-division multiplexing (TDM)*. As the name implies, TDM uses units of time to divide the signals from each source. These units of time, or *timeslots*, are approximately ⅛₀₀₀th of a second, which corresponds to the sampling rate of an analog voice call.

On a T-1, there are 24 carrier channels, each transmitting 8,000 timeslots/sec. The multiplexer is responsible for interleaving these timeslots so that the receiving device will be able to properly route the contents of each timeslot.

If four devices are all sending data through a TDM, the data is combined sequentially and sent down the T-carrier. At the receiving end, the order tells the de-multiplexer which device should receive the data. If a specific device has no data to send in a specific timeslot, then the multiplexer adds a null carrier to keep the ordering consistent.

Because TDM allows some timeslots to go unused, it is not as efficient as it might be. A newer multiplexing technology, called *Statistical Time Division Multiplexing (STDM)*, is being developed to fix this inefficiency.

Pulse Code Modulation Encoding

To carry a voice signal on a digital carrier, the voice signal needs to be converted to digital pulses. First, the signal is *sampled*, or measured many times per second. That measurement is then *quantized*, or converted into a number. The number is rounded to the nearest number that can be represented in an 8-bit byte. This process is called *Pulse Code Modulation (PCM)*.

While the human voice can produce sounds in the range between 50 and 1,500Hz, most of what we hear is between 300 and 3,400Hz. This 3,000Hz of bandwidth, plus 1,000Hz for separation between calls, gives a total of 4,000Hz.

The rate of sampling is determined by a rule called the *Nyquist theorem*. The Nyquist theorem states that, to ensure accuracy, a signal should be sampled at twice the rate of its frequency. In the case of voice signal, the proper sampling rate is 8K/sec.

Because each sample is 8 bits and samples are taken 8,000 times per second, the total bandwidth necessary to carry a digital voice signal is 64Kbps. This PCM requirement is the building block for both the DS0 channel size (described in "The Digital Signal Heirarchy" section of this chapter) and the ISDN B-channel size (described in Chapter 13, "ISDN").

Adaptive Pulse Code Modulation

A newer PCM standard promises to increase capacity even further by halving the amount of bandwidth needed to carry a voice signal. Adaptive PCM (ADPCM) predicts the next voice sample based on the level of the previous sample. The limitation of the technology is the inability to reliably transport analog modem traffic faster than 4,800bps.

Fractional Circuits

A fractional T-1 is nothing more than a standard T-1 in which only some of the 24 DS0 circuits are available to the end user. When a fractional T-1 is ordered, the carrier installs a full T-1 to the location, but provisions only the requested number of 64Kbps channels. The remaining channels are not configured. A fractional T-1 uses the same terminating hardware as a full T-1.

Fractional T-1s are useful when fewer than 1.544Mbps of bandwidth are needed, because they are less expensive than a full T-1. They are also useful when bandwidth needs are expected to grow. Because a full T-1 and the appropriate hardware are already in place, increasing a fractional T-1 requires only a phone call to your carrier.

T-Carrier Standards

In the world of digital communications, there have been two kinds of standards. AT&T, by providing much of the research into the area, has set de facto standards that other manufacturers have picked up. The other standards were more formalized, and were released periodically by associations and standards bodies. Two high-level standards which particularly affect T-carrier lines include the Digital Signal Hierarchy (DSH) and the OSI Network Model.

The Digital Signal Hierarchy

The different levels of bandwidth offered by the T-carrier system were standardized by the American National Standards Institute (ANSI) in the early 1980s. Table 16.1 shows the DSH.

Table 16.1. The Digital Signal Hierarchy.

DS Level	North American Bandwidth	Voice Channels
DS0	64Kbps	1
DS1	1.544Mbps	24
DS2	6.312Mbps	96
DS3	44.736Mbps	672
DS4	274.176Mbps	4032

The DSH is based on a core channel called the DS0 (digital signal 0). The DS0 is usually a 64Kbps channel, which is the amount of bandwidth needed to carry a single digitized voice signal. DS0 signals are aggregated to provide higher levels of bandwidth. Common DS0 levels include

- DS1. The DS1 is the most common digital signal size, and provides 1.544Mbps of aggregated data. A DS1 aggregates 24 DS0 channels, and can handle both voice and data traffic. The DS1 is commonly used to provide high bandwidth data service or trunk lines to a PBX.

- DS2. The DS2 is less common in the consumer market. This line uses 96 DS0 channels for a total of 6.312Mbps. This line was used primarily by the phone companies for high traffic trunk lines, but has been replaced by the DS3 in many applications.

- DS3. The DS3 is used for high bandwidth data transmission, with a total throughput of 44.736Mbps. A DS3 combines 672 DS0 channels.

In Europe, the DS0 standards were set by the International Telecommunication Union, and are therefore slightly different. While the core DS0 channel is the same size, the various levels are aggregated differently. As an example, the European equivalent of the T-1 circuit, called the E1, carries 30 DS0 channels instead of 24.

> **NOTE**
>
> You may hear people in the industry using the terms T-1 and DS1 interchangeably. Technically, the T-1 is the North American implementation of the DS1 standard. You're going to get your point across either way. In Europe, however, the DS1 service is called E1.

The T-Carrier and OSI

The T-carrier system addresses the first three layers (physical, data link, and network) of the OSI model. The higher layers are addressed by the hardware and software in the user's network.

The Physical Layer

The physical layer of the OSI model defines the hardware, wiring, connectors, and other electrical and physical characteristics of a network connection. In a T-carrier connection, this includes the cabling and Channel Service Unit/Data Service Unit (CSU/DSU) hardware. The CSU/DSU handles the physical and electrical termination of the connection and monitors physical line status.

The Data-Link Layer

The OSI data link layer handles connection maintenance and error correction. A T-carrier framing system (either D4, ESF, or M13) handles the data link functions.

The Network Layer

In the OSI model, the network layer defines signaling procedures between the network and users. In a T-carrier connection, the framing system provides the basic signaling pathway, and the CSU/DSU handles signal generation and management.

T-1 Wiring and Hardware

The hardware involved in a digital leased line has become progressively simpler as service became widespread. Today, the major hardware categories in a customer installation include cabling, service units, multiplexers and channel banks, and data terminal equipment.

Cabling and Connections

In an ideal installation, a T-1 operates over special low-capacitance shielded twisted-pair cabling. In many installations today, however, the phone company tries to use existing unshielded twisted pair. In these cases, extensive testing is required to ensure that the line is clean enough for T-1 use.

A typical T-1 line consists of two twisted pairs of copper wire. One pair handles data *to* the subscriber; the other pair handles data *from* the subscriber. These connections are usually terminated in an RJ48 jack.

Although analog signals over twisted pair can usually travel up to 18,000 feet from subscriber to central office without amplification, T-1s require cleaner lines. Repeaters are placed about every 6,000 feet to power the signal. The repeaters do not amplify the signal, but rather duplicate the digital signal to the next segment of the line.

The twisted-pair cable cannot, however, carry the increased bandwidth of the T-3 carrier. Both T-1 and T-3 carriers can be provided on alternate media, including coaxial, fiber, microwave, and infrared. Table 16.2 shows the approximate capacity of these other types of media.

Table 16.2. The Capacity of Various Media.

Media	T-Carrier Capacity
Twisted pair	Up to 1 T-1 circuit
Coaxial cable	Up to 4 T-1 circuits
Microwave	Up to 8 T-3 Circuits
Fiber optics	Up to 24 T-3 circuits

Service Units

Generally today, the functions of both the DSU and the CSU will be found in one device, commonly called the CSU/DSU. The CSU/DSU may be provided or recommended by your phone company. In some installations, you may find separate units, so we will describe the functions separately here.

Channel Service Units

The first piece of hardware in the customer premises is the CSU. The CSU serves a number of functions:

- The CSU physically and electrically terminates the connection to the telephone company.
- The CSU handles line coding, including bipolar violation correction and B8ZS signaling (described in the "Line Coding" section of this chapter).
- The CSU provides D4 or ESF framing, including error correction and network monitoring.

Data Service Units

The primary purpose of the DSU is to convert the standard unipolar digital signal from the multiplexer into a bipolar signal. The DSU also controls timing and synchronization of the signal.

Multiplexer

The *multiplexer* handles the combination and sequencing of several different devices into the signal. The earliest multiplexer was known as a *channel bank*. The channel bank had one hardware interface for each DS0 channel in the T-1 circuit. This fixed hardware configuration limited the channel bank; even if your application needed only 9.6Kbps, such as an older 9,600 baud modem, the channel bank would use an entire 64Kbps channel to pass this signal.

Today, a multiplexer can super-rate a channel for more than 64Kbps, or subrate a channel for less than 64Kbps. Multiplexers can take input from a variety of terminal equipment, and can be software-configured. A multiplexer may be able to provide internal PCM encoding for analog devices.

Routers/Bridges

Depending on your application, you may want to multiplex a number of different sources. These devices are referred to collectively as *terminal equipment*, and serve as the user interface to the network. Your terminal equipment might be a network router, a video conferencing system, or a PBX.

The most common piece of data hardware connected to a T-carrier line is a *network bridge* or *router*. A network bridge connects two dissimilar networks, providing the necessary protocol translation between them. The most common type of network bridge connects an CSU/DSU to an Ethernet local area network (LAN).

Most T-1-to-Ethernet bridges provide some sort of routing ability. *Routing* is a more complex version of bridging, where each packet is analyzed to determine if its destination is on the LAN or across the T-1 line. Depending on your specific hardware choice, you can find T-1-to-Ethernet bridges that route several different protocols.

Which protocol your hardware supports depends on your installation. If you are linking two AppleTalk LANs in different locations, you'll need a router which supports this protocol. Similarly, if you want to connect two Novell networks, you'll need a router that supports the IPX protocol. To connect your LAN to the Internet, you need to route TCP/IP.

Routers generally provide one serial connection for the CSU/DSU, and an RJ45 connection for your Ethernet LAN. Some vendors, such as Cisco, sell routers that have integrated CSU/DSU hardware. These pieces of equipment are the simplest way to connect your LAN directly to a T-1.

Implementing a T-1, Fractional T-1, or T-3 Solution

T-carrier lines are often the best choice for data applications with constant demand for a high level of bandwidth. If your application meets these requirements, you next need to secure a leased line solution.

T-1, Fractional T-1, and T-3 Carriers

T-carrier connectivity is provided by the regional Bell operating companies for short hauls, and by national telephone companies such as Sprint and AT&T for long-distance connections.

FCC regulations require that you provide the carrier with a certain amount of information when ordering service, including:

- A *service order code*, which specifies billing rates, service configurations, and total circuit bandwidth.
- A *jack designation*, which ensures that the carrier provides the correct physical connection. A typical jack designation might be the RJ48C or RJ48X.
- A *facility interface code*, which specifies your frame method. For the T-1 connection, the framing method is generally either D4 or ESF.

In addition, the FCC may require an affidavit certifying that your terminal equipment is compatible with the network you will be using. Your terminal equipment manufacturer may provide a sample affidavit for you to complete.

Circuit Costs

Costs of T-carrier circuits vary by provider, but generally are charged based on the length and total bandwidth of the circuit. Local circuits have a monthly cost per mile for a fractional T-1 circuit, with each additional 64Kbps channel activated adding to the cost, up to full T-1 bandwidth. For long distance connections, charges are generally a flat rate per month, and are costed by city pair. For example, a T-1 from New York to Los Angeles is a higher flat rate than a T-1 from New York to Baltimore.

If your application requires a fairly constant amount of bandwidth, a leased line is generally the most cost-efficient connection. If your bandwidth needs vary widely during the day, you may want to consider an ISDN connection, which charges by the minute per 64K channel in use. This method of call billing allows you to only pay for a high bandwidth connection when it is needed, instead of paying the full flat rate.

Accessing the Internet with T-Carrier Lines

A popular use of T-1 and T-3 lines are to connect a LAN or a server to the Internet. The T-1 line provides enough bandwidth for a large number of end users to send e-mail or browse the Web.

Internet Service Providers

If you do not have any connectivity to the Internet, consider using your Internet service provider (ISP) as a "one-stop shop." Most ISPs who provide leased line services have good relationships with the local digital service providers and can expedite your installation. In addition, an ISP will be able to assist with administrative functions such as domain name registration, IP address assignment, and network monitoring. Most ISPs also offer some other services, such as newsgroups access and Web hosting.

Network Security Considerations

Once you connect your LAN to the Internet via a digital leased line, the sensitive data on your computers becomes vulnerable to unauthorized access. Before getting "wired," investigate firewalls, router filters, and other methods of security. Your ISP should be able to assist you in securing your network, or can refer you to a network security expert.

> **TIP**
>
> The LIST features details on more than 5,000 ISPs.

Troubleshooting

T-1 lines are heavily tested upon installation, because there are so many places where failures can occur, especially in the local loop. Often, though, failures can occur after installation as well. Equipment failures, cable cuts, and electrical interference can cause total failure or distortion in the lines, even after months of excellent performance.

Many CSU/DSU devices include loopback testing functions that help diagnose these problems, but in general, there is little the end user can do to troubleshoot a T-1 line. If your connection is down, or you experience poor performance and connection failures, you should contact your carrier.

Summary

The explosive growth of the Internet has made high-bandwidth connectivity a widespread need. To answer this need, The T-carrier circuit has developed from a phone company proprietary trunk standard into a common WAN building block. Today, T-1s, fractional T-1s, and T-3s are widely available and affordable methods of interconnecting office LANs and connecting to the Internet.

Bandwidth, bandwidth, and more bandwidth. As new applications demand more capacity for data transmission, you can count on digital leased lines, including T-3s, to become even more common. But for applications requiring more than the 44Mbps of a T-3, several new technologies are becoming available.

B-ISDN

The broadband ISDN standards, which are still being developed, aim to provide true digital bandwidth-on-demand. B-ISDN supplies bandwidth in excess of 1.544Mbps, or faster than a T-1. B-ISDN will be found in three common forms:

- Frame Relay. Available today in 56Kpbs and 1.5Mbps lines, frame relay service is an example of a B-ISDN solution. Frame relay uses packet switching instead of the circuit switching protocols commonly used in ISDN.
- SMDS. The Switched Multi-megabit Digital Service provides packet-switched connectivity from 1.5Mbps to 45Mbps.
- ATM. Asynchronous Transfer Mode communication uses small, 53-byte "cells" to transfer data at up to 155Mbps and 622Mbps. ATM is commonly held as the future direction of B-ISDN services.

SONET

The other major standard that will affect digital service in the near future is the *Synchronous Optical Network (SONET)*. SONET uses a new standard for framing that allows massive aggregation of DS0 channels. As shown in Table 16.3, SONET is designed to provide bandwidth capacity in the gigabit range. While the technology is currently used only by the telecommunications companies, you can imagine that the service will follow the example set by T-1 and T-3 lines, and eventually become a public service for large companies.

Table 16.3. The SONET Hierarchy.

SONET Level	Maximum Bandwidth
OC1	51.84Mbps
OC3	155.52Mbps
OC9	466.56Mbps
OC12	622.08Mbps

Frame Relay

by Arthur Cooper

IN THIS CHAPTER

CHAPTER 17

Frame Relay is a technology that grew from an existing protocol and the need to improve upon it. The need in this case was to provide cheap, reliable network services for Local Area Network (LAN) users who need to pass data back and forth between other LANs that they do business with on a daily basis. This data passing between LANs is where Wide Area Networking (WAN) technology comes into play. In order to understand the background of Frame Relay technology, it's necessary to take a trip down the path of network history and the creation of the X.25 protocol.

Frame Relay: The Technology that Grew from X.25

The history of data networks begins in the 1960s in the United States. At that time, most computer systems were standalone behemoths that had no reason to interact with other computers. The U.S. government created the Defense Advanced Research Projects Agency (DARPA), which was mandated to fund projects concerning the development of emerging technologies. One idea was to connect dissimilar computer systems to each other to simplify the task of sharing data between those systems. Scientists involved with DARPA began to look at creating a standard protocol to be used between computer systems. In 1969, using four network switches or nodes, the first internetwork (network of networks) became a reality. This network was called the Advanced Research Projects Agency Network (ARPANET), and it was the seed that created today's modern Internet system. Frame Relay grew out of this technology.

The ARPANET was responsible for the creation of a new internetwork protocol. This protocol was called ARPANET 1822, but it soon became known as X.25 (a standard name assigned by the International Telegraph and Telephone Consultative Committee [CCITT]).

X.25 was the original packet-switching scheme that grew from the old ARPANET 1822 protocol. Several factors were present in those days that are no longer a problem today. Those factors were the driving forces that made X.25 look and act the way it did. The first factor is the lack of sophistication of the computers themselves. By today's standards, these systems were anything but sophisticated. IBM's biggest and most popular machine in those days was the old IBM 360 series mainframe.

The 360 was a staple among businesses that could afford computers, and it was a marvel in its day. However, the personal computers (PCs) of today hold more computing power in their small, desktop-sized cases than the old 360 computers did. All of the programs running on these old mainframes were simply used for data manipulation and storage of some type. The computers themselves were not smart enough, or capable enough, to screen the data being fed to them for accuracy.

Computer programmers and operators needed to ensure that error-free data was being put into these computers. The phrase "garbage-in-garbage-out," or GIGO, was formulated at that time. GIGO meant simply that you could not expect a computer to know if the data being fed to it was useful or full of errors. If the data being fed to it was indeed "garbage," the computer would still attempt to process the data as it normally would. The results of the processing would, of course, be of no value, and the computer itself could not be faulted for producing garbage from garbage.

The second factor that drove X.25's development was the quality of telephone lines and connections. The entire Public Switched Telephone Network (PSTN) was composed of mostly copper wire between switch points, and the old Frequency Division Multiplex (FDM) microwave radio systems that carried telephone signals over greater distances were prone to thermal noise and other variations in signal quality due to the equipment itself or the atmosphere these microwave signals traveled through.

These two factors, unsophisticated computer systems and poor quality telephone lines, together make up a formula for failure if X.25 is not capable of rising above them. The scientists on the ARPANET understood these two factors very well, and they decided to ensure that the protocol developed for their network could overcome these two obstacles.

The ARPANET 1822 protocol was the result of their labor, and it did compensate for unsophisticated computers by ensuring error-free delivery of data. X.25 performed error-checking at many levels and stops along the network's path. All of this was built into X.25 at a time when no real protocol layers or standards had been developed.

Now that you know the history of X.25, let's compare X.25 and Frame Relay (FR) technology.

Comparing Frame Relay to X.25

Although X.25 was the father of almost all modern network protocols, it adheres well to the OSI standard in that it uses the first three layers of the reference model. Figure 17.1 shows the X.25 layers.

FIGURE 17.1.
X.25 layers of the OSI model.

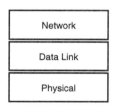

These three layers are called the physical, data, and network layers. Neat things are happening at each layer, as you will see later on, but the important thing to know is that X.25 uses these three layers at all times, and error checking occurs at each layer.

X.25 actually encompasses three protocols. There is one at each layer of operation, as shown in Figure 17.2.

FIGURE 17.2.

X.25 layers and their respective protocols.

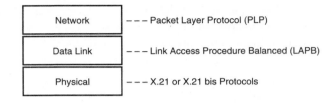

Network	– – – Packet Layer Protocol (PLP)
Data Link	– – – Link Access Procedure Balanced (LAPB)
Physical	– – – X.21 or X.21 bis Protocols

At the lowest layer of X.25, the layer at which there is a physical connection between a User-to-Network Interface (UNI) and the X.25 network itself, the actual protocol used that describes how the user and network tie together is called the X.21 or X.21bis protocol. X.21 is popular in Europe, whereas X.21bis is used in the United States. This protocol describes the actual physical data connection between the UNI and the network.

At the data or data link layer, X.25 uses a protocol known as Link Access Procedure Balanced (LAPB). Briefly, this is a software protocol that performs the function of decoding frames or collections of bits of information. These frames are collections of bits of information that the transmitting and receiving UNIs are trying to get passed through the network.

At the highest layer of X.25, the Network or packet layer, X.25 uses a protocol known widely as the Packet Layer Protocol (PLP). This protocol ensures that the frames from the second level are assembled into packets that can then be transmitted from one end of a network to the other.

Now that you have seen what X.25 is all about, what is Frame Relay? Frame Relay is simply the latest variation on the old X.25 scheme. The CCITT originally came up with the idea of using Frame Relay on Integrated Service Digital Network (ISDN) circuits. The ISDN circuits in use today are either a 2B & D arrangement or a 23B & D arrangement. The 2B & D uses 2 B, or bearer, channels that are 64Kbps circuits. The D, or delta, channel is a 16Kbps circuit used for signaling. The 23B & D is the same, except that there are actually 23 64Kbps circuits available.

When the CCITT came up with the original scheme for Frame Relay, they were not too sure how popular it would be, so they originally designed it to be used on the D, or delta, channel of an ISDN circuit. As you can see, 16Kbps is not a lot of bandwidth, so this idea was scrapped rather quickly. If you take a look at Figure 17.3, you will see that Frame Relay uses only the first two layers of the OSI Reference Model.

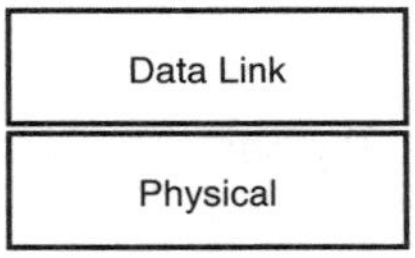

FIGURE 17.3.

Frame Relay layers of the OSI model.

| Data Link |
| Physical |

The lowest layer, the physical layer, describes the connection between the UNI and the Frame Relay network. The second layer shows the data, or data link layer, and this layer is used by Frame Relay for a few needed items to be discussed later. The interesting thing to note, however, is that Frame Relay has no need for the third layer as X.25 did. Frame Relay eliminates this layer completely.

Frame Relay technology makes a few assumptions about the environment it is operating within. First, it assumes that the computer systems being connected together by Frame Relay networks are by their nature intelligent devices. Second, it assumes that the telephone circuits carrying the data within a Frame Relay network are of above average, if not near-perfect, quality.

Examine these assumptions individually. As you know, today's modern computer systems do not in any way resemble the old mainframe systems in use during X.25's heyday. In fact, on most LANs today, the systems in use are powerful, sophisticated PCs with sophisticated operating systems and hardware. Why did X.25 have to assume computers were not too smart? If it did not, and it allowed error-ridden data to enter the computer after it had passed through the network, the computers in those days would simply have accepted and processed the data as if nothing was wrong.

Today's computer systems and LAN servers are smart enough to recognize garbage when it is being fed to them. If data being sent to a computer is incorrect, it is usually the function of the higher level peer processes in the programs themselves to recognize the bad data and request new data from the device, person, or computer providing the data. Frame Relay technology is counting on this ability to ferret out and ignore bad data.

The second assumption made by Frame Relay is also a valid and arguable one. Telephone circuits and networks have become extremely sophisticated and reliable in the past five to ten years. With the advent of modern fiber connections and extremely fast and reliable switching technology, line problems are really a thing of the past when dealing with data circuits and connections through the public telephone network.

Here's a quick comparison of X.25 and Frame Relay at each layer. Figure 17.4 provides a side-by-side look at the two technologies and their associated layers.

FIGURE 17.4.
Comparison of X.25 and Frame Relay layers.

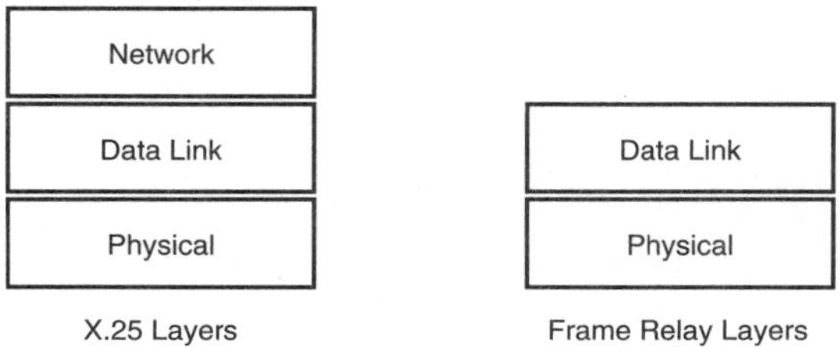

X.25 Layers   Frame Relay Layers

X.25 uses the physical layer through the implementation of the X.21 protocol discussed earlier. Frame Relay uses the physical layer in many different ways. In most cases, it will be a UNI such as a bridge or a router.

X.25 uses the data, or data link, layer with a protocol known as LAPB. This is a software-driven protocol that adds a lot of overhead to the data transmission taking place in the network. Frame Relay uses only a group of two octets (8 bits) at this level. This adds very little overhead to the transmission taking place.

Now look at the third level used by X.25. At the network, or packet, level, X.25 uses a device known as an X.25 Packet Assembler/Disassembler (PAD) to put all of the data into packet form. These packets, or bundles, of data contain all of the information to be transmitted through the network, but there are also overhead bits of information added by X.25 at this layer. These overhead bits include a section of bits known as the logical channel number (LCN). This number is then used by the distant end node of the X.25 network in order to identify what packets go where when receiving a sequence of packets.

It should be obvious to you now that Frame Relay is not even using this third layer at all. With that in mind, the following section discusses why Frame Relay is the logical choice for network managers to use when getting data from one place to another over wide distances.

Why Use Frame Relay?

Before moving into a discussion of the actual workings of Frame Relay technology, consider why Frame Relay is really a smart move to make when designing a WAN/LAN interface. In this author's opinion, the two major factors to consider when making any sort of networking choice are speed and cost. With that in mind and referring once again to Figure 17.4, take a look at the speed issue of X.25 technology. As you know, there is a lot of error checking and addition of redundant bits going on at the three levels of X.25 technology.

At the physical layer, the X.21 protocol does some Cyclic Redundancy Checking (CRC) of the data being passed back and forth, and this process takes time. At the data, or data link, level, X.25 uses LAPB in order to compile the data into frames. LAPB adds an enormous amount of overhead bits of information needed for general frame housekeeping as well as error detection. Even the addition of 2 bits/frame over the course of a large data transmission will slow down the transmission tremendously.

As the data approaches the network, or packet, layer, X.25 stuffs in a multitude of information as it performs the compilation of frames into what are known as packets. Bits are added to ensure that adequate error detection is performed at the packet level; bits are added to number, or sequence, the packets of a single transmission; and bits are even used to signal the fact that a packet was received in error. Again, all of these additional bits will slow the transmission down a lot.

How does speed relate to Frame Relay? At the physical layer, Frame Relay technology is usually a bridge or router connected to the user's LAN. There are many different physical protocols in use at this level, and Frame Relay technology does not specify a particular one to be used. Therefore, the fastest method of coupling a LAN with a bridge/router that serves as the Frame Relay network interface should, and could, be used.

At the data, or data link, layer, Frame Relay uses only a 2-octet field to pass its information from one end of the network to the other. What these two octets include is discussed later in this chapter, but for the purpose of this discussion, please note the small amount of information Frame Relay includes in the frames it assembles. Don't forget that Frame Relay does not even use the third layer.

Figure 17.5 compares the frames of X.25 and Frame Relay at Level 2, the data layer, of the OSI Reference Model.

FIGURE 17.5.

X.25 and Frame Relay frame comparison at Level 2 of the OSI Reference Model.

Flag	Address	Control	Actual data information	FCS field	Flag

X.25 Frame

Flag	Frame relay header	Actual data information	FCS field	Flag

Frame Relay Frame

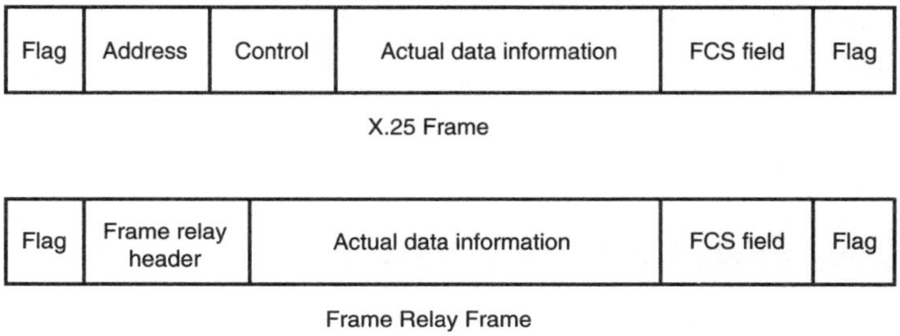

Notice the larger amount of information X.25 must place in all of its frames. Now, remember that Frame Relay has finished its job at this point as far as organizing and compiling frames is concerned. X.25 will be adding more bits and overhead information at Level 3, the network layer, of the OSI reference model. You can see why Frame Relay is really a speedier alternative to X.25.

The second determining factor for a network choice is cost. When Frame Relay became popular in the early 1990s, there were many companies who wanted to lead the pack and grab all of the Frame Relay customers they could.

One of the recognized leaders of the pack was a company called Williams Telecommunications (WILTEL) of Oklahoma. WILTEL prided itself on being one of the largest resellers of telephone and data bandwidth to America, but it actually was, and remains pretty much so today, a collection of leased fiber connections from coast to coast. WILTEL did not own a large portion of its network in the early 1990s, but they were still able to provide excellent coverage throughout the United States. They were able to do this by leasing Right of Ways from the various railroad corporations traversing the United States. For that reason, they decided to come up with a Frame Relay network and pricing package known as WILPAK.

17

FRAME RELAY

The only problem with this was that Frame Relay was in its infancy, and none of the major network companies including AT&T, MCI, as well as Sprint and others were too sure how it should be priced and sold. Today, most companies are clear on where the tariffs of pricing Frame Relay are concerned. In other words, most companies feel they can charge based on the committed information rate. In earlier days, many companies were not sure how to "explain and package" their pricing in terms the layman could understand. However, there are still some pretty difficult-to-understand and/or strange Frame Relay pricing schemes.

The moral of this story is that Frame Relay is a pay-as-you-use technology. X.25 was used primarily over expensive leased lines. Also, there was no system in place to look at the actual bandwidth being used, so X.25 lines were almost always never used to full capacity. Even when the ARPANET switched to a per/packet billing scheme for its major users, it was not very cost-effective. Frame Relay connections can be had quite cheaply today.

That's really it in a nutshell. X.25 is slower and in some, if not all, cases more expensive than Frame Relay. With that in mind, it makes more sense to go with a Frame Relay network connection between LANs if at all possible.

Frame Relay also has its problems. The next section of this chapter discusses the actual workings of Frame Relay step by step, including frame relay's limitations.

How Frame Relay Works

Frame Relay is not difficult to understand, and for the purposes of this chapter, we shall make every attempt to use layman's terms and concepts. Frame Relay is a wide area network (WAN) technology. It also happens to be a rather fast operating technology. X.25 is almost always used at speeds below 64Kbps, but Frame Relay is being used today at T-1 and even T-3 speeds.

> **NOTE**
>
> T-1 uses a 1.544Mbps data rate, and T-3 uses rates up to approximately 45Mbps.

With speeds such as this, it is easy to see why Frame Relay is sometimes referred to as *Fast Packet* technology.

Remember that X.25 was a packet technology that used logical channel numbers to get packets to the right addressee. X.25 did so by using Switched Virtual Circuits (SVC) and Permanent Virtual Circuits (PVC). X.25 was, and is, a full-duplex operation. This means that data is going back and forth in each direction on the network. The way X.25 got these packets delivered properly was through the use of end-to-end error and packet control. This was accomplished by the third layer used by X.25.

This layer, the network layer, ensured that if a message contained 500 packets, each packet was numbered 1–500 in sequence. At the receiving end of the transmission, the X.25 node on the network would be charged with the task of reassembling the packets in the correct order. If any of the packets did not arrive in sequence, the X.25 node would have to wait for the proper packet to arrive in order to pass the entire message on to the network computer requesting the transmission.

However, if any of the packets arrived with errors, the X.25 node would have to request a retransmission of errored packets from the node that originated the data transmission in the first place. This sounds good, but remember, this discussion covers factors that will eat up time during a data transmission. If the X.25 nodes are involved with error checking and retransmission requests as well as packet reassembly, then the transmission will be slowed down tremendously.

Frame Relay does none of this. First of all, Frame Relay does not use LCNs in order to assign packets to a destination address. Frame Relay uses a Data Link Connection Identifier (DLCI), which is covered later. The other nice thing about Frame Relay is that it also does no end-to-end error and packet control at the third layer. All it does do is some error checking at the frame, or second, level of the OSI Reference Model. At the data layer, Frame Relay does some simple error checking, and if a frame is full of errors, it does not ask for the frame to be retransmitted by the distant end. Rather, it simply discards the frame as no good, and goes on about its business of receiving and transmitting frames.

You may be wondering how frames can simply be tossed away after being determined to be laden with an error or errors. The answer relates to the sophistication levels of today's modern computers. Computers today can recognize and identify the fact that a frame was missing from the transmission. At that point, the request will be passed back through the Frame Relay network to the originator requesting the frame be sent again.

Frame Relay is also full-duplex, and there is indeed two-way transmission of frames from each end to the other. However, when the request is transmitted back to the originator to retransmit the frame that was apparently discarded by the Frame Relay network due to errors, it will look like any other frame to the Frame Relay network. In other words, the Frame Relay network does not get involved with the content of the frames being transmitted over it as deeply as X.25 did.

Frame Relay networks simply monitor the error checking information at the second level, and if there are errors, the network discards the errored frame or frames. This is not a big problem today, as the networks in use that carry Frame Relay transmissions are extremely stable and reliable. In all actuality, very few frames are discarded due to errors in today's modern Frame Relay networks. A much larger portion of frames are discarded due to traffic demands.

The frame format used by Frame Relay at Level 2 of the OSI model is shown in Figure 17.6.

FIGURE 17.6.
Frame Relay frame structure at OSI Level 2.

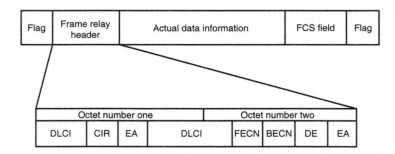

It's quite simple and makes a lot of sense. There are two octets used by Frame Relay at this point. These octets contain the information needed by the Frame Relay network to know where the frames are to be sent along the Frame Relay network structure. There is also some controlling information present. The first ten bits of these octets make up the DLCI.

The DLCI

The DLCI refers to the actual number assigned on the Frame Relay network to the user's port or system. When buying Frame Relay service from a vendor today, the circuit the vendor provides will determine what numbers are used as DLCIs at your location. If you are using the ten bits just mentioned, there is a possibility of 1,024 address combinations.

> **NOTE**
>
> The 1,024 combinations are created by forming a binary number between 0 and 1023 by using the 10 DLCI bits. 1111111111 would be 1023, and 0000000000 would equal zero. 0000000001 would equal one, 0000000010 would equal two, and so on.

Most of the vendors providing Frame Relay services today will use numbers between 16 and 1007 for DLCI address numbers.

Assume that you have a router connected to a Frame Relay circuit provided by a vendor. On this router, there are four ports in use. The vendor may decide that port one will be assigned a DLCI of 16, port two will be assigned a DLCI of 17, and so on for the remaining two ports. In this example, there would be four DLCIs assigned to your Frame Relay termination point.

At the other end of the Frame Relay network, there is obviously a system that will be communicating with your end through the network. Assume that it is another router with eight ports in use. The vendor may decide to reuse the DLCIs of 16, 17, 18, and 19 for the first four ports of this termination. Therefore, the last ports could be called 20, 21, 22, and 23. This would complete the eight port addresses.

How can the numbers 16 through 19 be reused? At the first termination point, the router would not be involved in sending frames to itself, so anything numbered as 16 coming in from its local ports would be sent to the first port at the other end of the Frame Relay connection.

This example may seem simple, but it explains the point that while the numbers 16 through 1007 are available on most DLCI configurations, the numbers may be used over again at each user location. The DLCI number 0 is reserved for call signaling by the Frame Relay network. Also, 1-15 and 1008-1022 are reserved at present and are not being used in most Frame Relay arrangements. DLCI address 1023 will be discussed later in this chapter.

The next logical question concerns itself with how a user of Frame Relay services is able to get data destined for a distant user or LAN to the right place. Within the routers and bridges themselves, there are static routing tables. In Frame Relay, most of today's users are connecting LANs together through Frame Relay technology. These LANs are almost always using a TCP/IP address scheme of sorts. Without going into a broad discussion of how IP addresses are created, let it suffice to say that each LAN will have a unique IP address.

It is the information concerning the IP address and their respective DLCI numbers that is entered into the static routing tables of routers and bridges that are in turn connected to Frame Relay networks. So, going back to the last example, if the LAN on DLCI port 16 at this end has an IP address of `207.102.88.1`, the tables in the distant end's router or bridge will know that anything coming in addressed to `207.102.88.1` should be sent to DLCI 16 at this end.

Now, with that discussion behind you, take a look at the concept of Committed Information Rate (CIR) and how it relates to Frame Relay.

CIR and the "Leaky Bucket"

The *committed information rate*, CIR, is the concept driving Frame Relay services and their pricing. When you purchase connectivity between your LANs from a Frame Relay vendor, they are going to help you establish a CIR rate to work with. This rate actually refers to the amount of frames you can blast down the Frame Relay pipe at any given time.

Figure 17.7 shows two pails of water. Believe it or not, Frame Relay technology uses an algorithm referred to as the *leaky bucket algorithm*. What this algorithm states is simple. When you purchase Frame Relay bandwidth at a certain CIR rate, you are assigned a timed buffer in each switch of the network along your frame relay's circuit path. Consider these buffers to be buckets of water, and the width of the buckets can be called the *time* or T_1 The height of the buckets can be called *committed burst* or B_1. By using these two symbols, you can see that the CIR rate would be equal to: $CIR = B_1 / T_1$.

Here's what this equation is saying. If the burst of data you are transmitting is small enough to be divided equally by the time of the buckets, or buffers, within each switch along the Frame Relay network, the data will be transmitted with no discarding of frames. In simpler terms, if you have been given a CIR rate of 64Kbps, and you transmit a burst of 56Kbps, this will divide by the time (T_1) which is actually a 1, and it will equal, of course, 56Kbps. Because this is smaller than the CIR rate you have been given, this burst of data should move through all of the switches in the Frame Relay network without any frames being discarded.

FIGURE 17.7.

Frame relay's bucket algorithm.

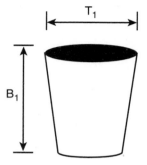

The basic bucket or buffer is set to the CIR rate you have been promised.

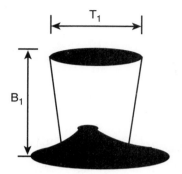

The leaky bucket or buffer may be able to save frames above the stated CIR rate.

Why is this math even needed? When you buy a Frame Relay circuit with a CIR rate of 64 or 128Kbps, you are gambling that your data may actually hover close to that figure at all times. Further, you are gambling that your data will want more bandwidth than that on several occasions. Now let's take the math a step further and explain the so-called leaky bucket.

The Leaky Bucket Itself

Whenever a customer's CIR rate has been surpassed at any switch within the Frame Relay network, there is a bit called the Discard Eligibility (DE) bit (refer to Figure 17.6) that will be set to a 1 in all of the frames above the CIR. As these frames move through the network, they may get discarded if traffic is heavy and the switch is in a position to meet the CIR rate only. The neat thing about Frame Relay is the so-called second, or leaky, bucket. This is used whenever a customer's frames have exceeded the CIR rate, and the DE bit has been set to 1.

This second bucket, the leaky bucket, is what makes Frame Relay so attractive. I will also refer to its width as T_1. However, I will refer to its height as B_2 for Bursts exceeding the CIR rate. This second bucket, or buffer, within the switches on a Frame Relay network will almost always be equal to the size of the first bucket. In other words, a CIR rate of 128Kbps would perhaps be able to accept bursts up to 256Kbps by filling the second bucket with data during T_1, but once again, if the demands of the network are great, the second bucket, the leaky one, may have no height at all. If this is the case, then all frames above the CIR of 128Kbps will have the DE bit set to 1 and will most likely get discarded by the switch setting the DE bit to 1 or the next switch along the network path.

Believe it or not, you can actually buy Frame Relay circuits today with a CIR rate of zero, but this will, of course, put all of the data you are putting on the network at risk. LANs are bursty by nature, and it behooves today's LAN administrators and network managers to attempt to determine the highest rates their LANs may need during the busy traffic periods of the average day. When using Frame Relay services, it makes sense to try a higher rate first and then lower the CIR rate after a trial period. If the lower CIR works, it may need to come lower still, but lowering the CIR can also be risky.

If a vendor's network has very little traffic on it when you first purchased your service, you may actually be exceeding your CIR on a regular basis without even realizing it. If this is the case, and you lower the CIR you require at the same time the network incurs more traffic, you may well create a monster. This monster will be the continual discarding of frames by the network. Each end of your Frame Relay connection will be in crisis as it attempts to request the discarded frames, and you could actually go dead in the water if it continues.

For this reason and many others, it's important to work closely with your Frame Relay vendor to ensure that the CIR rate you are paying for is cheap for you and profitable for your vendor. It's this marriage of cheap service combined with profitability for vendors that has made Frame Relay so attractive.

Congestion on Frame Relay Networks

Another area of Frame Relay that warrants explanation concerns the idea of node or traffic congestion. You have already learned how Frame Relay beats X.25 in terms of cost and speed, but there is one killer of Frame Relay services. That killer is congestion within the network itself. Frame Relay uses two methods of controlling and, hopefully, eliminating congestion.

The first method is called Explicit Congestion Notification (ECN). This method is used by the switches or nodes in a Frame Relay network to notify the User-to-Network Interfaces of congestion. Most UNIs are routers or bridges, so this notification is seen by the user's router or bridge. Refer to Figure 17.6, and you will notice there are two fields called FECN and BECN. These are called Forward Explicit Congestion Notification (FECN) and Backward Explicit Congestion Notification (BECN). Each of these fields is one bit in length, and the way they are used is as follows.

If a node along the path in the Frame Relay network realizes there is some congestion being experienced for frames being transmitted to a specific DLCI, the node will set the FECN bit to a 1 for all frames heading to that DLCI address. It is hoped that the UNI connected to the DLCI at the other end will see these FECN bits set to 1 and will attempt to communicate with the UNI at the originating DLCI and slow things down a bit.

At the same time, if any frames are seen going back toward the originator of the frames bound for the congested DLCI, the BECN bit will be set to a 1 on those frames. By doing so, the

17

FRAME RELAY

node is trying to tell the originator of frames bound for the congested DLCI that there is indeed congestion on the network. If a user's UNI sees the BECN bit set high to a 1, the UNI will know there is congestion going to the other end's DLCI, and hopefully the UNI will slow transmission to this congested site a bit.

There are a few things that will make ECN useless. If the routers or bridges that comprise the user's UNI do not even recognize or process the FECN and BECN bits, then there is no use in using this method. Likewise, if a user has completely surpassed the CIR rate for the Frame Relay connection in question, it is possible that traffic will simply halt and go dead in the water. If this occurs, naturally the ECN bits, both forward and backward, would be of no value.

For those reasons as well as others, another congestion control method is being used in some Frame Relay networks today. It is called Consolidated Link Layer Management (CLLM). This is used between the routers and nodes that comprise Frame Relay networks. It generally uses the DLCI address of 1023. The routers and nodes communicate via an established protocol called Link Management Interface (LMI) protocol.

There has been a lot of discussion lately as to where LMI should be sent and used, but most Frame Relay networks are using DLCI address 1023 to pass this information between nodes and UNIs. Some newer networks are using DLCI 0, but it really does not matter which address is used as long as the LMI data gets where it needs to be.

LMI will provide status messages to the UNI and node points along a Frame Relay network. These messages will contain information about what DLCIs are currently in use on the network, which ones are congested at present, and in which direction(s) the congestion is being experienced. No doubt future systems will put LMI to greater use than it is currently being used.

Summary

Frame Relay will no doubt be around for the next several years. For most users of X.25 network services, it is a simple task to upgrade to a Frame Relay network arrangement. A simple change of software in a user's router or bridge can make the transition from an X.25 to a Frame Relay-based service seem invisible to the users of the connected LANs. If these software changes are implemented simultaneously with a change of vendor to one who can provide Frame Relay services, the cost savings can be extremely large.

Frame Relay will provide users of network services a cheap, speedy, and reliable alternative to X.25 and other older network technologies. Some people have called Frame Relay simply a stop-gap on the way to Asynchronous Transfer Mode (ATM) technology. Although that statement may hold some truth, Frame Relay is proving itself to be anything but a stop-gap. As pricing becomes more uniform between different vendors, there will be less confusion about the CIR rate and how to determine monthly costs associated with Frame Relay. In fact, for most designers of enterprise TCP/IP networks, Frame Relay is the WAN technology of choice today.

ATM

by Arthur Cooper

IN THIS CHAPTER

Like Frame Relay, Asynchronous Transfer Mode (ATM) is another technology that grew from a need to improve local and wide area communications. This technology grew out of the old Integrated Services Digital Network (ISDN) package, as did Frame Relay when it appeared on the scene. The main differences between ATM and Frame Relay are the structure and speed arrangements of the two technologies. As you recall from the discussion of Frame Relay in Chapter 17, it was originally designed to be used on narrowband D channels of ISDN circuits.

Because these circuits run only at rates of 16Kbps, the idea was scrapped rather quickly. The various vendors and providers of Frame Relay service are providing whatever amount of bandwidth the customer wants and needs in order to operate. With ATM, the strategy was very different. When the CCITT started looking at ATM technology, the original intent was to allow ATM to be the actual transport method of moving data by broadband ISDN circuits from one point to another. The first U.S. carriers to really bring forward any offerings of ATM service were Sprint and AT&T. Both of these carriers started out by offering ATM service at T-3 and higher speeds.

> **NOTE**
>
> T-3 (or DS3) uses rates approximately 45Mbps.

The problem in the early days of ATM (1990–1993) was the fact that very few, if any, of the users out there had equipment capable of interfacing with ATM switches and circuits.

Any migrations to ATM in those early days of the technology would have been costly to potential users. As any network manager will tell you, the most important thing associated with network add-ons, changes, or upgrades is their cost. For this reason, ATM did not seem to be catching on as well as originally predicted.

Remember, ATM was originally conceived as a scheme for transporting broadband ISDN traffic. In the early 1980s, the ISDN standards were being developed. Unfortunately, there was never a solid agreement made between any of the large players in the ISDN market at an early point in ISDN's conception period. As a result, everybody in the business went off on their own and developed ISDN switches, phones, interface cards, and devices. The problem with this was that just calling something ISDN-compatible or ISDN-capable did not necessarily mean that it would operate or function with something else calling itself ISDN-compatible or ISDN-capable.

Just because you had an ISDN phone made by GTE, it did not mean that this phone would work with your AT&T System 85 switch, even though both of these devices were supposedly ISDN-compatible or ISDN-capable. This caused a lot of confusion in the marketplace. At the time, the U.S. Air Force purchased several ISDN systems, but it was an absolute nightmare because the phone switches and phone devices themselves were not compatible with each other.

Just because something was called ISDN in those days did not necessarily mean it would actually be compatible with any other device labeled ISDN. ATM has never had to deal with all of this confusion and frustration. When ATM began to come into its own as a new technology, an ATM forum was developed in order to avoid the fiasco that ensued following ISDN's introduction to the world.

The ATM Forum became a very important part of completing the puzzle as far as development of ATM was concerned. An e-mail list provided constant, efficient updates of the notes and minutes of any ATM Forum discussions, panels, or meetings. I believe that, as a result of the ATM Forum and its continued functioning, ATM will move forward with more momentum than other technologies have in the past. Once the issues of cost and availability have been properly addressed and handled, ATM will no doubt become a formidable foe to Frame Relay technology.

The next section compares Frame Relay and ATM, because Frame Relay really is the number-one wide area network (WAN) scheme being chosen for use today. ATM will no doubt surpass Frame Relay eventually, but for right now, it is important to look at ATM and Frame Relay on a comparative basis.

Comparing ATM to Frame Relay

As you recall from Chapter 17, Frame Relay is a new slant on the old X.25 technology. X.25 had reached the point where it had long outlived its usefulness as a WAN technology, so Frame Relay developed out of a need for an improved transmission scheme. ATM is really the next step as far as WAN and Local Area Network (LAN) technologies are concerned. X.25 and Frame Relay were simply WAN technologies, but ATM can bridge the gap between LAN and WAN.

ATM is a true border-crossing technology, as it will provide for LAN transmission schemes as well as WAN transmission schemes. In essence, ATM is an all-encompassing technology that will allow network managers to own a one-stop shop as far as network topology and transmission is concerned. Frame Relay does not do this. Frame Relay is a great method of connecting various LANs together. However, Frame Relay is not a technology that can be used between the various users, terminals, and equipment on a LAN.

ATM can do this and more. With ATM interface cards in user Personal Computers (PCs) and terminal equipment on a LAN, there can be a seamless flow of data through the LAN architecture and out into the WAN architecture as well (see Figure 18.1).

In other words, data that originates in a user's PC can flow through the ATM LAN topology to an ATM switch/router point on the same topological arrangement. From this ATM switch or router, the data can then be sent along either a Permanent Virtual Circuit (PVC) or a Switched Virtual Circuit (SVC) and arrive at a distant location on the ATM backbone.

18

ATM

FIGURE 18.1.
ATM LAN/WAN basic topology.

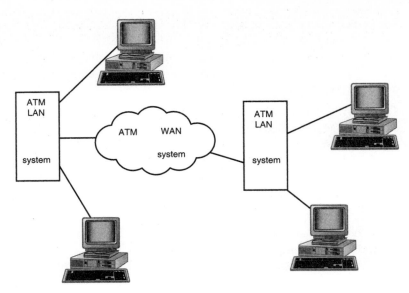

So what's the bottom line? ATM will do away with the distinction between a LAN and a WAN. By integrating LAN and WAN resources into one network, ATM is able to provide for the networking needs of everything from telephones to computer networks. Frame Relay is not suitable for doing anything in a LAN environment. Comparing ATM to Frame Relay is not really fair. It's sort of like trying to compare apples and bananas. The following section discusses some of the reasons why a network manager would want to use ATM technology.

Why Use ATM?

One of the first things any network manager needs to do when deciding on a network topology is to look at all of the pros and cons of each technology being considered. One of the first pros of ATM and a major reason why you would want to switch to it is that it obliterates the wall between WAN and LAN. This means that ATM networks are truly one-technology networks. Most of the enterprise networks in operation today are hodgepodges of different technologies. There may be some AppleTalk technology on some of the network's LANs, Windows NT on others, and perhaps Novell or something else on the remaining LANs.

When all kinds of different technologies are being used on each or all of the network's LANs, it means that the WAN portion of the network will be responsible for providing some commonality between the LANs on the network. This is where things can get a bit trickier. If the WAN portion of the network is using X.25, then most likely the speed of the WAN itself will play a big part in network congestion and problems. On the other hand, if the network's WAN is on a Frame Relay network, there may be no congestion problems right now. In the future, as Frame Relay networks become more crowded (depending on the vendor, the network used, and so on), there could be difficulties in meeting the needs of the WAN in terms of committed information rates (CIR).

NOTE

For a better explanation of Frame Relay CIR, see Chapter 17, "Frame Relay."

The point of this entire discussion is that WAN technologies prior to ATM can hardly compare with the speed of ATM as a WAN solution. Wouldn't it be easier to have a single technology that is capable of carrying your enterprise network's traffic from all points to all others? Think of the ease of upgrade. ATM technology is completely scaleable. In other words, as a network's capacity and requirements for more systems or bandwidth increase, additional ATM nodes running at higher speeds can simply be added to the existing network. This can all be done without having to redesign the existing network itself.

On present LAN topologies, whenever a hub or switch is added to the network, it's almost always done to accommodate the addition of new users, printers, or file servers. The beauty of ATM is the fact that when you add new switches, you increase the network capacity. When hubs and switches are added in present LANs, they do allow for more users and servers to run, but guess what? They do *not* add to the bandwidth capacity of the network as ATM does. In fact, they actually force all of the users, including the ones being added, to share whatever bandwidth resources the network already had. ATM's ease of expansion provides more bandwidth capacity as well as the ability to add more users, servers, or printers, and so on.

This ability to expand easily means that two very important things, time and money, are saved by using ATM. In terms of sheer speed alone, ATM can only improve the capabilities of any corporate network it is being used on. To top that off, whenever you decide in favor of upgrading your network and using shared media LANs, the existing network will need to be redesigned. When you are using ATM technology as your backbone, the network design remains the same, regardless of the size of the network.

Think of the time and effort that you can save by using ATM. Suppose that you are the administrator of a LAN/WAN setup used by a major corporation. Imagine that you have six sites with LANs and all of them are connected together by a WAN consisting of Plain Old Telephone Service (POTS) lines. You have speeds of 56Kbps on these POTS lines. Each LAN is using Ethernet technology behind their routers. Now, at one location, you are subnetting the LAN into smaller chunks of users (see Figure 18.2).

In Figure 18.2, five of the six LANs are depicted as simple, connected circles on the diagram. It is the sixth LAN that you are interested in looking at. LAN 6 has a router system tied to the back end of it. Let us assume there are other users tied off of these two routers, and that they are considered users of LAN 6. Suppose all of the Ethernet hubs on the back of router 1 are full and that the hubs on the back of router 2 (the subnetted portion of the LAN) are also full. Here's where the agony will come into play for any LAN administrator. One day, management will inform you there is a need to place five more users on the back of router 2. At this point, two things will happen. You will need to put a new hub on the back of router 2, and

18

ATM

now all of the bandwidth being used by router 2 to get over to router 1 will be shared by these five new users.

FIGURE 18.2.

Example LAN/WAN (six LANs with POTS WAN).

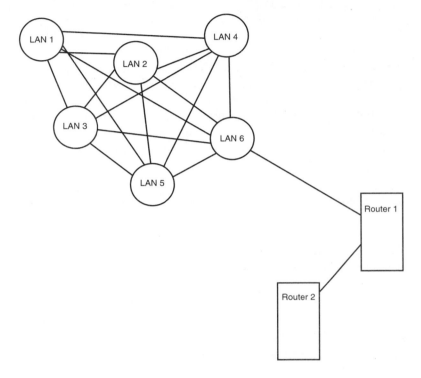

What just happened? By placing new hubs onto an existing LAN, that medium is shared by all. In other words, the users on this new hub will have to compete with every other user on all of the other hubs connected to router 2. Everyone just lost a little chunk of bandwidth on the Ethernet backbone of router 2. With ATM in the LAN, this is not the case. An ATM switch used on a LAN arrangement will provide each of the LAN's users with a switched connection. It's not a broadcast technology like Ethernet.

As the signal leaves each user's PC and is sent to the ATM interface device on the LAN, the connection is separate from each other user's connection. So, looking back at this little example, all of the users on router 2 will begin to experience longer delays when using the LAN. An ATM LAN would have not created this new delay as a result of adding five users (see Figure 18.3).

Suppose that instead of standard routers on LAN 6, the subnetted LAN 6 will have an ATM LAN covering the areas previously covered by routers 1 and 2. If you needed to place five new users onto this LAN, they would get their own direct connection into the ATM switch, hub, or bridging device. Further, when they are connecting with someone, either on the same LAN or across the WAN, they are given an actual individual connection across the ATM medium. They are not in a situation where they are sharing a broadcast medium as they would if they were on an Ethernet LAN. As you can see, this would make no impact on the speed and service of the new users as well as the existing users. All will get their own connection-based path through the ATM medium.

FIGURE 18.3.

Example LAN/WAN (LAN 6 improved with ATM).

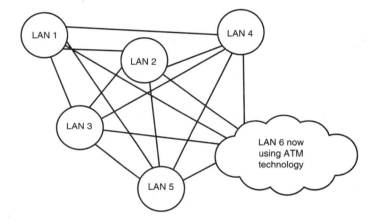

The next section discusses the inner workings of ATM and how it passes data from end to end based on connection-oriented services.

How ATM Works

ATM is not as big a mystery as some would have you believe. When ATM was first announced as the end-all, be-all of data networking WAN technologies, many people were afraid of the enormous costs associated with implementing it. Instead of trying to figure out what all the fuss was about, people decided ATM was beyond reach as a result of its enormous cost. If they had taken the time to learn how ATM works and how it is able to attain the enormous speeds with which it can transfer data, they might have thought twice before deciding ATM was beyond reach.

In a basic sense, ATM was conceived along the same lines as Frame Relay. It depends on clean, crisp data connections between service points on the network. Like Frame Relay, ATM does not involve itself in the business of verifying any errors in the data it is transferring from place to place. Also, like Frame Relay, ATM simply relies on the sophistication of the user equipment and endpoint devices on the network when it comes to error control and retransmission.

ATM uses fixed-size packets when transferring information. These packets are known as *cells* in the ATM world. Each ATM cell is actually a small packet of data exactly 53 bytes long. Within the 53 bytes, 5 bytes are used for address/header/descriptor information. More details on these 5 bytes are presented a little later. The remaining 48 bytes within the cell are used for the actual data, or information, being transferred through the ATM system. ATM is very adept at transferring voice, data, and video. The connections between two endpoints on an ATM network may use either a Switched Virtual Circuit (SVC) or a Permanent Virtual Circuit (SVC).

As you may recall from the previous chapter, Frame Relay also uses virtual circuits when transferring data from place to place. There is a big difference in the way ATM does the actual connecting of the virtual circuits. Whether the circuits are SVCs or PVCs, ATM will have pre-established the actual circuits ahead of time. Not only does this make it easy, but it is a major time-saver as well. The main benefits derived here are the processor and processing time factors, as both of these are greatly improved at the User-to-Network Interface (UNI) and the Network-to-Network Interface (NNI).

In the old X.25 days (as well as with Frame Relay), all of the connections were put up at subscription time with PVCs. This was an arduous process. It did take network time, which is valuable time. Likewise, if SVCs were going to be used, these connections would be made at the time of connection between points on the network. ATM does neither. It has a predetermined, mapped network to work with. All of the circuit information needed by ATM is preprogrammed before any data transference takes place. The ideal situation with ATM is when it is used on the Switched Optical Network (SONET). The reasons for this are, of course, speed and the fact that SONET also uses predestined addressing based on where the actual fiber connections physically exist. ATM fits well on OC3 SONET carriers, and it provides a preordained address scheme for the network it carries.

How does this addressing scheme operate, and how does ATM know to get the data where it belongs within the network? As you recall, ATM has a header that is exactly 5 bytes long. This header provides the information needed by ATM at the UNI as well as at the NNI (see Figure 18.4).

FIGURE 18.4.
ATM UNI and NNI cell headers.

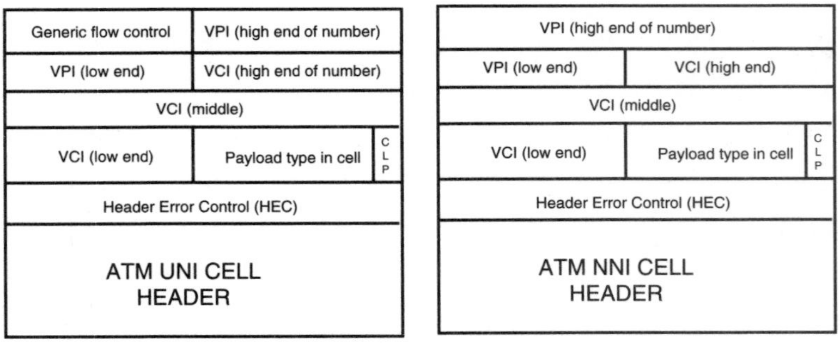

Generic flow control	VPI (high end of number)
VPI (low end)	VCI (high end of number)
VCI (middle)	
VCI (low end)	Payload type in cell	C L P
Header Error Control (HEC)	

ATM UNI CELL HEADER

VPI (high end of number)	
VPI (low end)	VCI (high end)
VCI (middle)	
VCI (low end)	Payload type in cell	C L P
Header Error Control (HEC)	

ATM NNI CELL HEADER

UNI Cell Header

At the UNI, one byte of eight bits provides a provision for 256 unique physical addresses. These physical paths are called virtual paths at the UNI. Within the header, the byte (8 bits) that describes these 256 paths is called a Virtual Path Identifier (VPI). Next, there are two bytes (16 bits) used to define up to 65,536 virtual circuits on each of these virtual paths. The diagram in

Figure 18.4 shows the order in which the bits are loaded into the header, in hierarchical order from top to bottom. You'll notice that some other fields are also used at the UNI level. One section of 4 bits is known as the Generic Flow Control (GFC) information field. There is also a 1-bit field called Cell Loss Priority (CLP). Three bits are reserved as the Payload Type field. However, at the NNI, this header information is definitely much different than it is at the UNI interface point.

NNI Cell Header

Reviewing Figure 18.4, you will notice that at the NNI, things are a little different. The VPI section of an NNI header (12 bits) will define 4,096 distinct paths. These VPIs will not refer to physical addresses as was the case in the UNI cell header structure. Rather, the VPI in an ATM NNI cell refers to network virtual paths between ATM switches on the ATM backbone network. The VCI is, once again, 16 bits long just as it was in the UNI cell structure. Once again, this means you have the capability of placing 65,536 virtual circuits on each virtual path. Also, there is a 3-bit Payload Type field and the 1-bit CLP field as was the case in the UNI cell header.

When comparing the two structures in Figure 18.4, you'll notice that the "bottom" 3 bytes of the cell headers are identical. It's the top 2 bytes of the cell that look different. This is, of course, due to the difference in the VPI (8 bits at UNI, 12 bits at NNI). The HEC field will be discussed in the section "The HEC: What Does It Do?"

The next section discusses the actual virtual circuits these ATM cells will follow. For the purposes of the following discussion, let's combine SVCs and PVCs and refer to the circuits in an ATM network simply as Virtual Connections (VCs). Each of these VCs will do the payload transference in the ATM network. Voice, data, and video can all be carried on ATM networks, but not at the same time. Each type of traffic will require an independent and unique VC.

What Keeps the VCs Straight in an ATM Network?

As traffic moves through an ATM network, it will no doubt traverse several network switches, hubs, or routers. As this traffic moves through the network, it will do so on one of these virtual connections, the VC referred to earlier. VCs, by nature of the header VPI and VCI information, are able to move through network nodes with ease, as each one of them will have separate and unique numbers contained within their headers. As you recall, ATM circuits are preordained before data is actually transmitted over them. At each node, buffers are assigned on the transmit and receive sides of the VCs passing through.

Therefore, there are certain characteristics we know all VCs will have. First, either a PVC or an SVC will comprise the trunk the VC resides on. Second, a VPI and VCI will be assigned at various nodes throughout the network in addition to the VPI/VCI assigned at the User-to-Network Interface (UNI) points. The third item refers to a cell speed or rate that will be accepted over the VC in question. These three items are what makes each VC unique within an ATM network. This is how the network can keep all of these cells (riding the VCs) straight.

ATM Rates and the "Leaky Bucket"

As you recall from Chapter 17, there was a so-called "leaky bucket" algorithm that allowed users to pass a certain amount of data through the Frame Relay network at any given time. ATM is no different. The only difference in an ATM network is the terminology used. Rather than calling it a Committed Information Rate (CIR) as in Frame Relay, we call it a Sustained/Sustainable Cell Rate (SCR) in ATM. ATM uses a timed buffer just as Frame Relay does.

> **NOTE**
>
> For a more detailed explanation of Frame Relay CIR, timed buffers, and leaky buckets, see Chapter 17.

There is a major difference, though. In ATM, the actual switching of the cells is done in hardware rather than in software. Because each cell is exactly 53 bytes in length, the buffers are much more efficient than in Frame Relay networks. The buffers can "know" exactly the length of each cell passing through. This allows for a more efficient leaky bucket to operate within ATM network nodes and equipment.

Remember the CLP bit shown in Figure 18.4? Well, that CLP bit does the same thing that Frame Relay Discard Eligibility (DE) bits do when a Frame Relay CIR rate has been surpassed. Frame Relay nodes would mark the DE bit in their packets when the packets had exceeded the CIR of the circuit. ATM does the same thing, but it uses the CLP bit. As you may have guessed, this happens when the SCR rate mentioned earlier has been surpassed.

The next section discusses the Header Error Control (HEC) byte contained in all ATM cell headers.

The HEC: What Does It Do?

Within each of the cell headers outlined in Figure 18.4, there was a byte (8 bits) called an HEC field. This field has a very important job within ATM networks. As cells are passing through the nodes on an ATM network, there is a little bit of poking around done as far as errors are concerned. Yes, it is true that ATM does not do any error checking per se. However, as each node "sees" cells passing through the network, if there are slight errors on the cells (usually involving only 1 bit), the nodes can use the HEC field and its associated 8 bits as a means to perform a bit of forward error correction.

Remember, this error correction can only work when there is a slight error in the cells passing through. It is rarely done, but the capability does exist. ATM does do a little tinkering when it comes to error control. This little bit of tinkering, coupled with the quality of today's high-speed transmission lines and ATM's speed, makes for an extremely stable means of transferring data.

This HEC field has a second use as well. As cells traverse the various nodes and points within an ATM network, the nodes themselves can use the HEC field as a good gauge of how well cells are "flying" through their ports. As long as the switches, or nodes, can constantly be allowed to monitor the HEC fields of cells passing through them (and they can), this can provide an excellent means of synchronization. Once again, the leaky bucket will apply here, but you can see where a steady flow of good HEC bytes in each cell could provide an awesome means of timing and synchronization for an ATM network.

The next section covers the actual payload section of ATM cells. After all, it is the data or payload of an ATM cell that must be reliably transmitted from place to place.

What Is This Thing Called the AAL?

Even though ATM is an extremely fast, reliable, and stable means of transmitting data from place to place, there is still going to be an amount of cell failure from point to point on the network. It simply can't be helped. This is why the ATM Forum mentioned at the beginning of the chapter has been so important in ATM's development cycle. The ATM Forum defined a set layer of ATM transmission known as the ATM Adaptation Layer (AAL). This layer is where all the rectification for bad, lost, or damaged cells with other errors takes place.

It's actually a software and/or firmware layer. It comprises two actual stages, or levels, of operation. The first stage is called the Convergence Sublayer (CS), and the second stage is called the Segmentation And Reassembly (SAR) Sublayer. The CS is actually the part that defines actual traffic types such as data, voice, or video. The CS will also take care of error control and the sequence and size of the information contained in the cells themselves. This is the first part of the process. After the CS has done its job, the SAR will come along and convert this raw data into the actual 48-byte-long pieces of data. These are the chunks of data that will make up each cell's payload section during transmission through the network.

The final part of the process is where the SAR earns its paycheck. The 5-byte header must be attached to each of these chunks the SAR just created. It is the job of the SAR to make sure that all of the information in the header is correct, in the right place, and properly attached to the 48-byte payload. After this has been done, a perfect, 53-byte cell has been created that is ready for transmission. As if we did not have enough acronyms to worry about, the ATM Forum saw fit to create five unique and independent AAL service structures. They are called AAL1, AAL2, AAL3, AAL4, and AAL5.

There's a reason why the ATM Forum came up with five adaptation layers. Each one is designed for different types of payloads. The AAL layers are put into place at the transmit node on an ATM network. It is the function of the receive node to simply receive the cells, break them down properly, and then hand them off to whatever process they belong to.

The following sections look at each of the five AALs and the types of traffic they handle.

18

ATM

AAL1

AAL1 is the basic service structure that handles voice traffic on ATM networks. You may think this is an easy task, but it does require a bit of work on AAL1's part. In order to keep voice competent from end to end, AAL1 must ensure that each cell being transmitted is done so in a perfect sequence. If any of the cells are out of order, the humans on each end would think each other was speaking a foreign language.

Further, if the cells are sent too close together, the humans would not be able to distinguish the beginning and ending of some of the words being spoken. AAL1 is ready for this natural pausing humans do when speaking. It ensures that the sequence numbers assigned to the cells it creates identify what parts of the cell(s) include voice traffic and what parts of the cell(s) include nothing due to silence. For this reason, many people refer to AAL1 and its ATM services as "streaming mode" ATM.

AAL2

This service structure concerns itself with video transmission service through ATM networks. Like AAL1, AAL2 must do sequencing and synchronization of the cells created by its process. However, there is also an added gimmick. There are error-checking codes called Cyclic Redundancy Checks (CRCs) used in the transmission of video. This is due to the large amount of information concerning each pixel of a video transmission.

AAL2 also does some labeling of each of the cells being transmitted. This cell labeling helps the end video device know where the information for each of the refreshed screens (or frames) of video starts and ends. This is extremely important in video transmissions. Each cell is either first, in the middle, or the last cell of each frame's transmission. When you look at the amount of pixel information transmitted during a video transmission through a network, it is dependent on how much movement is actually taking place. AAL2 can provide variable bandwidth on demand when handling video transmissions by using this labeling method. If there is little motion being made by the video's subject, then the amount of cells being transmitted will be smaller than when the video's subject is moving around a lot.

AAL3/AAL5

The reason I have grouped AAL3 and AAL5 together is that they are both designed to be used with Connection-Oriented Protocols (COP). A COP is a situation where an actual connection must be established between the sending and receiving members of a data transmission. A good example of this is the Internet, which uses TCP/IP. Whenever someone goes out on the World Wide Web and attaches to a certain resource or home page, he has put up that "connection" prior to any traffic being passed back and forth between the Web resource and himself. Hence, the term connection-oriented applies here.

Both of these AAL services will perform error control, sequencing, and identification within the cells as they are created for transmission. All of this information will be placed within the cell's structure, as the connection-oriented data process using these cells will need all of this information in order to pass data back and forth over the ATM network. AAL5 requires less overhead than AAL3, and relies on the fact that ATM is being used on clear, digital transmission facilities. For that reason alone, most ATM networks passing connection-oriented data will use the AAL5 structure when creating cells for transmission.

AAL4

This service is a lot different than AAL3 and AAL5. AAL4 is for connection-less transmissions of data. Naturally, this type of service would not work for either voice or video. Voice and video are indeed dependent on a distinct connection from end to end. Even if the connection is over an SVC or a PVC, that connection is in place. AAL4 does not rely on that connection. Instead, it just "releases" the data into the network and relies on the network to somehow get the data to its destination. There is actually a 10-bit field called a Multiplex Identifier (MI) that is used by AAL4 in order to get the data to its rightful destination.

ATM: Putting It All Together

Now that you know all about cells and such, imagine a situation from one LAN user to another through an ATM network. Assuming a non-perfect world, imagine a fictitious user (User A) on an Ethernet LAN in Chicago and a fictitious user (User B) on a Token Ring network in Colorado Springs. If the two LANs are being tied together by an ATM Wide Area Network (WAN), what will generally take place is shown in Figure 18.5.

FIGURE 18.5.

User A and User B example.

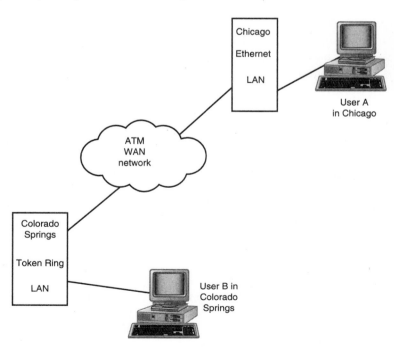

User A in Chicago will send out the data destined for User B in Colorado Springs. Say it's a picture/graphics file of some sort. Perhaps User A will compose an e-mail message on the LAN in Chicago using Microsoft Mail. He will then attach the picture/graphics file to the e-mail message. After Microsoft Mail has determined that this e-mail is not addressed to anyone on its LAN, it will send the e-mail message along to the router or domain controller in charge of its LAN's inward and outbound traffic.

This was all done over the Ethernet. Once the router receives the message from User A's PC, it will then recognize (through the use of its routing tables) that the message needs to be placed out on the WAN. Remember, this fictitious WAN is ATM-based. The router would send its data to an ATM "box" of some type that would contain the software/firmware/hardware needed to get the router's data into ATM-acceptable chunks. This box may be a Customer Service Unit (CSU) or it may be an actual ATM switch with built-in CSU functions. Either way, this ATM box will then convert the data into 53-byte cells.

These cells will be "zapped" out onto the ATM Virtual Connection (VC) predetermined between User A's location to User B's location.

> **NOTE**
>
> Remember, ATM uses predefined virtual circuits between each location on its network.

After these cells arrive (rather rapidly) at User B's ATM box, CSU, or switch, they will all be broken down again into a form of data User B's router can recognize. After the ATM interface equipment has done that, it will pass this data over to the router controlling inward and outward traffic on User B's LAN. At that point, this router will place the information out on the Token Ring LAN in Colorado Springs that User B is a part of. The LAN will deliver the e-mail to User B's PC, where he can then open the message and view the attached picture/graphics file. That's all there is to it. Although this example may seem simplistic, it is a good example of where ATM technology will fit into the picture.

Summary

Many organizations have LANs in place that will meet their needs for years to come. Simply replacing these LANs with ATM LANs in order to keep up with technology makes absolutely no sense. However, tying these LAN's together with ATM technology makes a lot of sense. Hopefully, as new organizations begin to create their own LANs in different locations, they will base the topology of their LANs on ATM technology. This makes for a very easy transition to ATM wide area service between newly formed LANs in an organization's structure. ATM technology will no doubt be as commonplace as the telephone in a few years, but for now, it still remains the "technophile's" network of choice and the manager's last choice when considering cost. ATM will progress a lot further than ISDN because it is being handled and "groomed" much better than ISDN ever was. The ATM Forum is seeing to that. All we can do is take a wait-and-see attitude.

ATM will no doubt be the LAN and WAN technology of the future. It only makes sense to use fixed-length data cells and to carry these cells from one user to another. After all, what is the main purpose of any network? We know that the effective and efficient transfer of data from one point to another can be accomplished by using one of many technologies. However, we also know that ATM is without a doubt the most effective and efficient way to do this. Once the costs of ATM interface boards for PCs, ATM switches, bridges, hubs, and routers have reached an affordable level, network managers will jump on the ATM bandwagon with both feet.

As you recall from the information given in this chapter, data from one user's PC will basically travel the entire network path to the other user's PC with very little interaction from software processes. Hardware and firmware processes do most of the processing and routing of data in ATM networks, and this is what makes the movement of data so fast and efficient. As the line between what constitutes a LAN or a WAN becomes blurred, it is ATM that will bridge the gap and provide network managers with a one-technology solution to all of their network traffic. This will happen very soon, and many vendors are poised to begin selling ATM hardware and equipment. ATM will become the network topology of choice.

18

ATM

IV
PART

IN THIS PART

The Right OS for the Job

CHAPTER 19

Selecting the OS to Meet Your Needs

by David Welk

IN THIS CHAPTER

The purpose of this chapter is to provide an overview of three major network operating systems (NOS) and to determine exactly how each of these platforms may fit into your high-performance network. I discuss three operating systems: Microsoft NT version 4, Novell NetWare, and UNIX/Linux.

In this chapter, I will talk about many of the real and often overlooked issues that exist in most organizations. The three major topics include the political agendas of senior management, the organization's culture, and the fiscal health of the company.

I will also discuss some real world examples of networks in small, medium, and large environments. In these discussions, I try to provide some insight into the use of network operating systems and the strengths and weaknesses of each. Detailed discussions will center around financial responsibility, investment protection, and future proofing.

Determining Your Needs

Before you can begin to analyze the information needs of your business, there are some organizational issues that you should consider. A company's senior management team will tend to set the organization's culture and they also have responsibility for the current fiscal trend of the business. These factors along with the current state of your network, which typically is the responsibility of your Information Systems (IS) group, are some of the elements that determine the business needs. A good understanding of available solutions, when matched with a strong understanding of the business' requirements, will help to define the appropriate high-performance network operating system solutions. Later in this chapter, a more in-depth explanation should fully address these sticky issues.

Where Do I Start?

The first step in trying to determine the needs of the business, is to analyze and understand just how the organization goes about doing business. Understanding the day-to-day operations of selling and buying products and services, as well as supporting mundane tasks like storing, shipping, and scheduling, is an important aspect of this process. Analyzing which people within the organization have access to the various kinds of information already available is also extremely important.

Is the required information entirely within the organization's control or are there some external connectivity requirements? In many situations, there are services being provided by second and third-party organizations. These organizations contract for access to certain areas of information. A significant part of the contractual agreements dictate which organization is responsible for establishing and maintaining connectivity. Security becomes very important when opening an environment to external access.

Is there a need to access external information databases and competitive companies' Web information? The easiest way to accomplish this has often been to allow modem access from individual desktops. The industry has taken note that there are unscrupulous individuals with the knowledge and capability to invade private networks through a single modem connection. This has lead to a dramatic increase in chassis-based, integrated remote access equipment. Security solutions have been rolling along hand-in-hand with the advancing remote access solutions, as the user community expands. The increase in telecommuting and Web browsing have also been instrumental in this increase in the dial-up community. Another very important issue is to develop an understanding of how your organization manages the various connectivity requirements and their related costs.

For the most part, the larger organizations have already determined the answers to these questions. Usually, improving support for existing business applications and the occasional implementation of a new business application drives these groups through their daily routines. In medium and smaller organizations, a business application typically comes along to force the migration initially to networking and then on to high-performance networking. These applications usually come with some advice from a consultant on how to host them. Investing the time necessary to research hardware platforms enables you to isolate the little things that help productivity improvements. There may also be recommendations on the type of infrastructure required to make the chosen hardware and software work effectively.

> **NOTE**
>
> Of course, all of this advice comes with a corresponding price tag. The evaluation of this price tag to determine your return on investment is necessary to ensure that a good business decision is being made.

After completing a reasonable amount of research and gathering most of the aforementioned information, you will have a good picture of your "environment." It is within the concept of this environment that you can begin to envision the need for high-performance networking and the relevant network operating systems to run the applications. In the past, if an information systems group decided to implement new technology for the sake of the new technology, the business eventually found some reason to use it. The Systems Department generally was responsible for the operating costs associated with this environment. Today, most corporations charge the individual business units for the use of the corporate network. The departments that fund any new projects are forced to do a careful analysis to guarantee suitable returns on their investment. Unfortunately, the business units might then not be forced to adhere to the prevailing corporate standards, if any exist. Such lack of adherence to standards creates a difficult job for centralized systems management people and is a strong argument for the local information systems group to have budget control.

Management Requirements

Management's requirements for the Information Systems people typically have three parts: individual political agendas, the culture of the organization, and the quality of recent revenues.

In organizations where money is tight, IS personnel are often transferred to other departments, or the slow replacement of former employees causes understaffing. In these same organizations, there is constant struggle over available investment money. With systems in place that seem to be doing an adequate job, the Information Systems group tends to get the short end of the budget stick.

Of course, there are always technically savvy individuals who reach the higher ranks and push for technical advantages such as a high-performance network. Those individuals may have difficulty driving changes within the organization, depending upon their individual abilities to sell technology to non-technical senior management. Organizations that historically have been conservative also tend to follow the tested and safe trends of network computing.

On the other hand, the leading-edge organizations are always testing and evaluating the latest and greatest hardware and software systems. The culture of these organizations dictates that they employ leading-edge capabilities throughout the organization. These companies tend to get and keep much of the brightest talent in the industry and often have tremendous funding for System's budgets.

Culture

I use the term "culture" in this chapter to refer to the way a company interacts with itself and with its customers and suppliers. Your company's culture can directly affect the type of network infrastructure and operating systems that your organization deploys.

In growing companies that are comfortable with taking risks, you typically find leading-edge networking technology, such as switching and high-speed connectivity. In older, more bureaucratic corporations, you are likely to see an array of various systems and aging software. Typically, older systems supporting only one function sit alongside newer platforms that can perform multiple functions for the business. IS groups spend countless hours trying to shift an application away from or working to delete these single-function pieces of equipment. In between these technological extremes are most of the rest of today's companies.

In the majority of companies, the concept of centralized management information systems, which is a legacy of mainframe environments, has been severely strained with the advent of the desktop personal computer (PC). Staffs have become larger and have fanned out to support high node-count and geographically dispersed networks. Previously, an administrator was able to do most of the work required to manage the network from a centralized console. Although not completely eliminated, IS staffs have been minimizing the usage of this management capability.

It is also not unusual to have at least a few PC-challenged senior managers who are typically averse to high risk, and therefore inclined to provide limited IS investment capital. For the most part, these IS groups are able to do just enough with their limited resources to get by each and every day. Systems have no strategic impact on these organizations' productivity or on improving development time to market a new product.

Political Issues

The job of figuring out networking project sponsors is usually not very hard. In today's typical corporations, there are very few senior-level executives who have spent any time within a desktop computing group. These few PC literate, project sponsors know a business cannot get along without high-performance network computing. Generally, there are one or at most a small group of executives who regularly use personal computers and believe in the capabilities of remote connectivity and high-performance networking. Learning who these senior managers are and working to satisfy their individual requirements is important to growing a systems department. These allies will fight to help you implement needed high-performance technology.

Business Trends

You need to measure the profitability of your organization by using the tools provided by corporate accounting. If your company is doing well financially, you'll have greater freedom to evaluate leading-edge technological improvements. Organizations that are doing well have probably already taken risks along the way and have found that doing so has paid off for them. The Information Systems people are strategically relevant in such a company.

In organizations that are exhibiting fiscal weakness, holding the line on costs and capital expenditures is routine. The requirement to support outdated systems, which often reside alongside newer equipment, with limited staff is increasing. Many times there is a high rate of turnover in the IS department. The problem of training new people combined with the loss of key knowledge, limits what any technical group can do to be effective. Such an organization will typically be very slow to implement any high-performance technology.

IS Personnel

A large part of the business community is in the process of thinning out Information Systems departments. Outsourcing of strategic pieces is becoming much more common. Turnover among technical employees has always been higher than in most other departments, often as the result of increasing salary offers on the free market. Technical personnel are prone to changing jobs anyway, so turnover within a slow-moving IS group is very common.

The good news for IS people is that there is a wealth of education and skill-enhancing information available. In many organizations, all it takes to receive advanced training is to show some inclination and a strong desire to learn. The overall attractiveness of the networking industry has brought larger amounts of new people into technical roles than have ever existed before. The amount of companies doing business in the industry, along with the networking industry itself, are growing at strong rates. Good, strong talent is always hard to find, so making yourself good at something is a means of job security.

Identifying Solutions

The theme of this book is high-performance networking, so as I initially discuss the following operating systems, I will slant the topics towards usage in a high-performance environment.

UNIX—Linux

This grandfather of network operating systems has several stepchildren and iterations. Versions continue to be updated and enhanced. Major manufacturers such as Digital Equipment Corporation, Hewlett-Packard, and Sun Microsystems offer customized versions of UNIX that work in conjunction with hardware workstations also developed by these companies. An ongoing question mark about UNIX continues to be whether and when it will be superseded by some PC-based operating systems. Microsoft and Intel are certainly working very hard to eliminate all competition, but there will always be room for multiple vendors who are able to bring strong products to market. There is an industry wide consensus that some "flavor" of UNIX will carry on indefinitely because of its tight linkage to the Internet.

UNIX operating systems were originally conceived and built to be robust and support networked equipment. This reason alone has allowed UNIX to survive many years as a niche solution. The UNIX operating systems' ability to support multiple tasks at the same time makes it a strong candidate for a high-performance network. The strong performance and portability of UNIX are additional reasons that it has been adapted to support the more powerful workstations. Examples of these more powerful computing stations are found in most engineering and research facilities.

Linux is the version of UNIX that has been adapted to run on the Intel processor. Much of the strength of UNIX has to be scaled down to run on this platform. As the Intel processors and their clones improve, you will begin to see strong Microsoft products that are almost as robust as UNIX, and infinitely easier to use.

Windows NT 4

Depending on your point of view, Windows NT 4 may be the end of UNIX as we know it or just another Microsoft operating system to control our lives. This third major version of the NT operating system comes in desktop and server variations. The big difference is the usage of the Windows 95 shell. There is a higher level of stability within this version of Windows also. A major focus for Microsoft is improvement of its support for external devices and enhanced Internet capabilities.

Although Microsoft has not labeled the newest version of DOS-based Windows as of press time, there is a renewed emphasis on Internet and intranet capabilities. Over time, the tight integration of these new capabilities will also be found in the updated versions of NT.

This is the network operating system that provides most of the same functionality as found in UNIX operating systems. Because it is not based on any underlying operating system and is in fact a multitasking environment, NT 4 has the capability of being extremely robust. It is important to remember that UNIX has been developed over almost thirty years, and NT is only a few years old. It will take time and experience for this operating system to become as strong as UNIX, but having the backing of corporate America may just speed that learning curve up dramatically.

NetWare

This market-leading network operating system is suffering from severe stagnation. By taking on more than they could handle a few years ago, Novell has lost considerable market momentum and mind share. Now that it has sold off its WordPerfect and Borland products, Novell's focus has returned to building a strong network operating system. Novell has always had good software, but the competition is getting better all the time.

Because the previous two network operating systems were true operating systems, NetWare still requires an underlying operating system. This was a conscious decision by Novell and may prove to be an insurmountable obstacle for Novell.

Novell's products are still very well represented within corporate America and have become integral to the network environments there. There are boatloads of thoroughly trained technical resources available that will continue to support and recommend these products.

The hardest perception for Novell to overcome will be that its products must be somewhat inferior to Microsoft's and others because it is losing market share. It still makes a highly reliable environment that can literally run for years. I would consider that high performance. Over the last year, Novell has been trying to adapt to the intranet craze. Its network operating system is perfectly suited to this kind of environment and is beginning to show itself in the marketplace. The advent and complete acceptance of browser technology is also finding Novell chasing the market a little bit.

Financial Responsibility

What are the cost elements associated with each of these operating systems? What are the costs associated with the required hardware to make these systems run effectively? What are some of the tools you can use to determine adequate returns on investment? What are some of the other financial factors to consider when evaluating a project's feasibility?

The simplest method of determining return on investment (ROI) is to use the "payback method"—totaling all the relevant costs to implement new technology and comparing that figure to the recurring savings. This calculation will reveal the amount of time necessary to recoup setup costs. Keeping this time factor under two years is usually good enough for the finance people. The technology industry does not wait around for ROI, and counting on realizing savings over a period longer than two years may be a risky business practice.

There are other factors to consider. Is the system a requirement for our business to function? Analyzing ROI in this situation does not really matter. At times some project sponsored by a powerful manager may not make sense financially. This high risk tactic either leaves the manager labeled a visionary or gets him fired.

Investment Protection

How do we as an organization go about protecting the investment we have already made in networking products? What do we need to think about as we plan our networking strategy?

The answers to these questions are improving all the time as the manufacturers begin to build products that have extendible life cycles. Using chassis slots and interface ports that accept differing technologies allows network managers to upgrade their hardware when needed. Having flash-ROM capabilities allows network engineers to upgrade operating code as new features and fixes come along.

Existing Infrastructure

What kind of infrastructure already exists? The analysis here pertains to the topology or physical media in place. Depending on the primary host computer, there might be Ethernet, Token Ring, or FDDI technologies in place. How well does each of these aspects meld into a high-performance environment? What do the next generations of switched technology expect to be able to do with the existing equipment?

Determining the Best Solution

In today's high-performance networking environments, switching technology is the preferred method of transporting data. Even long-time routed environments are starting to evaluate and implement switching technology. Improving the concept of fast bridging has lead switches to become mainstream technology today. This technology creates direct connections between communicating devices. This is important because it allows the network to service the next bits of data without having to wait for previous information to be processed. The ability of switching technology to scale up and add incremental bandwidth has been a blessing for network managers.

Another excellent feature is switching's ease of use. Few, if any, configuration and programming skills are required. Switches can literally be plug-and-play devices. Of course, like any effective high-performance networking component, there will need to be some advanced setup and configuration. As the technology advances and the price points continue to improve, functionality will increase, which will require high-level skill sets.

Layer 3 switching or fast routing will need to go through the same acceptance period that layer 2 switches recently endured. There are already competing technologies and methods for accomplishing layer 3 switching. This area of high-performance networking has yet to be truly tested and will bring a certain amount of pain with it. The concepts behind this method of transporting data are strong. The obvious requirement here again will be a high level of technical skill to properly configure and manage these devices.

What desktop operating systems work the best within a switched environment? My analysis section basically identified Microsoft Windows in the 95 or the NT form, or some consolidation of these two iterations, as logical selections. OS/2 already makes a strong multitasking operating system that works well in a switched environment. This feature gives an advantage to IBM in the server environment. The future of OS/2 as a desktop solution seems to be nearing the end of its life cycle.

The server side of your environment is the lucrative end of this marketplace. The hardware is typically high-end and very expensive. The costs associated with server operating systems and the appropriate licensing is significant also. All of the aforementioned operating systems have a role here. I will discuss that role and try to isolate the strengths and weaknesses of each in a high-speed networking environment.

Small Environments—Fewer Than 100 Users

The ease of use of the Windows environment makes this selection almost a no-brainer. Running Windows 95 on desktops as soon as possible as a replacement for Windows 3.1 is the state of the market today. On the server side, the options are Windows NT, Novell NetWare, UNIX, or OS/2. Microsoft might have an advantage here because of the similarity between its desktop and server operating systems. Analyzing the type of network usage is important in this environment, too. Novell does a very good job of supporting file and print services. These are the primary requirements for the majority of small network users. Microsoft NT has its advantages in an environment that loads and runs applications from a central server. UNIX does a fine job of both print and file support, as well as application sharing. Unfortunately this robust, IP-based operating system has its roots in the scientific community and is quite difficult to master.

The costs for licensing and supporting these environments is important to look at also. What kind of staff is in place to support these servers after they have been initially installed? Regular maintenance is required by certified technicians on all of these platforms.

Medium Environments

In medium environments, which I will define as greater than one hundred users and less than one thousand users, Windows 95 makes sense as the desktop operating system. It is more difficult for these organizations to update their entire user community and they have been slow to adopt Windows 95. The improvements over existing Windows 3.1 desktops make the pain associated with this major Systems change worthwhile.

From the server side, the picture gets more hazy. The quantity and quality of Systems personnel often dictates software decisions in these organizations. Novell still has the largest segment of the server market and is valiantly trying to reestablish itself in the Internet/intranet industry. Support for Novell-based systems is everywhere and usually good skills can be acquired for a reasonable cost.

Certainly, there will be specific applications that will dictate what types of operating systems are run. A good example of this would be OS/2 and its early support for the Lotus Notes environment. Much of this support is now slipping to Microsoft NT, and OS/2 must quickly become something very dramatic to change this phenomenon.

Microsoft's premier network operating system, NT 4, is being linked more closely to many mission-critical applications being rolled out in leading organizations. By providing integrated support for Novell and other internetworking protocols, this network operating system's graphically based ease of use is winning over customers.

The network operating system that has been around the longest probably does not enjoy its greatest success in the medium-level organizations. UNIX still requires highly paid support personnel and is closely tied to the Internet and scientific community. Certainly, these emerging organizations are approaching the Internet at a faster rate, but they are now able to do it with other more user friendly network operating systems.

Large Environments

The large environment, which I will define as greater than one thousand users, is typically spread out over some geographical area. In fact, in today's age of global communications, the environment may encompass several continents.

There is usually no easy answer to establishing a high-performance network within these environments. Certainly there is no single network operating system that will provide all the features and functions necessary to do business effectively today. Also, the combination of existing networks, typically Novell, as well as new applications, typically Microsoft-based, have caused a mixture of platforms for the network group to support.

In most of the networks that I have been involved with, printer and file services have been running under NetWare forever. The job is being accomplished adequately, so there has been no major push to change it. As new powerful applications are coming out, you will see a lot of platforms dependent on Microsoft NT.

From the network management perspective, most software platforms are being ported to Windows NT. The inherent weaknesses of DOS-based operating systems within a networked environment, along with the improved ease of use, are speeding NT to the forefront of application development.

Another large factor in Microsoft's favor is the integrated support for network protocols. Instead of following Novell down the proprietary protocol path, Microsoft has developed interfaces that work with Novell and TCP/IP. This integrated support further simplifies the use of this operating system. As the world approaches perfection and one network protocol, Microsoft is properly positioned to support it.

Of course Microsoft NT is not perfect. There are probably many of us who have had to support NetBios-based protocols within a network. As soon as the utilization begins to escalate, the performance in these environments degrades. This was never an issue in the early networks. As switching technology improves overall bandwidth, new bottlenecks are appearing that are exposing the weaknesses of network design and infrastructures.

The bottom line of this discussion is that supporting multiple protocols is here and will be for a long time. Choose the network operating system that has the features that are necessary for you to do business. If it becomes necessary to hire staff trained in multiple categories, so be it! There is no longer a good reason to follow one vendor down the path to glory. Find the products that fit your environment the tightest and effectively provide the kind of support necessary to do business. It is okay to mix and match; most large organizations are already doing it. This puts the burden back on the manufacturer to comply with standards and interoperate. In the end, this will be good for all of our environments no matter the size of the user community.

Summary

This chapter provided you with the necessary tools for selecting the right operating system (OS) to meet the business needs of your organization. All organizations have varying needs, and the right solution is often a combination of operating systems. Where appropriate, this chapter addressed and discussed the links of the operating system to high-speed networking. The first section of this chapter suggested some ways of determining the business needs of your organization. The second section contained brief discussions about the operating systems and their performance in various high-speed environments. A more detailed discussion of each of these operating systems made up the remainder of this chapter. I also integrated several management issues that affect the determination of the right OS for the job. Finally, I described some detailed solutions implementing the aforementioned operating systems.

As stated earlier, many of these solutions, especially in larger environments, consist of a combination of several operating systems. The end goal of this analysis is to find the right operating system or systems for the job. This chapter tries to take as many factors as possible into consideration.

UNIX/Linux

*by Frank C. Pappas
and Emil Rensing*

IN THIS CHAPTER

CHAPTER 20

In recent years, the rise in both popularity and performance of Windows and Macintosh networking products has irrevocably altered the role of UNIX in the world of corporate information systems. UNIX is no longer the *de facto* standard for the technology workplace, and the question of "Why UNIX?" has been transformed into more than simply an issue of satisfying the needs of demanding users, penny-pinching bosses, or technical neophytes. More to the point, the battle over enterprise-wide network operating system (NOS) solutions has been elevated to a quasi-religion, in which the believers—on both sides of the aisle—eagerly await any opportunity to reshape the opinions of "nonbelievers." This is especially the case among UNIX devotees, whose passion for UNIX (and disdain for Windows) is readily apparent in the jobs they accept, the recommendations they offer to management, and in the opinions they espouse on Usenet, in the media, and at industry conventions worldwide. It's important to understand why so many people have such strong and differing opinions when it comes to the UNIX versus Windows versus Mac debate, because it's anything but a simple issue.

Why Use UNIX?

First and foremost, UNIX is an incredibly powerful, flexible, and dynamic operating system, capable of handling almost any task that you care to throw at it. System administrators and programmers love it because it offers a wide array of avenues through which to address most Information Technology problems, including an obscene amount of processing power, renowned stability and reliability, powerful automation and scripting, and support for a variety of popular (and not-so-popular) programming languages.

After all is said and done, however, you're left with the big question: Why should you select UNIX as the NOS of choice for your organization?

This chapter takes a good, hard look at the question of "Why UNIX?" Specifically, the topics covered are the history and evolution of the UNIX OS, why it has become increasingly popular over the years (especially with the explosion of Internet services), and the various areas in which UNIX most often beats the pants off the competition. Finally, the chapter presents an overview of the six most popular "flavors" of UNIX currently in use around the world, complete with information on system-specific hardware and software requirements, where to find more information, and how to bring UNIX solutions to fruition.

The History of UNIX

With its development pre-dating even the earliest versions of Microsoft Windows and Apple's MacOS, the beginnings of UNIX can be traced back to the early 1960s and a computing project spearheaded by AT&T's Bell Labs. Working in cooperation with a consortium of leading technology R&D firms, the goal of AT&T's project was to develop Multics, an operating system capable of providing a powerful, robust, and reliable computing environment for large-scale deployment in communities throughout the United States. The creation of Multics was anything but an altruistic move on AT&T's part because the motive behind the project was to gain a monopoly in the computer services arena, similar to the regional monopolies enjoyed by AT&T in the telecommunications industry at the time. However, in mid-1969, Bell Labs terminated its support for the Multics project, which for a time left the development of such grand computing services with an uncertain future.

Drawing on the invaluable experience gained from their participation in the Multics project, a number of individuals within AT&T were determined to continue the development of a powerful operating system that could handle large-scale computing problems with ease. After they designed a workable file system that was first ported to the PDP-7 platform, the earliest version of UNIX began to earn marked support from within the ranks at AT&T. It became more popular when, following further development, it was ported to newer, more powerful hardware and successfully tackled the automation of a number of important functions within the company. However, despite the many accomplishments of the system, it was still bulky, unwieldy, and difficult to maintain, which left its designers, administrators, and users yearning for something more.

UNIX Begins to Evolve

AT&T would not have to wait very long for the radical shift in technology that would allow UNIX to be simultaneously made more efficient as well as more powerful. Only a few years after the second port of UNIX to a PDP-11 system, that "something" would take the form of the C programming language. With the introduction of C in the early 1970s—following a number of variants that pre-dated the "official" language—C was chosen by the architects of UNIX as the ideal way to solve a number of the nagging problems inherent in their initial design. With a complete rebuild utilizing the advanced resources of C, UNIX took a number of major steps toward becoming the premiere operating system for handling large-scale computing needs in business, academia, and government, especially because the new C-code foundation for UNIX brought the OS out of the proprietary age into the world of open standards.

Licenses were increasingly granted to universities at little or no cost, and the domination of UNIX was simply limited by how fast administrators could obtain the distributions and install them on their systems. By the late 1970s, the first commercial versions of UNIX were made available to the public, and UNIX began to infiltrate the world of business computing with systems deployed throughout corporate America at a breakneck pace.

Standards and Practices

As developers began to unleash a dizzying array of UNIX variants—not necessarily sporting even remotely similar levels of functionality—it quickly became apparent that a serious, official effort was needed to control the development of standards and features that would minimally define a system as a member of the UNIX family. After all, with the core strengths of UNIX residing in its unique combination of open standards and a common command set, the many dissimilar versions that had begun to pepper the market in the late 70s and early 80s were doing great harm to the uniformity of the UNIX crusade.

20

UNIX/LINUX

As the final arbiter of what is (and isn't) officially part of the UNIX game plan, the Institute of Electrical and Electronic Engineers (IEEE) established two committees that are responsible for regulating the development of the UNIX operating system and supporting software products. As the first of the two committees, POSIX.1 is tasked with maintaining a standardized C library interface for UNIX, so that developers (and users) can be assured that there will be a fairly reliable degree of portability among UNIX flavors for any particular program developed in C. The second of the committees, named (strangely enough) POSIX.2, is responsible for the front-end portion of UNIX, making sure that a basic command set exists that is native to all versions of the operating system, despite any particular eccentricities or proprietary features introduced by the various vendors. Despite this seemingly impossible job, the IEEE's POSIX committees have done a fairly thorough job at maintaining high degrees of compatibility between the different implementations of UNIX, with the features and performance of DEC UNIX, Linux, Solaris, SCO, and others significantly resembling one another.

Where UNIX Excels

Over the course of the past three decades, countless thousands of hours of blood, sweat, and code have been poured into the development of the UNIX operating system. After such a Herculean effort, one that is still in progress even today, you'd expect that UNIX would be able to perform far above the competition in a number of areas central to the field of networked computing. And you'd be right. Not only is UNIX a phenomenal choice to handle traditional corporate computing needs, but it has also risen to the task of providing superior solutions for Internet-based needs, including Web, Telnet, FTP, database access, and more! Because UNIX was designed to handle high usage loads and to integrate without much hassle into a networked environment, it almost always outperforms any other platform/OS combo attempting to perform such services.

But what, specifically, does UNIX do so extraordinarily? Three areas that really highlight the strength of the UNIX OS are closed TCP/IP networking, Internet and intranet services, and database manipulation. The next few sections cover these three areas briefly, touching on the main points and features of each.

Closed TCP/IP Networking

From the earliest days, UNIX was, has been, and forever shall be a *network* operating system. Unlike Windows and Mac, which evolved over time to include certain successful networking features, the foundation of everything that UNIX does relies on its ability to network speedily and efficiently. In order to understand the UNIX networking environment, you'll need to be familiar with the following six points.

Point One: TCP/IP or Bust

As you'll recall from earlier chapters, a variety of protocols can be used to join a group of computers together in a network. Although UNIX is able to easily and efficiently handle a number of different protocols in certain situations, the single most important pair of protocols to the success of UNIX-based networking is most certainly the combination of the Transmission Control Protocol (TCP) and the Internet Protocol (IP), most often referenced jointly as TCP/IP.

A UNIX system is wholly dependent upon TCP/IP to maintain its connectivity with the various hosts, workstations, and remote users who will want to access the system at any given time. You'll remember from your previous reading that IP has the ultimate responsibility for transferring data from one machine to another, TCP is the virtual traffic cop who makes sure that there's an available, safe route to get your information from `bungo.flyingmonkey.org` to `rango.fojfo.com`. And because TCP/IP connections are uniquely identifiable by virtue of their CLIENT[IP:PORT]/HOST[IP:PORT] values, the capacity exists for multiple simultaneous connections, given enough bandwidth and available memory.

Point Two: TCP User Services

Included among the UNIX bag of tricks are a variety of services designed to enhance the usefulness of the UNIX networking environment for users and administrators alike. After all, while TCP/IP is all well and good, it doesn't do anyone any good if the power of TCP/IP can't easily be harnessed and directed by the user. Two of the three most common UNIX services will be familiar to just about anyone who has ever logged onto a UNIX box in the past, namely Telnet and FTP. The third service, DNS (Domain Name Service) is geared toward system administrators and operators.

Telnet is a special communications service that allows a user to remotely connect to a machine, that is, they do not have to be physically present at the console to execute commands, check mail, administer servers, and so on.

FTP similarly allows users to remotely connect to certain machines, although instead of being able to execute the full array of shell commands, the users are limited to either sending or receiving one or more files.

Point Three: Administration Tools and Daemons

Administrators responsible for the maintenance and performance of UNIX machines are provided with a wide range of utilities to automate the most common and complex tasks generally encountered when dealing with the UNIX environment. Of this class of tools, network *daemons*—a special groups of processes that run silently in the background—assist the administrator by managing everything from routing, logging, and time synchronization to SMTP mail transmissions, talk requests, performance monitoring, and much, much more. UNIX really shines in this area, especially considering that neither Windows nor MacOS-based systems come with anything more than the simplest of network management tools, with large outlays of cash necessary to purchase comparable third-party network software packages.

Point Four: The UNIX Network File System

Of the many duties and responsibilities that a network administrator will face during the course of his employment, one of the most critical deals with maintaining a workable, secure, and reliable file system, ensuring the integrity of both system and user data.

UNIX once again far outpaces the competition in the file system arena (with the possible exception of WinNT's NTFS) with its *Network File System*, generally referred to as NFS. NFS is geared to allow administrators to quickly and easily construct a complete file system using all or part of local and, more impressively, remote directory trees, including directories residing on machines not necessarily running the UNIX OS. This gives the system administrator a great deal of flexibility because he is empowered to create file systems that don't strictly mimic the distribution of files physically on a given series of partitions. In this way, the administrator can tailor specific file systems to meet the special needs of various user groups, applications, or other processes, without having to purchase, configure, and maintain separate physical resources for various services.

Point Five: NIS and System Security

Once you've passed the initial steps of installing and configuring your UNIX network—or have decided that now is a good time to re-examine your existing network configuration—one of the most vital issues that you'll need to address is network security. As a fairly secure system—though not necessarily sporting the security certifications featured by other operating systems—the UNIX security system is of little use if improperly configured or simply misused.

The UNIX NIS is comprised of a series of administration utilities, daemons, and database tools that are designed to streamline the maintenance and optimization of multiple-host UNIX networks. NIS functions very much like the User Administrator for Domains in Windows NT, conceptually at any rate, in that UNIX NIS allows the system administrator to consolidate a number of security-critical files from two or more UNIX hosts into a centrally hosted security database, to which all future requests involving security information are passed. This is an extraordinarily useful feature for two main reasons. First, with all security information residing on one physical machine, you can keep close physical and electronic watch for illegal or otherwise unauthorized console or remote access. Second, because all changes to security information are written to the central NIS database, they are instantaneously available to all machines (NIS clients) validating logins and other requests against the NIS database (NIS host). This can potentially save the system administrator a lot of time, frustration, and record-keeping because he will no longer have to review and update the security information on all his machines following each employee termination, layoff, transfer, or resignation.

The files controlled by NIS are: passwd, group, hosts, ethers, networks, rcp, services, protocols, netgroup, bootparams, aliases, publickey, netid, netmasks, c2secure, timezone, auto.master, and auto.home.

Point Six: Resources for Troubleshooting the Network

As every experienced system administrator knows, Murphy's Law is about the only constant in the universe: If something *can* go wrong with your network, chances are it probably will. Generally, your network will fail horribly at one of three times: two o'clock in the morning; when vendors are back-ordered for the *specific* part of which you're in dire need; or when the security pad *and* physical lock to your network operations center have died and you can't even gain access to your machines. Unfortunately, the network diagnostic tools that accompany most UNIX distributions can't do much to combat these types of problems, but they can and do assist in resolving many common and not-so-common problems that tend to afflict TCP/IP networks. There are seven main tools (in addition to many third-party products) that can help you isolate specific problems and get you back on track in the event a network segment fails, an Ethernet card croaks, or a remote host goes down, which are illustrated in Table 20.1.

Table 20.1. UNIX–TCP/IP network troubleshooting tools.

Tool Name	Description
ifconfig	This command will report on the currently configured interfaces that are installed in a particular machine. Additionally, ifconfig will allow you to update the configuration of the interface if you believe it to be erroneous.
netstat	Netstat offers four very important diagnostic command options, -I (interface), -r (route), -a (connection), and -s (statistics). -I will report with a concise chart of the current interface status, with special attention to inbound and outbound packets, collisions, and errors. -r will display the current routing table, along with flags detailing the current status of each particular route. -a will provide current connection status on a port-by-port basis. -s varies slightly based on the vendor, but generally provides a fairly comprehensive breakdown of almost every conceivable (and measurable) value relating to the TCP/IP functions of the network.
nfsstat	nsfstat aids the administrator in isolating performance problems that may be the result of a degraded, dying, or improperly configured NFS system.
arp	arp will dump the current contents of the address resolution protocol cache to <STDOUT>. This information will allow you to confirm that each Ethernet address is properly associated with the correct IP address.

continues

20

UNIX/LINUX

Table 20.1. continued

Tool Name	Description
Ping	Ping can be an excellent tool to use when you are either unable or sporadically unable to reach a particular host. Ping will confirm that the remote machine is, in fact, responding to requests, and that there is a valid, functional route from your machine to the server.
Traceroute	Traceroute is a handy ask-and-answer utility that will query each hop (router, gateway, host, and so on) between two IP addresses to identify themselves. In this fashion, you can quickly learn if your problems are local, at an ISP, or somewhere at the host destination.
Snoop	Snoop is a last resort. Running Snoop will switch the NIC over to promiscuous mode, allowing the NIC to listen to (and analyze) all traffic that passes by on the network. This has some serious security implications attached to it, so be sure to check with your boss before you start snooping around.

Internet/Intranet

The second area in which UNIX has performed spectacularly is in providing both Internet and intranet services to large volumes of users through the Hypertext Transfer Protocol (HTTP). Due to the initially unprecedented (and now standard) growth in the online user community, everyone from college students to museums, corporations, and government agencies have tried to make as much information as possible available by the Internet. Most often, this information is available on the World Wide Web (WWW), the part of the Internet best suited for the simultaneous delivery of audio, video, and text files. Of course, information is still occasionally accessed through Telnet, FTP, and Gopher servers, though these delivery mechanisms have taken a back seat to the flashy, user-friendly nature of the Web.

UNIX has prospered as a Web platform for a number of reasons, primarily because the hardware configurations generally far outperform their Windows or MacOS competition when providing Web services. Additionally, for the largest of corporations seeking a Net presence, UNIX was more than likely already entrenched in their information services department, and it was a familiar platform on which to develop products for the Web.

What's more, the third-party software available for the UNIX operating system is exceedingly powerful and robust, which is a very enticing factor that usually sways companies away from the less powerful, limited applications available for Apple and Microsoft operating systems. From database systems to ad delivery and discussion software, virtually any service that can be run on Windows or MacOS can be accomplished with more versatility, increased speed, and can handle higher numbers of concurrent users when run under UNIX.

Database

Despite the fact that software vendors are constantly releasing new and impressive software for the Windows, Mac, and PowerPC platforms, the odds are that you'll be hard pressed to find a suitable enterprise-wide solution to your database needs among these offerings. Now, this may not necessarily be a bad thing, because the high-end database systems that run under UNIX are both extremely powerful and prohibitively expensive, meaning that if you or your company can't quite afford the software and the hardware for the UNIX solution, your computing needs probably don't require such blazing speed and flexibility.

However, for those of you who have access to the company till and do, in fact, have a need for the latest and greatest of the modern database systems, there are a number of companies that can provide excellent solutions, often tailored to meet your specific needs courtesy of on-site representatives.

Here are some resources you can use as a starting point:

- Informix—www.informix.com
- Sybase—www.sybase.com
- Oracle—www.oracle.com

Flavors of UNIX

The rise in popularity of UNIX as a server and workstation operating system has led to the need for UNIX to run on a variety of hardware platforms. Many large corporations and universities as well as smaller companies and personal users wanted to run UNIX on their existing hardware. From that need, several flavors of UNIX, all with the same core features, same core command set, same development tools, and extremely efficient, integrated networking capabilities were developed to run on a variety of hardware platforms—from the Motorola 68000 series processors found in some older Apple and Atari computers to MIPS processors found in today's high-end Silicon Graphics workstations and servers. In fact, it's safe to say that there is a version of UNIX that will run on any major, modern hardware platform, which makes UNIX a perfect choice for small LANs to huge, global WANs.

As an upgrade strategy for hardware and software platforms, UNIX is also an excellent choice. To say nothing of the portability of code and the breadth of applications available for different UNIX systems as discussed earlier in the chapter, the integrated networking features make UNIX an excellent entry-level and professional operating system solution. As your network infrastructure grows and upgrades to new and better technologies, integrating new protocols and hardware devices into your servers and workstations in a UNIX environment will prove to be an uncomplicated task (depending on the availability of the physical hardware devices, of course) that will deliver unparalleled networking performance. From 14.4Kbps modem dial-up networking to dedicated data services over T-1 lines, it is almost always faster on UNIX, regardless of the flavor.

20

UNIX/LINUX

UNIX for Free?

For those of you on a budget, several low-cost (free) versions of UNIX-like operating systems are available. They are referred to as UNIX-like simply because they are not fully POSIX-compliant; however, they do have all the features you would expect in a modern, fully functional version, including true multitasking, shared libraries, demand loading, proper memory management and integrated TCP/IP networking. NetBSD (not to be confused with BSDI, which will be discussed later) and Linux are the two major contenders in the free UNIX operating system market. The choice of which free version you choose will be based partly (if not entirely) on what hardware platform you choose (or currently own). Table 20.2 shows which of the free UNIX-like versions will run on which hardware platform.

Table 20.2. Platform availability for free UNIX variants.

Hardware Platform	*Linux*	*NetBSD*
Apple (PowerPC-based)	X	
Amiga/Apple/Atari (68000-based Systems)		X
Intel (386, 486, Pentium, and Pentium Pro)	X	X

> **NOTE**
>
> Many ports of Linux and NetBSD are available on a variety of hardware platforms from vendors like Atari, Commodore, and Digital Equipment Corporation. The list is always changing. For more specific information about what platforms support what flavor, head to the Web:
>
> Linux: `http://www.ssc.com/linux-int/Resources/linux-faq/section1.html#cpu`
>
> NetBSD: `http://www.netbsd.org/Ports/index.html`

It's important to remember that although these versions are free, they are most certainly not considered public domain software. The copyrights to much of the core code that comprises Linux and NetBSD are retained by their authors and distributed under specific, general release guidelines. It's very important that you check the documentation regarding copyright and licensing for the NetBSD and Linux distributions before you begin using the software in either a personal or commercial environment.

Solaris from Sun Microsystems

Developed by Sun Microsystems from its own SunOS, Solaris was designed to be a more "open" option for users of Sun RISC-based workstations and servers. Systems from Sun are certainly expensive, but they are also extremely powerful, fast, and flexible. Part of their success in speed can be attributed directly to their processor architecture. RISC-based processors can perform several tasks simultaneously. In fact, many Internet service providers choose servers and workstations from Sun that run Solaris because of the speed with which networking functions under Solaris. Many large corporations and universities base their entire network infrastructure on Sun systems because of the performance seen from Solaris under unusually heavy loads. Furthermore, Solaris is the most popular UNIX operating system found on the Internet today, which is a great testament to the ability of Solaris to network in a high performance fashion.

> **NOTE**
>
> For more information about hardware from Sun Microsystems, check out http://www.sun.com. For information about software from Sun Microsystems, check out http://www.sunsoft.com.

Although Solaris has also been ported to 486-based systems, Sun has seen little success with its sales, possibly because of difficult installation and confusing maintenance procedures, but more probably because of a mismatch of hardware and software. Solaris runs extremely well on systems designed to run Solaris. Solaris runs rather poorly on systems not designed specifically for it. Regardless, Solaris is an excellent choice and top contender on the high-end UNIX market.

HP-UX from Hewlett-Packard

Consumers know them for their printing and imaging systems. Scientists and industrialists know them from their analysis, testing and measurement systems, but MIS professionals know them for their network servers, workstations and high-performance hardware. That's right, Hewlett-Packard has their own version of UNIX: HP-UX.

Providing a highly reliable, standards-based foundation for companies to run and manage critical solutions, HP-UX can be argued as the industry's leading large-scale UNIX. Designed for the demands of large-scale operations that require both compliance to the standards of POSIX and a solution set that meets the demands of more specialized applications in the financial and technical industries, HP-UX is strict on its IEEE compliance but open enough to be applied to specialized applications in a variety of industries. HP-UX also boasts outstanding software scalability and value-added features. It is designed to run in environments ranging from desktop workstations, graphical engineering workstations, departmental servers, and enterprise server systems within the heart of large corporations.

HP-UX is also a leader in multi-vendor network operating environments, connectivity with other network operating systems, and mainframe connectivity. Thanks in part to Hewlett-Packard's wide variety of networking hardware products for its UNIX server and workstation hardware line as well as the additional "openness" found in HP-UX, it simply excels in network performance features. From 10base-T adapters to Asynchronous Transfer Mode adapters, HP-UX can talk the talk and Hewlett-Packard servers can walk the walk. Hewlett-Packard also goes the extra step by offering a rather extensive line of dedicated network hardware like high-speed hubs, network switches, and routers.

> **NOTE**
>
> For more information about hardware and software from Hewlett-Packard, check out `http://www.hp.com`. The list of protocols and hardware supported by HP is always growing! Be sure to visit their site for the most current information.

SCO OpenServer and BSDI

SCO OpenServer is today's leading commercial UNIX server operating system for Intel-based hardware platforms. OpenServer systems from the Santa Cruz Operation run crucial business operations for government agencies, large corporations, as well as small- to medium-sized businesses of every kind. OpenServer systems are excellent for running multiuser, I/O-intensive applications, communications and networking gateways, as well as mail and messaging servers in both host and client/server environments. Like other UNIX operating systems, OpenServer has networking that is extensible with existing LANs and WANs. SCO also boasts a 16-year history of bringing high-performance network computing operating systems and solutions to the Intel platform.

> **NOTE**
>
> For more information about software from the Santa Cruz Operation, as well as free licensing offers for non-commercial and educational uses, check out `http://www.sco.com`. SCO also has products for running DOS and Windows applications under UNIX, which makes for even tighter integration with existing DOS and Windows workgroups.

Berkeley Software Design, Inc. is the commercial supplier of the high performance BSD Internet and networking operating system software. Originally developed at the University of California, Berkeley, BSDI Internet Server operating system software integrates the complete 32-bit BSD/OS and its extremely efficient ultra-fast TCP/IP networking. All you need is an Intel 386 or 486, Pentium, or Pentium Pro server, and you're ready to go. Like products from SCO, BSDI Internet Server delivers world-class performance with advanced software and performance-optimized networking. The BSDI Internet Server takes full advantage of the wide range of advanced PC networking hardware available today, including 100Mbps Ethernet adapters and FDDI networking cards. The BSDI server integrates seamlessly with many existing routers. Also, BSDI server can act as its own router, which eliminates the expense and latencies associated with hardware routers. BSDI's unique built-in router has an excellent feature set. It is highly versatile and extremely efficient. It supports SLIP or PPP over a modem for inexpensive dial-up communications or high-speed synchronous interface cards at speeds up to fractional T-3.

NOTE

For more information about software solutions from Berkeley Software Design, Inc., check out http://www.bsd.com.

Digital UNIX from Digital Equipment Corporation

Digital UNIX is a modern, fully POSIX-compliant, 64-bit UNIX operating system from the kernel out. Designed to run on specialized hardware platforms from Digital based on Alpha processors, Digital UNIX delivers full, native 64-bit computing today. Digital UNIX features a robust networking feature set that you would expect to find in any UNIX including support for TCP/IP, Telnet, IP Multicast, Token Ring, SLIP, PPP, NTP, BIND name services, Streams, and sockets. Integrated FDDI support, Asynchronous Transfer Mode protocol, and specialized packet filter applications also make Digital UNIX an excellent choice for any high-performance network environment. Currently, Digital UNIX supports more standards than any UNIX, which makes coexistence with and migration from other, smaller-scale UNIX systems extremely easy. Digital UNIX brings excellent speed of networking and multiuser support into one extremely fast, scalable solution for any size environment or budget.

NOTE

For more information about Digital UNIX, check out http://www.unix.digital.com. Of course, if you find everything you need on the Web, you won't get to talk to Digital's world-class sales representatives or product resellers!

IRIX from Silicon Graphics

Often referred to as the MacOS of the UNIX world, Silicon Graphics is known for its easy-to-use-and-maintain UNIX workstations that specialize in multimedia production and computer graphics. IRIX is the version of UNIX from Silicon Graphics used on the systems that created the visual effects in movies such as *Twister, Independence Day*, and *Star Wars Special Edition* and used on Internet servers for some of the largest Internet service providers and Internet-online services in the world. With a proven 64-bit architecture for high-performance visual computing, I/O-intensive services, and high-performance, reliable networking functions, IRIX is the first desktop workstation-to-data-center server, 64-bit UNIX operating system. IRIX provides exceptional desktop multimedia production services, with extremely high-performance networking services and advanced data management for servers, plus extensive support for a variety of industry standards. IRIX offers industry-leading scalability across the specialized Silicon Graphics product line, with some servers that utilize as many as 36 processors. IRIX also provides a very interesting feature in software compatibility by providing binary compatibility with legacy versions of IRIX applications. Of course, recompiled 32-bit applications can take full advantage of the latest and greatest 64-bit MIPS performance features.

Silicon Graphics has also geared some of its desktop workstations to Internet and intranet users by combining the performance of a Silicon Graphics workstation with the power of the World Wide Web. Their O2 product line is the first system to provide bundled professional multimedia capabilities and Internet publication and authoring tools. With the Web integrated throughout the desktop interface, users can communicate their work more easily than ever before on company intranets and the Internet.

> **NOTE**
>
> For more information about Silicon Graphics comprehensive hardware and software product solutions, check out http://www.sgi.com. Because of SGI's target to the computer graphics industry, there is always something fun to see on their Web site!

Linux and NetBSD

Unlike most high-end software products that come with exorbitant price tags, the power and flexibility of UNIX operating systems offers significant advantages for more than just the largest, well-funded corporations and government organizations. As the benefits and promise of UNIX spread beyond these circles, the less well-funded scientists, engineers, and educators of the world decided that they needed an affordable UNIX solution. It was from that need—and perhaps some other secret desires—that free UNIX kernels and other UNIX-based tools were developed.

Linux

As mentioned earlier, freely distributable UNIX-like operating systems are available for certain hardware platforms. The most widely used and readily available is Linux, which is available for Intel 386, 486, Pentium, and Pentium Pro systems as well as Motorola PowerPC, Digital Alpha, Sparc, and MIPS systems. It is an implementation of the IEEE's POSIX specifications. Linux has an extremely wide range of software and services including the standard high performance TCP/IP networking that includes support for services such as SLIP and PPP and specialized hardware such as modems and ISDN adapters. Because the source code to the entire operating system is freely available under the GNU Public License, inclusion of modern networking hardware into the operating system is restricted only by your skills as a developer or your patience for the appropriate software to be written.

> **NOTE**
>
> The GNU Project was started in 1984 to help with the development of complete, free UNIX-like operating systems. Linux-based versions of products of the GNU system are widely used across the Internet on many different levels and for many different reasons. For more information regarding the GNU software project, be sure to check out `http://www.gnu.org`. For more specific information regarding the copyrights and licenses associated with Linux and its associated components, please consult the documentation that came with your software distribution.

Grown with the assistance and dedication of developers from around the world, Linux was created by Linus Torvalds at the University of Helsinki in Helsinki, Finland. Torvalds originally started playing with UNIX kernel code as a personal project that was inspired by another UNIX-like operating system called Minix. After significant development time and effort on his part, the first "official" version of Linux (version 0.02) was released on October 5, 1991, with a kernel that is 100% AT&T code-free. Over the next several years, a veritable slew of software developers have responded to the need for a free UNIX for Intel-based hardware.

> **NOTE**
>
> The following is a reprint of Linus Torvalds' original posting to the Usenet newsgroup `comp.os.minix`:
>
> Do you pine for the nice days of Minix-1.1, when men were men and wrote their own device drivers? Are you without a nice project and just dying to cut your teeth on an OS you can try to modify for your needs? Are you finding it frustrating when everything works on Minix? No more all-nighters to get a nifty program working? Then this post might be just for you.
>
> As I mentioned a month ago, I'm working on a free version of a Minix-lookalike for AT-386 computers. It has finally reached the stage where it's even usable (though it may not be depending on what you want), and I am willing to put out the sources for wider distribution. It is just version 0.02...but I've successfully run bash, gcc, gnu-make, gnu-sed, compress, and so on under it.

> **NOTE**
>
> `http://www.linux.org` is the site on the Internet for Linux information They have everything you will need to get started—from more information about Linux to what you need to get up and running, where to get it from, and what to do once you get it!

20

UNIX/Linux

Different versions of the Linux kernel are usually broken down into a package with other related binaries ranging from minimal root system installations to complete network-ready distributions with tools such as the XFree86 version of the X Window system and whole suites of services and applications. These packages are known as *distributions*. Various distributions of Linux are available.

The Red Hat Distribution

Red Hat Software is a computer software development company that sells products and provides services related to Linux. Available by anonymous FTP from `ftp://ftp.redhat.com/pub`, Red Hat's role in the Linux distribution game is to review, package, and develop new tools that are useful for computing professionals who do not have the time or interest to keep up with the cutting edge of development. For more information about the products and services provided by Red Hat, check out `http://www.redhat.com`.

The Slackware Distribution

Patrick Volkerding created the Slackware distribution of Linux and authored the official 1996 Slackware distribution CD-ROM set. Linux Slackware 96 turns your machine into a multitasking workstation with a full range of software development, text editing, image processing, and high-speed networking services and tools. Slackware can be also be obtained by anonymous FTP from `ftp://ftp.cdrom.com/pub/Linux/slackware`, or you can order Slackware on CD-ROM on the Web at `http://www.cdrom.com/titles/os/slack96.htm`.

The Debian Distribution

Debian GNU/Linux is yet another complete and powerful Linux-based UNIX-like operating system. It uses the standard Linux kernel, and includes hundreds of applications, services and tools, including most GNU software and the XFree86 version of the X Window system. Each package is an independent segment of the Debian distribution, in that it is not associated with any particular release of the complete system or distribution scheme. Anyone can create their own packages and even upload them to be made available with the distribution or as a part of the distribution. Debian is possibly best known for its upgradability. It is upgradable incrementally and "in place," which means that users can upgrade individual packages or entire systems when they become available without having to reinitialize disk drives and entirely reinstall operating systems. Debian may be obtained at `ftp://ftp.debian.org/debian`, or for more information, check out `http://www.debian.org`.

MkLinux

Apple Computer is supporting a project with the Open Software Foundation Research Institute to port Linux to a variety of Power Macintosh platforms. Currently supported in a prerelease fashion are Apple Power Macintosh 6100, 7100, 8100, 7200, 7500, 7600, 8200, 8500, and 9500 systems and PowerComputing 100 or 120 machines. The MkLinux distribution program is still in its infancy, so for information about how to obtain the software or to volunteer your services in shaping MkLinux, please check out `http://www.mklinux.apple.com`.

Once you have Linux installed and running and you have networking configured and performing at lightning speeds, you'll be ready to download additional software to run on your system. Listed following are the most popular FTP archives on the Internet for Linux software:

- `ftp://sunsite.unc.edu`   University of North Carolina at Chapel Hill
- `ftp://tsx-11.mit.edu`   Massachusetts Institute of Technology
- `ftp://ftp.funet.fi`   Finnish University and Research network
- `ftp://ftp.cc.gatech.edu`   Georgia Tech College of Computing

NetBSD

Resulting from an enormous collaborative effort on the part of software developers around the world, the NetBSD Project is dedicated to the production of a freely available and redistributable UNIX-like operating system, NetBSD. Based on a variety of free software products authored by various individuals and organizations, including 4.4 BSD Lite from the University of California, Berkeley, NetBSD has positioned itself as the most POSIX-compliant free UNIX for Intel systems. There are few known glitches in the POSIX compliance, but even if they were all fixed (either through additional development effort) or through revisions of the Posix standard, official compliance will probably never come to NetBSD (or any other free UNIX) simply because of the costs associated with certifications. Due to this stricter-than-average compliance for a free UNIX, it is highly interoperable with other systems. Furthermore, it is easy to port software to NetBSD, because of that same strict compliance.

> **NOTE**
>
> Similar to the GNU License that protects Linux, NetBSD is protected by a Berkeley-style license. However, some portions of the NetBSD source are protected by the GNU General Public License. For more specific information regarding the copyrights and licenses associated with NetBSD and its associated components, please consult the documentation that came with your software distribution.

NetBSD itself is highly portable and is distributed with complete source code. Like Linux, it has been ported to a large number of hardware platforms and like Linux, it has the same limitations of usability and integration of networking hardware.

Unlike Linux, which has taken a rather ambiguous distribution path, NetBSD is distributed in two easy-to-understand forms. Formal releases are done periodically and include well-tested binaries, source code, and installation tools, and the *NetBSD-Current*—a nightly distribution of the latest sources gathered from everyone who is currently working on the NetBSD Project. The NetBSD-Current releases are meant for hard-core users and serious kernel hackers who want to work with the absolutely latest software and are willing to help debug it. Each of these distributions can be obtained from `http://www.netbsd.org`.

Market Share

For years, the Internet was comprised primarily of servers running UNIX. More recently, advances in operating system technology and the decrease of the cost of hardware from vendors such as Intel, Apple, Microsoft, and Novell have shown a major increase in the usage of products such as Windows NT and Novell NetWare as internetworking operating systems. Although UNIX is still run on the majority of Internet sites and corporate networks, Windows NT and NetWare are rapidly gaining ground in the marketplace. Of course, with the availability of almost POSIX-compliant, free UNIX-like operating systems such as NetBSD and Linux that have well-implemented networking support, and a large supply of UNIX professionals in the world, UNIX will be around for some time.

Summary

UNIX *is not* the proper operating system for every computing need. Although many UNIX loyalists would prefer that were not the case, it is true that for most of the high-end systems, such as Solaris and HP-UX, not only will your company require a highly paid database administrator to run herd over the system, but a large infrastructure outlay as well, in order to acquire the associated machines, disk arrays, and other vital hardware. That being said, however, it's equally important to note that for every job for which UNIX *isn't* the proper solution, it's likely that there are a dozen or more that would suffer without the power and attractive feature set offered by any member of the UNIX clan.

From its early days as one of the first network operating systems to the overwhelming popularity that has encouraged the development of so many competing styles of the basic UNIX system, UNIX has evolved from a quirky operating system with a questionable future into a networking powerhouse that is respected by nearly every serious technology professional. If you're in a technology position and fail to consider UNIX as a viable solution to your company's computing needs simply because you like graphical interfaces or the Eep! Eep! of the Mac, heaven help you when your boss finds out—which he will about five minutes after your system fails to perform.

Windows NT 4

by James Causey

IN THIS CHAPTER

CHAPTER 21

The recent explosive growth of the Windows NT market is arguably the most heavily discussed and debated trend in today's enterprise marketplace. Windows NT has been described in myriad terms, ranging from "NetWare killer" and "the heir apparent to UNIX" to "another Wintel disaster" and "more marketing than meat."

Once the dust has settled, however, the question remains: "What *is* Windows NT and why should I use it, or not use it?" This is the question that this chapter attempts to answer.

Windows NT is a critically important product, incorporating features from desktop, server, and mainframe operating systems, while introducing some new wrinkles all its own. After reading this chapter, you should be able to evaluate NT's pros and cons and decide whether Windows NT can fill some of your computing needs (and if so, how).

Windows NT: A Brief History

In order to best understand Windows NT, its role in the market, and some of the terminology critical to designing and setting up an NT network, it's important to understand the legacy of network operating systems which led up to Windows NT, and which NT has inherited (see Figure 21.1).

FIGURE 21.1.

The Microsoft network operating system family tree.

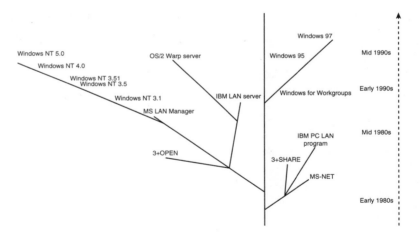

Early Microsoft Network Operating Systems

Microsoft has been in the networking operating system market longer than most people suspect. In the early to mid-1980s, the increasing popularity of using local area networks to connect desktop computers brought about the creation of a whole new subclass of the PC market: the PC-based network operating system. Networks with central, shared hardware using operating systems such as UNIX, VMS, and other such powerful network operating systems had been used successfully for quite some time, and the capability for a PC to both perform desk-top business tasks and replace dumb terminals dedicated to connecting to centralized systems proved to be a boon to companies investing in the new desktop computers. In addition, the shared network connections (typically using technology such as early Ethernet and Token Ring) allowed PCs to share resources, such as hard drives and printers.

In this burgeoning market, PCs dedicated to serving files, print queues, and applications to PCs quickly exploded in popularity. Operating systems such as Banyan's VINES (based on UNIX System V) and Novell's NetWare (a server operating system written from the ground up for Intel hardware) quickly gained success and early dominance. Microsoft, in an attempt to gain a share of this market, developed a primitive extension to MS-DOS called MS-NET, designed to give DOS networking file and print-sharing capabilities without running NetWare, VINES, or another competing product.

MS-NET had some serious flaws, however, the most important of which was the lack of multitasking in DOS. Without this capability, not only could an MS-NET server not process instructions or code executed locally on the server while processing network requests at the same time, but also it could not even service more than one network server request at once. This flaw severely limited MS-NET's usefulness and popularity. Though some third parties (such as 3COM, Microsoft's partner in competing against Novell in the early days of the LAN market) attempted, with varying degrees of success, to extend MS-NET with re-entrant server code to get around DOS limitations, the product was a market failure.

The Step up to OS/2

Microsoft did not give up so easily, however. Microsoft and IBM later partnered to develop OS/2, a revolutionary desktop operating system for Intel hardware. OS/2 was designed to ex-pand the vast popularity of MS-DOS by providing a new, pre-emptively graphical environ-ment. OS/2's new inherent abilities also made it a good candidate for extension into the role of a network operating system. Microsoft did just that, by developing Microsoft LAN Manager (or LANMAN, for short).

LAN Manager was designed around a model similar to NetWare: a centralized, high-powered server, providing file, print, and application services; and specialized client software running on each OS/2 and DOS client, to give those workstations the capability to take advantage of those network services. LAN Manager used NetBIOS, an IBM-designed protocol that pro-vides high-speed, efficient network services (though limited to subnet-only communications). IBM also licensed the LANMAN technology for their server product, IBM LAN Server, which was also based on OS/2.

Though OS/2 proved to be something of a disappointment to IBM due to its lackluster sales, LANMAN's popularity as a server operating system and an alternative to NetWare continued to grow; however, it never seriously threatened NetWare's dominance of the market.

The NT Project

Later on in the 1980s, however, Microsoft realized that OS/2 had some serious long-term flaws. OS/2 was wedded tightly to the Intel processor architecture (having been written largely in 286 assembly language), suffered from an unpopular user interface and poor market image, and lacked the necessary developer and hardware manufacturer support enjoyed by other operating systems. Microsoft decided to leave the OS/2 development effort entirely to IBM and follow its own path in developing the next generation of desktop network operating systems.

Microsoft hired famously talented operating system designer David Cutler, architect of such important operating systems as VMS, to lead this new effort. The project was dubbed "NT," standing for "New Technology" (though one of the most intriguing, and probably apocryphal, myths of this time describes Cutler's fabled choice of the letters "WNT," or "Windows NT," because each letter is the result of adding one to the ASCII codes for the letters "VMS," thus snubbing his past efforts on that operating system).

Windows NT was designed to build on the humble but important success of the LANMAN product line and provide an advanced, high-performance network operating system (see the "Windows NT System Design" section later in this chapter). In 1993, Windows NT came to market (see Figure 21.2 for a list of the NT product line).

FIGURE 21.2.
Windows NT product timeline.

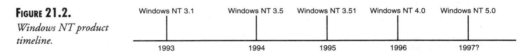

Microsoft chose to use the Program Manager interface used by their wildly popular desktop product, Microsoft Windows. To synchronize their product lines, the first version of Windows NT was released under version number 3.1, as the most recent version of Microsoft Windows was also 3.1. NT was available in two forms: Windows NT Advanced Server, or NTAS, to act as the server backbone for an NT network; and Windows NT Workstation, to provide a powerful desktop operating system using the same design features and core as the Advanced Server.

Windows NT 3.1 was seen by many in the industry as something of a disappointment. Although its architecture and design were impressive, it was a massive memory hog and ran quite slowly. In addition, hardware support was rather weak, due to its newness. With its next version, however, NT became a force to be reckoned with in the market.

Windows NT 3.5 was released in 1994, with the server product being renamed to Windows NT Server. The vast performance and application support improvements, as well as the new NT domain structure, made NT a much more popular operating system, and sales began to take off. A more incremental upgrade, version 3.51, was released in 1995.

Windows NT 4.0, released in late 1996, has once again energized NT's sales and popularity, by combining increased Internet/intranet integration and improved performance with greater

compatibility with other Microsoft operating systems (DOS and Windows 95, particularly) and the new Windows Explorer interface, introduced previously with Windows 95.

Now that you've looked at NT's legacy, let's examine NT's design goals.

Windows NT System Design

Windows NT was designed to be a modern operating system, incorporating lessons learned from the classic network operating systems (including the king, UNIX), as well as more modern and robust design elements. It achieves these goals through a highly flexible, stable, and secure design.

When the NT project was initiated, Microsoft wanted to ensure that NT would be an advanced network operating system, with the inherent modernity and flexibility to survive well into the future as their flagship networking product. To that end, they designated several important design goals: robustness, portability, compatibility, security, performance, and upgradability.

■ Robustness

Desktop operating systems have long earned a reputation for instability. Due to their design, applications or failed system services could easily lock up or crash the entire system or severely reduce system performance and stability. This vulnerability is simply not appropriate for a high-performance network operating system, which needs to be able to provide mission-critical network services or perform intense long-term computational tasks with a minimal risk of failure. Major network operating systems of the past, such as UNIX, incorporated this important fact in their design. Other network operating systems attempted to achieve these goals in a somewhat dubious fashion, reducing their stability and their usefulness outside of basic file and print sharing. The NT project, however, was driven from the very beginning by a desire to provide an extremely stable platform for enterprise network services, and such protective features as true pre-emptive multitasking and full memory protection were incorporated in the system. In addition, Windows NT includes a new, modern file system, known as NTFS, which is designed to allow efficient, rapid, fault-tolerant access to disk drives ranging from small IDE hard disks to large SCSI-based RAID arrays. NTFS utilizes transaction logging to prevent corruption of the file system in the event of a system failure.

■ Portability

One of the powerful advantages of an operating system like UNIX is its ease of portability to multiple platforms, making the operating system totally non-dependent on the design and performance of one vendor's hardware solutions. Windows NT was designed with portability in mind, with the vast majority of the operating system being written in easily portable C, with hardware-specific functions and calls being abstracted by a system-specific Hardware Abstraction Layer, or HAL (see Figure 21.3).

FIGURE 21.3.

An abstracted model of a Hardware Abstraction Layer (HAL).

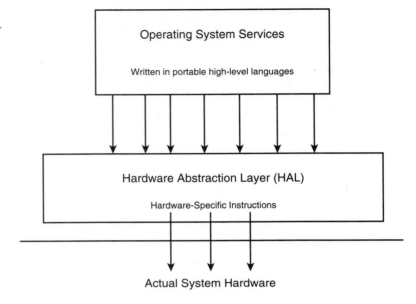

The use of a Hardware Abstraction Layer allows important hardware-specific calls that most greatly impact system performance to be written in fast, optimized assembly language, while still retaining the vast majority of the operating system in easily portable high-level languages.

This portability allowed Windows NT to be released originally with support for Intel x86, Digital Equipment Corporation Alpha, and MIPS RISC processors. With NT 3.51, support was extended to the IBM/Motorola PowerPC processor. Recent developments, however, have led Microsoft to limit its cross-platform hardware support to Intel x86 and DEC Alpha processors. NT still has the essential portability necessary to take advantage of future processor innovations, however.

■ Compatibility

In the vastly heterogeneous enterprise market of the 1990s and beyond, the ability to maintain a high level of compatibility with other products is critical to a network operating system's survival. Windows NT approaches compatibility from multiple perspectives.

First, NT maintains a high level of software compatibility. Windows NT's primary programming interface, the Win32 API (Application Programming Interface), is virtually identical across all Microsoft 32-bit platforms, making it simple for vendors to design 32-bit products that run on both the newer Windows consumer desktop operating systems (Windows 95 and the forthcoming Windows 97) and on Windows NT. Windows NT can also run most 16-bit Windows applications designed for

Windows 3.1*x* in a protected environment, allowing a high level of backward compatibility while still preventing those applications from crashing the system or other 32-bit applications and services. NT also has the inherent ability to run POSIX.1-compliant applications, requiring only that those programs be recompiled for the target hardware platform. Finally, NT can run applications written for OS/2 version 1.*x*.

Second, NT's ability to provide services over several network protocols gives it the flexibility to integrate with and provide services to networks running such disparate operating systems as NetWare, UNIX, OS/2, DOS, Windows 3.1*x*, and Windows 95, as well as providing Internet and intranet connectivity and support. Add-on products let NT provide gateways to entities such as IBM SNA mainframes.

Third, Windows NT's file system, NTFS, maintains multiple data streams within each file, which can be used to emulate many types of file systems (including the data fork/resource fork structure used by Macintoshes). In addition, Windows NT can access disk partitions using the FAT file system (used by MS-DOS, Windows, and Windows 95) and the HPFS file system (used by OS/2). As a result, an NT system can easily serve files to multiple platforms without impacting those platforms' functionality.

■ Security

NT was designed from the beginning with the potential to provide extremely secure network services. NT's object-oriented structure and integrated security manager authenticate actions and processes within the operating system on a per-access basis, giving system administrators a high level of flexibility in determining user and service rights and privileges. Windows NT 3.51 received the highly coveted Red Book C3 certification, designating it as an extremely secure operating system. NT 4.0 is currently in the evaluation process for C3 certification.

■ Performance

Operating systems such as UNIX have found wide acceptance not only as powerful servers and network service providers, but also as high-performance computational, design, and graphic workstations. In order to compete with these products in these areas, NT needs to provide a high level of system performance.

To this end, NT supports Symmetric Multiprocessing (SMP), the ability to split application threads over multiple processors. This allows customers to add CPUs to increase system performance.

NT's network stack is also optimized for high-speed networking, and when using high-quality hardware, it can achieve network performance similar to a UNIX workstation.

NT's native file system, NTFS, also includes features designed to enhance I/O performance, including powerful data-level caching and physical data location.

One of NT's weaknesses, however, from a performance standpoint, is its extreme level of hardware abstraction. Although hardware abstraction greatly enhances stability, it introduces layers of complexity to most system services, imposing a performance burden in the process. In order to reduce this performance burden, NT's designers have been carefully reducing the abstraction of certain key areas, such as the video subsystem (an important change in Windows NT 4.0), in order to significantly boost performance while not significantly impacting reliability.

- Upgradability

  An important feature of a modern operating system is the ability to extend or modify the system to respond to changes and advances in technology. NT provides this upgradability by being extremely modular. Individual components can be rewritten and redesigned without impacting the rest of the operating system as long as essential basic functionalities are still provided. This flexibility has been evidenced by the rapid growth in features and performance NT has shown through the life of the product.

You've seen NT's design mission, and in the process, two important questions arise: How did Microsoft achieve these goals, and how well did it do so? To begin to answer these questions, the next section looks at NT's system architecture.

NT System Architecture

As discussed earlier, NT relies on a series of interconnected modules, separated from direct hardware access by a Hardware Abstraction Layer. This section covers some of the specific architectural features relied upon by NT, and then describes the layout of NT's system architecture itself.

User Mode Versus Kernel Mode

One of the most important distinctions to understand when viewing NT's system architecture is the distinction between User Mode services and Kernel Mode services. In Kernel Mode, a piece of code has the ability to execute any instruction that a processor is capable of and can generally access all system resources. In User Mode, however, a piece of code has a much more restricted set of functionality and resources, in order to significantly reduce the danger to the operating system's stability posed by providing complete resource access. These modes are abstract modes, designated by Windows NT, but they're based on the ability of most modern processors to switch state between a full-access mode and a more restricted secure mode (see Figure 21.4).

NT takes advantage of these modes by placing application code and related components in User Mode. By doing so, NT both eliminates the potential of an application or related service to execute a bad instruction or perform a task that locks a resource designed to be allocated by the operating system itself, and makes certain that changes in basic interface and application components do not require changes in more sensitive Kernel Mode components.

FIGURE 21.4.
User Mode versus Kernel Mode.

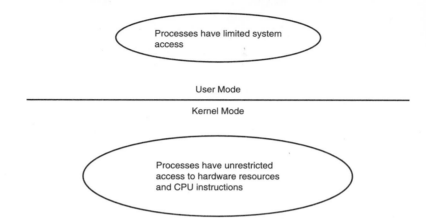

NT places those components in Kernel Mode only if those components require that level of privilege in order to execute, or if placing those components in User Mode would severely impact system performance. For example, in previous versions of Windows NT, video and printing services ran in User Mode, which eliminated the ability of a bad video driver or video-related instruction to crash the entire system, but the system overhead incurred by switching between User Mode and Kernel Mode constantly for video hardware access hurt NT's video performance. Moving those components to Kernel Mode has increased the risk that NT's stability could be affected by video-related functions and drivers, but has also significantly improved system performance.

> **NOTE**
>
> Are you concerned about the stability of Windows NT 4.0 in comparison to other versions of NT? Keep in mind that in earlier versions, a severe problem in the video subsystem could crash the entire Win32 subsystem, which all other application subsystems rely on for access to system services (this point is covered in more detail in the section "Environmental Subsystems"). Though a similar problem in NT 4.0 can crash the entire system rather than just the Win32 subsystem, there is little practical difference between the two types of crashes because a dead Win32 subsystem will prevent anyone from administering the system or running any applications. In both cases, it's critically important for video and printer driver designers to thoroughly test and refine their drivers before releasing them.

Object-Oriented Architecture

Another important feature of NT's design is the use of modular components, or *objects*. Objects are self-contained, self-controlling pieces of code that maintain all their procedures and data internally, while providing an abstracted set of *interfaces* to other objects and/or applications. Using objects makes maintaining and updating a program, particularly one as complex as an operating system, a much easier and more reliable process.

As an example, take a look at two different ways to implement file access in an operating system.

In a non-object-oriented OS (such as the one shown in Figure 21.5), the procedures of file access must be understood down to the lowest level by everyone designing portions of the operating system that rely on them. If the designers decide at some point to change how file access is performed, the file access code throughout the OS must be changed to reflect the new methods. This is a time-consuming, painstaking process, and one in which it is nearly impossible to avoid making errors or forgetting to change portions of the OS.

Figure 21.5.

Without objects, all components must understand every detail of file access.

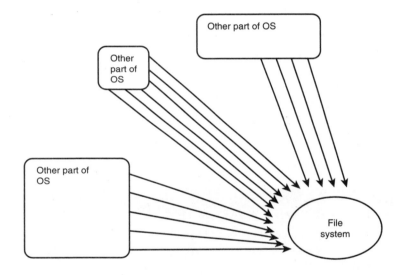

In an object-oriented OS, however, the details of file access are known only to the object handling those details (see Figure 21.6). That object presents a common interface of abstracted file manipulation functions to the rest of the operating system. In this model, should the particulars of file access need to be changed, the file access object can be modified, or even completely replaced, as long as it presents the same interface to the rest of the OS. If this basic interface requirement is met, the designers of the operating system can even provide new, enhanced functionality, as long as the old interface is maintained for backward compatibility.

Windows NT uses the object-oriented model throughout its architecture, from actual operating system components to individual manipulation objects (such as files, users, groups, processes, and the like). This not only makes it easier to code and maintain the OS, but also provides a superb framework for implementing many of NT's design goals. For instance, because each object maintains its own data, the operating system as a whole is, in theory, far more reliable because individual processes can't run roughshod over each other's resources. In addition, the use of objects makes it easy to enhance and revise the operating system because components can be rewritten, replaced, and added on, as long as the interfaces relied upon by other portions of the operating system are not altered. Portability is enhanced as well because any component that relies on the specifics of a particular platform (such as the HAL) can be replaced with a component designed for another.

Figure 21.6.

With objects, only the file access object needs to understand details of file access.

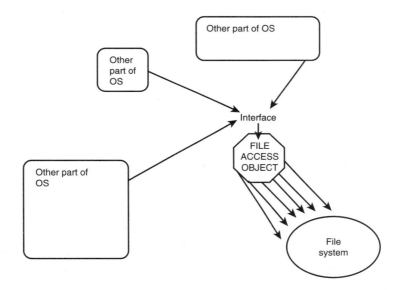

Operating System Components and Architecture

Now that you've examined some of the crucial concepts behind NT's architecture, take a look at NT layout itself. Figure 21.7 contains a complete diagram of the layout of NT's various components and subsystems.

The discussion of these various components begins by starting at the lowest level and working upwards.

HAL

As already discussed, the HAL performs the task of abstracting the CPU and other platform-specific resources, providing a generalized interface to higher-level system components for maximum portability. Windows NT includes a generic HAL for each major platform (Intel, x86, Alpha, and PowerPC), as well as other HALs provided by manufacturers for variations in hardware design. Manufacturers can also provide different HALs for application after NT has been installed, to maximize performance and reliability on specific hardware.

FIGURE 21.7.

*Windows NT 4.0
component layout.*

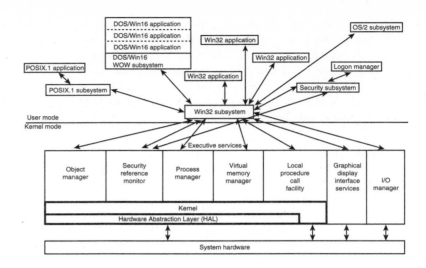

The Kernel

The Windows NT kernel is a *microkernel*, meaning that it performs only the scheduling and execution of instructions on the system's processor or processors. By using such a small system kernel, NT's designers hoped to improve both the system's performance and reliability; the kernel cannot be pre-empted by any other portion of the OS, so it is critical that it be both lightweight and extremely reliable. Limiting the kernel to these essential tasks provides NT with a great deal of inherent stability. The kernel does not determine how many threads a process has, nor does it determine precisely when to create or destroy them; those tasks are handled higher up, in the NT Executive.

Windows NT is a *threaded* operating system. A thread is a small, organic task or set of instructions. Processes running under Windows NT can each spawn multiple threads, in order to execute multiple tasks concurrently. The use of multiple threads can greatly enhance a process's speed and efficiency. Every process uses at least one thread, and threads are implemented by the kernel, which creates, schedules, executes, and destroys threads on the system CPU.

NT includes support for Symmetric Multiprocessing (SMP), meaning that if a system contains more than one CPU, the kernel can schedule threads freely on whichever processor is least burdened. SMP allows systems to be scaled for better performance under heavy processor load situations by adding more processors. NT comes with support for up to four processors, and system manufacturers can provide modifications to NT in order to support even more CPUs.

Executive Services

Above the kernel, but still in kernel mode, lie Windows NT's Executive services. The members of the NT Executive provide important operating system services needed by applications and other services to perform their allotted tasks. These services include:

■ I/O Manager

The I/O Manager, rather like the theoretical file access object from the earlier example, handles most hardware data input/output services for NT, ranging from such functions as disk access to network communications.

NOTE

Because this is a book on networking, you'll take a look at the network model for the NT operating system later in this chapter, in the section titled "Windows NT Networking."

It uses a series of administrator-configurable drivers to handle communications with those specific pieces of hardware. Because they deal so closely with hardware, these drivers have to be able to bypass the Hardware Abstraction Layer and communicate directly with hardware devices, lest the HAL become unwieldy and large and system performance suffer severely as a result.

■ Graphical Device Interface (GDI) Services

The GDI services include all services that control how data is rendered and displayed visually, both to the video card and to the printer. For maximum stability, previous versions of NT placed most of the GDI in User Mode. Unfortunately, system performance was severely impacted as a result of this decision.

For Windows NT 4.0, the system's designers decided to move all GDI services into Kernel Mode, to reduce the performance impact of those tasks. As discussed earlier, although this move does provide a threat to system stability, in practice it provides little or no significant stability impact.

■ Local Procedure Call Facility

The LPC module provides NT objects, applications, and services the ability to communicate with one another using named pipes. Maintaining this functionality within one object assures that any module written for Windows NT can use the same basic set of calls to communicate with other modules.

■ Virtual Memory Manager

The Virtual Memory Manager controls the allocation and manipulation of pages of application and system-wide virtual memory pools, which can consist of both high-speed RAM and the slower, but larger, system swap file. All processes under Windows NT have access to a virtual memory space of 4GB. When an individual process requires access to memory, the Virtual Memory Manager (with help from the I/O Manager) handles the actual movement of pages from RAM to disk (and back again) and provides a virtual interface to those hardware addresses that the individual process can manipulate, without having to know where its individual pages are located.

- Process Manager

  The Process Manager controls process objects, determining when they are created and destroyed. It also handles the creation and destruction of threads. It does not, however, directly schedule and execute those threads on the system's processor or processors; that task is handled by the kernel.

- Security Reference Monitor

  The Security Reference Monitor maintains the system-wide database of security rights, privileges, and identities, and is called upon by other modules of the operating system to verify an object's rights and privileges to other objects and tasks. This low-level, constant comparison and verification of object security are an important part of NT's C2-level security rating.

- Object Manager

  The Object Manager, appropriately enough, manages the identity of all objects within the system. It works closely with the rest of the operating system to maintain a database of all active objects, whether they be processes, files, users, groups, network resources, drives, or any other possible system object. It also maintains the database of available interfaces and methods for those objects and verifies attempts to access objects at that level.

NT's Kernel Mode modules provide the services you expect from an operating system, such as security, I/O, hardware control, and other basic services. The next section moves higher up NT's architectural model to look at the User Mode application services.

Environmental Subsystems

The most important, and most common, module that NT runs in User Mode is the Environmental subsystem. Environmental subsystems provide applications with a generic interface to the Executive services below. Individual subsystems can be designed to provide specific APIs, memory models, and other features an application expects. In this way, applications for other operating systems can be run under Windows NT.

The primary subsystem running under User Mode is the Win32 Subsystem. The Win32 API is Microsoft's 32-bit programming interface for applications written to run under Windows NT. It provides all features available under NT, including pre-emptive multitasking, protected memory, a flat 32-bit memory model, and so on. Every other subsystem running in User Mode is a Win32 application, each with its own memory space and input queue. All access to NT resources and Executive services takes place through the Win32 subsystem because each application and subsystem running as a Win32 application makes API calls, which are interpreted and passed on to the appropriate Executive module (see Figure 21.8).

No Win32 application can access another Win32 application's memory pool, nor can it interfere with its input. Because each Win32 application is pre-emptively multitasked, no one Win32 application can hog system resources and prevent others from accessing them.

FIGURE 21.8.

Every subsystem in User Mode is a Win32 application.

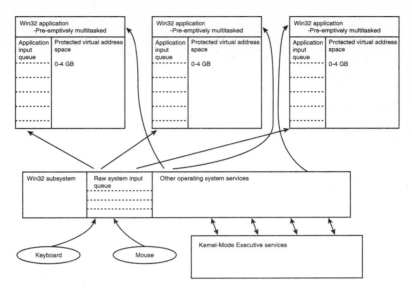

The Win32 API is standardized across all of NT's hardware platforms; an application written for NT in Win32 needs only to be recompiled for each target platform.

> **NOTE**
>
> Developer support for NT platforms other than Intel has been lackluster, outside of core products (such as the BackOffice suite). In order to get around this limitation, Digital Equipment Corporation has developed FX!32, a recompilation engine for Intel Win32 applications. When a Win32 application written for the Intel platform is first run on an Alpha, the Intel instructions are translated into equivalent Alpha code by an emulator. In the meantime, the Win32 instructions used by the application are recompiled into Alpha-native binaries and saved to disk. The next time that application is launched, those functions run natively on the Alpha, greatly improving their performance. Over time, more and more of the application is converted to Alpha-native code. This amazing innovation greatly enhances the viability of the Alpha platform for Windows NT.

Windows NT includes a number of other environmental subsystems, each a Win32 application in its own right, to run other types of applications. These subsystems include:

■ Win16 subsystem

The Win16 subsystem, or Windows On Windows (WOW) as it's commonly known, is a Win32 application that provides a virtual DOS/Windows 3.1 machine. MS-DOS and Windows 3.1*x* 16-bit applications can run in this subsystem, with access to the complete Win16 API, and standard 16-bit Windows memory models. Most 16-bit

DOS and Windows applications run perfectly within the WOW subsystem; the only exceptions are those applications that attempt to directly access system hardware and resources. Windows NT does not allow such applications to have direct access to those resources, in order to maintain system stability and performance (see Figure 21.9).

FIGURE 21.9.

The Win16 subsystem and Win16 applications within it.

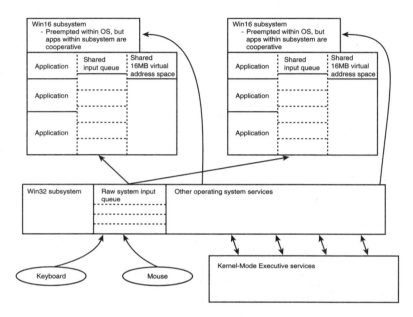

Each Win16 subsystem provides a complete emulated version of a DOS/Windows 3.1 machine, including all the limitations included therein. Within a Win16 subsystem, poorly behaved Win16 applications are multitasked cooperatively, and share one 16-bit virtual memory pool. A Win16 application can crash other Win16 applications within that subsystem, as well as the entire subsystem itself. However, because the Win16 subsystem is, in fact, just another Win32 application, the Win16 applications within it cannot crash the entire operating system, nor can they affect other Win32 applications. In fact, in order to provide more crash protection between multiple Win16 applications, users can start each Win16 application on their NT systems in a separate WOW subsystem.

> **NOTE**
>
> Because Win16 applications are written only for the Intel platform, versions of NT 4.0 for other operating systems run Intel emulators to allow those applications to be run. As with any software emulator, however, performance of those Win16 applications suffers on other platforms.

- OS/2 subsystem

  The OS/2 subsystem allows applications written for OS/2 versions 1.*x* to be run under Windows NT without being recompiled. This support is only provided on NT for Intel, however, and only command-line applications can be run, as the OS/2 subsystem does not include support for the OS/2 Presentation Manager interface.

- POSIX subsystem

  NT'S POSIX subsystem allows applications written to the POSIX.1 standard, a standard that defines application compatibility standards among various UNIX variants, to be run under Windows NT. POSIX.1-compliant applications need only be recompiled for the applicable NT platform in order to function under NT. NT provides additional compatibility features to meet POSIX.1 compliance, including providing the necessary file system functions needed by POSIX applications within the NTFS file system.

The Windows NT Registry

One crucial portion of NT's architecture not shown in Figure 21.7 is the Registry. The Windows NT Registry is a dynamically maintained system database. NT uses the Registry for a number of functions, including:

- Current hardware status and settings
- Individual user configuration settings and customizations
- Application preference data
- Operating system configuration settings

The Registry provides a valuable, efficient storehouse for many, many different types of data, used by both NT itself and the applications that run under it. Because the Registry can be accessed and manipulated by a standard set of APIs, its presence simplifies the tasks of programmers who need to retrieve or modify system data or store individual user or application preferences.

Now that you understand how NT is put together, it's a good opportunity to talk about the use of Windows NT as a network operating system (because this *is* a book on networking, after all).

Windows NT Networking

Windows NT was designed from the ground up as a network operating system. To understand its potential as a network OS, it's important to understand how NT can communicate on a network, and what features and protocols it supports. You'll also look at the model Microsoft has chosen for NT-centric networks, and how those networks can be integrated with other products.

The NT Network Stack

Windows NT's network stack was designed to allow multiple methods of communication, use different protocols, and allow myriad services to be used over those protocols. In addition, the basic NT network stack can be extended to use additional add-on network products.

Figure 21.10 illustrates the model used in the design of NT's network stack.

FIGURE 21.10.

The Windows NT network stack.

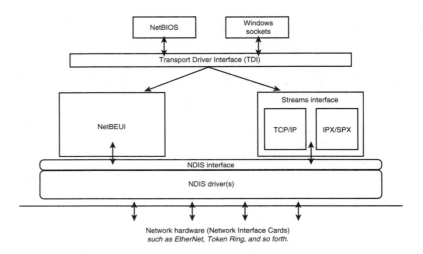

Rather than starting from the bottom, as with NT's system architecture, start at the top of this diagram.

The topmost level consists of networking APIs. These programming interfaces contain the actual function calls made by applications in order to communicate over the network and use those calls to perform network functions. Perhaps the most important of those network APIs is NetBIOS, the Network Basic Input/Output Interface. NetBIOS is the core API used by NT and LANMAN networking. When an NT system (or any other system, for that matter) communicates with other systems using Microsoft networking, the calls made are made to the NetBIOS API. NetBIOS can, through the NT network stack, perform those functions using other protocols, as you'll see in a moment. Other APIs live at this level as well, such as the Windows Sockets (or Winsock, for short), which provides standard TCP/IP Internet/intranet connectivity such as you've become accustomed to with UNIX and other operating systems.

Right below the network APIs themselves lives a component known as the Transport Driver Interface, or TDI for short. The TDI allows networking APIs such as NetBIOS, Winsock, or others to be written in a protocol-independent fashion, so that they can be bound to any lower-level transport protocol.

Underneath the TDI, you have the transport protocols themselves. Windows NT can, out of the box, use any of three primary protocols for Microsoft/LANMAN networking:

- NetBEUI
- TCP/IP
- IPX/SPX

NetBEUI is a proprietary protocol used for Microsoft/LANMAN networking only. NetBEUI stands for the NetBIOS Extended User Interface. NetBEUI is a fast, efficient, subnet-only protocol, designed for use in small workgroups using peer-to-peer or small server-based networks. NetBEUI cannot be routed, so it is suitable only for local subnet communication.

> **NOTE**
>
> Confused yet about the difference between NetBIOS and NetBEUI? Don't worry; many NT system administrators don't understand the difference.
>
> NetBIOS, when originally designed in the 1980s, was a network protocol into itself. It was later extended to provide more functionality, and renamed NetBEUI (NetBIOS Extended User Interface). Finally, in the late 1980s, NetBIOS and NetBEUI were split apart. NetBIOS became a generic networking API, and NetBEUI the network protocol. This is the state in which these two terms remain.

TCP/IP and IPX/SPX are the other protocols available for Microsoft/LANMAN networking under NT. They are available due to their many advantages; they can be routed across subnets, and they are very commonly used for other networks, so an administrator can design his NT network to fit best into his current LAN/WAN setup.

> **NOTE**
>
> In fact, if TCP/IP is used for a Microsoft network, an administrator can use the Internet itself as an extended Wide Area Network!

TCP/IP and IPX/SPX are encapsulated within an NT version of the Streams interface, originally designed for UNIX System V. Streams allows network component designers to easily wrap various network protocols in a standard interface, so that higher-level and lower-level protocols can plug into them seamlessly.

Beneath the transport protocols is the NDIS interface. NDIS stands for Network Driver Interface Specification. The NDIS interface provides even more modularity within NT's network stack, allowing the higher-level transport protocols to interface seamlessly with any type of lower data-link protocols (such as Ethernet, Token Ring, CDDI, or others) without being rewritten. Finally, underneath the NDIS interface itself lie NDIS drivers, written for specific network devices. These drivers also only have to be written once for NT because the abstraction provided by the NDIS interface allows that same driver to connect with higher-level protocols.

Microsoft Windows Networking Models

Like any network operating system, NT was designed to provide its network services in a number of specific ways. Many operating systems have been designed with one specific purpose, but NT networks can be modeled in two different fashions: a Microsoft *workgroup* or a Microsoft *domain*.

> **NOTE**
>
> Before moving on into the discussion of Microsoft network models, you need to understand the difference between the products in the NT product line: Windows NT Workstation and Windows NT Server.
>
> Windows NT Workstation was designed as an individual desktop workstation operating system, or as a peer-to-peer server for a very small workgroup. A Windows NT Workstation can connect to any other Microsoft operating system (whether NT Server, NT Workstation, a Windows 95 workstation, a Windows for Workgroups workstation, or any other Microsoft network-capable system). An NT Workstation can also connect to other operating systems for which it has clients; for example, NT Workstation has the ability (through the Winsock interface) to use TCP/IP Internet/intranet applications such as Telnet, FTP, and a Web browser, and can also connect to NetWare servers. In addition, Windows NT Workstation can serve connections to other Microsoft systems, or to Internet/intranet clients (or even Macintosh workstations). However, the license for Windows NT Workstation restricts its use to a maximum of 10 concurrent server connections.
>
> Windows NT Server, on the other hand, was designed as a central file, print, application, and Internet/intranet server. It has all the capabilities of Windows NT Workstation, with additional licensing and performance tuning options specifically aimed at use as a server operating system. NT Server can also provide authentication services for a Windows NT Domain.

A Microsoft workgroup is just that, a small workgroup of computers designed to perform simple network file, print, and application sharing. All Microsoft network-capable clients can be members of a workgroup, whether NT, Windows 95, Windows for Workgroups, or other. Within a workgroup, there is no centralized authentication for user or group resources; users must maintain an account, with appropriate privileges, on every system where they want to have access, either directly at the system console or over the network (see Figure 21.11).

For small groups of systems, a workgroup model can be highly useful. In very large organizations, however, the task of maintaining individual accounts and all the needed passwords across an entire group of mixed resources can quickly grow out of hand.

21

WINDOWS NT 4

FIGURE 21.11.
*The NT workgroup
model.*

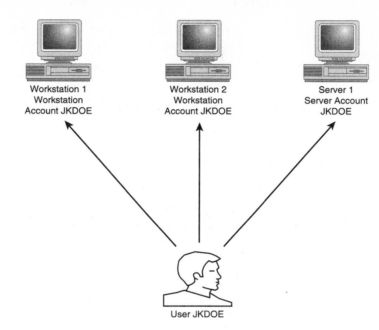

In order to simplify the management of large groups of network resources, Microsoft devised the Windows NT domain. An NT domain provides a centralized authentication service, with one security database containing all users and groups within an organization. Users authenticate once to that domain, and then can access any resource shared to their user account (or a group to which their user account belongs). Figure 21.12 illustrates an NT domain.

The security database for an NT domain is maintained on a Windows NT server that has been designated the Primary Domain Controller (or PDC) for that domain. To provide fault tolerance and better scalability, an NT domain can also use multiple Backup Domain Controllers (or BDCs), which are NT servers that maintain read-only mirrors of the domain's master database. When an authentication request is made, it can be tested against the database on any Backup Domain Controller as well as on the PDC, thus reducing the load on that PDC (see Figure 21.13). Should the PDC fail for whatever reason, any BDC can be promoted to replace it.

NOTE

A Windows NT server does *not* have to be dedicated solely to acting as a Domain Controller, whether used as a PDC or BDC. In small- to medium-sized domains, a PDC or BDC can also serve as a file, print, or application server. In larger domains, however, it can significantly increase domain performance to dedicate a server to those purposes.

FIGURE 21.12.

The NT domain model.

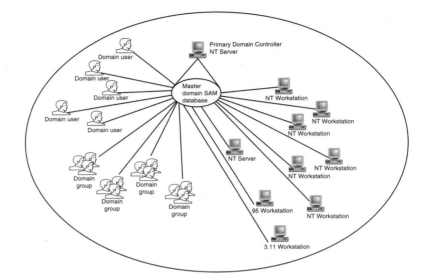

FIGURE 21.13.

Primary and Backup Domain Controllers in an NT domain.

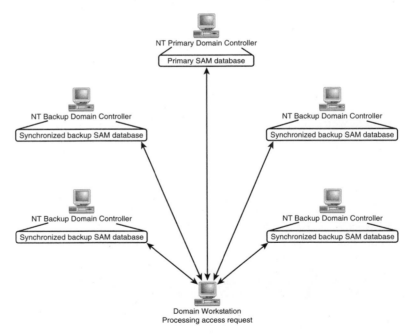

To further extend the domain model, domains can perform pass-through authentication of users to other domains, through a *trust relationship*. Trust relationships allow domains to establish secure communications through which authentication requests can be passed off to the domain controller responsible for that user's account. Using trust relationships, resources can be easily shared between organizations, while still maintaining centralized user authentication.

Integrating NT with Other Network Operating Systems

Windows NT has the capability, using both included services and add-on software packages, to integrate well with other types of networks. Its flexibility of protocol choice allows an administrator to select the protocol that best meets his needs for network simplicity, LAN/WAN management, and capabilities. In addition, NT computers have the ability to use resources from, and serve to, many different types of network operating systems, including:

- NetWare

  Windows NT 4.0 comes with a Client for NetWare Networks, which allows it to connect to NetWare servers using both Bindery authentication and NDS. In addition, an add-on product available from Microsoft allows an NT server to masquerade as a NetWare 3.*x* Bindery server, so that NetWare clients can take advantage of its resources.

- Macintosh

  Windows NT workstations and servers can run an included set of Services for Macintosh, which allows them to share files and printers to Macintosh clients using the AppleShare protocol. They cannot, however, connect to Macintosh clients without a third-party product (either an AppleShare client for NT, available from Apple, or a product that allows a Macintosh to share resources over LANMAN-standard protocols).

- UNIX Internet/intranet services

  Windows NT includes the Windows Sockets service, which allows it to connect over TCP/IP to standard Internet/intranet services such as Telnet, FTP, WWW, and other such services. In addition, Windows NT Server includes the Internet Information Service (IIS), which allows an NT server to act as an enterprise WWW, FTP, and Gopher server. Third-party products are also available from vendors such as Netscape to provide such Internet/intranet services, and Windows NT Workstation includes a less powerful version of IIS for peer intranet services.

  Additional third-party products allow NT systems to more directly interact with UNIX workstations and servers, using services such as X-Windows and NFS. There are also clients for UNIX systems (such as the shareware product SAMBA), which allow UNIX machines to take part in NT workgroups and domains, and share files and printers with Microsoft systems.

- Other network operating systems

  Windows NT also includes the DLC protocol, used by both many IBM mainframes and by Hewlett-Packard JetDirect print servers. NT can connect to both. In addition, products are available that allow NT servers to act as gateways to IBM SNA networks, such as Microsoft SNA Server.

All in all, Windows NT provides many different options for network connectivity and services.

High-Performance Networking with Windows NT

Windows NT's advanced network connectivity model has allowed the implementation of a number of high-performance networking systems on Windows NT. The range of available tools for some bleeding-edge technologies pales in comparison to those available on UNIX, which is the de facto development platform for advanced networks. However, most high-performance network technologies are available on Windows NT.

Perhaps the simplest and most common of all high-speed technologies is the use of 100 Megabit Ethernet. All common 100Mbps implementations, including 100base-T, have both interface cards and drivers compatible with Windows NT.

As the standards and implementations for ATM are sorted out, support for Windows NT is keeping up quite well. A number of major vendors, such as Digital and 3COM, provide interface cards for running ATM connections directly to a Windows NT server or workstation for use as a high-end computer or data server.

Multicast technologies for videoconferencing are also being made available for the NT platform; the most popular research multicast system, the MBONE, has clients and servers for Windows NT currently in beta-test. For more information on MBONE on Windows NT, check the ICAST Web page at `http://www.icast.com`. Other videoconferencing systems are available for NT as well, such as the non-multicast CUSeeMe package and proprietary systems from vendors such as Intel Corporation.

Wrapping It All Up: Should You Use Windows NT?

Now that you've seen where NT came from, how NT is designed, and some of what it can do, the decision remains: Can NT be useful to you?

First, it's important to evaluate NT Workstation and NT Server separately. NT Workstation is a very powerful, secure, stable workstation operating system. With its combination of an easy-to-use graphical user interface and a wide variety of available software programs (the library of software for Microsoft Windows is the largest on earth), an NT Workstation can serve as a reliable desktop solution, for tasks ranging from basic office automation (word-processing, spreadsheets, and the like) to software development to high-end computational tasks such as 3D modeling and statistical processing. Its combination of stability, performance, and flexible platform choice (particularly on the high bang-for-buck Intel platform) makes it an appealing alternative to more expensive UNIX desktop workstations (and can even exceed their performance when running on powerful hardware such as the Alpha), as well as a more advanced and more reliable alternative to other Windows and Macintosh computers. As more high-speed network implementations become available on NT, the ability to augment or replace UNIX systems with NT becomes a more viable option. For many, the decision to use Windows NT Workstation on the desktop is a no-brainer, particularly for organizations moving from other Microsoft operating systems.

Whether or not to use Windows NT Server is a much more complicated choice. Due to its advanced architectural design, simple interface, and rapidly growing industry support, a Windows NT server can work wonderfully in any number of roles, including:

- Domain controller for a Microsoft domain
- File and print server
- Application server

Windows NT servers can be used for a wide range of application services. Products from Microsoft, Sybase, Oracle, and other vendors exist to use an NT server as a SQL database server, for example. NT servers can also be used to maintain a centrally controlled source for most applications used by an organization, though this is simply another facet of file serving.

- Internet/intranet Server

  Due to their favorable cost/performance ratio, NT servers are seeing increasing use as World Wide Web, FTP, and other Internet service providers. Many of the Web's most used sites, including Microsoft's, run on NT Server, using either IIS or a third-party Web server product. NT servers can also act as DNS (Domain Name Service) servers multiprotocol routers and provide other services essential to a TCP/IP network.

- Messaging Server

  Many messaging and groupware products, ranging from simple SMTP servers to integrated products such as Microsoft Exchange and Lotus Notes, can be (and are) run on Windows NT servers.

  In these roles, an NT server can completely replace similar servers running other network operating systems, such as UNIX or NetWare.

Despite what Microsoft would have you believe, however, UNIX and NetWare still have their uses. Consider some of NT's disadvantages:

- NT is not a true multiuser operating system.

  At first glance, this statement may seem confusing. Windows NT can multitask, can't it? And it can serve multiple network connections, as well as an interactive console user, can't it? Well, yes, it can. However, NT is not designed to provide more than one interactive session at a time. UNIX machines are often used to allow multiple users to connect using terminal emulators (such as Telnet) and run interactive sessions on the system, to perform their computing tasks. NT is simply not designed to do this; NT machines are designed to allow one user to sit at the console and manage and use the machine for personal computing tasks, and/or to serve files, print queues, and applications to multiple remote users over client/server connections.

■ Windows NT uses a complex architecture.

When compared to more monolithic operating systems such as NetWare, the model used by Windows NT is extremely complex. These layers of complexity can reduce performance; when doing raw file transfers, for example, a Windows NT server can be somewhat slower than an equally equipped NetWare server (though NT 4.0 mostly eliminates this performance edge). The tradeoffs for this reduced performance, however, include better security and reliability.

■ Windows NT is a relatively immature product.

Windows NT is a very young product, particularly when compared to UNIX and NetWare. Because of this, some of its management tools are rather poorly designed. Managing a complicated structure of Windows NT domains can currently be a very complex, time-consuming task, as NT lacks some of the advanced management tools available to UNIX system administrators. NT is quickly closing these gaps, particularly when compared to NetWare, but it has a long way to go.

■ Windows NT has limited scalability.

Windows NT currently cannot scale to the degree that many operating systems, such as UNIX, can. For example, Windows NT supports only up to four processors out of the box. Although a server using four Pentium Pro or Alpha processors is an extremely powerful machine, there are times when huge megaservers with many, many processors and huge amounts of RAM and disk can be necessary, and NT is not suitable for such tasks. In addition, Windows NT is a 32-bit operating system, and some very rare, very large datasets can require the performance and memory access capabilities afforded by a 64-bit system architecture. Future versions of NT will address these issues, but for now, NT cannot serve as a megaserver or as a massively parallel server.

■ Windows NT is Intel-centric.

Though Windows NT is available for many hardware platforms, the vast majority of developer support focuses on Intel-based platforms (with slowly increasing support for the DEC Alpha). Recently, Microsoft has dropped support for future versions of NT running on MIPS and PowerPC processors, so the next version of NT will be available only for Intel and Alpha. On the plus side, Intel's expanded range of processors (including the Pentium, Pentium Pro, and MMX processors) does allow for many different price/performance ratios, and the DEC Alpha is still the world's fastest computer, making it suitable for very high-end tasks. However, if you do not want to be tied to a one- or two-platform solution, NT may not be right for you.

Summary

This chapter looked at Windows NT from a number of different perspectives, in order to let you see its advantages and disadvantages. NT is a powerful product, with many advantages and a great deal of increased future potential, and has the power of Microsoft's goliath development, marketing, and relations capabilities to help push it to new heights. There are still some areas, however, when your particular needs may require features NT cannot (and will not) provide. With the information in this chapter, you should have much of what you need to make that decision.

NetWare

by James Causey

IN THIS CHAPTER

CHAPTER 22

A glance at any current computer industry magazine will show you the recent upheaval in desktop system LAN/WAN (Local Area Network/Wide Area Network) products. Upstart products, such as Microsoft's Windows NT, have caused a firestorm of competition and activity in the PC networking market and have even threatened to encroach upon the territory of such high-end operating systems as UNIX.

However, such competing products all owe their market, and much of their history, features, and functionality, to the long-term reigning king of the LAN: Novell's NetWare. NetWare deserves the lion's share of the credit for elevating PC-based local area networks from being cute toys to providing powerful, reliable, and serious network services. NetWare was the first Intel-based network operating system to provide a serious alternative to mainframe-based server networks, providing critical reliability and security features needed in the modern enterprise.

Recently, Novell seems to be undergoing a great deal of difficulty competing with companies such as Microsoft in the server market. However, the vast majority of installed LAN servers still run one version or another of NetWare, and this will continue for some time into the future. NetWare can still be an excellent choice for use as a network operating system, and even if you choose to use another OS, chances are you will run into NetWare servers in the modern enterprise. This chapter will help you to understand the features and limitations of NetWare, both so that you can decide whether or not to go with NetWare as an NOS (Network Operating System) and so that you will be more prepared for future encounters with NetWare networks.

A Brief History of NetWare

Early on in the rapid expansion of the PC desktop market, it was realized that networking PCs together into a LAN would be a very good thing. It would allow the computing power on those desktops to be used not only to replace the networks of dumb terminals used to communicate with enterprise back-end mainframes, but creating LANs would also give users of those desktop systems a much easier way to share resources, such as files, applications, and printers.

One of the earliest vendors to innovate in this market was Novell. Novell's first NOS product was called S-Net. S-Net was an entirely proprietary NOS, relying on a star-based network whose center element was a specialized computer running the S-Net OS on a Motorola 68000 processor. Needless to say, this solution hardly revolutionized the market.

Novell quickly realized the inherent limitations of such a solution, however, and released the first product in the NetWare line: NetWare 86. NetWare 86 was designed from the beginning to provide a multitasking, centralized file, print, and application server, running on the IBM PC XT with an Intel 8086 processor. NetWare was, and still is, a custom-designed operating system, specifically written to perform the tasks of a central LAN server. It is not designed (nor is it suitable) for use as a workstation operating system; NetWare is a dedicated server operating system.

NetWare immediately provided a huge advantage over the competition at the time it was introduced: It was a multitasking operating system, allowing it to perform as a server for multiple connections at once. Competing products, such as Microsoft's MS-NET, could not perform in this role, based as they were upon MS-DOS. In addition, NetWare provided security comparable to that of mainframe systems, with user and group authentication, and file- and volume-level security restrictions. When compared to the rudimentary (or nonexistent) security implementations of competing LAN NOSs, this level of security proved a real boon to LAN managers.

NetWare rapidly took off and gained dominance over the PC LAN market. To take advantage of improvements in PC hardware architecture (see Figure 22.1 for a timeline), NetWare continued to be rewritten and revised to add more functionality.

FIGURE 22.1.

The NetWare product family.

NetWare's next major release was NetWare 286. For NetWare 286, Novell rewrote the OS in 80286 assembly language to take advantage of the performance and architecture advantages of that processor. In addition, a new version of NetWare was added to the product line: SFT (System Fault Tolerant) NetWare 286. SFT NetWare was designed to include still more features in a LAN server previously unseen outside the mainframe market: the ability to provide levels of fault tolerance. Standard NetWare 286 was retitled Advanced NetWare 286, and both products were available for some time.

By this time, other NOS vendors had risen to the challenge and released competing products to try to reduce NetWare's market dominance. Microsoft and IBM collaborated on LAN Manager (or LANMAN) based NOSs, running on top of their multitasking OS/2 operating system. LAN Manager-based NOSs enjoyed a great deal of success in many markets (due to the marketing power of Microsoft and IBM, and LANMAN's suitability and performance in some specific network configurations), but NetWare's feature set and better networking support helped it continue to lead LANMAN networks by a large margin.

NetWare's other major competitor at that time was VINES from Banyan. VINES is a NOS based on a highly modified UNIX System V core. VINES uses industry-standard internetworking protocols, such as TCP/IP, and as such performed better in integrated LAN/WAN situations than did NetWare. In addition, VINES included a directory service by which all network services could be accessed by a symbolic name with centralized management and user login, no matter where their location on the network. These features helped Banyan compete well against Novell in many markets, but NetWare continued to lead the market.

As the LAN market grew, interoperability between desktop operating systems became more and more important. Novell began to address this issue by adding the ability to serve files and printers to Macintoshes in a release of SFT NetWare 286. Novell also tried to take over the peer-to-peer networking market with a product called ELS NetWare, which eventually proved to be a market failure.

When Intel released the 80386 processor, Novell took a look at their product and made a number of significant changes to it. First, they realized that reliance on assembly language, while providing excellent performance, would make the process of updating their products more and more difficult as hardware architectures advanced and changed. In addition, Novell wanted the ability to port certain NetWare services to other platforms to increase NetWare's interoperability with other NOSs. In order to achieve this goal, NetWare was rewritten entirely in C for the 80386 and released as NetWare 386. NetWare 386 included all the features of NetWare 286, including the fault tolerance additions made to SFT NetWare. NetWare 386 also included the ability to more easily design and install add-on products called NLMs (short for NetWare Loadable Modules).

In order to reduce the confusion inherent in their vast array of products, Novell later merged and retitled their product lines. All versions of NetWare 286 were merged into a new version of NetWare designed primarily for 80286 processors, called NetWare 2.2. NetWare 386 became the NetWare 3.*x* series of operating systems. ELS NetWare was scrapped, and Novell released NetWare Lite to provide simple peer-to-peer NOS services between workstations. Figure 22.2 illustrates this merging of lines, with the latest version numbers of the merged products.

FIGURE 22.2.

The merging of NetWare's product lines.

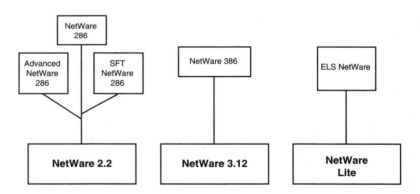

The next version of NetWare provided the most significant leap forward of any version so far. NetWare version 4 introduced a number of improvements to the OS itself, including better memory management and a vastly improved file system. Its most significant addition, however, was the introduction of NetWare Directory Services, or NDS for short. NDS was designed to compete with the directory services provided by products such as Banyan VINES, giving a centralized login and network management model for a NetWare network (we'll talk more about NDS later on in this chapter). This radical change in network design and management also caused the tools, both on the server and on the client, to change as well. NetWare 4 also required a new set of workstation clients in order to utilize the features of NDS (though Version 4 could emulate the network model used by 2.*x* and 3.*x* servers, and older clients could be used with that emulation). NetWare 4 required much more powerful hardware than did earlier versions of NetWare, and required a new set of installation, support, and administrative skills to be developed by the LAN administrator.

At the same time, the most significant competitor for NetWare yet to appear began rapidly gaining industry support and popularity: Windows NT. (For more information on Windows NT, see Chapter 21, "Windows NT 4.") Novell began seeing a sharp decline in sales and popularity as competitors such as Windows NT began to gnaw at their market share. While the majority of LAN servers still run Novell products, NetWare continues to decline in popularity compared to more modern operating systems. In order to combat this, and provide a competitive set of features, Novell recently released IntranetWare, a product designed to bridge the gap between LAN-centric NetWare networks and Internet/intranet services provided by OSs such as UNIX and Windows NT. It remains to be seen whether or not IntranetWare can stem the tide of shifting popularity. Novell has also worked with a number of vendors to port NetWare to other platforms, such as Apple's Macintosh Workgroup Server. Most of these porting efforts have been abandoned, while Novell focuses on their current core market: Intel-based LAN/WAN servers.

Despite Novell's current woes, NetWare is still a highly viable NOS product, with many advantages and features still not seen (or not implemented as well) in competing products. In order to better understand NetWare's pros and cons, let's take a look at the system architecture behind the current NetWare product line.

NetWare 3.*x* and 4.*x* System Architecture

NetWare's architecture is rather simple and easy to understand. It has been refined to provide a higher level of service and a greater level of reliability, but it still retains the simplicity of its original, dedicated server design.

NetWare utilizes a monolithic design model, much like operating systems such as MS-DOS. A NetWare server consists of only two major components: the system's kernel and additional application and service process NLMs. Figure 22.3 contains a depiction of NetWare's system architecture.

This simplicity belies one of the core architectural flaws in NetWare: there is no inherent modularity or protection for the operating system built into the system's design. A NetWare server's reliability relies on the proper behavior of each application; therefore, NetWare applications must be very carefully designed and debugged, lest they severely limit the reliability of a mission-critical NetWare server. This simplicity, however, allows NetWare servers to achieve very high levels of raw performance and throughput.

FIGURE 22.3.
NetWare's system architecture.

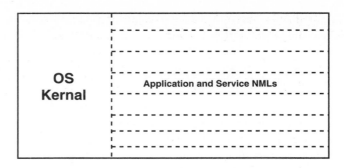

NetWare's sheer speed as a file and print server has been well respected for many years, and cannot yet be matched by competing products such as Windows NT Server; in fact, it was once said that on many systems, accessing files over a drive redirected to a NetWare volume was faster than accessing those same files on a local hard drive. This speed, however, comes at the potential cost of reliability and modularity.

The NetWare kernel provides the operating system's essential services. The services include such essential functions as process creation and destruction, memory allocation and release, hardware manipulation, and input/output functions. See Figure 22.4 for an illustration.

FIGURE 22.4.
The NetWare OS kernel.

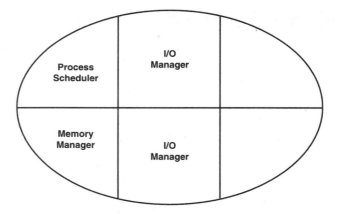

The kernel is responsible for management of individual processes, or instances of instructions that execute applications or perform services. These processes are cooperatively multitasked by the OS kernel; in this model, the kernel launches or awakens each individual process. Each of these processes, in turn, has a monopoly over the CPU and other system resources until they choose to release them, at which time the kernel awakens another process.

> **NOTE**
>
> This form of multitasking differs from *preemptive multitasking*, where the operating system has complete control over system resources and can actively switch resources between each running process. Each process receives a priority rating, which designates its access priority to and length of time for which it receives system resources. If an application locks up, hangs, or dies, the operating system can destroy that process and continue running. This form of multitasking is the most fair to each process, which is important in multiuser operating systems such as UNIX, as well as workstation operating systems where a user needs to run many applications at once.
>
> In a cooperative multitasking system, however, each process can monopolize system resources until done with them. This allows critical processes to complete essential tasks more rapidly, or in real-time if necessary. However, if a process hangs or dies while monopolizing those resources, the entire system can hang. According to Novell, cooperative multitasking is more appropriate for a server operating system, because it provides the highest level of performance; however, poorly written services or NLMs can crash the entire server. For this reason, it is critically important that NLMs be well written and very well tested.

Each process running on a NetWare server, whether a system service or a subprocess of an NLM, receives the same cooperative treatment, as well as having complete access to the server's entire memory pool. See Figure 22.5 for an illustration.

FIGURE 22.5.

NetWare processes have unlimited resource access.

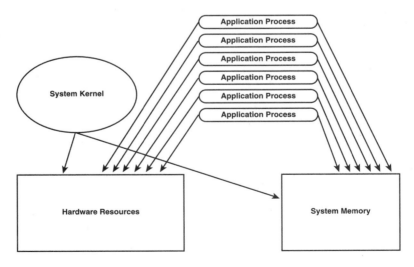

NetWare's lack of operating system-enforced memory protection is, again, an enhancement to performance, because each access to memory does not have to be verified by the OS as being part of an application's own memory pool. The possibility of an application modifying memory locations used by other applications, however, and therefore causing them to return unpredictable data or even crash is significantly increased.

Nonetheless, steps have been made to increase NetWare's reliability, at least from the perspective of memory management. First, let's look at how NetWare 3.*x* and 4.*x* allocate memory.

NetWare 3.*x* divides memory into six pools (see Figure 22.6).

FIGURE 22.6.

NetWare 3.x memory allocation.

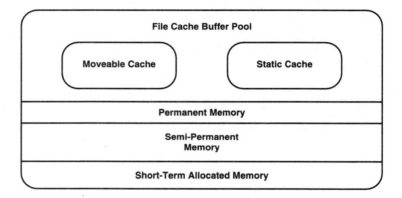

- The first pool is the permanent memory pool. This pool consists of memory that is allocated at system startup time for essential portions of the kernel and other services that need to remain running for the life of the server. Permanent memory cannot be reallocated.

- The second pool is the semi-permanent memory pool. Semi-permanent memory is memory that is allocated by application processes that needs to remain static during the life of the process, but that can be reclaimed once that process terminates.

- The third pool, the file cache buffer pool, is the largest on a NetWare 3.*x* server. The file cache buffer pool is memory used to form a cache buffer for individual blocks of data from disk, to speed client access for that disk data. The file cache buffer can be further subdivided into pools four and five: non-moveable cache, or cache that needs to be retained statically, and moveable cache, which can be reloaded with new data from disk as performance needs dictate.

- The sixth pool is the temporary allocated memory pool. Temporary allocated memory is a pool that allows processes to quickly allocate and discard memory for temporary stacks.

During the life of a system, however, these pools may need additional memory beyond that originally allocated to them. In order to provide for this growth, each pool can gradually take memory away from the file cache buffer pool. This memory is not, however, returned when the allocating process terminates. This has the effect of both impacting server performance (when the file cache buffer pool is severely depleted, fewer data blocks can be cached from disk, thus requiring more disk input\output) and potentially limiting stability (by making memory management tasks for writers of NetWare NLMs more difficult).

NetWare 4.*x* addresses this problem while not impacting performance. It does this by treating all memory as one contiguous memory pool (see Figure 22.7).

Figure 22.7.

NetWare 4.x memory allocation.

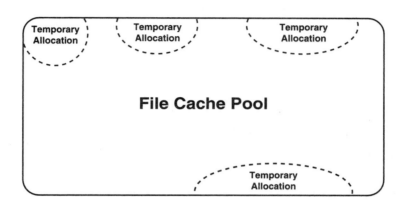

As processes are launched, they allocate memory by borrowing pages from the file cache buffer pool. When this memory is no longer needed, and/or the allocating process terminates, the allocated pages are returned to the cache buffer pool. The inexorable memory leakage found under NetWare 3.*x* is therefore eliminated, both reducing the damage to server file caching performance and allowing more efficient use of allocated memory by other processes. This simpler memory management is also faster, thus actually increasing memory management performance.

In addition, NetWare 4.*x* takes better advantage of the Intel processor family's design to provide better system memory protection. The Intel x86 processor family uses a series of hard-coded protection layers, called *rings*, in which applications can execute (see Figure 22.8).

Each ring provides a reduced subset of the processor's set of instructions; in addition, code running in a ring can only directly manipulate memory allocated to it and to other processes running within that ring.

NetWare 3.*x* does not take advantage of the memory and instruction security provided by this ring architecture; all processes on a NetWare 3.*x* server run in Ring 0 (see Figure 22.9).

Because all instructions are available to each process, however, and no context switches between rings have to be performed, NetWare 3.*x* servers perform CPU-intensive tasks very rapidly.

NetWare 4.*x* maintains the performance abilities of a Ring 0 operating system, while adding the ability to force individual NLMs to run in an outer ring (as illustrated in Figure 22.10).

22

NetWare

FIGURE 22.8.
*The Intel x86 processor
ring architecture.*

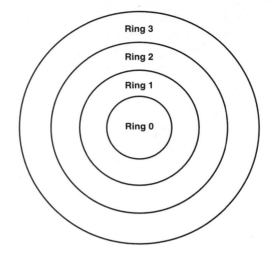

FIGURE 22.9.
*NetWare 3.x runs
entirely in Ring 0.*

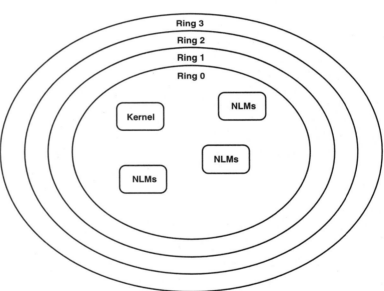

While those NLMs are then forced to perform context switches to access OS services, they cannot manipulate the memory used by the kernel, therefore increasing reliability. Once an NLM is proven to be reliable, it can then be moved to Ring 0 for better performance.

We've examined some issues behind NetWare's architectural design, as well as the pros and cons of those decisions. Now, let's examine NetWare's networking.

FIGURE 22.10.

NetWare 4.x can place NLMs in outer rings.

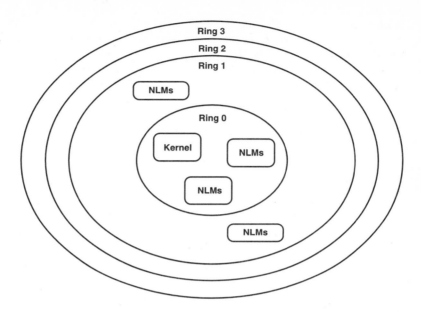

NetWare Networking

NetWare has been designed as a network operating system, and specifically, as a file, print, and application server operating system. In order to better understand its value as a server OS, let's take a look at how NetWare networking is performed. We'll look at a NetWare server's networking stack, examine the differing models for setting up a NetWare network, and discuss the issues involved in integrating NetWare with other network products.

The NetWare Network Stack

NetWare's network stack was originally designed for optimum server performance using Novell's proprietary IPX/SPX protocol. The vast variety of network card drivers, and the desirability of supporting other protocols (such as TCP/IP), later caused Novell to modify the NetWare network stack to be more modular.

NetWare 3.*x* and above uses a mechanism called the *Open Data Link Interface* (ODI) to layer and modularize its network stack. The ODI specification, developed by Novell and Apple Computer, allows vendors to provide protocol and network drivers that can plug into the ODI network stack without the need for protocol- or system-specific customization. This modularity makes the processes of designing and implementing network protocols and network card drivers simpler, and causes fewer headaches for the server administrator.

Let's take a look at the ODI stack NetWare uses, from the top down. Figure 22.11 contains an illustration of NetWare's network stack.

FIGURE 22.11.
The NetWare ODI network stack.

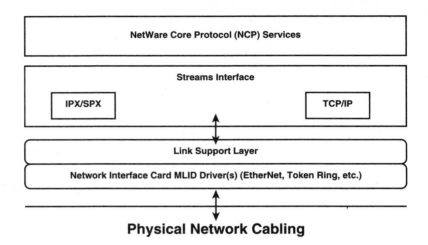

Physical Network Cabling

At the top of our diagram we have the NetWare Core Protocol (NCP) services. NCP is the application layer of the NetWare protocol stack, providing generic networking API that NetWare's services and NLMs can call to gain network access and to perform networking tasks. These basic services, originally oriented toward providing the services needed by a NetWare client/server network, have recently been expanded to also provide access to TCP/IP socket services, for performing Internet/intranet services such as serving WWW (World Wide Web) pages and acting as an FTP (File Transfer Protocol) server.

Directly below the NCP layer lies the Streams interface. The Streams interface was originally designed for UNIX System V. Streams provides a generic, modular interface for network and transport protocols, so that they can be plugged into a network stack without requiring protocol-specific programming either higher up in the stack or in the stack's lower levels. In NetWare 3.*x* and higher, the streams interface abstracts access to two protocols: the standard IPX/SPX, used most commonly for NetWare networks, and TCP/IP, used for Internet/intranet services as well as NetWare/IP (which we'll discuss later).

Beneath the Streams interface, we find the Link Support Layer (LSL). The Link Support Layer is one of the most important pieces of the ODI specification. The LSL acts to provide a virtual interface between network cards and card drivers and higher-level protocols. Before virtualizing layers such as the LSL became commonly used, operating systems required a new network stack for each network interface card, making administration of network operating systems (and the design and programming of network stacks) difficult and time-consuming. The LSL allows each vendor to design the drivers for their network cards to plug into a common interface, which in turn provides a common interface into which upper-level network stacks can be plugged. Designers of the various portions of the network stack do not need to be familiar with the exact design specifics of modules that lie at higher or lower levels in the stack, as long as they understand the virtual interfaces provided by those modules.

Finally, at the bottom of our stack, we have various MLID (Multiple Link Interface Driver) drivers. Each MLID driver is designed specifically to operate with a given NIC (Network Interface Card) or series of NICs and provides a common interface that the LSL can use to transfer data back and forth from the card to the operating system. The LSL allows multiple MLIDs to be loaded at once, allowing for servers that use multiple network cards (such as multiprotocol routers).

The NetWare 3.x Network Model

NetWare 3.x was designed to serve as a standalone file, print, and application server, using the IPX/SPX protocol. Individual groups and organizations can maintain individual NetWare 3.x servers, each of which has its own resources (such as data volumes and print queues). See Figure 22.12 for an illustration of this concept.

FIGURE 22.12.

An example of a NetWare 3.x network.

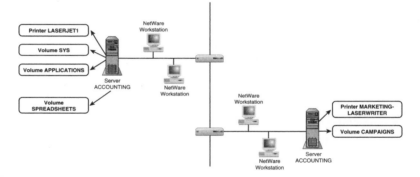

In addition, each NetWare server maintains its own security database, known as the *bindery*. The bindery contains users and groups, along with those users' passwords and rights to server objects (such as files, printer queues, volumes, and other resources). This model works fine when individual departments maintain their own IS departments, and each user only needs access to NetWare resources within their department. However, if those users need to access resources located on multiple NetWare servers, the administration of those users rapidly becomes complex. Each user needs either to maintain a long list of passwords for each server's resources, or the user will need to tackle the complex and difficult (and potentially insecure) process of synchronizing their various passwords across the network (see Figure 22.13 for an example).

Because of the rapid growth in popularity in large enterprise networks, Novell decided that the use of individual binderies on servers was impractical. With NetWare 4.x, Novell introduced a new network model: NetWare Directory Services (NDS).

FIGURE 22.13.

NetWare 3.x servers each maintain a local security bindery.

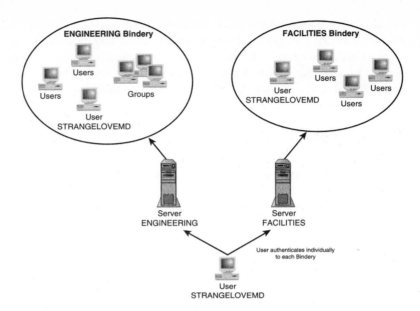

The NDS Network Model

NDS is designed to provide the same types of advantages as competing products, such as Banyan VINES: a single, global database of network resources accessible through one login. All network resources, whether users, groups, or servers, are treated as objects. These objects exist within a tree architecture (see Figure 22.14).

FIGURE 22.14.

An example of a NetWare directory services tree.

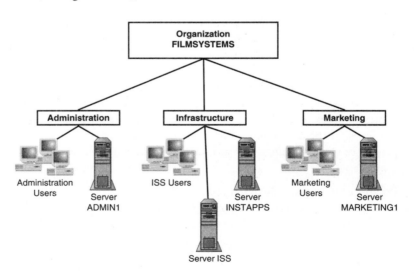

An NDS tree is organized into two different object types: containers, and resources. Containers can be used to organize resources by type (for example, you could have containers named users, printers, and servers), or by organization (as in Figure 22.14—administration, infrastructure, and marketing).

Each user in an NDS tree logs into the entire tree rather than logging into an individual server. When logging into the tree, users specify a default context, which defines the container in which their user object lies. For example, in Figure 22.15, user JOEBOBFRANK would specify the default context SALES.SANJOSE.USERS at initial login time.

Figure 22.15.

An example of a user logging into an NDS tree.

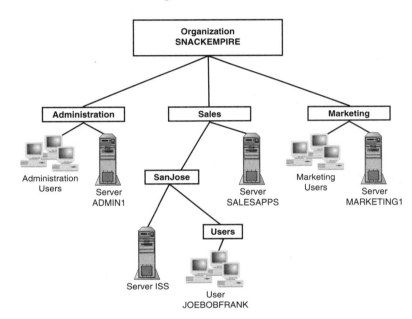

The NDS tree, and all objects within it, are stored in a database. This database is replicated to all servers within the tree, which enhances login performance (each user can be authenticated to the tree by the most local, fastest responding server) and makes the tree more fault tolerant (no one server failure can bring down the entire tree). See Figure 22.16 for an illustration.

Changes to an object, such as password revisions or server removals, can take a long time to be recognized by the entire tree, as the update is carried around from server database update to server database update.

Because of the many changes in network access brought about by the advent of NDS, newer network clients must be used on client workstations in order to authenticate to an NDS tree. In order to provide services to Bindery NetWare clients, a NetWare 4.*x* server can be run in bindery emulation mode, in which NDS database objects are translated into bindery objects, which can then be accessed with older NetWare clients. This process imposes a serious performance hit on any servers performing bindery emulation, however.

FIGURE 22.16.

Database replication in an NDS tree.

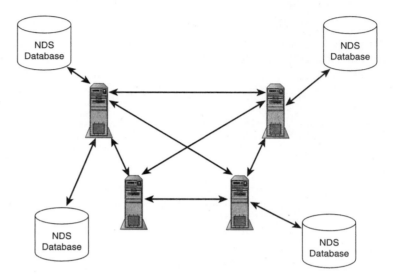

NDS provides a number of advantages. Network resources can be organized, viewed, and managed in a logical format, without regard to physical location. In addition, a single network login is available to all users within the tree, and resources from any container can be accesses by any user in the tree, as long as appropriate rights are granted. The complexity of this model, however, limits its scalability in very large organizations, as it becomes difficult for servers to manage and update the massive NDS databases. In addition, the complexity of the model, and its many differences from previous versions of NetWare, can make it difficult to manage, especially for LAN administrators familiar only with NetWare 3.*x* and older.

Interoperating with Other Network Operating Systems

NetWare's prevalence as a server operating system does not eliminate the utility, or necessity, of other major network operating systems. Though NetWare was originally designed to serve Intel-based MS-DOS and Windows clients, in order to make the product more successful Novell (and third-party companies) has added the ability to integrate NetWare servers and networks with networks using many other network operating systems:

- UNIX—Through the use of add-on NLMs, NetWare servers can easily be used in a mixed NetWare/UNIX environment. NFS (Network File System) services can be run over TCP/IP on a NetWare server as an NLM, providing UNIX clients the ability to map NetWare volumes as network file systems. In addition, bindery clients are available for most UNIX platforms, allowing users on UNIX machines to map

NetWare volumes as network file systems using the same IPX/SPX networking used by standard Novell NetWare clients. Novell also developed a product called UnixWare, which provided NetWare IPX/SPX client and server features on a UNIX System V platform (UnixWare has since been sold to the Santa Cruz Operation). In addition, NetWare servers can be configured to use NetWare/IP rather than IPX/SPX for NetWare networking, allowing administrators to reduce the number of protocols they must manage and maintain on their network. IntranetWare servers can also perform common TCP/IP Internet/intranet services, such as serving WWW pages and serving FTP (File Transfer Protocol), which are traditionally provided (and used) by UNIX-based systems.

- Macintosh—NetWare servers can serve files, print queues, and applications to Macintosh users. Bindery servers (both NetWare 3.*x* servers and NetWare 4.*x* servers running bindery emulation) can run AppleTalk File and Print Services, making them appear on an AppleTalk network as AppleShare servers. In addition, a NetWare server can manage print queues for AppleTalk network printers. Finally, in order to take advantage of NDS services, Macintosh clients can run MacIPX and MacNDS. Novell's Macintosh services have been plagued with minor problems, such as a lack of total compatibility with the Macintosh file system, but they can provide quality network services to Macintosh desktop users.

- Windows NT—The onslaught of Windows NT as both a server and a workstation operating system has become the greatest threat to Novell's dominance and market share. Novell has introduced new features for NetWare (such as IntranetWare) to directly combat NT's early advantages in features. However, Novell's efforts to discount Windows NT Server as a viable server product have failed, so they have wisely begun work on efforts to integrate networks running each product.

Novell has traditionally provided clients for all Microsoft desktop operating systems to access both bindery and NDS resources, and they continue to do so for Windows NT. Microsoft also includes products that allow NT users to access NetWare networks, but due to Novell's closed network architecture, they traditionally lack some functionality (for example, the Microsoft NDS client for Windows 95 cannot run NetWare Administrator, a graphical tool for managing NDS networks). Novell's products do not have these limitations, though they often face some issues with reliability and interoperability with other operating system modules.

Novell has also integrated Windows NT into their Windows desktop management products, such as ManageWare. Novell also produces an NT-based administration tool for NDS networks.

One very recent product from Novell addresses one of Windows NT's current weaknesses: the complexity and potential lack of scalability of Windows NT Domains (see Chapter 21 for more information). The Novell Administrator for Windows NT allows Windows NT resources, such as users, groups, shares, and print queues, to be integrated into NDS by synchronizing NT domain and workgroup SAM databases with an NDS database.

To NetWare or Not to NetWare?

The current wars that rage in the industry about the viability of NetWare as an operating system often obscure the facts. NetWare is an older, monolithic operating system, with an architecture and system design that lacks some modern features. However, Novell believes that some of these features (such as preemptive multitasking) do not belong on the file server. In any case, it cannot be argued that Novell servers, with proper care and the use of high-quality third-party products, cannot be used as reliable, high-performance network servers. Indeed, due to some of the architectural decisions we've looked at above, a NetWare server can often outperform any other competing product in raw throughput.

There are a few advantages to NetWare not currently provided by any other major competitor:

■ NetWare Directory Services—Currently, this is probably NetWare's most important advantage. NDS provides a centralized management interface as well as scalability unmatched by any other server operating system, including Windows NT.

■ Client Simplicity—Due to Novell's use of IPX/SPX, and long-term support for older operating systems such as MS-DOS, NetWare servers can often be a superior choice when an administrator needs to support a large number of MS-DOS and Windows 3.1 clients.

■ Vast Installed Base—Despite Windows NT's incredible, breakneck success, NetWare servers still comprise the vast majority of network file and print servers on the market. Because of this, support resources are often easier to find for NetWare, and there are more trained NetWare personnel than there are with competing products. NetWare management solutions tend to be more mature, and therefore more flexible and reliable, than many products available for newer competitors.

There are a few circumstances, however, in which NetWare may not be the right choice for you:

■ Enterprise Application Serving—NetWare's system architecture is inherently less protected, and therefore potentially less stable, than that of UNIX or NT Server solutions. For this reason, it is probably not the best choice for serving enterprise applications, such as databases, gateways, and mail servers. However, for serving shared copies of desktop applications, NetWare servers are perfectly suitable.

■ Mixed-Usage Computing—Because of NetWare's architecture, it is not suitable (or even usable) as a mixed workstation-server platform, as are UNIX and NT systems. NetWare is designed to be used as a dedicated file, print, and application server.

■ Cross-Platform Serving—Though NetWare has a great deal of support for multiple operating system clients, such as UNIX and NetWare, many have found the cross-platform abilities of competing products such as Windows NT to be superior, particularly with mixed environments of 32-bit Microsoft desktops (for example,

Windows 95 and Windows NT Workstation) and Macintosh systems. In addition, UNIX and NT systems have more mature, easier-to-manage Internet/intranet service packages.

■ Multiuser Shared Computing—NetWare is a dedicated server operating system, and cannot provide multiple shared-time interactive sessions, as can UNIX and other operating systems (such as VMS).

Summary

Novell's recent troubles, and the massive growth in popularity of Windows NT Server, have caused the industry to cast a disparaging light on NetWare-based network solutions. While NetWare currently suffers a number of disadvantages when compared to more modern operating systems, NetWare also has a number of advantages unmatched by any of its major competitors. Whether or not NetWare is right for you will depend on your specific needs and future plans.

22

NETWARE

V PART

IN THIS PART

Putting It All Together

Improving an Existing Network

*by Frank C. Pappas
and Emil Rensing*

IN THIS CHAPTER

The reality of networking in the 1990s is that everyone—from management and local users to the most distant of Web surfers—is demanding more and more from rapidly-aging legacy networks. Not to mention, of course, the hell that the poor souls tasked with keeping everything online and in tip-top condition must endure on a daily basis. It's almost a certainty that these ravenous bandwidth hogs will expect nothing less than miraculous improvements in network speed, access, and reliability, with only the most conservative of investments set aside for the upgrade of existing network components. Never mind the silly notions that may have been dancing (like sugarplums) in your head about actually expanding your network's processing and bandwidth capacity in order to accommodate the ever-increasing demands coming from your user community.

So what's a network engineer to do?

Starting from Scratch—NOT!

In an ideal world, every network engineer would be able to report to work on the first day of a new job and design a complete network from scratch, tailored specifically to meet—and beat—the many unique and demanding challenges that the particular computing environment has to offer. Of course, coupled with this carte blanche, every engineer would also be given ample money to purchase the best hardware (PCs, servers, hubs), software (network and client operating systems, client/server applications), and other networking essentials (cabling, external connectivity, and so on). And (considering we're fantasizing here) let's not forget a generous amount of time thrown in to build out the data center, run cable, and tweak, configure, and pray over every aspect of the network until there was nary a packet lost anywhere in the system.

Unfortunately, any veteran of the network world knows very well that this is hardly ever the case. The first days (sometimes weeks) spent with a new employer are most often spent analyzing the current network topology, services, and technology resources—at the same time that you're trying to get a handle on office politics, assess the skills of coworkers, and generally make a good first impression with the management team. Granted, little of this is particularly helpful in your quest to improve the company's network. Projects most often have to be accomplished in short spans of time and within the confines of ridiculously hobbled budgets, meaning that you'll have to be no less than a miracle worker in order to satisfy—let alone impress—the hand that feeds you.

Even for a synchronized and highly talented corporate infrastructure team, the threat of network death due to substandard or failing hardware and software is most certainly the single-largest drain on resources, leaving little in the way of spare time to plan—or build—for the future. Keeping the company's current systems intact and functional is, properly, the lifeblood of networking teams, especially because any degradation in network performance will most certainly be noticed by the users and bumped upstairs to management, often resulting in agonizing meetings with non-technical managers whose role—or so it would seem—is to know as little about the technology involved as possible, yet still have the final word in all serious decisions.

Consequently, the meager funding that is allocated to these groups is usually directed at stop-gap or "band-aid" upgrades (incremental memory upgrades, an extra processor or two, and so on) intended to hold things together only as long as it takes for the next relatively minor advancement to present itself. It is quite frustrating when you realize that you'll rarely find companies eager to set aside the requisite thousands or possibly millions of dollars needed to properly deploy the latest in high-speed gadgetry and telecommunications gear, especially when the network has been neglected to the point of obsolescence. Granted, sooner or later significant cash outlays and large-scale network reengineering will become the only viable options for many of the battered and decaying networks deployed today throughout the world, so network engineers are in for some fun times in the years ahead. But take heart, fellow network fanatics, because despite the overwhelming tasks that lie ahead, there is a light at the end of the tunnel.

Remember Where You're Headed

As impossible as it may seem, there are many productive avenues that you can explore in order to improve the general performance of your network. Keep in mind, however, that because of the heterogeneous and often baffling array of network configurations and user demands that has cropped up over the years, these options (or certain combinations) will yield markedly different results for each specific network in which they are implemented. There is no single fix that can account for every hardware, software, and (mis)configuration variable, so it's up to you to do a little brainstorming with your team before you proceed with anything drastic that may significantly impact your corporate networking environment.

Step 1: Identify the Problems Currently Affecting Your System

Identifying all of the problems affecting your network at any given time is anything but a simple task. To be completely honest, on occasion it can seem to be an easy task, though you should not necessarily stop after identifying one or more obvious problems after a cursory troubleshooting episode. Remember that networks—both literally and figuratively—are constructed from layer upon layer of heterogeneous hardware and software combinations, and the problems most readily noticed, while important, may be serving as camouflage for more serious issues buried deeper within your network.

From time to time, the problems you encounter may indeed be straightforward and resolved with relative ease. If you have a simple problem such as a lack of available ports to which to connect your users' PCs, and all other aspects of the network seem to be performing at acceptable levels, you may be able to get away with nothing more than running some additional cable and perhaps the installation/upgrade of a hub or two. Unfortunately, most network problems are far more insidious, requiring a significant amount of investigation and analysis before any serious plans-of-attack can be drafted or reinforcements deployed.

Step 2: Determine Your Ideal, "Golden" Network Configuration

The next step in "Magical Network Expansion Land" requires you to identify all the aspects of an ideal network that would make you, your users, and management happy, hopefully all at the same time. While this can be a nerve-wracking, hair-pulling experience, the ease of administration and general level of user satisfaction that can be achieved from a "golden" network is often well worth the effort.

Does this include the installation of new (or additional) cabling in order to increase internal bandwidth available network drops and decrease latency? Perhaps your company has a few *HAV*—high asset value—or mission-critical resources to which your network must provide access, such as color laser printers, RAID arrays, optical drives, or news feeds. In some cases, certain security products such as firewalls can prevent users from accessing certain types of data, especially Internet-related resources such as streaming audio and video, America Online, and UseNet newsgroups. Is a proxy server, then, the right solution for your troubles?

Once you get a handle on all the macro-level services and characteristics of your "golden" network configuration, you'll need to get approval (and support) from your superiors in order to transform your whims—um, carefully considered recommendations—into technical reality.

Step 3: Spec Out the System

It is to be expected that you are at this very instant daydreaming about the latest and greatest in AlphaServers, SparcStations, fiber optics, and the like. As nice as it would be to have such high-tech toys complementing and supporting your network, chances are that your boss will never fork over that much cash, especially for products and services that are not necessarily critical to the daily operations of your company.

In this business, the only way you get anywhere near the amount of money you need is to architect a plan that succinctly addresses the needs (read: wants) of your company as perceived by your user community and goes slightly beyond—say, 10 to 15 percent of the total cost—for additional capacity.

Step 4: Develop a Workable Implementation Plan

At this stage of the game, you've (hopefully) channeled much time, effort, and energy into the framing of a suitable plan for improving and/or expanding your network. Theoretically, at least, you've identified the major problems that you want to resolve, have drawn up specifications for your "golden" network configuration, and have received tacit approval and a blank purchase order from your boss. You're almost ready to begin implementing the many great upgrades that are sure to satisfy everyone involved. There's only one problem: Each user still needs to be able to access the network during the transition.

This is another one of the logistical nightmares that can sometimes catch network engineers and systems administrators unaware. It's a catch-22 of sorts: The essential services that allow the company to conduct business are in need of a little TLC, but these same services cannot be taken offline because they happen to be, well, essential services.

Certainly there are some companies that are less affected by this than others. Take, for example, a site like ABC's new flagship online presence, abc.com. If a particular piece of their internal network is taken down to accommodate the installation of new hardware or software, chances are that a good portion of their critical business resources—publishing systems, photograph databases—will go down as well, bringing production to a halt.

Because this is generally a bad thing, Internet administrators have to make sure that these upgrades are as transparent as possible, occurring at odd hours or on isolated segments of the network that can more easily or frequently be powered down. Of course, even in non-minute-by-minute organizations such as law firms, consulting houses, and universities, the reliability of the network, while not critical, is still quite important. Companies simply do not spend the amount of money necessary to install or upgrade advanced networks, only to find that the network is down for maintenance more than it is available for use.

Let me illustrate my ramblings with an example from my dark past. Back during the heyday of PoliticsNow, we suffered day after day with a quirky and altogether troublesome publishing system. This software failed countless times each day, but to our dismay it was the relative best of only a few products with the scalability and functionality that we required to produce the site. As our vendor's programmers—conveniently located in the Netherlands, Lake Titicaca, or some such place—churned out updates to both the server and client software, the tech team was constantly under the gun to evaluate and then install each supposed fix. Unfortunately, upgrading certain parts of the system required that the server-side database and publishing systems be disabled, or necessitated a seemingly unending series of complete reinstalls and subsequent reconfigurations of user workstations. The nature of the news business—especially the breaking kind—means that for every second you keep a user offline, you seriously and negatively impact the capacity of the company to do its work.

While it's not the most convenient of things for the technology staff, it is important to remember that the users come first. A partial or complete network outage can be scheduled ahead of time (with the appropriate approval from management—important!) and provides an excellent opportunity for small, easily implemented upgrades with minimal fuss.

A second, more risky option is to take the entire network down late at night, generally when network utilization is at a minimum. While this is often an excellent strategy for accomplishing larger-scale changes to your network (because you'll have more time and no immediate pressure to bring the system back online), it does have some rather unpleasant possible side effects.

While I don't want to harp on America Online, their troubles with such an issue illustrate my point quite nicely. At regular intervals, the technology people at America Online conduct what is known as a *bounce*, which is basically a complete shutdown of the system that occurs around 4 a.m. Eastern time. The bounce is a quick way to get everyone offline, thus opening a window for modem installations, software upgrades, or any of a number of possible alterations needed to keep a network of AOL's size running at peak efficiency.

Unfortunately, when AOL's systems went offline, so too did a system that monitors certain interactions with ANS, an AOL subsidiary that provides the majority of AOL's connectivity. Once the physical upgrades were completed and the servers restarted—all well within the standard span of a bounce—all hell broke loose because no one could access the service, thanks to errors on the AOL-to-ANS connection that would normally have been isolated and corrected by that non-running process.

While this wasn't directly caused by hands-on problems encountered by the AOL staff during the upgrade itself, it took the staff some 19 hours—an eternity during such a crisis—to get things fixed. I don't know if heads rolled in Reston because of this little problem, but rest assured that there are many bosses who'd go postal if their companies were damaged on a similar scale.

So what's the lesson here? Don't take anything for granted! While you may know almost everything there is to know about your network and its services, sometimes familiarity can breed carelessness. Be prepared for the unexpected, and don't be overly ambitious. Break large upgrades into easily achievable phases that can be implemented over the span of a few days rather than in marathon 38-hour weekend shifts. Know how your actions will affect not only your user pool but the rest of the network as well. And most importantly, know how (and be prepared) to undo your changes in case you reboot and find that your system has mysteriously become crippled or is trying to use Microsoft Bob for the shell.

Do I Need 10base-T?

Ask almost anyone who uses an office network about 10base-T, and you're sure to get a number of very interesting and humorous responses. As with many technologies, some terms and phrases become fashionable, and you'll hear *10base-T* bantered about quite often, especially in meetings where the participants want to be part of the "in" crowd. Unfortunately, knowing that 10base-T exists doesn't confer any other special knowledge on these people, who can become dangerous if not quickly cut off. But what *is* 10base-T, you ask?

10base-T is one of a number of designations used to differentiate between four main types of networks, as defined by the 802.3 specification issued by the IEEE (Institute of Electric and Electronic Engineers). The other types are referred to as *10base-5*, *10base-2*, and in the 100 Megabit genre, *100base-T4, 100base-TX,* and *100base-FX*, with each type providing varying levels of performance at different price points. In a moment, we'll take a closer look at each of the IEEE-specified network types, but let's talk about which network is right for you.

Unlike some of the other decisions that you'll have to make when building out your corporate network, you'll have some guidance when it comes to picking the network scheme. This is the case because each one of the specifications offers uniquely disparate functionality, giving each type its own niche market. If your plans call for extremely high speed networking, then 100base-T is your choice. If you only need to connect 10 PCs in a small office, you can choose from any of the options. As we've discussed, once you draw up your network requirements, the path to choosing the proper scheme will pop into view.

10base-5

According to the infinite wisdom of the IEEE, 10base-5 networks rely on a traditional 50-ohm thicknet (coaxial) cable to connect network devices. You can have a maximum distance of approximately 500 meters for the network bus, which must be terminated at either end with resistors similar in impedance to the cable itself.

Each device that is connected to the thicknet is attached with a transceiver, which in turn is itself connected to the backbone via a special tap that penetrates the coaxial shielding and connects to the internal wire.

10base-2

10base-2 networks are commonly referred to as *thinnet networks* because—strangely enough—they use a thinner, double-shielded variation of the traditional thicknet coaxial cable. Because these networks use a thinner cable—and therefore have a smaller amount of bandwidth—the maximum run length is significantly reduced from the 10base-5 specification down to approximately 185 meters. While the IEEE specifications do not support this, certain vendors have been known to release products capable of supporting much greater lengths, even up to 300 meters or so.

You'll connect all of your network devices via a combination of co-axial type BNC connectors and host adapters, which makes setting up the network a bit easier than with 10base-5. However, you'll only be able to connect up to 30 separate devices, due to the limitations of the cable itself.

10base-T

10base-T is by far the most widely installed network type, thanks to ease-of-use, reduced maintenance and troubleshooting time, and other important benefits that have been introduced as answers to the complaints and pleas of network administrators and engineers.

The new performance characteristics of 10base-T networks are many and varied. First and foremost is the fact that 10base-T networks rely on twisted-pair wiring to link network devices. *Twisted pair* is extraordinarily cheap, comes in a variety of pleasing colors and patterns, and is small and easy to work with—which is quite handy when running cable in confined spaces and around tight corners. Generally you'll connect the cable with 8-wire RJ-45 wall jacks, although you have some flexibility here if there is a pressing need or desire to be different.

What's more, while 10base-T networks allow only for cable runs of 100 meters between host and hub adapter, you'll benefit in the end because you can connect a virtually unlimited number of devices to this type of network.

Beyond 10 Megabits Per Second

As the need for faster network communications becomes more and more common, you may find yourself looking to technologies that offer significant performance over 10base-T. Sure, 10Mbps switching is a great building block for better network performance, but chances are you will find that some of your nodes or possibly an entire subnet (or two) will need more speed. If those systems are based around a PCI bus and have Pentium, Pentium Pro, or Pentium II processors, you are a prime candidate for faster 100Mbps Fast Ethernet networking.

There are currently three primary specifications for Fast Ethernet: 100base-T4, 100base-TX, and 100base-FX.

> **NOTE**
>
> Fast Ethernet is not the only 100Mbps topology available. Hewlett-Packard and a variety of other network hardware manufacturers offer a line of products that conforms to the 100VG AnyLAN specification. One of the major advantages of the 100VG technology (VG stands for Voice Grade) is a feature called Demand Priority. 100VG sends packets over four pairs of Unshielded Twisted-Pair cabling, and Demand Priority offers a way for certain network applications to receive priority on the network.

100base-T4

If you need Fast Ethernet performance on a limited basis and do not want to have to upgrade your network cabling or if you simply want to test Fast Ethernet, 100base-T4 might be for you. It can use the same type of LAN cable that you have in your current 10base-T network, either Category 3, 4, or 5. You will have to upgrade NICs in your systems and upgrade some of your hubs (depending on your specific network architecture), but you will not have to re-cable your entire network as you would have to do with other standards. Why would you want to upgrade to other standards that require costly re-cabling? Well, 100base-T4 requires four pairs of wire (hence the "4" in the name) at each node to attain these speeds. Because LAN cables contain only four pairs of wire, you are placing an extreme burden on your cable's integrity—which is not always possible, especially in older installations.

100base-TX

Similar in performance to 100base-T4 and in specification to 10base-T, 100base-TX LANs demand high-quality Category 5 cable throughout your infrastructure. In many cases, this requirement will force a large investment to upgrade your existing cable infrastructure. There is no other significant advantage to 100base-TX over 100base-T4 except for the reduced headaches of having a significantly more reliable infrastructure to push data through.

100base-FX

The 100base-FX offers the same network speed, with enhanced performance, but an even more costly investment in your cabling infrastructure. 100base-FX relies on fiber optic cable. This is great because it does a few things for you. It will dramatically eliminate almost all electromagnetic interference that can result in degraded network performance. Additionally, 100base-FX will extend the maximum cable run to over 1 mile, a significant increase over 10base-T and other Fast Ethernet standards that have significantly shorter distance limitations.

As with 100base-TX, the fiber optic requirement will place 100base-FX LANs out of the reach of most mere mortals. It is not uncommon for upgrades to fiber optic infrastructure to cost more than two or three times as much as an upgrade to a different category of network cabling.

Topology: Myth and Religion

As with just about everything else that we've covered in this book, the different network topologies—how your physical cabling and hardware are distributed throughout your offices to support your network—that you'll encounter each have fervent and protective camps of supporters who will do their best to convince you why Token Ring is better than star, or that everything should be wireless. Due to the fact that cable plays such an important role in the design of both LANs and wide area networks (WANs), there will be endless numbers of people who'll want to throw in their two-cents worth. Watch out for them. Seriously.

While you may not be able to separate the truth from the bottomless pit of marketing hype (at first, anyway), you should be able to get a clue as to how valid any advice is by evaluating the person who is advocating one particular technology over another. If the person with whom you're talking is a network engineer, you're probably getting very good technical advice that may or may not be the solution to your particular network needs. If, on the other hand, you've been cornered by a network supply vendor—and are without either taser or cattle prod—keep in mind that you're probably getting valid but highly biased information. After all, while the vendor probably has a good understanding of his product line, remember that his first duty is to move products out of the showroom and into your operations center, so be careful before embracing the solutions offered by overly interested parties.

What this all boils down to is that no one can give you a complete solution to building a network, nor should you accept one even if a reasonable one is proffered. After all, the whole reason that you're reading this book is that you've been given the task of upgrading or installing a new network. No one is as familiar with your company's needs, financial resources, and eccentricities as you happen to be, so it is up to you to marry that knowledge to an understanding of the available technology and make your bosses proud! What we're doing is providing the most important background information that you'll need to build an impressive network, essentially empowering you to combine technologies until your requirements are satisfied. Ready for more?

There are three central types of topologies that you're likely to read about: linear, ring, and star. However, only the latter two are widely found to be in use these days. Each of the topologies varies in the hardware and (sometimes) software that will be required, the services that will be supported, and in the maximum performance levels that can be achieved, assuming an optimally configured environment.

Type 1: Linear (Bus)

A *linear topology*, sometimes referred to as a *bus topology*, is a network in which all networked devices tap directly into one central run of cable, most often called the *backbone*. In this situation, every device is attached to the backbone by a transceiver that facilitates both inbound and outbound communication with the greater network (see Figure 23.1). Additionally, in order to decrease the possibility of signal loss or mangled data transfers, linear network backbones must be terminated at both ends using pairs of resistors that are equivalent to the impedance of the particular type of backbone cabling.

FIGURE 23.1.
An example of bus topology.

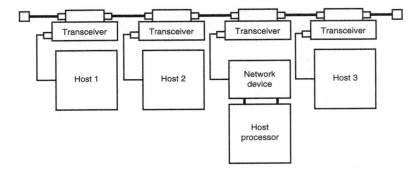

Type 2: Ring

If you happen to be familiar with the early-1980s Intellivision game Snafu, you're already familiar with the physical layout of a ring network topology. A *ring network* is a variation on the bus design, with the end of the cable run attaching itself to the beginning of the backbone in order to form a complete, unbroken ring.

Keep in mind, however, that Figure 23.2 is only a conceptual representation of a ring network; they're not really constructed in a circle. The function of a ring is achieved through the use of

MAUs, or *Media Access Units*, hardware to which other devices are connected in order to gain access to the network itself. Within each of their MAU boxes is a cable ring that allows data to pass by every node in the network during transmission, thus achieving the ring concept.

FIGURE 23.2.

An example of a ring topology.

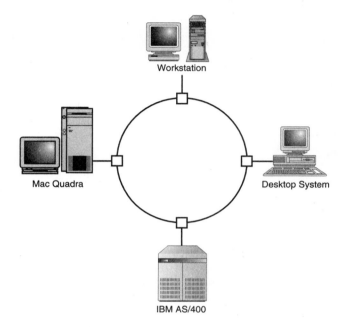

Workstation

Mac Quadra

Desktop System

IBM AS/400

Type 3: Star

Because both ring and bus topologies are unwieldy to install, maintain, and troubleshoot, it wasn't long before the star topology (see Figure 23.3) found its way into the mainstream network computing world. If you recall how you (probably) used to draw pictures of the sun in grade school, you'll begin to get an idea of the theory behind star networks. Imagine the heart of the sun as your hub, with the rays representing actual lengths of network cable that run out (depending on the type of cable used) and connect to individual PCs, Macs, network printers, and so forth.

The star topology's popularity is two-fold. First, it is significantly easier and less expensive to install and maintain, especially because it can mimic the physical distribution of other office wiring (telephony, intercom). Second, it has greater expansion potential than other topologies, in that you cannot run out of physical space on the backbone as with linear networks, nor do you have to worry about expanding an already huge ring in order to accommodate a new device.

FIGURE 23.3.
An example of a star topology.

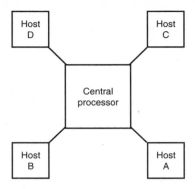

Choice of Cabling

After you've selected the overall topology that will best serve the needs of your budding network, the next step in the process is to decide on what type of cable will be most appropriate as the foundation for your network. You've got two main choices, fiber or copper, the choice of which will determine how well your network will eventually be able to handle the many services and other traffic that your organization will require.

Choosing between fiber and copper cabling is not the hardest thing in the world. In fact, you'll have much more trouble actually getting the cable installed than you will picking between the two. Chances are that the decision will be made for you, simply because fiber is prohibitively expensive and offers performance characteristics that will most often exceed all but the most demanding of network performance requirements.

There are three main criteria against which you should evaluate your need (or ability) to use copper or fiber cable when building your network:

- Cost
- Bandwidth
- Ultimate expansion capacity

You'll have to do some soul-searching to determine which characteristics are the most important to your project and then plan accordingly.

Fiber

If you can convince your company to go the extra mile and invest in a fiber-based network, you're going to be out a ton of cash in the short term. However, fiber soon makes up for this with higher performance specifications, including support for higher numbers of attached devices, as well much greater flexibility in the overall length of cable runs, on the order of n feet. You'll also reap two additional—and extremely enticing—benefits from cable. Because fiber optics are just that, *optical*, relying on light rather than electricity to transmit data, fiber networks are not susceptible to ambient EM (electromagnetic) energy radiating from other network devices or power lines or transmissions in the UHF (ultrahigh frequency), VHF (very high frequency), or other bands.

> **NOTE**
>
> It is important to understand that fiber and copper are not mutually exclusive terms. An excellent strategy for a dynamic and flexible network includes a fiber backbone that is connected to each individual device via less-expensive copper wire. This will give you a high-capacity backbone, yet still allow you to easily and affordably attach an almost endless number of network devices. Remember that the majority of a fiber network's price tag comes from attaching individual devices to the cable, not from the cable itself.

Coaxial/BNX

With the debut of the earliest Ethernet LANs back in the 1980s, the standard types of cable available at the time were anything but convenient. Unfortunately, the implementation of coaxial-based Ethernet didn't do much to help the situation, because coax is both quite expensive and difficult to work with due to rigidity and overall bulk, requiring obscene amounts of wall or duct space to install more than a few runs.

However, despite its limitations, coaxial cabling does have some interesting benefits, including a transmission capacity of 10Mbps to a maximum run length of nearly 500 meters! While you'll still find networks in use today that rely on coaxial cable for their inter-device connectivity, their numbers are steadily decreasing, thanks to newer, more network-friendly technologies that have been released in recent years.

Twisted Pair

Twisted-pair wiring is everywhere. You'd be hard-pressed to find a network environment in existence today—at least in professional environments—that doesn't have some form of twisted pair supporting at least a portion of the entire network. Twisted-pair wiring is comprised—coincidentally—of a helical strand of two insulated conducting wires. These strands are most often encased in a small sheath of plastic, and are referred to as UTP (unshielded twisted-pair) because the plastic does not serve as protection against ambient radiation or other signals that may interfere with the data transmission across your network. The second form of twisted-pair wiring is shielded much in the same way as standard coaxial cable.

In practical situations, twisted pair is an excellent choice for most networked environments, due primarily to its low cost, lack of rigidity, and excellent transmission quality.

Client and Server Hardware

The next area that you will need to examine in your quest to upgrade your existing network will be your client and server hardware. The computer systems connected to your network are often overlooked as a component of network performance. Certainly, applications will run at reduced speed and efficiency on slow hardware; the same holds true for a slow piece of hardware's capability to push data through your network. Nevertheless, your collective group of clients and servers, if poorly implemented, can drastically reduce network performance. Unfortunately, the same cannot be said about well-implemented systems. Ultra-fast systems with high-speed network interfaces using homogenized client access protocols across your Enterprise Level LAN will not greatly improve your performance—at least not above what is expected from a network that is functioning within normal operating parameters.

There are many things to consider when optimizing your networked computer systems. Like most of what you have already read about topology, the focus of your enhancement strategy will be on hardware. We have already talked about how you can improve your network topology. Most of that discussion focused on upgrading your cabling, re-segmenting your LAN, and adding faster hubs, routers, and switches. This section will be no different; hardware is what you want to examine first when trying to "speed up" your systems. Faster processors, more memory and, of course, faster LAN adapters—as well as how those systems are built and configured—are the most crucial components when discussing networking performance of your hardware.

As usual, software is a close second in the high-performance networking game. You do not want to run more protocols on your network than are absolutely required to satisfy the requirements of your users. Nor do you want to run more protocols on your network than you need to. Think about who needs access to what and how to minimize the protocols and services required getting there, just as you focused on minimizing routes in the previous section.

Finally, when upgrading your network, you have a third consideration: The users. Many, many LANs do not place a high enough value on what a user has to do to function on your network. Upgrades to your overall network operating system can greatly affect a user's ability to simply log on to the network, and that could wreak havoc come Monday morning when the same staff that has trouble using America Online shows up and does not recognize the new login procedure.

What Hardware Do You Have?

The first step in your hardware upgrade plan is to examine your collection of existing hardware. Do not look at your computer systems in a macroscopic sense; look at the specific hardware that comprises each of your systems. Inventory all of the internal components, such as individual SIMMs, processors, disk drives, video adapters, sound cards, network interfaces, backup devices, input devices, monitors—everything! Do not leave anything out.

Think about your systems not as a 486 DX4 100MHz system with 16MB of RAM, but as a mid-size tower case with an Intel 486 DX4 100MHz processor, 16MB of RAM with 2× 4MB SIMMs and 4× 2MB SIMMs. Then build another list of the systems that you need to assemble to fulfill the needs of your employees. (We will discuss how to do that in the next section.) Then redistribute your hardware as appropriately and as evenly as you can across your network, supplementing to reach a common level of hardware but not wasting the money on something that will be useless in six months when your boss will finally kick in the cash needed to purchase brand-new systems.

As you are doing this, you must always be thinking about the future. You do not want to spend money upgrading 68030-based Macintosh systems to 68040; you want to go straight to the PowerPC, if you can. You do not want to spend the money to upgrade the processor in your 486 DX 33MHz systems to 486 DX4 100MHz systems, if you will be able to buy Pentium 150MHz systems in six months. Of course, it is nearly impossible to predict what types of hardware will be available in six months to a year; your investment in Category 5 Ethernet cabling and interface adapters will be useless once the cost of fiber drops to $0.02 a meter. When will that be? Who knows?!

How Do I Get to Where I Want to Be?

Planning, planning, and planning! Oh, and money. As important as planning is in your endeavor to upgrade your network infrastructure, planning is equally important in your path to upgrade your client and server hardware. Careful analysis of the tasks that need to be performed in your computing environment and your ability to match hardware, software, and services to those tasks are of the utmost importance.

Remember to match your computer system upgrade strategy to the overall plan you have already established for your network. Consider all of your network users. What do they need to do? What are their needs? What services do you need to provide for them? Who needs the fastest machines? If you run a call center, chances are you will not need to upgrade your operators' systems much past a Pentium 100MHz. That should be plenty of horsepower to run your custom Delphi or Visual Basic applications. Putting them on the path to a 200MHz Pentium Pro might be fun, but it is probably overkill. If you have software developers all running on 486 DX2 80MHz systems or artists using Power Macintosh 7100, you will probably want to get those folks onto Pentium Pro or Silicon Graphics UNIX workstations ASAP! If you have a 486 DX 66MHz server running Linux that 25 to 50 users access for Internet Mail, News, and intranet Web services, adding more drive space, RAM, and faster network adapters for each segment of your LAN will probably be sufficient.

Stop upgrading systems that don't need to be upgraded! Let the administrative assistants, managers, and vice presidents have the older but adequate systems. Get your development staff, financial analysts, and graphic artists some machines with real power; they are probably performing the most time-intensive applications in your organization. If your business consultants get paid as much as mine, you don't want them to have to wait 60 seconds each time they hit your SQL server to get data, do you? You want these guys working—not waiting—and a new $3,000 piece of hardware might save you $10,000 over time, especially if your employees have to wait for machines to be fixed or to finish recalculating a spreadsheet.

Clients

If you are anything like most organizations, you probably are not starting from scratch. You might have a room full of shiny new Pentium or PowerPC-based computers, or you might have a bunch of dusty old 486/33 MHz, 486/50 MHz, or 68040 based computers. In any of these situations, you need to be thinking about the future. Of course, client software configuration will be of more interest to the owners of new systems in their endeavor to improve their existing network. Nevertheless, both groups will need to think about where they want to be in six months to a year with their hardware, even though it is nearly impossible to predict what will be available so far in advance.

I Thought that Everyone Needed Pentium Pros

No! Are all of your users doing real-time 3D modeling? Are they all compiling multi-megabyte applications? Are they all doing massive financial calculations? Chances are, they aren't. If anything, your users are probably playing a networked game of Quake and wishing that when they killed Mike that he died in a timely fashion.

> **TIP**
>
> Quake runs best on most LANs when using the IPX protocol. This is also the protocol of choice on LANs that primarily access Novell servers. Running a network game using the TCP/IP protocol, however, will make games more difficult to detect—especially if you use a port that is different than the default!

For the most part, your hardware decisions should be based entirely on what a particular member of your staff does for your organization. Most administrative assistant-level employees should be content with systems that can run your word processor, spread sheet, scheduling, and contact management software. In most cases, 486 DX2/80 MHz systems, with sufficient memory, will do the trick—even if your network clients run Windows 95. Of course, a Pentium 100 will be even better, but a high-end 486 will usually get you by, and it might be more cost effective to upgrade your existing supply of 486 DX2 33, 50, and 66 MHz systems to DX2 80 or DX4 100 MHz systems than to buy all new Pentium systems—especially if you do not think you will be able to upgrade much more in the next 12 to 18 months. You will have to do extensive testing. Depending on what office suite you use, depending on what workgroup scheduler, depending on what additional applications you use—it all affects what your clients will need. A free upgrade to the latest version of your office suite—though seemingly a bargain—might end up costing you thousands of dollars to purchase the additional CPU processing power needed to run it, especially if the next version runs as a Java applet!

Table 23.1 shows recommended general guidelines for equipment distribution. This might not be where your organization is today; however, it might be where you want to think about being a year from now. An amiable and possibly daunting goal, but one that might be worth sacrificing for.

Table 23.1. General guidelines for equipment distribution.

Job Title	Optimal System
Administrative Assistant	Standard Macintosh or standard PC
Sales Force, Marketers, and the like	Standard Macintosh or standard PC, optional portable system
Developer, Artist, and the like	High-end Macintosh and high-end PC
Analyst	High-end Macintosh or high-end PC
Management, Executives	Standard Macintosh or Standard PC, optionally only a portable system
Chairman of the Board	Whatever the heck they want, if you want to keep your job!

It is important that you always remember two things when delegating hardware to clients:

1. You need to set your ranges. You need to define what your users can accept as the bare minimum to run on your LAN. You need to define what is considered mid-range equipment. You need to determine what is a high-end system. This can only be done through extensive testing on your part with various types of hardware. This will be an extremely tedious and time-consuming process; however, if done correctly it will set the stage for your entire upgrade path. Table 23.2 will give you more general guidelines or a place to start your testing.

Table 23.2. General guidelines for client standards.

System Type	Description
Standard Macintosh	33 MHz 68040 processor, 16 MB of RAM, 500 MB hard disk, 15" monitor
Standard PC	66 MHz 486 processor, 16 MB of RAM, 500 MB hard disk, 15" monitor

continues

Table 23.2. continued

System Type	Description
High-End Macintosh	60 MHz PowerPC processor, 24 MB of RAM, 700 MB hard disk, 17" monitor
High-End PC	100 MHz 486 processor, 32 MB of RAM, 1.0 GB hard disk, 17" monitor
Standard Notebook	33 MHz 486 processor, 16 MB of RAM, 500 MB hard disk, 9" display
High-End Notebook	50 MHz 486 processor, 16 MB of RAM, 500 MB hard disk, 10" display

2. The other thing to remember is never get so caught up in your general guidelines of equipment distribution that you let it affect an employee's ability to do a job. If you have analysts that travel to different offices to collect data and analyze it, don't get a high-end desktop system for them! Get a powerful, portable notebook system. It might be something that you do not normally stock, it may take a while to arrive from the vendor, and it might be for a non-standard position, but it is the right tool for the right job!

Also, do not forget that you will need to supply your on-call staff with systems at home. In most cases, these can be any old things that you happen to have lying around. Depending on the employee, it might be more fun to give him a pile of parts that could be assembled into a computer and say, "Here. Put it together." These systems do not need to be the best—they will already be hindered by their slower than normal connection to your network, but they should be sufficient. Remember, the employee's inability to repair servers remotely might be directly tied to what hardware he has at home. An old 386 with a 14.4Kbps modem might be fine for a UNIX administrator dialing in to a UNIX host, but not for a Windows NT administrator expecting to make a Windows NT 4.0 dial-up networking connection.

Are My Macs Worthless?

Well, that depends on who you ask. Most competent Information Services professionals would say, "No! Of course not! What kind of ridiculous question is that?" However, many, many internal computing groups within most large organizations feel that a flexible, powerful, and easy-to-use personal computer might put them out of a job. Of course, there is no right answer, so it is probably wise to allow users (when possible) to make their own platform decisions. After all, they are the people who have to perform the real work on your LAN, and you want them to bother you as infrequently as possible—make it easy for them!

Most popular network operating systems can accommodate Macintosh clients with little or no modification. Windows NT, for example, has an excellent fileserver service for Macintosh. It can make available the same shared volumes that your Intel-based PC clients connect to using native Macintosh AppleShare networking. Microsoft also provides an extension to AppleShare that will allow authentication using Microsoft's secure protocols.

Although AppleTalk, Apple's network protocol, can be a bit "chatty" on your network, the increased activity makes for an extremely easy user configuration and operation. No Ethernet or IP address numbers to remember, no frame types to choose, no bindings to have to configure. Simply plug in your network cable, name your workstation, and away you go! Most Apple-Talk networks can function without routers of any kind. Simply plug your 10base-T or 100base-T Ethernet adapters into capable hubs, and you will be ready to go!

Software incompatibility is not really an issue any more. Most standard word processor, spreadsheet, and database file formats can be read by similar or competing Macintosh and Windows applications. Other file formats like images, digitized audio, and video can also be used among the different platforms. The only problem you might encounter is a Windows PC's inability to read a floppy disk formatted for a Macintosh, which is not really a problem if you are sharing common network space or if you use a PC-formatted floppy disk. Most modern Macintosh computers can effortlessly read PC floppy disks.

Getting back to improving existing hardware for you network, it is important to remember that a Macintosh investment, in most cases, is a wiser investment than an investment in a comparable PC. That is because most Macintosh computers can be upgraded with a lot less effort and expense than a Windows-based PC. For example, you may currently have some non-PowerPC-based Macintosh systems that use Motorola 68040 processors. If the upgrade path you want to take your organization on requires that all of your Macintosh users have PowerPC systems, you may not need to upgrade to brand new systems. There are PowerPC upgrades available for many Macintosh systems, available either directly from Apple or from third-party manufacturers such as DayStar Digital and Newer Technology.

The other major upgrade you might want to invest in, depending on the type of Macintosh you already own and type of network you are building, is the type of network adapter that is in your Macintosh. Similar to Windows-based PCs, the Macintosh has networking options to fit every price range. From inexpensive peer-to-peer connections running at serial speeds to the uncommon 100base-T or fiber optic transceiver running at more than 100Mbps, the Macintosh can handle most any type of networking infrastructure.

The Macintosh is also an Internet or intranet-ready workstation. The newest upgrade to the MacOS provides full TCP/IP network support across your Internet or intranet. It supports BootP, DHCP, and RARP IP Address allocation, and can support PPP connections as well.

What About UNIX?

For most organizations, the decision to use UNIX-based clients on its LAN is probably one of necessity rather than desire. Just as applications like word processors and spreadsheets run well on Intel- or Motorola-based systems, certain development tools and graphics packages simply run better on UNIX systems. Most UNIX systems require specialized hardware, and the flavor of UNIX you are running will dictate where you have to go for hardware upgrades.

NOTE

Chapter 20, "UNIX/Linux," has more in-depth information about many of the different versions of UNIX available and where to get information about hardware and software.

If you are running Linux, NetBSD, or SCO-based UNIX systems, however, you can use much of the same hardware as you use on your Intel-based PCs. It is important to remember that the requirements for running UNIX on Intel-based PCs vary greatly from the requirements you will find match your needs for clients running operating systems from Microsoft or IBM. Generally, you will find that the requirements to run UNIX are much more modest than the requirements to run Windows 95 or Windows NT. If UNIX systems are that important to your organization, you should include them in your general guidelines of equipment distribution, and if you have specialized UNIX hardware, get in touch with your sales representative about upgrade plans and stay close to that issue—it could be a very expensive one!

Your decision to run UNIX clients carries another important factor along—the presence of TCP/IP on your network. UNIX has very fast and efficient networking built right in to the operating system kernel, which is one of its many advantages. While most modern networks readily support the integration of TCP/IP among the clients, there may be some Internet, or intranet-phobic system administrators out there who do not want that protocol on the LAN. Alternatives are available in some cases, so check with your hardware and software vendors.

Future Clients

As technology advances and the price of hardware drops, the range of technology that is available to users increases at a breakneck pace. While it can be extraordinarily difficult to even begin to craft a long-term upgrade strategy for your network without worrying too much about advancements in current technology, "holding back" on the integration of brand-new technology such as Network Computers (NCI) from Sun Microsystems and Oracle or Pocket PCs from Casio or Philips might prove to be a very expensive experiment. The promise of new and exciting features from new and exciting products can prove to be too much for some Information Services professionals to resist. On a personal level, purchasing a U.S. Robotics PalmPilot might be a great investment, but the decision to purchase a PalmPilot for each member of your 1,000 employee sales force might prove devastating if the 6-month old product fails and you can no longer receive support or software from the vendor.

Be careful in your decision to include new technology. Don't exclude new technologies out-of-hand, but be sure to take a good, hard look at any infant technology before jumping in feet-first.

Personal Digital Assistants

Apple was one of the first to enter the PDA market with its Newton MessagePad. This small, hand-held device has a touch-sensitive screen where users can write notes and enter data into address books, calendars, digital checkbooks and games. The initial Newtons were slow, had poor handwriting recognition, and had many other shortcomings, but the ever-persistent Apple kept at it, improving the software and hardware. Apple's latest Newton, the Newton 2000, is laden with features, including a back-lit screen, wireless keyboard, and significantly improved hand-writing recognition. The PDA market has also seen entries from U.S. Robotics and Sharp. In its brief life, the U.S. Robotics PalmPilot has seen tremendous initial sales to and applications from many third-party software vendors.

Companies such as Casio and Philips have small, highly portable Digital Assistants as well. Commonly referred to as Pocket PCs, the Casiopeia and Velo 1 are both among the first generation of portable systems to run WindowsCE, a version of the Microsoft Windows 95 operating system designed for low-powered hardware. Not as reliant on handwriting recognition technology as the PDAs from Apple and U.S. Robotics, the Pocket PC might be just what the doctor ordered to spur increased sales in the PDA market.

As far as network connectivity is concerned, most PDA-type devices do not plug directly in to the network. They plug in to a standard desktop or notebook PC that becomes a host for file synchronization and data transfer of contacts, appointments, and e-mail messages.

The Network Computer

Oracle and Sun Microsystems have joined forces in an attempt to define the future of the modern network. Their diskless computer that plugs in to a regular television and high-speed network was designed to make client administration simple and error free as well as. All applications and data live on a centralized server, making your infrastructure investment even more important! All access to network resources is controlled from a central location, making Network Computer an excellent choice and logical decision for the client of the future.

Unfortunately, at this point in its development, Network Computer is too slow and too lean to be considered for any serious computing tasks. Very few third-party software developers are taking a serious interest in the Network Computer, and the availability of out-of-the-box software might be another weak area for it. Part of the speed issue concerning the Network Computer will undoubtedly be resolved once the speed of Java is improved.

The Zero Administration PC

Hot on the tail of Sun and Oracle is industry giant Microsoft. In his never-ending quest to dominate the market, Bill Gates has committed Microsoft to the development of the Zero Administration PC, which is in essence a system that runs a Windows 95-like operating system that can support most or all of current and future applications with the same ease of administration as the Network Computer. With the added functionality of self-diagnosing hardware that can notify a user or administrator of potential problems before they become too serious, the Zero Administration PC might just be the future of network computing.

Servers

From a networking perspective, a client can only be as useful as the services offered on the network. A client can only function on a network as fast as the services can handle the transactions required by the client. In this sense, the server plays an extremely important role in the performance of your network.

Depending on the types of services you require on your network, you may or may not need more than one server. Many types of services cannot coexist very effectively on the same machine. For example, if you are running Windows NT as your network operating system, you do not want to run filesharing and SQL database services on the same physical hardware. Those services have very specific and different optimal hardware configuration needs—needs that vary greatly based on traffic, the amount of data involved, and the distance the data has to travel. For the most part, server configuration is not something you want to skimp on. It is very different from client configuration; you probably do not want to play trial-and-error to find an optimal configuration for your servers. Rather, you want to consult with software and hardware vendors to get systems built to your exact needs, with the appropriate amount of disk drives, RAID arrays, RAM, and processing power. That is your safest and wisest bet, especially when running such dramatically different services on your servers.

On the other hand, you may have no choice but to determine your own optimal configuration for servers that run operating systems and services that are freely available. UNIX operating systems such as Linux are freely available and offer general guidelines for what hardware configurations will match what service and usage specifications, although those guidelines will vary greatly. As with Intel-based UNIX clients, Intel-based UNIX servers will generally have more modest hardware configurations to run similar services, as compared to network operating systems like Novell NetWare and Windows NT.

Connectivity Hardware

In all cases of computer hardware attached to your LAN, you want the fastest possible connection, regardless of the platform, service, and protocol. We have already discussed how simply resegmenting your network may dramatically improve performance of data transfers. We have also discussed how upgrading your cabling can enhance performance. To make the best use of that investment, you need to make sure that the interfaces between the network and your hardware are as fast as they can possibly be, and that can only be done through research and—you guessed it—trial and error.

The research phase is simple. Look at your hardware. Look at what type of LAN you have now. Look at what type of LAN adapter you have now. Think about how you are upgrading your infrastructure and match your components. Head to the Web, which is always an invaluable resource when preparing for upgrades and build-outs. Look at LAN adapters from vendors like 3Com, SMC, Hewlett-Packard, Digital Equipment Corporation, and Novell, and match up your needs with their product lines and availability. Get adapters that can "talk" with the data bus on your PC as fast as the bus can spew data. Make sure that your adapters can interact with your network as fast as your cable and servers will respond. Go as fast as you can possibly go! You should also consider data regarding vendors' services and past performance. How fast have they put out drivers for past upgrades to your operating systems? How long does it take to get an adapter repaired? How long have they been in the network hardware business? What is their dedication to the product line?

(Ethernet) Switches

If you haven't already plowed through Chapter 8, "Switches," and are experiencing a high degree of network congestion, it's a good idea to flip back to the earlier part of this book and give Chapter 8 a once-over before you move on. Ethernet switching, which is covered extensively in that chapter, can provide one of the most powerful and cost-effective solutions for reducing network problems such as lost connections, slow or corrupt data transmissions, and other connectivity issues by effectively managing the *flow* of data across the many subnets of your greater network.

Switching solutions provide a viable solution to many of the problems typically cited by network engineers when trying to re-architect anything but the smallest of LANs: They are a relatively inexpensive technology (although high-end, high-price models are available); the benefits derived from switching solutions are usually quite dramatic, including a reclamation of total network bandwidth; full-duplex (20Mbps) networking becomes a possibility; and switching solutions are faster, easier, and cheaper than a complete network redesign based on FDDI, Fast Ethernet, or other high-speed options, because switches allow you to retain the bulk of your current network infrastructure.

The network performance gains that are associated with switching solutions come from the manner in which switches are able to segregate various segments of your network into *subnets*, Ethernet segments that support the communication of only a small fraction of the total number of workstations connected to your network. By splitting the greater network into subnets, switches are able to free up valuable bandwidth for vital network communication because the machines—now isolated on their various subnets—talk only on their local segments. Of course, if a particular packet is destined for a host on a different subnet, the switch will route it to the proper subnet, generally with only minimal delay. In the end, switching becomes a prime candidate for network rebuilds because it has such a great price/performance ratio.

Price Competitively and Purchase Intelligently

Once you get some systems in to your testing lab (which you should obviously have built from your experiences in piecing together client and server hardware), run them through their paces. Test your operating systems and protocols on the adapter; see which ones perform the best.

Chances are that you will have a very difficult time finding a clear speed demon out of a pack of well-engineered adapters. More than likely, you will base a large portion of your decision on LAN adapters on the ease of installation and configuration in a host computer. That, coupled with a vendor's dedication to a product line, quality of support, timelines of repair, and your overall upgrade plan, will allow you to make an intelligent purchasing decision.

Protocols

"Less is More" is the name of the game when delving into the ever-exciting world of communication protocols. When you boot your PC, do you start the Microsoft Windows for Workgroups NetBEUI client, then load a series of drivers for IPX support to your Novell NetWare server, and then load your TCP/IP stack just before firing up Windows 3.1? Do you also have Macintosh clients and servers that are AppleTalking on the same physical network? This is a bad situation that, without question, is undoubtedly creating unnecessary and significant traffic with which your network must cope. Why do you need so many protocols on your network? The answer, generally, is that you don't.

Finding a lowest common denominator protocol—a single protocol that can satisfy the communications needs of all the services running on your network—can be time-consuming and frustrating, but the end result will be well worth it: a streamlined configuration that (you hope) will provide a significant boost in network speed. Elimination of excess chatter on your network will result in less packet collision, less waiting time for user requests, and faster data transfers. If you have any questions as to which protocol is currently the most widely used by the widest range of services, that's easy to say in a word: The Internet. OK, so it was two words, but the explosion in popularity, functionality, and desirability of the Internet has led to a flood of network services that requires the ability to be used across large distances and among various hardware combinations. From that explosion, TCP/IP has risen as clearly the most widely used by the widest range of services on the widest range of platforms.

So why not take advantage of this where you can? Fewer protocols for the same number of services equals less network traffic.

Supporting Your Clients

Do not forget the reason you exist. If you are vice president of information systems and technology, a SQL Server administrator, the senior network engineer, or the person who answers the phone at the help desk, your goal is servicing your users. You need to make things flexible, easy, and powerful for power users and the newbie user. Do not restrict things to the point where working is difficult. Do not be so unwavering in your stance to move printers from a Novell print server to a Windows NT print server for users who only need to run IPX and log in to a Novell directory tree for print services. That is not good for them, and it is not good for the traffic on your LAN!

Remember that when dealing with users you should be nice, especially when dealing with a "know-it-all." Be informative and listen carefully. Some "know-it-alls" might actually be able to help you! Ninety percent of all major problems you have on a large scale with your users can probably be avoided entirely by informing, instructing, and documenting changes ahead of time and getting those instructions into the hands of your users. Do not assume that they will pick up on even the most minor change in the operation of the network, even if things look similar on the screen.

Summary

With users screaming, crying, and (sometimes) becoming physically aggressive in response to less-than-impressive network performance, it is becoming increasingly necessary for businesses to upgrade and optimize their internal networks on a much more frequent basis than ever before. Unfortunately, taking your network to the next level of performance usually requires significant time, effort, and funding, which are not necessarily available or forthcoming from management, even in the most desperate of times. This means, unfortunately, that network engineers and systems administrators have to do more with less, and somehow try to address as many problems as they can in the most efficient and cost-effective manner available. This can involve incremental upgrades to aging and over-burdened server hardware and software, client systems, and other infrastructure items. In many instances, small but strategic upgrades will be able to resolve the most urgent (or visible) of network issues, allowing more time to address the underlying issues that prevent your network from achieving "golden" status.

Occasionally, of course, miracles do happen. Every so often there will be a little cash left in the corporate pot at the end of the fiscal year, which means that you can plan and implement large-scale infrastructure improvements targeted to alleviate current problems while simultaneously providing for additional performance and capacity in the future.

Whatever the case, remember that there are rarely any quick fixes that will make all of your network troubles magically disappear. With a significant amount of analysis and planning, you'll be able to determine what your requirements are for your optimal network and craft a package that is comprised of carefully selected hardware, software, and cable systems in order to make every person in your organization—from the boss right down to the secretaries—happy with the services that your network provides.

Now let's get busy!

Building a New Network from Scratch

by Richard Maring

IN THIS CHAPTER

The idea of computer networking is new to some people and almost always seen as a highly technical and rapidly evolving process. Every day, computer professionals are called upon by their employers to evaluate, judge, and implement the technologies necessary for the rapid communication of dissimilar groups in order to enhance productivity or lessen complexity within the organization's processes. Most see the task as a formidable one, and many feel they are not qualified or fully prepared to drive the creation of a Local Area Network (LAN) or Wide Area Network (WAN). The purpose of this chapter is to break this creation process into small digestible chunks, giving even the most inexperienced a blueprint for success.

Let's start with the term *networking*. Networking can be defined as a pathway. The term "network of tunnels" is an example. Networking is by no means a new concept or one exclusively restricted to technology. Whether it be a network of railroads or the telephone network, the same image comes to mind: a pathway by which something is transmitted. Thus a computer network is an electronic extension of the same concept. The purpose of a computer network is to link two or more "clients" together in order to exchange information.

There are three basic rules without which no computer network could be created. Although these three rules may seem trivial, they are the cornerstones for a successful development initiative.

In order to do computer networking, you must

1. Have a means to connect two or more "clients" together.
2. Speak a common language.
3. Determine the rules for a dialogue: Who talks first? Who responds? How are errors handled?

The majority of problems that most existing networks face are based on design factors: either they were ill-conceived or they were not proactively designed to allow for the existence of growth. Design is the most important ingredient if a network is to meet all the necessary milestones for success. Regardless of how limited the business requirements are or how many networks your group has built in the past, approach each new network as a challenge. Cutting the design time a week to shorten the schedule could add four weeks of re-engineering at the end of the project.

Documentation follows as a close second to design as a critical part of the network. Not only does the documentation validate the effort and time you put into the project, it also provides a built-in "sanity check," always setting the tone from the start of the project to its fruition. Proper documentation can save untold time just as a means to eliminate the endless routine of searching for that one piece of critical information necessary during a physical failure or preplanned upgrade. If the network has grown beyond the capabilities of your current IS department, documentation will provide the evidence to justify the increase in budget to gain the necessary resources and manpower.

As an additional primer to give the inexperienced a chance to test their decision-making skills without costing their companies untold amounts, included in the next section are three different company scenarios, allowing the reader to experience each step for themselves and evaluate their decisions. In computer networking, there are no "right" or "wrong" decisions, only "better" and "easier" implementations. What is listed in this book is one interpretation; critique it for yourself. It will be good practice should your IS group ever be called in to do a network upgrade of an existing system.

The purpose of this chapter is for you to gain enough confidence with the basic ideas and concepts of networking to make informed decisions. There are numerous books that devote several hundred pages to what will be covered in these few. Although not all the possible answers can be explained, if you walk away asking the right questions and know where to go for the answers yourselves, then your time spent on this chapter is well used.

Business Scenarios

Make it a practice to carry a highlighter with you to place emphasis on what elements must be applied to your design as you take notes talking to your user community. Non-technical people will often approach the idea of connecting their companies together from a business perspective. They will tell you what they want and what capabilities they feel would be good to have. It will be your job to determine what they really need and what the limitations of the technology will allow for their organization.

Scenario #1

You are a new hire as the third member of Acme's IS department. The 73-year-old company is expanding at a rate of 120% this year compared to last year. Due to the overwhelming demand for their products, Acme would like to implement a computer network to connect their corporate office with their remote offices and speed up the turn-around time necessary to distribute their products. Acme's president, Wallace Kiote, has an "old school" mentality, feeling that automation is unnecessary, and he would have preferred increased manpower to handle the new influx of orders. After discussing the idea with his Board of Directors, he agreed to provide the resources necessary to implement a limited network connecting the corporate office with two of the busiest offices. If this goes well, the total connectivity of the 11 offices will occur.

Acme Industries still uses typewriters and hand-processes every order. Their customer support center, although quite organized, has difficulty researching every problem presented to them in a timely manner. They spend a small fortune on the use of mailings from office to office. For important correspondence, they often rely on couriers to hand-deliver the materials.

Each department has its own internal hierarchy, having developed its own way of doing things as the departments have evolved. Although the departments do not resist the new technology, they are aware of the potential of possible problems or errors that they do not have in their current system.

Company Name:	Acme Industries
Employees:	217
Locations:	3 (1 corporate office and 2 remote offices)

Scenario #2

Your neighbor approached you during a cookout in the park. He heard you were into computers and wants to know if you would be interested in setting up a small network for his law office. He has a computer, as does his secretary. He wants to link together his other two partners in the firm who still write their case briefs by hand. He has two legal assistants in the field who fax him progress reports as they work on a case. He wants to connect all these people together and streamline his organization more effectively. He stresses that in his line of work he needs a secure computer environment where no one except the six of them will have access to their files. He tells you that only he and his secretary are fairly "computer literate."

Company Name:	Linux, Dynix, and Ultrix—Attorneys at Law
Employees:	6
Locations:	1 fixed at main office
	2 in the field on assignment

Scenario #3

You are a member of a 20-person IS department working for a multimillion-dollar health insurance brokerage. Your company has recently bought out a smaller competitor, and your purpose is to integrate the new company's existing network architecture into your own, allowing total communication between the two branches. The competitor's computer environments are using 8-year-old technology, and they were paying support to a company to maintain their custom-made proprietary systems. Each of the competitor's remote sites were using whatever technology they independently budgeted for. The sites range from a site with just a simple word processor to one of their larger remote sites, which had a small network installed. Upper management wants you to take a design team into the field and analyze the hardware, time, and money necessary to move the new holdings up to the company's standards. The personnel from the smaller company were retained; they see this acquisition as a good thing and will do whatever is necessary to work with the parent company. Management wants the acquisitions absorbed as soon as possible so they can incorporate their new patient files into their existing database.

Parent Company Name:	Best Care Inc.
Parent Employees:	600
Parent Locations:	8 (1 corporate office and 7 sales branches)
Child Company Name:	Better Care Inc.
Child Employees:	418
Child Locations:	6 (1 corporate office and 5 regional offices)

Business Scenario Summary

These three examples, while not the norm, provide a good cross section into the obstacles you would face going into a completely new situation. Each scenario presents its own challenges with multiple resolutions depending on what criteria your design stresses. For someone who has never done networking, they may seem unrealistic.

However, these three cases are actually based on jobs I once worked on at one time in my career. When I was learning networking, all the examples I read were these perfect, neat environments where everything pointed to one solution exclusively. To be good at networking, you need to be well informed of the technologies involved, and you need to be creative enough to adapt to the situation as it presents itself.

Assembling the Design Team

The design team is a *logical* breakdown of areas of responsibility that need to be addressed in order for each major piece of a network to be developed properly. Note the emphasis on the word logical. In many cases, one or two people will fill the roles of several of these areas of responsibility based on the relative simplicity of the network design or the lack of IS resources to commit to the development. Either way, remember to place equal emphasis on each of the areas of responsibility, for a lack of focus in any one area of responsibility could weaken the whole network.

The areas of responsibility are as follows:

Project Management

- Integrate with the company's management in reporting and budgeting issues
- Manage the team's resources and time schedules
- Create standards for the design process
- Handle issues that might hinder the development initiative
- Lead the design meetings and act as the focal point for information gathering

Business Responsibilities

- Monitor contact with the user community
- Help convert the users' needs into tangible project milestones
- Educate the design team as to the history and functionality of the company
- Prototype the network to determine its effectiveness before it is released to the user test group

Networking Responsibilities

- Closely monitor and coordinate all activities in the areas of network infrastructure and architecture design
- Ensure the logical business process flow is represented by a physical network topology that meets or exceeds needs
- Interface with vendors to provide product information as necessary
- Set standards for future network expansion

Hardware Responsibilities

- Create personalized hardware setups to meet current and future needs
- Interface with vendors to provide product information as necessary
- Set standards for future systems expansion

Applications Responsibilities

- Ensure there is continued emphasis on making the best choices of software available for the users' needs
- Verify that the network's hardware requirements meet the minimum allowable specifications for any software being used on the network
- Optimize the network to handle the traffic patterns that will be generated by the software selected

Security and Reliability Responsibilities

- Determine the level of physical and network security necessary to protect the company
- Set standards for network auditing and resource tracking
- Determine the level of fault tolerance and redundancy needed by the company
- Set policies for new/modified resource access

Training Responsibilities

- Determine the different levels of the users' computer and network experience
- Create training pathways to educate each of the levels defined above
- Provide feedback as to issues that might hinder the users' understanding of the training information
- Educate the users and track their comments about the curriculum

These areas of responsibility listings do not always cover all the uniquely possible design events that might occur; however, the breakdowns show that appropriate coverage of all areas of responsibility is necessary in order to maintain an understanding of all the factors involved. Once again, as mentioned above, these areas of responsibility may rest on the heads of a few based on many factors. Personnel, money, time, and other factors may make one to two people responsible for covering all of the areas.

Determining Business Requirements

Now that the design team is assembled, it's time to go to your customer and determine what his actual business needs are. Remember, the users that are polled to provide requirements rarely have the technical background that you have. They will usually speak in terms of the business side of the corporation. Before even speaking to the user community, take along this list of important topics. Although the topics will not be discussed directly, the design team should be able, at the end of the meetings, to meet and determine all the necessary components for the functional design. The key points are as follows:

1. Business Objectives
   - What does the company do?
   - Why do they think they need a network?
   - What divisions/departments would be impacted by the network?

2. Future Growth
   - What is the projected growth of the company?
   - Are new divisions/departments planned to be developed in the near future?
   - Where does the company see itself in one year? Five years?

3. User/Group Requirements
   - How will the network impact and improve user performance?
   - How will the network allow users to grow within their current roles?
   - What type and amount of resources must be available to each group?

4. Security
   - What are the levels of security within the company?
   - Are there different levels of security when dealing with outside sources?
   - What is the physical security in the company?

5. Fault Tolerance
   - If the company had a major network failure, what would the impact be?
   - How fast does the network need to be repaired in the event of a failure?
   - How critical is fault tolerance and redundancy for this network?

6. Existing Network Architecture
   - Does the company have an existing network?
   - Can that network be successfully upgraded or retained?
   - What would be the impact of replacing the legacy network?

7. Management

   ■ How much time and resource management is necessary to maintain the network?

   ■ What level of network management does the company expect?

The first step when venturing to a site location is to obtain an organizational chart of the corporation both at that location and for the whole corporation. This will usually give you a tentative breakdown of each site as most branches are set up with specific departments in mind. Focus on interacting with the layer known as middle management. These are the people who understand the purpose and vision of the corporation and at the same time can provide information as to daily operations and procedures. Make sure you ask questions as necessary to break the discussion down into as simple a workflow design as possible. The objective is to understand enough of their and their department's job function to make educated decisions as to what equipment they need.

Try if at all possible to have only one person from your design group interact with each department. Define these people as the support liaisons for their respective departments.

Breaking Down the Network

It's often easier, especially in large design initiatives, to break the network down into smaller pieces in order to focus on the user's needs more effectively. My recommendation is to make each location its own little site. Everything that connects the sites together is considered a WAN link. Everything inside the site is considered a LAN link. Because of the differences in technology and speed between WANs and LANs, this approach is usually best to spot inherent weaknesses in the design.

Creating a Logical Design

All the background information has now been gathered, and it's time to design a logical map of the company's proposed network environment. A logical map helps one understand the potential bottlenecks as well as what the areas of relative performance need to be to provide consistent performance evenly across the network.

This map is often designed at a high level, and then attachments are added to the map that logically map each site in greater detail down to individual segments.

The way I design a logical network like this is to draw out the logical map and print out three copies onto clear transparencies. Each transparency will hold a different segment of the network, and when they are held together, they provide a comprehensive guide to the network's logical flow. This way, each layer can be analyzed individually and optimized based on budgeting and time constraints to provide design alternatives. Figure 24.1 provides a possible logical mapping of the three scenarios described.

FIGURE 24.1.

The logical mappings for each of the scenarios.

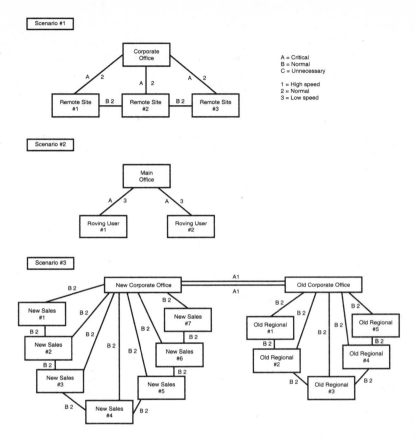

Creating the Physical Design

Whereas the logical design deals with the transfer and flow of information, the physical design deals with the logistics of users and resources. Questions like the following will commonly be asked:

- Where and how many users are located on each site?
- Are there multiple floors on each site?
- Where will the central location for all networking equipment be kept on each site?
- What are the power requirements of each site?
- Are UPS and backup generators necessary?
- Where will the users' workstations be located?
- What access to external devices (printers, modems, scanners) do the users need?

If at all possible, get each location's floor plan to help not only with the physical design but to aid in capacity planning for personnel and equipment. Once all the physical questions have been answered, draw connecting lines on the floor plan showing potential cabling pathways. Be aware that these connections may change repeatedly based on your choice of network model, network media, and the sophistication of the network's connectivity hardware. The hardware and network specialist usually work on this map as it deals with concrete physical equipment. Figure 24.2 gives a breakdown of each scenario with example remote offices for reference.

FIGURE 24.2.

An example of a physical mapping.

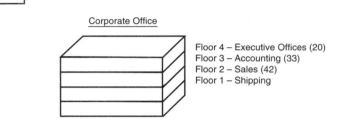

Scenario #1

Corporate Office

Floor 4 – Executive Offices (20)
Floor 3 – Accounting (33)
Floor 2 – Sales (42)
Floor 1 – Shipping

Power: Standard Current
UPS: Non-essential; Limited to specific systems
Workstation Locations: Floor 1: 20 pcs; Floor 2: 33 pcs; Floor 3: 42 pcs; Floor 4: 32 pcs
External Devices: Printers on each floor
                 Modems on floors 1, 3, and 4
                 Additional phone connections on floors 2 and 4

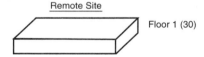

Remote Site

Floor 1 (30)

Power: Standard current
UPS: Non-essential; Limited to specific systems
Workstation Locations: Floor 1: 30 pc
External Devices: Printers, Modems, and Additional phone connections

Determining the Network Model

The network model is a set of implementation standards around which the network you design is built. Every network ever created follows one of these models; they govern where data is stored and define the information pathways from which the data is accessed.

There are basically four models that are currently being used in the network world to deliver applications and information to the user community:

1. Distributed or "mainframe" environment

   This model was the first of its kind and still popular today. It focuses all its resources into a server that handles all the data manipulation and storage for the company. Each user will "query" the server using video terminals or diskless workstations in order to start processes running on the server. Some advantages and disadvantages of the mainframe environment are listed here:

■ Single point of failure on the server.

■ No need to upgrade client workstations in the field to support new applications.

■ Server can become a bottleneck if its resources are overtaxed.

■ The server's proprietary solution may limit upgrade and expandability.

■ Security and physical access to the server can be maintained easily.

Figure 24.3 shows a sample of a mainframe environment.

FIGURE 24.3.

An example of a main-frame environment.

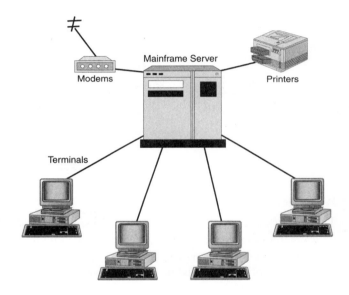

Mainframe Server

Modems

Printers

Terminals

2. Client/server environment

In this age of connectivity and information sharing, the client/server model has surfaced as perhaps the most popular and technically scaleable model available today. The basic premise is that of a main server similar to the mainframe environment. However, the server is simply used to provide applications and space to hold the data generated. All processing is done on the client workstations as a way to bypass the potential bottleneck caused by an overtaxed server. Some advantages and disadvantages of the client/server environment are as follows:

■ Involves more planning than the other models.

■ Client workstations can function even if the server is not present.

■ When an upgrade occurs, each workstation must be upgraded as well as the server.

■ Security can be an issue if all critical data is not kept on the server.

■ Scalable to an enterprise level.

Figure 24.4 shows a sample of a client/server environment.

FIGURE 24.4.

*An example of a client/
server environment.*

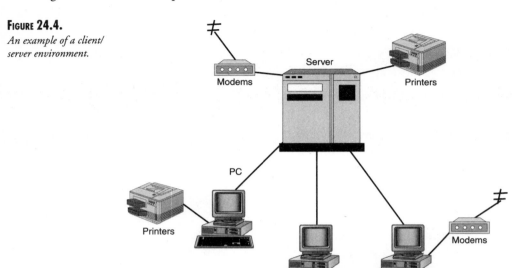

3. Peer-to-peer environment

   This model was created for a small (under 15 workstations) LAN environment typically found in a office setting. The premise behind it is to have every workstation as its own server, providing data and devices physically connected to it to whoever has been granted privileges to use it. The peer-to-peer environment offers the following advantages and disadvantages:

   - Cost-efficient due to the lack of a dedicated server or connectivity hardware.
   - Workstations must be left on to access all the resources available.
   - Lack of a centralized administration or security.
   - Not scaleable to larger networks.
   - Each machine has the potential of failure, crippling part of the network.

   Figure 24.5 shows a sample of a peer-to-peer environment.

FIGURE 24.5.

An example of a peer-to-peer environment.

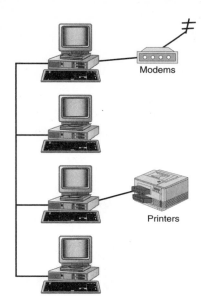

Modems

Printers

4. World Wide Web–based environment

This model is relatively new, having sprung from the influx of Internet activity over the past five years. The design is relatively similar to a mainframe type environment in that a central server delivers "pages" of information which users can view and interact with. Each user, however, has the potential of using these pages to start processing within their own session either on their local machine or back on a server. Some advantages and disadvantages of the World Wide Web-based environment are as follows:

- Cost-efficient in an LAN\WAN solution.
- Easy to install and deliver new versions of applications without visiting each client's workstation.
- Single point of failure on the Web server.
- May require multiplatform support.
- Security issues have not been reliably defined across the industry.
- Good for low-bandwidth or high-traffic environments.
- Integrates into the existing Internet.

Figure 24.6 shows a sample of a Web-based environment.

FIGURE 24.6.
An example of a Web-based environment.

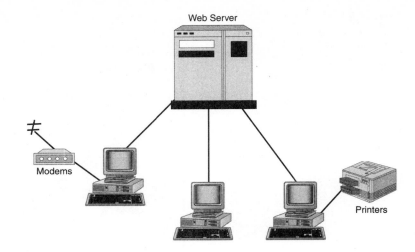

Making Some Final Choices

When you have reached this point in your development process, there are three important areas that merit careful consideration. First, you must choose the various applications your network will use. Second, you must decide upon a network operating system. Last, but not least, you will finalize all your decisions concerning hardware requirements.

The network model will drive the location and types of applications needed to meet the users' requirements. However, the following basic guidelines/areas must be adhered to:

■ Cost and licensing scheme

■ Ease of installation/configuration

■ Ease of use

■ Level of technical support available

■ How well the application interacts with other applications on the network

■ What network operating systems support the desired network application

After you choose the preferred network model and the list of application options that you and your users feel are necessary, the intersection of these two sets of data should lead to a list of potential network operating systems (NOS). Issues to address are very similar to those of a application perspective, including:

■ Cost and licensing scheme

■ Ease of installation/configuration

■ Ease of use

■ Maintainability

- Level of technical support available
- Hardware supported
- Upgradability
- Level of third-party vendor support
- Avenues for education for the onsite system administrators

Be careful not to get trapped in a proprietary NOS solution, which only supports hardware, software, and services all coming from one company (Apple and IBM during their heydays are examples of these principles). Although the level of functionality between the software and hardware is higher, you end up paying more due to a lack of competition. Also, if the company's support services do not adequately meet your network's repair and functionality needs, there is no other place to get support. In most cases, the NOS will be the one that either the company currently has running as a different site or one that the design team agrees on as the best choice.

Hardware requirements constitute three classifications:

- Server hardware
- Workstation hardware
- Peripheral hardware (printers, modems, scanners, and so on)

Server hardware is determined by the Network Operating System that is selected. My recommendation is to always go with the industry leader that is well supported. Some system administrators try to push the envelope and buy the absolute fastest, coolest, most feature-packed hardware they can find. *Always* make sure that the hardware company has updated drivers for all the hardware you purchase on the NOS that was chosen. Check to see how they handle problems and if the hardware vendor has any known incompatibilities with any other hardware.

Whereas server hardware was based on the NOS, workstation hardware is based on the applications that will be run on them. I usually recommend that when you choose a workstation solution, you test it thoroughly to work all the compatibility and functional bugs out of the planned desktop setup. If a choice of components is given, stick with the companies who will be providing your server hardware as a point of guidance. When I select a vendor, I usually have them create specifications for three different profiles: the average user, the power user, and the developer. If at all possible, get these three systems in house and try to "break" the desktop setup. Ask the following questions during the assessment to validate your findings:

24

BUILDING A NEW
NETWORK FROM
SCRATCH

- Does the system run out of resources (memory) at any point?
- How does the system benchmark relative to other systems in its price range?
- How easy is it to upgrade and repair components within the machine?

The final point to cover is that of the peripheral hardware. This is usually driven both by the business needs of each department as well as the physical site map. An example of this would be that there is a need in a department for a printer. Based on the business needs of the group, the relative complexity/expense can be determined. (Does it need to print graphics? Does it need to be high speed? Does it need to print color?)

Once a specific series of printer is selected, the model can be selected by the number of users who are going to be physically using it daily. The physical map also allows physical placement of the printer to make it accessible to the greatest percentage of its user community.

Although there are many little details in the selection, validation, and finally implementation of system hardware, follow the standards, and don't be afraid to ask a vendor to describe in detail the standard their products support. Just be aware that their job is to sell their product, so analyze everything they say carefully and always get a second opinion from other sources as necessary.

Developing a Test Laboratory

This step is often left out due to either budgeting issues or time constraints placed on the implementation. Depending on the simplicity of the design or the ability to modify the network design while in production, this step may not be necessary. It is recommended usually as a second check to verify that what the hardware and software vendors specified as far as compatibility and performance was correct. This step can also be utilized to allow users the first look at the functionality of the applications to gauge their reactions to the implementations. Various pieces of hardware and software can be "swapped" in and out of the test laboratory in an effort to find the optimal configuration. At this point in your process, it will be necessary to allow users a chance to see and possibly use the beta systems you put into operation in your test lab. However, make sure you explain to the users that the speeds and operations being attained may not necessarily be the same as what will occur when the actual network is assembled. No matter how effective you are at putting together a test lab, it can never duplicate the "real thing." However, it is a good idea to ensure all the pieces of the puzzle "fit" together and work with each other the way they are supposed to.

The test laboratory is also a useful staging ground for training support and installation personnel who will aid in the implementation effort but are not part of the support team. Although written documentation can sometimes be enough for a remote site to upgrade their systems, it is often more beneficial for the support person to visit the test lab and do an entire installation/ upgrade from beginning to end. This allows the support professional to ask any questions or address their site specifics in detail. These extra little details may provide more insight and help to focus the testing initiative.

As a basic test lab design, set up two individual subnetworks with a router or bridge linking the two together. Place two workstations on each of the subnets to be used for application testing/ benchmarking. One of the workstations will be set up with the standard user client profile, and the other will have network monitoring/sniffing software installed on it. This allows for passive monitoring, which will not impact network traffic and cause the monitoring software to read more traffic than what is really on the segment. Figure 24.7 gives a logical diagram of such a test network.

FIGURE 24.7.

The test laboratory.

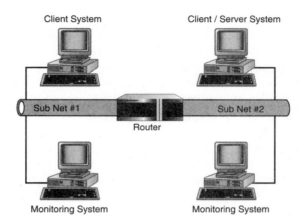

Evaluating Bandwidth Needs

After the final configuration has been determined, it is sometimes desirable, especially in larger networks, to evaluate the bandwidth needs in order to determine scaleability and in what places network devices (routers, bridges, gateways) should be placed to load-balance the potential traffic. To do this most effectively, connect a network protocol sniffer to the test laboratory and run the applications from different workstations, first singularly and then together, to gather preliminary time and bandwidth needs. Based on this data, the following questions can be answered:

- Are the data packet sizes small or large?
- Is the data packet stream for each application bursty or constant?
- Does one application limit the effectiveness of another?
- Are there options within the application that impact packet performance?
- How many users will use the application, and what will be the effect on the whole network?
- What is the frequency of execution for the application (once a week? daily? hourly?)

With these questions answered, you can define options to limit application activity to the area where it is used in order to limit performance degradation across the entire network. If you determine that an application that is very bandwidth-intensive will be run all day across the whole network, it may be best to add redundant routes within each segment to allow the delivery of packets more effectively to the server.

Selecting Connectivity Hardware

The other chapters of this book will do a good job educating the user as to the various connectivity hardware options (routers, bridges, gateways). Instead of going over the definition of these tools, I am going to go from a design perspective and show where the hardware should be implemented based on the network traffic patterns. Start by going back to the instructions in the section "Breaking Down the Network." A network device will primarily be placed where the LAN areas meet other WAN areas. This will keep all local packet traffic within each area or segment and allow only the traffic that needs to traverse the WAN link out. Connect the transparency that you created in the section, "Creating a Logical Design," with the application benchmark and bandwidth data captured according to the instructions in the section, "Evaluating Bandwidth Needs." Place additional network devices within every LAN segment based on the three criteria defined in the section, "Creating a Logical Design." If the data needs to be fast and the application takes up a lot of network bandwidth, perhaps the segment needs to have a switch or multiple routes to get from point to point. Ultimately, the purpose of connectivity is to meet the needs of the user community. Just remember, the more devices that are implemented to enhance performance, the more that need to be configured and supported.

I have included the following guidelines from my experience as a way to aid in the decision as to whether to implement a router or a bridge for a given network situation. Even experienced networking specialists will argue among themselves as to what the best implementations are.

- Bridges are good for smaller networks with fewer slow WAN links.
- Bridges must be used in certain situations where the protocols cannot be encapsulated or tunneled.
- Bridges usually are more cost-effective; in a cost-to-speed ratio, a low-end router is more expensive than a low-end bridge.
- Routers require human intervention in that they need to be set up, whereas bridges are plug-and-play.
- Routers handle larger networks with different speed links better.
- Routers are better at filtering things such as broadcasts and bandwidth utilization.
- Routers are more intelligent and can make decisions based on upper OSI layer sections of the packet.

Documentation

Throughout this chapter, the emphasis on documenting and drawing the networking structures has been obvious. At this point in the creation process, the design phase should be completed. The whole network should be laid out with knowledge of both the needs and expectations of the user community as well as issues of support, performance, and reliability. It is time to pull all the research and documentation together in order to prepare a business proposal that allows the project manager to educate the management of the company as to its needs and the final results to be expected. Go back through each of your pieces of documentation starting with the first one. Was there anything you would like to change in the design based on what you learned? Are there alternative solutions that will meet the needs of each step more efficiently or more cost-effectively? Before finishing the final documentation, revisit the options and redesign the whole network as necessary. It is better at this point to lose time redesigning than to be caught in the middle of an implementation that does not meet all the users' needs. On each step, add additional documentation as to why each specific choice was made and what the alternatives were. In most cases, before management will provide a budget for the project, they will interrogate the project manager as to how he determined the best solution. Make sure the project manager has plenty of information to support the team's decision.

At a minimum, the documentation should include the following:

- Detailed user requirements
- Logical map
- Physical map
- Specifications on the applications chosen (connect back to the user requirements)
- Specifications on the network operating system chosen
- Specifications on the hardware requirements (do a breakout by server, the three workstation requirements, and the peripherals involved)
- Specifications on protocol and media options
- Reports that describe the application's benchmark times and characteristics
- A logical map with the added network connectivity options included

Determining Cost/Time to Implementation

Once all the data has been documented and collected, it is time for the final project design meeting. The topics of cost-effectiveness and determination of rollout method should be discussed in great detail from all members' perspective to get an overall view of the necessary resources that need to be made available. The following is a list of usual weaknesses in an implementation plan that could be missed. Consider their impact carefully before presenting the final plan to the management of the company.

- Are onsite personnel in remote offices able to troubleshoot the installation?
- Will the upgrade be delivered as a static image, which can just be updated, or a full install, which will take a dedicated support person's time?
- How much of the installation can be automated?
- Will the vendors be onsite to respond to any inconsistencies in the delivered equipment?
- How many installs can the onsite personnel perform in a day?

- What departments have priority to have the installation done?
- If the users have questions/problems after the installation, who should they call?
- Will additional resources need to be hired to complete the installations within a specified time period?

Once the project manager feels secure about all phases of the implementation and that all issues have been properly addressed, the manager will present the findings to the management of the company in order to get proper funding for the purchase of equipment and additional manpower to complete the implementation. The project manager *must* present the findings using the most English-like language and analogies as possible to convey the message. Management may not always have as much computer literacy as you would like. Make sure to emphasize the benefits in productivity both in the time saved by using automation as well as the security and greater reliability.

Go through the documentation packet, educate the management as to why that is the best choice for each level and stand by the decision the group delivered. If money in the budget becomes an issue, present them with the possible alternatives and make them aware upfront what the negatives to the alternative will entail. Have management sign off on the official proposal in order to place responsibility for the project in their hands.

Selecting a Beta Test Site

Once management signs off on the project proposal, the design team shifts focus to plan, prepare, and implement the rollout schedule. The first phase of this rollout schedule is to select a beta test site in the field where all the systems that were designed in the test laboratory are field tested. If at all possible, try to set the first site near the test laboratory in case there are inconsistencies between the two sites. When engaging in a beta test site, always provide the user group with a comprehensive description of how the system works as well as polling them periodically to get their feedback on various facets of the network. These users will not only be able to provide valuable information as to how well the network design meets the business needs, but they in turn will reinforce the points that were made to management when the project's budget was approved. Key points to emphasize and discuss with the user community during this initial period include

- Does the network design presented to them allow the flow of data within their department?
- Do the applications that were selected adequately replace the manual processing or applications that had been used previously?
- What security would be appropriate for their data?
- What additional benefits have manifested that were not in the initial design requirements?
- How important is the data they are currently dealing with?

■ If the data were destroyed, what would be the impact on the company?

■ How long would it take to re-create data if it were destroyed?

Give the users time to adjust to the new system while you are compiling the results of the preceding questions. If any major or obvious problems appear within the system, repair them and update the systems for the beta test site. An important thing to note is that no matter how well crafted the network is, the users will always ask for more and more functionally. The need to determine a cutoff point is important to the success of the project. After this "stable" platform is configured (usually takes at least two weeks), follow up the finalized survey before proceeding to the next phase. This survey will provide more personalized points including

■ Does the network meet your expectations and needs?

■ How much training do you feel is necessary to become functional on the new system?

■ Does the network remove a degree of difficulty in your job, allowing more time to focus on more business issues?

■ What additional recommendations do you have?

The first set of comments meets the technical needs of the network, allowing the improvement in the design and functionality. The second set of comments provides insight as to the amount of user training and future enhancements that may be addressed in future releases. Remember, with the implementation of any type of organized or automated system, the effort levels to do the hardest tasks will usually be reduced from days to hours. This extra time can directly enhance the productivity of each department.

Creating Standards

If the beta test site is a successful installation and both the design team and the beta users feel that the implementation goals were met, then the next move is to create a standards sheet for the installation and maintenance of the new network. This allows groups other than the design team to install, troubleshoot, and maintain the new network. Opinions vary as to whether this milestone is really necessary because it does not directly impact the project. Standards are most useful for connecting to external networks outside the one that is being designed or in the case where an existing internal network is being upgraded. If the network will lack a centralized IS department, opting instead for an onsite support person who will maintain that piece of the network, then standards allow the support person to communicate effectively with the other members of the support structure in the case where a problem or difficulty is beyond their comprehension or technical competence. Based on the feedback from the user community when the entire project is done, the standards provide a valuable framework on which current design considerations can be re-evaluated, and the next network upgrade will have a baseline for installation.

The following list gives some specifications for a standards document. Based on the level of security, replication, or the variety of technologies on each site, these specifications will help with the selection of vendors, determine important network administration roles, and preserve/ enforce a consistent plan for all future changes to the network.

- Desktop Hardware
    - Systems make and model (list all three systems separately)
    - CPU
    - Memory
    - Hard drives
    - Monitor
    - Network interface cards

- Server Hardware
    - Systems make and model
    - CPU
    - Memory
    - Hard drives (list redundancy methods: mirroring, duplexing, RAID level)
    - Network interface cards

- Additional Peripherals
    - Make/model of peripheral
    - Site-specific settings
    - Interfaces used (serial, parallel, proprietary)

- Software
    - Operating systems supported
    - Memory requirements
    - Space necessary on workstation
    - Space necessary on server
    - Site-specific configuration parameters

- User Management
    - User naming conventions
    - New hire/termination guidelines

- Information Management
    - Volume naming conventions
    - Directory structure (applications, user directories, department directories)
    - Directory size restrictions (these are optional)

- Network Management

    Server naming conventions

    Routing and gateway information

- Security

    Password restrictions

    Login hours

    Department rights/login scripts

    Auditing (file, directory, user)

- Problem Tracking/Resolution

    Standard naming conventions for problems/resolutions

Take all the standards information and bind it together to form a notebook that contains all relevant information from the preceding list. This will help to isolate/troubleshoot complex problems as well as dealing with purchasing and replacement (RMA) issues. Keep it at the same location onsite where all the server equipment will be kept. Add the following to aid in the event of problems:

- Vendor contact information

- Support/contract agreements (useful when on the telephone with manufacturer support)

- System-specific configurations (IRQ, DMA, I/O address)

- Internal support personnel contact list (phone/beeper numbers)

- Recovery tools (boot disks, sector editors, server-specific configuration files, and so on)

Network Administration

"Network administration" is usually a catchall phrase that encompasses every facet of the network's user/group and file/directory setup and maintenance. Although the term network administrator usually carries the same meaning in most network environments, network administrators are very different from site to site.

All have different levels of technical skill and job experience. The best that you can hope to achieve is consistency in the administration practices. Whereas the previous section dealt with issues and standards to consider when implementing the network, the network administration section deals with applying those standards. The following is a list of responsibilities that fall into the network administration phase:

- What is the procedure for adding new users?

- What is the procedure for removing existing users?

- What is the volume structure on the server?
- What directories fall into which volumes?
- What is the predetermined backup schedule?
- Are there any specialized needs/configurations at the site that are not present elsewhere?
- What is the security for each specific department/user directory?
- Will data be replicated to a central location for reliability in case of site failure?
- When are patches/fixes applied to the servers?
- How are irregularities in the server's operation documented?

Although this list may lack other job functions found at existing sites, it comprises a general area of user and system-based responsibilities that must be instituted to maintain the site's integrity.

Developing a Disaster Recovery and Maintenance Plan

A network is no good if it is not running. The company spends money to design, develop, and propagate its usage; if it is not running or there is a failure, the network is useless. To combat this, develop a strong disaster recovery and maintenance plan. A typical disaster recovery plan will include

- Identify levels for all the applications and systems (necessary, vital, critical)
- Identify assumptions about environment systems (electrical, heating/cooling)
- Identify the groups that will be responsible for a failure and when they will be called in
- Identify what support the groups will provide
- Identify the hardware profiles (copy from the standards book you created)
- Evaluate and rank contingency plans (downtime, replacement, offsite processing)
- Determine who will be notified in case of a failure
- Determine how to handle nonstandard issues (fire, bomb threat, natural disaster)
- Determine the schedule for downtime and testing of all vital systems

These issues, even though they might seem trivial or outrageous, are the key to both protecting the network and the career of the network administrator.

The way a failure is handled in a properly planned and documented network is as follows:

There is a serious failure, but the person who found the failure documents what has happened. What is the level of severity? Is the failure in the software or the hardware? Additional on-site support people are pulled from their other duties as needed to combat the failure. The support group consults the disaster recovery plan to review the options in the event the problem cannot be remedied immediately. A call to management is made making them aware of what the situation is and how it will impact the environment. Management is told what the support personnel are in the process of doing and what realistic time schedules for network restoration will be. The company has invested in critical replacement hardware and has it onsite in case of total failure. If an agreement has been made with the vendors, the vendors will provide support in a preset timely manner and report the status to management as necessary. The network is restored, and management feels that they were kept informed. The problem is handled effectively, and there is no wasted effort or miscommunication.

The bottom line, when dealing with equipment that is used in a production environment, is that failures can occur. They may take a year to manifest themselves, but they will occur. It is better to plan for them and define clear guidelines as to how they will be handled before the system is even implemented. If the development team has determined that additional equipment needs to be purchased to provide a better response time, the requests are taken to management and approved as management decides. In the event of a failure, the decisions management makes will be the level of support that can be provided. The better the network functions, the better the IS department functions.

Network-Based Problem Tracking System

Not all problems that occur on a network will be covered in the disaster recovery plan. If a user's printer jammed or they cannot connect to the network, the network's productivity does not stop, only the individual user's. However, if enough problems occur and the users do not feel that their needs are being met in a timely manner, a user's perception of the network and the IS department is impaired. Even if the users just have questions about what they are doing on the network and need reassurance, they have to feel secure. Always create a tracking system and have support people prepared to help. A problem tracking system can be as simple as having a central number that all users call if they have problems. A secretary enters the information into a database or simply writes it down on a trouble form and sends the "trouble tickets" to the support group who follow up with the users, based on their availability and the severity of the issue. It does not need to be sophisticated, but it has to be there when the first users in the field are installed. Within the user manuals are procedures for the users to follow in the event of a problem. These should be emphasized to make sure the users feel comfortable with the procedure.

The following is a list of suggested fields that should be included. Each environment is different and depending on the availability of support personnel, whoever is taking the call should be able to selectively screen the problem to keep the IS people from doing nothing but handling problems all day. The fields include:

- User's name.
- User's location.
- User's department.
- User's telephone number or connection information.
- What type of problem is this (failure, question, request)?
- Is the problem software- or hardware-related?
- What products are involved?
- What is the application/hardware failure (not always identifiable)?
- Is this a recurring problem?
- Is the user unable to continue working?
- Are other users in the area impacted (potential network application failure)?
- The resolution (used when the trouble ticket is resolved).
- How long did the resolution take?

It's important to track these problems. Databases are always useful because if the tickets are entered using a standard naming convention, then a count of failures of a certain type can be made and a trend analyzed. (Is certain equipment faulty? Are there factors in the application's stability that were not determined during testing?) The analysis could lead to decisions being made for future upgrades or network environment replacement as necessary.

The other element often overlooked is one of effort. At the end of the year, if the group is running around trying to handle a workload of problems and not getting anything else done productively, then more personnel may be needed. By polling the database and determining the person-hours spent in support broken down by problems in a monthly basis, it will show management the commitment to the user community and the need to continue this commitment by allowing the hiring of additional personnel. The IS department group is often seen but not always heard; in most cases, someone in management will try to determine if all the expensive skilled manpower is really necessary once the network is stable. Consider the problem tracking system as job security.

Implementation

This section more than any other is one of communication. An implementation is like a battle. The purpose of the battle is to place troops and equipment at key locations to create an "information supply line." The opposition is the user community, whose ignorance of technology and focus on current systems make it difficult to gain ground quickly. Consider the following "battle plan" before deploying the troops and resources:

- Determine the plan of attack (implement all at once or in phases).
- Send out scouts (have the users who viewed the system in the test laboratory advise as to the best way to implement at their site).

- Contact the home base for reinforcements (let management know the plan to implement and ask for additional manpower as necessary).

- Move the armies coherently (failure to do a single step in an implementation can cause the whole implementation to fail).

- Keep in contact with the divisions (do status checks periodically to determine how the sites/departments are doing and at what level they are in the implementation).

- Add reinforcements to areas of resistance (if a problem occurs at a site/department, be ready to filter additional resources at the problem to resolve it).

- Verify success (have all sites coordinate when they have completed the implementation and provide a status as to any problems or potential problems that might occur).

- Organize (make sure that all sites have followed the standards documentation and that the support personnel are in place to handle immediate user needs as necessary).

- Report (let management know of the completion of the implementation and any problems that might occur in the future).

With these basic factors in mind, every implementation will occur seamlessly and all problems will be dealt with before they escalate into crisis.

User Training

Although most sites decide to send their personnel offsite to handle the issues of training their workforce on the new network and the applications run in it, this is not always necessary. Based on the feedback from users who participated in the beta test site, the development team should have an idea as to what problems the average user might encounter and be able to both offer tailored internal training as to the operation of the new equipment as well as answering common questions the users might have. When the new system is being installed, it is often useful to provide each user with a user handbook that details their new desktop system and discusses issues such as

- Definition and structure of the network
- Description of the three client workstation profiles (user, power user, and developer)
- A user FAQ (Frequently Asked Questions)
- List of support personnel for their area
- How a problem or question is resolved with the problem tracking system
- Example templates to be used for new users/termination of accounts on the network
- A summary about each application with a shortcut sheet to help the users to start working with the applications immediately

The important thing is not to overwhelm the users. It is often better to divide the applications into two courses instead of one. The first course will address starting the applications and using their common functionality. The second class will deal with the more advanced features of the application as well as issues such as troubleshooting and personalized customizations. About 80 percent of the users will be happy with the first class, allowing their experience to lead them into the additional functionality as they need to learn it. The remaining percentage will take the advanced classes. This group of people includes power users, developers, support personnel, and technical management who want to have an overall understanding of the application.

> **NOTE**
>
> If multiple departments are located at the same remote site, it is often useful to form user groups among the power users and developers at the site to allow for the free flow of information and aid.

Analyzing User Feedback

How the network functions is different from its perceived functionality. If the users feel their needs were met, they will usually continue to work uninterrupted. If there is a problem, the IS department is the first to know. In a large user community, it is often very hard to determine how well the network is received. A need for feedback is essential to validate the network and determine any weaknesses or unplanned events that the original design team and design constraints did not take into consideration. Sometimes this feedback will take the form of accommodations for different departments as to how well the support team has performed. It could be that the users send their comments to their department head or manager who passes it to the IS manager. It could simply be an e-mail from a user to a support person thanking them for a job well done. Regardless of what form it takes, both management and the IS department need to know that what they had planned, designed, and provided is making a difference in the user community and if there are weaknesses or problems in the design, how they can be remedied.

Design "Post Mortem"

The implementation has been completed. The users have all been installed and trained, and problems for the most part have been resolved. It's time to reflect on what was done and whether it could have been done differently. Have the IS department get together (success parties are a common theme) to discuss the different phases of design, development, and implementation. The project manager (or project leader) should take notes to determine the following:

- Was the project a success?
- Was the project a perceived success by the users (something very different from the first point)?

- At what points did the design and planning fail?
- Were there areas that were not properly supported or emphasized?
- Did the team feel the goals of the initial design were met? (Reread the goals to help the group focus.)
- Did unexpected benefits come out of the design that were not known about?

Ask the group one final question, "If you were doing the same project now, knowing what you know now, what would you have changed?" Have each group member answer this independently based on their area of specialty. Then as a group collectively, determine what areas the group can improve upon for future upgrades/installations. The purpose of this type of "post mortem" exercise is to both learn from mistakes made and focus on the core set of success factors that make for a properly built network.

Summary

Designing a network from scratch is not an easy job. A lot of factors go into a successful network, and many are out of anyone's control. The emphasis throughout should be on documentation and communication. It is better to have a well-documented network that fails and needs additional resources than a network which, although functional, has an IS department afraid to touch it for fear that it will break and they will have no way to troubleshoot it. Many of the key points are not technical but organizational. The project manager is a pivotal figure in the entire scheme; if the project manager is not sufficiently prepared or does not have the necessary support from the group, the initiative has failed. Technical problems are rarely the cause of a network project's failure because everyone on the design group usually has a highly technical background and has learned the methodology to handle the technical problems. Never lose sight of the fact that the network is a tool with which the user community can become more productive. Productivity and reliability are always the ultimate byproducts of a well-functioning network, and a well-functioning network is the best scenario that can ever be achieved.

Internetworking Operating Systems

*Frank C. Pappas
and Emil Rensing*

CHAPTER 25

IN THIS CHAPTER

There once was a time when networks—as we've grown to know and love them—simply didn't exist. Imagine that: a time when all of the hardware for which you were responsible was under your control, generally under lock-and-key in a central computing facility and away from the tinkering and meddling hands of those pesky users. Of course, even if the users *did* manage to get their hands on a terminal, chances were that nothing bad happened simply because the systems themselves were too darn complicated and confusing. This was nothing short of a technical nirvana for network managers across the country, a workplace in which upgrades stayed upgraded, fixes fixed, and where the only screw-ups were due to vendor error—or so they'd have management believe. Unfortunately, a number of factors—that were mostly out of the network administrator's control—began to conspire toward the goal of shattering this computing paradise and replacing it with an open networking environment.

A Brief History

The first step that contributed to the demise of this ideal computing atmosphere occurred, ironically enough, with the introduction of the earliest forms of networked computing back in the 1960s. The situation was anything but ideal for the users or, truth be told, for the system administrators who had to manage the users *and* the hardware. After all, the systems in use at the time were not particularly powerful, quite restricted in their functionality, and fairly difficult to use. This, on top of the fact that there were only a few ways of interfacing with the mainframe, with the most common—dumb terminals—being a scarce and often busy resource. All of this made users and administrators yearn for something more, both in ease-of-use and overall performance, though (thankfully) it didn't sour them on the general concept of networked computing.

The second factor that prompted a serious re-thinking of the networking concept flowed from a wholly different set of motivations. For years, corporate IT managers had to deal with a significantly unpleasant challenge on a daily basis: proprietary systems. In the early days, prior to the development and wide-spread acceptance of the OSI open-standards reference model, nearly all computing and network systems were *proprietary*. Proprietary systems are designed in such a way as to only allow communications with similar hardware and software combinations, for example, Digital Equipment Corporation's early hardware could communicate only with other DEC equipment, but not with products developed by Hewlett-Packard, IBM, or other vendors.

Proprietary systems caused two main headaches for IT managers. First, computing infrastructure expansions were limited by the product lines of a particular company's main vendor. If your company relied on Big Blue for your hardware needs, you pretty much had to depend on IBM for any and all add-on products in order to handle new services, increase capacity, or to accomplish anything other than what your current systems already facilitated. Unfortunately, these closed systems often crippled the technology manager's ability to quickly and appropriately address performance or usability issues relating to corporate computing systems. Granted, technology companies weren't stupid—there was a reason that OSI took so long to take hold. Whenever you wanted to add on to a proprietary system, you generally needed to call in a vendor's representative or authorized consultant who—for a charming fee—would help you re-architect your system in order to accommodate the new and improved hardware. Because this had a significantly negative impact on the corporate pocketbook, executives looked for another avenue for designing and implementing technology upgrades. Most often, these financial concerns were allayed by building-out a complete and usually overly-powerful system which, as a major capital investment, was designed to meet the company's computing needs for more than a few years. Because hardware and software were (and still are) developing at a break-neck pace, it was generally felt to be a better idea to completely replace all IT infrastructure with new, exciting, and more powerful products once the current systems reached obsolescence. However, while these two factors were huge influences in the transition to an open networking environment, there was one final trend that was necessary to spell the death-knell of centralized computing: the PC.

Introduced in 1981, the PC was the final influence that convinced everyone—from vendors and developers to management and users—of the need for an efficient, relatively cost-effective method for connecting multiple computers, printers, and other devices together in order to facilitate local or wide area communication. The debut of the PC introduced a new world of possibilities, including higher processing power and significantly greater usability than had been found in the terminals of the time. However, these same PCs didn't quite match up to the power of the mainframes connected to the *other* end of the dumb terminals, so complaints of inadequate memory, insufficient processing power, and overall frustration soon began to filter up from the user community. The first attempt to remedy this situation was more of a stop-gap measure than anything else. PCs became front-ends for the muscle-machines themselves, becoming, in essence, high-tech and rather expensive dumb terminals. While this was a step up in the world, it too lacked the ground-shaking results that had been expected from the revolutionary technology.

As the months and years passed, many pieces of the PC puzzle that had for so long hobbled its role in the corporate computing arena finally achieved a breakpoint of power, price, and performance, signaling that the PC was *finally* a serious player in the networking game. Nearly every aspect of the PC had experienced tremendous advances, from memory and clock speed to storage, bus width, and graphics capacity. What's more, not only had the hardware itself grown beyond it's modest beginnings, so too had the array of third-party applications and various operating systems (network and otherwise) matured to such an extent as to be ready for prime-time network operations. And, thanks to the development of both the Ethernet/IEEE802.3 and TokenRing/IEEE802.5 standards back in the 1970s, the entire groundwork was seemingly in place for the birth of the modern network.

Can't We All Just Get Along?—Internetworking Protocols

Choosing the right hardware for your network is one of the most important considerations that you'll make when drawing up your network "game plan." Unfortunately, even after all those long hours analyzing and evaluating cable, processors, and architectures, there's still a good amount of work left to be done before your network can achieve greatness—or even function, for that matter. Hardware is only 50 percent of the network equation. While it is all well and good that your hardware and cable are top-notch, how in the heck are all those computers, printers, and storage devices going to communicate with one another? As we've discussed, in the earliest days they simply couldn't. DEC spoke DEC, HP understood HP, and so on. The power of modern networking comes from the fact that nearly any hardware from any manufacturer can—given enough time and patience—be made to communicate efficiently with any other piece or pieces of hardware. But how did we manage to get from forced homogeneity to the flexibility of heterogeneous networks? Three simple letters: OSI.

Open Systems Interconnection

In order to move beyond the closed, proprietary systems that had been frustrating technology managers on and off for years, the International Standards Organization (ISO) released in the late 1970s a framework for computer communication that, if adopted, would allow systems using this framework to communicate with one another. This standard, referred to as the Open Systems Interconnection (OSI) Reference Model, segregates network communication into seven distinct layers, with each layer responsible for handling specific steps in the process of cross-network data transmission. Of course, there's much, much more to the OSI model that we can realistically talk about in the next few pages, but you'll get a general idea as to the role of OSI, why it is important, and how it functions in the overall scheme of networked computing. If you're just itching to delve deeper into OSI, a trip to your local bookstore will reward you with a number of fine titles dealing strictly with OSI, it's history, and specifications.

The bottom-most layer of the OSI model is known as the *physical layer*. The physical layer is responsible for communicating directly with the transmission media (ISDN, twisted pair, and so on) the actual encoding/decoding of the data, and determining and accounting for specific connectors, line voltage issues, and so on.

Moving up through the layers, we next encounter the *data link layer*. The data link layer is the communications conscience of the OSI model, in that its job is to maintain the integrity of the transmission between various nodes. It accomplishes this by providing error control (via CRC) for all data transmissions, as well as helping to ensure that source and destination nodes are clearly identifiable by appending source and destination addresses into each frame.

The *network layer* is the traffic cop of the OSI, making sure that all data has a clear and efficient path to travel between the sending and receiving nodes. This is achieved by managing the transmission of packets across the network through a combination of switching, routing, and flow control.

The *transport layer* is charged with delivering messages from the top-most layer of the OSI model, known as the *application layer*. While it works in a fashion quite reminiscent of the data link layer, the transport layer's main function is to make sure that outbound transmissions are segmented in such a manner (into packets) as to be readily interpreted at the destination address.

As the fifth (from bottom to top) layer of the OSI scheme, the *session layer* manages inter-process communication between various hosts. This includes name resolution, inter-host synchronization, or any other variable necessary to control the general progression of the communication.

Sixth in line, the *presentation layer* acts as the interpreter for network communication. The presentation layer prepares the data for transmission by using one (or more) of a number of resources, including compression, encryption, or a complete translation of the data into a form more suitable for the currently-implemented communications methods.

Finally, the *application layer*, as the highest of the OSI levels, is tasked with providing the front-end of the computing experience for the user. The application layer is responsible for everything that the user will see, hear, and feel in the course of the networking process—everything from sending and receiving electronic mail, establishing Telnet or FTP sessions, to managing remote network resources.

Behind Every Great Network Is a Protocol...

Now that you have a better idea of how and why various combinations of hardware and software are able to communicate—thanks to OSI and the variety of other modern-day networking methods—the next important step is to take a look at the various protocols that serve as the non-physical foundation for network communication. Each protocol will offer its own unique combination of strengths and weaknesses, so it is important that you have a clear understanding of the services that are (or will be) provided by your network so that you can optimize the type and number of protocols running simultaneously on your network.

> **NOTE**
>
> While it is possible to have NetBEUI, TCP/IP, AppleTalk, or a variety of other protocols all bound to the same NIC, it probably isn't doing any favors for your overall level of network performance! Remember, determine the services that your network *must* provide to fulfill its role for your organization, then find one or two common-denominator protocols that will support the breadth of your needs. You'll save hours of troubleshooting, have fewer support headaches, and will enjoy significantly increased network response and performance.

AppleTalk

Introduced more than a decade ago as Apple's first contribution to the field of networked computing, AppleTalk was designed using the same "computing for the masses" philosophy that had been so completely successful (at least initially) for their Macintosh line of computer systems. It was easy to implement, featured relatively simple administrative requirements, and in general caused fewer headaches for network administrators than did the other network protocols popular at the time. Fortunately, the designers at Apple chose to conform to the OSI open-standards model, which has made it much easier to administer, troubleshoot, and to use networks running AppleTalk as their primary protocol.

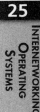

What has come to be known as Phase 1, Apple's first implementation of the AppleTalk networking protocol, sports a variety of features that make it distinctly different—and less flexible—than later versions of AppleTalk. Phase 1 of AppleTalk supports two separate protocols, one proprietary and one open. The LocalTalk Link Access Protocol (LLAP) is a proprietary serial communications protocol that enables network communications at the less-than-fantastic speed of up to 230Kbps. Additionally, Phase 1 supports the EtherTalk Link Access Protocol (ELAP), Apple's implementation of the IEEE's 802.3 Ethernet frame, supporting the much more familiar and impressive rate of 10Mbps. At the time, Phase 1 did much to increase the power, ease, and flexibility surrounding the installation and maintenance of local and wide area networks. However, as the weeks and months passed, certain services and features that were not supported by AppleTalk Phase 1 required Apple to return to the drawing board.

While AppleTalk soon gathered a substantial following, there were a number of advances in networking technology that necessitated a newer, more feature-laden version of AppleTalk. Apple, of course, was more than happy to oblige; new systems meant (with any luck) increased profitability. After a few years of research and development, Apple in mid-1989 released a new and improved version of the AppleTalk networking standard, generally referred to as Phase 2.

Phase 2 went above and beyond the achievements of Phase 1 by including support for a number of important technological advances, most notably Token Ring networks. Apple achieved the advances for Phase 2 through the implementation of the TokenTalk Link Access Protocol (TLAP), essentially as described by the IEEE's 802.5 frame standard. TLAP faced mixed emotions in the networking community, for while it could support a low-end speed of 4Mbps or an Ethernet-crushing maximum of 16Mbps, the infrastructure needed to support Token Ring networks was administratively and financially more demanding that either LocalTalk or traditional Ethernet networks. Additionally, Apple used the opportunity to introduce augmented variations on the standard ELAP and TLAP frame standards, based on a number of specifications included in the IEEE's 802.2 Logical Link Control (LLC) header, adding increased reliability and efficiency to AppleTalk's bag of tricks.

VINES

The Virtual Networking System (VINES), courtesy of Banyan, is one of a number of other networking environments that have competed for market-share alongside AppleTalk. Unlike many of the other systems that perform similar functions, VINES diverges in a number of regards, with the most interesting being that VINES is based on the UNIX operating system. At the time of its introduction, VINES was a fairly revolutionary entrant into the networking arena. It was multi-tasking, robust, flexible, and quite powerful—just about everything you'd ever want in a computer system. However, while the VINES server is dependent on UNIX, clients are available for a variety of the more popular desktop operating systems, supporting Macintosh, DOS, OS/2, and others.

Of course, Banyan didn't want to be left behind in the proprietary protocol field. Just as Apple decided to supplement the IEEE-sanctioned protocols with LocalTalk, Banyan decided to go hog-wild and include a significant number of additional (and proprietary) protocols as part of their networking environment. Fortunately for the rest of us, however, Banyan *did* stick quite closely to the seven layers of the OSI model, so despite the proprietary nature of many of their protocols, it is still quite easy to understand the function and importance of each piece of the protocol stack.

Based partly on it's UNIX lineage and partly on the ambition of it's designers, VINES can tackle just about any networking job that you'd care to throw at it. Thanks to a particularly flexible physical layer supplemented by a robust data link layer, VINES is capable of supporting an incredible variety of networking hardware. You'll find that VINES will support both LAN and WAN connections, including everything from High-Level Data Link Control (HDLC) and Link Access Procedure-Balanced (LAPB) to the more familiar implementations along the IEEE/802.x standard, including Ethernet, Token Ring networks, and so on.

Of course, the lower layers are useless if not complimented by equally powerful higher layers. VINES' upper layers are quite the dichotomy, insofar as they can be readily separated into two distinct categories, proprietary and open. Banyan chose to implement a number of protocols that mimicked—sometimes superbly, sometimes not—the publicly available protocols that are part of TCP/IP. VINES' network layer includes specific protocols for address resolution (VARP), a proprietary flavor of IP (VIP), and of TCP (VICP), among others. Of course, also supported by VINES' network layer are all the protocols that you've come to know and love—TCP/IP, ICMP, ARP, and so on. This proprietary/open mix works its way up through the entire OSI model, featuring a combination of VINES-only implementations alongside the more common DOS, Macintosh, and OS/2 protocols.

Token Ring/SNA

Token Ring and SNA networking have survived and prospered by the good graces of Big Blue. Throughout their development in the 1970s and 1980s, IBM was one of the staunch supporters for the IEEE's 802.5 Token Ring network specification, and this support blended with IBM's Systems Network Architecture (SNA) scheme to achieve a remarkable synergy in the networked computing arena.

Token Ring networks are designed in such a way as to create a continuous loop for data transmission. This is most often not in the form of a physical loop, but rather a closed electrical circuit that travels in and out of every device that is attached to the network at a given time. Unlike traditional Ethernet networks that rely on the collision avoidance routines of CSMA/CD, the designers of Token Ring decided to avoid the possibility of collisions entirely by implementing a game of network 'hot potato.' It works like this: Station one receives the token, giving it the opportunity to send data across the network. Assuming that station one has data, it will encode the data onto the token, add destination and other information, and send the token (with the new data) ahead to the destination. Once the destination machine receives the token, it will strip off the data and return the token to the originating station, who will strip any remaining information away from the token and release it back into the loop, providing subsequent stations the opportunity to transmit their information.

The attraction (for some, anyway) of Token Ring networks comes from its unique routing methods, which diverge rather significantly from other architectures, especially Ethernet/IEEE 802.3. Token Ring networks use the Source Routing Protocol (IEEE 802.1) that allows the originating station to determine the optimum route to its designated recipient. This is facilitated by one of two separate methodologies, specifically the *All Routes Explorer* (ARE) and the *Spanning Tree Explorer* (STE), which rely on the broadcast transmission of multiple TEST and XID frames. ARE, which is the preferred method utilized by SNA, broadcasts its frame, along with a destination address, to all of the rings of the network, accumulating routing information along the way. Once the frame reaches the destination address, it is returned to the sending machine—complete with all the collected routing information—allowing the host to select a path to the destination. STE works in a similar fashion. STE will send a single TEST or XID frame to each ring, where the destination host will respond with a data set including all available routes known between source and destination. The originating station will then select a route and retransmit the route to the destination, allowing both sides of the connection to be aware of the intended route.

The SNA architecture is quite similar to the seven layers of the OSI reference model. The minor differences in the layer names and layer functionality are due to the fact that SNA predates the release of the ISO's open-standards initiative, with it's release in 1974 pre-dating OSI by nearly a decade. However, despite this divergence, there remains a nearly one-to-one relationship between the OSI and SNA layers, though some of the functions delegated to specific OSI layers are somewhat shifted in the SNA stack.

NetWare

NetWare is probably the most popular network operating system (NOS) that is currently available anywhere in the world. It controls the lion's share of the networking market with an impressive (even mind-staggering) number of installations, despite the recent increase in popularity of Microsoft's Windows NT product line. This strength has come, in part, from a great marketing and promotional scheme. More to the point, the popularity of the NetWare NOS has been earned as a result of the strong and versatile suite of protocols that serve as the foundation for Novell's networking flagship.

Over the years, Novell has extensively rebuilt NetWare in response to the changing needs of the networking community. In it's earlier 286 incarnation, NetWare used a variety of protocols to enable network communication. These included the NetWare Control Protocol (NCP) as the heart of the NetWare product, which controlled file services; the Sequenced Packet Exchange (SPX) protocol that facilitated application-level communication; the Routing Information Protocol (RIP), Internetwork Packet Exchange (IPX) protocol, and the Service Advertising Protocol (SAP) for the routing of data. As time progressed and Novell found the need to support additional functionality and services, new protocols were integrated into the system in order to keep up with the increasing pace of internetworking.

NetWare 3 built upon the earlier version based on the 286 architecture, adding increased capacity for workstations, increasing the customization options for the NetWare file services, and expanding upon the overall number of communications methods that were previously supported by Novell's products. One of the strengths of the NetWare 3.x products centers around the Open Data-Link Interface (ODI) which substitutes for the physical and data link layers as developed by OSI. The ODI facilitates multi-protocol communication between LAN and WAN hardware and other adapters, allowing one or more protocols to be bound to the same host adapter. The ODI has greatly contributed to the success of NetWare, due primarily to its ability to integrate a wide variety of open and proprietary network and transport layer protocols into the NetWare environment, including: TCP/IP; AppleTalk; IPX/SPX; as well as others. NetWare 4 goes just a bit further, though it supplements some mildly enhanced protocols with additional core functionality, robustness, and overall performance.

TCP/IP

Although NetWare is probably the most widely implemented *proprietary* network operating system, there can be no doubt as to the king of the protocol hill: TCP/IP. Not only is TCP/IP probably the best-known of all networking protocols, it is also the most widely implemented, for the simple reason that it is a truly open standard. The benefits of TCP/IP are many: Everyone has access to the protocols themselves; documentation is easily obtainable; it is eminently flexible; and is supported by many legacy products as well as almost every new product developed in recent years. Additionally, because it is the heart and soul of the Internet, the future of TCP/IP is anything but dim.

The TCP/IP stack (also known as the DoD protocols) follows the OSI seven-layer model in function, though not strictly in form. Where OSI divides the stack into seven distinct layers, TCP/IP subdivides into only four, though the functionality of these four layers extends across the full range of the OSI model. The TCP/IP *network access layer* serves double-duty, filling in for both the physical and data link layers of OSI. Moving up, the *Internet layer* is the TCP/IP equivalent of the OSI network layer, with OSI's transport layer replaced by the TCP/IP *host-to-host layer*. Finally, the higher-level function of the OSI model are combined into the TCP/IP *process/application layer*.

The strengths of TCP/IP are many and varied. As we've discussed, it is extraordinarily flexible, supporting a variety of network interfaces, including: Ethernet; ARCNET; FDDI; and broadband networking options. A number of dynamic routing protocols are an integral part of TCP/IP as well, using the Xerox-designed *Routing Information Protocol* (RIP) and (later) the *Open Shortest Path First* (OSPF), which would incorporate load-balancing and other optimization functions into the process of data routing.

Moving to the heart of the matter, the two Host-to-Host level protocols that keep the TCP/IP process moving along are the *Transmission Control Protocol* (TCP) and the *Universal Datagram Packet* (UDP). TCP is the protocol used for transmissions that require highly reliable connections, including electronic mail services (SMTP), file transfer (FTP), and so on. TCP works in a *streaming* environment, breaking each data stream into 65K segments (octets). These segments are then tracked and transmitted, allowing the stack to provide the data-integrity services such as flow and error control. The downside to TCP is that there is a tangible tradeoff for the increased reliability of the connection: overhead. All TCP transmissions require a header whose length must be a minimum of 20 octets, which—depending on what you're sending across the network—may or may not be a reasonable amount of extra work for your machines.

UDP, on the other hand, is a perfect choice for certain applications that do not require extreme degrees of reliability. UDP sacrifices flow control, error detection and handling, as well as other functions to achieve a *maximum* header size of 8 octets, which allows for significantly improved network performance for certain functions.

As we move into the higher TCP/IP layers, we find that the process/application layer of the TCP/IP stack controls a number or protocols essential to the proper functioning of TCP/IP-based networks. These protocols include: the electronic messaging *Simple Mail Transfer Protocol* (SMTP); file transfer (FTP); the foundation of the World Wide Web, *Hypertext Transfer Protocol* (HTTP); as well as network management via *Simple Network Management Protocol,* or (SNMP). These protocols enable the feature-by-feature functionality that allows users and administrators to interact with the lower layers and obtain the information that they need.

Bridging the Gap—Internetworking Operating Systems

Before you can set up an effective network comprised of multiple operating systems, there are a number of issues you'll need to consider, including whether your internetwork will be a local (LAN) or wide area (WAN) network, how the networks will be physically connected, and how you will enable communication across multiple operating systems and hardware types. Let's take a quick look at some of the more important topics involved when preparing to connect multiple networks into one grand network. There are literally thousands of pages written on the subject, but the single-most important factor involved will be an intimate understanding of your network, the role that it plays within your organization, and the goals that you have set for yourself in your internetworking activities.

Whether your internetwork will be a LAN or a WAN is a choice that is made for you, due simply to the nature of the two beasts. LANs, by definition, are local; WANs are widely separated. This will also determine, in part, how you will physically connect networks of different types. No two networks are alike. In your particular case, the unique combination of hardware, applications, and operating systems that comprise your network will necessitate certain design considerations, including bridges, hubs, routers, gateways, and other similar equipment.

To give you a leg-up on the role of some of the most essential tools in the network engineer's arsenal of hardware, let's talk briefly about the role of some of these items. The simplest device, the *repeater*, is used to extend the length of a particular cable run beyond the maximum length as specified in the IEEE standards. For example, a run of twisted-pair cannot exceed 100m from hub to host. If you need to extend that run, you can insert a repeater at the end of the first 100m of cable, which will enhance the signal strength and prevent it from degrading as it covers the remaining distance on the far side of the repeater.

A *bridge* is a device that is used to segment various portions of a greater network into more easily controlled regions, much like the phone company divides the national network into subsets of area codes. The bridge is a useful tool when connecting a variety of networks that need to be in frequent contact with one another.

A *Bridge/Router* (*Brouter*) is a somewhat more advanced device, generally due to enhanced software, that not only segments networks into more easily controlled subsections, but also manages the overall flow of data across the network. The brouter accomplishes this based on a number of possible factors, including internal routing algorithms, specifics of the higher-layer protocols, or other factors as defined by the administrator.

These devices can all be used to make the connection between networks. But what are your options for implementing internetworking? While there are a number of options, the three most prevalent offer you the best chance for an easy and cost-effective implementation.

Your first option is to install multiple-host adapters into one server, with each host adapter handling a specific type of information provided by the upper-levels of the network operating system. One adapter could be speaking to an Ethernet network while the other communicates strictly for a Token Ring (802.5) network. This way allows you to maintain a minimum of server hardware while still supporting multiple network types.

A second option would be to install a hardware bridge between two networks. While this has been proven to work in many cases, it is far and away one of the most difficult solutions that you can implement. Unfortunately, there are many incompatibilities between the Ethernet and Token Ring standards that must be accounted for, such as frame size, addressing methodologies, and routing procedures. These can be handled with hardware and software configurations, but it can prove to be a constant headache trying to accommodate such internetworks.

Far and away the best option, as mentioned previously, is to find a common-denominator protocol that will facilitate the spectrum of services your network needs to provide for your users. While this used to be a problem when limited to the less-than-compatible offerings of LocalTalk, VIP, or IPX, the development of OSI and TCP/IP have proven to be an excellent option for an LCD-protocol, due to its popularity, ease-of-use, and huge base of installed servers. While it is not always possible to find one single protocol that will satisfy your internetworking needs, the concept itself is still quite valid. If you are able to reduce the number of protocols running on your network to the bare minimum, you'll reap endless rewards in troubleshooting, support, and general performance. If, for some reason, you *want* to have five or six protocols bound to your adapter at any given time, perhaps you should seek counseling. If not, spend some quality time analyzing your network, clients, services, and other eccentricities until you come up with a combination, say NetBEUI and AppleTalk, that does the trick!

Operating Systems

The key to having various network operating systems running on various hardware platforms successfully inter-operate lies solely in their ability to communicate. For the most part, "data" is cross platform, providing the application software used to manipulate the data can access and understand the type of file in question. The hard part, however, lies in extending the extension to your operating system that allowed network communication in the first place.

The goal in internetworking any group of operating systems is based entirely on the vendor of your network software. Certain operating systems simply do not support the additional protocols needed to participate in a multi-protocol environment, or the operating system is not popular enough to have third-party developers enhancing its functionality. Whatever the case, when you need two or more network operating systems to communicate, you need to have the network operating systems speak each others' protocols or (optimally) you can have each operating system speak the same protocol. In many enterprise-level operations, this can be a very intimidating and daunting task—especially if you're running older systems that require extremely proprietary communication. However in more small scale operations, internetworking various operating systems can be a rather easy task, especially if you have planned your infrastructure carefully.

As you may have already guessed, the easiest and possibly the most efficient way to have different operating systems internetwork is to have them speak the same protocol, as opposed to having each network operating system speak all of the protocols you are using. From reading past chapters, it is also probably already clear to you that because of its popularity, TCP/IP is probably the most popular protocol and most widely available across the most operating systems. In addition, from reading past chapters, you may also realize why you would take this approach. This lowest common denominator approach to internetwork communication will also aid you in your never-ending quest to optimize your network performance. Sure, it may be possible to have every operating system you run speak every communication protocol you support, but that approach increases network traffic significantly and degrades the performance of the systems that have to load four or five different protocols.

You may think that building an intranet for your organization might be more trouble than it is worth. However, if you already run TCP/IP on your network you are more than halfway there. The additional benefit you get from having all of your operating systems talking to one another—along with the performance benefit of having fewer protocols in use—will more than make up for any initial difficulties in implementing this strategy.

MacOS AppleTalk

AppleTalk, released in 1985 by Apple Computer, was the network architecture used by the Apple Macintosh product line. AppleTalk was a simple-to-use and simple-to-configure peer-to-peer networking add-on to the Apple Macintosh Operating System that provided an excellent set of networking features. The hardware was all *plug-and-play* and the configuration was simple, making AppleTalk an excellent workgroup-sized Network Operating System. A revision of the AppleTalk architecture, known as AppleTalk Phase 2, was released in 1989 and added increased functionality and support for new standards.

The physical and data link layers of the AppleTalk protocol support a variety of networking hardware. The older revision of AppleTalk, which became known as AppleTalk Phase 1, supported EtherTalk, Apple's name for Ethernet, and LocalTalk, Apple's proprietary Data Link protocol. LocalTalk was a 230Kbps connection that used the standard serial ports found on all Macintosh systems, meaning that if you had a serial port on your Macintosh and the ability to run the AppleTalk software, you could participate in a small workgroup networking environment. AppleTalk Phase 2 added support for larger-scale internetworks and Token Ring—Several IEEE standards—specifically, 802.2, 802.3, and 802.5 support. Additionally, the ability to connect to IBM SNA and Digital Equipment Corporation DECnet architectures became available from third-party vendors.

There are many vendors of Macintosh networking hardware. Companies like Dayna and Farralon, have excellent network adapters and interconnectivity hardware, such as hubs. Apple, however, is the primary vendor of internetworking software that enhances Macintosh connectivity to other systems. Products to allow TCP/IP services, Remote Access, and X.25 and OSI protocols are among Apple's featured internetworking products.

The latest revisions of Apple's MacOS provide integrated TCP/IP networking support. The protocol stack that runs on the Macintosh workstation implements IP, UDP, TCP, ARP, RARP, ICMP, BOOTP, RIP, and DNS. The Macintosh will also allow for remote TCP/IP network services over standard PPP or SLIP dial-up connections. With this new standard, native implementation of TCP/IP has allowed for easy internetworking with TCP/IP and made it an easy operating system to integrate into most internetworking environment. Apple is currently planning to implement native AppleShare network services to run over TCP/IP. This will allow Macintosh systems the ability to participate in a network environment and run only the TCP/IP protocol, making it an extremely flexible and highly desirable network operating system.

There are currently several products from Apple and third-party vendors to allow for connectivity to other network operating systems, as well as enhancing current network services. The Apple IP Gateway, for example, allows users running Apple's Remote Access, LocalTalk, or any standard AppleTalk interface to connect with an Ethernet-based TCP/IP network. In its first operating configuration, the Apple IP Gateway allows a network of Macintosh computers running AppleTalk to connect to an IP network. When used with the Apple Internet Router software, it can provide TCP/IP access to any Macintosh system that is also part of the same router. Although freeware and shareware PPP and SLIP clients are readily available for most Macintosh computers, the Apple IP Gateway, when used in with Apple's Remote Access Server, can provide dial-in with access to AppleTalk networks as well as TCP/IP networks.

While we are on the subject of remote access, the AppleTalk Remote Access Server and Client products allow Macintosh computers to communicate with another Macintosh computer or an entire network of Macintosh computers. Using standard dial-up, ISDN, X.25, or even

25

INTERNETWORKING OPERATING SYSTEMS

cellular connections, the Apple Remote Access family of products provides a simple, easy, and efficient way to telecommute.

Apple also provides options for SNA connectivity. Using the SNA*ps Gateway, SNA*ps 3270, or SNA*ps 5250 will turn your Macintosh computer into an integrated 3270, 5250, advanced program-to-program, or advanced peer-to-peer networking gateway. The software is built in to a NuBus-based Token Ring, SLDC, or coaxial network adapter, thus freeing the systems main processor to run other applications. The 3270 software delivers full-function 3270-display terminal emulation, which allows any Macintosh system to communicate with IBM mainframes. The emulation software will work with a variety of network interfaces. Option-ally, the emulation software may connect to an SNA*ps Gateway over an AppleTalk network. Similarly, the SNA*ps 5250 product will allow access to IBM AS/400 systems.

Apple also provides a connectivity product for X.25-based network connections. MacX.25 is a software product that provides all of the necessary software to link a Macintosh to an X.25-based network. MacX.25 may also be used in conjunction with other Apple products, like the Apple Internet Router, to internetwork AppleTalk networks over wide area X.25 networks. MacPAD is the MacX.25 component that allows other Macintosh systems to use a system running the MacX25 server component as a gateway. MacX.25 also includes a software com-ponent that is an OSI stack. MacOSI Transport is a component to either MacX.25 or TCP/IP to allow the operation of OSI services over TCP/IP internetworks.

Microsoft Windows

Microsoft has learned a great deal about networking from its past ventures. The OS/2 LanManager product that they developed for IBM gave them the experience they needed to create their own networking products for their own operating systems, as well as the founda-tion to build their own highly advanced, extremely scaleable network server product. In addi-tion to their own efforts to build networking services for their operating systems, the insane popularity of their operating systems has lead to the availability of many, many third-party networking products, making Microsoft operating systems an excellent choice for workstations and servers of all caliber in any network operating environment.

For the most part, software vendors have done an excellent job in extending the MS-DOS and Microsoft Windows operating systems by providing support for many network protocols and services. SNA Gateways, IPX/SPX clients, and TCP/IP services are all available for the 16-bit Microsoft operating systems. Windows for Workgroups is a special version of the Microsoft Windows operating system that has integrated peer-to-peer networking, optional TCP/IP, and remote access clients as well. Windows for Workgroups filled the void of not having a truly powerful Windows-based network operating system on the PC until Microsoft was ready to ship its Windows95 product.

Internetworking the 16-bit Microsoft operating systems is not really a challenge, at least not as far as networking is concerned. The same rules apply to planning the internetwork connec-tions as they do with any other group of operating systems, but, as far as finding the protocols and services to run, it is not a very difficult challenge. The real difficulty comes in finding the vendor who publishes the client access software or the manufacturer who builds the appropriate network adapter. In addition, since networking is not native to the 16-bit network operating systems, you will have a bit more freedom in establishing your standards and practices.

Windows 95 takes things even a bit more seriously by implementing networking with the same ease-of-use and configuration as the rest of the operating system. Offering *Plug-&-Play* configuration for most network interfaces, and an easy way to install and configure protocols and services, Windows 95 networking truly accentuates Microsoft's overhaul of the Windows computing environment. Additionally enhancing the networking environment of Windows 95 is the standard inclusion of many protocols from a variety of vendors. Protocols such as TCP/IP, IPX/SPX, and even NetBEUI are included in the Windows95 distribution, and the peer-to-peer file sharing services provided by Windows95 can run using most of these protocols. Windows 95 also provides a very open architecture for adding new and better as well as legacy protocols to the operating system. Third-party products to allow participation in AppleTalk environments, as well as DECnet networks, are already available.

Windows NT is the next generation in the Microsoft Windows–based operating system family. Distributed in a workstation and server version, Windows NT is intended for a more advanced type of user and professional computing environment. Providing all of the networking features of Windows 95 with a bit more power, control, and performance, the network-centric focus of Windows NT is poised to take on the current heavy hitters in the network operating market. Again, the open architecture of the Windows NT operating system allows for future expansion and additions to the operating system.

Recognizing that connectivity to legacy systems is an extremely important feature for a network operating system, Microsoft publishes a product that allows Windows NT to act as an SNA gateway to mainframe systems from IBM. It can allow an entire network, running most any protocol that can "see" the gateway server, to connect to multiple SNA hosts. The Windows NT server product also provides an integrated multi-port remote-access server that allows Windows clients access to a single server or an entire network. The remote access server and client products can also support SLIP and PPP remote dial-up networking protocols.

As you can see, from the earliest days the Microsoft family of operating systems has lent themselves to the successful implementation of various network client services and protocols, making them a powerful addition and flexible basis to any internetwork.

Novell NetWare

Novell NetWare is a network operating system that is designed to integrate heterogeneous hardware and protocols into one cohesive network operating system. Although the primary focus of NetWare is their server product, that provides file-sharing services, Novell offers a number of workstation client services for DOS and Windows systems as well as Macintosh, UNIX, and OS/2.

NetWare's Open Data-Link Interface is what allows the network adapters to communicate with the higher protocol layers of NetWare's architecture. ODI allows multiple adapters in the same workstation, or server, to interact with multiple protocols and network frame types exclusive to a single adapter or shared among multiple adapters. NetWare's OSI Network and Transport layer protocol options include, TCP/IP, AppleTalk, or IPX/SPX, Novell's own protocol derived from the XNS protocol.

> **NOTE**
>
> IPX/SPX stands for Internetwork Packet Exchange/Sequenced Packet Exchange. It is an extremely fast protocol and requires few system resources. In many ways, it is as simple to use as AppleTalk, but may require more configurations.

The architecture of the NetWare file server is divided into modular components that can be loaded and unloaded without having to take the server down. The NetWare Loadable Module (NLM) architecture can be used to implement additional functionality not found in the standard NetWare server, thus extending the functionality of your NetWare server. NLMs can provide new services for your network environment, or new interfaces for programming, to really extend the NetWare server.

Recent advances to Novell NetWare have continued to build on Novell's foundation and dedication to multi-platform internetworking. The release of NetWare Directory Services (NDS) for Novell NetWare provides a system to manage all of the resources on your network. Everything from users to printers to servers to applications to shared volumes can be tracked using NDS. NDS is also revolutionary in its approach to setting the permissions of resources on the network. Based on rules instead of exceptions, NDS presents network security management in a straightforward, easy-to-use way unlike anything else available today. NDS also changes the paradigm for network authentication. By logging into the Directory Tree as opposed to a specific server, users can find and use any of the resources that they have permission to use without having to authenticate themselves to other servers, printers, or any other resources.

Much of the internetworkability of the NetWare server can be implemented using NLMs on the server. The NetWare server is primarily a file server. It serves volumes of files to systems so that a client can mount them as drives on their system. This provides an extremely easy way for people to use the network to share files across hardware platforms. This not to say that the NetWare server is merely a file server. There are many NLMs available for NetWare servers that provide numerous services such as FTP server services, SNA gateway services, and even Web-server services—many of which ship with Novell's Intra-NetWare.

While the promise of homogenous client connectivity seems like a nirvana to some extent, Novell has faced many obstacles reaching toward that goal. Novell provides client access services for many platforms including DOS, Windows, Windows 95, Windows NT, OS/2, MacOS, and even UNIX. The more current Novell clients use an architecture similar to the Novell server's

NLM architecture. *Virtual Loadable Modules* (VLM) are the client-side equivalent of the NetWare Loadable Module. Like their server-side counterpart, VLMs can be dynamically loaded and unloaded, as they are required. This is an extremely important feature in your quest to optimize client performance. Loading only the features of your network client that you need can greatly enhance client performance. However, in some cases Novell has met much difficulty. Their Macintosh client for Novell Directory Services does not rely on Apple's native AppleTalk implementation. This essential "add-on" approach to the MacOS NDS client is often fraught with system conflicts making Macintosh systems with the Novell Directory Service client very unstable. This, however, only effects NDS clients. The AppleTalk and AppleShare NLMs are excellent in terms of performance and reliability. Novell also has an IPX/SPX client for the MacOS that allows Macintosh clients to access certain resources over an IPX/SPX connection. Their UNIX client also tends to be very unstable on certain systems. This is, of course, the direct result of having so many variants of UNIX to support.

UNIX

Internetworking UNIX systems fits in quite nicely with what we have been discussing. UNIX systems support a variety of network hardware and network protocols, however, UNIX has TCP/IP networking integrated very closely into the operating system kernel. It would be extremely foolish not to leverage TCP/IP in your implementation of UNIX systems in your networking environment. For the most part, UNIX systems have the fastest implementation of TCP/IP, making it an extremely powerful and flexible system to have on your network.

If your organization has a very well-built intranet, your investment in UNIX workstations and servers can only enhance it. UNIX from most vendors has the core intranet services built-in and that can make it a powerful asset to have on your network. Because many of the services are built-in or freely available, you should have no problem sharing files with other network operating systems, providing they have the necessary client access tools such as a Web browser or FTP client.

If you do need to run additional protocols on a UNIX system, you have that option. SNA gateways, as well as IPX/SPX gateways and AppleTalk, are all available for many UNIX systems. However, because there are so many flavors of UNIX from so many different vendors, you should probably contact the vendor directly for complete, comprehensive information.

Implementation

When it comes right down to it, the best way to ensure your ability to successfully internetwork your computing environment is to plan carefully. Like most aspects of networking, planning and always focusing on the big picture will help tremendously in the immediate and distant future. The internetworking aspect of your overall network implementation plan is just one small component that should be integrated as you see fit. You may not need internetworking services at the launch of your network, but you may in the future. Therefore, you should always have your internetworking plan in the back of your mind.

25

INTERNETWORKING OPERATING SYSTEMS

With today's modern network operating systems, the task of implementing an internetwork can be quite easy. The recent infusion of TCP/IP networking products for most network operating systems can be used to your advantage.

Planning Your Internetwork

The following steps are ones that may or may not find their way into your plan. You need to decide which of the outlined steps below, or what additional steps, need to be in your plan.

Define the Requirements for Your Internetwork

Not all internetworks are created equal, partly because they will not be used equally. Deciding to internetwork a group of different operating systems can open a whole new world of services and applications to your network, or it can just be a big waste of time and money. The first and most important step in building your internetwork is deciding if you need to build one in the first place! You need to make sure that the additional connectivity will provide useful services for your users. If there is nothing to be gained from connecting groups of Windows-based PCs to a group of UNIX workstations, then do not do it! However, if establishing an SNA gateway from your mainframe to your existing PC and Macintosh network will allow you to remove dedicated terminals throughout your organization that will result in cheaper cabling maintenance and lower hardware costs, you might want to consider it.

Oh, and always remember to plan for the future. Upgrading and scaling are very, very important here, in networking, as well as in most aspects of computing, as you are more than already aware!

Develop a Network Management Strategy and Implementation Plan

Don't just start loading protocols on clients and routers. Think about how you can optimize the protocols on your LAN. Do not just haphazardly start running protocols; remember your network optimization plan. This step should complement that plan, not counteract it!

Test Your Management System, Network Applications, and Interconnectivity

Before you begin rolling out your new features to your users, make sure you can manage the additional resources efficiently. While centralized network management features are built-in to most modern network operating systems, other network operating systems will require third-party management tools. Make sure they work before you begin rolling out new features to your enterprise-wide computing environment.

The interconnectivity of your internetwork implementation plan is also of the utmost importance. Give yourself enough time to plan and implement your interconnectivity, and use standard analysis tools (as we will discuss later) to make sure that data is being sent appropriately. Getting your data packets sent and received by the appropriate piece of network hardware may take some time and tweaking, but it is the core of what your internetwork will become. Make sure it is functioning correctly and efficiently.

Make sure the network applications function correctly. Just because your gateway is up and your protocols are routing, does not mean your client applications for accessing these new resources will work correctly. Do not leave it to chance or blind faith, and do not leave it to the last minute to test.

Begin Training Support Staff

When users have problems, questions, or simply general concerns about their workstation or network they will call your support staff, not you. You need to make sure that they are appropriately equipped to handle any additional situations that may arise from the implementation of your new group of internetwork connectivity.

Additionally, quality operating procedures you have already established for your network should be updated and enhanced to account for the new architecture. Just as you need to make sure that your support staff can handle the new technology that they have, you need to make sure that the quality of your overall operating procedures remain consistently high.

Begin Training Users

Do not forget about your users! Adding new services for your users will do no good if they cannot access the new features. Even the most elementary of procedures for accessing services can baffle most users, and it is your responsibility as a network administrator to make employees using your LAN as efficient as they can be. NDS makes your job as a network manager easier, but someone unfamiliar with NDS on a UNIX workstation may need additional information. Of course, this does not mean that you have to teach all of your users how to use simple applications., It does mean, however, that you are responsible for making sure that services that can enhance productivity are being used.

Summary

The job of internetworking operating systems is anything but an easy one. There are an endless number of variables that must be taken into consideration before implementing even the most basic of internetworks: servers, clients, hardware, software, protocols, and many, many more. It's a daunting task, for certain. If done correctly, the creation of a multi-protocol network can be an impressive and incredibly useful feat. If implemented poorly, however, you may soon find yourself staring head-on at a pink slip!

Over the course of developing your internetwork, you'll be required to spec out the required hardware and software configurations, request bids from vendors, hire (and train!) network engineers and administrators, create fail-safe and backup plans, and negotiate contracts for support, connectivity, and other services.

Of course, the important thing to remember (and we continue to emphasize!) is that book learning only goes so far in designing internetworks, or in any technical arena for that matter. It takes a certain combination of experience, seasoning, technical aptitude, some reading, and a little luck before you'll be able to bring all the pieces together in the right order. It's a lot like fortune-telling. Anybody can take a crack at it, but it takes a special knack to do it well. Good luck!

Clustering

by Mark Sportack

IN THIS CHAPTER

Clustering is a computing technique that has slowly, but steadily, been gaining popularity at all levels of computing. Originally a data center-grade technology, the last 20 years have witnessed support for clustering being added to mid-range UNIX processors and, today, to low-end client/server computing architectures. For all its heritage, clustering remains a vague concept that all but defies definition. This chapter examines clustering techniques, identifies their relative strengths and weaknesses, and explores the ways that high-performance networking can be used to support clusters.

Overview of Clustering

The concept of clustering computers dates back to 1982 when the Digital Equipment Company (DEC) introduced its VAXCluster. The VAXCluster offered more economical computing by decoupling the input/output (I/O) devices from any single CPU. Instead, all CPUs could access the devices, and their contents, by way of a star topology bus and coupling device, as shown in Figure 26.1. This simple form of clustering is still useful today, although it has been refocused to provide scalability and/or fault tolerance rather than simple device sharing.

FIGURE 26.1.
The typical VAXCluster configuration.

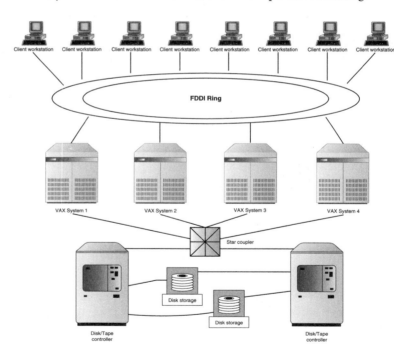

The original clustering product, the DEC VAXCluster, allowed "clusters" of VAX systems to share I/O devices.

From this rather humble beginning, clustering has grown into a confusing aspect of parallel computing that almost defies definition. Numerous factors contribute to this. First, there is no standard for "clustering" computers. Clusters can be implemented in many different ways. They can be designed and engineered to solve many different business problems, assuming numerous different topologies in the process.

There is also no standard platform to build a cluster on. Uniprocessor and multiprocessor machines from all vendors can be mixed and matched in clusters, too. Even the choice of microprocessor is not limited. Clusters can also be built using either Reduced Instruction Set Computing (RISC), Complex Instruction Set Computing (CISC), or even Very Large Instruction Word (VLIW) processors.

RISC processors and UNIX-based clustering products have been available for some time. It is the relatively recent introduction of products based on the "Wintel" platform that is generating excitement in the marketplace. Given the relatively low cost of the x86 CISC microprocessors, and the broad knowledge base that the various Microsoft Windows operating systems enjoy, clustering software for this platform can greatly reduce both the acquisition and operation costs of a cluster without compromising scalability, availability, or functionality. Thus, clustering appears poised for the mass market.

But, you may point out, we haven't really identified what a cluster is yet! All we've done is identify some of the potential physical platforms that clusters can be built upon. Clusters are a distributed form of parallel computing. Implementations and topologies can vary significantly in the degree of parallelism, functionality, physical platform, operating system, networks, and so on.

Not surprisingly, clusters are frequently confused with two other forms of parallel computing: Symmetric Multiprocessors (SMPs) and Massively Parallel Processors (MPPs). As Figure 26.2 illustrates, clusters demonstrate a significant overlap with both SMPs and MPPs. This is to be expected, given that they are all forms of parallel computing, yet they are not completely interchangeable.

This diagram, though not scientifically derived, visually demonstrates the partial overlap of clustered computers with uniprocessors, symmetric multiprocessors, and massively parallel processors relative to each one's trade-offs between scalability and availability. Clusters are capable of broader simultaneous support for scalability and availability.

Despite the functional similarities, there is one important architectural distinction between clusters and both SMPs and MPPs. Clusters are distributed. SMPs and MPPs are self-contained within a single computer. Therefore, even though they can redistribute workloads internally in the event of a CPU failure, they are vulnerable to downtime from failures in other parts of the computer. Clusters are capable of greater availability rates because they have fewer single points of failure. They distribute the processing across multiple separate computers that are networked together.

FIGURE 26.2.

*Functional overlap
with SMPs and MPPs.*

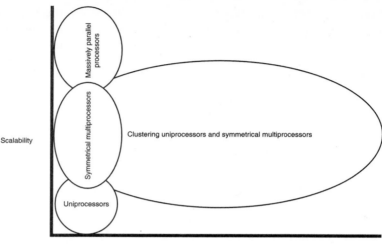

System architects who are considering clusters must also decide whether one of the myriad commercial cluster products will suffice, or whether they need to cobble their own cluster with a pastiche of hardware, software, and networking products. The availability of "canned" cluster solutions only adds to the confusion about what clustering means because of their great dissimilarities. Vendors are intentionally trying to differentiate their clustered solutions in the marketplace either by focusing on specific niches or by concentrating on feature- and/or performance-based competition.

The physical separation and redundancy of computers within a cluster lends itself to architectural creativity. Clusters can be implemented in so many different ways, and for so many different purposes, that one would be hard pressed to find anything in common between some types of clusters.

In short, there is no single, coherent definition for clustering. It is, rather, a generic concept for configuring multiple computers to perform the same set of tasks. Consequently, many people use clusters and cluster products every day, without recognizing them for what they are.

Basic Cluster Architectures

Given that there is no consensus on the proper way to design, or even use a cluster, it is not surprising that numerous topologies have appeared. By examining some of the potential cluster topologies, their strengths and weaknesses should become apparent. An understanding of each topology's strengths and weaknesses is essential to developing effective clustered computing solutions.

Contemporary clusters tend to embrace one of two architectures: shared disk or shared nothing. Both of these architectures are subject to a seemingly infinite array of variation and combination.

The following figures demonstrate some of the more common examples, albeit in an intentionally generic manner. The network technologies indicated in the following figures are somewhat arbitrary, but functional.

Shared-Disk Clustering

Shared disk clustering is a close relative to the I/O sharing VAXClusters. Ostensibly, the primary difference is that the computers illustrated in Figure 26.3 are all performing the same application work, although this is not an absolute. As the computers in that figure are likely to be sharing the same data, an access manager is needed to coordinate the access, modification, deletion of the shared data.

FIGURE 26.3.

Shared-disk clustering.

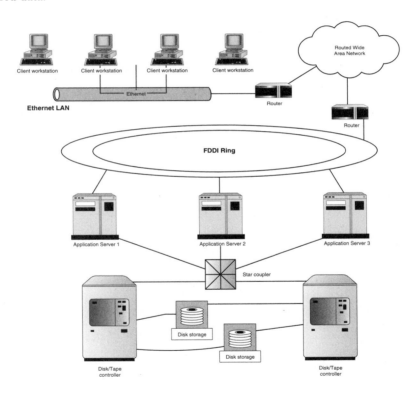

Clusters that share disks, and their contents, are directly descended from the original VAXClusters. Unlike the hosts in Figure 26.1, these hosts are dedicated to the same task and must coordinate access to, and modification of, the data. This requires interhost communication that can be satisfied through the local area network (LAN) that connects them to their wide area network (WAN).

Several companies have introduced products based on the shared disk cluster configuration, albeit with a slight variation. The clustered hosts access the shared disks directly, without a physical disk access management device. This variant is illustrated in Figure 26.4. Disk access management is still critical to the successful operation of the cluster, but is performed in the application layer rather than embodied in a physical device.

FIGURE 26.4.

Shared-disk clustering without access management.

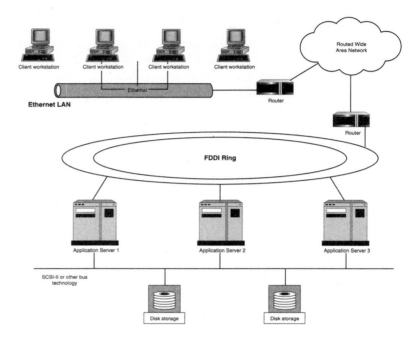

Single-application clusters that access shared disks rely directly upon database management or other software to coordinate access to disks and data.

Shared-disk clustering, in general, excels at satisfying I/O-intensive requirements, maximizing aggregate system performance, and load balancing. This approach is often used in conjunction with other mechanisms that provide auto-recovery from failures within the cluster.

Shared disk clusters, in general, are the least scalable of all clusters. Their limiting factor is the coordination of sharing disks and, more importantly, their *contents.* The coordination chore becomes increasingly complex as more computers are added to the cluster. Another limitation is that it may not be possible to share disks over great distances. Technologies exist that can network geographically dispersed disk drives for sharing, but they may be expensive to implement and operate. Geographic dispersion of the data also complicates and increases the time required to coordinate access to the data.

Shared-Nothing Clustering

The second cluster architecture is known as a *shared-nothing* cluster. This type of cluster, despite its somewhat oxymoronic name, is more scalable and has greater potential for delivering fault tolerance and auto-recovery from failures than shared-disk clusters. To achieve scalability and availability, shared-nothing clusters may compromise application performance. This type of cluster can be built in two major variations: close proximity and geographically dispersed. Figure 26.5 presents the close proximity form of a shared-nothing cluster. The geographically dispersed version is illustrated in Figure 26.6.

FIGURE 26.5.
Shared-nothing clustering.

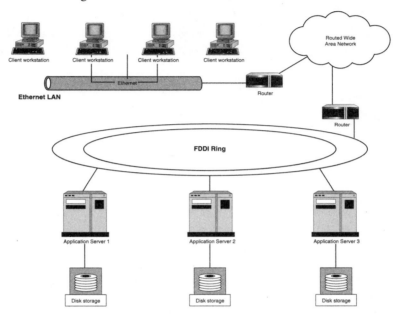

Shared-nothing clusters eliminate shared drives as a single point of failure. This degree of re-dundancy increases both the cost and complexity of building and operating a cluster.

The shared-nothing approach to clustering eliminates the scalability problems faced by shared-disk clusters. Each computer in the cluster has its own disk(s). Whether the client request for data can be resolved locally, or requires making an I/O request of another host in the cluster depends on how the application, and its database subsystem, was designed and implemented.

The shared-nothing clustering also enables clusters to be distributed geographically. This per-mits taking availability to an extreme by creating options for disaster recovery.

Shared-nothing clusters can also be dispersed geographically. This provides a degree of avail-ability that is impossible to achieve with any system, clustered or not, that is wholly contained in a single location. It is also possible for the hosts in this figure to be clusters, rather than in-dividual computers.

The flexibility of a geographically distributed cluster comes at the cost of performance. The WAN facilities will, almost certainly, be slower than any LAN technology. Attempts to use geographically dispersed clustered hosts for load balancing of a single application is doomed, as the participating hosts may need to ship I/O requests to other computers within the cluster. For example, if Host A in Figure 26.6 receives a request from a client for data that resides on Host B's disk, it must ship the I/O request across the relatively low-bandwidth wide area network to Host B for fulfillment. This is a substantially slower process than retrieving data from a local disk drive.

This negative performance delta is probably sufficient to warrant limiting this clustered arrangement to batch processing, disaster recovery, or other applications that are tolerant of long waits for I/O requests.

FIGURE 26.6.

Geographically dispersed shared-nothing clustering.

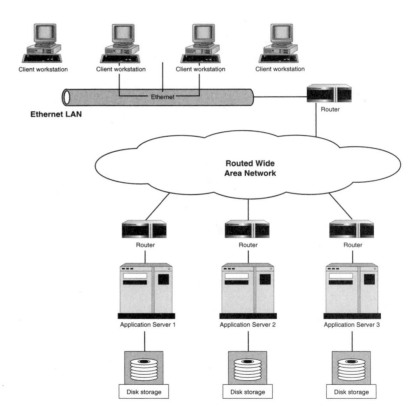

Topological Variations

Other topological variations on the shared-disk or shared-nothing architectures can be developed by customizing clusters for specific purposes. For example, contemporary clustering products typically focus on providing specific functionality, such as scalability, fault tolerance, failure recovery, performance, and so on. This functionality is provided by varying either the shared-disk or shared-nothing architecture, or even by offering a combination of the two. Although numerous subtle differences exist, the key difference between the various cluster products lies in the specialized software that coordinates activity between the clustered hosts.

Fail-Over Clustering

There are numerous specialized, high-availability clustering products designed for automatic failure recovery. These are known as *fail-over systems*. In a fail-over configuration, two or more computers (or clusters, for that matter!) serve as functional backups for each other. If one should fail, the other automatically takes over the processing normally performed by the failed system, thus eliminating downtime. Needless to say, fail-over clusters are highly desirable for supporting mission-critical applications. Figure 26.7 presents the basic fail-over cluster topology.

FIGURE 26.7.

Fail-over clustering.

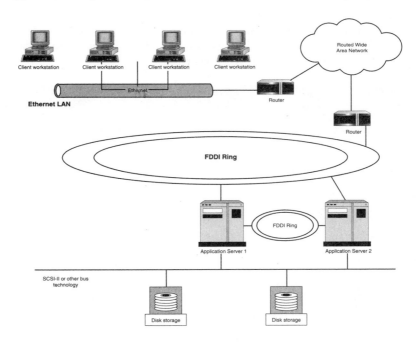

The shared-disk fail-over cluster typically requires an extra, dedicated high-performance network that is used solely for communication and coordination between the clustered hosts.

Traditionally, building a fault tolerant system meant buying two complete systems. One would be used to actively support the application while the second sat almost unused, except for keeping its copy of the application software and data up to date. In the event of a failure, the idle system would be pressed into service, buying time for the stricken host to be repaired. This approach tended to be fairly expensive and, depending upon how it was implemented, could still result in downtime and/or the loss of data.

Fail-over clusters take a more active approach to redundancy. The redundant hosts continuously monitor each other's health and have contingencies in place that will allow the cluster to recover from a failed host almost immediately. This monitoring mechanism also permits system architects to establish some load balancing between the hosts, provided that CPU utilization remains below 50 percent on all hosts.

Regardless of how they are implemented, fail-over clusters can be designed to provide high levels of availability without high levels of hardware inactivity.

Scalable Clustering

Designing clusters for scalability, too, has direct implications on the cluster's topology and functionality. Commercial clustering products that emphasize scalability tend to have stronger cluster management software. They also are more aggressive at load balancing than fail-over products. This requires all clustered hosts to have equal access to all data, regardless of where the data resides, or how that access is provided.

> **NOTE**
>
> Highly scalable clusters absolutely require the elimination of systemic performance bottlenecks. Given the current combinations of technologies in any given "system," slight mismatches are inevitable. The impacts of these mismatches are magnified by scale. The most obvious bottleneck component is I/O. Therefore, highly scalable clusters made from low-end processors will remain unattainable until technological advance closes the gap between the speed of I/O and processors.

Despite the availability of commercial products, designing scalable clusters can be difficult. The biggest trap that awaits anyone designing a scalable cluster is not compromising aggregate system performance for the sake of future scalability. Essentially, the cluster must be designed so that managing access to shared disks and data is not compromised by increases in usage volumes, or the cluster growth that should follow any such increases. Given that managing disk and file access becomes more complex as additional computers are added to the cluster, one easy way to avoid this trap is to build the cluster using expandable (that is, not fully configured) SMPs. This enables the entire cluster, regardless of architecture, to scale upwards by simply adding microprocessors to the existing SMPs.

While this solution may seem somewhat glib, consider the architectural alternatives and their risks. Servers in a poorly designed shared-disk cluster spend an unacceptable amount of time negotiating for permission to disk files as the cluster grows. Using a shared-nothing architecture may provide erratic performance, as perceived by the clients. Requests for I/O that can be satisfied locally are, typically, fulfilled very quickly. Requests for I/O that must be shipped to other servers in the cluster take considerably longer to fulfill.

Another alternative may be available, *if* the system or application that is being clustered, lends itself to task separation. In such cases, the cluster may be designed so that certain hosts have primary responsibility for specific functions. If this task separation enabled a similar separation of data, this type of cluster could be best implemented with a shared-nothing architecture, as (under normal circumstances) most requests for I/O would not have to be shipped to a different host. Applications that offered task separation, but not data separation, would probably perform best in a shared-disk cluster.

Properly designed, scalable clusters offer numerous benefits. Technological change, upgrades, and even maintenance can occur without disrupting service. This genre of cluster tends to have a greater need for high-speed I/O and access to shared storage devices.

Multitiered Clustering

Clusters can also be designed to satisfy numerous other objectives and can be implemented in combinations of the illustrated models. For example, multiple logical tiers of clustering functionality can be added through commercially available software without altering the physical cluster topology. Relational database management software, transaction processing management software, queuing management software, and so on, usually contain some provisions for either fail-over or load balancing.

A physically distinct topological variation of the multitiered cluster can best be described as a client/server/server. As Figure 26.8 demonstrates, a cluster of application servers can share access to a server that "owns" the data and database subsystem. This configuration enables one class of machines to focus on database management and another to be dedicated to performing application work.

Using a two-tiered server model physically decouples the application from the data, while permitting scalable growth of the application and its host. The small, private FDDI ring that interconnects the three servers is used to segregate inbound traffic from I/O requests. This network may also be used for interhost communications, if a fail-over mechanism was installed.

Given that each type of work imposes different requirements on their host, this arrangement offers system architects the ability to customize each server's configuration according to its specialized function. For example, the application servers can be optimized for either transaction processing or computation, depending upon the nature of the application. Similarly, the data server would be equipped with high-speed I/O capabilities and large disks.

For applications that cannot afford a single point of failure, the cluster's data server may be clustered, too. Thus, two or more fully redundant servers could function interchangeably as the cluster's server for database management.

FIGURE 26.8.

Client/server/server clustering.

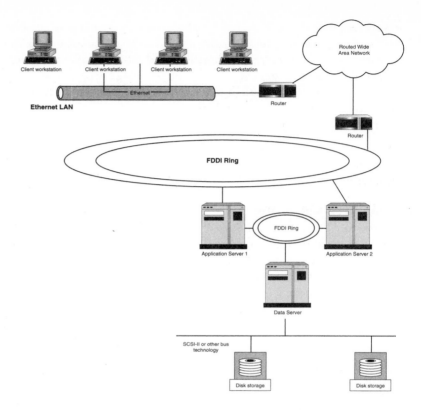

In Figure 26.9, the single point of failure evident is eliminated by introducing a fail-over cluster in the role of the primary cluster's data server. Depending upon usage volumes, either a more robust and/or separate LAN may be required to further segregate "keep alive" communications from I/O requests.

The last variation of a basic cluster topology that this chapter addresses is a form of the remotely distributed, shared-nothing cluster. Properly planned and implemented, this topology can provide application-level disaster recovery. It requires that clustered servers, and their storage facilities, meet certain criteria. These criteria are as follows:

- They must have sufficient spare capacity to instantly absorb the processing and I/O demands of the application that they are backing up.

- The LANs and WANs that interconnect the user base and the clustered hosts should have adequate spare capacity to automatically accommodate the shift in traffic patterns that will result from implementation of the disaster recovery contingency plans.

- The servers should be geographically separated from each other to ensure that regional disasters do not simultaneously impact both an application's primary and backup hosts.

- Provisions must be made for maintaining current copies of the application software and data at the emergency host.

FIGURE 26.9.

Client/server/server clustering, with internal cluster.

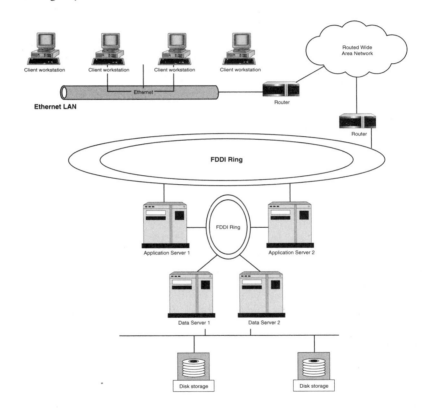

Figure 26.10 depicts a typical disaster recovery cluster.

Using a variation of the remotely distributed, shared-nothing cluster enables system architects to accommodate disaster recovery requirements, without incurring the costs normally associated with fully redundant, emergency backup systems.

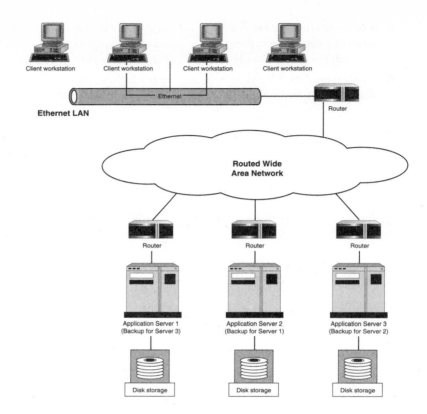

FIGURE 26.10.
Clustering for disaster recovery.

Summary of Cluster Varieties

This collection of typical clustering configurations, though by no means complete, should adequately convey the degree of flexibility that clustering affords. Topologies and their variations can be mixed and matched and even nested together to accommodate business requirements. Individual computers within a cluster can also be tailored to meet specific performance and functional requirements.

A slightly more subtle purpose of these examples, however, is to demonstrate the extent to which data networking supports clustering. If data networking were a homogenous quantity, this chapter could end here. Alas, it is not. Networks are almost as varied in their design and implementation as clusters.

Selection of Network Technologies

Given that interhost communications are essential to all clustering configurations, network technologies *must* be selected to ensure an optimal fit. This requires an understanding of the cluster's mechanics and performance requirements, as well as the various network technologies' performance specifications. Failure to use the right networking tool for the right job directly, and negatively, affects the performance of the cluster.

Network Functional Areas

Clustering may require network connectivity for one or more of three network functional areas:

- Client to cluster
- Cluster host to cluster host
- Cluster host to shared storage device

A fourth network functional area exists, intracomputer communications. The choice of technology for this function is determined by its manufacturer.

Each network technology must be evaluated relative to the unique demands and constraints of each of these functional capacities.

Client-to-cluster connectivity depends a great deal on where the clients are located, relative to the location of the cluster! If, for example, they are all located in the same location, WAN technologies need not be discussed. On the other hand, if the users are geographically dispersed, a combination of LAN and WAN technologies will be required. Fortunately, for the purposes of clustering, this aspect is likely to impose the least stringent network performance requirement.

Cluster host-to-cluster host connectivity also depends on whether or not the hosts are co-located. The performance requirements for this network component depend directly on the nature of the cluster. For example, fail-over clusters will require this to be a high-speed, non-contention-based network that is dedicated solely to interhost communication. This enables the quickest possible identification of a failed host and, subsequently, the quickest auto-recovery.

> **NOTE**
>
> Of all the network functional areas, cluster host-to-cluster host networking has the most impact on the aggregate performance of the cluster. This highly specialized network is best described as a *Cluster Area Network* (CAN). Technological innovations will soon render this network functional area a semi-internal function of the clustered processors. Such new technologies will bypass the I/O bus and feature direct memory-to-memory connectivity of the clustered nodes.

Scalable clusters, depending upon the actual implementation, typically impose more demanding performance requirements for I/O than they do for intracluster host communications. As a result, scalable clusters may be able to use the same network used for client-to-cluster host connectivity for all its interhost communications.

Finally, *cluster host-to-shared-storage device* always require high-speed connectivity. The distances between the cluster hosts and the storage devices, as well as the expected number of hosts that comprise the cluster, dictate the choice of network technology.

Network Technologies

Some network and/or bus technologies that can be used in a cluster are: 10Mbps Ethernet, 100Mbps Ethernet, FDDI and CDDI, ATM, ESCON, SCSI-II and III, Fibre Channel, as well as numerous other LAN, WAN, and bus technologies. Each has its own strengths, weaknesses, and peculiarities that must be considered against the clustered system's performance requirements. A quick survey should reveal just how different network technologies can be. Strengths and weaknesses should amply demonstrate the criticality of network technology selection for each network functional area of a cluster.

Given that all network technologies must abide by the laws of physics, each one represents a different balance struck between speed and distance, varying by the physical media that they are implemented with. Two other differences between network technologies that also serve as key metrics for comparisons, are sustainable throughput and latency. Both of these are a function of the network's protocols for media access and packet handling. These are the metrics that should be applied to each technology to assess its viability in the cluster configuration.

10Mbps Ethernet

10Mbps Ethernet is an extremely mature and stable technology. As defined in the IEEE's specification 802.3, there are four different physical layer specifications for transmission media. Table 26.1 presents the distance limits and data rates that can be achieved with each of the physical layer specifications.

Table 26.1. Ethernet's distance limitations.

Physical Media	Max. Distance	Data Rate
10base-2 thin coaxial cable	Up to 185 meters	10Mbps
10base-5 thick coaxial cable	Up to 500 meters	10Mbps
10base-T unshielded twisted pair	Up to 100 meters	10Mbps
10base-FL fiber-optic cable	Up to 2000 meters	10Mbps

Ethernet uses a variable length packet to transmit data that can vary from 64 to 1500 octets. This is an extremely efficient means of transporting bulk data, as the packet-to-payload ratio can be optimized automatically. Ethernet's effectiveness in bulk data transport renders it incapable of providing consistently low latency levels for time-sensitive traffic.

For its access method, Ethernet uses Carrier Sense, Multiple Access with Collision Detection, also affectionately known as CSMA/CD. This is a contention-based media access method.

Devices connected to the LAN must compete for empty packets. This competition may result in the collision of packets, especially if the network is heavily used. Collisions between packets result in a retransmission of those packets.

The net effect of Ethernet's flexible packet sizes and competition for bandwidth, is a protocol that is incapable of gracefully accommodating heavy traffic volumes. At utilization rates in excess of 20 percent, performance begins to degrade quickly. Thus, its sustainable throughputs are limited to less than 3Mbps. Using switched Ethernet bolsters the performance of this technology by increasing the amount of bandwidth available to switch-connected devices.

100Mbps Ethernet

100Mbps Ethernet (or *Fast Ethernet*) is a recent extension to the 802.3 specification. It presents a graceful migration path from, and ready interoperability with, its slower sibling. Unfortunately, it also retains all of Ethernet's shortcomings, albeit at a faster transmission rate. Table 26.2 shows the distance limits and data rates for 100Mbps Ethernet.

Table 26.2. Fast Ethernet's distance limitations.

Physical Media	Distance	Data Rate
62.5 micron multimode fiber-optic cabling (100base-FX)	Up to 412 meters	100Mbps
Category 3 unshielded twisted pair (100base-T4)	Up to 100 meters	100Mbps
Category 5 unshielded twisted pair (100base-TX)	Up to 100 meters	100Mbps

Given an order-of-magnitude-faster clock than its predecessor, Fast Ethernet is capable of sustaining approximately an order of magnitude more throughput, that is, about an aggregate of 20Mbps to 30Mbps, before it begins experiencing performance degradation. Implementing port-switched Fast Ethernet effectively reduces competition for packets on a segment to just two devices: the hub port and the computer that it serves. This means that each switch-connected device can use at least 40Mbps to 60Mbps, rather than competing for that bandwidth with all the other devices, and their respective hub ports, on the LAN.

FDDI and CDDI

FDDI and CDDI are 100Mbps token-passing local area networks that use a ring topology. Network access is highly deterministic as it is governed by a "token" that passes around the FDDI loop. Decreasing network latency is easily accomplished by reducing the size of the ring, that is, the fewer devices connected, the more frequently each device gets the token.

FDDI also features a dual, counter-rotating, ring topology that can "splice" logically to heal a broken cable. The drawback to this self-healing capability is a sudden increase in propagation delay in the event of a cable break. This is a minor price to pay for a network that can auto-recover. Table 26.3 shows the distance limits and data rates for FDDI.

Table 26.3. FDDI and CDDI's distance limitations.

Physical Media	Max. Distance	Data Rate
62.5 micron multimode fiber-optic cabling	200 total kilometers (100 per "ring")	100Mbps
Category 5 unshielded twisted pair	> 100 meters	100Mbps
Type 1 shielded twisted pair	> 100 meters	100Mbps

FDDI, and its wire-based sibling CDDI, are designed to provide high levels of sustainable throughput, approximately 60Mbps to 80Mbps. This is due largely to the regulated media access method.

ATM

Asynchronous Transfer Mode, ATM's proper name, was originally developed as an asynchronous transfer mechanism for Broadband Integrated Services Digital Network (B-ISDN). It is a high-bandwidth switched protocol that uses a 53-byte packet that includes 48 bytes of payload with a 5-byte header.

Although essentially a connectionless protocol, mechanisms have been implemented that enable ATM to function in a connection-oriented mode. ATM was initially touted as a grand unifier in the world of networking, capable of seamlessly integrating LANs and WANs. Predictably, ATM was implemented in numerous data rates that were designed specifically for a LAN environment. For example, data rates as low as 25.6Mbps were developed for client connectivity, whereas 155.52Mbps was intended for initial implementation a LAN backbone technology, as well as for servers and high-end client connectivity.

This protocol is, in theory, scalable up to approximately 2.4 gigabits per second, although LAN products are currently only available up to 622Mbps. The norm for host connectivity is the 155.52Mbps interface. Distance limits and data rates for ATM appear in Table 26.4.

Table 26.4. ATM's distance limitations and data rates.

Physical Media	Distance	Data Rate
Category 3 unshielded twisted pair	Up to 100 meters	25.6Mbps
Category 5 unshielded twisted pair	Up to 100 meters	155.52Mbps
62.5 micron multimode fiber-optic cabling	Up to 2 kilometers	155.52Mbps

Given that ATM is an inherently switched technology, its sustainable throughputs should be fairly close to its data rate. ATM also uses a fixed-length packet. This makes it a low latency protocol, ideally suited to time-sensitive applications. Conversely, it has a high overhead of packet frame to payload. Thus, it might not be as efficient at bulk data transport as a protocol with a flexible-length packet, yet it operates at a higher data rate than either Fast Ethernet or FDDI.

ESCON

ESCON (Enterprise Server Connectivity) is an IBM channel technology. It provides 17.1Mbps sustainable throughput. Due to its protocol and packet structure, ESCON excels at bulk data transfer. It does not handle short transactions or interactivity well at all. Attempts to use ESCON for a high volume of small transfers results in a premature deterioration of its performance, causing it to fall well short of its potential. The distance limits and data rates for ESCON appear in Table 26.5.

Table 26.5. ESCON's distance limitations.

Physical Media	Distance	Data Rate
50 micron multimode fiber-optic cabling	Up to 3 kilometers	200Mbps
62.5 micron multimode fiber-optic cabling	Up to 3 kilometers (9 with repeaters)	200Mbps

SCSI-II

Small Computer Systems Interface, version 2, known as SCSI-II, is a moderately high-bandwidth bus technology. It was designed for peer-to-peer connectivity of peripheral devices and at least one host. Its major limitations are the number of devices that can be connected, and the short distance that the bus can span. These limitations make SCSI-II useful only for connecting cluster hosts to storage devices. Table 26.6 shows the distance limits and data rates for SCSI-II.

Table 26.6. SCSI-II distance limitations.

Physical Media	Max. Total Distance	Data Rate
Ribbon cable (16-bit SCSI-II)	25 meters	10Mbps
50-pin shielded cable (16-bit SCSI-II)	25 meters	10Mbps
Ribbon cable (32-bit SCSI-II)	25 meters	40Mbps
50-pin shielded cable (32-bit SCSI-II)	25 meters	40Mbps

For asynchronous transmissions, the actual data rates achieved are a function of aggregate cable length and implementation. Synchronous transmissions are a function of cable length and SCSI implementation. For example, 32-bit SCSI-II buses are capable of transmission speeds of up to 40MB per second and 16-bit SCSI-II can transmit up to 10MB per second.

Fibre Channel

Fibre Channel was originally developed by IBM as an optical channel technology for mainframes. Its specification provided for a transmission rate of one gigabit per second! Given that mainframes are not likely to support time-sensitive applications like voice and videoconferencing any time soon, flexible-length packets were used.

Fibre Channel has since been implemented as a LAN technology. The physical layer specification for this technology provides for a variety of speed and distance trade-offs over most common transmission media. Table 26.7 shows the distance limits and data rates for Fibre Channel.

Table 26.7. Fibre Channel's distance limitations.

Physical Media	Distance	Data Rate
9 micron single-mode fiber-optic cabling	Up to 10 kilometers	1062.5Mbaud
50 micron multimode fiber-optic cabling	Up to 1 kilometer	531.25Mbaud
	Up to 2 kilometers	265.6Mbaud
62.5 micron multimode fiber-optic cabling	Up to 500 meters	265.6Mbaud
	Up to 1 kilometer	132.8Mbaud
Video coaxial cabling	Up to 25 meters	1062.5Mbaud
	Up to 50 meters	531.25Mbaud
	Up to 75 meters	265.6Mbaud
	Up to 100 meters	132.8Mbaud
Miniature coaxial cabling	Up to 10 meters	1062.5Mbaud
	Up to 20 meters	531.25Mbaud
	Up to 30 meters	265.6Mbaud
	Up to 40 meters	132.8Mbaud
Shielded twisted pair	Up to 50 meters	265.6Mbaud
	Up to 100 meters	132.8Mbaud

This technology provides for an automatic scaling back of the clock rate if it begins to experience transmission errors. Thus, the values listed in Table 26.7 should be considered the maximum data rates that can be supported.

Summary of Network Technologies

Once the technologies have been identified for each required networking function, equal due diligence must be paid to their implementation. Networks must be considered a functional extension of the cluster. Thus, it is critical that they be implemented so as to reinforce the intended functionality of the cluster. For example, if the cluster supports a mission-critical application designed for 100 percent availability, the network, too, must be capable of 100 percent availability. This means selecting hardware that supports hot-swapping of circuit boards, protecting all the network's electrical components with uninterruptible power supplies (UPSs), and having fully redundant network paths to all clustered hosts. Otherwise, the cluster may find itself experiencing service outages that it cannot fix with a fail-over.

Similarly, if the cluster is designed for scalability, the network must be designed to scale upwards as gracefully and easily as the cluster. Ideally, the networks would be over-engineered relative to the cluster's initial loads. Thus, the additional ports for connectivity and bandwidth would be available in advance to support the cluster's growth as it materializes.

Another important implementation issue is addressing. Many of the network technologies mentioned are also available in a switched form. Switching is a technique that improves network performance by dividing the LAN into smaller segments, thereby providing greater overall bandwidth across the network. This performance gain brings with it additional cost and complexity in addressing. Is switching necessary and/or desirable in terms of the cluster's projected network requirements?

Switches work like high-speed bridges. They use tables to collate physical ports with addresses. Host naming and addressing must be worked out so that it can support the functionality of the planned cluster. For example, you need to ensure that, when a fail-over occurs, all network routing and switching tables are updated automatically to reflect the failed host's unavailability. Ideally, clients access the cluster using a single mnemonic and do not need to know any specific addresses. Properly planned and implemented, the network automatically routes around failed hosts without the clients' even knowing a failure occurred.

Summary

Clustering uniprocessors and SMPs is an exciting aspect of computer parallelism. It can be used to provide both fault tolerance and disaster recovery for mission-critical applications, as easily as it can support graceful scalability. By distributing the processing workload, clustering enables smaller, less expensive computers to simulate the processing power of larger, more expensive computers. Their distributed nature makes clusters absolutely dependent upon data networking technologies. If the wrong network technology is chosen, even in just one of the three identified functional areas, the results on aggregate cluster performance can be disastrous.

Matching network technologies to functional areas may seem trivial. After all, it is relatively easy to examine network technologies from an academic perspective and to select the ideal candidates for each network component of a planned cluster. This is especially true if the comparison is based on a limited number of obvious criteria, that is, the distance limitations and transmission speeds for various physical media. These are good, tangible criteria for a "paper" evaluation that can be used by anyone with a passing familiarity with data networking.

However, network selection criteria cannot stop there. There are many more subtle, yet significant criteria to consider. For example, is the network's maximum sustainable throughput capable of accommodating the traffic load? Will the network(s) scale upward with the projected growth of the cluster? Are there any hardware and/or software dependencies dictated by your cluster's platform, that is, availability of network interface cards (NICs) and software drivers, that would preclude the use of any network technologies? Is the network capable of living up to the cluster's expected availability rate?

In real life, numerous other variables, many of them subjective and/or non-technical, must also be factored into the selection of network technologies. Existing skill sets, training costs, budgetary constraints, vendor relationships, and so on, are all important constraints that must be considered when selecting technologies.

This may begin to resemble an impossible dilemma and, in fact, that's partially true. There is no single correct answer. Don't despair, the correct answers vary from project to project, and from company to company. To find your correct answers, start with a fundamental appreciation for the business goals and performance requirements of your cluster. Identify the expected intensity with which the cluster's resources, that is, CPU cycles or I/O, will be consumed by *each* cluster component.

Next, identify all the network technologies that may be appropriate for each network functional area required. Then, use the realities of your particular situation, including the local techno-politics and all the other soft criteria, as the final criteria for matching your short list of network technologies to your cluster's performance requirements.

Multimedia Communication

by Mark Sportack

IN THIS CHAPTER

CHAPTER 27

The ever increasing amount of processing power at the Desktop has spawned wave after wave of technological innovation. Each innovation has sought to exploit this power. One of the more compelling but elusive challenges of desktop computing has been multimedia processing and communication. Ultimately, all forms of information, regardless of their current media, will be digitized and transmitted over a single network infrastructure. Unfortunately, that day is a long way off. In the meantime, numerous challenges face anyone seeking to integrate other media types onto a network designed specifically for data transport.

Multimedia applications impose very different performance requirements upon the network than do the traditional applications types that networks were designed to support. Besides being potentially bandwidth-intensive, multimedia applications are also usually time-sensitive. Traditional networks and protocols are designed to deliver packets of guaranteed integrity, rather than guarantee a timely delivery of packets. Significant progress has been made in this direction in communications technologies and protocols.

This chapter explores the various technologies that are driving multimedia communication, and identifies network performance issues and technologies that are being developed to address those issues.

Overview of Multimedia Communication

In the past, separate infrastructures were required to support different types of communication. Most workstations are still equipped with both a telephone and a personal computer (PC) to support voice and data communication. The telephone is the user's front end to the Private Branch Exchange (PBX) or other telephony switch, while the PC is an intelligent device that uses LANs and WANs to communicate with other devices.

Technological innovations have slowly, but steadily, eroded the long-standing distinctions between previously distinct communication technologies. Advances in component technologies have enabled the development of increasingly sophisticated and specialized applications. Multimedia communication, for example, owes its existence to advances in microprocessors and magnetic storage media. Microprocessors are continuing to increase in power and speed while steadily becoming more affordable. Similar advances have been made in the various types of magnetic storage devices.

These advancements encouraged creative attempts to exploit their potential. One creative attempt was the digitization of data that traditionally existed in other forms. Today, numerous data types converging into a common format: digital encoding. Integrating multiple application types that use digitally encoded data into a single host platform, that is, a computer, has become euphemistically known as "multimedia computing." Figure 27.1 illustrates one form of multimedia computing.

FIGURE 27.1.

Integrating different application types into a common platform, that is, the PC, constitutes multimedia computing.

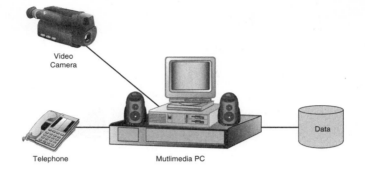

Video Camera

Telephone   Mutlimedia PC   Data

Some of the more common multimedia applications include

- Computer-based telephony
- Video conferencing
- Video transmission
- Audio transmission
- High-density graphics

Although some of these may seem so closely related as to be virtually identical, they differ in one critical aspect: the network performance that they demand.

Multimedia communication can be equally difficult to define. For the purposes of this book, *multimedia communication* means the integration of multiple data types into a common bit stream. This is illustrated in Figure 27.2.

A subtle but important point is that multimedia computing and multimedia communication are not completely synonymous. For example, a LAN can support client machines that are used exclusively for traditional forms of data communication and also provide networking for machines that are dedicated to providing video or audio service for external clients. Consequently, the LAN can be simultaneously transporting multiple media types with extremely different performance requirements, even though no true "multimedia" computers are directly connected to it. This is illustrated in Figure 27.3.

NOTE

A common misconception is that multimedia computing is live, interactive videoconferencing. This is, perhaps, the most compelling and resource intensive of the multimedia applications. However, it isn't the only one. Many other more subtle forms of multimedia applications will diffuse throughout the client population first. Consequently, you will need to consider ways to integrate support for multimedia communications long before the network infrastructure is ready to support the "killer" videoconferencing application.

Figure 27.2.

Integrating different data types into a common network, such as the LAN, constitutes multimedia communication.

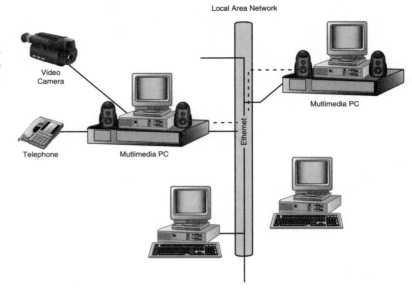

Figure 27.3.

A network can be required to support multiple, mixed media types without having to support any "multimedia" computers.

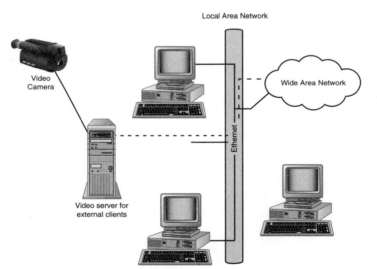

Trade publications have fixated on multimedia computing to the almost complete exclusion of multimedia communication. This has resulted in an inappropriate focus on the integration of multiple media types at the application layer, without regard for preparing networks to accommodate multiple media and application types.

At the physical layer of the OSI Reference Model, all forms of communication, regardless of whether they are ASCII-encoded data or a live video conference, are nothing more than a stream of 1s and 0s. It is only at the application layer that the distinctions are obvious.

Given that the network moves packets or frames filled with 1s and 0s, transporting a stream of digitally encoded speech or video should be easy. Unfortunately, this is not the case. Network technologies have lagged behind the various computing technologies' advance rates. This is evident when one compares the network's ability to perform against the performance requirements of contemporary multimedia applications.

At the risk of oversimplifying, multimedia applications typically impose two basic types of performance requirements: latency and bandwidth.

Latency

Latency is defined as the minimum amount of time required for a packet to clear any given network device, such as a router, a hub, a switch, and so on. Time-sensitive applications like live voice or video conferencing require low-latency connections throughout the entire network. A low-latency connection, ideally, provides a low *and consistent* delay between the transmission and receipt of a packet. Low but inconsistent delays can result in jittery images, choppy sounds, or otherwise degraded performance of networked multimedia applications.

LAN Access Method

The cumulative latency of a network is affected in many ways. The first, and most obvious, is the LAN's access method. LANs that feature a contention-based access method (for example, all "flavors" of Ethernet) are likely to have a higher, and less consistent, latency due to the vicissitudes of competing for empty packets. LANs that use a deterministic access method (for example, Token Ring and FDDI) have a lower latency, but remain inconsistent and unpredictable.

Deterministic networks offer the ability to improve performance by decreasing the number of nodes connected to each segment or ring. This statistically decreases the amount of time before any given node receives permission to transmit, thereby decreasing latency somewhat. Unfortunately, this cannot provide a highly consistent delay as frame sizes used by these protocols are highly flexible.

A good way to improve the latency of both contention- and token-based networks is to implement them using switching hubs. Switches are very fast forwarding devices that function completely at Layers 1 and 2 of the OSI Reference Model. A LAN based on switching hubs enjoys a lower innate latency than one based on repeating hubs simply because the switches forward packets faster than conventional repeating hubs.

> **NOTE**
>
> The use of a full-duplex, switched version of any of the Ethernets will also help reduce latency by eliminating the effects of contention for media access. Full-duplex connections permit the simultaneous transmission and reception of data. Traditional Ethernet is only half-duplex: A device can either transmit or receive, but not both simultaneously.
>
> In a full-duplex switched Ethernet, there are only two ports on the segment, the switched hub port and the device it connects to. Each has its own dedicated wire path for transmission and reception. Consequently, there is absolutely no contention for packets on the wire; latency is effectively reduced.

Each port on a switch represents a separate segment or ring. That is, an 802.3 Ethernet switching hub provides a number of ports, each acting as a standalone collision domain, that are members of the same broadcast domain. Devices connected to a dedicated switched port still must compete for empty packets, but the competition is limited to that device and the hub port it is connected to. Switching is rapidly displacing traditional broadcast Ethernet hubs. It is even being implemented in Token Ring and FDDI versions.

Routing

Another aspect of a network's cumulative latency is whether or not routing is used. Routers, an integral part of virtually all WANs, operate at Layer 3 of the OSI Reference Model and require software-driven table lookups to forward packets. This means that they cannot forward packets as quickly as a switch. Thus, they directly increase the cumulative latency of a network.

Frame and Packet Structures

Latency is also directly affected by a network's frame structure. Many of today's more common and mature network protocols also use flexible frame and packet sizes. Flexible data fields excel at transporting traditional data types by minimizing the packet-to-payload ratio. Unfortunately, this has the exact opposite impact on time-sensitive applications. Forcing such applications to intermingle in the bit stream with indeterminate packet sizes adversely affects time-sensitive applications by introducing inconsistency to the network's cumulative latency.

Packet Discrimination

Given that conventional networks are designed explicitly to support the transport of data, the time-sensitive packets of multimedia applications require non-standard handling. Networks must be able to

- Identify packets that require special handling.
- Be capable of accommodating those special requirements.

A mechanism that can provide networks with the ability to discriminate between packets, based on their performance requirements, is known as Quality of Service (QoS). QoS has two distinct facets: network and application. Valid application QoS parameters include image size and quality, frame rate (if the application is video), start-up delays, reliability, and so on. The network, however, has a very different set of QoS parameters. These include: bandwidth, loss rate, and delay. Users are not allowed to specify network QoS parameters. A QoS-capable protocol, such as RSVP, provides the translation between application and network parameters.

Obviously, the relationship between these sets of parameters is very complex. In theory, QoS will enable the different application types to receive the special handling that they require. Applications that require guaranteed integrity of packet contents can receive that, while others that need low delay and/or response times can tell the network about those requirements through QoS tags, too.

In order for QoS to work, both the network and the networked multimedia applications must conform to a common standard for QoS. Unfortunately, this uniformity has yet to develop. QoS must be supported throughout the full spectrum of the networked computing infrastructure. It can't work unless all the network hardware, client platform, and applications support a common set of QoS tags.

The good news is that almost all of the major players in these technology areas are committed to implementing RSVP, a networking protocol with native QoS support. The bad news is that, until a critical mass is achieved, QoS is useless.

Conventional networks are artifacts of the recent past. Their access methods, route-calculation and packet-forwarding techniques, and even their frame structures make them well suited to guaranteeing the integrity and sequence of delivered packets. Conversely, they are ill-prepared for guaranteeing the timeliness with which those packets will be delivered. Rectifying these deficiencies, with respect to the low-latency demands of time-sensitive applications, is not a trivial task. The use of QoS is just one of the ways that existing networks can be retrofitted to provide some measure of support for time-sensitive applications.

Bandwidth

In addition to the timeliness of delivery, there is another challenge that must be overcome to successfully transport multimedia communication. This challenge is the sheer quantitative challenge of transporting the volume of data generated by multimedia applications. Applications that are not time-sensitive, like high-density graphics or non-streaming audio and/or video transmissions, can be transported better by conventional networks. Their only performance requirements are the guaranteed integrity of packet contents, and re-sequencing upon arrival. However, they can be extremely bandwidth intensive.

Bandwidth Conservation

Perhaps the best way to increase the amount of usable bandwidth is to conserve the consumption of existing bandwidth. There are numerous techniques for conserving bandwidth, most of which are automatically built in to multimedia applications software.

Compression is an invaluable tool for conserving bandwidth. Compression algorithms vary, based upon application and data type. For example, video conferencing software can compress data streams by transmitting only the pixels that have changed since the previously transmitted frame (in other words, motion). Other forms of compression may be based upon character strings or repeated patterns.

Non-interactive transmissions may also be effectively stored and forwarded, thereby conserving bandwidth during peak demand periods.

Regardless of which technique is used, conservation makes better use of the existing, available bandwidth. It may even forestall the need to reinvest in network hardware.

Increasing Available Bandwidth

The other way to increase the bandwidth available for multimedia applications is to increase the speed of the network. Fast Ethernet, Gigabit Ethernet, ATM, FDDI, Fibre Channel, and so on, may all be used to substantially increase the available bandwidth on a LAN. Upgrading an existing network to these technologies may require a substantial investment in station wiring, network interface cards, hubs, and so on, and involve a considerable amount of planning and work to implement.

Often referred to as a "fork lift upgrade," very little, if any, of the previous network's components are retained. Such upgrades are expensive and non-trivial undertakings. They should be considered a last resort for increasing bandwidth.

More modest upgrades can be effective at increasing the supply of bandwidth. A typical, incremental, upgrade might be to implement a high-speed LAN backbone using ATM, FDDI, or Fast Ethernet, and then selectively introduce a switched variant of the existing LAN technology as a segmentation device.

FIGURE 27.4.

Improving LAN performance with Switching.

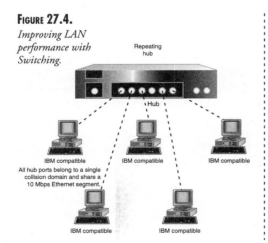
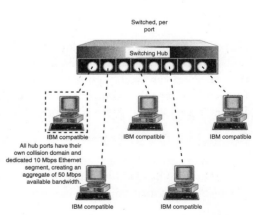

Segmentation increases usable bandwidth without increasing a network's velocity by creating multiple collision domains or logical rings within a common broadcast domain. This type of upgrade allows the retention of the station wiring and network interface cards.

High Bandwidth with Low Latency

Certain applications, like video conferencing, simultaneously require low latency and high levels of throughput to operate successfully. Unless a network is intentionally and severely over-engineered, adding such applications to an existing network may tax the network's abilities, and reduce overall performance for all the applications that rely upon the network for transport.

Given the various contributors to a network's cumulative latency, the surest way to provide high bandwidth *and* low latency is to select network technologies that are specifically designed for this tandem purpose. Some specific examples include ATM and isochronous Ethernet.

Bandwidth Reservation

Bolstering the available LAN bandwidth is not without risks. If a suitable LAN technology can be identified, and the embedded base of premise wiring is adequate, a successful LAN renovation may only create a greater mismatch between the LAN and the WAN. WANs typically are constructed with routers (antithetical to low-latency networking) and transmission facilities that are at least an order of magnitude "smaller" than the LANs they interconnect. Larger transmission facilities are available, for example, DS-3 and fiber-based MANs, but their cost may be prohibitive.

Multimedia applications require the lowest, and most consistent, cumulative latency possible. Upgrading or renovating LANs, without considering the WANs that interconnect them, may well be an expensive exercise in futility.

One way to avoid this trap is to use protocols that can reserve bandwidth. RSVP, for example, is an emerging network protocol that can reserve the amount of bandwidth that will be needed by establishing a temporary but dedicated virtual circuit between the source and destination machines.

The obvious danger inherent in bandwidth reservation schemes is that once bandwidth is reserved by an application, it is unavailable to other machines and their applications. A WAN comprised of T-1s will quickly exhaust its bandwidth if users start reserving 128Kbps virtual circuits for their videoconferencing sessions.

Reflections on Multimedia Communication

Multimedia communication imposes a combination of performance requirements that are beyond the abilities of many of today's mature LAN and WAN technologies and protocols. The difficulty is in simultaneously satisfying the *combination* of performance parameters using a platform that is more legacy- than future-oriented.

New internetworking protocols are emerging that may enable existing platforms to more effectively transport mixed media types, but they are not panaceas. They are designed to either identify specific packets as having priority over others, or provide a more or less guaranteed level of service by reserving bandwidth between the endpoints engaged in multimedia communication. The fundamental deficiencies remain unresolved.

The key to unleashing the power of high-performance networking by supporting multimedia communication lies in understanding the different types of multimedia communication, as well as their specific performance requirements. This knowledge provides a context for evaluating the potential of LAN, WAN, and application technologies to support multimedia communication.

High-Density File Transfers

Multimedia communication includes some applications that generate traffic that can be merely a quantitative challenge to transport. This type of traffic can include everything from low-resolution, cartoon-like images up to full-color, high-resolution photographs, as well as recorded streams of audio and/or video signals. High-density file transfers include three categories: graphics, audio, and video transfers.

They share common network performance requirements: guaranteed integrity of packetized data upon delivery, without regard for the sequence or timing of that delivery. In fact, failure to retransmit damaged or dropped packets will likely result in noticeable degradation of files. These files are no different than any conventional data file when being transferred. They require the transport protocol to provide error detection and correction, as well as resequencing of the received packets. Once this is accomplished, the transport protocol hands the packets to the appropriate application for storage.

Graphics File Transfers

Graphics files vary in size based upon the compression algorithm used, that is, the file's format, physical size, and pixel and color density. Graphics have become a readily accepted form of computing since the advent of graphical user interfaces. This integration has been so successful that most users do not consider graphics to be "multimedia." Additional evidence that supports this assertion is that this form of transmission is easily accommodated with conventional network technologies. Graphics file transmissions do not require timeliness of delivery. Damaged packets can be retransmitted and resequenced without adversely affecting the application.

One possible exception to this could be the World Wide Web (WWW). Web pages are a notorious example of the quantitative challenge of adding a new, bandwidth-intensive, multimedia application to an existing network.

This type of traffic is likely to contain in-line graphics embedded in text files, and users are likely to be waiting for the graphics to be delivered. Large, complex graphics and/or animation may require multiple retransmissions before being successfully reassembled by the user's browser.

This may take more time than the user is willing to wait. Though not technically a time-sensitive application, this example demonstrates the difficulty of constructing categories to define a spectrum of uses. Fortunately, this type of multimedia communication is readily abetted by carefully selecting graphics formats for their effectiveness in compressing the file.

Audio File Transfers

Prerecorded audio files can be encoded in several different formats and contain speech, music, sounds, and so on. A transferred file can be stored either on disk or in memory. Once received in its entirety, the file can be played back.

Audio transfers, by virtue of having been prerecorded, can effectively utilize transmission error detection and correction mechanisms. Temporarily storing them to disk or memory upon receipt provides the user with a more error-free file and smoother sound quality than is possible if the file were played back immediately upon receipt.

This temporary storage provides the time needed for damaged or dropped packets to be identified, and re-sent. This implies that this method can create a greater volume of overall network traffic than a streaming audio transmission would.

Video File Transfers

Recorded video files can also be encoded in a variety of formats. They may or may not contain supplemental audio tracks. Those with accompanying audio will be marginally larger than a similarly sized and same duration video-only file, but they require synchronization of audio and video. Any errors in the received file will be more obvious due to the temporary disruption in the continuity between image and sound.

Prerecorded video files, like their audio-only counterparts, can take advantage of transmission error detection and correction mechanisms. Storing them to disk (memory is probably not a viable storage option, given the likely sizes of even "small" video files) upon receipt provides the user with a more accurate replication of the original file than would have been possible if the file were being viewed immediately.

Temporarily storing, or buffering, the file provides the time needed for damaged or dropped packets to be re-sent and resequenced.

Audio Communication

Audio communication can take three distinct forms, each with a slightly different set of network performance requirements. Specific application categories include: computer-based telephony, audio conferencing, and audio transmission.

Computer-Based Telephony

Computer-based telephony uses PCs and LANs/WANs to integrate voice telephony into a data network. The client PC buffers inbound transmissions and plays them using its sound card and speakers. This buffering can "smooth out" the sound quality of the transmission somewhat, despite its having traversed contention-based LANs using error-correcting protocols.

Audio communication is not bandwidth intensive. Audio can be delivered over dialup facilities as slow as 14.4Kbps using Point-to-Point Protocol (PPP). This form of communication, however, is extremely susceptible to corruption from packets delivered late or out of sequence. Any such packets are discarded because, by the time a successful retransmission can be made, the stream being played back will likely have progressed beyond the point at which that packet was needed. Thus, re-inserting it late creates a second disturbance that is readily detectable by the user.

Computer-based telephony suffers from two significant limitations. Transmissions are, to date, half-duplex only. Half-duplex transmissions mean that only one party can "talk" at a time, much like "push-to-talk" walkie-talkies. Telephones are full-duplex mechanisms. Both parties on a telephone call can talk and listen simultaneously. They might not be able to communicate effectively this way, but the technology supports their ability to try.

The second limitation is that computer-based telephony is capable of providing sound quality on par with an AM radio. The combination of half-duplex transmission and relatively low sound quality renders this technology more of a curiosity or techno-toy than a business tool.

Interestingly, the bandwidth requirements for half-duplex audio can be as little as one percent of a video communication session. Thus, this technology is far easier to implement and may not require re-investment in the network infrastructure. Unfortunately, it may also be the least useful. The greatest impediment to this multimedia communication technology is the well-established base of higher-quality telephony equipment. Why use a networked PC to emulate a walkie-talkie when there's already a telephone on every desk?

Computer-Based Audio Conferencing

Audio conferencing differs from computer-based telephony only in that it is used in other than point-to-point sessions. Conferences tend to be multipoint-to-multipoint in the case of a collaborative conference of peers, or point-to-multipoint for broadcasts of major events.

Given the half-duplex nature of this technology set, point-to-multipoint unidirectional broadcasts may be the best use of this technology. The network must have some mechanism for this form of multicasting. Multicasting is the transmission of a single stream of packetized data with an address that is recognized by more than one workstation. This is far more bandwidth-efficient than transmitting multiple simultaneous streams, each destined for a single, specific end-point. End-points that belong to a multicast group "listen" for both their unique Internet address, and the address of their group.

Streaming Audio

Streaming audio transmissions are unidirectional transmissions of a stream of audio data. It uses a host that either records audio in real-time, or uses prerecorded audio media. In either case, packets stream out onto the network as soon as they are generated. Recipients listen to them as they arrive, generally without buffering them. Dropped or damaged packets are usually left out of the playback session; some of the newer streaming audio products on the market, however, offer the opportunity to attempt a retransmission.

Streaming audio, like most audio-only multimedia applications, is relatively easy to support in a LAN/WAN environment. It is low bandwidth, and benefits from but does not require low network latency. Perhaps the most important attribute of streaming audio technology is that it does not pretend to be a bi-directional audio transmission technology. Therefore, its practical applications are much more readily determined. Streaming audio can be used to distribute, on demand, either a feed from a live speech or copies of recorded speeches, Question and Answer sessions, or even the latest disk from your favorite group.

Video Communication

Video communication is the acid test of any IT platform. It requires a fairly high-powered computer and can also be extremely bandwidth intensive. It also benefits greatly from low-latency network components. At a minimum, it should use network protocols that can reserve bandwidth at the time of call setup.

Video communication can occur at surprisingly low levels of throughput, given the right compromise of picture size, quality, and refresh rate. The ideal rate of refresh is 30 frames per second. At this rate, known as "full motion," the picture appears smooth, and movement is smooth, not jerky. Unfortunately, even using a small picture size, like 288 pixels by 352 pixels, the uncompressed stream is approximately 500Kbps! This represents a generous portion of a T-1's available bandwidth. It is also a sizeable portion of the useable bandwidth on most LANs.

Dropping the refresh rate to 15 frames per second dramatically reduces bandwidth consumption, but only marginally degrades perceivable performance. The use of sophisticated video engines, like those that offer compression "on-the-fly," can further reduce the bandwidth consumption, albeit at an increase in CPU cycle consumption.

Decreasing the number of colors recognized can also greatly reduce the size of the transmission stream. Similarly, reducing the size of the picture, as measured either in inches, pixels, or fractions of a screen (for example, full-screen, quarter-screen, eighth-screen, and so on) can also greatly reduce the transmission stream.

Unfortunately, compromises in refresh rate, color density, pixel density, and so on, effectively translate into degraded video picture quality. An overly aggressive bandwidth conservation effort can easily result in a jerky, tiny, "talking head" of a video image. This defeats the very purpose of video conferencing by failing to capture the body language and other subtle non-verbal communication that can be gleaned from face-to-face interactions.

The trick is to understand the limitations of the networking that will support the video transmissions, and strive for an optimal combination of tunable parameters that doesn't have adverse affects on the network.

Video communication includes video conferencing and streaming video transmissions. Although very similar, they have distinct functionality sets and, consequently, different network performance requirements.

Video Conferencing

Real-time, bi-directional transmissions between two or more points is known as video conferencing. The accompanying audio can be handled "in-band" or "out-of-band." In-band audio transmissions bundle the audio signals with the video signals in the same bit stream. This requires the video conferencing system to have its own speakers and microphone or to interface with those already installed in the computer.

Out-of-band audio relieves software from having to capture and play back the audio signals. It also means the video conferencing system doesn't have to synchronize the audio and video. Rather, the video conferencing system ignores the audio signals and requires conferees to establish a second communication link over conventional telephony.

Because a video conference entails a bi-directional transmission, the network interconnecting the conferenced end-points must be capable of supporting *two* separate video streams. If both conferees opt for full-screen, full-motion video and use 17-inch monitors set for 1024×768 dots per inch (dpi) resolution, most networks will be extremely hard pressed to deliver the desired level of service.

Proprietary video conferencing hardware and software bundles have been available for quite some time. Numerous transmission technologies are supported by these bundles, including ISDN at 128Kbps. Ostensibly, the controlling software is smart enough to understand the limits of the selected network, and throttles maximum quality settings accordingly.

Streaming Video

Streaming video differs from video conferencing in that it is not bi-directional. Nor does it have to be live. The streams can be either live or prerecorded, but are transmitted, multicast, or broadcast uni-directionally.

As is the case with streaming audio, streaming video does not benefit from a network protocol's ability to detect and correct errors, or resequence received packets. Rather, the packets are played back immediately upon receipt. Compared to video conferencing systems, streaming video transmission systems are fairly crude.

Although it lacks the functionality and sophistication of a video conferencing system, streaming video may be even more useful just by virtue of being more useable. Video libraries can be maintained of public events, speeches, meetings, and so on, and played back on demand.

Assuming the picture size and quality were carefully managed, the streams can be supported on as little as 128Kbps, although a vastly superior video would result from connections of 384Kbps or higher.

Summary

It is inevitable that the currently separate, and redundant, voice, data, and video communication infrastructure will eventually integrate into a single, broadband, multimedia communication infrastructure, with a common user interface and vehicle. This integration is only just beginning, and will take years to complete. It is already clear that the LAN is capable of incrementally growing into the role of multimedia communication network. In the interim, it is being used to support fledgling attempts at this degree of integration: today's multimedia applications.

Some of these applications require levels of performance that are difficult to achieve in a conventional LAN/WAN environment. For example, any of the live, interactive applications like computer and video telephony, or video conferencing, require that packets be delivered on time, in sequence, and intact! Packets that are damaged are simply discarded without generating a request to the sender for a retransmission. Similarly, packets that are delivered intact, but are delivered late or out of sequence are also discarded without requesting retransmission.

Today's LANs, WANs, and their protocols, are not well suited to transporting the time-sensitive data of many multimedia communication technologies. Contemporary networks and protocols are better suited to the transport of traditional data. They can guarantee the integrity of each packet's payload upon delivery, and are more efficient at transporting bulk data than they are at guaranteeing timeliness of delivery.

Even if the LANs have been engineered to support high-bandwidth and/or low-latency applications, WAN links can be the kiss of death. They use high-latency routers, which function at the relatively slow Layer 3 and in conjunction with relatively low-bandwidth transmission facilities (DS 1 or less). This can be a vexing problem as it is widely accepted that the business value of multimedia applications, like video conferencing, is directly proportional to the geographic distances separating the end-points. In other words, today's networks are least capable of delivering time-sensitive applications in their highest-value scenarios.

The good news is that today's data networks have the potential to evolve incrementally into a true multimedia communication infrastructure. The introduction of switching in both LANs and WANs, the development of bandwidth reservation protocols, Quality of Service protocols, increases in the network's transmission rates, and even prioritization protocols all contribute to making the network infrastructure increasingly multimedia capable. As a network designer, you must maintain a focus on the customer's performance requirements, and develop a forward-looking plan for introducing the appropriate network support mechanisms for multimedia applications.

Similar evolution of application software and hardware will complete this evolution. Until true multiple-media communication technologies are available, remember the benefits of open standards. They apply universally throughout the information technologies. Proprietary, single-function "multimedia" products, regardless of how well they perform, are likely to impede interoperability of multimedia applications.

In the Meantime...

There are, however, numerous multimedia applications that can be supported over networks today.

One example of how today's open standard components can be assembled to support a multimedia application and can be used with videoconferencing over ISDN. The recent trends toward telecommuting and virtual offices have created both near-ideal conditions and a legitimate business need for videoconferencing.

Telecommuters, particularly those in small offices or home offices, are often deprived the luxury of a dedicated leased connection (such as T-1 or fractional T-1) to the company's networked computing resources. Rather, they must use lower cost dial-up facilities. ISDN has finally found a legitimate market in providing these small offices and home offices with more robust connectivity than they would otherwise enjoy. With the right hardware, software, and drivers, telecommuters can enjoy a 128Kbps connection to other ISDN-connected users. This is more than ample to support a videoconference or even collaborative development of documents.

Using an inexpensive video camera, PC, and an ISDN connection permits these otherwise isolated workers to maintain visual contact with their managers, peers, and the like. The added benefit of this arrangement is that other company applications are not impacted. They continue to traverse the company's WAN, and are completely separate from the ISDN network. Until QoS and other network technologies mature, this approach is probably the best way to begin supporting multimedia communications without incurring any performance penalties for other networked applications.

VI
PART

Maintaining Your Network

Monitoring Your Network

by Frank C. Pappas
and Emil Rensing

IN THIS CHAPTER

Congratulations! By now you've probably become quite familiar with all sorts of networking topics, including hardware and software selection, network topologies, cabling options, and much, much more. In fact, you're probably itching to drop this book and begin planning the creation or rebirth of your own corporate super-network. But wait—you're not ready to solo just yet! *Almost.* But not quite. There are just a few more important issues that we need to cover before you'll be ready to assemble your team, call or fax hardware vendors and systems consultants, and provide a wide array of important and amazing network services for your managers, colleagues, secretaries, and interns.

The chapters that you've covered so far throughout this book have given you a number of vital tools to help you build or, just as importantly, rebuild—a corporate local- or wide-area network from the ground up. No expense has been spared; we've covered everything from the physical connections between the computers to the various protocols that allow the many different network and client operating systems to be joined together in vast heterogeneous internetworks. So, truth be told, you probably are just about ready to go out and architect a Grade-A system that would make us (and you!) proud. After all, you've put in a lot of effort reading this book from cover to cover, have invested lots of time researching vendors and their offerings, and have used all of your education, experience, and intuition to spec out a system that meets and exceeds every desire, expectation, or daydream that your techno-geek boss may once have verbalized.

However—and here's the kicker—have you stopped to consider what will happen to that magnificent creation of yours a week, a month, or a year down the road? What will you do when this testament to high-tech corporate communications begins to develop quirks or, worse yet, becomes the very nightmare it was designed to replace? Taking a good deal of poetic license with the words of an actor whom we feel can't quite act his way out of a wet paper bag: When your network begins to fall apart at the seams, "What do you do? What do you do?"

The answer itself is simple: You make sure that your network never degrades to the point that people will start asking questions (or start building a gallows). To avoid the lynch-mob, you'll need to be proactive when it comes to systems maintenance. What's more, you need to be especially vigilant when it comes to problem detection and resolution, knowing where, when, and (most importantly) *how* to look for those bottlenecks, malfunctions, and other assorted quirks that will undoubtedly develop over the life of your network, as well as how best to resolve them when they do crop up. Unfortunately, keeping abreast of every aspect of your network can be a daunting task. How do you know when there's a problem? Well, just as realtors the world over will tell you that the most important feature of any house is "location, location, location," network engineers and systems administrators have their own axiom for making sure that your networks don't get out of hand: "monitor, monitor, monitor!" This way, you can be sure that your networks will always be *preventing* headaches instead of *causing* them.

The Mother of All Network Problems

Without a doubt, a corporate network can be one of the most complex technology environments you'll ever be required to support and maintain. Of course, we're not saying that you'll never take a job over at MAE-East troubleshooting backbone problems, or that you'll never get that dream job with the Air Force connecting, via T-1 lines, all of the SAC missile silos in North Dakota. The chances are, however, that the ragged mix of state-of-the-art and hand-me-down hardware, software, and cable that you call a network is in dire need of a good dose of tender loving care. Your job, as a skilled network engineer or systems administrator, is to make sure that your network is optimally configured so that it can, well, be all that it can be.

Now, as any seasoned network administrator will tell you, when you receive a report of network trouble, there's one thing that should be done immediately: Blame the User (BTU). Ninety percent of all supposed network trouble is actually the result of users doing something they shouldn't be doing, such as installing inappropriate or uncertified software and hardware, tinkering with Registry settings, folding or yanking on the CAT5 that's running into their NIC, and other such frustrating mischief. This is especially the case when only a few workstations are afflicted by the mysterious network malady. While we'd love to give these users a good spanking or send them to bed without dinner, the BTU policy is an excellent way of simultaneously keeping your network on its toes and responding to user problems in a timely and efficient manner.

Of course, BTU won't be of much help to you unless you follow a few highly important tips. First, *never, ever* let the user know about the BTU system—they'll probably get mad and throw something hard at you (such as a monitor). Second, remember that almost all BTU-related problems are either fixed, or at least identified, within the first ten minutes or so after you've responded to the call for help. If, after the first ten or fifteen minutes, neither you nor the user can come up with even the foggiest of ideas as to why the network is acting up—or if any more than a few machines are affected—it may be time to regroup and start looking for a more pervasive cause somewhere on your server or in your spider web of hubs, routers, and cable.

TIP

If you're stumped as to the cause of a single-workstation network outage, be sure to check the cable running between the network drop on the wall and the network interface card (NIC) at the back of the client workstation. While this most likely will seem absurdly obvious, you'll be surprised how often this three-second procedure will be the answer you need. Chances are that the cable was inadvertently yanked or twisted and no longer has a good connection in one of the two sockets. If that doesn't work, try swapping in a new section of cable; every so often network wiring will just mysteriously die.

28

MONITORING
YOUR NETWORK

Things To Look For

It is of the utmost importance to remember that your network is more that just a simple collection of highly expensive hardware linked together via some fancy protocols and a bunch of wiring. The utility—and frustration—involved with modern corporate networking comes from the fact that they are such complex systems, where multiple protocols run across different hardware types, with each particular brand of hardware often hosting a unique combination of software and services. While providing a robust, reliable, and efficient networking solution for your company may seem like magic to your user community, we all know that you'll most likely lose a few nights of sleep (and some hair) in the process. Because there's a slight chance that we may end up working together in the same network operations center (NOC) one of these days, we're here to provide you with some monitoring tricks, tips, and pointers so you can effectively manage a top-notch network, keep your good looks, and (hopefully) never go crazy!

In the most general sense, there are five areas that can provide their own unique set of serious (that is, non-BTU) network problems: cable, routers and hubs, hardware, software, and operating systems. We've already covered some of these topics throughout the course of this book. Chapters 6, "Hubs," and 8, "Switches," provide a bit of information on the proper role of hubs and switches in a networked environment so you can be extra confident that you're using the right tools for the right job.

How You Can Analyze Your Network

There are a number of different methods that you will use to analyze your network. While some utilize specialized (also known as expensive) hardware and software reminiscent of an episode from your favorite science-fiction television show, there are other avenues you can explore that are anything but high-tech or prohibitively expensive. Even if you (or your company) can't quite justify spending $10,000 on the latest button-and-light–covered LAN analyzer that once graced the cover of *Network World*, take heart. While these gadgets certainly perform some wonderful tasks that help to speed up network troubleshooting, systems administrators and engineers were resolving complex network problems long before these products came to market. In other words, with a little bit of sweat and a pinch of luck, you'll muddle through!

If, however, you're still a bit unsure as to how you'll be keeping track of your network following are some rules of thumb that should be of tremendous value.

Listen to Your Users

As your first line of defense against the evils of network trouble, be sure to listen to the troops. The guys and gals on the front line (the users) are probably more sensitive to network trouble than, say, a systems administrator, programmer, or network engineer, and they're almost sure to come a hollerin' at the first sign of trouble. This is the case simply because the network administrator and other related tech-types probably spend the majority of their time working directly at the server console, not at a remote workstation at the other end of the building where problems tend to be exceedingly more pronounced. Remember that when users gripe about seemingly insignificant problems, it's still worth a few minutes of your time to investigate. BTU notwithstanding, every once in a while a user will spot something that's indicative of a budding catastrophe, and you'll be thankful that you followed up on that trouble ticket!

Listen to Your Network Operating System

As important as it is to listen and respond to the requests, gripes, and queries that filter up from the unwashed masses, it's equally important to listen to what your network operating system(s) (NOS) has to say about its impressions of network performance. Posh! Silly author, you think. How can my operating systems talk to me? Two words: server logs.

As overwhelming as they can often be, server logs are, in fact, your friends. Depending on your operating system, you'll have anything from a handful of services intermittently reporting on their status to full-blown administrative tracking systems that record every error, warning, or informative flag that is raised by the many applications, services, and hardware that comprise your network. The key here is to not only know where to look, but also *what* to look for and *how* to respond to the specific warning(s). This is a sufficiently complex enough issue to easily demand its own book. What will (hopefully) save the day is your understanding of the various components of your network, how they interrelate, and the dependencies between each service and between particular services and specific hardware. Once again, it's experience over book-learning that will separate the men from the boys when it comes to monitoring networks via system logs.

The locations and contents of these logs vary from NOS to NOS, based partially on the operating system itself as well as administrator-defined configuration preferences (most often specified at installation). On servers running any of the many flavors of the UNIX operating system, you'll find logs scattered throughout the directory structure, reporting on everything from mail services and Web traffic to disk/volume status and security information. Windows NT networks, on the other hand, offer one of the most comprehensive and easy-to-use logging tools that is provided, at no additional charge, as part of the operating system itself. The Windows NT Event Viewer monitors and records status messages from all NT services, security data, and other applications, providing a consolidated viewer to review all logs.

Beware Obsolescence!

The third major defense that you wield against the scourge of network trouble is the patch. Thanks to the poking and prodding of users and administrators around the world, it isn't long before deficiencies or omissions in operating system releases are identified and publicized. This includes the entire gamut of operating system parts, from security features to file system eccentricities to resource-hungry graphics subsystems. So that their products continue to function as advertised (and don't lose market share), many vendors, including Digital Equipment Corporation, Microsoft, Novell, Sun Microsystems, and many others, offer frequent patches (upgrades) to their operating systems to remedy these noticeable and sometimes unknown bugs. Monitoring the version numbers on your firmware, network operating system, and applications will allow you to be ahead of the curve when it comes to keeping the network running all day, every day. These patches are generally made available on the particular NOS manufacturer's Web site and are generally provided at little or no charge. You can also keep up-to-date on the newest revisions for these products by monitoring the various Usenet news groups that are relevant to your particular hardware and software.

Use Your Operating System's Native Diagnostic Tools

A common mistake that network administrators often make is that they reject, out-of-hand, the suites of diagnostic tools that are frequently integrated into, or are occasionally bundled with, network operating systems. This is more often the case with administrators running Windows NT, who are generally less than impressed with the appearance of PerfMon, the freebie Windows NT diagnostic utility. However, don't judge a book by its cover.

The reality of the Windows NT performance monitor is altogether different. While some third-party packages will include a more attractive front-end or some flashy monitoring wizards, the NT performance monitor allows you to track just about every service, application, and byte of data that passes though or around your NT network. If you spend some time learning how PerfMon does its stuff, you'll find that it is an excellent tool that can handle perhaps 80 percent (sometimes more) of your network monitoring needs, depending entirely on the size and complexity of your internetworking environment. If you are using Windows NT as your network operating system, Bill Gates and his minions in Redmond, WA have been thoughtful enough to provide you with a second set of tools—command line options—that can be used to supplement the information gathered in a Performance Monitor session. These options (such as Net statistics, Net file, Net session, and so on) can be executed at the command line to give you an instant snapshot, and control, of a variety of internetworking-related systems running on your NT server.

UNIX also provides an exhaustive set of tools and other utilities designed to help you help yourself when it comes to monitoring your network. While UNIX diagnostics may not always be as attractive or as user-friendly as you'd like, you'll be hard-pressed to find a set of standard, affordable tools that can compete with the amount of information that the UNIX monitoring utilities will provide. If you'd like, you can skip right ahead to the UNIX section and read up on some more specific information relating to UNIX monitoring.

These four steps should provide you with just about every bit of information that you'll need in order to keep a watchful eye over your network. Should things start to get a little out of control however, you can start bringing in the heavy artillery—LAN analyzers.

Using a LAN Analyzer

If, for one reason or another, the steps that we've previously covered haven't helped you solve your particular set of network problems, your next move will be to employ a dedicated LAN analyzer and cross your fingers! While LAN analyzers are most often quite expensive, they're usually more than worth their cost if you plan on maintaining anything more than a simple, one-protocol network. Because networks and internetworks are becoming increasingly complicated—running multiple protocols, supporting wider arrays of software and hardware, and providing for ultra-high bandwidth connections—sometimes the standard sets of monitoring and diagnostic tools that are included with network operating systems simply aren't up to the task. After all, these NOS-specific suites were designed to monitor a specific type of homogeneous (often single-protocol) network, not the complex, heterogeneous monstrosity that you have installed in your office.

LAN analyzers are basically network therapists. Once you've connected the device (anything from a full-blown PC to a hand-held unit) to your network, it listens to all of the information that passes between the various network nodes, taking note of a number of transmission statistics. In earlier days, LAN analyzers simply gathered this information and presented it in a predefined format via any of a number of display devices, just like the good therapist, without offering any concrete advice. At that point, it was up to the network administrator to figure out how best to interpret the data and what actions, if any, were needed in order to address the perceived problems.

Unfortunately, this passivity would only be acceptable for so long. As networks have become increasingly more complex, so too have the feature-sets of LAN analysis devices grown beyond their early and limited incarnations. Today, most dedicated LAN analysis systems require high-end RISC or x86 processors, significant amounts of memory, and quite a good deal of money. A large portion of the analysis tool market is comprised of proprietary hardware and software combinations that are often designed as portable, hand-held devices that support a variety of protocols, architectures, and network types. What's more, the growing complexity of internetworks has forced these advanced monitoring devices to incorporate the latest developments in artificial intelligence and expert systems in order to streamline the process of monitoring and troubleshooting networking issues. Not only will the most recent LAN analysis tools monitor network traffic and build reports containing nearly every type of information available, they'll also use their on-board knowledge of IEEE standards, protocol specifics, and other networking issues to offer possible avenues of action based on what *they* see as the most serious network issues.

Operating System Analysis and Tuning Tools

Although conceptually the same from network operating system to network operating system, the actual implementation of monitoring and tuning tools is quite different. This is not necessarily the result of different developers working for different software vendors who are building competing products, but from the low-level differences in the actual implementation of networking, and to some extent the other abilities of an operating system. Additionally, these tools will leverage other abilities of an operating system in the overall tool design. For example, most monitoring tools for Windows NT are full-screen applications that make use of the Windows GUI, while UNIX tools are primarily command-line tools that write to standard output or standard error. In this section, we will discuss the primary monitoring and tuning tools for both Windows NT and UNIX operating systems.

Windows NT

Windows NT networks can be fun and (relatively) easy to work with, especially when they're working according to spec. Unfortunately, when things go wrong they tend to go wrong in a big way.

THE BLUE SCREEN OF DEATH

If you ever show up to work and find one of your critical NT servers displaying some hexadecimal identifiers and a bunch of (seemingly) nonsensical letters and numbers on a blue background, be prepared for a long day. Whenever the NT kernel is critically unable to deal with hardware or software (kernel-specific) errors, Windows NT will come to a halt and display this blue screen and the associated characters, which actually are providing some clues as to the cause of the crash. Your first step is to reboot the machine via the power switch. You can ignore the specific characters on the screen if the problem goes away after your reboot. If the machine blue-screens again, however, take note of the characters and get in touch with your support representative.

A lot of times such problems will be related to NT as an operating system, exclusive of its role as a part of your greater network. This will include file system problems, interrupt conflicts, print failures, and other hardware hiccups. However, based on your system and network configuration, you may find that NT isn't performing as well as you'd like as the brain of your network, or is perhaps failing altogether. In cases where NT's networking functions are involved, there are a number of monitoring tools at your disposal that you can use to resolve network trouble.

Event Viewer

The Windows NT Event Viewer hasn't changed much over the years. This three-tiered system records System, Security, and Application event information for later analysis. System events occur when a driver fails during operation or cannot load at boot time. The Security log tracks login attempts and other security information, allowing you to detect and repel possible attacks. Finally, the Application event log will capture any information from NT-based applications, from third-party Web servers to database or communications software.

Network Monitor

As one of the most exciting additions to the tools suite of Windows NT 4.0, the Network Monitor provides what at one time was only available as a third-party application or as part of an expensive LAN analysis hardware package. The Network Monitor provides a host of network statistics, from frames, broadcasts, and multicasts detected to adapter-specific traffic data. You are able to run in either normal or dedicated capture modes and can save the data for later analysis.

Performance Monitor

The Performance Monitor is a graphical tool that allows you to measure the performance of nearly every aspect of your Windows NT network operating system, including the server and remote workstations. The Performance Monitor will also provide charting, reporting, and alerting services to inform you if and when predefined performance levels are reached, such as %Processor Time, Packets Transmitted/sec, and so on.

Remote Access Administrator

If you are providing remote access (RAS) services for your network and trouble arises, your first stop should be at the Remote Access Administrator. The Remote Access Administrator will provide a quick view of your overall RAS status, including: available and busy ports, inbound and outbound byte and frame rates, CRC, time-outs, framing, hardware, buffer errors, and identification data for the remote workstation.

Server Manager

The Windows NT Server Manager is a resource that will allow you to administer Windows NT domains, as well as settings on specific computers. You can view a list of users connected to certain machines, view machine-specific resources (shared and open), control directory replication, configure services, and broadcast alert messages to connected users. Additionally, you can manage primary domain controllers (PDCs) and backup domain controllers (BDCs), synchronize servers with the PDC, and add or remove machines from the NT domain.

28

MONITORING
YOUR NETWORK

Built-In Diagnostics

The built-in suite of NT diagnostics named, aptly enough, Windows NT Diagnostics, provides a comprehensive look at the configuration and environment variables that your NT box is currently using, in any of nine categories, including: Version, System, Display, Drives, Memory, Services, Resources, Environment, and Network. The category tabs will provide you with the following information:

> Version—OS version and build numbers, 20-digit registration number, and personalized registration data
>
> System—HAL type, BIOS type and version, and types of processor(s)
>
> Display—BIOS date and type, current settings, memory, chip and DAC types, and driver-specific data
>
> Drives—Access to and information on all drives connected to the machine
>
> Memory—Pagefile space, physical and kernel memory, handles, threads, processes, commit change totals
>
> Services—All installed services and their current states (running, stopped, paused)
>
> Resources—IRQs, Buys number and type for all devices attached to the server
>
> Environment—Processor type, architecture, level, and revision; Windows Path; OS
>
> Network—Four categories of data: General (access rights, workgroup/domain name, LAN root), Transports (type, address), Settings (time-out values, read-ahead, buffers, and so on), and Statistics (bytes sent/received, cache, failed reads, and so on).

Internet Service Manager

With the recent addition of the Microsoft Internet Information Server as an integral part of the Windows NT network operating system, Microsoft has added the Internet Service Manager as a front-line tool for managing NT-based Internet services running on boxes located anywhere on your local area network.

The Internet Service Manager allows you to easily access any local Windows NT servers providing HTTP, FTP, or Gopher services, view their current status (running, stopped, paused), and reconfigure specific service properties in response to current or anticipated network trouble. While ISM monitoring functions are fairly limited, they can, when coupled with the ability to remotely start, stop, and configure net services, be a godsend for systems maintenance!

NT Networking Hotspots

There is an almost endless number of subsystems that work in concert to provide the robust networking environment that we have come to know as Windows NT. However, when it comes to NT networks, there is a number of very important features of which you need to be made aware. Once you know where they are and what to look for, you should have a much easier time trying to resolve latency issues and other performance bottlenecks.

Monitoring the NT hotspots will always require you to use the NT Performance Monitor (PerfMon). While you'll usually end up complementing your PerfMon analysis with other monitoring tools, PerfMon is generally the best and most enlightening place to begin your investigations. Depending on the services and other additional features that you have installed with your NT server or workstation, you'll have your choice of monitoring a number of PerfMon objects, including: browser, cache, FTP Server, HTTP Service, ICMP, IP, Memory, NetBEUI/ NetBEUI Resource, Network Interface/Segment, Paging File, Physical Disk, Process, Processor, RAS Port/Total, Redirector, Server/Work Queues, System, TCP, Thread, and UDP. While each of these factors can contribute to the success or failure of your network at a particular moment, it is important to pay special attention to a minimum of four objects. While these four objects can vary, depending on your specific configuration, they can be broadly categorized into: default network protocol, interface hardware, memory, and server.

During the course of preventative or responsive troubleshooting, you should remember to monitor the default network protocol that connects your various nodes. In some cases this can be achieved through a combination of the TCP and IP objects, or perhaps as a function of the NetBEUI object. Collisions, byte and packet rates, time-out values, and other important information can be examined and evaluated based on ideal and/or anticipated performance levels.

Interface hardware deals with the state of your current host adapter and its overall performance in terms of sent and received packets, errors, queue length, and so on. You can (and should) rely on this object to help you determine when network outages are the result of an improperly configured NIC, adapter failure, or even bad CAT5.

Memory, quite simply, will provide performance data for the currently installed system memory, including read and write errors, faults, copies, available memory, and so on. You can use this object to determine whether network services are being degraded by faulty memory (indicated by high numbers of errors/faults), insufficient memory (large paging files and frequent disk access), or an improperly configured Paging File.

The server object is the last central object to which you'll immediately turn for signs of network trouble. You can measure everything from permission and system errors to additional data on the status of available physical memory. Also, the Bytes Total/Sec. value can provide invaluable data as to how busy a particular machine is under different circumstances (especially useful for file servers) and can be of great help when trying to perform load-balancing calculations.

UNIX

For the most part, network troubleshooting in the UNIX world will focus on TCP/IP, which is a communications protocol, and NFS, which is a network file system. In addition, you must be constantly aware of the implementation of the rest of your network infrastructure, which is an additional source of potential problems. Every decision you make in building your infrastructure will affect the capacities and capabilities of your network. Your inability to send heavy traffic across your network can be detected using many different monitoring tools (not just

28

MONITORING
YOUR NETWORK

those found on UNIX systems) but the source of your problem may lie elsewhere—not in the hardware of the systems that are dropping the data packets.

The majority of networks in the world today with UNIX systems attached are based on 10base-T, twisted-pair Ethernet technologies. Although 10base-T is usually thought of as a 10Mbps medium, the actual speed of the network that can be used by applications is usually significantly less. Even with the tightly integrated networking features within the UNIX operating system, it is not uncommon for UNIX hosts on 10base-T networks to see realized speeds of only 4Mbps. At first look, you might think that 4Mbps is still enough speed to function. However, that number can continue to shrink as your network grows. As actual demand begins to exceed capacity, all the users on your network will know it, even if they are running UNIX. In addition, it only takes one system on an Ethernet network to bring an entire network to a grinding halt. Continually transferring large files across the network is just one example of an activity most any user can perform that will have an impact on your network performance. Remember, as with any of the other resources on your systems, network capacity is a resource you may run out of.

UNIX users, however, have an additional advantage in the world of network monitoring. They have very powerful and informative tools built into their operating system. With a little instruction from you, users can quite easily detect capacity problems. A quick comparison of the execution times of simple commands executed locally versus the execution times of simple commands executed using rsh, for example, can indicate that your network has problems.

Before we begin talking about detailed network monitoring, let's do a quick test to make sure you are connected to a network. To do this, you need to know the name or IP address of a second machine on the network. You will use the `ping` command to send a single packet to a remote system and time how long it takes the remote system to send the packet back to you. In its simplest form, `ping` (shown in Listing 28.1) accepts a machine name or IP address as its command line parameter. In the example in Listing 28.1, the host `dole` cannot seem to find `whitehouse`, another host on the network.

Listing 28.1. An unsuccessful `ping`.

```
dole % ping whitehouse
ping: whitehouse: Unknown host
```

In the event that resolution of the second system fails using a name, try using an IP address (see Listing 28.2).

In this example, `dole` has found `whitehouse` using its IP address and is sending and receiving data 100% error free. `ping` will keep sending data until you break the loop by pressing Ctrl+C.

Listing 28.2. A successful ping.

```
dole % ping 198.137.240.92
PING 198.137.240.92 (198.137.240.92): 56 data bytes
64 bytes from 152.163.41.3: icmp_seq=0 ttl=254 time=8 ms
64 bytes from 152.163.41.3: icmp_seq=1 ttl=254 time=2 ms
64 bytes from 152.163.41.3: icmp_seq=2 ttl=254 time=1 ms
64 bytes from 152.163.41.3: icmp_seq=3 ttl=254 time=2 ms
----198.137.240.92 PING Statistics----
4 packets transmitted, 4 packets received, 0% packet loss
round-trip min/avg/max = 1/3/8 ms
```

Monitoring Using spray

spray is a UNIX command used to deliver a burst of data packets to another machine and report how many of the packets made the trip successfully and how long it took. Similar in scope to its little brother ping, spray can be used more effectively to monitor performance than ping because it can send more data. The results of the command, shown in Listing 28.3, will let you know whether the other machine was able to successfully receive all of the packets you sent.

In the example shown in Listing 28.3, a burst of data packets is being sent from the source machine (dole) to the destination machine (clinton).

Listing 28.3. Using spray to monitor your network.

```
dole % spray clinton
sending 1162 packets of lnth 86 to clinton ...
        no packets dropped by clinton
        5917 packets/sec, 508943 bytes/sec
```

In the example above, the destination machine (dole) successfully returned all of the data sent to it by the source machine (clinton). If clinton were under heavy load, caused either by network traffic or other intense activity, some of the data packets would not have been returned by clinton. spray defaults to sending 1162, 86-byte packets.

spray supports several command line parameters, shown in Listing 28.4, that you can use to modify the count of packets sent, the length of each packet and the number of buffers to use on the source machine. These parameters can be helpful in running tests that are more realistic.

Listing 28.4 shows the spray command used with the -c option, which delivers 1,000 packets, and the -l option, which sets each packet to 4096 bytes.

Listing 28.4. Using variable packet counts, spray can be used to more closely simulate realistic network traffic.

```
dole % spray -c 1000 -d 20 -l 4096 clinton
sending 1000 packets of lnth 4096 to clinton ...
        no packets dropped by clinton
        95 packets/sec, 392342 bytes/sec
```

28

MONITORING
YOUR NETWORK

Simulating network data transmissions with spray can be made more realistic by increasing the number of packets and the length of each packet. The -c option will let you increase the total count of packets that is sent and the -1 option lets you set the length of each packet. This can be helpful in mimicking certain transmission protocols. The -d option is used to set the delay between the transmission of each packet. This can be useful so you do not overrun the network buffers on the source machine. Listing 28.5 shows what a problem might look like. In this case, the source machine (dole) overwhelms the destination machine (carter) with data. This does not immediately indicate that a networking problem exists, but that the destination machine (carter) might just not have enough available processing power to handle the network requests.

Listing 28.5. spray can be used to isolate failing network hardware.

```
dole % spray -1 4096 carter
sending 1162 packets of lnth 4096 to carter ...
        415 packets (35.714%) dropped by carter
        73 packets/sec, 6312 bytes/sec
```

In the event that your tests with spray result in packet loss, your next step would be to take a closer look at the destination machine you have been testing. First, look for a heavy process load, memory shortage, or other CPU problems. Anything on that system that might be bogging it down can cause degraded network performance. In the event that you cannot find anything wrong with your test system that might be causing a delayed network response, sending a similar test back to your initial test machine might indicate a larger network problem. At that point, it is time to start checking your routing hardware and your infrastructure with the analysis hardware.

Monitoring with `netstat`

The simplest way to check the network load on a particular system is to use the netstat command. When executed without any command-line parameters, the command displays a list of active sockets for each protocol. Listing 28.6 shows the output of netstat running on a Silicon Graphics Indy workstation. In this example, the host dole has several open connections. The only potentially problematic entry in the list is the connection from the system named dukakis. However, because it is a modem connection, the depth of the send queue is expected to be slightly higher.

Listing 28.6. Using `netstat` to monitor active network connections.

```
dole % netstat
Active Internet connections
Proto Recv-Q Send-Q  Local Address          Foreign Address          (state)
tcp        0      0  dole.telnet            reagan.431025            ESTABLISHED
tcp        0      0  dole.telnet            nixon.9031               ESTABLISHED
tcp        0      4  dole.telnet            dukakis.ppp.1036         ESTABLISHED
tcp       56      0  dole.1060              ftp.watergate.ftp        CLOSE_WAIT
tcp       52      0  dole.1799              news.washngtnpost.nntp   CLOSE_WAIT
```

In the standard `netstat` report, the only field that is significant in your monitoring operation is the Send-Q, which is reporting on the depth of your network send queue, that is the amount of data in bytes that is waiting to be sent (or received if you are looking at the receive queue). If the numbers in your send queue for connections across a particular network segment are already large and getting larger, that particular network is probably inundated with excess traffic. If single entries are appearing with high send queue entries, it is possible that there is a problem with the particular host.

Perhaps the quickest way to determine the integrity of your network—are packets reaching their destination as quickly as they can—is by using `netstat` with the `-i` command line parameter. All of the systems attached to a particular segment of your network share it. When more than one client or server system attempts to utilize the network at the same time, a collision occurs when the packets from one machine meet the packets from another. This is actually not an uncommon condition on most networks; however, when the number of collisions becomes a significant percentage of all of the network traffic, you will start to see performance degradation. In addition to collisions caused by simultaneous broadcast on the network, various other extenuating conditions might cause errors in transmission or reception of data. Faulty hubs, malfunctioning interfaces, or even other electromagnetic fields from devices not physically connected to a network (such as motors for the elevators in a building) might be to blame for high rates of packet collisions. As the number of collisions and other errors on your network increase, the performance of the network degrades.

When used with the `-i` command-line parameter, `netstat` will report on how many packets each of the network interfaces in your system has sent and received and whether the number of errors and collisions is anything to be concerned about. Listing 28.7 shows a `netstat` report for all of the adapters in `dole`. As you can see, `dole` is on a very high-traffic network, and has seen many collisions since it was last rebooted. However, because the number of collisions is less than 2.25% of all packets sent, this network is not really saturated with traffic. If the percentage of all packets sent were constantly in the double-digits, you probably have a problem with network traffic.

Listing 28.7. Using `netstat` to monitor individual packet and error rates for each network interface.

```
dole % netstat -i
Name Mtu   Network    Address      Ipkts     Ierrs  Opkts     Oerrs  Coll
ec3  1500  207.221.40 dole         45223252  0      953351793 0      21402113
lo0  8304  loopback   localhost    2065169   0      2065169   0      0
```

Table 28.1 shows the values of the output from the `netstat` command.

Table 28.1. The information returned by `netstat`.

Value	*Data*
Name	The name of the network interface (naming conventions vary among UNIX)
MTU	The maximum packet size of the interface
Net/Dest	The network that the interface connects to
Address	The resolved Internet name of the interface
Ipkts	Number of incoming packets since the last time the system was rebooted
Ierrs	Number of incoming packet errors since the last time the system was rebooted
Opkts	Number of outgoing packets since the last time the system was rebooted
Oerrs	Number of outgoing packet errors since the last time the system was rebooted
Collis	Number of detected collisions

TIP

Cheat sheet for interpreting the results of a `netstat -i` command:

- The number of input packet errors (`Ierrs`) should never be more than 0.25% of all input packets (`Ipkts`) for a particular adapter. If that is the case, you probably have a network that is extremely saturated with traffic.

- If the number of output packet errors (`Oerrs`) is anything but 0, you may have a hardware problem with that particular adapter. You should monitor that interface a bit more carefully.

- If the number of collisions (`Collis`) seen by a particular interface continually is greater than 5% of all the packets that it sends (`Opkts`), that is an indicator that your network may be on its way to becoming highly saturated with traffic. The obvious sluggishness of network performance should also be another indicator.

In the previous example, you see that the percentage of collisions detected on the network is less than 2.25% of all the packets sent. As discussed earlier, if collisions were continually in double digits, your network is probably suffering from a capacity shortage. Also of note in the previous example is the input to error and output to error ratios. Both are insignificantly low, which is another indicator that the network that `dole` is attached to, as well as the system itself, is functioning normally.

If you suspect that network problems are to blame for your degraded system performance, you should repeat this command often. Active, healthy systems will have input and output packet counts that are continually on the rise. If Ipkts increases and Opkts does not, your system is probably not responding to all of the requests it receives, indicating that your system may be overloaded or is having transmission problems. If the number of input packets never increases, your system is not receiving any network data.

When the -s command line parameter is used with the netstat command, statistical log information associated with each of the supported components of TCP/IP is displayed. In Listing 28.8, IP, ICMP, IGMP, TCP, and UDP are displayed in the output of netstat -s as it is executed on dole.

Listing 28.8. The output from the netstat -s command.

```
dole % netstat -s
ip:
        41887 total packets received
        0 bad header checksums
        0 with size smaller than minimum
        0 with data size < data length
        0 with header length < data size
        0 with data length < header length
        0 with bad options
        0 fragments received
        0 fragments dropped (dup or out of space)
        0 fragments dropped after timeout
        39820 packets for this host
        4240 packets recvd for unknown/unsupported protocol
        0 packets forwarded  (forwarding enabled)
        2067 packets not forwardable
        0 redirects sent
        84436 packets sent from this host
        0 output packets dropped due to no bufs, etc.
        0 output packets discarded due to no route
        36140 datagrams fragmented
        175925 fragments created
        0 datagrams that can't be fragmented
icmp:
        24 calls to icmp_error
        0 errors not generated 'cuz old message was icmp
        Output histogram:
                echo reply    : 4
                destination unreachable : 24
        6 messages with bad code fields
        0 messages < minimum length
        0 bad checksums
        0 messages with bad length
        Input histogram:
                echo reply    : 8
                destination unreachable : 4230
                echo    : 4
                time exceeded    : 2
        4 message responses generated
igmp:
        0 messages received
        0 messages received with too few bytes
```

continues

Listing 28.8. continued

```
              0 messages received with bad checksum
              0 membership queries received
              0 membership queries received with invalid field(s)
              0 membership reports received
              0 membership reports received with invalid field(s)
              0 membership reports received for groups to which we belong
              6 membership reports sent
tcp:
          28744 packets sent
                  14789 data packets (8274385 bytes)
                  34 data packets (10276 bytes) retransmitted
                  8351 ack-only packets (6314 delayed)
                  0 URG only packets
                  5 window probe packets
                  3975 window update packets
                  1591 control packets
          25848 packets received
                  3973 pcb cache misses
                  10891 acks (for 8261734 bytes)
                  1048 ack predictions ok
                  307 duplicate acks
                  0 acks for unsent data
                  20905 packets (8099738 bytes) received in-sequence
                  12465 in-sequence predictions ok
                  65 completely duplicate packets (37613 bytes)
                  4 packets with some dup. data (174 bytes duped)
                  628 out-of-order packets (423912 bytes)
                  2 packets (2 bytes) of data after window
                  2 window probes
                  46 window update packets
                  49 packets received after close
                  0 discarded for bad checksums
                  0 discarded for bad header offset fields
                  0 discarded because packet too short
                  0 discarded because of old timestamp
            826 connection requests
            50 connection accepts
            790 connections established (including accepts)
            871 connections closed (including 41 drops)
            82 embryonic connections dropped
            11120 segments updated rtt (of 11337 attempts)
            67 retransmit timeouts
                  0 connections dropped by rexmit timeout
            0 persist timeouts
            387 keepalive timeouts
                  0 keepalive probes sent
                  1 connection dropped by keepalive
udp:
          9728 total datagrams received
          0 with incomplete header
          0 with bad data length field
          0 with bad checksum
          24 datagrams dropped due to no socket
          38 broadcast/multicast datagrams dropped due to no socket
          0 datagrams dropped due to full socket buffers
          9666 datagrams delivered
          55475 datagrams output
```

When looking at the overall statistics, you should pay close attention to the checksum fields. They should always show extremely small values. If they are large, that indicates that your network is handling extremely large amounts of traffic.

Running `netstat -s` on your original destination system (that is now targeted at your source system), in combination with `spray` on your source system, can help you determine whether data corruption caused by faulty hardware or network traffic caused by high demand is to blame for your degraded network performance. If you see similar numbers in the count of packets lost between systems, chances are you are faced with a network integrity problem. If you see packets being lost only on one system, you should begin to examine your hardware more thoroughly.

> **TIP**
>
> If your tests with `netstat -s` and `spray` lead you to believe that you have a network integrity problem, you can verify this by running `netstat -i` on your destination machine.

Monitoring with `nfsstat -c`

NFS is an extremely powerful tool. It gives users an easy way to share files among UNIX systems by mounting directories on remote volumes as local drives. With this power also must come increased responsibility and education. Users should be taught how to appropriately use NFS volumes. It is important to point out that things will be generally slower when accessing files across the network using NFS, especially if the file is large. Accessing the same file directly on the remote machine by using a remote login will result in an operation that will execute in a more timely fashion. However, certain functions such as editing and copying files that are of a more reasonable size is perfectly fine—that is what NFS was designed for. Your users should be very careful when using NFS and they should know how to use it appropriately. That is how you can best monitor NFS performance on your network.

For those who need an actual tool, `nfsstat` is just what the doctor ordered. `nfsstat` is used to display communication statistics between NFS clients and servers. The `-c` command line parameter is used when you wish to display client statistics and the `-s` command line parameter is used to display server statistics.

> **TIP**
>
> If you feel the need to reset the counters used by `nfsstat`, try executing the command with the `-z` command line parameter. This may be useful when attempting to determine when a particular error condition occurred. Remember that the NFS counters can only be reset by root.

NFS is based on synchronous procedures commonly referred to as RPCs. RPCs, or Remote Procedure Calls, allow the client making the call to wait for successful completion of the operation on the server that is handling the request before continuing. If the server fails to respond to the RPC, the client will simply transmit the request again. Remember that, when dealing with network communication in general, as the communication between systems degrades due to packet collisions, traffic on the network will increase. In addition, as we all know, the more traffic that exists on the network, the slower the network will perform and the greater the possibility of having even more collisions increases. So if the NFS re-transmission count is high, you should look for servers that are functioning under heavy loads, high collision rates that are delaying the packets sent between clients and servers, or Ethernet devices such as routers, hubs or interfaces that are simply dropping packets. Listing 28.9 shows sample output from the nfsstat command when used with the -c option. The client data displayed shows a healthy use of NFS. Pay close attention to the ratio of time-outs to calls.

Listing 28.9. Sample output from the nfsstat command when executed with the -c parameter.

```
bush % nfsstat -c
Client rpc:
Calls      badcalls      retrans      badxid      timeout      wait      newcred
➡timers
231893     0             101          0           101          0         0         122
Client nfs:
Calls      badcalls      nclget       nclcreate
229114     0             229114       0
null       getattr       setattr      root        lookup       readlink     read
0   0%     16038   7%    1    0%      0    0%     2930   1%     0    0%      1456  0%
wrcache    write         create       remove      rename       link         symlink
0   0%     210784 92%    176  0%      1    0%     0    0%      0    0%      0    0%
mkdir      rmdir         readdir      statfs
0%      0  0%         322  0%      12   0%
```

The output from the nfsstat command shows the following values:

Table 28.2. What nfsstat shows you.

Data returned by nfsstat	Description
calls	Number of calls sent by a client
badcalls	Number of calls rejected by the NFS service
retrans	Number of re-transmissions made
badxid	Number of duplicated acknowledgments received
timeout	Number of service time-outs
wait	Number of times no client handler was available on the server

Data returned by `nfsstat`	*Description*
`newcred`	Number of authentications that were automatically refreshed
`timers`	Number of times a time-out was reached
`readlink`	Number of times a symbolic link was read/resolved on an NFS server

If the ratio of time-outs to calls is high, you may have found a problem with either an over-worked NFS server or a larger problem with your network. Either the packets are delayed in reaching their destination or the NFS server is unavailable to handle the request being made by the client. In the example above of the system named `bush`, there are very few time-outs in relation to the number of calls being made by the client to the NFS server. As the number of time-outs grows toward 5% of all calls being made, it will become time for you to act. If the number of duplicated acknowledgments received by a client is approximately equal to the number or re-transmissions being made, the problem probably lies with an over-burdened NFS server. If the number of duplicated acknowledgments received is much smaller than the number of re-transmissions being made and/or the number of time-out conditions being reached, it is logical to assume that you have a problem with your network that is causing the requests to be sent again.

Summary

Monitoring your network from other operating systems can be a little bit more of a challenge. Networking is not as "integrated" to most other operating systems the way it is under Windows NT and UNIX. The standard distributions of most other operating systems do not contain protocol stacks, nor do they contain analysis tools. Therefore, it may be more difficult for you to find software tools to deliver the analysis features you are looking for.

There are many commercial and public domain monitoring tools available for MS-DOS, Microsoft Windows, IBM OS/2, or the Apple MacOS that will track the number of packets sent and received. Additionally, there are tools that report on the percentage of output packets that result in a collision as well as tools to historically track the results of network performance.

America Online users can find may such network utilities in the Computing & Software channel, or you can search for them directly at Keyword: FileSearch. If you do not have access to America Online, or would rather find things on the Internet, clnet maintains a large database of links to many large, popular FTP sites around the world at `http://www.shareware.com` and `http://www.download.com`.

Administering Your Network

by Phillip T. Rawles

IN THIS CHAPTER

CHAPTER 29

Network administration is a multifaceted area. Unlike other network functions, network administration focuses primarily on what happens after the network is installed. While it is true that administration tasks and issues must be considered in the design and implementation phases of a network installation, administration is primarily an operations issue.

This chapter focuses on the basic network administration tasks and functions common to all networked systems. Although the functional implementation of administrative tools varies among network operating systems (NOSs), each NOS provides a means of accomplishing these basic administrative functions. In this chapter, tasks are arranged in the order that an administrator installing a new network operating system would typically need to address them.

Network Administration Functions

Network administration tasks include installing and configuring network workstations, creating and maintaining user accounts, backing up the system, distributing software across the networked workstations, and providing end user support. Each of these tasks serves a specific purpose in the administration of a networked system. However, one task can have an impact on several other tasks. In order to gain insight into how these tasks are interrelated, they are commonly grouped into functional areas. The International Standards Organization (ISO) Network Forum has divided network administration and management tasks into five basic functional areas: Fault Management, Configuration Management, Accounting Management, Performance Management, and Security Management.

Fault management is the process of locating and correcting network problems. A fault is defined as any anomaly that adversely affects network operations. Common faults include broken network wiring, disk errors, and memory failures. The fault management process begins when a suspected fault is reported. An analysis of the reported symptoms is performed to identify the problem. After the problem is identified and defined, the root cause of the fault situation must be isolated to ensure that proper corrective action can be taken.

Fault management is an exercise in troubleshooting. Some problems are easily identifiable, but others may be caused by the interaction of several factors. Even for those problems that have a single cause, the troubleshooting process can be difficult if the problem is intermittent. Once the root cause of the problem is identified, the administrator can take corrective action.

Fault management is the most important network administration task. Without proper fault management procedures, network administrators can find themselves spending all of their time trying to keep the network functional. By implementing good fault management procedures, network administrators can reduce the amount of time spent "firefighting," freeing them to focus their efforts on improving network operation and performance.

Configuration management is the process of gathering information from the network and using that data to manage and optimize network devices. Common configuration management tasks include the assignment of network addresses to network devices and maintaining an up-to-date inventory of equipment installed on the network. Configuration management is a prerequisite function to performance management.

Accounting management is the process of managing the use of network resources. Basic accounting management tasks include the creation and maintenance of user accounts and groups and the assignment of access rights to users and groups. Ensuring that adequate network resources are available to network users and documenting the usage of such resources is also an accounting management function.

The activities associated with maintaining and improving network speed, responsiveness, flexibility, and adaptability are collectively known as *performance management.* Typical performance management tasks include system tuning, overall capacity planning, and performance troubleshooting.

Networked systems allow for information to be distributed rapidly throughout an organization. Although networking allows productivity gains and quicker information access, it creates the possibility of sensitive information being destroyed or accessed by unauthorized personnel. The process of protecting against such events is known as *security management.*

Network Address Management

One of the first tasks that you must perform when you install a new network is the assignment of network addresses to the stations on the network. Although this is technically a network installation task, maintaining a list of addresses and making changes in station configurations over time is a network administration function. Before considering the various methods available for network address assignment, let's consider the role of network addresses.

Each station on a network requires an address that uniquely identifies it to the other stations on the network so that messages can be addressed to it. Fortunately, such an address is automatically etched on each network interface card (NIC) by the manufacturer. This address, called the media access control (MAC) address or physical address, consists of 16 hexadecimal digits. The first eight digits represent the manufacturer of the NIC, and the last eight digits are assigned in succession, much like a serial number. A network may contain network interface cards from various vendors that were manufactured at various times, thus yielding a near random list of MAC addresses. Although each address is unique, you have no logical means of determining which station is at which address or how to get to that address.

To illustrate the problem, consider a small town of 50 houses. Each house has a unique house number consisting of random digits assigned to it, such as 579432467. The letter carrier for this town has several letters to deliver. However, all they have to identify the destination is the house number. How can they locate the correct house without driving down every street until they happen upon it?

In order to make the houses easier to identify, it would be helpful to assign each house a logical address that provides more information to the letter carrier. Logical location numbers arranged in ascending numerical order combined with street names (such as 121 Wood Street) would make it significantly easier for the letter carrier to find the correct house. After finding the house by this logical address, the letter carrier could verify the physical house number with the address on the message to ensure that the letter is being delivered to the correct location.

Just like the letter carrier in this example, networks use logical addresses to identify stations and facilitate the delivery of messages between networks. These logical addresses are commonly referred to as *network addresses*. Just as a street address consists of a street name and a house number, a network address consists of a network number and a station number. The network number uniquely identifies the network segment the station is on, and the station number uniquely identifies the station on that segment.

Each network protocol uses its own logical network addressing scheme. In the case of IPX, the network number and station number are handled separately. For TCP/IP, the network number and station number are run together into a single IP address. The IP address is parsed by looking at a second parameter called the subnet mask.

IPX

Network address assignment for networks based on the Internet Packet Exchange (IPX) protocol typically requires little administrator intervention. Each network segment is assigned a network number at the server. Most network operating systems randomly choose a network number, although the network administrator always has the option of assigning a specific number to a network. Station number assignment is performed automatically at boot time by the network operating system.

IP

Network address management for networks based on the Internet Protocol (IP) is significantly more involved. Rather than having separate network numbers and station numbers, the IP protocol combines both into a single composite IP address. The network address and station address portion of the IP address are determined by consulting a key that indicates which part of the composite address represents the network address and which part represents the station address. Both an IP address and a subnet mask are required for two stations to communicate through the IP protocol.

If the two stations are located on separate network segments, a third parameter is required to provide a means of internetwork communication. This third parameter is the default gateway, sometimes referred to as the default router or gateway router. The default router represents the door from one network to other networks. The default gateway is similar to the out-of-town slot at the post office. If a station wants to send a message to a station on another network, it sends it to the default router.

Unlike IPX, the IP protocol does not automatically assign any portion of the composite IP address. All configuration parameters must be assigned by the network administrator. You can assign configuration parameters manually or through one of two automated methods: the bootstrap protocol and the dynamic host configuration protocol.

The bootstrap protocol (BootP) was the first method developed to automate the IP configuration process. The basic procedure used by BootP is as follows: At boot time, the station makes a broadcast message to the network and asks if anyone has IP configuration information for it.

A BootP server located on the same network segment examines the MAC address of the requesting station and consults a table of known MAC addresses. If the MAC address is in the server's table, the server returns the IP configuration parameters associated with the MAC address to the station. If no server answers the station's request, the BootP process fails and the station is unusable until an alternative address assignment method is successful.

The bootstrap protocol is a static addressing protocol. Each station on the network always gets the same IP configuration parameters, barring action by the network administrator. The static nature of BootP requires that an IP address be reserved for the exclusive use of every network device that might connect to the network. There is also no automatic check performed by the BootP server to ensure that the administrator has assigned functionally correct IP configuration parameters.

> **NOTE**
>
> The static nature of BootP can be limiting in modern computing environments. Laptop computers that are only occasionally connected to the network require a network address to be reserved for them at all times. Because there are a limited number of network addresses available on a network segment, this can artificially limit the number of stations that can be connected.

Another shortcoming of BootP is the administrative workload required. Whenever a new network device that requires configuration through BootP is placed into service or a device is moved to a new network, the administrator must edit the address records on the BootP server containing the MAC address of the affected device. Because the BootP protocol uses a station's MAC address for identification, replacing a network interface card in a station requires the BootP server to be updated to reflect the new MAC address associated with the station.

In order to solve these problems with BootP, a new automatic IP address assignment strategy was developed. The dynamic host configuration protocol (DHCP) provides a means of dynamically assigning IP configuration information. The operating premise of DHCP is that a station will once again send a broadcast message to the network asking for configuration information. Upon receipt of the request, the DHCP server checks to see if it has a static address defined for the requesting MAC address. If it does, it returns the predefined IP configuration parameters for the requesting MAC address. If there is no static address defined, the DHCP server will select an address from a list of available addresses and return it to the requesting station.

The dynamic address returned by the DHCP server is called a *lease address* because it has a time limit associated with it. The requesting station can only use the leased address for a certain period of time (commonly 72 hours). At the end of the lease, the station must contact the DHCP server and request an extension to the lease. By using dynamic address assignments, the number of IP addresses required is limited to the number of available physical network connections rather than being artificially limited to the maximum number of devices that could require connection to the network. The amount of administrator overhead required to manage the server is also reduced because new stations no longer require modification to the server.

> **NOTE**
>
> Even if a DHCP server is used for IP address assignment, there are certain types of stations that should be mapped to static addresses. In general, all servers should be assigned static addresses. Network operating system file and print servers, database servers, and any Internet servers such as FTP servers or HTTP (World Wide Web) servers all fit into this category. Dynamic addresses should be reserved for use with client stations. However, because most stations on a typical network are clients, there is a considerable benefit to the use of dynamic addressing.

IP Name Services

The IP address is the address used by the network to route messages from one station to another, but most stations have alphanumeric names that are used by the users to identify them. The hostname is used at the local level as a means to identify a station in a manner easy for humans to remember. These names (commonly referred to as hostnames or domain names) are immediately resolved to their IP addresses by the local workstation for use by the network.

Just as in IP address assignment, there are static and dynamic methods for resolving domain names to IP addresses. The first method developed for host name resolution is the Domain Name Service (DNS). The Domain Name Service is a static mapping of host names to IP addresses. When a user enters a destination host name, the station asks the DNS server for the IP address associated with the host name. Upon receipt of the destination IP address, the station sends the message to the destination station. Due to the static nature of DNS, it can only be used when network stations have static IP addresses obtained through manual configuration, BootP, or DHCP in static mode.

At this time, there is no open standard for handling host name resolution for dynamically assigned IP addresses. In order to facilitate the use of dynamic IP addresses in Windows networks, Microsoft developed a proprietary protocol called the Windows Internet Name Service (WINS). In a WINS environment, each station contacts the server at boot time and gives the server its IP address and host name. The server then consults this dynamic table when asked for the IP address for a specific host name. Due to its dynamic nature, WINS can be used with any IP address assignment method. Stations with statically assigned IP addresses will always provide the same information to the DHCP server.

The Internet Engineering Task Force (IETF) is currently working on an open standard for dynamic IP address host name resolution. The project, tentatively called Dynamic DNS, aims to add support for dynamically assigned IP addresses to the existing DNS standard. Microsoft has pledged to support Dynamic DNS in place of WINS upon completion of the new standard.

User Accounts and Authentication

The first computers were only capable of running one operation at a time. In order to use the system, you had to be sitting at the computer's console. From the system's perspective, everyone at the console was the same user.

This single-user approach contradicts the basic fact that different people have different computing needs. They need access to different files, applications, and varying rights to the system's configuration. Without the ability to distinguish between users, the system cannot provide for such varying needs. This leads to basic concerns in terms of data security and ease of use.

If the payroll system runs on the same physical computer system as the maintenance system, there needs to be a way to ensure that maintenance personnel do not have access to the payroll system and that payroll personnel do not have access to the maintenance system. It is equally important to ensure that both the payroll and maintenance personnel do not have access to the system's configuration information unless they happen to be the system administrator.

In order to meet the varying needs of the people using the system, the concept of user accounts was developed. Accounts refer to the capability of a computing system to differentiate between various people using it and to customize the information and the way information is presented to the user. Although the system may still only support one user at a time, it can grant access to files, applications, and configuration information based on profiles associated with each user account. This section details the issues associated with implementing and maintaining user accounts.

User Identification

In order for a system to distinguish among users, there must be a unique means of identification for each user. This identification method serves as the computer system's means of knowing who is accessing the system and what system resources they are able to access. There are many possible means of identifying users, but the most common technique is the use of a string of characters known as the User Identification Code (UID).

User Identification Code requirements vary from system to system, but they usually consist of a single string of characters with a maximum length. The longer the UID becomes, the harder it is to remember and the easier it is to mistype. For this reason, it is good administrative practice to set a maximum UID length even if there is no limitation from the network operating system. A common maximum length for user identification codes is eight characters.

There are several approaches to assigning user identification codes. For large systems or accounts that are used only for a finite period of time, such as class accounts in an educational environment, administrative overhead can be greatly reduced by assigning arbitrary codes such as "abc123." Although codes of this type are easy to create and manage, they are not descriptive.

For long-term user accounts, a code based at least in part on the user's name has the advantage of being easy for both the user and system administrator to remember. This is especially important in systems where UIDs are used for electronic mail because users must know each other's code to send mail. For a small departmental system, the user's first name can be used. However, problems can arise when there is more than one person requiring access to the system with the same first name. What if there are two Freds in the department? For this reason, first-name–based UIDs are too ambiguous for most systems. A more formal method of user identification must be developed.

There are two commonly used user identification strategies based on combinations of the user's first and last names. The first strategy is to take the user's last name and append their first or first and middle initials to it, yielding a user identification code that is easily associated with its owner. This approach has the additional benefit of providing easy alphabetical ordering by last name. However, problems can arise if last names are longer than the maximum number of characters allowed in the user identification code. For instance, John Allen Smith might easily resolve to `smithja`, but Herbert James Gaither-Weiss creates problems. Should Herb's UID be `gaitherh` or `gaithewh`? Another problem with this method is that it is difficult to determine where the last name stops and the first initial begins. For instance, the UID `fells`, which belongs to Sheri Fell, might be thought to belong to Sheri Fells.

Another strategy is to use the first and middle initials of the user's name combined with however many characters of the last name will fit within the user identification code length guidelines. Assuming an eight-character UID limit, John Smith would become `jasmith` and Herb Gaither-Weiss would resolve to `hjgaither`. This approach is easier to remember, although the resulting user identification codes are no longer alphabetized by last name.

Regardless of the algorithm you use to develop user identification codes, it is imperative to use it consistently. This is especially important if the resulting user identification codes are going to be used for electronic mail. By providing a consistent strategy, both users and administrators will be able to easily determine UIDs of other users.

Passwords

The second part of user authentication is proving to the system that the user is who he or she claims to be. The most common means of providing this assurance is by using a password. If good password rules are implemented and steps are taken to ensure users follow these rules diligently, passwords can be a very effective means of user authentication.

The main problem with implementing effective password security is combating human nature. People typically use a password only a few times daily. This may not be often enough to readily memorize the password. Because of this, people have a tendency to choose passwords that are easy for them to remember. Unfortunately, passwords that are easy for them to remember are also easy for someone else to guess. Commonly used passwords that provide low levels of security include names of family members or pets, birthdates, and special interests such as a favorite sports team.

The key to implementing effective passwords is to use rules that combat this predisposition and require the passwords that are chosen to be secure. Password rules should reflect the environment and the importance of the resources being protected. Rules protecting a bulletin board system can and should be less stringent than rules protecting a company's research and design information.

Many strategies to increase password effectiveness are included in most network operating systems. The most effective rule for increasing the effectiveness of a password is to institute a minimum password length greater than six characters. In general, the longer the password is, the lower the chances of its being compromised by someone looking over a shoulder and catching it as it is typed into the system. Most network operating systems can define a minimum password length.

Similarly, the longer a password is used, the higher the probability that it may be compromised. Forcing periodic password changes can reduce the risk of a password being stolen or restore security to an account that has had the password compromised. Unfortunately, if password changes are required too frequently, users will have a hard time remembering their new passwords. A nice balance of security and user needs is to require password changes be limited to no more than once every 30 days. Once every 90 days is a good rule of thumb for most systems. Most network operating systems can force periodic password changes.

> **TIP**
>
> If periodic password changes are implemented, the system should be capable of remembering the last few passwords used and disallowing their reuse. This prevents a user from simply alternating between two passwords, effectively negating the benefit of periodic changes. Although this feature is not common in network operating systems, some UNIX systems and database systems provide this capability.

Another means of increasing password effectiveness is to require mixed case or the use of nonalphabetic characters in the password. By using capitalization, you can make a fairly short password more secure, especially if the capitalized letter comes in the middle of the password rather than at the beginning. Another highly effective password rule is requiring a punctuation mark to be included in all passwords.

A good password construction strategy is to combine two short words separated by a punctuation mark. You can enhance the security of this technique by including mixed case, yielding a password such as baT$boot. This is especially effective if the words bear no particular relationship to each other. The capability to force mixed case and special characters in passwords varies among network operating systems, although most will provide at least one of these options.

Although these strategies greatly increase password effectiveness, the best password rules will not prevent unauthorized access if the user does not take an active role in securing and valuing her password and the information it protects. Common sense items such as not writing passwords down and not giving passwords to others are all too frequently ignored. In the long-term analysis, user education is the most important component determining overall password effectiveness.

Groups and Access Control

Many users share common requirements in terms of applications and data access. One of the most effective administrative strategies is to create groups of people that share common needs and provide access based on the group rather than the users in the group. You can create a group of users that contains all members of the accounting department who need access to the payroll system. As each user in the group inherits the rights of the group, you can grant access to the system to the entire group at one time.

This approach also increases overall system security by providing consistency for all members of the group. If the access needs of the group changes, the administrator can make the change in one place rather than changing each user on an individual basis. New users requiring access to the system gain all the appropriate rights by simply being added to the group, and users who no longer need access can simply be removed from the group.

Although the use of groups eases administrative overhead, there is at least one case when it is not appropriate. Each user should have a home directory to which he has exclusive access. Some network operating systems provide the capability to prevent the system administrator from gaining casual access to a user's home directories. Administrators can still gain access to home directories by changing the security profile, although such action leaves a security trail for the owner of the directory. This capability helps prevent network administrators from unknowingly accessing sensitive information stored in personal directories.

Disaster Prevention and Recovery

No one wants to think about network disasters. However, it is a network administrator's responsibility to take action to ensure that the organization can continue to function in the event of a disaster. Creating an effective disaster prevention and recovery plan is complicated by the sheer number of potential disasters. The catastrophic failure of a network component, earthquakes, tornadoes, and acts of terrorism such as the World Trade Center bombing are all examples of network disasters.

Regardless of the nature of the disaster, the primary objective of disaster prevention and recovery is to minimize the period of time that information services are not available to the organization. Taken to its logical extreme, the best option is for the users to not realize that a disaster has taken place.

Uninterruptible Power Supplies

The most common cause of system failure is damage caused by electrical power fluctuations. Electrical power fluctuations have many causes, ranging from surges to lightning strikes to brownouts caused by overburdened circuits during the air conditioning season.

Regardless of the cause of power fluctuations, they pose a serious risk to network equipment. The simplest method of protecting against damage from high voltage electrical spikes such as lightning strikes is to install surge protectors. However, surge protectors cannot supply power to devices in the event that electrical power is lost, resulting in improper system shutdown cycles. Failure to properly shut down network servers and equipment can have disastrous repercussions on system functionality, especially if they occur during system upgrades or backup procedures.

In order to prevent system damage from line surges, brownouts, and blackouts, the use of uninterruptible power supplies (UPS) is required on all servers. The most basic type of UPS passes the incoming power directly to the attached devices while monitoring for power failures. In the event of a power failure, the device is switched to battery-supplied power. This type of UPS is best used for workstations or network communications equipment.

Advanced units constantly supply power to the devices from the batteries, which are constantly charged by the incoming power. This type of UPS is preferable for server installations because it provides better protection from power fluctuations while effectively eliminating the time lag and potential cycle flux resulting from the change from line power to battery power. Regardless of the type of UPS selected, it must be carefully sized to ensure it is capable of providing adequate power to the attached devices. The use of undersized units will result in lower than expected runtime and potentially "dirty" power.

Power protection systems that protect servers and other complex systems should also provide a means of communicating to the device they protect. This communications capability allows the protected device to realize that it is running off battery power and to shut itself down properly prior to exhaustion of the battery. Most UPS devices are equipped with an RS-232 serial communication port that provides this capability. The device being protected must have a compatible communication port and must be capable of running a service that constantly monitors the communications port and notifies the system of updated conditions in the UPS system. All modern network operating systems support such services either from the operating system itself or from third-party drivers that commonly ship with the UPS system. Some advanced systems also provide a means for the system connected to the UPS communications port to inform other devices that might be powered through the UPS of its condition.

System Backup

The data on most networked systems is far more valuable and difficult to replace than the systems themselves. It is this inherent value of data that makes modern information systems economically feasible. The most important part of disaster prevention is providing a means of protecting this information through system backup. In order to recover from a failure, you must have a good system backup to recover. The first step in implementing an effective backup program is to determine what data you need to back up and how often it needs to be backed up. Some data is fairly static and might only need to be backed up on a monthly basis, whereas other data is changed on a minute-to-minute basis and may need to be backed up every few hours to ensure system stability upon restoration.

Some common examples of data types and their typical backup schedules are as follows: System configuration files and applications typically are updated very rarely and only need to be backed up when they are altered through administrative action. User files are changed more often and should be backed up at least once every working day.

The best time to back up these files is during night hours when the system can be secured to ensure that there are no open files that would not be saved on the backup. A good time to schedule daily backups is 2:00 a.m. This is late enough that most users who might be working overtime have completed their work and early enough to complete the backup process before users who come in early arrive.

Database files containing vital operating information are constantly changing and should be backed up every few hours. Database applications pose another issue in terms of system backups. The files associated with the database application are always open while the application is in service. Therefore, a file-based backup system will not be able to save these files as they are already open by another application. In order to solve this problem, a specialized piece of software, known as a backup agent, is used to interface with the database management system and provide access to the data.

There are three basic types of backups: full, differential, and incremental. As its name suggests, a *full backup* is a backup of all files regardless of whether they have been changed since the last backup. A *differential backup* saves only those files that have been changed since the last full backup, whereas an *incremental backup* saves only those files that have been changed since the last backup of any type.

Each backup type presents different issues in terms of restoration. If the most recent backup is a full backup, all that needs to be done to return the system to operation is to restore the full backup. If differential backups are used, the last full backup must be restored followed by the last differential backup. In the case of incremental backups, the last full backup must be restored followed by each incremental backup taken since the full backup in the same order they were saved.

Several different media options are available for system backup including floppy disks, Zip drives, and writable CD-ROMs. However, for network backup purposes, the best solution is magnetic tapes. Available in several different formats, these tapes can hold in excess of 10 gigabytes at a cost of a few cents per megabyte of capacity.

Common tape formats include quarter-inch tape (QIC) and digital tape. Quarter-inch tape equipment is typically designed to work on the computer's floppy diskette bus, yielding performance that is relatively slow compared to the digital tape alternatives. For this reason, quarter-inch tape should only be considered for use in workstation or peer-to-peer network backup. The actual QIC tape media is also significantly more expensive than that of digital tape, yielding a higher operating cost.

Digital tape systems differ from quarter-inch tape in several important areas: The tape drive hardware is typically designed to work on a small computer system interface (SCSI) bus, yielding significantly faster data transfer rates than quarter-inch tape. Digital tape formats also offer higher capacity than QIC tapes at a lower per tape cost.

There are two basic digital tape formats: 4mm and 8mm. Four millimeter tape systems are based on Digital Audio Tape (DAT) standards, whereas 8mm tapes are based on 8mm video tape standards. At the current time, 4mm tape is the more common media with several manufacturers manufacturing tape drives compliant with the standard. Exabyte Corporation is the only current manufacturer of 8mm tape systems. Regardless of the type of digital tape used, data grade media should always be used, and tape drives should be cleaned on a regular basis to ensure data reliability.

> **TIP**
>
> Regardless of the type used, magnetic tape is not errorproof. Just as floppy disk drives and hard drives can develop errors, backup tapes are susceptible to data loss. In order to guard against such data loss, the contents of a backup should always be compared against the actual data immediately after the tape is written. The network administrator should check the backup logs on a daily basis for errors or other anomalies that could indicate that the backup set is not complete.

It is also important to rotate tapes to ensure that if a single tape fails, there is another backup set to restore. The most basic tape rotation technique is to simply use each tape once and archive it. Although this has the advantage of ensuring that all data ever backed up is available, it requires a significant investment in tapes and greatly increases media storage requirements.

Another technique primarily used for single servers or small departmental networks is to rotate at least two tapes on a weekly basis. Each tape begins with a full backup followed by daily incremental or differential backups for the remainder of the week. Although this technique eases restoration concerns because all backup sets are on the same tape in the order they were taken, up to a full week's data is at risk in the event of tape failure. If this technique is used, it is recommended that the last tape each month be kept for at least a year for archiving purposes.

A more comprehensive technique commonly used in larger networks is known as the Grandfather, Father, Son tape rotation method. In this technique, a different tape is used for each day of the week that a weekly backup is not performed. For an organization that backs up every night, there would be six daily tapes labeled by day of the week. There would also be three tapes that are rotated each week on the seventh day of the week. These three tapes are labeled one, two, and three. On the day of the last weekly backup of each month, twelve tapes are rotated. These tapes are labeled for the month they are used. This technique provides an automatic archiving method to save data for up to a year as part of the standard tape rotation procedure.

> **TIP**
>
> Regardless of the tape rotation technique used, it is important that proper maintenance be performed on the tape system. Tape drives should be cleaned on a periodic basis per manufacturer's specifications. Tapes should be periodically replaced as they approach the upper limit of their expected service life as defined by the tape manufacturer.

Another area of concern is the location of the backup system. The most common approach on small departmental networks is to locate the tape drive in the primary file server. By installing the tape drive in the server, you can copy data to the tape drive at system bus speeds. Besides being much faster than copying the data across the network, this technique has the advantage of not impacting available network bandwidth.

However, placing the tape drive in the file server creates a greater demand on the server's processing and data bus capacity. In addition to serving files to the network clients, the server must also run the backup software. Another potential downside to this approach is the risk of a total system failure in the event of a failure in the backup system. If a tape drive fails, it could bring down the entire system with it, effectively creating the type of catastrophic system failure against which it was meant to protect.

A second approach is to place the backup subsystem in a client workstation. This approach isolates the backup devices from the file servers, effectively eliminating the chances of crashing the servers during the backup process. A backup agent may be required on the network server to allow the client-based backup system to read configuration information and other special files. Another issue with this approach is that it places a high demand on network bandwidth. If you use this approach, you should schedule backups for a time when there are few users on the system.

A third approach is the implementation of specialized backup hardware. Designed for the express purpose of backing up enterprise networks, these systems provide fast, reliable system backup capabilities for all devices on the network. However, these solutions are usually quite expensive and are best implemented when a centralized backup point for multiple servers is required.

Dealing with Faults

Regardless of the amount of care you take to ensure that the system is running properly, faults will always occur. Components such as hard drives, memory, and power supplies are the most common sources of system faults. The key is to minimize the service interruption caused by the failure of these components. The best-case scenario is if the failure of a component can be dealt with by the system automatically in a manner such that the user does not notice that a fault occurred. Systems that provide such capabilities are referred to as being *fault tolerant*.

The most basic level of fault tolerance is to implement redundant systems (also known as hot backups). Redundant systems consist of at least two devices, a primary device to routinely perform the required function and at least one secondary device to monitor the primary device and take over if a fault occurs. Examples of redundant systems are backup routers and duplicate network lines.

Redundant systems typically lend themselves to devices that are static in configuration. Another obstacle to redundant systems is cost. Implementing redundant systems typically more than doubles the cost of implementing a single system due to the instantaneous monitoring requirements.

For those devices that are mission critical, but difficult to duplicate, such as file servers, subsystems that may be prone to failure should be identified and duplicated. This practice is referred to as *redundant subsystems*. A common implementation of redundant subsystems in network servers is in hard disk arrays.

Redundant Arrays of Inexpensive Disks (RAID) is a system that uses several physical hard drives clustered to provide a single logical drive to the network operating system. The data stored on the individual drives is mirrored on other drives so that in the event of the failure of an individual drive, the data remains accessible. Most RAID subsystems include the capability to remove and replace drives in the system while the system remains online. When a drive fails, it can be replaced, and the system will automatically replace the data that was on the failed drive from the copy on the other drives.

Other examples of fault-tolerant subsystems include multiple power supplies and error–code-correcting memory systems. These fault-tolerant subsystems allow the overall system to remain highly available even if a fault occurs. However, it is imperative that the system administrator consistently monitor the systems to ensure that they are working properly. If a power supply fails and the system switches to a backup unit, the failed unit needs to be replaced as soon as possible for the system to remain fault tolerant.

As you might expect, fault-tolerant systems are expensive and should only be used when the opportunity cost of the system being out of service long enough for repair exceeds the cost of the fault tolerant system. Fault tolerance is usually reserved for mission-critical servers and network hardware such as routers and bridges. Individual workstations are usually not candidates for the application of fault-tolerant equipment.

There are usually several devices that, although mission critical, are not candidates for redundancy for one of the reasons already listed. These devices may be candidates for warm backups (also known as warm swaps). Warm backup refers to the practice of keeping a backup device on hand. If a device fails, a technician replaces the failed device with the backup device to restore service as quickly as possible. Examples of devices that are good candidates for warm backup consideration include network concentrators and bridges. Warm backups are especially cost-effective because a single warm backup device can back up several production devices.

Regardless of whether a device is fault tolerant, when a fault occurs, the affected device must be repaired. There are two repair options: on-site and off-site. On-site repair can either be performed by personnel from within the organization or by a third-party service provider under service contract. When looking for service contract providers, be sure to analyze response time to ensure that the service provider can accommodate your needs. Off-site repair is most commonly used for specialized devices such as concentrators and low volume printers. If an off-site repair strategy is selected for a device, ensure that adequate backup hardware is available to allow time for shipping in addition to the time required to repair the device.

Software Administration

One of the most time-consuming activities associated with network system administration is the management of application software. Whereas the host-based systems that preceded them used a central application program, today's personal computer network-based systems distribute software throughout the stations on a network. Maintaining some degree of consistency in such a distributed system poses a serious network administration challenge.

Software Metering

Software license fees represent a large investment for an organization. Although volume purchases and site license agreements can reduce costs, license fees can still exceed $1,000 per workstation. Fortunately, most license agreements limit the number of copies that can be run concurrently rather than the number of workstations capable of running the software.

It is highly unlikely that every workstation on a network will be running the same application at any given time. Therefore, minimizing software license fees becomes an issue of determining the maximum number of concurrent licenses required to meet the organization's needs and limiting the number of workstations that can run the application concurrently to the number of licenses available.

Software metering systems provide these capabilities. Metering packages specifically include the capability to determine the number of workstations accessing an application and a means of preventing workstations from accessing an application when the number of licenses is eclipsed. All metering packages work on server-based applications, and some can be configured to meter client-based software as well.

Software metering packages are available from a number of vendors for most network operating systems. Implementation methods vary, although solutions that are wholly server-based are preferable to solutions requiring an agent on each client due to the added complexity and management requirements of an agent-based system.

Software Distribution

The key to easing management of a personal computer software base is to centralize the software. Whenever possible, install software to a file server. This provides a greater measure of consistency across the network and a single point for software maintenance. Installing and configuring software to run from a file server was once an art form. Fortunately, most software developers now provide applications that are capable of running from a file server or at least are network-aware.

When installing a server-based application across a network, use a two-part process. First, you must install the application files to the file server. For small applications, you can accomplish this by simply copying them to a directory on the server and setting appropriate file permissions to allow execution on the client workstations. Larger applications may include a specialized server installation mode that automatically configures the software for a server-based environment.

Second, after you install the software on the server, the client workstations must be configured to run the server-based software. For simple programs, this can be as straightforward as creating a shortcut to the application's executable file on the server. More complex applications may require specific files, such as dynamic link libraries (DLL), to be housed locally on the workstation. In that case, the appropriate files must be marked and copied. Some network-aware applications provide a workstation installation program that automatically configures the workstation to run the application from the server. Always check the application's installation documentation to see if such a mode is supported before beginning installation.

Regardless of whether a client installation program is available, manually configuring each workstation can be a time-consuming task. Although you can complete the installation of an application across a departmental network containing a few workstations in a relatively short period of time, the same cannot be said of an enterprise network containing several hundred or even thousands of workstations. In addition to being time-consuming, manual configuration is also error-prone, especially if there are several people configuring workstations.

In order to reduce the time required and propensity for errors associated with manual client installation, a means for automating client installation is desirable. The first means of easing the burden of software installation is creating scripts to automate manual tasks. Some client software installation programs can also be configured to take input from a script file, thus removing the burden of entering configuration information from the administrator installing the software.

Taking advantage of such scripting techniques can reduce the time and likelihood of error, but an administrator must still physically visit each workstation, execute the script, and test the installation. This represents a serious investment of resources, time, and money in large organizations. Imagine having to send someone to install software on 5,000 workstations located in 12 buildings in 10 different cities. Later in this chapter, in the section titled "Network Management Platforms," I discuss solutions that will assist in further automating software management.

Software Audits

One of the least appealing responsibilities of a network administrator is auditing the software contained on client workstations. Due to the distributed nature of network workstations, it is

29

ADMINISTERING
YOUR NETWORK

difficult to determine what versions of which software packages are installed. This presents a significant issue when new software is required. Is the other software on the workstations compatible with the new software? Can upgrade versions of the software be installed, or must completely new licenses be purchased? A network administrator needs quick accurate answers to these types of questions.

The difficulty of answering these questions is compounded by employees who have installed personal software on their workstations. Most personal software is designed to run on standalone computers rather than on networked workstations. Installation into a networked environment can create software incompatibilities and render the workstation unusable until a network administrator can repair the damage. Even if the software presents no compatibility issue, it consumes system resources such as hard drive space.

Although the potential of personal software to degrade workstation performance is of considerable importance, there is a larger issue involved with the installation of personal software. By installing software on a corporate workstation without a license for the software, the user is placing the company into a software license noncompliance situation. This problem is magnified by the human desire to share. If a single user in the accounting department gets a new screen saver for Christmas, half the accounting department could be running illegal software by New Year's Day.

Software license noncompliance or software pirating is a serious issue. The Software Publishers Association (SPA) investigates corporate software license with relentless efficiency. If an organization is found with illegal software, the minimum penalty is a fine equal to the purchase price of the illegal software coupled with an order to remove the offending software. If the software in question is required by the business, they must then purchase legal copies of the software. Many network administrators have lost their jobs over software license noncompliance issues.

To ensure that these issues are properly addressed, a network administrator needs a comprehensive audit of software installed on all workstations on the network. In order to provide such a comprehensive listing of software on a large network in a practical manner, some means of automatically querying the workstations is required. Such capabilities are included in most network management platforms.

Network Management Platforms

To assist in the management of distributed networks, a new type of network management tool has been developed. These new tools represent a comprehensive approach to providing management tools for the maintenance of distributed network systems. Designed to work in a distributed environment, these tools utilize a manager/agent approach. A central manager coordinates the activities of agent software installed on each client workstation.

Network management platforms provide a wide range of functions. As already mentioned, they provide a means of installing software rapidly onto distributed workstations. In order to gain the maximum benefit of this capability, the structure of each workstation's hard drive should be identical. The agent must know where to find and place each file associated with the software being installed. Without such consistency, the effectiveness of a network management platform is seriously compromised.

Another major functional area of management platforms is the capability to gather and store configuration information from the network workstations. In addition to automatically performing application software audits, network management platforms include the capability to report a wealth of information about a workstation's hardware, such as

- The type of network card installed in the system
- Interrupt and I/O port usage
- Memory installed in the system and its current usage
- Amount of disk space installed and the amount of free disk space
- Video card type, supported modes, and current mode
- Processor type and speed
- Communication port availability and configuration

By collecting and analyzing this information, you can make software upgrade decisions from a more informed perspective. A network administrator preparing for a major upgrade could easily identify which workstations are not adequately configured to support the new software. By using this information, you can make accurate projections of the amount of funding required to upgrade the hardware to support the software.

Management platforms also include several functions to improve the efficiency and quality of user support. Real-time communications sessions (commonly called chat sessions) can be launched between administrators and users to discuss user problems. In a typical chat session, the screen is divided into two sections: one for the user's input and one for the administrator's input. This feature is particularly valuable to organizations that have workstations located in branch offices that would otherwise incur a long-distance telephone fee to contact.

Most network management platforms also include the capability to interact with the remote workstation through a command prompt. Administrators can check configurations, remove or add files, or launch programs directly over the network, without traveling to the location of the workstation. It is even possible to remotely reboot workstations to activate changes made in configuration files.

Taking the concept of remote access one step further, some network management platforms include the capability to control the remote workstation. Remote control differs from a remote command prompt in that in a remote control scenario, the network administrator sees the exact same screen as the local user. Both the user and administrator can enter characters into the system or use the mouse in graphical user environments. This capability allows the user to show the administrator the exact symptoms of the problem. The administrator can then perform problem resolution activities remotely and show the user how to operate the system properly.

> **NOTE**
>
> Remote control can present a serious security concern. You must take care to put procedures into place that prevent network administration personnel from connecting to remote workstations covertly and "eavesdropping" on users as they work. Ideally, a remote control program would announce to the user on the remote workstation that someone wants to share control of their workstation and give the user the ability to accept or deny the request. However, some commonly available packages do not include this capability, so you should be careful when selecting a package.

Network management platforms usually include capabilities to manage network devices such as hubs, switches, and routers. Although this capability is beyond the scope of this chapter, it is an important feature in an internetworked environment.

Network Security

The process of protecting data and equipment from unauthorized access is collectively known as network security. The importance of implementing good network security procedures is highlighted when you consider the ramifications of not taking such precautions: data can be accidentally or intentionally erased from the system; a competitor can gain an unfair advantage by accessing confidential data; and the use of network resources can be lost, yielding a corresponding loss of productivity.

It is the role of network administration to take preventive action to ensure that the risk of such losses is minimized. However, care must be taken to balance the reduction of security risks against the ensuing loss in ease of use and availability of the networked systems. Security procedures and system flexibility are diametrically opposed concepts. Every step taken by a network administrator to prevent unauthorized access creates another step that an authorized user must take to gain access to the data. It is important to analyze each system on a network and place appropriate security restrictions on an individual basis.

Security Threats

The first step in evaluating security risks is to determine the threats to system security. Although the term network security has been commonly categorized as protecting data and system resources from infiltration by third-party invaders, most security breaches are initiated by personnel inside the organization. Organizations will spend hundreds of thousands of dollars on securing sensitive data from outside attack while taking little or no action to prevent access to the same data from unauthorized personnel within the organization.

Although the media commonly present exotic tales of espionage through computer systems, most information theft occurs through traditional means. Even when the source of the threat is an outside force, the instrument is usually in the form of an inside operative. From the perspective of an outside entity wanting to gain access to sensitive information, it is usually much easier to find an employee who is willing to help than it is to attempt to break into the target company's systems. The compromised employee can usually gain access to the data more rapidly than an outside attack could yet is considerably more difficult to trace.

The most common scenario for information theft is disgruntled employees or employees who are leaving the organization. Whenever an employee resigns or is released, immediate action should be taken to protect information assets to which the employee might have had access. Their computer accounts should be disabled. If it is not possible to disable the employees' accounts, security rights should be re-examined to ensure that the risk of a security breach is minimized. Passwords to any administrative accounts the employee might have had access to should be changed immediately. Many ex-employees report being able to access data at their old firms for years through accounts that were never secured after their departure.

Systems administrators and database administrators present an even larger security risk. By necessity, these employees have greater access to data and systems than any other user. For this reason, it is best if systems administration is performed by at least two people rather than a single administrator. Whenever there are multiple administrators, the likelihood of detecting improper administrative action is increased greatly.

It is also a good practice to create users and grant them administrator rights for daily systems administration rather than using the administrator account itself. The password for the administrator account should then be sealed and placed in a safe location. If all other administrator access level accounts are disabled for some reason, the administrator account will still be available and can be used to restore access to the system.

Although internal threats represent the majority of security threats, a significant number of threats originate from outside the organization. Hackers, competitors, vendors, and government agencies have all been known to attempt unauthorized access to computer systems.

The threat from hackers has been largely overstated. Individuals who fit into this group have more of a Robin Hood mentality than a destructive mentality. Most hackers, or crackers as they prefer to be called, are more interested in the thrill of breaking into the system than they are in causing damage once they succeed in gaining access. Unfortunately, there is an increasing trend for hackers to be employed by other entities as an instrument to gain access to systems.

As the amount of critical data stored on networked systems has increased, the appeal of gaining access to competitors' systems has also increased. In highly competitive industry segments, an entire underground market exists in the buying and trading of product and sales data. By gaining access to research and development information from a competitor, millions of dollars and years of research can be eliminated.

Another external threat is that of government intrusion, both from the domestic government and from foreign governments. Agencies such as the Federal Bureau of Investigation and the Internal Revenue Service can have vested interests in gaining access to critical tax and related information. Foreign governments are especially interested in information that could represent an economic or national defense advantage.

Network Operating System Security

Regardless of the source of the threat, there are several measures you can take to increase the security of a network operating system. The first step is to physically secure all network equipment. If you can lock it up, lock it up. Servers, hubs, and switches should always be installed in a location that provides physical security to prevent tampering and unauthorized access to the network.

It is equally important to educate users on the importance of maintaining security and basic security techniques. Concepts as simple as not leaving workstations that are logged into the network unattended can be overlooked if the employee does not think about the ramifications of his actions. Anyone who has physical access to these unsecured systems by extension has access to the data stored on the host system. This problem is exacerbated if the workstation in question is located in an open office or cubicle-based environment.

Educating network users to log off the system or to lock their workstations when not at their desk can greatly reduce the security risk. Some operating systems allow the use of screen savers that automatically lock the workstation after a few minutes of inactivity. This can be a powerful tool to force users to adhere to good security practices.

> **NOTE**
>
> An organization that spends several hundred thousand dollars on the latest firewall technology may not even think about protecting against data being copied onto floppy diskettes or laptop computers. This is the easiest method for transporting stolen data. To reduce this risk, many organizations are now removing floppy drives from workstations or installing drive locks that prevent the floppy drive from being accessed by the user. This approach has the added benefit of reducing the risk of a workstation contracting a virus from a contaminated diskette.

Firewalls

Although the majority of network security threats come from within the organization, there is a growing threat of outside infiltration. This threat is greatly increased by connection of private networks to public networks such as the Internet. In order to reduce the risk of outside parties gaining access to a private network, you can install a firewall.

As the name suggests, a firewall is a network security device that blocks certain data from coming through. There are three basic types of firewalls: packet filters, circuit-level gateways, and application gateways. Packet filters, also known as router firewalls, limit the types of packets that can pass through the firewall. In this manner, communication through the firewall can be limited to specific session types. For instance, a packet filter can allow e-mail (SMTP) packets to pass through but prevent file transfers (FTP) from occurring.

Circuit-level gateways provide greater flexibility than packet filters. Like packet filters, a circuit-level gateway can limit the types of packets that can pass through the firewall. However, a circuit-level gateway works by stripping the network layer header and footer from the incoming packet and replacing it with a version appropriate for the other side of the firewall. In this way, a circuit-level gateway can connect private IP networks to the Internet without re-addressing the private network to Internet standards.

Application gateways provide the best security because stations inside the firewall and those outside the firewall never actually communicate with each other. The outside station sends a message to the application gateway, which reformats and retransmits the message to the destination inside the firewall. Unlike packet filters or circuit-level gateways, both workstations view the firewall as the final destination of the network traffic.

Regardless of the firewall technology implemented, one of the most common misconceptions in network security is that a firewall solves all network security concerns. A firewall merely represents a first line of defense. Just as warring factions create multiple lines of defense, a network administrator should ensure that proper security measures are taken inside the firewall.

Remote Access Security Considerations

One of the fastest-growing areas of network computing is that of remote access. Sales representatives, technical support personnel, and telecommuters all require access to centralized network resources from remote locations. These communication links are usually made through the public telephone network. Unfortunately, extending the corporate network to remote locations through the public telephone system represents a large security risk.

To reduce the security risk of remote access, several safeguards should be implemented. Use a communications protocol that provides encryption for user identification codes and passwords. For example, the Point-to-Point Protocol (PPP) should be used whenever possible rather than the Serial Line Internet Protocol (SLIP).

To maintain system security, passwords should never be stored in local password cache files, especially on portable computers. Although password caches have the benefit of reducing the time required for a user to access data on the network, they effectively bypass all security if a computer falls into the wrong hands. A thief who steals a laptop in an airport could simply plug the computer into a telephone, tell it to dial the preconfigured number, pass the stored password to the server, and have access to the system.

Another means of providing additional security is to implement call-back rather than dial-in.

In a call-back environment, the user calls the server and instructs the server to place a call to the workstation to initiate the remote access session. The server can be configured to always return the call to a specific phone number or have the user enter a number to place a return call.

For remote users who attach to the network from a consistent location, such as telecommuters, the remote access server should be configured to place the return call to a predefined telephone number. For mobile users, call-back offers a means to create a log of locations and phone numbers from which the user is accessing the system. This log can then be scanned in real time for any nonstandard locations. Another advantage to a call-back implementation is the potential to reduce toll charges by originating the call at the central site rather than in the field.

Viruses and Other Computer Parasites

Viruses and other computer parasites represent a huge productivity threat to organizations regardless of size. Experts estimate that the loss of productivity resulting from computer virus infections is measured in billions of dollars annually.

A *computer parasite* is any program or task that destroys data or prevents a computer system from being used as intended. Computer parasites range from the benign, such as the Stoned virus that displays a message to the user of an infected computer about legalizing marijuana, to the extreme, such as the Hari virus that destroys all data stored on a system.

There are three major types of viruses. *Boot sector viruses* attach themselves to the system code of the infected system. The first type of virus to be developed, boot sector viruses always reside in the infected system's memory and are fairly easy to detect and remove from a system. Examples of boot sector viruses include Stoned and Michelangelo.

File infectors attach to executable files rather than the system's boot sector. Therefore, file infectors affect system performance only when the infected file is resident in memory. This can make detection and removal of file infectors more difficult than boot sector viruses. Examples of file infectors are Vienna, Jerusalem, Dark Avenger, and Frodo.

The latest virus threat comes from *macro viruses*. Unlike other virus types that are transmitted through the infected executable programs, macro viruses are hosted in documents. Although the manner of infection differs, the result of a macro virus infection can be just as destructive. In some respects, macro viruses represent a larger threat as they attack data files rather than executables. Although executable files can be easily replaced by reinstalling the affected software, documents are irreplaceable unless they have been backed up onto other media.

As use of the Internet expands, another virus threat is emerging. World Wide Web browsers are evolving to include new technologies designed to increase the capability of browsers to perform application tasks. These technologies provide an automatic means for executable software, commonly referred to as applets, residing on a server to be downloaded to the local workstation and executed automatically when a link is pressed. Many times, the user is not aware that the applets are being installed on the workstation. As these technologies continue to mature, a means of ensuring that their capabilities are not used for destructive purposes is an industry-wide concern.

Virus hoaxes, although not technically a computer parasite, can represent as much of a threat to productivity as real viruses. The best known virus hoax is the "Good Times" virus. The hoax consists of an electronic mail message stating that a new computer virus has been developed that can destroy the contents of a hard drive simply by opening an electronic mail message with the subject line Good Times. In the spirit of helpfulness, users forward the "warning" to all of their friends and coworkers, thus overwhelming network resources in the process of perpetuating the hoax.

In addition to viruses, the field of computer parasites includes Trojan horses and worms. *Trojan horses* are viruses or other destructive programs that are masquerading in the guise of application software. The user launches what she thinks is an application, and the parasite is unleashed. *Worms* are programs that attack memory rather than files. A typical worm infection results in tasks being launched until the system becomes so overloaded that it ceases to function effectively. Fortunately, worm attacks can usually be cured by shutting down and restarting the affected system.

The best defense for computer parasite attacks is a good offense. Rather than waiting for an infection to occur, and then taking steps to remove the infection, you should take preventive action to ensure that the risk of infection is minimized. The most important preventive measure is the implementation of sound system and user policies:

- Make all system and executable files read-only. Although some viruses can change the read-only file attribute, new operating system implementations counteract this threat by providing a means of preventing applications from changing file attributes.

- Limit the use of floppy diskettes whenever practical. Locks that prevent the use of diskette drives are now on the market for under $20. As previously mentioned, this has the additional benefit of increasing overall data security by preventing sensitive data to be copied.

- Education on the risks of parasite infection and preventive measures should be required for all users. An alert user can recognize suspicious program activity and report it before the problem propagates throughout the enterprise.

In addition to the implementation of sound system and user policies, virus-scanning software should be installed on all workstations and servers within the enterprise. Many capable virus-scanning packages are available on the market. Key features to look for when searching for a virus-scanning solution include cost, cross-platform compatibility, and the available of timely updates as new viruses and their derivatives are discovered every day.

29

ADMINISTERING YOUR NETWORK

Help Desk and Trouble Ticket Systems

The most visible and often time-consuming responsibility of network administration is supporting end users throughout the organization. Network administrators often feel more like firefighters running from one user problem to the next than administrators. In many cases, administrators can be so busy responding to end user problems that they cannot take action to prevent such problems from occurring in the first place.

This problem is made more frustrating by the fact that most problems users experience do not require systems administrative action to resolve. Printers that do not work, application programs that do not work as expected, and computers that will not boot can often be traced to simple operational issues.

The establishment of a help desk to serve as the initial point of contact for end users improves this situation from both the end user and administrator's perspective: The end user has a single point of contact for all problems associated with the use of the network, and the network administrator is freed to concentrate on those problems that represent operational issues.

A help desk is a single point of contact for end users to report any computing problems they might be experiencing regardless of their nature. Personnel at the help desk take the call and make an assessment as to which of four main categories the user's problem falls into: application questions, workstation installation issues, network administration issues, or system faults.

The majority of calls to a typical help desk will be application questions. Questions such as "How can I add a chart to a word processing document?" and "How do I print to the color printer?" fall into this category. The help desk personnel are usually capable of handling these questions internally either over the phone or by a visit to the user's workstation. Through the use of remote control software as detailed in the systems management platform section of this chapter, it is even possible for most problems to be taken care of directly from the help desk.

Workstation installation issues include workstations that are not properly configured to meet the user's needs. Examples of this type of problem would include a user whose spreadsheet program does not have the statistical analysis package installed or a workstation that does not have appropriate printer drivers. These problems can also be solved directly by help desk personnel.

Network administration issues are those problems whose root cause lies in the management of network resources. Examples include users who do not have adequate access rights to network resources or requests for new users or new groups. The help desk personnel usually forward network administration issues to the network administrators for appropriate action.

If the problem appears to be caused by a system fault, the problem is immediately escalated to the network administration personnel. Problems of this type are usually identified quickly because the problem often affects multiple users in the same way at the same time, resulting in a rash of calls to the help desk. By taking care to note who is affected by the problem, help desk personnel can greatly aid systems administration personnel in solving the problem quickly and efficiently.

In order to ensure that each problem reported to the help desk is resolved, a trouble ticketing system can be implemented. Trouble ticket systems are a formalized methodology of tracing a help call through the problem resolution process from the initial report to problem resolution. Trouble ticket systems provide many benefits:

- Problems that are not resolved in one shift are documented for the action on the next shift.
- Common problems that represent user training needs can be identified.
- Intermittent problems can be tracked to determine the underlying cause.
- Resources that create an unusual amount of help desk traffic can be identified and examined.
- A database of common problems and their solutions can be built.

Although manual trouble ticket systems are adequate for smaller networks, several automated trouble ticket systems are available for larger systems. These automated systems provide many benefits, including the capability to automatically search for similar problems from previous trouble tickets, the capability to interface directly into electronic mail systems, comprehensive search capabilities, and automated reporting functions.

Regardless of whether a trouble ticket system is manual or automated, it can be effective only if it is kept current. Each problem should be logged in to the system no matter how insignificant it may seem. Often these small problems when looked at on a macro level are indicative of other, more serious problems in the network system.

Documentation

One of the most important tools for supporting and maintaining a network system is proper documentation. Unfortunately, most network administrators would rather concentrate on the next project rather than on carefully documenting the work just completed. Good documentation should be considered a vital part of each network administrative task rather than a separate task to be completed when the "real work" is completed. To put it another way, documentation is an integral part of the administration process rather than a separate task.

The importance of good documentation is emphasized by considering the results of poor documentation. A system installed for a long period of time needs to be upgraded to a newer version of the operating system. Before the upgrade process can be started, the network administrator needs answers to several questions about the system and its configuration: What are the current settings on the device? What version of the operating system or firmware is installed on the device? These questions increase in importance if the administrator who initially installed the device has since left the company.

The network documentation process begins with the management of documentation from software and hardware vendors. Instructions that detail jumper settings, installation procedures, system requirements, and copies of any software that may be required for configuration should be carefully stored. This information is invaluable when a change needs to be made to a system. A copy of all user documentation should also be kept at the help desk for users to use as reference material.

There are three basic areas that should be considered when documenting network systems: hardware configurations, software configurations, and network wiring diagrams. Hardware configuration is one of the most important documentation areas. In the event of hardware failure or a proposed upgrade, you must analyze the current configurations and read the manufacturer's documentation to ensure that replacement equipment is compatible with installed equipment. Examples of hardware configuration information included in the systems documentation includes:

- CMOS configurations
- Jumper settings
- Driver settings
- Memory maps
- Installed component types and versions

Software configuration information should also be carefully documented. The client/server environments that are becoming commonplace require considerable configuration at both the client and server ends. In order to make the system as self documenting as possible, a consistent strategy should be used for the assignment of software configuration information such as station names. Software configuration information includes

- Directory structures used for applications and user files
- Application serial numbers, license codes, and proofs of purchase
- System startup and configuration files

Network wiring and cables also require careful documentation. Due to the dynamic nature of networked systems, the destination of a cable can quickly become lost in a "rat's nest" of wiring. Each end of all cables should be descriptively labeled and color-coded. Network maps detailing the locations of servers, workstations, network communications equipment, and the wiring that connects them should be kept current. Some network management platforms include the capability to create and update logical network maps in real time. Although these products do not explicitly determine the location of the device, they do show how the equipment is interconnected. The issue of physical location can be addressed if the network devices are named in a manner that represents their location, such as smith_101 for a workstation located in room 101 of the Smith building.

Summary

Network Administration is a never-ending operations issue. There are five basic network administration functions: fault management, configuration management, accounting management, performance management, and security management. By addressing each of these functional areas, a network administrator can ensure that data and applications stored on the network are secure and available for use.

By being diligent in the creation and implementation of network policies, a network administrator can greatly reduce the time spent "firefighting" and increase the time spent planning for the future needs of the network system. In short, the more time spent developing a comprehensive plan to administrate your network, the less time spent actually performing network administration.

CHAPTER 30

Looking to the Future

by Mark Sportack

IN THIS CHAPTER

Looking into the future is always a risky proposition. Fortune tellers make a living by predicting the future for those gullible enough to believe them. The good ones can surmise enough about their customer, based on appearance, mannerisms, and even their statements, to make open-ended but educated guesses about that customer's future. If all else fails, they can always claim that only time will tell if they were right and, as long as there is hope for a tomorrow, there will always be hope that their predictions will still materialize. The future of high-performance networks is no exception.

Trade publications abound with speculation from "experts" about what the future holds. Nevertheless, there are only two certainties in networking. The first is constant change. The second is that constant change will be driven by the customer's constantly changing requirements. Given this, it seems prudent for the techno-fortune teller to study the customer's present and recent past for clues about the future.

These clues can be found in the trends that have emerged in the networked computing industry during the past few years. Specific topics that warrant investigation are the recent evolutionary history of networked clients, distributed servers, and their application software and operating systems. The networking impacts of these trends can be identified and used as a basis for extrapolating future expected changes. This exercise creates a "window" for looking into the future of high-performance networking.

Net Trends

The first networked computing trend that can't be ignored is the Internet phenomenon. Commercialization of the Internet has proven to be a virtual Pandora's box. The millions of new Net users, both personal and corporate, have permanently altered the Internet in ways that are only now being understood.

The Internet, and its protocol the Internet Protocol (IP), were originally designed to facilitate research by interconnecting academic sites with government and private research centers. They were not designed for interconnecting millions of highly dispersed individual users nor were they prepared for the explosive growth that accompanied their commercialization.

This influx of new users threatened both the Internet and IP. The Internet found itself struggling to add capacity fast enough to meet demand, while the Internet Engineering Task Force (IETF) scrambled to develop ways to make the existing supply of IP addresses last longer and add longer-term support for expanded network layer functionality.

More importantly, commercialization of the Internet has generated a flurry of interesting new technologies, and new applications of some old technologies, that can only increase demands for bandwidth.

The Internet

The Internet itself suffered from commercialization's severe growing pains. It wasn't engineered for the massive increases in usage volumes that it experienced. Internet service providers found the booming business challenging, if not impossible, to keep up with. Consequently, the World Wide Web quickly turned into the World Wide Wait.

The Internet hype affected more than technologically proficient individuals. Even corporate America succumbed to the lure of the Internet. The Internet was viewed by many companies as a new, passive channel for reaching a focused and desirable market segment. Marketers in these companies scrambled to establish a presence on the World Wide Web (WWW or Web), lest they appeared to be "behind the times."

Numerous lessons had to be learned about using this new electronic channel. Providing too little information, or presenting it in an uninspired manner, could turn off potential customers. Providing too much information could be overwhelming and result in time-consuming access. Failure to keep the site updated could also reduce the effectiveness of the site.

As companies struggled to learn how to take advantage of the commercial Net, a greater internal issue arose: Is having a Web site worth the cost? This generated an even greater frenzy to either directly generate revenues from Web sites or, at the very least, attribute some portion of sales to it. Unfortunately, if the Web site is just an electronic billboard, this can be almost impossible.

Expanding the functionality of a corporate Internet presence beyond passive advertising was, and still is, fraught with other risks for both customers and companies. For example, using a Web site as an active marketing and/or sales tool requires some degree of integration with existing systems and applications. Database and software vendors are doing their best to enable this integration by supplying the tools necessary for accessing databases from a browser.

Unfortunately, the data contained in, and used by, these systems is usually extremely sensitive and proprietary. Companies would have to make a "hole" in their corporate network's perimeter defenses to enable any advanced marketing or customer care functionality.

Customers, too, are subjected to an increased risk just by using the Internet for commerce. To conduct any transaction, or even query an account for status, requires them to transmit enough personal information, such as Social Security Numbers or Personal Identification Numbers (PINs), to uniquely identify themselves. Plus, if they are making purchases, they may have to provide a credit card number. This sensitive personal information must traverse an unsecured morass of networking facilities.

The "net" (pardon the intentional double entendre) effect has been an increased emphasis on network perimeter defenses, like firewalls, with sacrificial machines placed outside the firewall to proxitize inbound requests for data. In the future, these physical firewalls and proxy servers may go "virtual" as their functionality becomes embedded in the network layer protocols and mechanisms. Widespread use of X.509 certificates, in conjunction with network and host layer authentication, could enable customers to directly access and perform limited manipulation of their account data. Expect this to occur later rather than sooner.

Internet Protocol (IP)

The Internet Protocol is currently at revision level 4 (IPv4). It is rapidly approaching functional obsolescence on several fronts. This protocol was originally developed nearly two decades ago as a means of interconnecting the emerging Internet's computers. The total projected growth of this original Internet was optimistically estimated in the millions of computers. Thus, IP's 32-bit addressing scheme was deemed excessive: It is mathematically capable of supporting over four billion possible addresses. Therefore, address classifications could afford to have gaps between them measured in orders of magnitude. Other inefficient practices, too, helped to squander much of IPv4's theoretical scaleability.

Beyond the address limitations, routing issues are also driving the development and deployment of a new IP protocol. IPv4 is also hampered by its two-level addressing hierarchy, and its address classes. Its addressing hierarchy consists of a host and domain name. Even with provisions for subnetting, this simply does not allow construction of efficient address hierarchies that can be aggregated by routers on the scale that today's, much less tomorrow's, global Internet requires.

Obsolescence also threatens the current IP from a functional perspective. Increasingly complex applications continuously impose new, unforeseen network performance requirements that traditional IP cannot deliver efficiently. Mobile users, individual users, streaming video and audio broadcasts, and the need for improved security are straining the limits of IPv4.

The next generation of IP, commonly known as IPng (Internet Protocol Next Generation) but more correctly identified as Internet Protocol Version 6 (IPv6), resolves all of these issues. It will offer a vastly expanded addressing scheme to support the continued expansion of the Internet, and an improved ability to aggregate routes on a large scale.

IPv6 also contains support for numerous other features such as real-time audio and/or video transmissions, host mobility, end-to-end security through network layer encryption and authentication, as well as auto-configuration and auto-reconfiguration.

Despite the potential benefits of IPv6, the migration from IPv4 is not risk-free. The extension of the address length from 32 to 128 bits automatically limits interoperability between IPv4 and IPv6. *IPv4-only nodes cannot interoperate with IPv6-only nodes because the address architectures are not directly compatible.*

Most companies' IP networks will be impossible to "flash cut" to IPv6. The number of users, devices, and applications that use IP makes this a logistical impossibility for all but the smallest companies. Instead, the usual processes of acquisition and maintenance will probably result in

IPv6-capable devices being deployed in a highly decentralized, piecemeal fashion. It is equally likely that some individuals and/or organizations within companies will want to take advantage of IPv6 functionality before the network infrastructure is ready for it. This can result in widespread breakdowns in network connectivity that can severely disrupt connectivity and potentially cripple operations.

Given that operators of large, distributed IP networks can expect lengthy migrations from IPv4 to IPv6, this address incompatibility has the potential to severely disrupt service across the network if the conversion is not carefully planned and implemented!

This issue requires the attention of system architects, application developers, and anyone else who uses an IP network, *now!* IPv6 products won't be out for some time yet, but they *are* coming. Getting up to speed on IPv6 features and migration issues now will afford the opportunity to integrate one or more of IPv6's many powerful new features into future application development efforts.

More importantly, because IPv4 is not directly compatible with IPv6, an understanding of the differences and the various transition mechanisms will facilitate the planning of a graceful migration of clients, systems, and applications without experiencing service outages.

Intranets

As companies were experimenting with using the Internet as a marketing tool, a funny thing happened to their internal IP Wide Area Networks. They began turning into "intranets." Users, once accustomed to gathering the hyperconnected information available on the Internet's World Wide Web, began to experiment with developing and publishing their own Web content. This content, usually resident behind firewalls or other perimeter defense mechanisms, could not be accessed from outside their company's domain. Therefore, it couldn't really be considered part of the World Wide Web. For that matter, their private WAN couldn't be considered part of the Internet. The new hybrid was dubbed "intranet."

Intranets underwent a transition that brought them from their nascent days as a techno-toy/ Internet access mechanism to an undeniable business tool. This transition was facilitated by the increasing availability of Web-based tools. Software manufacturers realized that the real money to be made in Internet technologies was held by companies, not individual users. Consequently, they targeted this market aggressively, and developed everything from graphical user interface tools for the creation and management of sites and their content to new programming languages specifically designed for the Web environment. Database companies, too, provided APIs for their products, as well as middleware that would enable users to extract data from their databases using a browser.

In the future, the browser will become the ubiquitous, business-oriented presentation layer for virtually all applications on a company's intranet. This is due, in large part, to the ability to develop an application that can run on every client workstation without customization or modification. Rather than the user interface of custom-developed application software being

30

LOOKING TO
THE FUTURE

developed for specific physical platforms, the browser becomes the client's logical presentation layer. Additionally, this paradigm can even off-load some of the server workload to the clients. Small but repetitive tasks can be made into "applets" that are downloaded to, and executed at, the client workstation, rather than consuming a server's relatively more expensive CPU cycles.

Extranets

The next subtrend in the ongoing Internet saga is likely to be the evolution of extranets. An *extranet* is an extension of the internal intranet (that is, access only to specific, required business systems) to external business partners. In other words, a limited trust is defined and established between the networked computing resources of two or more companies. This arrangement is a hybridized compromise between using firewalls and the unsecured Internet for internetworking, and directly connecting the two companies' WANs.

Any companies with interlocking business processes, such as joint ventures, partnerships, customers and suppliers, and so on, may benefit from an extranet. Properly designed and implemented, extranets offer maximum performance internetworking between the networked computing resources of different companies, with limited risk to both parties. The key words in the preceding sentence are: "properly designed and implemented."

Given the open nature of IP, extending connectivity to other IP WANs can be an extremely risky proposition. Even using a point-to-point private line to interconnect two or more IP wide area networks creates one big IP WAN, unless access is carefully restricted at each end of the interconnecting transmission facility, using something more stringent than just router access lists. Access can be inadvertently extended (or surreptitiously gained) to all the other IP domains, and their networked computing assets, that each business partner may have access to. This can have disastrous results. However, the potential benefits can be significant enough to warrant the risks, especially because the risks can be minimized through careful planning and network management.

In the not-too-distant future, extranets will emerge as the preferred interconnectivity vehicle between business partners. In the longer term, the distinctions between the Internet, intranets, and extranets are likely to be almost completely erased by technological advance. Improvements in network layer authentication, certification, and (to a lesser extent) encryption will probably give companies the ability to tear down their firewalls and other physical perimeter defenses of their WANs. In their place will be logically defined intranets and extranets. When this happens, we will have come full circle. The various nets will have reintegrated into a single, ubiquitous Net with logical, not physical, subdivisions.

Hyperconnectivity

Yet another Internet-related trend that will have further impacts on networking in the future is *hyperconnectivity*. Hyperconnectivity is the enabling technology that was responsible for the success of the World Wide Web by making the Internet accessible to the masses. Hyperconnectivity uses predefined hyperlinks to specific data.

Hyperlinks are the electronic cross-referencing of networked information. Hyperlinked documents "fetch" additional information for the user with a single mouse click. With this technology, a user can transparently navigate through a complex sequence of hosts searching for information without knowing anything about the host.

Although this is the very essence of hyperconnectivity's value, it is also its Achilles' heel. The user is almost completely insulated from any appreciation of the network intensity of each request. Files are accessed in exactly the same manner, regardless of whether they reside locally or reside half a continent or half a world away. The only clue that the users may receive about the network intensity of any given request is the amount of time required to fulfill their requests.

Network intensity consists of two components: the amount of bandwidth required, and the total amount of switches, routers, hubs, and every transmission facility that will support the requested transmission. Given that the Web is multimedia-capable, these requests can be for anything from another "page" created in the Hypertext Markup Language (HTML) that contains nothing but more hyperlinks, to data files to executable applets to high-resolution, true-color graphics files, audio or even video clips. In the hyperconnected World Wide Web (WWW), the user simply points at an active, or "hot," spot on the browser's screen, and the data is retrieved automatically and somewhat anonymously without any regard for network intensity.

This has already proved problematic for many companies whose WANs bogged down under the sudden traffic increase. The problem will soon get worse. Hyperconnectivity will soon transcend the Web and become *the* accessibility technology of the late 90s. Like the mouse a decade earlier, it has helped the masses overcome a technological barrier. It has already expanded the ranks of Internet/intranet users, driving up the demand for connectivity and bandwidth in the process.

In the future, hyperconnectivity will become the operational model for the User Interface (UI) of client operating systems. This is as dangerous as it is powerful. Having a "browser" as the operating system's UI means that a communications program is no longer a nice feature. It is *the* interface to all applications and data, regardless of where they reside. In fact, the contents of a user's hard drive and the contents of everything else connected to his network are presented to the user as if the sum total were resident locally.

This means that the network intensity of any given request will be almost completely shielded from the user by this UI. Such hyperconnected operating systems will almost certainly be accompanied by a significant increase in demand for LAN, and possibly even WAN, bandwidth.

Agents

The most recent branch of artificial intelligence (AI), agent software, joins the ranks of internet-related trends that can drive future network performance requirements. Agents are small, autonomous programs that the user can customize to perform very specific tasks.

In a Web environment, an agent can be used to automate routine information retrieval. For example, an agent can automatically fetch headlines from your electronic news service. Some types of agents are even capable of self-learning. These agents can recognize their user's patterns of responses, such as always deleting political stories without reading them, and learn to not fetch things that will only be deleted.

Artificial intelligence, in the form of agent software, may have finally found its niche in the marketplace. Almost every existing means of information distribution in companies requires the sender to identify the recipients and "push" information through the infrastructure to the recipients. The single exception is the Web. The Web relies on hyperlinks that are established by site/content owners in anticipation of someone needing them. Users must find these links to information and use them to "pull" information through the networked computing infrastructure.

This "pull" paradigm has been used relatively successfully to date, but is not scaleable. Finding and retrieving information will become much more difficult as the universe of available information expands. Evidence of this is found in the success of commercial search engines. These services have proven themselves invaluable in assisting the search for information.

Current engines, however, require the development and maintenance of a key word index. Intersite search engines typically launch a self-replicating, mobile process that explores links and looks for content. This process, commonly referred to as a "spider," forwards everything it finds back to the originating host. This host stores all content until the discovery process finishes. Then, the engine's cataloging facility develops its index. This process is simultaneously and extremely disk, CPU, and network intensive. Consequently, it is impractical to keep the index up to date in anything near real time. This limits the search engine's timeliness, usefulness, and scaleability.

An intelligent agent can be used for highly individual information discovery. The result of such a search is much more up to date and focused. This use of agents would consume less bandwidth, CPU cycles, and disk space on the search engine's host. Without an automated and individual search tool, people will be hard pressed to maintain their information discovery and retrieval tasks in addition to performing normal work responsibilities.

Regardless of how they are used, agents will leverage a user's time and increase both the efficiency and effectiveness of Web usage. As the volume of Web-based information grows, an agent may well become essential.

Though agents are not limited to Internet/intranet applications, the way they are used for these applications will determine what kind of impact they will have on networks. Properly used, they will save time and network/computing resources. Unfortunately, the degree to which agents are automated can easily be misused. Even modest misuses can cause increased consumption of bandwidth across both the LAN and WAN, even when their users/owners are not at work.

Multimedia Communications

Multimedia communications, as described in Chapter 27, include voice and/or video transmissions. These technologies have long been viewed suspiciously by management as having dubious business value (that is, more "toy" than "tool"). After all, why use a networked PC to emulate a walkie-talkie when there's already a telephone on every desk? Similarly, the quarter-screen "talking heads" of desktop videoconferencing over conventional LANs and WANs is slow and jerky. Worse, it doesn't really capture the body language and other subtle non-verbal communications that can be gleaned from face-to-face interactions. So there remains little compelling reason to invest in an expensive "toy."

Part of the reason behind the limited capabilities of current generation multimedia communications technologies has to do with the networks that must support them. Neither today's LANs and WANs nor their protocols are well-suited to transporting the time-sensitive data of a multimedia communications session. In such a session, packets that are delivered late, or even out of sequence, are simply discarded.

Today's network protocols tend to be much better at guaranteeing the integrity of each packet's payload, and more efficient at transporting bulk data than they are at guaranteeing timeliness of delivery. Error checking mechanisms ensure that, when an errored packet is discovered, it is discarded and the originating host notified of the need to retransmit.

Many of today's more common network protocols also use a flexible packet size. The larger the stream of data, the better the ratio of packet-to-payload can be, as the protocol simply expands the total size of the packet. This is wonderfully efficient at transporting conventional application data, but can wreak havoc on a time-sensitive application. Therefore, today's networks are 180 degrees out of phase with the performance requirements of multimedia communications by forcing them to share the network with packets of indeterminate size, and therefore indeterminate transmission durations.

Today's networking hardware is also ill-suited to multimedia communications for two basic reasons: access method and usable bandwidth. Contemporary LANs, in particular, force networked devices to either wait their turn for an empty packet, or compete fiercely in a broadcast environment for an empty packet. Neither form of shared access is conducive to the latency requirements of multimedia communications.

The second reason that today's networks are ill-prepared for multimedia communications is that these applications can be extremely bandwidth intensive. These sessions, in addition to the "normal" workload of the LAN and/or WAN, can degrade the network's performance substantially.

To be fair, there are numerous other non-network-related factors that also impede the acceptance of multimedia communications technologies. Some of these other reasons include primitive

30

LOOKING TO
THE FUTURE

drivers, lack of adequate desktop computing power, and the proprietary vendor product "bundles" that prevent communications with other brands. The net effect of all these factors is that multimedia communications technologies tend to be perceived as expensive "toys," rather than serious and legitimate business tools.

In the future, all the factors that are currently hindering the acceptance of multimedia communications will be removed. When this happens, it will be essential to already have a high-performance network in place that will be equally capable of satisfying the low latency requirements of multimedia communications and the data integrity requirements of traditional networked applications.

Higher performance LAN technologies will be needed that can provide the same high data rates to all connected devices, without forcing them to share, or compete for, available bandwidth. Simultaneously, they will lower network latency to support time-sensitive applications. This combination of high data rates and low latency will allow voice, data, and video communications to share the same infrastructure.

Extremely High-Performance Networks

Extremely high-performance, highly specialized "networks" will also appear in the not-too-distant future. Currently, networking computers requires several physical layers, as indicated in Figure 30.1.

FIGURE 30.1.

Connecting computers to the LAN requires a sequence of physical layers, beginning with the CPU, memory, and I/O of each computer plus the LAN.

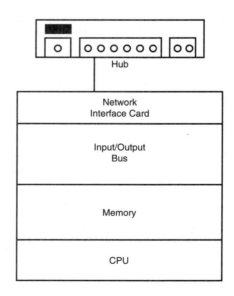

Of all the layers depicted in Figure 30.1, the LAN layer results in the greatest performance degradation. For example, a computer with a PCI bus is capable of raw I/O at just over 1Gbps.

Connections to the LAN constrict this down as far as 100 or 10Mbps, depending upon the LAN technology. The computer's network interface card (NIC) is responsible for providing the protocol conversion between PCI and the LAN, as well as buffering the PCI bus down to LAN performance levels.

In the short run, this performance bottleneck will be addressed through numerous attempts at increasing the clock rate of LAN technologies. Today's 100Mbps LANs will become adequate only for general desktop connectivity. The more bandwidth-hungry servers will absolutely require several times this quantity. Consequently, LAN technologies with raw bit rates of approximately 1Gbps will emerge.

Ultimately, however, this paradigm will become obsolete by implementing a switched connection directly at the I/O layer through extension of the computer's bus. This is known as *I/O switching*. I/O switching transfers responsibilities for protocol translation and speed buffering to the switching hub. This relieves the computer of a substantial burden, thereby freeing it up to perform more germane duties. Figure 30.2 illustrates how I/O switching can expedite I/O by partially eliminating the LAN.

FIGURE 30.2.

Connecting computers to the LAN using I/O switching is done by extending the computer's bus to the switching hub.

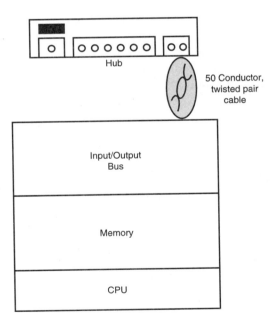

Later, switched connections directly to computer memory banks (called Direct Memory Access or DMA by one hardware manufacturer) will begin to proliferate in computer clusters and possibly even for inter-host communications within "server farms." Both I/O switching and DMA are highly specialized, high-bandwidth mechanisms that require very close physical proximity of the hosts they interconnect. Unlike I/O switching, DMA will likely only be used for inter-host communications in clustered computers.

Both of these technologies are subject to stringent distance limitations, therefore they will be limited to niche roles in larger high-performance networks. They both, however, point out the fact that today's LAN and WAN technologies are already woefully mismatched against the computers that they interconnect. And those computers will continue to experience increases in both speed and power at a fairly rapid pace for the foreseeable future.

Vision of the Future

These trends, and numerous others not mentioned here, demonstrate that the future of networks will be filled with at least as much radical change as they have experienced in the past decade. The changes will be necessary if networks are to keep pace with the rest of the information technologies.

These examples should also show that there is no single "killer app" that will determine the shape and substance of future networks. Unfortunately, that would be too easy. Instead, there will be numerous "minor" applications that will continuously push the development of ever higher performance networks.

The problem is that there will be several different definitions of the word *performance*. Multimedia applications will require very low-latency networks and guaranteed levels of service, whereas traditional application types will continue to place an emphasis on data integrity. Networks must become flexible enough to accommodate the many different types of applications, regardless of how conflicting their network performance requirements may be. Thus, they must simultaneously become capable of satisfying very dissimilar network performance requirements.

Today, the typical company maintains multiple communications infrastructures: one for voice, and at least one (possibly more) for data. In the future, there will only be a single, multimedia communications network infrastructure.

The multiple existing communications infrastructures will consolidate slowly, but steadily. Numerous upgrades to the LAN/WAN infrastructure will need to occur. WAN transmission facilities will eventually transition over to switched facilities. WAN routers, too, will eventually be replaced with a relatively small, high-bandwidth switch that functions as the multi-media communications vehicle at the premise edge. A premise edge vehicle is a device that interconnects the LAN with the WAN. The routing function will be driven to the edges of the network: the clients and servers.

LANs will continue to increase their switched port densities until there are no more "shared" LAN segments. They will complete their evolution into high-bandwidth switching hubs (or mini-PBXs, depending upon your perspective) when they embrace a network protocol that was designed as a high-speed, low-latency, port-switched protocol. These switching hubs will be distributed throughout the building. Installing them in telephone closets will minimize the distance to the desktop, thereby permitting higher bandwidth over most of the existing premise wiring.

This single multimedia infrastructure will contain familiar elements of today's LANs and PBXs. The PBX will become a software-driven premise edge switch responsible for "off-network" communications, that is, phone calls to destinations outside of the corporate network. Switching hubs will remain in the telephone closets and provide multimedia communications service to the users. These distributed switches will provide connectivity to a combination of telephony-capable computers. They will also interconnect with the PBX for "off-network" voice-only communications.

The users' stations will undergo a similar transformation. Currently, the user station features separate devices for access to the two communications infrastructures. These devices, the PC and telephone, will merge. They will integrate into a single multimedia information appliance. This information appliance will provide the user with an integrated platform for manipulating and sharing all types of information. Traditional desktop computing will be augmented by telephony applications, and both will enjoy a single connection from the information appliance into a common multiservice network.

These desktop telephony applications, for example, call management, voice mail management, and audio and video communications, will be available through a hyperconnected graphical interface through the PC, or a networked server. This represents the maturation of "multimedia computing" into a legitimate business tool. These applications will also drive the incremental integration of computing and telephony until a single infrastructure satisfies user requirements for both.

Having a physical networking infrastructure that is ready to meet the future expected challenges is not enough. These physical preparations must be complemented by the evolution of network protocols. As previously demonstrated, network protocols must be capable of simultaneously accommodating time-sensitive applications and legacy bulk data, queries, and transactions. These protocols also must be capable of scaling to higher transmission rates, and support migration away from routing in favor of switching across the WAN.

The emerging technologies and trends described in this chapter, as well as numerous others, all promise to make the future of high-performance networking even more exciting and dynamic than its past. The nature of the new demands that will be placed on networks are such that they can't be satisfied by following the historic precedent of simply increasing the network's clock rate. This might be adequate for some of the applications, and might even be necessary to accommodate the increased aggregate traffic load, but it is not a panacea.

The networks of the future must also provide native support for new features and functionality. These networks will be expected to provide Quality of Service (QoS) guarantees for time-sensitive traffic, network layer authentication and encryption for sensitive applications and data, as well as the continued ability to transport conventional data. As the future unfolds, networks that are not flexible and extensible and cannot be easily adapted to satisfy ever-changing customer performance requirements will quickly founder.

I

INDEX

A V I A C O M   S E R V I C E

The Information SuperLibrary™

Bookstore

Search

What's New

Reference

Software

Newsletter

Company Overviews

Yellow Pages

Internet Starter Kit

HTML Workshop

Win a Free T-Shirt!

Macmillan Computer Publishing

Site Map

Talk to Us

CHECK OUT THE BOOKS IN THIS LIBRARY.

You'll find thousands of shareware files and over 1600 computer books designed for both technowizards and technophobes. You can browse through 700 sample chapters, get the latest news on the Net, and find just about anything using our massive search directories.

All Macmillan Computer Publishing books are available at your local bookstore.

We're open 24-hours a day, 365 days a year.

You don't need a card.

We don't charge fines.

And you can be as **LOUD** as you want.

The Information SuperLibrary
http://www.mcp.com/mcp/   ftp.mcp.com

MACMILLAN COMPUTER PUBLISHING USA

A VIACOM COMPANY

 Support:

If you need assistance with the information in this book or with a CD/Disk accompanying the book, please access the Knowledge Base on our Web site at **http://www.superlibrary.com/general/support**. Our most Frequently Asked Questions are answered there. If you do not find the answer to your questions on our Web site, you may contact Macmillan Technical Support **(317) 581-3833** or e-mail us at **support@mcp.com**.

Windows NT 4 and Web Site Resource Library

— Sams Development Group

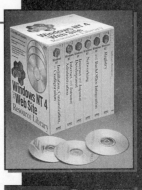

This comprehensive library is the most complete reference available for Windows NT and Web administrators and developers. Six volumes and more than 3,500 pages of key information about the Windows NT Registry, Web site administration and development, networking, BackOffice integration, and much more.

Three Bonus CD-ROMs include networking utilities, third-party tools, support utilities, Web site development tools, HTML templates, CGI scripts, and more!

$149.99 USA/$209.95 CAN
ISBN: 0-672-30995-5

User Level: Accomplished–Expert
3,200 pp.

Robert Cowart's Windows NT 4 Unleashed, Professional Reference Edition

— Robert Cowart

The only reference Windows NT administrators need to learn how to configure their NT systems for maximum performance, security, and reliability. This comprehensive reference explains how to install, maintain, and configure an individual workstation as well as connecting computers to peer-to-peer networking. Includes comprehensive advice for setting up and administering an NT server network, and focuses on the new and improved administration and connectivity features of version 4.0

The CD-ROM includes source code, utilities, and sample applications from the book.

$59.99 USA/$84.95 CAN
ISBN: 0-672-31001-5

User Level: Intermediate–Expert
1,044 pp.

Windows NT Troubleshooting and Configuration

— Robert Reinstein, et al.

Written for system administrators, this book details how to use Windows NT with the other components of the BackOffice suite. It includes coverage of NT design, system management, Registry modification and management, troubleshooting, Internet support, and security issues.

This book teaches readers how to use NT with BackOffice and as a Web server with Internet Information Server and Microsoft's other Internet tools and contains a complete troubleshooting section outlining problems and their solutions.

The CD-ROM contains scripts and source code from the book.

$59.99 USA/$84.95 CAN
ISBN: 0-672-30941-6

User Level: Accomplished–Expert
1,120 pp.

Deploying Windows NT 4.0 in the Enterprise

— Jim Plas

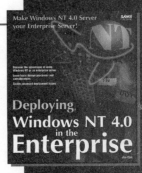

NT is quickly becoming a recognized contender in the enterprise arena, and this must-have guide specifically addresses NT as an enterprise server—from LANs and WANs to multi-platform networks. This book provides comprehensive coverage of server standardization, workstation standards, alternative clients, SNA connectivity, advanced trust relationships, and more. It also discusses the challenges that are particular to large systems using the newest technologies, such as ATM and ISDN.

$55.00 USA/$77.95 CAN
ISBN: 0-672-31038-4

User Level: Accomplished–Expert
500 pp.

Paul McFedries' Windows 95 Unleashed, Professional Reference Edition

— Paul McFedries

Essential for all Windows users, *Paul McFedries' Windows 95 Unleashed, Professional Reference Edition* takes readers beyond the basics, exploring all facets of this operating system, including installation, the Internet, customization, optimization, networking multimedia, plug-and-play, and the new features of Windows Messaging System for communications. This title, which covers enhancements since the initial release of Windows 95, has been updated with additional reference material. Coverage includes Internet Explorer 4.0 and bringing the "active desktop" to Windows 95. The CD-ROM contains 32-bit software designed for Windows 95 and an easy-to-search online chapter on troubleshooting for Windows 95.

$59.99 USA/$84.95 CAN   *User Level: Accomplished–Expert*
ISBN: 0-672-31039-2   *1,648 pp.*

Lotus Notes and Domino Server 4.5 Unleashed, Second Edition

— Randall A. Tamura, et al.

Lotus Notes is a versatile "groupware" package that offers document management, e-mail, and other features across multiple operating environments, including OS/2, Windows, NT, Macintosh, UNIX, and NetWare. Because of its complex development platform, it is difficult for uninformed users to manipulate and customize the various products. This book shows the 4.5 million registered Notes users how to work with and customize Lotus Notes 4.5 and demonstrates how to maximize Notes in a networked environment. The CD-ROM contains various utilities, toolkits, and two best-selling books in HTML format.

$55.00 USA/$77.95 CAN   *User Level: Accomplished–Expert*
ISBN: 0-672-31004-X   *1,152 pp.*

Domino Server 4.5 Unleashed

— Rizwan Virk & Thomas Fredell, et al.

Targeted toward the administrator of a Domino Server, this book goes beyond the Lotus documentation and takes users from job responsibilities and planning to implementation of Domino and performance monitoring. This title provides extensive coverage of the physical components of the environment, administrating the systems, tuning, optimizing, and maintenance. The CD-ROM includes various utilities and toolkits.

$49.99 USA/$70.95 CAN   *User Level: Accomplished–Expert*
ISBN: 1-57521-259-5   *600 pp.*

Maximum Security: A Hacker's Guide to Protecting Your Internet Site and Network

— Anonymous

Now more than ever, it is imperative that users be able to protect their system from hackers trashing their Web sites or stealing information. Written by a reformed hacker, this comprehensive resource identifies security holes in common computer and network systems, allowing systems administrators to discover faults inherent within their network and work toward a solution to those problems. This book explores the most commonly used hacking techniques so users can safeguard their system, and includes step-by-step lists and discussions of the vulnerabilities inherent in each operating system on the market. The CD-ROM is loaded with source code, technical documents, system logs, utilities, and other practical items for understanding and implementing Internet and computer system security.

$49.99 USA/$70.95 CAN   *User Level: Accomplished–Expert*
ISBN: 1-57521-268-4   *928 pp.*

Add to Your Sams.net Library Today
with the Best Books for Internet Technologies

ISBN	Quantity	Description of Item	Unit Cost	Total Cost
0-672-30995-5		Windows NT 4 and Web Site Resource Library (6 Books/3 CD-ROMs)	$149.99	
0-672-31001-5		Robert Cowart's Windows NT 4 Unleashed, Professional Reference Edition (Book/CD-ROM)	$59.99	
0-672-30941-6		Windows NT Configuration and Troubleshooting (Book/CD-ROM)	$59.99	
0-672-31038-4		Deploying Windows NT 4.0 in the Enterprise	$55.00	
0-672-31039-2		Paul McFedries' Windows 95 Unleashed, Professional Reference Edition (Book/CD-ROM)	$59.99	
0-672-31004-X		Lotus Notes and Domino Server 4.5 Unleashed, Second Edition (Book/CD-ROM)	$55.00	
1-57521-259-5		Domino Server 4.5 Unleashed (Book/CD-ROM)	$49.99	
1-57521-268-4		Maximum Internet Security: A Hacker's Guide to Protecting Your Internet Site and Network (Book/CD-ROM)	$49.99	
		Shipping and Handling: See information below.		
		TOTAL		

Shipping and Handling: $4.00 for the first book, and $1.75 for each additional book. If you need to have it NOW, we can ship product to you in 24 hours for an additional charge of approximately $18.00, and you will receive your item overnight or in two days. Overseas shipping and handling adds $2.00. Prices subject to change. Call between 9:00 a.m. and 5:00 p.m. EST for availability and pricing information on latest editions.

201 W. 103rd Street, Indianapolis, Indiana 46290

1-800-428-5331 — Orders   1-800-835-3202 — Fax   1-800-858-7674 — Customer Service

Book ISBN 1-57521-187-4